D0599157

SCREAMING MONKEYS

SCREAMING MONKEYS

Critiques of
ASIAN AMERICAN IMAGES

EDITED BY

M. EVELINA GALANG

— IN COLLABORATION WITH —
NONFICTION EDITOR SUNAINA MAIRA
POETRY EDITOR EILEEN TABIOS
ART EDITOR JORDIN ISIP
FOUND IMAGES EDITOR ANIDA YOEU ESGUERRA
AND MONKEY'S COMPANION CONTRIBUTOR LESLIE BOW
WITH ASSISTANCE FROM AIMEE BROWN,
TOIYA KRISTEN FINLEY, AND LAURA VASSER

COFFEE HOUSE PRESS
MINNEAPOLIS

COPYRIGHT © 2003 by M. Evelina Galang
COVER ILLUSTRATION © Jordin Isip
COVER & BOOK DESIGN by Linda Koutsky

The rights to the individual works are held by each author, or their publisher. Permissions information and credits can be found in the back of this book.

Coffee House Press books are available to the trade through our primary distributor, Consortium Book Sales & Distribution, 1045 Westgate Drive, Saint Paul, MN 55114. For personal orders, catalogs, or other information, write to: Coffee House Press, 27 North Fourth Street, Suite 400, Minneapolis, MN 55401.

Coffee House Press is a nonprofit literary publishing house. Support from private foundations, corporate giving programs, government programs, and generous individuals help make the publication of our books possible. We gratefully acknowledge their support in detail in the back of this book.

LIBRARY OF CONGRESS CIP INFORMATION
Screaming monkeys : critiques of Asian American images / edited by M. Evelina Galang ; in collaboration with . . . [et al.].
p. cm.
ISBN-13 978-1-56689-141-7 (alk. paper)
ISBN-10 1-56689-141-8 (alk. paper)
1. American literature—Asian American authors. 2. American literature—Asian American authors—History and criticism. 3. Asian Americans—Literary collections. 4. Asian Americans—Intellectual life. 5. Asian Americans in literature. 6. Asian Americans. I. Galang, M. Evelina, 1961– II. Tabios, Eileen.

PS508.A8S37 2003
810.9'895—DC22   2003061251

10   9   8   7   6   5   4   3   2

Printed in Canada

Maraming Salamat sa Inyó

This anthology, this dialogue, would not have been possible without the help of many. First and foremost thanks to Ann Christenson who opened the conversation with her article, "Philing Station," and Manuel R. Galang for being the first to scream and pass the story on to the community.

Thanks too to *Milwaukee Magazine*'s John Fennell.

For Angelica Varona and her family. Maraming salamat sa inyó.

Special thanks to Eileen Tabios and Nick Carbó as well as poets and writers of FLIPS, a Filipino/Fil-Am listserv of writers who kept the dialogue flowing. Tabios and Carbó helped conceive this book in a fury of e-mails and wild conversations. FLIPS disseminated the story to our colleagues around the globe and got everybody writing.

A big loud shout—what am I saying—a SCREAM—to the contributing editors—Sunaina Maira, Anida Yoeu Esguerra, Jordin Isip, and Eileen Tabios. For their patience, devotion, and most of all their time.

To the found images and text crew that worked many hours gathering, processing, choosing, and delivering material to us. We couldn't use all of it, but you sure gave us plenty to choose from. Thanks to these behind-the-scenes researchers in Chicago: Anna Kong, Daphne Kwok, Gita Reddy, Mario Santos, Jr., Sean Butay, Aya Seko, Sophoan Kheun, Jay Monteverde. And to the lone researcher in Milwaukee, thank you, Miguel T. Galang.

Thanks to Leslie Bow for coming on board and sifting through the material to make sense of all this screaming. Your contribution is an awesome way to enter this text.

A special thank you to editorial assistants Toiya Kristen Finley, Aimee Brown, and Laura Vasser. You kept the monkeys from drowning. You kept the monkeys from chewing up their tales.

To all our contributors—thank God for your voices—beautiful and angry and forgiving and scholarly and visual and visionary, and so many other things I have not space to list—Thank God we are not all the same (no matter what they say).

To Coffee House Press—Maraming Salamat.

And to Jane Davis, Oliver de la Paz, and José F. Grave de Peralta who have heard the monkey scream—not always so prettily—but always with great passion.

Lastly, thanks to Miguel and Gloria Galang for teaching me the value of the voice—how to make it sing, how to make it scream!

MAKIBAKA!

MAKIBAKA!
*for our ancestors, our teachers, the land we call home,
and this divinity of Grace*

CONTENTS

MEN

WAR

TRANSCENDENCE

SCREAMING MONKEYS

APRIL 1998 $3.00

Milwaukee

Philing Station

FAVORITE find

A few words about Shorewood's unusual new deli.

"People don't know where the Philippines is," Angelica Varona tells a customer at deli **Mango Wango Tango**. We do know, silly. It's in this teeny storefront at 1808 E. Capitol Dr. The customer is looking away from the coconut and stuffed monkey (decorative touches) and tuning out the rambunctious little monkey (Varona's young son) flicking light switches on and off. It's a strange place, but let's give it the old college try. The customer is looking at an ube sponge cake (my God, it's purple!) made from dark yams and a cassava cake topped with beans and jackfruit. Yum, the sponge has a delicate crumb. Num, the cassava has a dense crumb.

"I'm making sweet rice boiled in banana leaves," Varona is saying. The leaves look like sheets of green paper and lie on a cutting board in the kitchen. A broom leans against the sink near some cans of mango juice. Entrées under the cold counter are wrapped in cellophane – a salady chicken/mango dish, meatballs in carrot sauce. A crêpe is folded between wax paper and dropped into a paper sack for the customer. "I just made them," she says proudly. "You put these vegetables inside [cabbage, carrots, string beans] and roll them up with garlic sauce. They're called lumpia." Thailanders coined a different term – spring roll. Apritada is American beef stew, and her pot of meat, potatoes and carrots in rice tastes standard. But she has plans for red snapper and squid like the scattered banana leaves. "Come back and tell me what you think," she calls, the boy hanging on her waist. Only if you promise to make dessert.

Kicking and Screaming

I was a foreigner in Iowa. My experience as an American, my perspective as a woman of Filipina descent, and the history of my ancestors—migrant workers who harvested the fields in California or factory workers in the canneries of Alaska, Navy cooks who went to war for America, and doctors who settled in places no other Anglo doctor would venture—my ancestors and their contributions to American history were foreign to most locals because they've never had access to this perspective.

In a community of mostly fifth, sixth, and seventh generation Dutch, Danes, and Germans, it was easy for a woman like myself to be seen as a foreigner long before I opened my mouth. I am a 5'-9" Pinay who was born in Pennsylvania, raised in Wisconsin, and is at home in the city of Chicago. So even after I spoke it was hard for some to believe I am American.

From 1999 through 2000, I served as an Assistant Professor of English/ Creative Writing at Iowa State University. During my first year, three senior faculty cornered me in the hall, grinning wildly. We were discussing some department politics and they wanted my opinion. My back was literally up against a wall when I asked them to back off. One of the professors folded her hands in prayer, stepped away, bowed to me, and said, "I'm sorry, but in my culture when we're listening to someone and we pay them respect, we look them in the eye." This full professor was born and raised in the South and had traveled to China on a Fulbright Scholarship. She should have known better—but there she was, bowing to me like I was some China doll from the "Orient."

Most Asian Pacific Island and Southeast Asian Americans living in the United States experience similar incidents of foreignness. During the early nineties, a Filipino American family moved from Illinois to Virginia. Because of the Navy base in Norfolk, the Tidewater area has the highest concentration of Filipino Americans on the East Coast. But the two youngest kids in a family of four—a sixteen-year-old boy and his younger sister—found themselves at a high school in Virginia Beach where they were among the only Filipino Americans. The teens didn't look too different than other kids in the early nineties—his head was shaved, maybe he had an earring. He wore baggy jeans and oversized shirts. She was a quiet girl, a baby sister with four brothers. In true Filipino style, she lived a well-chaperoned life. For a year, the principal would call the brother and sister into the office and interrogate them, "Tell me what gang you belong to. Don't lie. Tell me." When the boy left school the following year, administrators banned him from returning—he wasn't even allowed to pick his sister up. They told him they'd arrest him if they saw him. Meanwhile, the principal continued to bring the girl into the office, "What gang, come on—what gang do you belong to?" Neither kid belonged to a gang, and the interrogation was relentless. Eventually, the girl transferred out of that school. Graduated elsewhere.

And during the fall of 1998, students from the Filipino Student Association at Rutgers University requested a public service announcement for one of their events. In true Howard Stern fashion, co-hosts from WRNU's *The Little Mike and Dave Morning Show,* poked fun at the organization: "Filipino Student Ass—Student Ass . . . Filipino Student Ass . . . ho. Ah never mind if you're not Filipino don't bother," is how alumnus Adam Diaz remembers it. The co-hosts—Little Mike and Dave—were of African American and Korean American descent, but that didn't stop them from joking around. Diaz recalls that David—the d.j. of Korean descent—didn't think that Filipinos looked Asian, but half-Chinese and half-Mexican. *What's up with that,* he wanted to know.

When the Filipino Student Association called the d.j.'s on their remarks and filed complaints with university officials—an administration which consisted of three deans of African American descent—the administrators listened, nodded their heads, sentenced the disc jockeys and the radio station to diversity sensitivity training, but never held them to it. When the student organization persisted, somehow the tables turned and the culprits became the Filipino Student Association and its advisor, Adam Diaz. Eventually, Diaz was banned from campus and the student organization was forced to drop it. Diaz says the incident is a testimony to the double standards culture has when it comes to race issues. "If this had happened to a Black or Latino student group, you know it would have blown up . . . It goes to show how API (Asian Pacific Islanders) are not taken seriously, even when we speak out."

During my second year of teaching at ISU, I was featured in the English Department newsletter. The publication was meant for students, faculty, and staff, as well as Iowa State alumni, donors, and other university offices. For this issue I had been asked to provide materials for a short profile. I gave the grad student in charge my author press kit: a bio, a photo, an interview from *Pacific Enterprise Magazine,* an article from *Filipinas Magazine,* and two book reviews for my short story collection, *Her Wild American Self*—one from *The New York Times Book Review* and one from MS. Despite this information, the article states that I joined the "Literature and Creative Writing faculty, specializing in multicultural literature." I was hired to teach the writing of fiction. My Bachelor of Arts is in Radio-TV and Film, and my MFA in writing has a concentration in fiction, yet in this article, I had been redefined as the department's multiculturalist. Not only was I hired to teach the writing of fiction, but I didn't have the academic degrees that would have qualified me as a multiculturalist. The article assumed I was an expert in multicultural literature because—of what—the color of my skin? My black-and-white photo? In the profile, there was no mention of my true area of concentration, nor was there any mention of my publications or my book, the strongest evidence of my expertise. This stereotyping of faculty of color in academia happens more often than many of us would like to admit. The graduate student and the faculty advisor chose to ignore the facts of my hire, the focus of my research, and the information I submitted.

In a single paragraph my identity and my role at the university had been distorted, my professional credentials discounted, and I had become another example of what it means to be misrepresented because of the color of my skin. In the end, they wrote retractions, apologies, and corrections, and sent them out to some 3,000 newsletter recipients.

Part of the problem is that too much of our Western culture remains ignorant about the historical, cultural, and social realities of most Americans of Asian and Southeast Asian descent and so begin the faux pas. The "oops I didn't mean to insult you" conversations, the "I didn't know," and the "you speak good English" asides that come with the miseducation of American history—Asian American, African American, Indian American, Latino American—you know—American history.

Screaming Monkeys is born of such faux pas.

In April of 1998, my brother Manuel Galang, an attorney in Milwaukee, Wisconsin, sent me a copy of *Milwaukee Magazine*. There was a food review of a Filipino deli called Mango Wango Tango. The review, titled, "Philing Station: A few words about Shorewood's unusual new deli" by Ann Christenson, was to recommend or pan the food.

She began the piece this way:

> "'People don't know where the Philippines is,' Angelica Varona tells a customer at deli Mango Wango Tango. We do know, silly. It's in this teeny storefront at 1808 E. Capitol Dr. The customer is looking away from the coconut and stuffed monkey (decorative touches) and tuning out the rambunctious little monkey (Varona's young son) flicking light switches on and off. It's a strange place, but let's give it the old college try. The customer is looking at an ube sponge cake (my God, it's purple!) made from dark yams and a cassava cake topped with beans and jackfruit. Yum, the sponge cake has a delicate crumb. Num, the cassava has a dense crumb."

One could argue over the voice and tone of the article (condescending, objectifying, and exoticizing vs. cute, witty, and entertaining, for example), but what's clear, what's concrete is this: Christenson called a Filipino/African American child a monkey and this affront carried with it historical baggage, a racial slur first cast toward Filipinos by American soldiers during the

Spanish American War and then here in the States, when our first Filipino elders, U.S. nationals, arrived on the Northwest coast of America. The fact that the child was also black deepens the injury. Whether Christenson meant to make the racial slur or not isn't the point. The editors let it slip, and once it slipped from the pages of *Milwaukee Magazine* and into my computer, I sent it out to a number of listservs—FLIPS, a national list of Filipino American/Filipino writers, and KAPATID, a list of politically hungry Filipino American youth, and then I sent it to everyone I knew. And all those people sent the article out to their lists, lists that crossed borders reaching Canada, the Philippines, Europe, South America, and Australia. *Milwaukee Magazine* was bombarded via electronic mail and fax machines and snail mail. They must have gotten a history lesson that they never intended to receive.

Editor John Fennell e-mailed me his response on April 13, 1998:

> "Thank you for your letter. Obviously, had we been aware that we were going to offend, we would never have published the short piece on Mango Wango Tango in the form you saw. Ann Christenson is not a racist. She does try in her copy to reach beyond standard writing solutions. But obviously in this case, an attempt to create a visual impression of what she saw led to misinterpretation by Filipino Americans who read the piece on an internet site."

So first, Fennell apologizes, and then in the same missive he attempts to quell the dispersal of the piece with a subtle threat, thereby stripping all the sincerity out of his apology. He implies that the reproduction of the article, read by readers beyond their subscribers was illegal:

> "I'm not sure if the person responsible for putting up our review on the Internet is aware of this, but it is illegal to republish copyrighted material in any venue (print or electronic) without permission. As we plan to be more sensitive about our cultural references, I trust whoever is republishing this material will realize they are breaking the law and will take corrective action, as we will do in future cultural references."

But the truth is, the Fair Use Act, which covers not only the discourse back in 1998, but the discourse throughout this anthology, allows us to read, reproduce, and comment on works for the specific intent to educate, to provide social commentary, and to react in order to set things straight. *Screaming Monkeys* would like to contribute to the dialogue.

We would like to help set things straight.

Fennell's apology/threat only served to anger Filipino Americans further. And when an apology of sorts—vague and dismissive—was buried on page 12 of the May 1998 issue of *Milwaukee Magazine*, the community across borders and now across ethnic backgrounds came out kicking and screaming. The editors had an opportunity to use the incident as way of not only apologizing for the remark, but also educating its readers by explaining why Filipino Americans "misinterpreted" Christenson's remark. But Fennell didn't even name the article, "Philing Station," he referred to it by its section's name, "Favorite Finds." He wrote that the magazine, "unintentionally made a racially insensitive reference about a local food shop," not that they cast a racial slur with a historically based context—calling Filipinos monkeys—against the owner's son (not the food shop). So if you didn't read the article, you'd have no idea what he was talking about. And if you did read the article, and you didn't know the historical context of the remark, you'd think that some people were just being too sensitive.

The community's anger grew. The letters kept coming. Filipino Americans from the Milwaukee community met with Fennell, hoping to get not only a more sincere apology in the June issue of *Milwaukee Magazine*, but to also have pages devoted to an explanation of that historical context and a representation of the numerous letters they had received. Because the June issue was committed to covering the summer activities in Milwaukee, Fennell did not address the matter in their June issue.

In July of 1998, Fennell finally published a longer version of his apology, never really saying sorry the magazine called the child a monkey, never really educating the readers about the historical context of what it means to call a Filipino a monkey. They did, however, publish excerpts (milder versions) of the letters sent to them. Some of these are included here as found articles. A selection of missives can also be found here under the title, "Scream Monkeys, Scream."

Still, for many of us in the Filipino American and Asian American community, it hardly seemed right. Though seemingly a small incident, relative to the greater historical injustices against Asian Americans, this matter posed its own significance we could not so easily dismiss. Poet Eileen Tabios and I had a furious exchange of e-mails debating the issue. In the end, we concluded that the reason things like this happen is because our history books— and I mean our American history books—do not cover this, our Asian American history—the atrocities, the accomplishments, the contributions, the acknowledgment that we are a part of this America, not visitors, not ghosts, not foreigners, not monkeys. While there has been groundbreaking work written on the history of Asians in America, most of that work has an elite audience, students who specifically seek Asian American Studies, but these lessons, integral to the development of America are still mostly omitted in our American history books, our courses and our records. What if Ann Christenson had studied the history of the first wave of Filipino U.S.

Nationals? What if her editors at *Milwaukee Magazine* had been as familiar with the history of Asian immigrants in America as they are with the history of immigrants on the *Mayflower?* Someone would have seen the mistake, caught it, erased it, and never let it see the printed page. As it turns out, not only did the writer and editors of *Milwaukee Magazine* let the racial slur run, they didn't fix the problem, they didn't explain.

We decided to use this event in our recent history as a leaping point, as a place to begin an exploration of Asian image in America. We convinced writer/editor Sunaina Maira to join us, to help us gather the fiction, nonfiction, and poetry that speaks to the representation of our collective communities. Creating *Screaming Monkeys* meant going beyond the traditional anthology. We wanted to look at the facts, the evidence that documents the way America knows us, the way America presents us, and in some cases refuses to look at us. So we looked not only to our history, but to mass media—to headlines and articles and advertisements. We wanted to see how we, as a community, render our images, how the assault of racial profiling, of innocuous exotification, and of stereotyping us as "model minorities" has affected the way Asian Americans cast their own identities. We asked graphic designers Anida Esguerra and Jordin Isip to join our team of editors. Anida Esguerra—whose last name in Tagalog means *war*—gathered a small crew of researchers and they found images and articles that speak to our past, and to our current presence in the media. Jordin Isip—his Tagalog last name means *thought*—has brought the visual images of how Asians and Southeast Asians see themselves and the way they see America portraying their people.

Finally, once we compiled the manuscript, we sent it off to scholar Leslie Bow at the University of Wisconsin-Madison where she is a professor of Asian American Studies, and she read through the book to cull questions, themes, and exercises to guide readers, educators, and students through the text and images of *Screaming Monkeys*.

Our goal was not only to document negative or positive representations of Asians in America, our goal was to seek any or all representations, to find out what is out there. Because this book is only a book, we were not able to use all the material we found, we were not able to speak to all the cultures of Asia America, but we tried to cast a range of perspectives in our disparate collective. Not only was our mission to record the images, but it was to begin the gathering of our histories in America. And the collection of words, of stories, of images here forces us—editors, artists, and readers—to make the fine distinctions between the reality, the stereotype, and the racism. We were not only interested in the way the dominant culture sees Asia America, we were wondering how much of our reality is a direct result of how the West adopts us, appropriates us, denies and revises who we are. And that is why *Screaming Monkeys* explores not only the external faces we have been assigned, but also documents historical events, statistics, and political histories—evidence of how we got here, how we've survived, and how far we have to go despite the railroads, the internment camps, the constant allegations—spies, traitors, mongrels, savages, eternal foreigners.

The book also examines our own tendency to rely on stereotypes, prejudice, and self-loathing because it is inevitable that no matter how strong the resistance, how high the pitch of the scream, or the desire to rise above the hate, we too can become infected by the misinterpretations, the anger, the distrust, the very denial of our existence as a viable, visible community of American citizens. As I explore these issues in my own life, feeling alienated and out of place in the middle of America, I see that in order to get to the other side, a place of reason, or analysis and understanding, we must—along with the rest of America—go through this painful process—all of us, especially people of color. And part of this process is primal, a scream so loud, so pure, so full of wretched agony the screaming leaves us weak. We have to be willing to look at what's ugly, what's painful, what's positive too. We have to be willing to let the anger dwell, erupt, and leave our bodies. This issue, like all issues that have to do with the marginalization, dehumanization, and elimination of a community are volatile and affect not only our minds, but the hands, the feet, the very core that houses our spirits. If you ignore the need to scream, then how do you go on?

So the book gives us permission to say what cannot be said, hasn't been said, and to use what has wronged us as a tool of activism, an opportunity to educate, a way to initiate discussion, and, we're hoping, a way to contribute to the act of change.

As I studied the different contributions to the anthology, I began to see a pattern in the way certain genres attack, explore, deconstruct, and re-define the image of the Asian American collective. Found images, found articles, and statistics act as hard evidence and a way of tracking not only a historical presence but a skewed identity of what it means to be American and more importantly, what it means to be an American of Asian descent.

The nonfiction essays deconstruct many of the images found in *Screaming Monkeys* while the stories and poems are ways of entering the interior lives of our collective experience. Even the artwork in the book serves a role that poems, stories, and articles cannot fill. They are the abstract response to traditional stereotypes and expectations Western culture has stamped across our foreheads.

Esguerra and her team of researchers looked into the archives of old libraries and historical museums, digging up not only historical misrepresentations of Asians in America, but present-day distortions too. Esguerra and the found images crew revealed that some things are not changing. For example, we took to reading walls, graffiti screaming anti-Asian sentiment.

In 1930, a photographer in California shot a picture of a wall upon which someone had scribbled, "WORK NO FILIPINOS OR WE'LL DESTROY YOUR CROP AND YOU TOO." The remark comes from a time in history when Pinoy laborers worked the fields in California. The comment attacks not only Filipinos, but those who supported them. Sixty-nine years later, the same anger is directed to Korean Americans on the other side of the country. In 1999 a photographer captured "NO MORE KOREANS!" on a wall in Palisades Park, New Jersey. In both photos, one can see the rage in the hand that's written these cries—irregular capital letters, etched, and angry. To look at these walls, you'd think nothing has changed.

Some things have. Slowly things are changing. You can see the difference by the way our American presidents cast their gaze upon us. After the Spanish American War, President McKinley stayed up half the night wondering what to do with the Philippines and the natives on those seven thousand islands. In this passage, he tells the world about how he got down on his hands and knees, waiting for God to answer his prayers. The answer came to him, civilize and Christianize the Filipino, (forget about the 300 years of Catholicism that came with the Spanish), tame that savage. This sentiment is a far cry from President Clinton's initiative on Asian Americans. On April 14, 2000, he honored the loss of Filipino American postal worker Joseph Ileto who was shot dead because of his color. Clinton's statement reads:

> "During the last year, we have all been shaken by violent acts like the murder of Joseph Ileto, acts that strike at the very values that define us as a nation. Now is the time for us to take strong and decisive action to fight hate crimes, and I call on Congress, at long last, to pass strong hate crimes legislation. It is time for us all to raise our voices against intolerance and to build the One America that our hearts tell us we can be."

As the population of Asians in America grows and second, third, and fourth generations are coming into their own, we found the communities have begun to fight back. Asian Americans are no longer letting the insults go. They are calling America to be responsible for their words and for their depictions of the underrepresented. Consider the Skyy Vodka ad where a beautiful blonde lies with an arm outstretched, waiting for her handmaid, a sexy Asian woman in a traditional Chinese dress—only shorter and tighter—to pour her another. In response to the ad, *Gidra*, a magazine out of Los Angeles, depicts the same Asian woman dousing a bottle of vodka onto the blonde.

As these found images reveal America's perspectives, scholars and writers in *Screaming Monkeys* are responding through the deconstruction of this evidence. These essays, analytical and theoretical discussions of representation, are grounded in the historical, political, and economic reading of the way Asians are assigned specific roles. What's interesting is that much of what America knows of Asian Americans is not drawn from fact or history, but through assumptions made from movies, ads, and the violence portrayed in the media. So Helen Zia's chapter, "Surrogate Slaves to American Dreamers," acts as a reality check for all of us, as she calls us to hear the political history of many Asian immigrant groups. Through the documentation of this history she begins to deconstruct some of the unspoken realities for many Asian Americans. Many of the essays look to history and to a survey of historical evidence to ground the reader and challenge our expectations, pointing out what has not been said, what has not been considered.

But the fiction attacks the matter from a different gaze. Much of the fiction in *Screaming Monkeys* critiques the desire for Asian Americans to lighten up and whiten up. Perhaps fiction allows us to paint the ugliness that we might otherwise avoid. Whether or not Lois-Ann Yamanaka wants to marry a Haole is beside the point. The point is that her character Livvy does, and it is the exploration of Livvy's voice and Livvy's desire to make a better life for herself by discarding her ethnicity through marriage—specifically the name she calls herself—that we are able to explore the way our youth respond to the pressures of being American. Through Livvy's story we are able to see the effects of the pressure to fit in, to be "American" and to lose the culture of our immigrant ancestors. Fiction can bring us to the places we won't go on our own, or can't go, or perhaps we are too ashamed to go without a guide, a character who may be a composite of our various realities.

The poetry in *Screaming Monkeys* works in many of the ways fiction does, bringing us to places that are too difficult to attend otherwise. This screaming, stylized and primal, works on the levels of subtext and language. The voices are sophisticated cries, shadows of innuendo and abstractions, some of the voices are loud and angry and accusatory while others record their protest and illuminate their ideas through lyrical lines and visceral images. These poems are examples of our most primal scream. Here the artists' voices are wide and play on every emotion—anger, rage, sarcasm, sadness, and humor.

When Li-Young Lee responds to Ralph Waldo Emerson's statement that Chinese are " . . . not even as good as the Africans, who are at least willing to carry our fine wood. They have no culture to speak of, no music, no literature . . ." by cleaving Emerson's head and devouring it, he demonstrates through the most visceral and violent sarcastic response the dehumanization of a people and the anger that accompanies these moments. The screaming that occurs in the poetry of this anthology is the result of hundreds of years of silence. If we do not let the scream resound, what happens to the body? Where will it surface if not in lines like these, where Li-Young Lee exacts revenge, eating "Emerson, his transparent soul, his soporific transcendence." The way the artists respond to misrepresentations and accusations is as fractured and layered as the Asian American collective's definitions are of culture, of religion, of family, and the roles men and women are expected to play out. The artwork in *Screaming Monkeys* is perhaps the most abstract, the voice that is deepest inside us that has the longest route to travel before it can be heard. When Coffee House editor Allan Kornblum and I looked through the collection of artwork Jordin Isip gathered, we considered going through each piece and writing about it. But as I continued to work on this anthology and as I have been living a life among a people who continue to see my perspective as alien and sometimes imagined ("Sometimes I think you exaggerate this race thing," said a poet, a nice woman, a Southerner.), I realized that no amount of explaining will help the situation. What we need to do is let the piece exist and to study each one and weigh one against the other. So what does Kimura mean when he rests a giant fly on a map of America, wings spread fat across the East and West Coast, insect belly hovering just above the heartland? Weigh the image against Claire Dane's remarks about the Philippines, "The place just fucking smelled of cockroaches . . ." or baseball player John Rocker's statement in *Sports Illustrated:* ". . . the biggest thing I don't like about New York are the foreigners. You can walk an entire block in Times Square and not hear anybody speaking English. Asians and Koreans and Vietnamese and Indians and Russians and Spanish people, everything up there. How the hell did they get in this country?" Against the other pieces of evidence in the book, the image of the fly, the dirty garbage-dwelling-fly, takes on meaning. In the end, the art is the documentation of each of these artists, and no one can really translate their meaning—not the art editor, Jordin Isip, not me, not anyone, except the one who is viewing the piece at the moment. Each reader brings with him or her the understanding of experience and his or her understanding of Asian American culture (as if there's only one). And if that is not enough, there are the examples within the binding of this book that may guide the reader gently, gently guiding but not explaining the position and juxtaposition of the images, stories, and facts. Perhaps the artwork is the most difficult to translate, and yet it's as visceral as the pounding of a fist against a mattress, against a wall, through a glass window.

I know a rhetorician—white, male, and gay—who is earnest in his pursuit of understanding the differences between race, gender, and sexual orientation. He thinks he wants to know, but there are times the discussions become too much like an anthropological dig, where he treats people of color like specimens under a light and comments like, "There's no real negative connotation with being Asian in America," make me snap. The anger flies out of my mouth so fast, the words are an attack. He doesn't mean anything insulting by his comments, I know that, but the point is that this issue is not purely an intellectual discussion, it is an issue close to the bone, integral to many of our lives. So I snap and often he resents not only my emotional response, but the answer to his questions. There are two ways to survive this discussion: ignore it or deal with it. I could suppress my response, or allow it to exist. Scream. And after the scream, evaluate. Perhaps this is why this discussion of history and race is often passed over—the emotions are too volatile, too closely connected to the heart, too messy, and no one wants to be shouted at, no one wants to say the wrong thing, no one wants to be the bad guy. To move forward, to be honest, means to risk hearing answers that make us feel uncomfortable. Sometimes the answers are angry.

In the end, the struggle here is not between us (Asian Americans) and them (dominant mainstream culture). And the book is not an attempt to define Asia America because one of the truths is that we come from too many places in Asia to have one face, one experience and certainly one identity. The nature of Asia America is a fractured one full of complexity, contradictions, and cultural differences, differences that come with our various mother countries, our disparate histories, our changing priorities. It is as if our identities have been tied up too neatly under this umbrella we've been given, this Asian American umbrella we have been asked to huddle under. The conflict in this book is an internal struggle as America continues to work through her own identity issues. As I've worked with the youth of Asian American communities in Norfolk, Chicago, in pockets of California, and Ames, Iowa, one thing is clear: the struggle starts within each of us. Then comes the struggle that is not often explored, the struggle that comes between the generations and the confrontations of one Asian American community against another. Finally there is the struggle of Asia America and the American community at large. This book is about all of this. We are all struggling to define this identity, this America that has been built not by some of us but by all of us.

You will see some images in this book and you will think—how obvious is that—how could anyone in this day and age call the marriage between a white woman and a Filipino man a case of bestiality? And then there are some things you will look at and think—what's wrong with that? So last year's fashion trends were influenced by India. Why isn't that good? How do you know when it's not cool? Who draws the lines? What makes the offense? There's no concrete answer and it's not for me or the co-editors to decide. We are not experts, teaching some sort of Truth. But what we can do is record the stories, document the faces America renders of our brown and yellow brothers and sisters. We've invited everyone to participate, so the works come from writers and artists of various backgrounds—writers of prominence, writers in mid-career,—and writers who are fresh, but well on the way. You'll find works from Arthur Sze, Mei-mei Berssenbrugge, Maxine Hong Kingston, Jessica Hagedorn, Bienvenido Santos, Nick Carbó, Geeta Kothari, Bino A. Realuyo, Vijay Prashad, and Eugenio Matibag, Luba Halicki, Jon

Pineda, Oliver de la Paz, Dennis Sangmin Kim, and others. Some of our writers contribute their pieces from other rooms in the house, other perspectives—Molly McQuade and Denise Duhamel for example. This book is a community of writers, artists, and scholars, coming from our fractured American experience, working to educate, to explore, to respond, and learn. The making of this book is a testimony to community, not possible without the contributions of Ann Christenson and *Milwaukee Magazine*. Had Manuel Galang not felt a responsibility to bring the article to our attention, this anthology would not exist. "Philing Station" was a wake-up call to all of us. And *Screaming Monkeys* is the response, hopefully a beginning. We wanted to see how far we've come and how far behind we truly are. And after we show you this evidence—everything from the poems on transformation, to the images of Madonna's subservient geisha, to the histories of violence against Asians in America—after all this, it will be up to the reader. The reader who listens to the voices, whispering, sighing, chanting, and shouting from the pages of *Screaming Monkeys* will be the one to begin the critical process of defining differences and nuances. After reading this anthology, which will hopefully encourage you to continue your research of the missing American histories—my hope is that understanding will begin. Perhaps by considering the evidence and weighing that evidence against a traditional Anglo American education, people will start to see for themselves the effect untold history has on America. How should we react to those who commit crimes against our hearts and bodies—willingly and unknowingly? I'm hoping you hear the voices and let your bodies react, let your hearts follow, and maybe then there will come some clarity.

There are historians, elders in our community, who have been building a record of evidence, who speak to the presence of Asians in America—isn't it time to incorporate these stories into the larger autobiography that is America? The history present in this book is a smattering of our lives, there isn't room to document even a tenth of what has never been told, what has been ignored, what has been flat-out omitted. Even so, this book is a place to begin the process of change. We have to be willing to confront the ugliness that has been a part of the history, the anger, the acts of violence, and the innocence of ignorance. We have to be willing to be uncomfortable. We must take a deep breath and dive right into it before we can begin to understand, to come into our own, kicking and screaming all the way.

M. Evelina Galang, editor
January 17, 2003
Miami, Florida, USA

Letters and Found Images from Milwaukee Magazine

An apology: In "Favorite Finds" in the April issue of Milwaukee Magazine, *we unintentionally made a racially insensitive reference about a local food shop. We would like to extend our sincere apology to the owner of that establishment, Angelica Varona, to her family and to any reader we offended because of our carelessness. Although there was no malice meant, we should have been more sensitive and regret our error. – The Editors*

Milwaukee Magazine, apology from the editors, May 1998

LETTER FROM THE EDITOR

In the April issue of Milwaukee Magazine, *we published in "Favorite Finds" a short review of Shorewood deli Mango Wango Tango under the title "Philing Station." In describing the deli, reviewer Ann Christenson referred to a decorative stuffed monkey in the shop and carried the metaphor further by referring to the owner's son in a way meant to show his active nature.*

Subsequently, the review was distributed via the Internet and many readers, concerned by that comment and other references they felt were derogatory, sent e-mail responses or responded to other e-mails. A selection of those letters is published here. Though it was unintentional, the review offended many people, and in the May issue we apologized. These letters serve as a reminder that ethnic heritage is a very sensitive issue – one that calls for discussion and understanding.

John Fennell, Editor

July 1998

FOOD AND CULTURE CLASH

Even if you aren't aware of where the Philippines is, you should probably know that the complexities, culture, economics and politics of any country cannot be confined to a "teeny storefront window." That sort of condescension only proliferates narrow-minded racist perspective.

Even if you aren't aware of the historical racist remark you have allowed in naming the young Filipino boy in your article a "rambunctious monkey," please be aware that out of respect for any persons, it's wise to refrain from calling them monkeys, pigs, rats... you get the picture.

People from Thailand are not "Thailanders," they are Thai. Fresh lumpia is not the same thing as spring rolls, which, by the way, are actually po peo. Spring roll is a Western translation created to appease mainstream America.

Apritada is not an American beef stew, though it may resemble it. Apritada has its roots in Spain (hence the Spanish name for the dish) and the conquistadors who first took the islands hundreds of years ago.

Filipino Americans are the largest Asian-American population in the United States today. The first Filipinos came to America as U.S. nationals when, 50 years ago, U.S. troops landed and occupied the Philippines. Maybe you don't know about it because this act contradicts America's philosophy of independence, of democracy, and our history books are too embarrassed to teach this history....

M. Evelina Galang
Chicago, IL

...How could *anyone* not realize that calling a child a monkey... would be offensive.... Granted, Ms. Christenson was probably not aware of the historical basis of this racist remark... (Filipinos were referred to as "monkeys without tails" by American soldiers sent to the Philippines during World War II), but it was an ignorant remark nonetheless....

Marlo Tingzon Tan
Alachua, FL

...It's obvious the author didn't have any malicious feelings toward the proprietor... or her son – she's just a little unworldly and ignorant. There are worse crimes – but come on.... Editorial should have caught that....

Eleanor Reagh
San Francisco, CA

...It's articles like this that keep me from believing my culture is being accepted here in a country supposedly meant for *all* cultures.... It may be the case that [it] was meant to be a term of endearment, but read between the lines, it can be misunderstood....

Lisa Madrinan
University Park, PA

...I am not offended at any remarks nor feel there were racial overtones. In fact, [the review] made me hungry!...

How many times have we called children little whatevers? I called... [owner] Angelica Varona [and asked] if she was offended by Ms. Christenson calling her son a little monkey. She said she was concerned, but it did not offend her. She went on to say there are bigger things to talk about or to be concerned about than that statement....

She, along with other Filipino entrepreneurs, have my respect and admiration for facing the challenges of bringing a little taste of home to the States. I look forward to my little trip up I-94....

Rey A. Requiron
Chicago, IL

...It is the responsibility of [the] editorial staff to ensure that articles are written with a specific goal or objective in mind. [Here,] the objective... was to provide a critique on... Mango Wango Tango. To have laced the article with racially insensitive and offensive remarks clearly did not meet that objective. It is even more troubling to think this occurred in... Milwaukee, home to many prominent Filipino Americans....

Philippine Medical Association of
Wisconsin Auxiliary, New Berlin

...If the food's no good, say so. If the place is not clean (is that what the broom reference suggests?), criticize it. The problem is not negativity but ethnic/racial condescension. The problem is not cuteness but an author unaware that other cultures are not, by virtue of their difference from U.S. culture, cute.

Mary Beth Gallagher
St. Louis, MO

While I realize from the way [the article] is written that the author clearly had no idea that the content and assumptions presented are offensive, it is important that you know that for many of us, it is offensive.

> Cyndi Harris
> St. Louis, MO

In all the years I have read your magazine, I do not recall any mention of the Philippines, Filipino Americans or our culture.... I understand that the magazine's focus is local in nature. However, Filipino Americans have a strong social, cultural, academic and professional presence in Milwaukee.... It is unfortunate... that the first reference I have seen is condescending and derogatory. When you write about a country and culture your magazine knows nothing about, there is a higher risk of writing something offensive....

> Manuel R. Galang
> Milwaukee

...Is this supposed to be a food review?... [Christenson]... makes no effort to educate your readers, who, by the way, might *really* be interested in knowing about the cultural influences of Filipino food (Malaysian, Chinese, Muslim, American, Spanish).... Such ignorance... does not do Ms. Varona's store any service whatsoever except to let readers know that an "ube sponge cake" is "purple...."

> Reynila Calderon-Magbuhat
> San Diego, CA

...What a shame that after all these years of hard work by leaders like Martin Luther King... writers still remain ignorant to racial slurs.... Did you not know Filipinos were in this country since the 16th century, before this land became the United States? Did you not know that Filipino veterans who served for this country during World War II have been fighting for citizenship until now?...

I urge you and your writers to invest wisely in more detail history of all people of color.

> Steven A. Yagyagan
> San Diego, CA

...I am an immigrant and I want to say that I do not find the article racist at all. *There is nothing wrong with the article!* Don't ever feel you have brought the Filipino community down.... You have my support if you ever decide to write a follow-up article when [owner Angelica] Varona invites the writer back with the ready dessert!

As I told the [Internet] group, my "little monkey" gives me the worst of headaches as he romps and runs around our place!

> Joel Melgarejo
> Bakersfield, CA

...The Filipino culture is rich, diverse and deeply spiritual. Filipinos have made major contributions to this culture.... This article treats this tradition as "strange" and "little." What is strange and small is Christenson's ability to find words that honor and respect another culture.

> The Rev. Dr. Martin J. Rafanan
> National Conference for Community
> and Justice, St. Louis, MO

...I think your writer was not alert... [that she] sounded condescending and provincial. Did she think the food was going to bite back? Did she like it? It is hard to tell....

> Kim Persson
> Denville, NJ

...I know that there is a fine line... between making a good joke and making someone wince in pain, but I hope that, especially regarding jokes that could be considered racist, you will consider their far-reaching impact. As editors, you have an important role in setting the standard for what people may regard as acceptable things to say and write....

> Sue H. Kim
> Bloomington, IN

...No matter how [Christenson] tried to adapt a flippant style,... the condescending piece oozed with malice and racism. After all, the little boy (of Filipino/African-American descent) had nothing to do with the food.... Your magazine has not only insulted Ms. Varona's family but has likewise belittled the Filipino and African-American communities....

> B.J. Agoncillo-Ramos,
> Editor, *Bulalakaw*, Greendale

Scream Monkeys, Scream!

A sampling of electronic missives from the Filipino-American community to *Milwaukee Magazine*

April 11, 1998
Dear Ms. Christenson:

Your article, "Philing Station" has come to my attention. I live in New York City, where a good number of "monkeys" live and breed, except here we have iron tails, so that articles like yours with racist tones will not go unnoticed. No, you don't know where the Philippines is, silly. Because if you did, you'd probably be aware that this is the 100th anniversary of our first encounter during the Spanish-American war. Because if you did, you would probably understand that in those 100 years, your so called monkeys have come and lived in the United States, cooked Apritada and lumpia to your people's delight, amid the unforgiving racial tension that has been our history from that time MacArthur landed on our war-stricken soil. (Lucky you, you weren't the first one to call us monkeys—there were others who thought we lived in trees). Good that you don't live here, silly. Because if you did, and not in your little suburbia decorated with your magnificent taste for the exotic and unparalleled condescension, there would be a protest outside your little home, with all kinds of monkeys that would enter your limited imagination: ube-eating monkeys, politically-driven monkeys, monkeys who run for office, monkeys who hold offices, monkeys who run many many lumpia selling stores, medical monkeys and literary monkeys who love to write with their iron tails and all of us monkeys who are so tired of being referred to as such.

And no, silly, you WISH you knew where the Philippines is.

Bino A. Realuyo
a monkey from New York

* * *

Date: Sun, 12 Apr 1998
Salutations Ms. Christenson,

I really dug your piece on exotic Philippines foods. Being a second generation Filipino American myself, I also enjoy swinging through a rainforest in my spare time, hurling spears at wild boar while boiling American tourists and explorers in a big, black cauldron.

With all due respect, please be more cautious in your language. No one can afford to think or write the way you do these days.

And, as an L.A. County resident, I always say this to folks who have problems with Filipinos living in the U.S.: If you're not comfortable with us living in the country which we've helped build over the last 400 years (we've been here since 1587, by the way), YOU HAVE THE POWER AND THE RIGHT TO MOVE THE HELL OUT OF AMERICA. (This isn't directed at you, per se, it's just FOOD for thought)

Silly me, Allan G. Aquino
North Hills, CA

* * *

Mon, 13 Apr 1998 17:11:40
Dear Editors of *Milwaukee Magazine* and Ms. Christenson:

As a writer of my own publication, I understand how important it is to voice out concerns and make those opinions available to those who may not have access to them. Even if they are controversial.

However, I am not writing to you to identify with your publication and your practices; but to let you know that as the widely distributed magazine that you are, it is your responsibility not only to be factually accurate (let's bring up Ms. Christenson's skewed view that young Filipino children are "monkeys"), but to also disallow perpetuating racist assumptions that people of color, in this instance, Filipinos, have been fighting against for years.

16

I am not going to bother with a history lesson on the Filipino culture, that is not my responsibility. That is something *Milwaukee Magazine* needs to address on its own time.

But I would like to make some things clear:

- Filipino-Americans, and other people of color, are not monkeys;
- keep in mind that many of us were born in the US, are part of American culture, and have been for years;
- the term "exotic" should be strictly used for rugs (although not a term overtly used in the article, it is quite clear from Ms. Christenson's use of words at discovering the "strange place" at the "teeny storefront at 1808 E. Capitol Drive" to the "My God! It's purple!" sponge cake);
- your writers need to get out more and realize that there is life past White suburbia and a tiny store that supposedly represents all of the 7,000+ Philippine Islands;
- we are past the time of Margaret Mead and the examining of "savage cultures" as "a find," and I am hoping the *Milwaukee Magazine* will recognize that movement.

If I sound somewhat dissatisfied with the approach of the above article, I am. As an Asian-American woman who is fighting to create and validate her own space in this racist land of America, it is hard enough when hitting the glass ceiling at work, much less uncovering tiny articles that perpetuate the "exotic accommodating island savage" stereotype of Filipinos, and the rich White suburbia that patronizes them in their effort to appear cultured.

Ms. Christenson may not have intended to offend; however, her ignorance has. It is frightening to know that the Editors of *Milwaukee Magazine* and Ms. Christenson herself are so clueless as to the article's inherent racist undertones.

I do hope your future articles will be more responsible. Otherwise, you may find more than just a few "monkeys" on your back. Just a little something to think

about from my part of the jungle.
Margarita Alcantara-Tan
Editor/Producer, *Bamboo Girl*
* * *

Date: Mon, 13 Apr 1998
After reading your article "Philing Station," I'm finding it very difficult to refrain from screaming like a monkey—call it an internal struggle between my Caucasian (condescension?) genes and my Filipino (Vine-swinging tendencies) genes. My father was born and raised in the Philippines (some squat dump of land in some ocean, I don't know. Forget about it.), and after he mastered the art of picking fleas and vermin off of my little brown relatives, he decided to try his luck in the U.S., opening "de-lousing stations" throughout many of the northern states.

Unfortunately for you, his enterprise never made it to Wisconsin. I wish it had, then maybe he could have offered you all his services, not to mention receiving an intelligent and responsible "write up" in the process. Am I being "silly"?

Just another monkey,
Jon Marcelino Pineda
* * *

Date: Tue, 14 Apr 1998
Dear Mr. Fennell:
One word: BOYCOTT!
Second: Just where is the misinterpretation in this passage from the *Milwaukee Magazine*, April issue?

"The customer is looking away from the coconut and stuffed monkey (decorative touches) and tuning out the rambunctious little monkey (Varona's young son) flicking light switches on and off."

It's a factual description of events in the store where your Food Section writer describes the Filipina woman's son as a MONKEY! There are no sophisticated literary devices such as metaphor, simile, metonymy, synecdoche, or even hyperbole. It's a stated fact, the boy is called MONKEY. What do you not understand?

Third: In your defense of the article and the magazine you indicate that the Filipina store/deli owner may not be necessarily offended by the article and she is indeed "very pleased" with the story.

"Though we obviously offended some people, it's curious that the owner of the Mango Tango Wango called to thank us for our coverage. She was very pleased with the story. However, we would like to apologize to anyone we did offend."

Is this an attempt to absolve yourselves of the offense to "some people" by claiming the principal referent was not offended by the story? Did you or any of your staff point out the above passage to Ms. Varona where your writer called her son a "monkey?" Did you apologize to her and her son? If not, you and your staff have not been honest and the sincerity of your apology is very suspect. To claim that Ms. Varona was happy with the story carries with it the implication that she was also happy that your magazine called her son a monkey. Is this a misinterpretation of your words, Mr. Fennell? Or did you really mean to insult us (the Filipino American community) further by implying a collusion in such an insidious act?

Fourth: This veiled threat at legal retaliation for the "posters" of the article in the internet completely negates the sincerity of your apology and proves that you still feel there is something to be proud about the article, its authorship, and its intellectual ownership. Is this your half-hearted attempt at "damage control" and media spin? Are you trying to censor some people's freedom of speech and the right to access and receive information by this statement?: "I'm not sure if the person responsible for putting up our review on the internet is aware of this, but it is illegal to re-publish copyrighted material in any venue (print or electronic) without permission. As we plan to be more sensitive about our cultural references, I trust whoever is republishing this material will realize they are breaking the law and will take corrective action, as we will do in future cultural references."

Lastly: You will have to prosecute millions of Filipino Americans and Filipinos living in the Philippines for "republishing" this material because we have copied your magazine's article and exponentially sent it to everyone who is confronting racist remarks, racist magazine articles, and racist thinking. Because of your magazine's racist reference to a Filipino boy as a "monkey" and your dishonest and unsatisfactory apology: WE ARE BOYCOTTING MILWAUKEE MAGAZINE! Millions of us!

Sincerely,
Nick Carbó

∗ ∗ ∗

Date: Tue, 14 Apr 1998
Dear Mr. Fennel:

I was extremely disappointed by your response to Ms. Galang's letter and am appalled by the undisguised act of intimidation your response conveyed. Allow me to inform you that the said article was quoted in a list serve (not a web site) which is sent to a number of Filipinos in the United States, Europe, South Africa, and the Philippines. As far as I know, there is no legal infraction involved in quoting a story particularly if it is for the purpose of discussion on the Internet, which obviously your story warranted. Allow me also to say that I feel it is unfortunate when editors themselves threaten to quell open discussion specially of a subject as clearly racist as the story your paper ran. The article contained a racial slur, Mr. Fennell, make no mistake about that. And no amount of intimidation will stop the protests that you have obviously brought upon yourselves.

Eric Gamalinda
New York City

∗ ∗ ∗

Date: Tue, 14 Apr 1998

I want to thank you for reinforcing my continuing awareness towards the arrogance, insensitivity and selective ignorance of those who dispense so casually the written word. You and your editors belong to a tribe of writers who cannot inspire and therefore make it your vocation to depress the national psyche with your insidious stories in the guise of light journalism.

You contribute to violence-building in small and sure ways. Good work! You wake up sleeping vengeance and wreak havoc so casually on generations who are born here and build their lives here. What lessons have you learned from the debilitating effect you and your kind have engendered on past minorities of a different color who are not your prosperous kind? And if you haven't—when will your time come?

Your power with the written word is contributing to the rise in small thinking, mediocre attitudes, narrow mindedness. No one learns from you. All imbibe your poison and you wonder why the reaction to your piece!

If you can't write without putting down people, put down your pen! Don't even wash dishes, just take the dog for a long, long walk and digest why your masterpiece rubbed this people the wrong way.

Reme Grefalda,
A proud Filipino in
Washington, D.C.

* * *

Date: Wed, 15 Apr 1998

What a shame that in today's day and age, a publisher will print such insensitivity to Filipino Americans. What a shame that a writer like Christenson will refer to a Filipino American child as "a little monkey." What a shame that after all these years of hard work by leaders like Martin Luther King, who fought for civil rights, writers still remain ignorant to racial slurs.

Did you not know that Filipinos and Filipino Americans were called "little brown monkeys" in the past just as blacks were referred to as "niggers?" Did you not know that racism is up 20% according to CNN last month. Did you not know that Filipinos were in this country since the 16th century, before this land became the United States? Did you not know that 10th and 11th generation Filipino Americans live in the Bayous of Louisiana? Did you not know that Filipino Veterans who served for this country during WWII have been fighting for citizenship until now?

My father, a first generation Filipino American, fought for this country and settled in this country in 1946. My grandfather, a first generation Samoan American, fought for this country and died a Marine

Sergeant with honors. My father-in-law, a Filipino American, served this country during the Korean and Vietnam wars and retired with honors after 26 years.

I am an American of Filipino and Samoan ancestry. I am proud of my country, the United States, and of my ethnic heritage. I am not proud of the ignorance that still exists today, especially in the media, where writers can affect the readers' image of people. I urge you and your writers to invest wisely in more detailed history of all people of color. After all, we are not second class citizens. We are just as mainstream American as anyone else. And, we are definitely more civilized than "little brown monkeys."

Steven A. Yagyagan

* * *

Date: Thu, 16 Apr 1998
Dear Flips:

Poor Mr. Fennell must be wondering what hit him (including Mang Artemio's metaphorical kampilan). Perhaps he could use a little primer on Fil-American history. As far as I'm concerned, Ms. Christenson's only real offenses were her ignorance and poor writing. I don't believe she intended to make racist remarks. (In this day and age, you'd have to be really dumb to take any sort of stance that might even remotely be construed as racist.) But tough luck for her: even IF she had deliberately set out to be insulting, she could not have chosen a more unfortunate, ill-advised, inflammatory epithet for a Filipino (particularly in describing a child).

Perhaps Mr. Fennell could be clued in on some of the objectionable etymology behind linking monkeys with Filipinos. He ought to know by now that it is deeply offensive to Filipinos, though he may not know the specific reasons why it's repugnant to us: not merely because of its racist implications, but particularly because it is derived from a racial slur whose roots are embedded in the history that our two countries share. We Filipinos have all heard, resentfully, that little ditty which is commonly attributed to the American Expeditionary Forces that were sent by the government of President William McKinley as a colonizing army to the Philippines. The song, which is known by its first line, "Where the monkeys have no tails/In far Zamboanga," is believed to have been originated by the American soldiers, who were frustrated and angry at their inability to quickly subdue "the little brown brother" (to use another infamous phrase; this spoken by Mr. McKinley). "Little brown brother" is a phrase that encapsulates the complexity of the prevailing American attitude of his time, in all its stunning—albeit inadvertent—condescension, its assumption of manifest destiny, and its apparently sincere Christianizing motive. The so-called "Philippine Insurrection" of 1898–1902 is described by historians as being the United States' precursor to Vietnam: the conflict, by the reckoning of such historians as Stanley Karnow, "had not been inexpensive to America"—while as many as 200,000 Filipino civilians may have died, as much from starvation and war-related illness as from atrocities committed by the American forces.

In retrospect, the song, "Where the Monkeys Have No Tails"—far from being a derogatory, racist slur—can also be construed by Filipinos as a proud reminder of our unwillingness to capitulate to America's first, failed experiment in empire-building. They had to resort to calling us names because they couldn't hold us down.

Ms. Christenson could not reasonably be expected to be familiar with our country's infamous little footnote to the history of American racism. Her careless writing is a testimony to her ignorance. Her utterances show her to be poorly informed about her subject. Her attempts at levity make this reader cringe at their clumsiness. Her tone of breezy insularity reinforces another unfortunate stereotypical assumption: namely, that certain Americans tend to be ignorant of other cultures, and are willfully, fecklessly satisfied to remain so.

Mr. Fennell's responses do little to obviate that perception. His poorly veiled attempt at intimidation merely confirms that other, infamous epithet, describing the eponymous hero of the novel by William J. Lederer. Mr. Fennell can look it up.

Rowena Torrevillas
International Writing Program
University of Iowa

* * *

Date: Fri, 17 Apr 1998
To the Senior Editor,

A friend of mine recently passed on to me a copy of the article written by Ann Christenson in your most recent issue. I was deeply saddened to see this derogatory form of journalism offered in a publication such as yours in 1998. As I have visited Milwaukee and worked with local people there who are concerned about racism and multiethnic dialogue, I was also surprised that it would appear in your community where conscious efforts are being made in the arena of race relations.

I have visited the Philippines, and found her references to Filipino culture offensive and even racist, although it may have been in an ignorant context. First off, her use of the term "little monkey" was outright despicable, and your editorial staff must be questioned for letting such a blatantly racist reference in our nation's history be used in your periodical. But even more generally, the context in which she paternalistically related indigenous Filipino dishes to "spring rolls" and "American beef stew" shows an outright disrespect for anything "other" than the limited world-view in which Ms. Christenson amazingly exists.

If she is some sort of food critic for your magazine, perhaps she should stick to going to "American" diners . . . stuff with which she might be familiar.

I would urge you to print an apology from either the editorial staff and/or the author, to both your reading audience and (sent directly) to the owner of that establishment. It is the least you can do for that woman and the Filipino community.

Faithfully, Ethan Flad

* * *

Date: Tue, 21 Apr 1998 21:27:58 EDT

... In all the years that I have read your magazine, I do not recall any mention of the Philippines, Filipino Americans, or our culture in your magazine. I understand that the magazine's focus is local in nature. However, Filipino Americans have a strong social, cultural, academic and professional presence in Milwaukee. Yet, your magazine does not explore such a presence. It is unfortunate, though not surprising, that the first reference I have seen is condescending and derogatory. When you write about a country and culture your magazine knows nothing about, there is a higher risk of writing something offensive than when you write about subjects or cultures you do know something about. One suggestion: research.

Regarding Ms. Christenson, I personally do not believe that her article pigeonholes her as a racist. There is no denying her ignorance and insensitivity or her arrogance for concluding that a description of a "teeny storefront" deli can summarize an entire country and its culture. Furthermore, although I do not consider myself a literary expert, I did not see her "reach beyond writing solutions" in her article "Knick at Night." Her tone was quite different, respectful. Her "attempt to create a visual impression of what she saw" regarding her monkey reference can only be interpreted one way. To Ms. Christenson, there was a visual similarity between the "stuffed monkey" and the "rambunctious monkey." To suggest that there be any other interpretation to that is quite a stretch. I could expound on the historical significance of calling a Filipino a monkey but from reading my e-mail, others have taken on that task ...

... I am not sure you are aware of this, but republishing copyrighted material without permission under certain circumstances is legal. I do not specialize in copyright law. However, as a lawyer, I do have experience interpreting codes, statutes and case law. The U.S. Copyright Act, Section 106, gives your magazine exclusive rights to copyrighted works.

That is clear and undisputed under most but not all circumstances. Section 107, Limitations on exclusive rights: Fair Use, allow republication of copyrighted material under certain circumstances. Section 107 reads as follows:

Not withstanding the provisions of section 106, the fair use of a copyrighted work, including such use by reproduction in copies or phone records or by any other means specified by that section, for purposes of criticism, comment, news reporting, teaching (including multiple copies for classroom use), scholarship, or research, is not an infringement of copyright. In determining whether the use made of a work in a particular case is a fair use the factors to be considered shall include:

1. the purpose and character of the use, including whether such use is of a commercial nature or is for nonprofit educational purpose;
2. the nature of copyrighted work;
3. the amount and substantiality of the portion used in relation to the copyrighted work as a whole; and
4. the effect the use upon the potential market for or value of the copyrighted work.

Section 107 covers the posting of your review on the internet for criticism, comment, new reporting and teaching and is specifically meant for circumstances such as this. Again John, one suggestion for you (and Ms. Christenson): research. Then you can write intelligently. I trust that whoever is doing research for you will realize they need to do a better job and will take corrective action. ... It is ironic that this year marks the 100th year since the United States invaded and colonized the Philippines. There will be activities throughout the Filipino community that will observe the event. I am hopeful that positive press comes from the event and the contributions of Filipino Americans have made to this country the past 100 years and before.

Manuel R. Galang
Milwaukee, WI

The American Enterprise, Volume 9, No. 4, July/August 1998.

The Cleaving

He gossips like my grandmother, this man
with my face, and I could stand
amused all afternoon
in the Hon Kee Grocery,
amid hanging meats he
chops: roast pork cut
from a hog hung
by nose and shoulders,
her entire skin burnt
crisp, flesh I know
to be sweet,
her shining
face grinning
up at ducks
dangling single file,
each pierced by black
hooks through breast, bill,
and steaming from a hole
stitched shut at the ass.
I step to the counter, recite,
and he, without even slightly
varying the rhythm of his current confession or harangue,
scribbles my order on a greasy receipt,
and chops it up quick.

Such a sorrowful Chinese face,
nomad, Gobi Northern
in its boniness
clear from the high
warlike forehead
to the sheer edge of the jaw.
He could be my brother, but finer,
and, except for his left forearm, which is engorged,
sinewy from his daily grip and
wield of a two-pound tool,
he's delicate, narrow-
waisted, his frame
so slight a lover, some
rough other

might break it down
its smooth, oily length.
In his light-handed calligraphy
on receipts and in his
moodiness, he is
a Southerner from a river-province;
suited for scholarship, his face poised
above an open book, he'd mumble
his favorite passages.
He could be my grandfather;
come to America to get a Western education
in 1917, but too homesick to study,
he sits in the park all day, reading poems
and writing letters to his mother.

He lops the head off, chops
the neck of the duck
into six, slits
the body
open, groin
to breast, and drains
the scalding juices,
then quarters the carcass
with two fast hacks of the cleaver,
old blade that has worn
into the surface of the round
foot-thick chop-block
a scoop that cradles precisely the curved steel.

The head, flung from the body, opens
down the middle where the butcher
cleanly halved it between
the eyes, and I
see, foetal-crouched
inside the skull, the homunculus,
gray brain grainy
to eat.
Did this animal, after all, at the moment
its neck broke,
image the way his executioner
shrinks from his own death?
Is this how

I, too, recoil from my day?
See how this shape
hordes itself, see how
little it is.
See its grease on the blade.
Is this how I'll be found
when judgement is passed, when names
are called, when crimes are tallied?
This is also how I looked before I tore my mother open.
Is this how I presided over my century, is this how
I regarded the murders?
This is also how I prayed.
Was it me in the Other
I prayed to when I prayed?
This too was how I slept, clutching my wife.
Was it me in the other I loved
when I loved another?
The butcher sees me eye this delicacy.
With a finger, he picks it
out of the skull-cradle
and offers it to me.
I take it gingerly between my fingers
and suck it down.
I eat my man.

The noise the body makes
when the body meets
the soul over the soul's ocean and penumbra
is the old sound of up-and-down, in-and-out,
a lump of muscle chug-chugging blood
into the ear; a lover's
heart-shaped tongue;
flesh rocking flesh until flesh comes;
the butcher working
at his block and blade to marry their shapes
by violence and time;
an engine crossing,
re-crossing salt water, hauling
immigrants and the junk
of the poor. These
are the faces I love, the bodies
and scents of bodies

for which I long
in various ways, at various times,
thirteen gathered around the redwood,
happy, talkative, voracious
at day's end,
eager to eat
four kinds of meat
prepared four different ways,
numerous plates and bowls of rice and vegetables,
each made by distinct affections
and brought to table by many hands.
Brothers and sisters by blood and design,
who sit in separate bodies of varied shapes,
we constitute a many-membered
body of love.
In a world of shapes
of my desires, each one here
is a shape of one of my desires, and each
is known to me and dear by virtue
of each one's unique corruption
of those texts, the face, the body:
that jut jaw
to gnash tendon;
that wide nose to meet the blows
a face like that invites;
those long eyes closing on the seen;
those thick lips
to suck the meat of animals
or recite 300 poems of the T'ang:
these teeth to bite my monosyllables;
these cheekbones to make
those syllables sing the soul:
Puffed or sunken
according to the life,
dark or light according
to the birth, straight
or humped, whole, manqué, quasi, each pleases, verging
on utter grotesquery.
All are beautiful by variety.
The soul too
is a debasement
of a text, but thus, it

acquires salience, although a
human salience, but
inimitable, and, hence, memorable.
God is the text.
The soul is corruption
and a mnemonic.

A bright moment,
I hold up an old head
from the sea and admire the haughty
down-curved mouth
that seems to disdain
all the eyes are blind to,
including me, the eater.
Whole unto itself, complete
without me, yet its
shape compliments the shape of my mind.
I take it as text and evidence
of the world's love for me,
and I feel urged to utterance,
urged to read the body of the world, urged
to say it
in human terms,
my reading a kind of eating, my eating
a kind of reading,
my saying a diminishment, my noise
a love-in-answer.
What is it in me would
devour the world to utter it?
What is it in me will not let
the world be, would eat
not just this fish,
but the one who killed it,
the butcher who cleaned it.
I would eat the way he
squats, the way he
reaches into the plastic tubs
and pulls out a fish, clubs it, takes it
to the sink, guts it, drops it on the weighing pan.
I would eat that thrash
and plunge of the watery body
in the water, that liquid violence

between the man's hands,
I would eat
the gutless twitching on the scales,
three pounds of dumb
nerve and pulse, I would eat it all
to utter it.
The deaths at the sinks, those bodies prepared
for eating, I would eat,
and the standing deaths
at the counters, in the aisles,
the walking deaths in the streets,
the death-far-from-home, the death-
in-a-strange-land, these Chinatown
deaths, these American deaths.
I would devour this race to sing it,
this race that according to Emerson
managed to preserve to a hair
for three or four thousand years
the ugliest features in the world.
I would eat these features, eat
the last three or four thousand years, every hair.
And I would eat Emerson, his transparent soul, his
soporific transcendence.
I would eat this head,
glazed in pepper-speckled sauce,
the cooked eyes opaque in their sockets.
I bring it to my mouth and—
the way I was taught, the way I've watched
others before me do—
with a stiff tongue lick out
the cheek-meat and the meat
over the armored jaw, my eating,
its sensual, salient nowness,
punctuating the void
from which such hunger springs and to which it proceeds.

And what
is this
I excavate
with my mouth?
What is this
plated, ribbed, hinged

architecture, this *carp head*,
but one more
articulation of a single nothing
severally manifested?
What is my eating,
rapt as it is,
but another
shape of going,
my immaculate expiration?

O, nothing is so
steadfast it won't go
the way the body goes.
The body goes.
The body's grave,
so serious
in its dying,
arduous as martyrs
in that task and as
glorious. It goes
empty always
and announces its going
by spasms and groans, farts and sweats.
What I thought were the arms
aching *cleave*, were the knees trembling *leave*.
What I thought were the muscles
insisting *resist, persist, exist*,
were the pores
hissing *mist* and *waste*.
What I thought was the body humming *reside, reside*,
was the body sighing *revise, revise*.
O, the murderous deletions, the keening
down to nothing, the cleaving.
All of the body's revisions end
in death.
All of the body's revisions end.

Bodies eating bodies, heads eating heads,
we are nothing eating nothing,
and though we feast,
are filled, overfilled,
we go famished.

We gang the doors of death.
That is, our deaths are fed
that we may continue our daily dying,
our bodies going
down, while the plates-soon-empty
are passed around, that true
direction of our true prayers,
while the butcher spells
his message, manifold,
in the mortal air.
He coaxes, cleaves, brings change
before our very eyes, and at every
moment of our being.
As we eat we're eaten.
Else what is this
violence, this salt, this
passion, this heaven?

I thought the soul an airy thing.
I did not know the soul
is cleaved so that the soul might be restored.
Live wood hewn,
its sap springs from a sticky wound.
No seed, no egg has he
whose business calls for an axe,
In the trade of my soul's shaping,
he traffics in hews and hacks.

No easy thing, violence.
One of its names? Change. Change
resides in the embrace
of the effaced and the effacer,
in the covenant of the opened and the opener;
the axe accomplishes it on the soul's axis.
What then may I do
but cleave to what cleaves me.
I kiss the blade and eat my meat.
I thank the wielder and receive,
while terror spirits
my change, sorrow also.
The terror the butcher
scripts in the unhealed

air, the sorrow of his Shang
dynasty face,
African face with slit eyes. He is
my sister, this
beautiful Bedouin, this Shulamite,
keeper of sabbaths, diviner
of holy texts, this dark
dancer, this Jew, this Asian, this one
with the Cambodian face, Vietnamese face, this Chinese
I daily face,
this immigrant,
this man with my own face.

—LI-YOUNG LEE

1876–1932 — Caricature of an Asian reprinted in *Amerasia Journal* (Fall/Winter 1982) under the title of "Racism & Anti-Chinese persecution in Senora, Mexico from 1876-1932," Volume 9, No.2, p.21.

1904 — Dubbed the "overlord of the savage world," anthropologist W. J. McGee supervised the display and study of two thousand "primitive peoples" at the 1904 St. Louis World's Fair. "Human culture is becoming unified," wrote McGee, "not only through diffusion, but through the extinction of the lower grades."

The Century by Peter Jennings and Todd Brewster, 1998, p.19.

1876–1932 — Caricature of an Asian reprinted in *Amerasia Journal* (Fall/Winter 1982) under the title of "Racism & Anti-Chinese persecution in Senora, Mexico from 1876-1932," Volume 9, No.2, p.22.

Salvaging the Savage

On Representing Filipinos and Remembering American Empire

A Taste of Empire

Several months ago, while riding the bus to the University of Minnesota, I saw the billboard for the first time. Perched high on the corner of the busy intersection at Franklin Street and Hennepin Avenue, the advertisement for the new restaurant named Chino Latino consisted of a seemingly simple phrase spelled out in larger-than-life letters: "As exotic as food gets without using the dog." In a moment of double consciousness[1], a stream of images entered my mind: Filipino, savage, dogeater, monkey. I wondered who else on the bus had looked at this advertisement. I wondered if they were looking at me, a Filipino, savage, dogeater, monkey.

While the term Chino Latino historically refers to the longstanding presence of Chinese in the Americas, the peoples of mixed heritage there (such as Chinese Cubans and Chinese Peruvians), and the intermixing and fluidity of cultures, the Minneapolis restaurant Chino Latino reduces this complex history to a trendy, exotic menu of dishes inspired by cuisine from different parts of Asia and the Americas. Restaurant Chino Latino is the latest successful venture of Parasole Restaurant Holdings. Parasole's company partners—Don Hays, Pete Mihajlov, and Phil Roberts—own several restaurants in Minneapolis's downtown and its trendy Uptown neighborhood.

As an American historian who specializes in Asian American Studies and as a Filipino American woman, I interpret the advertisement as one form of the persistence of U.S. colonial narratives of white supremacy and Filipino inferiority in contemporary everyday life. The racist narratives implied in this particular advertisement are no accident. This billboard is only one piece of the restaurant's cohesive advertising strategy that exoticizes and degrades Asians and Latinos. Several days later, I see another Chino Latino billboard in another busy intersection of Minneapolis' trendy Uptown neighborhood. This one reads: "All the flavors without all the vaccines." Translation: You (meaning you white young adventurous Americans) can eat the delicious "street foods from the hot zone" (Chino Latino's tag line) without having to go through the trouble of visiting those diseased (meaning backward and uncivilized) places. As yet another insidious billboard points out, these places exist ambiguously somewhere out there to provide mysterious, yet tasty dishes for "your" pleasure. It proclaims that the restaurant specializes in "hard to pronounce food from hard to pronounce places."

Restaurant reviews construct a favorable image of Chino Latino as hip and cool precisely because of its global features without critiquing the unequal and exploitive power relations this globalization entails. As one review claims:

> Arguably the cleverest new restaurant in town, Chino Latino drew hipsters, foodies, and Uptown neighbors alike to its opening week-end in mid-February 2000. . . . bring your pals . . . The wild, complicated décor is a perfect match for the global menu . . . It's crowded and loud and wild like a street festival.[2]

I imagine that the owners of the restaurant, the creators of the advertisement, and the reviewers of the restaurant might vigorously disagree with my analysis above. I imagine that they will insist that some of their best employees, customers, and friends are Asian and Latino. They may rely on historical amnesia: "We don't even know anything about u.s. imperialism in the Philippines! How could our advertisements about street foods from the hot zone have anything to do with that?" And they would not be alone. In general, American scholars across disciplines have denied the existence of u.s. imperialism and its important connections to American culture. u.s. history textbooks barely mention the Spanish-American War of 1898, which led to the u.s. annexation of the Philippines, the Philippine-American War, and four decades of u.s. colonial rule in the archipelago. As Amy Kaplan has astutely observed, three salient absences contribute to this ongoing pattern: "the absence of culture from the history of u.s. imperialism; the absence of empire from the study of American culture; and the absence of the United States from the postcolonial study of imperialism."[3]

I imagine that the owners of Chino Latino might also refute my claims above by arguing that Chino Latino has nothing to do with Filipinos specifically. Its "street foods from the hot zone" include dishes from many different parts of the globe bordered by the tropics of Cancer and Capricorn. Its "Philippine Paella" is only one dish among the "carne asada ala moreliana," "Montego Bay jerked chicken," and "Bali fertility feast." However, this lumping of Asian and Latino cultures is especially dangerous as it restructures, but ultimately strengthens our historical amnesia, what Matthew Frye Jacobson has referred to as "the modern art of forgetting."[4] It erases the salient uniqueness of Filipino culture and history (in particular its colonial relationship with the United States)[5], while reminding us of the oppression that groups of racialized peoples share in America.

At first glance, some of these contemporary representations seem to have nothing to do with Filipino bodies because they make these bodies invisible through the focus on white Americans' adventure and consumption of exotic food, for example. Yet Filipino bodies are central to the narratives implicated in such references as "all the vaccines" and "using the dog." In the early twentieth century, the quarantine and vaccination of Filipino bodies paralleled U.S. colonial military aggression and control in the archipelago, and American medical personnel and scientists constructed Filipino bodies as carriers of disease. At the 1904 St. Louis World's Fair, exposition organizers exhibited Igorots (one group of Filipino indigenous peoples) and newspaper accounts highlighted their dogeating rituals to educate American masses about Filipino savagery as well as American "civilization."

This essay uncovers some of the pivotal moments of the representation of Filipino as savage in twentieth-century American history. Specifically, it traces this representation to the oppressive use of U.S. science and medicine by American colonizers in the Philippines and the exhibition of Filipinos in the 1904 World's Fair at St. Louis. In these historical contexts, the words and the images of savage, monkey, and dogeater are inextricably linked to racism, resistance, and violence. I then connect colonial narratives of the Filipino as savage with Filipino men's experiences of racism in the 1920s and 30s in the American West and the persecution of two Filipino immigrant nurses (Filipina Narciso and Leonora Perez) who were accused of conspiracy, poisoning, and murder in the mid 1970s in Ann Arbor, Michigan. The examples I present here by no means comprise a comprehensive historical study of Filipino representations as savage. I have chosen these examples specifically in order to illustrate how racialized images have shaped the experiences of different groups of Filipinos across class, gender, and time.

In this essay, I argue that it is politically imperative to "salvage the savage," to remember the history of representations of Filipino bodies as savage, subhuman, inferior, and to contest the irresponsible perpetuation of these representations. By salvaging the savage, I refer to the importance of rescuing the representation of Filipino as savage from contemporary historical amnesia about America's violent imperialism in the Philippines. While this history is ugly and painful, it helps us identify the racist traces of U.S. imperialist ideology in contemporary representations and provides a foundation for strategies of resistance. Through salvaging the savage, we learn a language with which to critique these representations, strip them of their innocence, and construct counter-narratives that challenge the imperialism and racism that inflict our everyday lives.

I will tell you that as I write this essay, I am physically and emotionally tired. As an assistant professor, wife, and mother of an infant, I find that the hours of the day are never enough to take care of work, family, myself, let alone protest successful restaurant owners and advertisement executives. When I saw the first Chino Latino billboard, I wanted to scream, to petition, and to picket. One of my colleagues in American Studies told me that she wrote the restaurant owners and criticized their advertisements, but they did not respond. Her experience reminded me of the importance of employing multiple strategies of resistance. So in writing this essay, I chart the intersections between the personal, the popular, and the historical in the hope that this is one small, but integral step that contests contemporary racism. This essay is my scream.

The Social and Scientific Construction of the Savage Filipino Body

Disease and "suffering" among Filipinos as well as Americans in the Philippines justified American colonial intervention in the Philippines in the form of medical practice. After American victories over cholera in the United States in the 1830s and 1850s, an outbreak of cholera in the Philippines in the early 1900s gave the u.s. colonial government represented by its American military surgeons and sanitation personnel a righteous purpose in their surveillance of the islands.[6]

The perception of Western science and medicine as progressive is so pervasive that even Filipino anti-colonial, nationalist writers have praised u.s. colonial health projects in the Philippines. For example, Teodoro Agoncillo and Milagros Guerrero documented the bloody Filipino struggle to defend their independence in the Philippine-American war of 1899–1902, but then later noted:

> When the Americans came, they immediately set to work to minimize the spread of diseases and to improve, on the other hand, the health of the people. Epidemics that used to migrate to the Philippines were either prevented or minimized by the establishment of the Quarantine Service supervised by competent American doctors and public health officers.[7]

However, Warwick Anderson and Reynaldo Ileto have persuasively argued that American scientific and medicine-related practices, such as laboratory studies, vaccination, and quarantine, furthered u.s. colonialism in the Philippines and racialized Filipino bodies.[8] My research on the development of Philippine professional nursing further revealed that Americanized nursing justified the white woman's (as well as man's) burden in the Philippines and imposed physical and social control on Filipinos.[9] American nurses actively participated along with other medical personnel in constructing a cultural and racial hierarchy with Americans on top and Filipinos below by imagining and contrasting their "progressive," "clean," and "modern" ways with the "backward," "dirty," and "primitive" practices of Filipinos.

Steeped in their belief in their "power" to heal, American medical personnel simultaneously linked Filipino social practices to ignorance and societal backwardness and Western ones to intelligence and civilization. An American chief quarantine officer contrasted Filipinos who ignored American anti-cholera measures such as quarantine with "intelligent Americans or Europeans."[10] Although the introduction of American nursing in the Philippines differed from previous American medical intervention as it involved the agitation and participation of American women in the Philippines, nursing education reinforced many of the functions and beliefs of previous forms of colonial medicine. In her history of Americanized nursing in the Philippines, Lavinia Dock reified the beliefs of other American medical personnel that medical knowledge was elusive to Filipinos as a result of interrelated factors such as "native stupidity" and "dirty" indigenous social practices. According to Dock, young Filipino women who were targeted to train as nurses suffered from a lack of "rudimentary knowledge" about sanitation as a result of the prevailing Filipino "primitive customs."[11]

Colonial medicine penetrated the colonized's bodies through statistical and laboratory studies, and then used these studies to authenticate cultural and racial hierarchies. In the early 1900s, the U.S. colonial government had established laboratories to study Filipino and American bodies in the archipelago. American scientists in government laboratories in the Philippines conducted studies of Igorots' stools in order to study parasites. These laboratory studies then linked native bodies to dirt and disease. For example, Philippine Commissioner of Health Victor Heiser referred to Filipino bodies as "incubators of leprosy."[12] At the same time, these studies enabled American medical personnel to biologically and socially re-invent American bodies and social practices. Colonial laboratory studies "re"-discovered American bodies as a resilient racial type and concluded that American bodies could survive the tropical climate, once thought to be the source of the "white man's grave."[13] Thus, the denigration of Filipino bodies was inextricably linked to the "health" of white Americans.

Displaying the Savage, Consuming the Savage

The knowledge of Filipino savage bodies was not confined to American colonial medical personnel and other officials. Rather, they shared the results of their scientific and personal observations with American masses in the United States through popular representations in travel literature and public exhibits. As Fatimah Tobing Rony astutely notes, "the exotic is always already known."[14] She refers to the "average museum goer" who "views a group of Hopi dancers handling snakes," but does not see these images for the first time. Rather, he or she has become familiar with these images through narratives that link indigenous peoples with the exotic. Similarly, the Filipino savage is always already known by the "average American." In the late nineteenth and early twentieth centuries, the conditions that made this knowledge possible involved the popularity and mass consumption of travel literature and photography. During this time period, travel literature and U.S. colonial agendas in the Philippines were linked in a mutually beneficial relationship.

Photographs of Filipino bodies on postcards and in books, magazines, and newspapers were an integral part of this travel literature. They functioned as "spatial and temporal bridges" from the Philippine colony to the imperial United States, enabling masses of Americans to consume the Philippines and its peoples visually.[15] In their visual consumption of the Philippines, "average Americans" imbibed American colonial officials' construction of the Filipino savage. For example, Fred Atkinson, the first General Superintendent of Education in the Philippines, shared his purportedly accurate and comprehensive observations about Filipinos in his book, *The Philippine Islands,* published in 1905. According to Atkinson, non-Christian Filipino tribes—Negritos, Igorots, Moros—comprised the archipelago's savage races. Photographs including those of a scantily clad Negrito boy shooting a large bow and arrow and a group of Igorots drumming and dancing wildly in a circle reinforced Atkinson's descriptions of their savagery through their illustration of stereotypically primitive social practices.[16] Other photographs of squatting Negritos and Igorots depicted them as subhuman and monkey-like.[17]

Atkinson's written text reaffirmed the narratives of savagery in the photographs. He characterized the Negritos, for example, as "true savages": "These people seem to be the survival of the unfittest, and are physical and mental weaklings; their legs are like broomsticks; their feet are clumsy and large, and their bodies are covered with tattoo marks in the form of long gashes" (241). Again, the use of the Filipino body to illustrate u.s. colonial narratives of diseased, and thus racially inferior, Filipino savages is foregrounded in these representations.

Colonial travel literature and photography were not the only modes of the corporeal colonization of Filipinos. Late-nineteenth and early-twentieth-century World's Fairs exhibited Filipino bodies in ways that reaffirmed Filipino savagery and American civilization for the average fair goer. Exposition directors displayed Filipino bodies at multiple fairs throughout the United States. However, the Filipino display at the 1904 World's Fair in St. Louis was unprecedented in its scale. At that fair, exposition directors, with the full support of the federal government, organized the Philippine Reservation, which displayed nearly twelve hundred Filipinos living in villages on a forty-seven-acre site. According to Robert Rydell, the exhibits of the Filipino "wild tribes"—Bagobos, Negritos, Igorots, and Moros—were the most popular displays of the reservation. Newspaper accounts of these displays exoticized Filipino savagery by highlighting the dogeating rituals of Igorots. As one account of the Filipino exhibit claimed: "See the Igorotte. . . . To the Igorotte a Dog with any other name will taste as sweet. . . . After the Igorotte gets hold of a dog it is Dog-Gone."[18]

While such accounts popularized Filipino savagery through the veil of humor, Americans' inhumane treatment of Filipinos resulted in the disease, deaths, and dismemberment of Filipino bodies. Two Filipinos died on a train while traveling to the St. Louis fair after train crewmen turned off the heat in their cars despite freezing weather. Others died from disease contracted during the fairs. Furthermore, American academics and museum officials strategized about the dissection and distribution of these Filipino corpses' body parts. According to Rydell, after discussions with Columbia University anthropologist Franz Boas, Aleš Hrdlička (the head of the Department of Physical Anthropology at the United States National Museum) "proposed obtaining as many corpses as he could lay hands on and dividing the bodies in such a way that Columbia and the American Museum would receive 'the soft parts' and skeletons while the United States National Museum would receive the brains" (Rydell 165).

In other parts of the United States, university officials expressed interest in obtaining Filipino body parts. During the research for his acclaimed experimental documentary, *Bontoc Eulogy*, about Filipinos' experiences at the 1904 St. Louis World's Fair, Marlon Fuentes came across a letter from University of Minnesota President Cyrus Northrup to the War Department's Bureau of Insular Affairs. Northrup inquired about the possibility of obtaining the skeletons of Filipino natives buried in St. Louis and justified his request with the belief that "they were buried where their friends would never visit their graves, and the matter may be carried through without arousing a sentimental cry in objection."[19] Northrup's letter reveals one important historical connection between Minnesota's imperial interests and Filipino bodies as well as the significance of memory—and, more specifically, a purposeful forgetfulness—in American imperial agendas. The absence of a "sentimental cry in objection" to this inhumane treatment of Filipino bodies is justified by the inability of the Filipino dead's family members and friends to visit, and thus remember through this act, their loved ones. Equally important, the absence of objection is also based on Americans' purposeful forgetfulness, their denial of Filipino humanity through the commodification of Filipino bodies. Ultimately, the Smithsonian obtained three Filipino brains and, according to Fuentes, the presumption is that the brains are from three Igorots who died of pneumonia in the Philippine Reservation. In the early twentieth century, Americans displayed and consumed Filipino bodies living and dead.

The (In)dispensable Savage

Throughout the twentieth century, Filipinos have comprised an indispensable labor force in specific American industries. However, despite these important contributions, Filipino workers faced racist hostility from white workers in the forms of jeers, slurs, exploitation, and violence. Filipinos' lived experiences of racism in America have been inextricably linked to the social and scientific constructions and popular representations of their savagery.

In the 1920s and 1930s, the numbers of Filipinos in the mainland United States increased exponentially from 5,603 in 1920 to 45,208 in 1930.[20] As U.S. nationals (given the U.S. annexation of the Philippines), these Filipinos—primarily young, male, and working class—comprised an inexpensive, yet crucial labor force in American agricultural, canning, and service industries after U.S. racist legislation had excluded the entry of Chinese, Japanese, Korean, and South Asian migrants. During this time period, most Filipinos worked in agriculture, planting and picking various crops, such as tomatoes, celery, and in particular, asparagus. Farmers viewed them as ideally suited for "stoop labor,"[21] a belief that hearkened back to late nineteenth-century stereotypes that cast native peoples' posture and gestures as racially inferior. As ideal stoop laborers, Filipinos were expected to tolerate highly exploitive, dehumanizing labor conditions that punished their bodies. As one laborer recalled, "I worked about six hours that first day. . . . my back was hurting . . . the next day I could hardly sit down because my back and all of my body was sore."[22] Another described conditions of one of the camps where Filipino migrant workers were housed during busy agricultural seasons. These conditions reveal that employers provided these Filipinos in America with subhuman, animal-like living quarters. He explained, "The bunkhouse . . . was crowded with men. There was no sewage disposal. When I ate swarms of flies fought over my plate . . . I slept on a dirty cot: the blanket was never washed."[23]

While Filipinos increasingly suffered from violent attacks by white workers in the late 1920s, one must not underestimate the pain of the day-to-day racism Filipinos faced in the United States. The racism of ordinary life sheds light on the intersecting politics of food, labor, and discrimination that challenges the perception that food is used innocently for entertainment and pleasure. During this time period, Filipinos planted and picked food for Americans, but were excluded from some American restaurants. They suffered from racist segregation practices, which denied them access to hotels and swimming pools. As one hotel sign in Stockton, California during the 1930s emphasized: "POSITIVELY NO FILIPINOS ALLOWED."[24] Furthermore, Americans publicly taunted Filipinos during this time period by calling them "monkeys." As George Pimentel recalled, "Some would stare. . . . They would even call us monkeys."[25] According to Ray Corpuz, even American children participated in these racist jeers: "At school, my schoolmates as young as they were, wouldn't talk to me. Mostly every other day we fight. They don't address me directly. They tell me, 'Hey, where did that monkey come from?'"[26]

While the difficult economic conditions of the Great Depression hastened the repatriation of Filipinos and, ultimately, their exclusion from the United States, American exclusionists justified their actions by referring to Filipinos' savage and unsanitary ways. For example, in 1930, Justice of the Peace D.W. Rohrback endorsed a resolution that proclaimed, "The unrestricted immigration into the

State of California of natives of the Philippine Islands is viewed with alarm both from a moral and sanitary standpoint while constituting a menace to white labor."[27] In an interview for a local newspaper, Rohrback characterized Filipinos as "little brown men about ten years removed from a bolo and breechcloth . . . fifteen of them will live in one room and content themselves with squatting on the floor eating rice and fish."[28] In the 1920s and 1930s, Filipinos may have supplied an integral source of labor, but American exclusionists refused to incorporate them into the life and culture of the United States. Perceptions of Filipino savagery ultimately rendered them dispensable at least until other labor shortages necessitated future migrations.

A Savage Is a Savage

While men dominated Filipino migration flows to the United States in the 1920s and 1930s, Filipino women began to migrate in significant numbers by the second half of the century. Many of these Filipinas entered the United States as occupational migrants who ameliorated critical labor shortages in the United States. During this time period, the most visible occupation of Filipino women in the United States was nursing. Post-World War II critical nursing shortages in the United States, the passage of new American immigration legislation in 1965 (which encouraged the migration of nurses and other professionals to the United States), and the implementation of Philippine labor export policies in the 1970s shaped a significant Filipino international nursing labor force. By the late 1960s, Filipino nurses comprised the overwhelming majority of foreign-trained nurses in the United States, replacing decades of numerical domination by nurses from Canada. Thus, Paul Ong and Tania Azores have argued that "a discussion of immigrant Asian nurses, indeed of foreign-trained nurses in general, is predominantly about Filipino nurses."[29]

Studies about more contemporary migration flows from the Philippines often emphasize that, unlike early-twentieth-century Filipino migrants, newer migrants are highly educated and professional. Although this difference is important, the common perception of a professional is of someone who is judged on his/her training, credentials, and expertise, and not on his/her race or national origin. While some histories have foregrounded how classism and racism have shaped the development of the nursing profession,[30] little scholarly attention has been paid to the barriers faced by Filipino nurses in the United States. The case against Filipina Narciso and Leonora Perez illustrates how the stereotype of the Filipino savage has persisted in the second half of the twentieth century.

Between July and August of 1975, approximately thirty-five patients suffered from respiratory arrest at the V.A. Hospital in Ann Arbor, Michigan and approximately ten of these patients died.[31] Because the V.A. is a federal institution, the

FBI launched an investigation and accused two Filipino nurses, Filipina Narciso and Leonora Perez, of committing the crimes. In June 1976, Narciso and Perez were arrested and indicted for ten counts of poisoning, five counts of murder, and one count of conspiracy.

At the time of her arrest, Narciso was a thirty-year-old permanent resident who had applied for U.S. citizenship. She arrived in the United States from the Philippines in May 1971 and worked as a registered nurse at University of Alabama Hospital before she began working at the V.A. in Ann Arbor in November 1972. Perez was a thirty-one-year-old permanent resident who had also applied for U.S. citizenship. She arrived in the United States from the Philippines in March 1971. At the time of her arrest, Perez was married to Epifanio Perez, Jr., also a Filipino-American permanent resident, and they had a three-year-old son, Christopher. Perez was also four months pregnant. Neither Narciso nor Perez had a criminal record, and during the initial stages of the investigation, they cooperated with the investigation by testifying before a grand jury on two occasions and appearing in a line-up.

Assistant U.S. Attorney Richard Delonis admitted from the beginning of the investigation that the case was "highly circumstantial" as murder weapons, direct eyewitness testimonies, confessions, and fingerprints were unavailable and/or non-existent. However, the U.S. government's strong motivations for solving the case of the V.A. murders, its use of seemingly unlimited resources of money and manpower, and racist stereotypes about Filipinos helped shape a powerful case against Narciso and Perez.

At the beginning of the case, defense lawyers for Narciso and Perez were optimistic. Attorney Thomas O'Brien believed that Narciso and Perez "looked innocent."[32] Even the prosecuting attorneys admitted that it would be difficult to prove that Narciso and Perez—"small, soft-spoken, young women"—could be involved in such a crime.[33]

However, these positive images of Narciso and Perez co-existed with negative ones conjured by mainstream news media and a popular non-fiction book. Narciso and Perez's gender, race, and national origin could invoke multiple and dangerous images of savagery. Such images became popularized in a non-fiction book by Robert Wilcox entitled *The Mysterious Deaths at Ann Arbor* published in 1976. In this account, Wilcox highlighted the nurses' Philippine origins and linked them to stereotypes of savagery. Although Wilcox acknowledged that Narciso was a U.S. permanent resident, he emphasized that "in plain language, until [U.S.] citizenship is granted, she is an alien" who "in the meantime . . . retains her Filipino citizenship."[34] Both Narciso and Perez were from the Philippines, which Wilcox described as "for the most part, jungly, hot, and steamy."[35] And the image of "jungly" savage natives committing the V.A. murders appeared in the opening chapter in which Wilcox informed his readers that Pavulon, the poison allegedly used in the crimes, was "a poison derived from special tropical plants and used, for instance, by South American jungle Indians on the tips of darts shot to kill game."[36] Wilcox concluded that the nature of the v.a. murders suggested "a real and monstrous savagery in the killer."[37]

In the popular narratives of America's benevolent colonialism in the Philippines, American nurses and doctors trained young Filipino women to create a healthy and modern nation, and saved them from continuing their native, dirty, and backward ways. Yet although Filipino nurses may have clothed their native bodies in white uniforms, the symbol of professional expertise in their field, they were still savages. Their academic degrees enabled them to practice professionally, but the potential for these professional women to act as deadly natives remained in Americans' imagination.

These stereotypical images of Narciso and Perez as dark, deadly natives were not confined to Wilcox's text, but also made their way into mainstream publications, prosecution witness testimony, and the prosecution attorneys' questions and statements in court.[38] For example, mainstream magazines such as *Time* also referred to the drug Pavulon as jungle poison, "the lethal plant toxin used by South American Indians to tip poison darts."[39] Despite the presentation of "highly circumstantial" evidence, the jury convicted Narciso and Perez of conspiracy and three counts of poisoning in July 1977.

In February 1978, a new u.s. Attorney dismissed the case against them after the defense team successfully appealed the verdict. However, Narciso, Perez, and other Filipino nurses in the United States endured incalculable hardship as the result of the indictment, trial, and short-lived conviction. In a *Detroit Free Press* interview before the trial commenced, Filipina Narciso characterized her experience as a "nightmare."[40] Leonora Perez revealed the painful ways in which her husband and son had been affected by the publicity of the case. Her son was "too young" to understand what was happening with the investigation of the v.a. murders, but old enough to see his mother's arrest on television. "You can't erase it from his mind," she lamented. As for her husband, "he just cried and cried and shut off the tv."[41] In late 1976, as they awaited trial in their homes, both women had their phones disconnected after receiving harassing phone calls.[42]

After the jury convicted Narciso and Perez in July 1977, Filipino nurses across the United States suffered from public doubt about their nursing abilities and public suspicion about their professional intentions. One v.a. hospital nurse in Philadelphia reported that she received a phone call from someone who threatened to kill the Filipino nurses of the hospital.[43] Filipino nurses across the United States reported instances of patients refusing to take medication from Filipino nurses and of hospitals developing policies not to hire Filipino nurses. Stereotypes of Filipino savagery had buried the very important professional contributions of these Filipino nurses out of view, rendering them invisible and forgotten.

On Recollecting the Buried and Forgotten

In his analysis of Filipinos in the United States and their literature of exile, Oscar Campomanes critiqued what he argued to be "the repetitious and unreflective use of the modifier 'forgotten'" to describe Filipino invisibility in American history. He queried, "What is being forgotten?"[44] In this essay, I have argued that what is forgotten is the exploitation of Filipino bodies through American medicine, popular representations, and Filipino immigrant labor, and, as a result of this exploitation, the material and psychological benefits of racial superiority and inexpensive labor reaped primarily by white Americans. The present day Chino Latino advertising I analyzed at the beginning of this essay is only one disturbing example of how "what is forgotten" is reconstructed to be humorous, trendy, and chic. Thus, it is politically imperative to confront what is forgotten by analyzing the history of American imperialism and its connections to contemporary everyday life. For me, the salient question then becomes: After recollecting what has been forgotten, how can we sustain these very important memories?

—CATHERINE CENIZA CHOY

Notes

1 Reflecting on a childhood memory, W.E.B. DuBois argued that a young person of color in the United States is forced to develop a double consciousness, the "sense of always looking at one's self through the eyes of others." DuBois, W.E.B. *The Souls of Black Folk*. New York: Bantam Books, 1989, 3.

2 "Chino Latino: editorial profile." <http://twincities.citysearch.com/E/V/MINMI/0009/34/06/>.

3 Kaplan, Amy. "Left Alone With America: The Absence of Empire in the Study of American Culture." *Cultures of United States Imperialism.* Ed. Amy Kaplan and Donald Pease. Durham: Duke Univ. Press, 1993, 11.

4 Jacobson, Matthew Frye. "Imperial Amnesia: Teddy Roosevelt, the Philippines, and the Modern Art of Forgetting." *Radical History Review* 73 (1999): 116–127.

5 The dish, Philippine Paella, for example, with its jumbo shrimp, adobo chicken, mussels, chorizo, calamari, and saffron-anatto rice, reflects an exoticization of the colonial mixing of Spanish and Filipino cultures. However, a similar dish that combines u.s. and Filipino cultures is not to be found on the menu. The feature of Philippine Paella and the absence of Philippine Apple Pie, for example, reveal our modern selective memories as well as our forgetfulness about imperialism.

6 Ileto, Reynaldo C. "Cholera and the Origins of the American Sanitary Order in the Philippines." *Discrepant Histories: Translocal Essays on Filipino Cultures.* Ed. Vicente L. Rafael. Manila: Anvil Publishing, 1995, 60-61.

7 Teodoro A. Agoncillo and Milagros C. Guerrero, *History of the Filipino People.* Quezon City, 1977, qtd. in Ileto, Reynaldo C. "Cholera and the Origins of the American Sanitary Order in the Philippines," 51-52.

8 See Reynaldo C. Ileto, "Cholera and the Origins of the American Sanitary Order in the Philippines," and Warwick Anderson, "'Where Every Prospect Pleases and Only Man Is Vile': Laboratory Medicine as Colonial Discourse," *Discrepant Histories: Translocal Essays of Filipino Cultures.* Ed. Vicente L. Rafael, 51-81, 83–112.

9 I have analyzed some of the ways in which American colonialism and its use of medicine in the Philippines functioned similarly to British imperialism and its application of medicine in Africa and India in the nineteenth- and early-twentieth centuries. See Catherine Ceniza Choy, "The Usual Subjects: Medicine, Nursing, and American Colonialism in the Philippines," *Critical Mass: A Journal of Asian American Cultural Criticism* 5:2 (Fall 1998): 1-28.

10 Ileto, Reynaldo C. "Cholera and the Origins of the American Sanitary Order in the Philippines," 58.

11 Dock, Lavinia L. *A History of Nursing: From the Earliest Times to the Present Day with Special Reference to the Work of the Past Thirty Years,* vol. 4. New York: G. P. Putnam's Sons, 1912, 313-314.

12 Anderson, Warwick, "Where Every Prospect Pleases and Only Man Is Vile," 100.

13 Ibid., 84, 95-99.

14 Rony, Fatimah Robing. *The Third Eye: Race, Cinema, and Ethnographic Spectacle.* Durham: Duke Univ. Press, 1996, 6.

15 Ibid., 81.

16 Atkinson, Fred W. *The Philippine Islands.* Boston: Ginn & Company, 1905, 239, 241.

17 As Rony noted, a French physician writing in the late nineteenth century concluded that race is written on the savage body through posture and gesture: "Savages squat whereas Civilized people sit, explained the doctor: a Batak, [for example] because of

this is akin to a monkey," Fatimah Tobing Rony, *The Third Eye,* 3.

18 Rydell, Robert W. *All the World's a Fair.* Chicago: The Univ. of Chicago Press, 1984, 195–196.

19 Blumentritt, Mia. "Bontoc Eulogy, History, and the Craft of Memory: An Extended Conversation with Marlon E. Fuentes." *Amerasia Journal* 24:3 (1998): 81.

20 Takaki, Ronald. *Strangers from a Different Shore: A History of Asian Americans,* rev. ed. Boston: Little, Brown and Company, 1998, 315.

21 Ibid., 320.

22 Ibid., 319.

23 Ibid., 320.

24 A photograph of this hotel sign is pictured in Fred Cordova, *Filipinos: Forgotten Asian Americans.* Seattle: Demonstration Project for Asian Americans, 1983, 114.

25 Ibid., 114.

26 Ibid., 121.

27 Ibid., 116.

28 Ibid.

29 Ong, Paul and Tania Azores. "The Migration and Incorporation of Filipino Nurses." *The New Immigration in Los Angeles and Global Restructuring.* Ed. Paul Ong and Edna Bonacich and Lucie Cheng. Philadelphia: Temple Univ. Press, 1994, 165. For a history of Filipino nurse international migration, see Catherine Ceniza Choy, *Empire of Care: Nursing and Migration in Filipino American History.* Duke University Press, Durham: 2003.

30 See, for example, Barbara Melosh, "The Physician's Hand": *Work, Culture, and Conflict in American Nursing.* Philadelphia: Temple Univ. Press, 1982 and Darlene Clark Hine, *Black Women in White: Racial Conflict and Cooperation in the Nursing Profession, 1890–1950.* Bloomington: Indiana Univ. Press, 1989.

31 Different accounts offer several different sets of statistics regarding the number of respiratory arrests and related deaths at the V.A. Hospital during the summer of 1975. According to defense attorney, Thomas O'Brien, 35 patients suffered from unexpected breathing failures on 51 occasions between July 1 and August 15 and 10 of those patients died. See Thomas C. O'Brien, "The V. A. Murders," *The Advocate* 28:4 April 1985: 12. *The Detroit News* reported that 56 arrests had occurred and 16 patients had died. See Charlie Cain, "Hospital Probe Called Nearer," *The Detroit News,* 19 October 1975. *Time* magazine claimed that 27 patients suffered respiratory arrests and that 11 of them died. See "The Michigan Murders," *Time,* 22 March 1976, 47. And *The New York Times* estimated that between 51 and 63 patients suffered respiratory failure and that 13 of them died. See Martin Waldron, "Trial Starts Today for Nurses in Michigan Hospital Death," *The New York Times,* 1 March 1977, 12.

32 O'Brien, Thomas C. "The V. A. Murders," 12.

33 Cheyfitz, Kirk. "Trial to Revive V.A. Nightmare." *Detroit Free Press,* 22 August 1976: 6A.

34 Wilcox, Robert K. *The Mysterious Deaths at Ann Arbor.* New York: Popular Library, 1977, 161.

35 Ibid., 159.

36 Ibid., 8-9.

37 Ibid., 184.

38 For a more detailed analysis of the case, see chapter five in Catherine Ceniza Choy, *Empire of Care: Nursing and Migration in Filipino American History.* Duke University Press, Durham: 2003.

39 "The Michigan Murders," *Time,* 22 March 1976: 47.

40 Cheyfitz, Kirk. "Trial to Revive V.A. Nightmare," 3A.

41 Ibid., 6A.

42 Simpson, Esther. "Narciso-Perez Hearing Postponed." Ang Katipunan 16 Dec.–15 Jan. 1977: 8.

43 "Filipino Communities Organize Support," Ang Katipunan, 1-15 August 1997, p. 7.

44 Oscar V. Camponanes, "Filipinos in the United States and Their Literature of Exile," in *Reading the Literatures of Asian America.* ed. Shirley Lim and Amy Ling, Philadelphia: Temple Univ. Press, 1992, 53.

Interracial Marriages

§60. Marriages. Illegal. All marriages of white persons with negroes, Mongolians, or mulattoes are illegal and void. [Amendment approved 1905; Stats. 1905, P.554.]

California's Anti-Miscegenation Law of 1880 was amended in 1905 to include the word "Mongolians." The above law is cited from the Civil Code of the State of California Division I, Part III, Title I, Chapter I, Article I, section 60, p.30.

Illinois 2000

BESTIALITY!

Behold, Brother and Sister, the abomination demonstrated by the newspaper excerpt below! A "wedding" of the blond White woman with the mongrel "Filipino" animal savage! Such a "union" can only be considered a form of bestiality—bestiality that is causing the death of our people. It is high time that each and every White man, woman, and child speak up and loudly against this genocide (mongrelization) of our Kind!

That the Mayor of Pekin, Illinois, Dave Tebben, would sanction giving his daughter to an animal reveals his own perversity as well. What is wrong with this man? How could he raise his daughter to have such hatred for her own Kind that she would be ready and willing to accept the seed of a half primate? Absolutely sick!

Further, no minister worth his salt would perform such a vile marriage, and therefore the "Rev" Johnson must be CONDEMNED for sanctifying this act.

Excerpt from a flyer denouncing the marriage of a Pekin, Illinois couple. The flyers were produced and distributed in July 2000 by a White supremacist group called The World Church of the Creator.

Transaction

In 1992, my mother opened an envelope
from the White House. A decade before,
Vincent Chin swung open doors
of a Detroit strip club, slapped down
a ten for a beer. In Seattle, I tucked
a crisp five in the belt of a Jamaican dancer.
Two men, 2,000 miles apart, thumbing through wads of cash:
the checkered strobe and women clenching poles,
spiked heels scissor-kicked in blinking indigo.
$20,000 and an apology, signed by the President.
They spelled my name wrong she muttered.
A white father and son, lacquered in piston grease,
fired from the plant. *My name's Francine* she whispered
as she snapped my bill, swiveling her hips
to Motown. They swilled gins,
Four years in the camps my mother said,
raising her check to the light.
Damn Jap they thought aloud as Vincent downed a Miller.
I'll spend it on you, Loren and your Dad, she said.
Francine did the splits as I followed her hips.
We'll split it four ways.
The father and son gulped flasks of whiskey.
My mother sealed the check in the envelope.
They crouched behind cars, clenching bats.
When the song ended, I searched my pockets—
pennies and nickels, stubs and receipts.
Vincent walked out, the cool oak
opening his skull like a piggy bank.
My mother stuffed the money in a safe.
I cracked my billfold. *Nothing can pay
me back*, she said. I fumbled
through emptied space. *Four years,
coming back to an empty home.*
The father and son paid $3,000, 3 years probation.
I packed my wallet in my denims and slid out *The Sands*.
My son was Chinese Vincent's mother wept.
They were provoked the judge said.
My mother tore out checks for tuition,
Nothing can take that away she told us.

I stumbled among years and models.
She signed for a four-door Honda Civic.
I don't regret what we did the father said,
He had it coming said the son.
Which car is mine? I wondered in the dark lot.
Come again Francine's voice echoed
as I unlocked my Ford, swiveled the key in the ignition.
I strapped my belt and palmed my crotch.
I saw big crowds, the electricity of dancing
or swinging a bat. I dreamed of respect and money,
the best way to act when hitting a home run.

—BRIAN KOMEI DEMPSTER

America Is in the Heart

—an excerpt

Chapter XIX

It was now the year of the great hatred: the lives of Filipinos were cheaper than those of dogs. They were forcibly shoved off the streets when they showed resistance. The sentiment against them was accelerated by the marriage of a Filipino and a girl of the Caucasian race in Pasadena. The case was tried in court and many technicalities were brought in with it to degrade the lineage and character of the Filipino people.

Prior to the *Roldan vs. The United States* case, Filipinos were considered Mongolians. Since there is a law which forbids the marriage between members of the Mongolian and Caucasian races, those who hated Filipinos wanted them to be included in this discriminatory legislation. Anthropologists and other experts maintained that the Filipinos are not Mongolians, but members of the Malayan race. It was then a simple thing for the state legislature to pass a law forbidding marriage between members of the Malayan and Caucasian races. This action was followed by neighboring states until, when the war with Japan broke out in 1941, New Mexico was the nearest place to the Pacific Coast where Filipino soldiers could marry Caucasian women.

This was the condition in California when José and I arrived in San Diego. I was still unaware of the vast social implications of the discrimination against Filipinos, and my ignorance had innocently brought me to the attention of white Americans. In San Diego, where I tried to get a job, I was beaten upon several occasions by restaurant and hotel proprietors. I put the blame on certain Filipinos who had behaved badly in America, who had instigated hate and discontent among their friends and followers. This misconception was generated by a confused personal reaction to dynamic social forces, but my hunger for the truth had inevitably led me to take an historical attitude. I was to understand and interpret this chaos from a collective point of view, because it was pervasive and universal.

From San Diego, José and I traveled by freight train to the south. We were told, when we reached the little desert town of Calipatria, that local whites were hunting Filipinos at night with shotguns. A countryman offered to take us in his loading truck to Brawley, but we decided it was too dangerous. We walked to Holtville where we found a Japanese farmer who hired us to pick winter peas.

It was cold at night and when morning came the fog was so thick it was tangible. But it was a safe place and it was far from the surveillance of vigilantes. Then from nearby El Centro, the center of Filipino population in the Imperial Valley, news came that a Filipino labor organizer had been found dead in a ditch.

I wanted to leave Holtville, but José insisted that we work through the season. I worked but made myself inconspicuous. At night I slept with a long knife under my pillow. My ears became sensitive to sounds and even my sense of smell was sharpened. I knew when rabbits were mating between the rows of peas. I knew when night birds were feasting in the melon patches.

One day a Filipino came to Holtville with his American wife and their child. It was blazing noon and the child was hungry. The strangers went to a little restaurant and sat down at a table. When they were refused service, they stayed on, hoping for some consideration. But it was no use. Bewildered, they walked outside; suddenly the child began to cry with hunger. The Filipino went back to the restaurant and asked if he could buy a bottle of milk for his child.

"It is only for my baby," he said humbly.

The proprietor came out from behind the counter. "For *your* baby?" he shouted.

"Yes, sir," said the Filipino.

The proprietor pushed him violently outside. "If you say *that* again in my place, I'll bash in your head!" he shouted aloud so that he would attract attention. "You goddamn brown monkeys have your nerve, marrying our women. Now get out of this town!"

"I love my wife and my child," said the Filipino desperately.

"*Goddamn* you!" The white man struck the Filipino viciously between the eyes with his fist.

Years of degradation came into the Filipino's face. All the fears of his life were here—in the white hand against his face. Was there no place where he could escape? Crouching like a leopard, he hurled his whole weight upon the white man, knocking him down instantly. He seized a stone the size of his fist and began smashing it into the man's face. Then the white men in the restaurant seized the small Filipino, beating him unconscious with pieces of wood and with their fists.

He lay inert on the road. When two deputy sheriffs came to take him away, he looked tearfully back at his wife and child.

I was about to go to bed when I heard unfamiliar noises outside. Quickly I reached for José's hand and whispered to him to dress. José followed me through the back door and down a narrow irrigation ditch. We crept on our bellies until we reached a wide field of tall peas, then we began running away from the town. We had not gone far when we saw our bunkhouse burning.

We walked all the cold, dark night toward Calexico. The next morning we met a Filipino driving a jalopy.

"Hop in, Pinoys!" he said. "I'm going to Bakersfield. I'm on my way to the vineyards."

I ran for the car, my heart singing with relief. In the car, José went to sleep at once.

"My name is Frank," said the driver. "It is getting hot in Imperial Valley, so I'm running away. I hope to find work in the grape fields."

It was the end of spring. Soon the grapevines would be loaded with fruit. The jalopy squeaked and groaned, and once when we were entering Los Angeles, it stalled for hours. Frank tinkered and cooed over it, as though the machine were a baby.

I wanted to find my brother Macario, but my companions were in a hurry. In Riverside the jalopy stalled again. José ran to the nearest orange grove. In San Bernardino, where we had stopped to eat pears, José took the wheel and drove all through the night to Bakersfield.

We found a place on a large farm owned by a man named Arakelian. Hundreds of Filipinos were arriving from Salinas and Santa Maria, so we improvised makeshift beds under the trees. Japanese workers were also arriving from San Francisco, but they were housed in another section of the farm. I did not discover until some years afterward that this tactic was the only way in which the farmers could forestall any possible alliance between the Filipinos and the Japanese.

Some weeks after our work had begun rumors of trouble reached our camp. Then, on the other side of town, a Filipino labor camp was burned. My fellow workers could not explain it to me. I understood it to be a racial issue, because everywhere I went I saw white men attacking Filipinos. It was but natural for me to hate and fear the white man.

I was nailing some boards on a broken crate when Frank came running into the vineyard.

"Our camp is attacked by white men!" he said. "Let's run for our lives!"

"I'm going back to Los Angeles," José said.

"Let's go to Fresno," I insisted.

We jumped into Frank's jalopy and started down the dirt road toward the highway. In Fresno the old car skidded into a ditch, and when we had lifted it back to the highway, it would not run any more. Frank went to a garage and sold it. I told my companions that we could take the freight train to Stockton. I knew that the figs were about ready to be picked in Lodi.

We ran to the freight yards, only to discover that all the boxcars were loaded. I climbed to the top of a car that was full of crates and my companions followed me. The train was already moving when I saw four detectives with blackjacks climbing up the cars. I shouted to my companions to hide. I ran to the trap door of an icebox, watching where the detectives were going.

José was running when they spotted him. He jumped to the other car and hid behind a trap door, but two more detectives came from the other end and grabbed him. José struggled violently and freed himself, rolling on his stomach away from his captors. On his feet again, he tried to jump to the car ahead, but his feet slipped and he fell, shouting to us for help. I saw his hands clawing frantically in the air before he disappeared.

I jumped out first. Frank followed me, falling upon the cinders almost simultaneously. Then we were running to José. I thought at first he was dead. One foot was cut off cleanly, but half of the other was still hanging. Frank lifted José and told him to tie my handkerchief around his foot. We carried him to the ditch.

"Hold his leg," Frank said, opening a knife.

"Right." I gripped the bleeding leg with all my might, but when Frank put the sharp blade on it, I turned my face away.

José jerked and moaned, then passed out. Frank chewed some tobacco and spread it on the stump to keep the blood from flowing. Then we ran to the highway and tried to hail a car, but the motorists looked at us with scorn and spat into the wind. Then an old man came along in a Ford truck and drove us to the county hospital, where a kind doctor and two nurses assured us that they would do their best for him.

Walking down the marble stairway of the hospital, I began to wonder at the paradox of America. José's tragedy was brought about by railroad detectives, yet he had done no harm of any consequence to the company. On the highway, again, motorists had refused to take a dying man. And yet in this hospital, among white people—Americans like those who had denied us—we had found refuge and tolerance. Why was America so kind and yet so cruel? Was there no way to simplify things in this continent so that suffering would be minimized? Was there no common denominator on which we could all meet? I was angry and confused, and wondered if I would ever understand this paradox.

We went to the hospital the following morning. José was pale but gay.

"I guess this is the end of my journey with you fellows," he said.

"For a while," Frank said. "You will be well again. We will meet you again somewhere. You will see!"

"I sent a telegram to your brother," I said. "He will be here tomorrow."

"We've got to go now," Frank said.

"We have a long way to go," I said.

"You are right," José said.

"Good-bye till we meet again," Frank said, taking José's hand affectionately.

I looked back sadly. It was another farewell. How many others had I met in my journey? Where were they now? It was like going to war with other soldiers; some survived death but could not survive life. Could I forget all the horror and pain? Could I survive life?

I walked silently beside Frank to the highway. I was tired and exhausted and hungry. Frank and I had given all our money to José. We walked several miles out of town and took the first freight train going north. I did not care where we were going so long as it was away from Bakersfield. I shrank from tragedy, and I was afraid of death. My fear of death made me love life dearly.

We jumped off in Fresno where Filipinos told us that trouble was brewing. Frank wanted to proceed to Alaska for the fishing season, but I told him that conditions there were intolerable. The east was still an unexplored world, so we agreed to take a freight train to Chicago.

When we arrived in Idaho, I changed my plans. The pea fields decided me. Why go to an unknown city where there was no work? Here in this little town of Moscow were peas waiting and ready to be picked. So Frank and I worked for three weeks picking peas. But his heart was already in Chicago. He could not work any more.

I took him to the bus station and gave him a little of my money. I hate slow partings. I patted him on the back and left. I met some Mexican families on their way to the beet fields in Wyoming. I rode on a truck with them as far as Cheyenne, where they stopped off to work for a month.

I went to town and walked around the premises of the Plains Hotel, hoping to see some workers there who might have come from Binalonan. I tried to locate them by peering through the windows, but gave up when some women looked at me suspiciously. I was too dirty to go inside. And I was afraid. My fear was the product of my early poverty, but it was also the nebulous force that drove me fanatically toward my goal.

I caught a freight train that landed me in Billings, Montana. The beet season was in full swing. Mexicans from Texas and New Mexico were everywhere; their jalopies and makeshift tents dotted the highways. There were also Filipinos from California and Washington. Some of them had just come back from the fish canneries in Alaska.

I went to Helena and found a camp of Filipino migratory workers. I decided to live and work with them, hoping to put my life in order. I had been fleeing from state to state, but now I hoped to gather the threads of my life together. Was there no end to this flight? I sharpened my cutting knife and joined my crew. I did not know that I was becoming a part of another tragedy.

The leader of our crew was a small Filipino called Pete. He walked lightly like a ball. When he was thinking, which he seldom did, he moved his head from side to side like a cat. He had a common-law wife, a young Mexican girl who was always flirting with the other men. I do not know what tribe he came from in the Philippines because he spoke several dialects fluently.

Every Saturday night the men rushed to town and came home at dawn, filling the house with the smell of whisky and strong soap. Once I went with them and found out that they played pool in a Mexican place and bought cheap whisky in a whorehouse where they went when the poolroom closed at midnight.

I was distracted by Myra, Pete's wife. She was careless with herself, in a house where she was the only girl. I noticed that she was always going to town with Poco, a tubercular Filipino who loved nice clothes and dancing. One afternoon when it was my turn to cook, I saw Myra come to the kitchen with her suitcase.

"I'm going now," she said to Pete, looking at the other men, who were eating at the table.

Pete was at the far end of the table, his bare feet curling around the legs of the chair. He stopped the hand with the ball of rice in mid-air and leaped to the floor. Then he placed the rice carefully on the edge of his plate.

"Are you going with Poco?" Pete asked.

"Yes," Myra said.

"You can't go with him," he said.

"You are not married to me," she said, picking up her suitcase. Pete grabbed her with one hand and struck her with the other. Then he dragged her to the parlor like a sack of beets, beating her with his fists when she screamed for Poco. Myra's lover was waiting in a car in the yard. Pete pulled off Myra's shoes and started beating the soles of her feet with a baseball bat, shouting curses at her and calling her obscene names.

I could not stand it any longer. I stopped washing the dishes, grabbed a butcher knife and ran into the parlor where they were. But Alfred, Poco's cousin, leaped from the table and grabbed me. I struggled violently with him, but he was much stronger than I. He struck me at the base of my skull and the knife went flying across the room. It struck a pot in the sink.

When I regained consciousness, I heard Myra moaning. Pete was still beating her.

"So you want to run away!" he kept saying. "I will show you who is going to run away!"

I got up on my knees and crawled to a bench. Pete threw Myra on the floor and went back to his plate. Alfred grabbed Pete's neck and hit him on the bridge of his nose with brass knuckles. Pete fell on the floor like a log and did not get up for minutes. When he regained consciousness, Alfred was sitting in the car with Poco. Pete resumed eating silently, but the blood kept coming out of his nose. He stopped eating and bathed his nose in the sink. Then he went to the parlor and began washing and bandaging Myra's feet.

I gathered the plates and continued washing. I heard Myra laughing and giggling softly. She was in bed with Pete.

"I won't do it again, honey," she kept saying.

"Will you be good now?" Pete asked her.

"I love you, darling," she said, laughing. "I love you! I love you!"

I cursed her under my breath. What kind of a girl was she? I cursed him, too. Pete bounced suddenly into the kitchen, rolling from side to side. I did not look at him. He was preparing something for Myra to eat. Then he carried the plates to her bed, walking lightly like a cat. I looked up from the sink. He was feeding her with a spoon, holding her head with one hand. Myra reached for Pete's neck and kissed him.

Suddenly Poco came into the house and started shooting at them. I ran out of the house terrified, shouting to Alfred. But he opened the door and told me to jump into the car. Poco showed his face at the door.

"Run away, Alfred!" he shouted to his cousin. "Run away and don't come back! I will kill them! Go now!"

Alfred hesitated for a moment; carefully he put the key in the lock and shifted the gear. Then we were driving furiously down the dirt road.

"The damn fool," Alfred wept. "That damn fool is going to be hanged—and all for a prostitute!"

I grabbed the front seat for fear I would fall out when we turned a corner. I could tell by the stars in the wheeling sky that we were driving west. I was going back to the beginning of my life in America. I was going back to start all over again.

—CARLOS BULOSAN

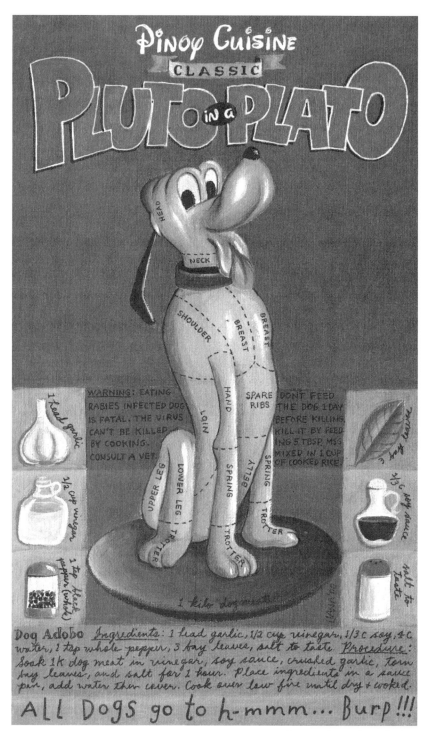

Pluto in a Plato, art by Dindo Llana

SCREAMING MONKEYS

Chin

I wasn't his friend, but I wasn't one of the main kids who hounded him up onto the shed roof, either. Sure I'd lob a rock or two, but this was our stage of life back then, someplace between the arm and the fist. Not to chuck nothing would have been against nature, and I never did him one he couldn't duck easy, especially being as fast as he was—basically the fastest kid in the ninth grade, and one of the smartest besides, smarter even than yours truly, the official class underachiever. I tested so high on my IQ that the school psychologists made me take the test over, nobody could believe it. They've been hounding me to apply myself ever since. But Chin was smart, too—not so much in math and science as in stuff like history and English. How's that for irony? And he was a good climber, you had to give him that, the only kid who could scale that shed wall, period. Because that wall didn't have no handholds or footholds. In fact, the naked eye would've pronounced that wall plain concrete; you had to wonder if the kid had some kind of special vision, so that he could look at that wall and see a way up. Maybe where we saw wall, he saw cracks, or maybe there was something he knew in his body about walls; or maybe they didn't have walls in China, besides the Great Wall, that is, so that he knew a wall was only a wall because we thought it was a wall. That might be getting philosophical. But you know, I've seen guys do that in basketball, find the basket in ways you can't account for. You can rewind the tape and watch the replay until your eyeballs pop, but finally you've got to say that obstacles are not always obstacles for these guys. Things melt away for them.

Gus said it was on account of there was monkey feet inside his sneakers that the kid could get up there. That was the day the kid started stockpiling the rocks we threw and raining them back down on us. A fall day, full of the crack and smell of people burning leaves illegally. It was just like the monkeys in the zoo when they get mad at the zookeepers, that's what I said. I saw that on TV once. But Gus blew a smoke ring and considered it like a sunset, then said even though you couldn't see the kid's monkey feet, they were like hands and could grip onto things. He said you've never seen such long toes, or such weird toenails either, and that the toenails were these little bitty slits, like his eyes. And that, he said, was why he was going to drown me in a douche bag if I threw any more rocks without paying attention. He said I was fucking arming the ape.

We didn't live in the same building, that kid and me. His name was Chin or something, like chin-up we used to say, and his family lived in the garden apartment next door to ours. This was in scenic Yonkers, New York, home of Central Avenue. We were both stuck on the ground floor, where everyone could look right into your kitchen. It was like having people look up your dress, my ma said, and they were smack across the alley from us. So you see, if I'd really wanted to nail him with a rock, I could've done it anytime their windows were open if I didn't want to break any glass. And I could've done it any time at all if I didn't care about noise and commotion and getting a JD card like the Beyer kid got for climbing the water tower. Of course, they didn't open their windows much, the Chins. My ma said it was because they were Chinese people—you know, like Chinese food, from China, she said, and then she cuffed me for playing dumb and getting her to explain what a Chinese was when they were getting to be a fact of life. Not like in California or Queens, but they were definitely proliferating, along with a lot of other people who could tell you where they came from, if they spoke English. They weren't like us who came from Yonkers and didn't have no special foods, unless you wanted to count fries. Gus never could see why we couldn't count fries. My own hunch, though, guess why, was that they just might be French. Not that I said so. I was more interested in why everybody suddenly had to have a special food. And why was everybody asking what your family was? First time somebody asked me that, I had no idea what they were talking about, but after awhile, I said, Vanilla. I said that because I didn't want to say we were nothing, my family was nothing.

My ma said that the Chins kept their windows shut because they liked their apartment hot, seeing as how it was what they were used to. People keep to what they're used to, she liked to say, though she also liked to say, Wait and see, you know your taste changes. Especially to my big sister she was always saying that, because my sis was getting married for real this time, to this hairdresser who had suddenly started offering her free bang trims anytime. Out of the blue, this was. He was a thinker, this Ray. He had it all figured out, how from doing the bang trim he could get to talking about her beautiful blue eyes. And damned if he wasn't right that a lot of people, including yours truly, had never particularly noticed her eyes, what with the hair hanging in them. A real truth-teller, that Ray was, and sharp as a narc. It was all that practice with women all day long, my ma said. He knows how to make a woman feel like a queen, not like your pa, who knows how to make her feel like shit. She was as excited as my sis, that's the truth, now that this Ray and her Debi were hitting the aisle sure enough. Ray was doing my ma's hair free, too, every other day just about, trying to fine-tune her do for the wedding, and in between she was trying to pitch a couple of last You knows across to Debi while she could. Kind of a cram course.

But my pa said the Chins did that with their windows because somebody put a cherry bomb in their kitchen for fun one day, and it upset them. Maybe they didn't know it was just a cherry bomb. Who knows what they thought it was, but they beat up Chin over it; that much we did know, because we could see everything and hear everything they did over there, especially if we turned the TV down, which we sometimes did for a fight. If only more was in English, we could've understood everything, too. Instead, all we caught was that Chin got beat up over the cherry bomb, as if they thought it was owing to him that somebody put the bomb in the window. Go figure.

Chin got beat up a lot—this wasn't the first time. He got beat up on account of he played hooky from school sometimes, and he got beat up on account of he mouthed off to his pa, and he got beat up on account of he once got a C in math, which was why right near the bomb site there was a black-board in the kitchen. Nights he wasn't getting beaten up, he was parked in front of the blackboard doing equations with his pa, who people said, was not satisfied with Chin plain getting the correct answer in algebra, he had to be able to get it two or three ways. Also he got beat up because he liked to find little presents for himself and his sis and his ma. He did this in stores with-out paying for them, and that pissed the hell out of his pa. On principle, peo-ple said, but maybe he just felt left out. I always thought Chin should've known enough to get something for his pa, too.

But really Chin got beat up, my pa said, because Mr. Chin had this weird cheek. He had some kind of infection in some kind of hole, and as a result, the cheek shook and for a long time he wouldn't go to the doctor, seeing as how in China he used to be a doctor himself. Here he was a cab driver—the worst driver in the city, we're talking someone who would sooner puke on the Pope than cut across two lanes of traffic. He had a little plastic sleeve on the passenger-side visor where he displayed his driver's license; that's how much it meant to him that he'd actually gotten one. But in China he'd been a doc-tor, and as a result, he refused to go to a doctor here until his whole cheek was about gone. Thought he should be able to cure himself with herbs.Now even with the missus out working down at the dry cleaners, they were getting cleaned out themselves, what with the bills. They're going to need that boy for their old age, that's what my pa said. Cabbies don't have no pension plan like firemen and policemen and everybody else. They can't afford for him to go wrong, he's going to have to step up to the plate and hit that ball into the bleachers for them. That's why he gets beat, so he'll grow up to be a doctor who can practice in America. They want that kid to have his M.D. hanging up instead of his driver's license.

That was our general theory of why Chin got the treatment. But this time was maybe different. This time my pa wondered if maybe Chin's pa thought he was in some kind of a gang. He asked me if Chin was or wasn't, and I said no way was he in anything. Nobody hung with Chin, why would anybody hang with the guy everyone wanted to break? Unless you wanted them to try and break you, too. That's when my pa nodded in that captain of the force way you see on TV, and I was glad I told him. It made me feel like I'd forked over valuable information to the guy who ought to know. I felt like I could relax after I'd told him, even though maybe it was Mr. Chin who really should've known. Who knows but maybe my pa should've told Mr. Chin. Though what was he going to do, call him up and say, This is our theory next door? The truth is, I understood my pa. Like maybe I should've told Gus that Chin didn't actually have monkey feet, because I've seen his feet top and bottom through my pa's binoculars, and they were just regular. But let's face it, people don't want to be told much. And what difference did it make that I didn't think his toes were even that long, or that I could see them completely plain because his pa used to make him kneel when he wanted to beat him? What difference does it make what anybody's seen? Sometimes I think I should've kept my eyes on the TV where they belonged, instead of watching stuff I couldn't turn off. Chin's pa used to use a belt mostly, but sometimes he used a metal garden stake, and with every single whack, I used to think how glad I was that it was Chin and not me that had those big welts rising up out of his back skin. They looked like some great special effect, these oozy red caterpillars crawling over some older pinkish ones. Chin never moved or said anything, and that just infuriated his pa more. You could see it so clear, you almost felt sorry for him. Here he had this garden stake and there was nothing he could do. What with his cheek all wrapped up, he had to stop the beating every now and then to readjust his bandage.

My pa used a ruler on me once, just like the one they used at school—Big Bertha, we called it, a solid eighteen inches, and if you flinched, you got hit another three times on the hands. Naturally, Chin never did, as a result of the advanced training he got at home. People said he didn't feel nothing; he was like a horse you had to kick with heel spurs, your plain heel just tickled. But I wasn't used to torture instruments. We didn't believe in that sort of thing in my house. Even that time my pa did get out the ruler, it broke and he had to go back to using his hand. That was bad enough. My pa was a fireman, meaning he was a lot stronger than Chin's pa was ever going to be, which maybe had nothing to do with anything. But my theory was, it was on account of that he knew he wasn't that strong that Mr. Chin used the garden stake on Chin, and once on the sister, too.

She wasn't as old as my sister, and she wasn't that pretty, and she wasn't that smart, and you were just glad when you looked at her that you weren't her gym teacher. She wore these glasses that looked like they were designed to fall off, and she moseyed down the school halls the way her pa did the highway—keeping all the way to the right and hesitating dangerously in the intersections. But she had a beautiful voice and was always doing the solo at school assembly. Some boring thing—the songs at school were all worse than ever since Mr. Reardon, the math teacher, had to take over music. He was so musical, people had to show him how to work those black stands; he didn't know you could adjust them, he thought they came in sizes. To be fair, he asked three times if he couldn't do study hall instead. But Chin's sister managed to wring something out of the songs he picked somehow. Everything she sang sounded like her. It was funny—she never talked, this girl, and everybody called her quiet, but when she sang, she filled up the whole auditorium and you completely forgot she wore these glasses people said were bulletproof.

It wasn't the usual thing that the sister got hit. But one day she threatened to move out of the house, actually stomped out into the snow, saying that she could not stand to watch what was going on anymore. Then her pa hauled her back and beat her, too. At least he left her clothes on and didn't make her kneel. She got to stand and only fell on the floor, curled up, by choice. But here was the sad thing: It turned out you could hear her singing voice when she cried; she still sounded like herself. She didn't look like herself with her glasses off, though, and nobody else did, either. Chin the unflinching turned so red in the face, he looked as though blood beads were going to come busting straight out of his pores, and he started pounding the wall so hard, he put craters in it. His ma told him to stop, but he kept going, until finally she packed a suitcase and put the sister's glasses back on for her. Ma Chin had to tape the suitcase with duct tape to get it to stay shut. Then Ma Chin and the sister both put on their coats and headed for the front door. The snowflakes by then were so giant, you'd think there was a closeout sale on underwear going on up in heaven. Still the dynamic duo marched out into the neighborhood and up our little hill without any boots. Right up the middle of the street, they went; I guess there being two of them bucked up the sister. Ma Chin started out with the suitcase, but by the time they'd reached the hill, the sister'd wrestled it away from her. Another unexpected physical feat. It was cold out, and so dark that what with all the snow, the light from the streetlights appeared to be falling down too, and kind of drifting around. My pa wondered out loud if he should give our neighbors a friendly lift someplace. After all, the Chins had no car, and it was a long walk over to the bus stop. But what would he say? Excuse me, I just happened to be out driving?

He was trying to work this out with my ma, but she had to tell him first how Ray would know what to say without having to consult nobody and how glad she was that her Debi wasn't marrying nobody like him. Ray, Ray, Ray! my pa said finally. Why don't you go fuck him yourself instead of using your daughter? Then he sat right in the kitchen window, where anybody who bothered to look could see him, and watched as Ma Chin and the sister stopped and had themselves a little conference. They were up to their ankles in snow, neither in one streetlight cone or the next, but smack in between. They jawed for a long time. Then they moved a little farther up the incline and stopped and jawed again, sheltering their glasses from the snow with their hands. They almost looked like lifeguards out there, trying to keep the sun out of their eyes, except that they didn't seem to know that they were supposed to be looking for something. Probably their glasses were all fogged up. Still my pa watched them and watched them while I had a look at Chin and his pa back at the ranch, and saw the most astounding thing of all: They were back at the blackboard, working problems out. Mr. Chin had a cup of tea made and you couldn't see his face on account of his bandage, but he was gesturing with the eraser and Chin was nodding. How do you figure? I half-wanted to say something to my pa, to point out this useless fact. But my pa was too busy sitting in the window with the lights on, waiting for the Chin women to shout Fire! or something, I guess. He wanted them to behold him there, all lit up, their rescuer. Unfortunately, though, it was snowing out, not burning, and their heads were bent and their eyes were on the ground as they dragged their broken suitcase straight back across our view.

—GISH JEN

On Teaching Filipinos

"I find this monotonous work, trying to teach these monkeys to talk. The more I see of this lazy, dirty, indolent people, the more I come to despise them. I am becoming more and more convinced that for years and years to come, the only business Americans ought to have over here is to rule them with severity."
—Harry Newton Cole, teacher on the island of Leyte Philippines, 1903

My Country Versus Me

—an excerpt

Trouble came roaring into my safe and steady world on December 23, 1998, like the kind of flash rainstorm up in the mountains that can turn a placid fishing trip deadly. Yes, I had weathered a previous storm when the FBI came into my life 16 years earlier, but that was more like an ominous rumbling, not the full-blown thunderboomer I was staring at now. Plus, I thought that the other incident, in 1982, had been over and done with long ago. In my straightforward scientific way of thinking, once a problem is solved, it is finished and there is no need to check if one plus one might suddenly yield a different answer. But I was beginning to see how one encounter with the FBI could keep coming back to haunt me, as if their asking the same question over and over might indeed yield a new solution. Looking back, I can see that with each iteration, new and unrelated events were thrown into the mix, mutating it into a more virulent inquiry and magnifying what were once simple questions by significant multiples.

Two days before Christmas, I was called into the security office at the Los Alamos National Lab. I had just returned home from a three-week trip to Taiwan that very morning, and I went directly to work at my office in the "x Division," where nuclear weapons research takes place. It was the last workday before the lab closed for the holidays, and I had a lot of work to do. My children were coming home for the week. Chung had arrived already and Alberta was flying in that evening from North Carolina. I wanted to get home to prepare their favorite foods, something that gave me great pleasure.

Getting called in for a security check is not such an unusual event at Los Alamos National Lab, or LANL, as it is also known. Anyone hoping to work at a national laboratory like LANL knows that an extensive background clearance review is required. For classified work involving national security, it can take many months of waiting until the investigation is complete. Everybody knows somebody who is getting a background investigation done. I held a "Q clearance" for twenty years, the highest level of security clearance. While not every scientist at Los Alamos needs to have a Q clearance, most do because the majority of research done at Los Alamos is related to the design, testing, manufacture, and maintenance of nuclear weapons, the purpose behind the lab's founding in 1943. Scientists at Los Alamos also conduct major unclassified research on oceanographic and atmospheric issues, the human genome, space travel, astrophysics and other endeavors, but nuclear weapons are LANL's bread and butter.

For many years I worked in the Applied Physics Division of LANL, also known as the x Division. I was a hydrodynamics code physicist—a "code developer"—working on several of the complex computer programs that simulate the detonation of thermonuclear weapons—atomic bombs and hydrogen bombs. I can't give specific details about my work because of its classified nature. But I can say that my job was to make sure the various computer simulation programs for nuclear bombs correctly reflected the hydrodynamic changes that occur inside a bomb during a nuclear explosion. Hydrodynamics describes the changes and extreme stress occurring to the metals—such as uranium or plutonium—in the moments after a detonation, microsecond by microsecond.

I spent my career using mathematics and physics to develop the equations and computer codes that would solve problems with these simulation programs. My solutions were part of the proper functioning of our nuclear stockpile as well as conventional weapons. In my unclassified research, I have calculated the shape and force of conventional ordnance that can pierce a 6-foot-thick wall of steel, and my equations were used in the Persian Gulf War in 1992. Earlier in my career I worked on the hydrodynamics of nuclear reactor safety—to ensure against Chernobyl-type accidents, for example. My research on the numerical modeling of nuclear reactors and reactions has been used in many countries, and I was proud that my work contributed to America's safety and to global nuclear security. I enjoyed my research and took it very seriously—if I didn't do my job well, the consequences could be dire.

There was another side to being part of this nuclear brotherhood. Like every other employee working in LANL's classified environment, I consented to a high degree of scrutiny and also agreed to inform on any security infractions made by my coworkers. I gave up the right to talk about certain aspects of my work with my children, family, and friends—or anyone who wasn't Q-cleared with a need to know. I had regular security debriefings with counterintelligence officers whenever I went overseas to present a talk on my published, unclassified research or to attend a scientific conference—for which I obtained advance approval from LANL.

It is also true that for many scientists, there are times when security procedures seem arbitrary or create an unnecessary burden and interference with our research work. For example, at LANL there was the two-hour rule: If you were leaving your office for more than two hours, you had to shut down your computer. This created a bind, because some complex programs took more than two hours to finish the calculations that they were performing. In addition, information that has long been in the open literature and printed in newspapers-for example, some of the details related to my case—are still considered—classified, and scientists are required to lock such information in vaults. Situations like these have been a regular topic of complaint among scientists who work in classified environments, whether at the national laboratories or among defense contractor facilities. A report by the President's

Foreign Intelligence Advisory Board that came out in June 1999 described attitudes in the labs and the DOE as "saturated with cynicism, an arrogant disregard for authority, and a staggering pattern of denial." This constant pull and tug between security and scientific inquiry was part of the culture of classified research, and I was a product of that culture.

After I got the call from LANL's counterintelligence chief, I headed to the security office. I didn't really think there was anything unusual with the call. After all, I had just returned from an overseas trip, and there might be some routine question that came up, even though it was a personal trip. Or it could be a question related to another LANL employee.

I walked quickly through the long corridors of enamel-painted cinder block and fluorescent lights from x Division to the administrative area. x Division and LANL's administrative and executive offices are located in the same H-shaped building, known as the Admin Building, at the lab's main driveway. Other LANL divisions are spread across 44 square miles of lab property, stretching from the finger mesas of Los Alamos into Bandelier National Monument.

Within minutes I reached the office of Ken Schiffer. Ken, probably in his early 60s, was new at LANL. He had taken over the counterintelligence duties not a month earlier, after retiring from a 35-year career with the FBI. His predecessor was newly retired Bob Vrooman, a former CIA guy. I didn't really know Ken, but Bob had questioned me about my travels several times over the years. He had also been my son Chung's soccer coach.

Ken was waiting for me with Terry Craig, another LANL counterintelligence officer, and a third man I didn't recognize. They began questioning me about my trip to Taiwan.

They asked me why I had gone to Taiwan, who I saw, what we talked about, where I stayed, what I did, and many details about the trip. Every answer prompted another round of inquiry: I tried to be helpful and to tell them what they wanted to know. It was an unpleasant but necessary exchange, rather like a trip to the dentist spent wishing for a quick and painless conclusion. It was soon evident that this wish would not be granted.

I had gone to Taiwan on personal business, related to a terrible family tragedy. I went to enroll my 28-year-old nephew William in a Chinese Christian rehabilitation center after his mother and younger brother were killed. They were shot and murdered in 1997 during a break-in of their home in the Los Angeles area. It was the kind of shocking event that no one ever expects to happen to one's own family. William was the son of my older brother Wentou. The killings appeared to be gang related, and my siblings and I thought it would be best to remove my nephew from this negative environment and enroll him in a school in Taiwan, to keep him out of trouble. My wife, Sylvia, and my kids were fearful that I was getting involved in my nephew's problems, and were concerned that I was making such a long trip twice in one year. But my extended family is very close, and we take our responsibilities to each other very seriously. Because I was able to take time off from work, I was elected to make the trip with my nephew. We chose a rehab center in Taiwan because we felt he would be safer there and because other family members would be close by.

I was born in Taiwan in 1939, the seventh of ten children. My father had come to the island in the early 1900s when he was a small boy; my mother also was born in Taiwan. After I came to the U.S. as a graduate student in 1964, some of my siblings also immigrated to the U.S., but three still lived in Taiwan. During the twenty years I worked at LANL, I visited Taiwan periodically, especially to honor my parents' graves. My visits were spaced every two years or so. Later, when I was accused of being a spy for several countries, including possibly Taiwan, some politicians and reporters made it sound as if I had been to Taiwan an extraordinary number of times. I don't think my visits were excessive at all, but I also wouldn't have returned so soon had it not been necessary to help my brother's family through their hardship.

After I got my nephew settled at the rehab center, I visited some of my scientific colleagues. One had invited me to give a talk at the Chung Shan Science and Technology Institute, a government-sponsored research facility similar to our national laboratories. I did some occasional consulting for Chung Shan, presenting my unclassified research papers there, just like other LANL scientists who did outside consulting, with full LANL and DOE approval. I had received an honorarium and payment for expenses for previous talks I gave at the institute. But on this most recent trip to Taiwan, LANL did not approve my request to give a talk at Chung Shan Institute, and so I followed LANL procedures and did not make a presentation.

I sat in the LANL security office, recounting the story of my trip to Taiwan, and spent two hours going over all of this in detail with Ken, Terry, and the third man. My inquisitors were particularly interested in what I did at the institute and how much money I received. Suddenly they told me they wanted to give me a lie detector test, right away, without explanation. I was surprised and alarmed, because even though security checks were a routine procedure, polygraphs were not. I knew I must be under suspicion. For what, I didn't yet know. Though I felt anxious, I trusted the security officers to be fair with me. In all my years at LANL, I never heard of anyone getting disciplined without a lengthy and careful review, and I expected a full and fair review for whatever I was suspected of doing. Most important, I felt I had done nothing wrong and so had no cause for concern.

In a large conference room near Ken's office, the polygraph testing equipment was already set up and a polygraph technician was on hand from Wackenhut, a private security contractor that the DOE used to administer polygraph tests. It all had been planned for me. At the time, I had no idea that my interrogation was being observed from outside the room by other counterintelligence agents, including an FBI agent who was standing by, ready to arrest me. I later learned that this polygraph was ordered from the highest rungs of the DOE, by a top FBI official, Edward Curran, who recently had been appointed chief of counterintelligence at the DOE headquarters in D.C. It never occurred to me that powerful politicians in Washington were watching me, convinced I must be a spy. At the same time, it didn't seem to occur to them that I might actually be innocent.

The polygraph examiner attached the sensors to the fingers of my left hand, applied a blood pressure cuff to my right arm, and fastened wires to my waist and chest. Meanwhile, Ken Schiffer explained the topic of this test: espionage. He explained the "elements" of espionage to provide a framework for me to discuss whether I had disclosed any classified information to unauthorized people, especially foreigners; if I had ever been asked to commit espionage or to disclose information that is classified or sensitive, related to weapons, or harmful to the U.S.; if I had clandestine or secret contacts with foreigners; or if I had ever offered to do any of these things.

Being a Taiwan-born, naturalized American citizen who had attended many international conferences, both in the U.S. and abroad, I knew lots of foreigners, beginning with members of my own family but also including my friends and classmates from college and graduate school, and my colleagues at LANL and around the world. For the next six hours, I wracked my brain to remember every potentially bad or "unusual" encounter I've ever had with foreigners.

During this polygraph exam, I discussed several topics. We spent a lot of time talking about my first encounter with the FBI in 1982, when they administered my first lie detector test. I told Schiffer and Craig about the first time I came under FBI suspicion in 1982, more than 16 years ago. It was the time when I made a phone call to another nuclear scientist who worked at the Lawrence Livermore National Laboratory, in Livermore, California, outside of San Francisco. My phone call led the FBI to me. As I later learned, this scientist was suspected of giving secrets to China about the neutron bomb, and his phones were being tapped by the FBI as part of a surveillance operation. I learned through many newspaper reports and from many Congressional hearings that this operation was called "Tiger Trap." That Livermore scientist was never charged with committing any wrongdoing, and I won't publicize his name here even though some reporters printed his name after this incident came up in my case. But his name never became as public as mine has, and I hope that he has been able to rebuild his life without a media spotlight.

Back in 1982, I didn't know that the FBI monitored Chinese American scientists. I had never even met this Livermore scientist before. But I read about him in a popular Chinese-language magazine. An article said that a

Taiwanese nuclear scientist was fired from Lawrence Livermore because he gave lectures in China and Taiwan. They printed the name of this scientist. Of course this news caught my attention, since I, too, was planning to present a paper in Taiwan.

In those days, Taiwanese in America had to worry about being spied on by the military regime of the Kuomintang (KMT) Party in Taiwan. It was well known that the KMT government used many spies and informants against its own citizens and even against Taiwanese in the U.S. Their actions could be ruthless, as in the execution-style killing of Henry Liu, a Taiwanese American journalist who was shot to death in 1984 outside his home in Daly City, California, for his outspoken criticism of the KMT government.

I had never had much interest in politics, maybe because I grew up in Taiwan at a time when getting involved in politics was so dangerous. I stuck to science and math, which are much more fascinating to me and have a clear benefit to humanity. They are also far less volatile than politics. But I couldn't help wondering if someone in the Taiwan government was making trouble for the Livermore scientist for some reason, perhaps because he gave a talk. I was also planning to give a talk in Taiwan about nuclear reactor safety. Though my upcoming trip and my talk had the approval of my superiors at LANL, I was worried that what had happened to him could happen to me. I found the man's phone number in a telephone directory and I contacted him. When I reached him, he wasn't interested in speaking with me, so I hung up after a brief conversation

It turned out that the Livermore scientist was not in trouble with the KMT but with the FBI, which had a wiretap on his phone as part of their Tiger Trap operation. The FBI monitors picked up my call to him. About a year later, in November 1983, three FBI agents came to Los Alamos. They asked me to meet them at their hotel room at the Los Alamos Inn on Trinity Drive. I met with them, and they questioned me for three or four hours about my contact with the Livermore scientist. One agent was from the Albuquerque FBI office; the other two might have been from San Francisco.

Shortly after they questioned me, the FBI wanted me to help them with their investigation of the Livermore scientist. They asked me to go to California and approach the scientist in person with some questions. Of course I felt that I should assist the FBI and visit the Livermore suspect. LANL paid for the airplane ticket to California and the rental car. In December 1983, I went to the scientist's home near Livermore in the San Francisco Bay area, introduced myself, and told him that someone was trying to frame him. I spoke with him for a half hour or so, and then I left. I reported this conversation to the FBI.

About a month later, in January 1984, some FBI agents asked me to go to the Los Alamos Inn again. They polygraphed me there in the hotel. It was the first time I had been subjected to a lie detector test, but it wouldn't be the last.

After attaching sensors to my fingers, arm, waist, and chest, the polygrapher spent a half-day asking me many questions. One of the questions they asked me was, "Did you pass any classified information to an unauthorized person?" I answered no. When the test was over, the FBI agents told me that I passed the polygraph with flying colors. I felt that the FBI accepted the fact that I was truthful. I believed them when they said their investigation of me was closed.

My role in the Tiger Trap investigation was over and my life at LANL returned to normal. I felt that the polygraph had verified that I had told the truth and that I also had proven my loyalty by assisting the FBI—and that was the end of the story. Until, of course, this new suspicion that I had committed espionage. Today the FBI claims that I lied to them when they asked me if I called the Livermore scientist. In many later Congressional hearings and in the news media, it was reported that I denied calling the other scientist and that this was evidence of my deceptive nature. My attorneys and I would later learn that the FBI had lost their file on me for their 1983 and 1984 meetings with me—and that they had had to "reconstruct" the information. I don't agree with the FBI version of the story, but it has been repeated many times as though it were a proven fact—and this reconstructed account would be used over and over again to justify the espionage allegations against me.

∗   ∗   ∗

Now, on December 23, 1998, so many years after that first encounter with the FBI, I found myself being polygraphed again, this time in the LANL conference room. I tried to think of any other incidents that might be useful to these security officers. I told them about a strange incident that had happened only a few months earlier, in August 1998. I received a call at my office late in the afternoon from a Chinese-speaking man who was at the Hilton Hotel in Santa Fe. He said his name was Wang Ming-Li. I didn't know him. He said he was a diplomat from Beijing on vacation in Santa Fe and that he wanted to meet me. I explained that I could not meet him without lab approval. Then he told me about a Chinese American scientist named Peter Lee who had once worked at LANL. Peter Lee was not related to me. He had pled guilty in 1997 to giving classified information about submarine research to China in a lecture during his visit there in 1985. Peter Lee's case didn't receive much attention, and he was sentenced to a halfway house and to perform community service. This strange caller, Mr. Wang, asked me, "Does the Peter Lee case result in any consequences to the Chinese at the laboratory?" I told him that nothing had happened to Chinese scientists at LANL because of Peter Lee, and hung up.

The same man called me again the next day, and asked me if I had any papers or reports I wanted to give to China, because he would be willing to take them back. I told him I had nothing for him to take back. Then he gave me a Santa Fe phone number and said that if I wanted to reach him, I could call him at any time.

After I got this strange phone call, I reported the episode to the LANL counterintelligence officer, Terry Craig—the same Terry Craig who was sitting there in the conference room, listening to me retell the story to the polygrapher. I had been very upset by the call.

Looking back, I feel like a fool to have told this story to LANL security and the FBI, because it turned out that this call from "Mr. Wang" was a "false flag" operation by the FBI to entrap me. All of the people sitting and listening to me relate this confusing incident must have been laughing at me. I didn't take the bait from "Mr. Wang," but at this point, no one bothered to enlighten me. I only found out later, while I was sitting behind bars, that this whole thing had been a setup. What happened to the Livermore scientist was now happening to me, only it was much worse than I could imagine.

* * *

My impromptu pre-Christmas polygraph test went on for six hours, past the time I would normally go home, past the time I had intended to leave to pick Alberta up at the airport. But the polygrapher kept pushing for any other events or incidents. I don't know why or how I thought of this, but suddenly I remembered something else when the examiner asked again if foreigners had ever approached me for classified information.

I recalled an incident that occurred when I was in China in June 1988, ten years earlier. I had been invited with other scientists from LANL and elsewhere to attend an international conference on computational physics in Beijing; I was to present a paper I had written. It would be only the second time I had ever visited China, and I went with my wife. I also was asked to present the same paper to China's Institute of Applied Physics and Computational Mathematics, China's nuclear research facility. The lab had approved both visits as well as the unclassified paper I was to talk about.

One day, when my wife was out and I was alone in my hotel room in Beijing, two Chinese scientists—Dr. Zheng Shaotong and Dr. Hu Side—visited me. Dr. Zheng did the talking, and after a few pleasantries, he asked me a question related to whether we use a certain number of explosive detonation points in a nuclear warhead of a certain size.

In response to Dr. Zheng's question about the number of detonation points in a certain-sized nuclear warhead, I replied that I didn't know and that I was not interested in discussing that topic. He just let it pass and talked about other things. Dr. Hu said nothing. When I returned to Los Alamos, I submitted a routine trip report and listed a number of the Chinese scientists I encountered, but I did not include this incident. I didn't mention it after I returned because I remembered the trouble that followed my phone call to the Lawrence Livermore scientist in 1982. Even though nothing had happened in the hotel room, I was afraid that if I reported their visit, I would be subjected to the kind of FBI questioning I'd received before. But now, as I was being polygraphed on suspicion of espionage, I told everything I could think of, so that any doubts about me could be cleared.

Little did I realize that by telling what had happened to me in that hotel room in 1988, the fact that I hadn't mentioned it earlier became the "proof" of my suspected espionage activity. Officials at the lab, the FBI, the DOJ, the DOE, politicians in Congress, and the media would later cite my recollection of this 1988 incident as evidence that I was deceptive, a liar, and therefore a probable spy. I didn't "fail to mention it" during my 1998 polygraph in the LANL conference room—I'm the one who brought it up. Only now, the fact that I reported it would become ammunition to be used against me.

The long hours of interrogation and polygraphing were exhausting. Finally, the Wackenhut examiner asked me four specific questions.

"Have you ever committed espionage against the United States?"

"No," I answered.

"Have you ever provided any classified weapons data to any unauthorized person?"

"No."

"Have you had any contact with anyone to commit espionage against the United States?"

"No."

And, "Have you ever had personal contact with anyone you know who has committed espionage against the United States?"

Again, I replied, "No."

Within about 30 minutes, I was told that I had passed the polygraph exam. Unknown to me then, the same message was given to the FBI agent who had been waiting to arrest me in case I failed the exam. So I wasn't arrested that day, and you might even say I was cleared, but I didn't feel any particular thrill —because I had fully expected to pass. I had not done the things they asked me about, so the test couldn't show that I had lied, could it?

Despite my "passing grade," I was handed some serious and bad news. I was told that my access to X Division was being suspended and that when I reported to work after the holidays, I should report to the Theoretical Division. The T Division, as it is known, focuses on basic research questions that are not classified. I would no longer have the necessary access to work in the X Division.

I was allowed to go back to my office to clear out my things. By the time I got there I was shaken, stunned by the events of the day. What had happened to provoke this interrogation? Why was I suspected of espionage? Why was I losing my access if I passed the polygraph? Every LANL scientist knew how much office politics affected who was in favor, who was to be shunned, and who worked on what projects. And I was not the sort who could play office politics—I didn't even try. My wife and my friends teased me for being a rough country bumpkin, and I suppose there is some truth to that. In 1993 I had received a notice that I had been on a list to be laid off for an anticipated potential "Reduction In Force." To even be on this "RIF" list at all was a sign that I was out of favor; yet when a later list appeared, in 1995, I wasn't on it.

In the quiet of my office, I was filled with the anxiety of not knowing. My specialized work for the last 20 years had involved classified information. A nuclear scientist without necessary access to X Division is a fish without fins. Of course I could perform productive research in the T Division. The numerous papers I had published over the years involved unclassified applications of the mathematics I used in the classified nuclear weapons field. But T Division would not make the best use of my expertise, and I would be that much closer to getting laid off or fired.

There was another reason for me to worry about this transfer to the T Division. At Los Alamos, the classified work areas were physically set apart from the unclassified areas by a fence—a high steel cyclone fence that is topped by coiled razor wire. The fence is patrolled by an armed security force, and watchtowers keep an eye out for potential violators. Sometimes SWAT teams practiced repelling mock invaders, though, to my best knowledge, there have never been any attempts to storm the fence. People with access to X Division, which is noted on the omnipresent ID badges we all wore, are among those permitted to work "inside the fence."

Most of the T Division, including the part to which I was assigned, was located outside the fence. This posed some immediate practical problems because so many of my own papers, books, files, computer programs—my "portfolio" and work product, to which I no longer had access—contained classified material that I could not bring with me into the T Division. Without access to X Division, I wasn't even supposed to have classified materials in my possession. As I went about the tedious process of sorting through what to take along with me to the T Division when the lab reopened after the week-long holiday break, I began to delete and destroy the classified material I no longer had the permission to possess. I will say more about this later, because these were the downloaded files that I was accused of giving to a foreign country—and the reason I was arrested, denied bail, and forced into solitary confinement.

* * *

It was very late when I got to my home in White Rock, the small subdivision of Los Alamos on one of the lower mesas. My daughter, Alberta, had fallen asleep on the living-room couch, but she got up right away when she heard me come in. Her eyes were round with fear. "Ba," she said to me, using the Chinese word for "Dad," "Ba, Mom says you're in some trouble at the lab." I knew that my wife was terrified about this new FBI attention, and she wouldn't be able to hide it from Alberta. I didn't know what to say to my daughter.

"Ba, are you going to be fired?" she asked.

"Mei-mei, I don't know." That's all I could manage to reply. "Mei-mei" is Chinese for "Little Sister," and it is the family name we call Alberta. I could see from the look on her face that my answer frightened her. I was the one who always had the answers in this family. She had never heard me sound so uncertain.

We did our best to celebrate Christmas in 1998. I did not grow up in the Christian tradition, but we always celebrated the holiday with our children. I'd get a tree-cutting permit and go with Chung into the Jemez mountains to find the best and biggest piñon tree; my tall, strong son would cut it down and we'd carry it home. Piñon trees are plentiful in New Mexico, and they have the most beautiful fragrance. Our home would smell like the forest for the months we kept the piñon tree because we hated to throw it away. Alberta was the artistic one in the family, and she had a special talent for decorating the tree—so that was her task. Sylvia always prepared a delicious roast duck for Christmas. That was her specialty, and it was our way of adding our Chinese heritage to our traditional dinner. On Christmas Eve we joined in with all the neighbors on our street each year by setting out luminarias along our house—the Mexican tradition of lighting the way with paper bags weighted down by sand and set aglow with candles. We had done this ever since we moved to White Rock twenty years ago. We are a close-knit family, and my kids and I could talk about anything, but this Christmas I did my best not to let the worry show.

Each year, LANL is closed between Christmas and the New Year. The official reason for this is to cut down on energy, but Los Alamos tries to foster a university-like setting for our research. That was the vision that J. Robert Oppenheimer had when he founded the lab, and it is what makes Los Alamos special among the national labs. Individual scientists can work in their offices during the holidays, if they choose.

I went back to the lab several times to try to finish moving my office. But my security swipe card no longer worked to admit me into the x Division. I needed to get in because I wanted to continue working on the scientific paper I was preparing for publication. I tried several times to get in, including late at night on Christmas Eve. Somehow I thought that the swipe card might work again at off hours. I also knew that I wasn't supposed to be trying to get into the x Division, and I was less likely to run into other people. Later, my attempts to get to my office would be used as another example to show that I was deceptive—and therefore must be a spy.

Alberta was urging me to get a lawyer. I didn't feel I needed a lawyer because I wasn't a spy and I hadn't done anything wrong. I also knew how expensive it could be to fight the lab. A friend of mine, Bob Clark, had taken LANL to court, and his legal bills were astronomical, more than what my house was worth. In fact, I had testified in court on his behalf—and was the only one at the lab who was willing to say the lab management was wrong. I wondered if that was being held against me now. But Chung agreed that I didn't need a lawyer. I thought it would all pass in time, the way my first polygraph had after I was questioned in 1984. Alberta tried very hard not to worry me, but she is the emotional one in our family, and I knew she was extremely upset by this. I tried to reassure her. "Don't worry, it will all be over soon. They'll find out the truth, and I'll be back at work like normal."

In hindsight, I was very stupid. I know now what a mistake it was for me to be so certain that nothing was wrong, and to keep talking to all the investigators from LANL, the FBI, DOE, and DOJ without counsel. I figured that all I had to do was tell the truth, since I was smart enough to answer their questions by myself. I could tough it out on my own. But I didn't even know that I didn't have to talk to the FBI. My wife sometimes says I am too stubborn, too proud, and too bullheaded. Some people say that Taiwanese people are known for being stubborn, proud, and bullheaded. I don't think it makes sense to generalize about a whole group of people, but it is true that I can be very stubborn.

Had I known that a trap was being set for me—had I the slightest inkling that my words could and would be twisted against me—I would have refused to participate in this cat-and-mouse game. I would not have given the many hours of voluntary interviews and submitted to the polygraphs that were still to come, even though I surely would have been fired on the spot. But I didn't know I could refuse to answer the questions, and I certainly didn't know that they were the cat and I was the mouse. So I just tried to be as helpful as possible.

I don't pay attention to any music that was produced after 1911, when Gustav Mahler died. I would fill the airwaves, elevators, waiting rooms, and shopping malls with classical music if I could. At the time, however, I found some small irony in the words of one Christmas song: "He knows when you are sleeping / He knows when you're awake / He knows when you've been bad or good. . . ."

The FBI had come to town.

—WEN HO LEE

Statement by Judge Parker to Wen Ho Lee, September 13, 2000

Following is a transcript of a statement by Judge James A. Parker of Federal District Court in Albuquerque to Dr. Wen Ho Lee, who pleaded guilty to mishandling nuclear secrets, as recorded by the court reporter. At one point the federal prosecutor in the case, George Stamboulidis, defends his dealings with the defense lawyer Mark Holscher.

JUDGE PARKER: Dr. Lee, you have pled guilty to a serious crime. It's a felony offense. For that you deserved to be punished. In my opinion, you have been punished harshly, both by the severe conditions of pretrial confinement and by the fact that you have lost valuable rights as a citizen.

Under the laws of our country, a person charged in Federal Court with commission of a crime normally is entitled to be released from jail until that person is tried and convicted. Congress expressed in the Bail Reform Act its distinct preference for pretrial release from jail and prescribed that release on conditions be denied to a person charged with a crime only in exceptional circumstances.

The Executive Branch of the United States Government has until today actually, or just recently, vigorously opposed your release from jail, even under what I had previously described as Draconian conditions of release.

During December 1999, the then United States Attorney, who has since resigned, and his Assistants presented me, during the three-day hearing between Christmas and New Year's Day, with information that was so extreme it convinced me that releasing you, even under the most stringent of conditions, would be a danger to the safety of this nation. The then United States Attorney personally argued vehemently against your release and ultimately persuaded me not to release you.

In my opinion and order that was entered December 30, 1999, I stated the following: "With a great deal of concern about the conditions under which Dr. Lee is presently being held in custody, which is in solitary confinement all but one hour of the week, when he is permitted to [be] visited [by] his family, the Court finds, based on the record before it, that the government has shown by clear and convincing evidence that there is no combination of conditions of release that would reasonably assure the safety of any other person and the community or the nation."

After stating that in the opinion, I made this request in the opinion right at the end: "Although the Court concludes that Dr. Lee must remain in custody, the Court urges the government attorneys to explore ways to lessen the severe restrictions currently imposed upon Dr. Lee while preserving the security of sensitive information."

I was very disappointed that my request was not promptly heeded by the government attorneys.

After December, your lawyers developed information that was not available to you or them during December. And I ordered the Executive Branch of the government to provide additional information that I reviewed, a lot of which you and your attorneys have not seen.

With more complete, balanced information before me, I felt the picture had changed significantly from that painted by the government during the December hearing. Hence, after the August hearing, I ordered your release despite the continued argument by the Executive Branch, through its government attorneys, that your release still presented an unacceptable extreme danger.

I find it most perplexing, although appropriate, that the Executive Branch today has suddenly agreed to your release without any significant conditions or restrictions whatsoever on your activities. I note that this has occurred shortly before the Executive Branch was to have produced, for my review in camera, a large volume of information that I previously ordered it to produce.

From the beginning, the focus of this case was on your motive or intent in taking the information from the secure computers and eventually downloading it on to tapes. There was never really any dispute about your having done that, only about why you did it.

What I believe remains unanswered is the question: What was the government's motive in insisting on your being jailed pretrial under extraordinarily onerous conditions of confinement until today, when the Executive Branch agrees that you may be set free essentially unrestricted? This makes no sense to me.

A corollary question I guess is: Why were you charged with the many Atomic Energy Act counts for which the penalty is life imprisonment, all of which the Executive Branch has now moved to dismiss and which I just dismissed?

During the proceedings in this case, I was told two things: First, the decision to prosecute you was made at the highest levels of the Executive Branch of the United States Government in Washington, D.C.

With respect to that, I quote from a transcript of the August 15, 2000, hearing, where I asked this question. This was asked of Dr. Lee's lawyers.

"Who do you contend made the decision to prosecute?"

Mr. Holscher responded: "We know that the decision was made at the highest levels in Washington. We know that there was a meeting at the White House the Saturday before the indictment, which was attended by the heads of a number of agencies. I believe the number two and number three persons in the Department of Justice were present. I don't know if the Attorney General herself was present. It was actually held at the White

House rather than the Department of Justice, which is, in our view, unusual circumstances for a meeting."

That statement by Mr. Holscher was not challenged.

The second thing that I was told was that the decision to prosecute you on the 39 Atomic Energy Act [counts], each of which had life imprisonment as a penalty, was made personally by the President's Attorney General. In that respect, I will quote one of the Assistant u.s. Attorneys, a very fine attorney in this case—this was also at the Aug. 15 hearing.

This is talking about materials that I ordered to be produced in connection with Dr. Lee's motion relating to selective prosecution. The first category of materials involved the January 2000 report by the Department of Energy task force on racial profiling.

"How would that in any way disclose prosecutorial strategy?"

Miss Fashing responded, "That I think falls more into the category of being burdensome on the government. I mean if the government—if we step back for just a second—I mean the prosecution decision and the investigation in this case, the investigation was conducted by the FBI, referred to the United States Attorney's Office, and then the United States Attorney's Office, in conjunction with—well, actually, the Attorney General, Janet Reno, made the ultimate decision on the Atomic Energy Act counts."

Dr. Lee, you're a citizen of the United States and so am I, but there is a difference between us. You had to study the Constitution of the United States to become a citizen. Most of us are citizens by reason of the simple serendipitous fact of our birth here. So what I am now about to explain to you, you probably already know from having studied it, but I will explain it anyway.

Under the Constitution of the United States, there are three branches of government. There is the Executive Branch, of which the President of the United States is the head. Next to him is the Vice-president of the United States. The President operates the Executive Branch with his cabinet, which is composed of secretaries or heads of the different departments of the Executive Branch. The Vice-president participates in cabinet meetings.

In this prosecution the more important members of the President's cabinet were the Attorney General and the Secretary of the Department of Energy, both of whom were appointed to their positions by the President.

The Attorney General is the head of the United States Department of Justice, which despite its title, is a part of the Executive Branch, not a part of the Judicial Branch of our government.

The United States Marshal Service, which was charged with overseeing your pretrial detention, also is a part of the Executive Branch, not the Judicial Branch.

The Executive Branch has enormous power, the abuse of which can be devastating to our citizens.

The second branch of our national government is the Legislative Branch, our Congress. Congress promulgated the laws under which you were prosecuted, the criminal statutes. And it also promulgated the Bail Reform Act, under which in hindsight you should not have been held in custody.

The Judicial Branch of government, of which I am a member, is called the Third Branch of government because it's described in Article III of our Constitution.

Judges must interpret the laws and must preside over criminal prosecutions brought by the Executive Branch. Since I am not a member of the Executive Branch, I cannot speak on behalf of the President of the United States, the Vice-president of the United States, their Attorney General, their Secretary of the Department of Energy or their former United States Attorney in this District, who vigorously insisted that you had to be kept in jail under extreme restrictions because your release pretrial would pose a grave threat to our nation's security.

I want everyone to know that I agree, based on the information that so far has been made available to me, that you, Dr. Lee, faced some risk of conviction by a jury if you were to have proceeded to trial. Because of that, I decided to accept the agreement you made with the United States Executive Branch under Rule II(e)(I)(c) of the Federal Rules of Criminal Procedure.

Further, I feel that the 278 days of confinement for your offense is not unjust; however, I believe you were terribly wronged by being held in custody pretrial in the Santa Fe County Detention Center under demeaning, unnecessarily punitive conditions. I am truly sorry that I was led by our Executive Branch of government to order your detention last December.

Dr. Lee, I tell you with great sadness that I feel I was led astray last December by the Executive Branch of our government through its Department of Justice, by its Federal Bureau of Investigation and by its United States Attorney for the district of New Mexico, who held the office at that time.

I am sad for you and your family because of the way in which you were kept in custody while you were presumed under the law to be innocent of the charges the Executive Branch brought against you.

I am sad that I was induced in December to order your detention, since by the terms of the plea agreement that frees you today without conditions, it becomes clear that the Executive Branch now concedes, or should concede, that it was not necessary to confine you last December or at any time before your trial.

I am sad because the resolution of this case drug on unnecessarily long. Before the Executive Branch obtained your indictment on the 59 charges last December, your attorney, Mr. Holscher, made a written offer to the Office of the United States Attorney to have you explain the missing tapes under polygraph examination.

I'll read from that letter of Dececember 10, 1999.

I quote from that letter: "Dear United States Attorney Kelly and First Assistant Gorence, I write to accept Mr. Kelly's request that we provide them with additional credible and verifiable information which will prove that Dr. Lee is innocent.

On the afternoon of Wednesday, December 8, Mr. Kelly informed me that it was very likely that Dr. Lee will be indicted within the next three to four business days. In our phone conversation, Mr. Kelly told me that the only way that we could prevent this indictment would be to provide a credible and verifiable explanation of what he described as missing tapes.

"We will immediately provide this credible and verifiable explanation. Specifically we are prepared to make Dr. Lee immediately available to a mutually agreeable polygraph examiner to verify our repeated written representations that at no time did he mishandle those tapes in question and to confirm that he did not provide the tapes to any third party.

"As a sign of our good faith, we will agree to submit Dr. Lee to the type of polygraph examination procedure that has recently been instituted at the Los Alamos Laboratory to question scientists. It is our understanding that the government has reaffirmed that this new polygraph procedure is the best and most accurate way to verify that scientists are properly handling classified information."

At the inception of the December hearing, I asked the parties to pursue that offer made by Mr. Holscher on behalf of Dr. Lee, but that was to no avail.

MR. STAMBOULIDIS: Your Honor, most respectfully, I take issue with that. There has been a full record of letters that were sent back and forth to you, and Mr. Holscher withdrew that offer.

THE COURT: Nothing came of it, and I was saddened by the fact that nothing came of it. I did read the letters that were sent and exchanged. I think I commented one time that I think both sides prepared their letters primarily for use by the media and not by me. Notwithstanding that, I thought my request was not taken seriously into consideration.

Let me turn for the moment to something else. Although I have indicated that I am sorry that I was led by the Executive Branch to order your detention last December, I want to make a clarification here. In fairness, I must note that virtually all of the lawyers who work for the Department of Justice are honest, honorable, dedicated people, who exemplify the best of those who represent our Federal Government.

Your attorney, Mr. Holscher, formerly was an Assistant United States Attorney. The new United States Attorney for the District of New Mexico, Mr. Norman Bay, and the many Assistant United States Attorneys here in New Mexico—and I include in this Mr. Stamboulidis and Mr. Liebman, who are present here today—have toiled long hours on this case in opposition to you. They are all outstanding members of the bar, and I have the highest regard for all of them.

It is only the top decision makers in the Executive Branch, especially the Department of Justice and the Department of Energy and locally, during December, who have caused embarrassment by the way this case began and was handled. They did not embarrass me alone. They have embarrassed our entire nation and each of us who is a citizen of it.

I might say that I am also sad and troubled because I do not know the real reasons why the Executive Branch has done all of this. We will not learn why because the plea agreement shields the Executive Branch from disclosing a lot of information that it was under order to produce that might have supplied the answer.

Although, as I indicated, I have no authority to speak on behalf of the Executive Branch, the President, the Vice-president, the Attorney General, or the Secretary of the Department of Energy, as a member of the Third Branch of the United States Government, the Judiciary, the United States Courts, I sincerely apologize to you, Dr. Lee, for the unfair manner you were held in custody by the Executive Branch.

Andrew Cunanan or
The Manhunt for Philippine America

What does a serial killer look like? The answer is: he could look like any one of us. A man. A woman. A man dressed up like a woman. Tonight, in a special Dateline *hour, we track suspected serial killer, Andrew Cunanan. His picture is everywhere, but what does he look like now? Who is this man wanted for the murder of fashion designer, Gianni Versace and four others? What touched oV the killing spree, and is it over?*
—Stone Phillips, DATELINE, July 21, 1997

So many faces. But, were the faces simply masks hiding a man no one ever really knew? Could a smile so warm conceal evil so cold?
—voice-over, DATELINE

Philippines: Where Asia Wears a Smile!
—Philippine Tourism Campaign

Apparently, even a good Filipino altar boy wearing a smile can grow up to become a serial killer. On July 27, 1997, a *New York Times* headline read "Suicide Brings Relief and Normality." The suicide in question was that of Andrew Cunanan, San Diego party boy responsible for the violent deaths of five people in Minnesota, Illinois, New Jersey, and Florida. His killing spree began on April 29 when he beat and murdered Naval Academy graduate Jeff Trail with a claw hammer. A few days later he killed a friend David Madson, and then tortured and slayed Chicago tycoon, Lee Miglin. On May 9, he struck again in New Jersey killing a caretaker, William Reese, and stealing his red pickup. Gay communities were alerted from San Francisco to New York to South Beach. The shooting of Gianni Versace on July 15 brought the "spree killer" to international attention. A week later, South Beach police found Andrew Cunanan dead. The nation let out a sigh of relief; the summer's cross-country manhunt was over. With his face horribly disfigured from the self-inflicted gunshot, Cunanan lay in the bedroom of a gleaming white houseboat. Thus, did most Americans leave him—in glaring, if not blinding, whiteness, unaware that he was Filipino.

When I read about Andrew, I was appalled and, yes, I admit it, titillated by this news-making, "shape-shifting," "over-the-hill" Filipino rent-boy with a reportedly "genius IQ." Perusing local Filipino American papers and the national media in those few weeks in 1997, I was struck by how Andrew Cunanan was portrayed in the national and the mainstream Filipino American community presses. Both savored the True Crime story elements of the tragic events: gory murders, sadomasochism, hustlers, an Italian fashion designer, and gay men, lots of them. However, the national American media, busy reveling in the mysteries of the gay demimonde, barely mentioned his Filipino heritage. Meanwhile, the mainstream Filipino American press could talk about nothing else.

Like the Filipino American newspapers, I was compelled to mark and remark upon his Filipino-ness. While watching CNN in my living room I anxiously awaited a brief small-screen glimpse of the Filipino father during the FBI and media manhunt. Was it simply my voyeuristic desires that compelled me to look for Andrew's Filipino father in the national media? I wanted to see the Filipino face to drive it home for me. I wanted to see the familiar broad Filipino nose on Andrew and to hear what the news might say about his Filipino background, rather than his possibly Irish roots. This Celtic assumption was a source of irritation for some reason. Perhaps, my perverse compulsion stemmed from a longing to be reflected in the small screen in this American media sensation. Filipinos would in some manner be part of an American drama. Any American drama.

It struck me that the non-mutual recognition—the disjuncture between the Filipino American press and the national coverage—characterized the relationship between Filipino Americans and the American public-at-large. The national media's obsession and inability to recognize Andrew's supposed masks and alleged "shapeshifting," as *Newsweek* and *Prime Time* liked to report, laid bare not only the American dis-ease with queerness, but pointed to the blind limits of the U.S. racial imagination and America's misreading and incomprehension of its imperial history. By the same token, the Filipino community papers' continual marking and remarking upon Andrew's Filipino-ness certainly bespoke of a fondness for the sensational but also of a desire to be part of that sensation by claiming and disclaiming him. A headline in the *Filipino Reporter*, "Cunanan Mourned and Reviled by Fil-Ams," underscored this schizophrenic relationship Filipino Americans had to their non-native son. The Filipino community papers' identification and simultaneous disavowal of Andrew signaled the conflicted position of Filipinos as postcolonial and ethnic Americans concerned with their public presentation. The mainstream Filipino American press depicted Andrew as having embodied the promise of assimilation by passing—socially, economically, and racially—into the white American world, yet Andrew's was an act of passing gone wrong.

In the few short weeks that Andrew captured national attention, the mainstream Filipino American press ran weekly reports on this Filipino American run amok. "Killer on the Loose" announced the *Filipino Express* headline, followed immediately by another piece entitled "Cunanan's Father Found." The FBI had alerted Philippine authorities who in turn put Andrew on an immigration blacklist. Furthermore, the FBI asked Philippine police to monitor relatives in case he would attempt to hide out in the country. The FBI and the media reached across the Pacific to the Philippines. In the Filipino American press, finding the Filipino father forged the connection, desired or not, between Andrew and Filipino American communities. The disclaimer was not far behind. "Publicity on Cunanan Tarnishes FilAm Image," lamented *Philippine News.* The lament was curious. Was it possible that this man of many faces caused Filipino American groups to lose theirs? Filipino gay men might have appeared on the community pages before but never one so lurid and sensational as to "tarnish" a whole group's image in the eyes of an imagined American public.

When Andrew committed suicide, the first sentence of the *Filipino Express* report read: "Andrew Cunanan is remembered by his relatives as an altar boy." Andrew's altar boy past invoked a mainstay in Catholic Filipino iconography tugging at parental heartstrings. Combined with his estranged father, he fit the facile image of the lost Filipino son. If only he had a good home . . . A week later, the same paper curiously informed its readers that there would be "No Philippine Burial for Cunanan" as if anyone ever saw the need to consider this possibility. Would this native burial have brought closure to his broken home, broken promise, broken story, broken body?

In the meantime, most of the national media fixated upon a more delectable milieu producing a flurry of articles about the gay underworld. Television news magazines predictably showed shots of frenzied gay men dancing in clubs engulfed by darkness, drowning in heavy hypnotic bass. Weekly magazines included short pieces on the gay "glamour after dark," supplemented by blurry photos of more dance clubs. The national press would have relegated Andrew to the middle pages as another tragic gay story were it not for Gianni Versace's murder. Concern then burst from the confines of gay communities onto the international scene. The police looked for a white male. One *New Yorker* commentator described the tense atmosphere around Miami while Cunanan was at large: "every white male between eighteen and fifty walking the sandy streets drew stares . . ." Andrew, construed as a "white male between eighteen and fifty," seemed elusive despite the sloppy trail of clues he left behind—a passport, a signature, a stolen red pickup, and video images.

Some national magazines marveled at his ingenious shape-shifting abilities. On July 21, a *Time*s article reported: "For one thing, Mr. Cunanan, a 27-year-old native of San Diego has a face so non-descript that it appears vaguely familiar to just about everyone." Indeed, it was his ordinariness that made possible his blending that led Stone Phillipps on *Dateline* to speculate that "he could look like any one of us." Being "5'–10", slim, olive skin, well-educated, well-dressed, very articulate" made him "average." But, lurking behind this facade of "normality" was a killer, engaged in "dark" sexual practices, as

SCREAMING MONKEYS

evidenced by porn tapes found in his room. He was a societal aberrant who looked like one of "us," presumably olive-skinned Americans. Andrew passed in American society in many ways. He passed across racial, social, class, and sexual lines.

To Filipinos who held a different racial schema which allowed for mestizaje, he looked like one of "us," Filipinos. He had the mestizo Filipino good-looks featured often in Filipino and Filipino American magazines, newspapers, and movies that Filipino Americans consume in Flushing or Jersey City. He could have easily been featured in the center pages of the *Filipino Reporter* and *Filipino Express,* both based in New York, or the *Philippine News,* based in California. An interviewee in the *Filipino Express* bemoaned his death. "Andrew Cunanan is such a waste. He's an altar boy, a straight-A student, handsome, intelligent, articulate." His picture could have been in those social pages along with beauty queen Miss this-or-that from Chicago, New Jersey, Los Angeles, or San Francisco. He could have been, but he was not.

In the mainstream Filipino American presses, his looks and profile appeared to embody all the mythic desires of the Filipino immigrant, yearning for that fantastical, 100-year-old promise of American assimilation. The Filipino American coverage of Andrew's story attempted to integrate him into the assimilationist promise, but something had gone awry. Perhaps, the "mourning" and "reviling"—the sense of loss and denial—exposed the inability of the Filipino immigrant narrative to reconcile his many masks, especially the queer one. The traditional narrative for a smart altar boy could not piece together fully Andrew's masks and story. His became a cautionary tale. At what point did that Filipino American face stray from that promise? Unfortunately, that smiling face, horribly disfigured in the end, refused, or perhaps, could not sustain, that promise.

Andrew's face bore the trace of the ambivalent century-long relationship between the Philippines and the United States. If we try to re-read the FBI manhunt with this relationship in mind, we're on the trail of Filipino America. How could a Filipino enter the United States without leaving the Philippines? By joining the U.S. Navy, usually filling the menial jobs reserved for Filipino enlistees. The American Dream may be realized by way of the U.S. military and its neo-colonial presence in the Philippines. Modesto Cunanan was a retired Navy man. Like other Filipinos he joined the U.S. Navy in the Philippines and wound up in San Diego, a military port city with a considerable number of Filipino residents. There, he married Mary Ann Schillaci, an Italian American, descended from an earlier wave of American immigration. They had four children, Chris, Elena, Gina, and the youngest and brightest, Andrew.

The father's favorite, Andrew, the one with the most promise, the chosen one, was sent to an elite prep school, Bishop Academy, in the tony section of

San Diego. There are two ways to further realize the American Dream—hard work and education or social climbing—though the two may not be so different in the end. Choosing the latter, Andrew spent much time and money attaining and improving upon his social capital—social skills, connections, money, and looks. A San Diego columnist commented: "He knew about the arts, the right kinds of fork to use, the right cognac to drink." In addition he offered sex and his sexuality. His social and sexual maneuvers obtained for him economic patronage from rich, older gay gentlemen, and no less important, an essential part of the American dream, astronomical credit limits on his platinum cards which he unfailingly put to use. He had class mobility, as long as his looks held out.

With his bi-racial heritage and "olive-skin," he passed himself off as a scion of a wealthy Jewish family or son of a Mexican or Filipino plantation owner. Mexican. Filipino. Jew. Andrew occupied the hazy but all too familiar territory of brown-ness that the American racial schema cannot successfully apprehend, literally and figuratively, in its little brown brothers. The u.s. nation-state polices borders, as Filipinos know only too well, and one of those borders is the color line. In many parts of the country, this line insists upon a peculiar binaristic black and white race paradigm. Sometimes, the binary is simply reduced to white and the not-white. Historically, the u.s. has had to legally contain this blurry, beigey, marshy bog of brownness. Latinos and Asian Americans (and in the past, Jews and Italians) fall in this yellow-brown category, a category reserved for, what Asian American historian Gary Okihiro termed, "custodial citizens." When strict categories, racial or sexual, fail to regulate identities and behavior such as Andrew's, stories remain incomplete. However, Andrew's "passing" narratives revealed another story.

Like the passport, the pickup and signature Andrew's masks also leave a trail of clues to America's past. Two of Andrew's "masks"—the Mexican and Filipino—hearken back to the United States's imperial past: 1848, the Mexican-American War in which northern Mexico was ceded to become California and the American Southwest; and 1898, the Spanish-Philippine-American War, which ceded the Philippines to become American territory. When a *Time*s article puzzled over Andrew's enigmatic unrecognizability—"Mr. Cunanan appears to be everywhere and nowhere"—this national media blindness could have also described Filipino presence in the United States.

Like Andrew, Filipino Americans have left many clues to their existence and live as testament to America's imperial past. Traces of this imperial past are indeed "everywhere," as the many pockets of Filipino communities evince, and "nowhere," as American public memory and vision effectively overlook the Filipino and absentmindedly ask, "what American Empire?" Despite 100 years of colonial and neocolonial relationship and exchange between the Philippines and the United States, the Philippines is virtually invisible in the American visual field, but America looms large in the Filipino imagination. American Studies scholar Amy Kaplan has suggested that "the invisibility of the Philippines in American history has everything to do with the invisibility of American imperialism to itself."

The Filipino wavers in and out of American vision and memory. The 1934 Tydings-McDuffie Act promised independence to the u.s. colonial outpost of the Philippines, and bestowed commonwealth status on the islands. At the same time, it gave Filipinos the uneasy status of American nationals, but not citizens. This awkward positioning as neither citizens nor aliens remained in place until the u.s. granted formal independence to the islands in 1946. For this reason, perhaps, the Philippines and its diaspora has, to echo Vicente Rafael, an uncanny effect on the American psyche to which Filipinos have a close and uncomfortable linkage. Colonies, like repressed memories, have a return effect on the metropole; they leave a ghostly, and sometimes bloody, trail that haunts the center.

Perhaps, this explains part of Andrew's enigma. Andrew's Filipino American story and Filipino American coverage, however, signal how Filipino identities and identifications go beyond the boundaries of the u.s. nation-state and its designated categories. The social pages in which Andrew would have appeared are usually found between articles about how horrible the situation is "back home" ridden with peso devaluations and typhoons, or about the plight of domestic workers in the Middle East and Southeast Asia. Because of global economic shifts, pockets of Filipino communities exist all over cities in North America, Southeast Asia, Australia, Oceania, the Middle East, and Europe. Filipinos as subjects and Filipino-ness are formed not only by the u.s. racial classification system but through identifications, good, bad, or ambivalent, with the stories of other Filipino communities and the images these produce. The drama-filled identifications with other spaces of labor and tragedy within and without the u.s. national borders form and inform Filipino/Filipino American identity.

Because of ever changing historical and geographical contexts, stories, and categories of race, identity, sexuality, and ethnicity cannot be taken for granted. Rather, the channels of power and multiple sources of these stories produced by imperialism complicate easy identifications with a single national narrative. Yet, these multiple identificatory sites also suggest a wider terrain of political alliances and action, making the manhunt for Philippine America that much more elusive and illusory.

What happens to a gay altar boy with a gun? What happens to a Filipino gone bad? Does he simply die in a blaze of whiteness, as did Andrew? No, with money, glamour, sex, and celebrities involved, he becomes the stuff movies are made of. In the Philippines, Modesto Cunanan sold the film rights to the filmmaker who made *Rizal sa Dapitan,* a story about the

Philippine national hero, José Rizal. In the u.s., Mary Ann Schillaci Cunanan sold movie rights of her son's life, and a b-movie was made in 1997, soon after the tragedy. How would two historically and psychically linked nations on either side of the Pacific tell Andrew Cunanan's story to themselves? Is it an American story? Is it a Filipino story? Is it a Filipino American story? Is it a tragic, "gay" story? Or is it all of these with traces of America's empire?

—ALLAN ISAAC

vegetarian

man-eater

mix accordingly

Hennessy
VERY SPECIAL
COGNAC

Back cover of *Premier*, Volume 14, No. 1, September 2000.

Untitled Art by Phung Huynh

Surrogate Slaves to American Dreamers

—an excerpt from Asian American Dreams

In my childhood photo album, there is a tattered brown news clipping taped to the inside cover. It features me as George Washington, looking as earnest as a seven-year-old in shorts can. I'm pointing straight ahead across a make-believe frozen river, leading other girls who are pulling imaginary oars. "Charades," the caption reads. ". . . Helen Zia, as Washington."

When the *Burlington County Times* photographed our tableau of George and the fateful crossing, no one seemed to care that this Revolutionary War hero was a Chinese girl, in a rice-bowl hairdo and razor-edge bangs. The role seemed natural enough to me. I was steeped in the stories of the ragtag Colonial Army and how it outsmarted the British and the Hessian mercenaries on Christmas night.

Each year, my history classes followed a predictable rhythm. September began with the Leni-Lenapes, the local Native American Indians who had vanished long ago. By midyear we were into Manifest Destiny, the Gold Rush, and the "settling" of the West. The Civil War came and went, and slavery was finally abolished. In the spring, we zipped through Woodrow Wilson, the League of Nations, and World War II. In this whirlwind treatment of history, there wasn't a single Asian American to be found. I hadn't a clue that people like me might have contributed to the building of America, the land of my birth.

The Second World War brought Asian faces into my textbooks, but that was hardly cause for celebration. My school chums would turn and squint at me, the face of the enemy. In American history texts, Asian people were either invisible or reviled. It was just like the real-life choice we faced, our Asian American dilemma. Was it better to choose invisibility and a life in the shadows than to be treated as a despised enemy? Or was acquiescent invisibility just another form of self-loathing?

My father wanted us to have a deeper understanding of history that included our Chinese heritage. As a young man he had translated and published several Western texts, including Georg Hegel's *Lectures on the Philosophy of History* from German into Chinese. His greater challenge was to imbue his American-born children with a similar devotion to knowledge. To accomplish this, he employed the teaching methods favored by many Asian immigrant parents: force feeding and strict discipline. He also bought the *Encyclopaedia Britannica* from a door-to-door salesperson and assigned sections for my brothers and me to read. Then he'd quiz us with his own written and oral exams. Oral were worse. If we did well, we might be rewarded with a nickel, but the real incentive was to avoid the humiliation that came with failure.

Dad was not happy with the *Britannica*. He found the sections on China to be outdated and inaccurate; he bristled at the Western romanizations of important Chinese words and was driven to fury by Western arrogance toward Chinese people. He took issue with the title of Will and Ariel Durant's *Story of Civilization,* which in one volume covered five thousand years of Asian civilizations and devoted eleven volumes to European cultures. But he respected the knowledge they presented, and wanted us to study such books critically.

To supplement the shortcomings of Western texts, Dad lectured his children on China's glorious past. One of his favorite stories was about Cheng Ho, the Chinese explorer. Cheng Ho made seven voyages from Suzhou to Java and to various points around the Indian Ocean during the Ming dynasty. His enormous fleets of huge junks carried ten thousand armed men and were laden with fine silks. Cheng Ho's final voyage was launched in 1431, decades ahead of Christopher Columbus, centuries before the *Mayflower.* Dad always ended his lesson in frustration, saying, "If only Cheng Ho had turned left across the Pacific instead of turning right toward India, America would be Asian, not European."

Cheng Ho's wrong turn was Dad's link between Chinese and American history. Though he mused about the land bridge across the Bering Strait during the Great Ice Age ten thousand years ago, my father had little else to say about Asians in America. In spite of his great interest in history, there was no body of knowledge for him to teach his Chinese American kids.

One day Dad brought home an old book from a flea market, *The Pictorial History of the United States.* Of the four hundred pictures, one showed Asians in America: terrified Chinese, fleeing persecution from murderous white mobs in Denver, Colorado. A few pages later was a photo marking the completion of the transcontinental railroad. All the workers were white, as though there had been no Chinese railroad workers.

In college I found some of the missing stories—not in textbooks, but from young scholars and activists who launched a movement to find our lost history, to give faces and names to Asian American pioneers, and to place them in history books with George Washington, Columbus, and the *Mayflower.* From them I learned that Asian American faces had been deliberately obscured. As their American stories came to light, I found that I didn't have to choose between invisibility and revulsion. Instead, I discovered dramatic moments in the nation's history with Asian Americans at center stage, a history of which every American could be proud.

Long before the thirteen colonies declared their independence from Britain, Asian people could be found in the Americas. The first Asian Americans appeared as early as the 1500s. From 1565 to 1815, during the lucrative Spanish galleon trade between Manila and Mexico, sailors in the Philippines were conscripted into service aboard Spanish ships. A number of these seamen jumped ship for freedom, establishing a settlement on the coast of Louisiana; today, their descendants live in New Orleans.

In the 1600s, a thriving Chinatown bustled in Mexico City. The Chinese American success led Spanish barbers to petition the Viceroy in 1635 to move the Chinese barbers to the city's outskirts. Even then Asians were seen as a threat in the New World.

At the Continental Congress of the new United States of America in 1785, our nation's founders discussed the plight of some Chinese sailors stranded in Baltimore by their U.S. cargo ship, the *Pallas,* which had set sail for China. Meanwhile, the Reverend William Bentley of Salem, Massachusetts, wrote in his diary in 1790 that he spied a "tall, well-proportioned, dark complexioned man from Madras," India, walking about the town.

The first known Asian American New Yorker was born in 1825, the son of a Chinese merchant seaman who married an Irishwoman. In 1850, a young Japanese sailor was rescued at sea by an American ship; he learned English and became a U.S. citizen, adopting the name Joseph Hecco. He went to work in the office of a U.S. senator, met three U.S. presidents: Pierce, Buchanan, and Lincoln—and served as an important adviser in the establishment of United States-Japan relations. In 1854, a Chinese man by the name of Yung Wing graduated from Yale College and established an educational mission from China to the United States.

It is hard for most Americans to imagine Asian people on the scene in George Washington's day. Even today, prominent Asian Americans are thought of as foreign, alien. In 1984, Congressman Norman Mineta, a second-generation Japanese American who served in the U.S. House of Representatives for ten terms, was a guest speaker at the opening of an auto plant in his California district surrounding San Jose, the first joint venture between General Motors and Toyota. During the ceremony, a senior vice president of General Motors and general manager of Chevrolet said to the congressman, "My, you speak English well. How long have you been in this country?"

The real story of Asians in America is inextricably bound to several of the driving forces of American history—the westward expansion to the Pacific and beyond, the growing nation's unquenchable need for cheap labor, the patriotic fervor of a young country in the throes of defining itself, and the ways in which race and racism were used to advance those ends.

Our Asian American migration begins with the Anglo-American moral dilemma over slavery. In 1806, one year before Britain officially ended the slave trade, two hundred Chinese were brought to Trinidad, a small offering to assuage the insatiable demand for plantation labor in the New World.

Using the same ships that brought slaves from Africa, the flesh merchants rerouted to Asia. They indentured "coolie" labor from China and India to perform the same work, under the same conditions, as the slaves; in the case of Cuba, which continued the practice of slavery until the end of the nineteenth century, the Asian coolies worked alongside African slaves.

Despite the similar treatment, it is important to note that the Asian workers were not slaves; according to Professor Evelyn Hu-DeHart of the University of Colorado at Boulder, the coolies themselves insisted on the distinction between their status and that of the slaves. The Asians worked knowing that they would be free men after they served their eight-year contracts and paid off their indebtedness for their passage, food, clothing, and other necessities—which often extended their servitude for years. With China and India in political and economic chaos resulting from Britain's imperial expansion, a vast pool of desperate Asian workers became available as commodities. This reliance on Asia for cheap labor was the start of a global trend that continues to the present.

Over several decades beginning in 1845, more than 500,000 Asian Indians were shipped to British Guiana (now Guyana), the West Indies, and various French colonies. Importation of Chinese began in earnest in 1847, first headed to Cuba, where more than 125,000 Chinese eventually supplemented the shrinking African slave labor force. Peru and other parts of South America also became major markets for human cargo from Asia. Most of the laborers were men, setting a pattern of Asian bachelor societies for the next hundred years.

The Pioneers from Asia

"Strangers from a different shore" is how historian Ronald Takaki, of the University of California at Berkeley, characterized the perception of immigrants from Asia, in his book by the same title. When gold was first discovered at Sutter's Mill in 1848, fewer than a hundred Chinese, mostly merchants and traders, were living in California. Plans to import Chinese labor to the territory were already in the works when news of gold reached China. Men from the villages near Canton in Southern China took off with dreams of making it in "Gold Mountain," their name for America. In 1850, some 50 Chinese arrived; the next year, 2,716. By 1860, some 41,000 Chinese had come to the United States. These Chinese were not coolies but "semifree" men who were deeply in debt from high-interest loans for their passage to America, according to K. Scott Wong and Sucheng Chan in *Claiming America: Constructing Chinese American Identities during the Exclusion Era.* By comparison, nearly 2.5 million Europeans immigrated during that same ten-year period.

Initially, the Chinese were welcomed to San Francisco, and some even participated in California's statehood ceremonies in 1850. The reception quickly turned cold, however, as new laws and taxes singled out the Chinese. A foreign-miners tax targeted Chinese miners, not Europeans. The tax gave way to complete prohibition of Chinese from mining. Laws forbade Chinese to testify in court, even in their own defense. Special zoning ordinances were selectively enforced against Chinese. Hair-cutting ordinances forced Chinese to cut off the braids, or queues, that the emperor required as proof of loyalty—ironically, making it harder for workers to return to China. In San Francisco, special license fees were levied solely against Chinese laundries.

The discriminatory treatment of the Chinese was overtly racist: the California state legislature declared that "Negroes, Mongolians, and Indians shall not be admitted into public schools." When the vote became available to African American men after the Civil War, citizenship was specifically denied to Chinese, because, it was reasoned, Chinese were neither black nor white.

Then came the killings. White gold diggers seized Chinese miners' stakes by beating, burning, and shooting the Chinese. Mass kidnappings and murders of Chinese took place, leading the *Shasta Republican* to report in 1856, "Hundreds of Chinamen have been slaughtered in cold blood during the last five years by desperadoes that infest our state. The murder of Chinamen is almost of daily occurrence, yet in all this time we have heard of but two or three instances where the guilty parties have been brought to justice and punished according to law."

Expelled from the goldfields, the Chinese miners found work with a railroad company hungry for workers. By 1865, Thomas Jefferson's dream of a transcontinental route was finally within reach. The Central Pacific Railroad was contracted to build the difficult half from the Pacific, through the Rocky Mountains; within two years, 12,000 Chinese were hired—about 90 percent of the company's workforce.

The Chinese workers shoveled, picked, blasted, and drilled their way through boulders, rock, and dirt, often suspended from mountain peaks high in the Sierras, even in the harsh mountain winters. It is estimated that one in ten Chinese died building the railroad. In return, they were paid sixty cents for every dollar paid to white workers. Chinese workers went on strike to protest the brutal conditions, going back to work only when Charles Crocker, superintendent of construction for the Central Pacific, cut off their food supply. In the meantime, the railroad made plans to ship several thousand black workers from the East in case the strike continued.

When the transcontinental railroad was completed in 1869, Chinese workers were barred from the celebrations. The speeches congratulated European immigrant workers for their labor but never mentioned the Chinese. Instead, the Chinese men were summarily fired and forced to walk the long distance back to San Francisco—forbidden to ride on the railroad they built.

The Driving-Out Time

In the late 1870s, the anti-Chinese "Yellow Peril" movement gripped the West. Cities erupted in riots against the Chinese—homes, laundries, and shops were burned to the ground. Murders and lynchings of Chinese were commonplace. Chinese women—the very small number who were admitted to the United States—were molested by angry gangs of whites. In rural areas, white farm workers set fire to the barns and fields where Chinese lived and worked. These egregious acts established a particular brand of American racism that would be directed against Asian Americans into the next century.

The Chinese called this the driving-out time. The illustration of terrified Chinese men I had seen as a child stemmed from this period. The Workingmen's Party in California, a white labor party with a large Irish following, adopted the slogan "The Chinese must go!" One of its ideas was to drop a balloon filled with dynamite on San Francisco's Chinatown. The "Chinese question" framed the labor stance for Democrats and Republicans: while Democrats exploited the race hysteria to win the support of labor, Republicans supported the business ideal of an unlimited supply of second-class, low-wage labor. Caught between the racism of both political parties, the Chinese were used to inflame and distract white workers, frustrated by rising unemployment and an economic depression.

From Los Angeles to Denver, from Seattle to Rock Springs, Wyoming, Chinese were driven out. In Tacoma, Washington, hundreds of Chinese were herded onto boats and set adrift at sea, presumably to their deaths. Mobs burned all the Chinese homes and businesses in Denver in 1880. Newspapers from *The New York Times* to the *San Francisco Chronicle* stirred fears that the Chinese, together with the newly freed black population, would become a threat to the Republic. Years earlier, orator Horace Greeley had captured the sense of the intelligentsia: "The Chinese are uncivilized, unclean, and filthy beyond all conception without any of the higher domestic or social relations; lustful and sensual in their dispositions; every female is a prostitute of the basest order."

The anti-Chinese fervor led Congress to pass the Chinese Exclusion Act in 1882, not only barring Chinese from immigrating but forbidding legal residents from becoming citizens, a prohibition that would inhibit Asian American political development for decades to come. The ugly legislation was also the first ever passed by Congress targeting a group based on race.

Against this tide of Yellow Peril fever, Chinese Americans organized early civil rights groups—the Native Sons of the Golden State, later becoming the Chinese American Citizens Alliance, in San Francisco, and the Chinese Equal Rights League in New York. The Chinese Six Companies, formed in 1854, fought the Chinese Exclusion Act of 1882 all the way to the u.s. Supreme Court, which ultimately ruled against them in 1889. Seventeen lawsuits by

Chinese Americans went to the Supreme Court between 1881 and 1896, with a few setting important civil rights precedents. In 1896 *Yick Wo v. Hopkins* established that "race-neutral" laws could not be selectively enforced against a particular group, as the city of San Francisco did against Chinese laundries, in violation of the Fourteenth Amendment of the Constitution. In 1898 the principle of u.s. citizenship by birthright was affirmed after native-born American Wong Kim Ark was denied reentry into the United States because he was Chinese. Through Wong's appeals, the u.s. Supreme Court ruled that all persons born in the United States are citizens by birth. Many of these cases became precedents that broke down barriers for African Americans and others during the civil rights movements of the twentieth century.

Nevertheless, after the Chinese Exclusion Act the population of Chinese plummeted to 71,531 in 1910. After building the West and contributing to the national economy, the Chinese men were confined to work as domestics, or in laundries and restaurants. The few crowded Chinatowns offered Chinese Americans some protection from racial terrorism and violence, but the numerous race restrictions prevented most Chinese from starting families and putting down roots in America.

An Elusive Dream

Though the gates to America closed for Chinese, other Asian nations still offered a source of labor for the backbreaking work that white workers were unwilling to do. American labor brokers introduced in consecutive stages Japanese, Indian, Korean, and Filipino workers. Ethnic hostilities were used to pit the Asians against one another. Each successive immigrant group came with the expectation that *they* would avoid the problems of their predecessors and succeed in becoming American.

In 1888, the first 75 Japanese workers were brought in for the California harvest. Within two decades, more than 150,000 Japanese men and women immigrated. Like China, Japan was in deep economic crisis. Widespread starvation prompted many to take their chances as indentured laborers in America. By the 1920s, the Japanese American population reached 220,596— almost double the Chinese population. But the Japanese government, unlike China's, took an active interest in its citizens' welfare, viewing the emigrants as its representatives to the world.

The Japanese government was confident its citizens could avoid the fate of the Chinese, whom they thought responsible for their own misfortunes in America. "It is indeed the ignominious conduct and behavior of indigent Chinese of inferior character . . . that brought upon [them] the contempt of the Westerners and resulted in the enactment of legislation to exclude them from the country," the Japanese consul to the United States reported in 1884. The government of Japan screened all early émigrés. Many were literate and more educated than their Chinese or European counterparts. Women were also encouraged to emigrate because of their stabilizing family influence.

In 1900, there were about one thousand Japanese women in the United States, but that number increased until 39 percent of Japanese immigrants were female. A "picture bride" system developed, allowing matchmaking to take place through photo exchanges, an imperfect system that frequently involved outdated or even fake photos, often to the great disappointment of the bride. The u.s. government refused to recognize the legality of the Japanese picture bride marriages, and the public derided Japanese women as immoral, even though photo matchmaking was common and tolerated among European immigrants. By 1920, more than 60,000 Japanese women were living in the mainland United States and Hawaii and 29,672 children had been born. American citizens by birth, these children—the Nisei, or second-generation Japanese Americans—made up the first Asian American baby boom.

The growing Japanese population on the West Coast and in Hawaii became a new target for the strong racial hatred directed against the Chinese only a few years earlier. While the racial slur "Jap" became part of everyday speech, Japanese immigrants also encountered the phenomenon of racial "lumping" of Asians: anti-Chinese slurs were routinely directed against them as if there were no difference between the two peoples. Despite the Japanese government's efforts to see that its overseas citizens would be treated equally, new laws were written against the Japanese.

The Japanese were condemned as more dangerous than the Chinese because of their willingness and ability to adopt American customs. Whereas the Chinese were attacked for not assimilating, the Japanese were reviled because they readily integrated. By 1913, a number of states west of the Mississippi River already prohibited Chinese and Asian Indians from owning land. The situation for Japanese immigrants in California was ambiguous until 1920, when a more comprehensive Alien Land Law was passed, preventing anyone of Asian ancestry from owning land.

In 1922, a Japanese immigrant who had become Americanized in every way but citizenship brought a challenge against the citizenship ban to the Supreme Court in *Ozawa v. United States*. Takao Ozawa attended high school in California and studied at the University of California for three years. He belonged to an American church and had no dealings with Japan or Japanese organizations. He married a Japanese woman who, like him, had been educated in the United States. Their family spoke English at home and the children attended American schools. But the u.s. District Court rejected his application for citizenship in 1916, ruling that Ozawa was "in every way eminently qualified under the statutes to become an American citizen" but for his race. The u.s. Supreme Court upheld the decision that Ozawa was not entitled to citizenship because he was not Caucasian.

The decision was a big setback to the Japanese, who were caught in a cruel vise—under constant attack both for being "foreign" and for being "too ready to adapt." In the Kingdom of Hawaii, a number of Japanese had become naturalized citizens, but when Hawaii was annexed by the United States in 1898, becoming a territory in 1900, the territorial government refused to recognize them as u.s. citizens. Newspaper publisher V.S. McClatchy testified before Congress: "Of all the races ineligible to citizenship, the Japanese are the least assimilable and the most dangerous to this country . . . They come here . . . for the purpose of colonizing and establishing permanently the proud Yamato race. They never cease to be Japanese."

For the Japanese, the final blow came when Congress passed the Immigration Act of 1924, which was worded in a veiled way to sound applicable to all immigrants. It barred anyone who was "forbidden to be a u.s. citizen" from immigrating at all. The real intent of the law was to halt Japanese immigration, which had reached a total of 275,000 over a thirty-year span. While white nativists complained of the "huge waves" of Asian immigrants, by comparison, 283,000 Italians arrived in a single year, 1913–14.

With the population of Japanese immigrants increasing, plantation owners in Hawaii and labor brokers in the mainland United States feared that the growing community might organize for more money and better working conditions. To keep the workforce fragmented, the labor brokers looked to India for workers.

In 1900, some 2,050 Asian Indians resided in the United States. Most of these earliest Indian immigrants were professionals, students, merchants, and visitors in the northeastern states. However, between 1906 and 1908, nearly 5,000 Asian Indian emigrants from the Punjab region arrived in Canada, which quickly established regulations that would prevent "hordes of hungry Hindus" from entering the country. In reality only a small fraction of the Indians were Hindu, most being Sikhs and about one third Muslim, but the misnomer stuck. Discouraged from entering Canada, many of the Indians headed south to Washington and Oregon. Others ventured to the farmlands of California, where they were contracted specifically to counter the labor power of the Japanese workers. Intra-Asian hostilities arose between the Japanese and Asian Indian laborers working next to each other in the California farmland.

Prevailing race theories included Asian Indians with the Caucasian race. European Americans acknowledged them as "full-blooded Aryans." This led many Asian Indians to believe that they were a cut above the other Asian migrants and could avoid the prejudice that the others faced. Citizenship was actually granted to some sixty-seven Indians, in seventeen states, between 1905 and 1923. The 1790 Naturalization Law allowed "free white persons" to become U.S. citizens, and Asian Indians were thought to be part of the "Mediterranean branch of the Caucasian family."

Nevertheless, their dark skin and willingness to work for low wages made Asian Indians a threat to white society. The Japanese and Korean Exclusion League, established in 1905, later changed its name to the Asiatic Exclusion League to include the Punjabis. Agitating against the "Indian menace" and the "tide of turbans," they succeeded in barring Asian Indians from entering the United States between 1908 and 1920. A magazine writer of that time warned: "This time the chimera is not the saturnine, almond-eyed mask . . . of the multitudinous Chinese, nor the close-cropped bullet-heads of the suave and smiling Japanese, but a face of finer features, rising, turbaned out of the Pacific." Whites forced seven hundred Asian Indians from their community in Bellingham, Washington, across the border into Canada in 1907. A few months later Asian Indians in Everett, Washington, were rounded up and expelled. Indian immigration was short-lived, ending with the Immigration Act of 1917.

In an effort to tear down citizenship barriers for Asian Indians, Bhagat Singh Thind took the issue to court. Thind had been granted citizenship in 1920 by an Oregon court, on the grounds that he was Caucasian, but the federal government disagreed and appealed in 1923. Arguing his case before the U.S. Supreme Court, Thind reasoned that Indians are Caucasians, not Asians, and therefore should be accorded full rights of citizenship, including land ownership and suffrage. But the Court determined in *United States v. Bhagat Singh Thind* that it was not enough to be "Caucasian." It ruled that it was also necessary to be "white." Since Indians were not white, they could not become citizens, nor could they own land or send for their wives from India.

The decision in the *Thind* case was applied retroactively, and the citizenship of the naturalized Indian Americans was revoked. One Indian American committed suicide, writing in a note that he tried to be "as American as possible," but "I am no longer an American citizen . . . I do not choose to live a life as an interned person." The small Asian Indian population declined after the *Thind* decision, but a few thousand stayed on. A majority of the Asian Indian men in California married Mexican women and established successful farming communities. Other Sikhs, believing that discrimination was stronger against Asian Indians, abandoned their turbans and tried to pass as Mexican or black.

Korea offered yet another pool of cheap labor for the United States, as political and economic instability resulting from Japanese aggression sent many Koreans into exile. From 1903 to 1907, about 7,000 Koreans came to the United States, mostly to work as contract plantation laborers to Hawaii.

Over 1,200 women and children also made the journey. Unlike the other Asian contract laborers before them, the first Korean immigrants came from cities, and were working, for example, as police officers, miners, clerks, even monks. Some 40 percent were Christians, encouraged to come to the United States by American missionaries.

Because their numbers were small, the Koreans didn't develop communities or settlements, as the earlier Asian immigrants had. Instead, they deliberately sought to become integrated into American society, learning English as quickly as possible, worshipping as Christians, and expressing their gratitude to America. Many Koreans felt that both the Chinese and Japanese were to blame for the hate they received from whites. They thought they could avoid the same fate. According to the Korean newspaper *Kongnip Sinmun*, "The reason why many Americans love Koreans and help us, while they hate Japanese more than ever, is that we Koreans gave up old baseness, thought and behavior, and became more westernized." Nevertheless, Koreans in America were subject to the same anti-Asian laws barring citizenship, land ownership, and equal access to education and housing.

Korean migration to America ended within a few years. Japan, which had occupied parts of Korea since the late 1800s, cut off Korean immigration to Hawaii in 1907, fearing that Korean labor would hurt the Japanese in Hawaii. The government also wanted to halt the overseas Korean independence movement. But this became moot when the Immigration Act of 1924 ended all immigration from China, Japan, India, and Korea. Although the Asian immigrants failed to connect with one another, u.s. policy and the prevailing anti-Asian racism subjected them all to the same treatment.

The last significant migration of Asians to the United States in the early twentieth century came from the Philippines. Because the Philippines was a u.s. territory and its residents were u.s. nationals, Filipinos carried u.s. passports and could travel freely within the States—they were the only Asians eligible for immigration after 1924. Hundreds of Filipinos came to the United States as college students beginning in 1903, on scholarships set up by the United States after it annexed the Philippines, ceded by Spain after the Spanish-American War. After 1907, more than 70,000 Filipino laborers arrived in Hawaii as contract laborers. Between 1920 and 1929, some 51,875 Filipino workers arrived on the mainland—many via Hawaii—to work in the fields and in other low-wage jobs on the West Coast, doing the same work as other earlier, excluded Asian immigrants.

Filipino immigrants, too, thought they could circumvent the troubles of the other Asians. In 1933, Filipino Salvador Roldan sought the right to marry outside his race by challenging California's 1880 antimiscegenation law that prohibited marriage between whites and "Negroes, mulattoes, or

Mongolians." Roldan argued that Filipinos are actually "Malay," not "Mongolian," and therefore not subject to the 1880 law. The California Court of Appeals agreed that Filipinos were not Mongolian and allowed him to marry his white fiancée. The California legislature immediately voted to add the "Malay race" to the forbidden list. Once again, an attempt by one Asian group to separate itself from the others had failed.

Anti-Filipino prejudice continued to grow, with vigilantes attacking, even burning, the camps where the Filipino laborers lived, the very land that Chinese had made arable before they were driven out nearly two generations earlier. "This Is a White Man's Country" was the message on a sign in Salinas, California. With Filipinos, white nativists focused on the menace that a bachelor society posed to white women. Testifying before the House Committee on Immigration and Naturalization in 1930, newspaper publisher V.S. McClatchy, a consistent voice against the "Yellow Peril," said, "You can realize, with the declared preference of the Filipino for white women and the willingness on the part of some white females to yield to that preference, the situation which arises . . . California in this matter is seeking to protect the nation, as well as itself, against the peaceful penetration of another colored race."

The white exclusionists strategized that there was only one way to end Filipino immigration: the United States would have to grant "independence" to the Philippines. Their racially inflamed arguments persuaded Congress to pass another law specifically targeting Asians, the Tydings-McDuffie Act of 1934, converting the Philippines to a commonwealth. Immediately, all Filipinos were reclassified as aliens and prohibited from applying for citizenship because they weren't white. Only fifty Filipinos from any nation of origin would be permitted to immigrate each year, except for plantation labor to Hawaii. As with the Japanese in Hawaii, Filipinos were debarred from leaving the Hawaiian Territory for the mainland. Congress even offered to pay for workers' fare to the Philippines if they agreed never to return; the *Los Angeles Times* urged Filipinos to "go back home." Fewer than 5 percent took the offer—in spite of the elusiveness of citizenship, the rest wanted to stay in America, as Americans.

Working on the Fringes of America

Of the approximately 489,000 Asians living in the United States when immigration from Asia was shut off after 1934, perhaps 99 percent had come to work as laborers, or were the offspring of laborers. Although these immigrants were overwhelmingly working-class, like those from Europe, they found no openings for solidarity with other workers in the burgeoning labor movements of the day. Rather, their status as "aliens ineligible for citizenship" who were neither white nor black turned them into objects of hostility and revulsion who could be used as a racial wedge by unionists and capitalists alike.

While Denis Kearney of the Workingmen's Party made driving out the Chinese his rallying cry, Samuel Gompers, founder and president of the American Federation of Labor, also maintained a special antipathy toward Asian workers. He refused to issue a charter to an early effort at multi-racial labor organizing by the Japanese Mexican Labor Association with the admonition "Your union will under no circumstance accept membership of any Chinese or Japanese." When Asian Indians became a farm labor presence, in 1908 Gompers added them to his prohibited-from-membership list.

California's business leaders acknowledged in the late 1800s that the state's industries could not have developed without Chinese labor to build the railroads, to drain the delta swamps of the Sacramento and San Joaquin rivers, to build the vineyards and work in its main manufacturing industries of shoes, woolens, cigars, and sewing. But they found another purpose for Chinese workers: the low wages paid to them could intimidate both white and black workers. Using Asian workers as a racialized wedge set a powerful model for a future role that Asian Americans could play.

Businesses in other parts of the country tried to duplicate California's labor machinations. Southern plantation owners imported Chinese to Mississippi, Arkansas, and Louisiana in the 1870s to "punish the Negro for having abandoned the control of his old master." Chinese were also brought to factories in Massachusetts, New Jersey, and Pennsylvania to keep the wage rates down. The presence of Asian workers in Hawaii and the West served another function: they gave white labor the possibility of upward mobility by subordinating the Chinese. As railroad builder Charles Crocker observed, "After we got Chinamen to work, we took the more intelligent of the white laborers and made foremen of them . . . they got a start by controlling Chinese labor on our railroad."

In Hawaii, Asian workers made a special contribution to American labor history. With the Native Hawaiian population decimated by illnesses introduced by its colonizers, plantation developers relied on imported Asian labor. Hawaii was the first stop for many Asian immigrants to America. Labor contractors scoured Asia, Europe, and the Caribbean for cheap labor, bringing in Portuguese, Puerto Rican, and African American workers, but the vast majority were Asian. By 1920, the contractors had imported more than 300,000 laborers from Asia, who comprised 62 percent of the islands' population.

American business interests were busy creating a sugar plantation system that would turn Hawaii into an economic colony of the United States. To do so, they embarked on a labor strategy of racial and ethnic antagonism. In *Strangers from a Different Shore,* Ronald Takaki chronicled the labor strategy of the plantation owners: "Keep a variety of laborers, that is different nationalities, and thus prevent any concerted action in case of strikes, for there are few, if any, cases of 'Japs,' Chinese, and Portuguese entering into a strike as a unit," advised one plantation manager. The Asian workers were mere commodities on supply manifests: "Bonemeal, canvas, Japanese laborers, macaroni, a Chinaman," read one plantation receipt. Foreign labor was imported to "set an example" for the Native Hawaiian workers; Chinese were hired to "play off" against Japanese, while Portuguese were brought in to offset the Chinese. As whites, the Portuguese were paid more than the Asians and took on the role of *lunas,* or overseers.

When Japanese workers organized for higher wages and better working conditions, plantation owners turned to Korea, sure that Koreans would never join any Japanese strike efforts. After Japan closed off Korean immigration, Filipinos were imported into Honolulu in order to put the Japanese "in their place." Inter-Asian resentments inevitably led to fights and even riots in the labor camps. The strategy of divide and conquer was effective, especially with newer immigrants who were less willing to risk changing the status quo. Despite the deliberate attempts to provoke ethnic friction, unity was eventually achieved. In 1920, Filipino and Japanese plantation workers decided to join ranks against the plantation owners; 3,000 members of the Filipino Federation of Labor and 5,000 Japanese workers went on strike after their demands for higher wages were rejected by the owners. Representing 77 percent of the plantation workforce, they brought sugar production to a halt, leading to a $12 million production loss. The strikers were joined by Portuguese and Chinese workers in the first united, interethnic labor action in Hawaii. Their action ultimately resulted in a 50 percent wage increase and paved the way for a strong trade union movement tradition that continues in modern-day Hawaii.

In the Western states, Filipino workers were in the vanguard of farm worker organizing, forming the Filipino Labor Union. They contributed significantly to the American labor movement, building interethnic solidarity with Mexican and white workers. In 1936, the Filipino Labor Union led a strike alongside Mexican workers. Their joint union received a charter from the American Federation of Labor—finally overcoming the barriers set by union founder Samuel Gompers against Asian workers in the unions. It is a little-known footnote to American history that Filipino labor activists initiated the United Farm Workers' grape pickers' strike that Cesar Chavez would build into a movement.

The labor and creativity of Asian Americans were responsible to a significant degree for developing the economies of California, Hawaii, Washington, Oregon, Alaska, and elsewhere in the growing nation. Many Asian Americans left the West Coast to find opportunities in less hostile locations in the Eastern and Midwestern states. Chinatowns and Japantowns sprang up as centers of commerce and social life, providing basic services to their separate and unequal communities. Even faced with the multitude of inhospitable barriers, Asian

Americans found ways to build lives in America. They formed their own political and cultural organizations, and sometimes they were able to beat city hall—as they did in 1906 in Butte, Montana, where Chinese successfully fought a boycott aimed at driving them out of town.

In addition to their labor, the Asian immigrants made significant contributions to their adopted homeland. In 1875, Ah Bing developed the Bing cherry in Oregon, and in 1886, Lue Gim Gong produced the frost-resistant Lue orange, which became the foundation of Florida's citrus industry. In Hawaii, Japanese workers created irrigation systems throughout the islands. In 1921, two Koreans, Harry Kim and Charles Kim (not related), invented the nectarine, the "perfect, fuzzless peach," in Reedley, California, and opened a successful orchard business, Kim Brothers. In California's Central Valley, Asian Indians found that the region resembled the Punjab and used their expertise with irrigation methods and specialized crops to make the land productive. In Louisiana, the descendants of the Filipino sailors who escaped the Spanish galleons introduced the process of sundrying shrimp to the region.

As the Asian immigrants had children, they were able to find ways around laws that forbade them to own or lease land. Japanese in particular were able to establish families because women had immigrated in significant numbers, but other Asians were also able to wed Asian women who made it into the country or women of other races. Their American-born children were American citizens by birth and therefore not subject to the "alien land" ownership prohibitions. Many immigrant Japanese parents bought farmland in their children's names. Farmers without children paid other families with Nisei—second-generation—children to use their names as fictitious landowners. In this way, Asian immigrants were able to create thousands of acres of productive farms across the West.

Although the American-born generations were entitled to the privileges of American citizenship, they continued to be treated as foreigners. Still subject to segregated housing and unequal treatment, young men and women who made it through high school and college could find work only as field hands and domestic workers, in the same limited occupations as their immigrant parents. Though the various Asian American ethnic groups experienced similar prejudices and were lumped together by other Americans as equally undesirable, each group suffered separately and in its own enclave.

Infamy

World War II changed everything. Suddenly, the events in Asia and the political realignment of the United States and Asian nations dictated a new social order among the separate enclaves of the various Asian American groups.

Years before the bombing of Pearl Harbor drew the United States into war with Japan, the different Asian communities in America were engaged in war relief efforts. Many Korean Americans took part in a resistance movement against the harsh Japanese military rule of Korea, which had fallen under increasing Japanese control since the late 1800s until it was formally annexed in 1910. Japanese aggression against China that began in 1931 sparked demonstrations by Chinese Americans, who raised $56 million for China war relief between 1937 and 1945.

On December 7, 1941, Japan bombed Pearl Harbor, and seven hours later, Japanese planes turned the Philippines into a war zone. Suddenly China and the Philippines were important allies of the United States against Japan. Almost overnight, the much maligned Chinese and Filipino "rat-eaters," "monkeys," and "headhunters" were praised as though they were much beloved—especially compared to Japanese.

Two weeks after Pearl Harbor, *Time* magazine gave readers tips on how to distinguish between a Chinese "friend" and Japanese "enemy," complete with photos:

HOW TO TELL YOUR FRIENDS FROM THE JAPS
Virtually all Japanese are short. Japanese are likely to be stockier and broader-hipped than short Chinese. Japanese are seldom fat; they often dry up and grow lean as they age. Although both have the typical epicanthic fold of the upper eyelid, Japanese eyes are usually set closer together. The Chinese expression is likely to be more placid, kindly, open; the Japanese more positive, dogmatic, arrogant. Japanese are hesitant, nervous in conversation, laugh loudly at the wrong time.

Time magazine's Henry Luce was part of a powerful pro-China lobby—a prominent group that included public figures and other publishers. Chinese were resurrected from the depths of demonhood and elevated to sainthood—a switch so swift that Chinese Americans wondered how long it would last.

Knowing that Asians "all look alike" to most other Americans, the Chinese posted signs saying "This is a Chinese shop" and wore buttons that said "I Am Chinese" and even "I Hate Japs Worse Than You Do." Filipinos and Koreans did the same. Koreans, to their great horror and despite their own hostility toward Japan for occupying their country, were classified by the U.S. government as Japanese subjects and therefore "enemy aliens." In Hawaii, Koreans were required to wear badges designating them as Japanese; they retaliated by wearing other badges that read "I'm No Jap."

Many Asian Americans jumped at the chance to enlist as American GIs to demonstrate their patriotism. Their service offered another benefit: foreign-born GIs could become naturalized citizens. The demonization of Japanese Americans allowed other Asian Americans to become Americans. The nation's leaders worried about America's image in Asia, where the exclusionary laws were an obvious insult to the Asian allies—a point frequently made by Japan in its anti-American propaganda. India was also strategically important in the fight against Japan, and the same arguments were made for the Philippines. In 1943, the laws that excluded Chinese from immigration were finally repealed; Chinese could become naturalized. In 1946, the laws that barred Filipinos and Indians from citizenship were also overturned. For Japanese and Koreans, the ban would remain until 1952. Asian immigration was placed on a quota system, as European immigrants were, except that the Chinese quota was 102 Chinese from anywhere in the world and for Filipinos it was 50 per year. In contrast, 6,000 Polish and 65,000 British immigrants were allowed per year.

If the status of Chinese, Filipinos, and Indians improved somewhat as the United States went to war with Japan, the lives of Japanese Americans were destroyed. Japanese in America—including the thousands of Nisei youngsters who were native-born American citizens—became the personification of the enemy. On the day war was declared, hundreds of Japanese living on the West Coast were arrested by the FBI, including leaders of community groups, language teachers, Shinto and Buddhist priests and nuns, and journalists.

Using "confidential" Census Bureau survey reports, the FBI was able to compile addresses and information on all Japanese Americans along the Pacific coast. Those who worked for local, state, or federal government offices were summarily fired. Bank accounts were frozen. Japanese Americans already serving in the military were reclassified to menial duties; in Hawaii, Japanese American soldiers were disarmed and put to work digging ditches under armed guard. When politicians advocated that "all Japanese, whether citizens or not, be placed in inland concentration camps," some West Coast nativists admitted their eagerness to seize Japanese American-owned farmland for white farmers.

Even before Pearl Harbor, a secret report analyzing Japanese American loyalty was submitted to President Franklin D. Roosevelt. The report concluded that Japanese Americans posed no security threat; FBI director J. Edgar Hoover also stated in a separate report that a mass evacuation of Japanese was unnecessary. Lieutenant General Delos Emmons, who was in charge of Hawaii, was certain that the Japanese on the islands had nothing to do with the attack. But Lieutenant General John DeWitt, head of the Western Defense Command, concluded, "The Japanese race is an enemy race and while many second and third generation Japanese born on United States soil, possessed of United States citizenship, have become 'Americanized,' the racial strains are undiluted . . . Along the vital Pacific Coast over 112,000 potential enemies of Japanese extraction are at large today. The very fact that no sabotage has taken place to date is a disturbing and confirming indication that such action will be taken."

DeWitt's arguments were readily espoused by the media. Many newspapers throughout the West Coast, including the powerful Hearst chain, adopted the same tenor as this *Los Angeles Times* editorial: "A viper is nonetheless a viper wherever the egg is hatched—so a Japanese American, born of Japanese parents—grows up to be a Japanese, not an American." Even distinguished CBS news commentator Edward R. Murrow said, on January 27, 1942, "I think it's probable that, if Seattle ever does get bombed, you will be able to look up and see some University of Washington sweaters on the boys doing the bombing."

On February 19, 1942, President Roosevelt issued Executive Order 9066, which authorized the evacuation and internment of Japanese Americans. Soon after, all Americans of Japanese descent were prohibited from living, working, or traveling on the West Coast. Families were given no more than a week to somehow dispose of all their household goods and property before moving to points unknown with only what they could carry in clothing, bedding and linen, kitchen and toilet articles, and "personal effects."

With numbered tags tied around their necks, the Japanese Americans were packed onto buses and trains with blinds drawn down. They were sent first to racetracks and fairgrounds, which became makeshift assembly centers; they were forced to live in filthy animal stalls. There they awaited a more permanent incarceration at one of ten internment camps in the barren hinterlands of California, Idaho, Wyoming, Utah, Arizona, Colorado, and Arkansas. About half of the incarcerated were children. At the internment camps, the families were told they needed barbed wire and armed guard towers for their own protection—but the guns pointed inward. Families lived in prison-style blocks with communal latrines and showers.

Individual Japanese took up lawsuits and acts of civil disobedience to challenge the evacuation and various orders imposed on them because of their ancestry. At the Manzanar camp in California, protests and strikes led to the killing of two internees and the imposition of martial law; in Topaz, Utah, an elderly Japanese internee was shot and killed by guards. But most Japanese cooperated with the military to show that they were loyal Americans.

When the U.S. government required that the imprisoned Japanese Americans sign loyalty statements forswearing allegiance to the Emperor of Japan, bitter divisions broke out over how to answer. The second-generation Nisei—who were American citizens by birthright—had no such allegiance to disavow. If their first-generation parents renounced their Japanese citizenship, they would become stateless persons, since U.S. citizenship was prohibited. About 4,600 Japanese Americans resisted by refusing to give the expected yes to the loyalty tests; many were sent to federal penitentiaries, while other "troublemakers" were forced to move again to the harshest camp,

Tule Lake, in the desolate mountains of Northern California. But the majority of internees answered yes to the loyalty tests, while thousands of eligible Nisei men responded to the recruitment drive for an all-Japanese American combat team. The loyalty issues drove a deep wedge into the Japanese American community that continues to this day, pitting internees against each other and tainting groups such as the Japanese American Citizens League, which many viewed as collaborating with the u.s. government.

All together, some 23,000 Japanese Americans served in the u.s. Army during World War II, the majority in the segregated 442nd Nisei Regimental Combat Team, the most highly decorated unit in u.s. military history for its size and length of service. In a 1944 battle to break the German ring in France, Japanese American soldiers in the 442nd incurred 800 casualties, with 200 deaths, in order to save 200 Texans of the 141st Regiment. Young Nisei men wrote home about their loyalty: "Sure we're called Japs—the more to fight to show them we're Americans . . . Prove to them and they'll change their minds! That's why I volunteered! Yes-sir! To fight for the rights of my parents, myself, and kid-brothers and sister."

Ironically, near the end of the war in Europe, the Japanese American GIS of the 442nd broke through the German defensive "Gothic Line" in northern Italy, and were among the first to liberate the Nazi concentration camp in Dachau, Germany. However, the u.s. military commanders decided it would be bad public relations if Jewish prisoners were freed by Japanese American soldiers whose own families were imprisoned in American concentration camps. As with the transcontinental railroad photographs seventy-five years earlier, the Japanese American soldiers who liberated Dachau were MIH—Missing in History.

When World War II ended, about 45,000 Japanese Americans were still interned. Many were unsure where to go, their homes and livelihoods lost and their communities poisoned by neighbors who had turned against them. Some followed children or relatives to the Midwest or the East Coast, while others received only train fare to go back to their old homes on the West Coast, which they often found dilapidated, vandalized, or destroyed, and farms wasted. The old racial hatreds were still alive and active, as American Legion outposts, anti-Japanese union leaders, and politicians agitated against them. When future u.s. Senator Daniel Inouye of Hawaii returned from the war as a hero in uniform with only one arm, a barber refused him service, saying, "We don't serve Japs."

Nevertheless, the thousands of veterans of Chinese and Filipino as well as Japanese descent returned home as bona fide American heroes. They made use of the GI Bill to attend college, and some were able to buy homes outside their ethnic ghettoes. They also returned from the war as citizens, which gave them the right to find a wife in Asia if they chose and to bring her to the United

States—a right that had been denied to previous generations of Asian American men. The wives were not subject to the immigration quota restrictions, and for the first time in Asian immigration to the United States, more women arrived than men. The gender imbalance of the bachelor societies began to shift. In addition, several thousand war brides of non-Asian GIs were permitted to immigrate, a phenomenon that would continue in the subsequent wars the United States would fight in Asia.

In the years following the war, the newly created families brought a spirit of change—the notion that Asians could be part of America if they proved their loyalty as worthy Americans. This reinforced the flip side as well, that to stand apart from the American mainstream could be disastrous. The old Japanese adage "The nail that sticks out gets hammered down" was never felt to be more true.

Menace and Democracy

It was not long before this sensibility would be tested. This time, the Communist revolution in China turned the newly beloved ally extolled in *Time* magazine only a few years earlier into a "Red Menace." In 1950, the Korean War, fought by the United States to "contain" Communism, raised the specter of two other Asian enemies—China and North Korea. The Chinese American population, under particular scrutiny from the FBI, became fearful that they, too, could be rounded up and incarcerated. Sharp divisions formed between Chinese Americans over the question of Communist rule in China—with a clear awareness of the trouble it might bring them in America. The more conservative community organizations mounted their own anti-Communist campaigns to prove, preemptively, that Chinese were loyal Americans.

Their fears were not unfounded. Congress passed a bill in 1950 authorizing another internment, the McCarran Internal Security Act, to lock up anyone suspected on "reasonable ground" that they would "probably" engage in espionage. The immigration service posted signs in Chinese in Chinatowns publicizing a "Confession Program," which encouraged people to inform on friends and relatives in exchange for legal immigration status; thousands participated, including more than 10,000 in San Francisco alone.

FBI director J. Edgar Hoover was convinced that Chinese Americans posed a domestic Communist threat. In 1969 he warned, "The United States is Communist China's No. 1 enemy . . . Red China has been flooding the country with propaganda and there are over 300,000 Chinese in the United States, some of whom could be susceptible to recruitment either through ethnic ties or hostage situations because of relatives in Communist China."

With hostilities directed toward the Chinese, citizenship exclusions for Japanese and Koreans were finally lifted in 1952, allowing many first-generation

Japanese immigrants, now elderly, to become citizens. The Japanese American Citizens League actively sought to eliminate the laws that had impugned the loyalty of Japanese Americans, and tried to restore some of the property that they had lost. In 1956, Japanese Americans successfully led a ballot initiative in California to repeal all alien land laws that had for nearly a century prevented any Asians from settling down in America.

As the movement for racial equality swept the nation following the 1954 Supreme Court decision in *Brown v. Board of Education,* Asian Americans were inspired to civic consciousness and involvement, after having been so long forbidden to exercise the privileges of citizenship in a democracy. A contingent of Asian Americans from Hawaii joined the Reverend Martin Luther King, Jr., in Selma, Alabama, bringing him the lei he wore during the march. The first Asian American entered Congress when Dalip Singh Saund, an Indian immigrant, won election in 1956 in the mostly white district of California's Imperial Valley, ultimately serving three terms in the U.S. House of Representatives. He was soon joined by representatives from Hawaii, which was granted statehood in 1959 after years of opposition in the U.S. Senate. One of the primary concerns raised by Strom Thurmond and other senators from the South was the fact that Hawaii's population was mostly "nonwhite," whose Asian ancestry posed an "impassable difference" with the European ancestry of whites.

Statehood brought a Chinese American senator, Hiram Fong, a Republican, under the Capitol dome. In 1963 he was joined by Daniel Inouye, a Democrat and decorated hero of the 442nd Japanese American Regimental Combat Team. For a time Fong and Inouye were the only people of color in the Senate. In 1964, Patsy Mink became the first woman of color to be elected to the House of Representatives. The presence of Asian Americans in Congress was a tremendous leap from the days of exclusion from American public life.

A Myth and a Movement

In the 1960s, a new stereotype emerged on the American scene. As urban ghettoes from Newark, New Jersey, to Watts in Los Angeles erupted into riots and civil unrest, Asian Americans suddenly became the object of "flattering" media stories. After more than a century of invisibility alternating with virulent headlines and radio broadcasts that advocated eliminating or imprisoning America's Asians, a rash of stories began to extol our virtues.

"Success Story: Japanese American Style" was the title of an article that appeared in *The New York Times Magazine* on January 9, 1966. A few months later, *US. News & World Report* produced a similar piece entitled "Success Story of One Minority Group in the United States," praising Chinese Americans while making transparent comparisons to African Americans: "At a time when Americans are awash in worry over the plight of racial minorities, one such minority, the nation's 300,000 Chinese Americans, is winning wealth and respect by dint of its own hard work . . . Still being taught in Chinatown is the old idea that people should depend on their own efforts—not a welfare check—in order to reach America's 'Promised Land.'"

The radical attitude shift was a too familiar experience for Asian Americans who had seen many iterations of the "friend today, foe tomorrow" treatment. Nor was the link to urban uprisings an accident. Where Asians had previously been the economic wedge to distract labor unrest, in the 1960s they were refashioned as a political and social hammer against other disadvantaged groups. The "model minority" was born.

The new stereotype proved tenacious, surfacing like clockwork whenever the Westinghouse Science Talent Search winners or other scholastic prizes were announced, with tales of stunning accomplishment by Asian immigrant youngsters who had just learned to speak English. The "model minority" myth presented its own quandary: should Asian Americans accept, if not embrace, this "good" stereotype as an improvement over the "inscrutable alien enemy" image of the previous hundred years?

In the 1960s, a new generation of Asian Americans was preparing to reject all stereotypes, preferring instead to find its own self-definition. One of the unacknowledged consequences of the civil rights movement and the war in Vietnam was their impact on the consciousness of the postwar generation of Asian Americans—primarily the second- and third-generation Japanese, Chinese, and Filipino Americans. The call by African Americans for equality resonated among Asian American youth, appealing to their sense of justice as well as their own experiences as a racial minority.

The young Asian Americans, inspired by the movement for Black Power, declared "Yellow Power" and "Yellow is beautiful." They believed that the various Asian immigrant groups had common interests and experiences in America that transcended cultural differences and historical animosities from centuries of war and conflict in Asia. This was a radical departure from the views of the immigrant generations that identified more closely with "over there." It was a declaration that, for Asian Americans, our identities and futures held much in common with other Asians in the United States. The burgeoning Asian American student movement found a target in the Vietnam War. Asian Americans were outraged at the government's willingness to dehumanize and reduce Vietnamese people to mere body counts on the evening news.

Nineteen sixty-eight marked the coming out of this new movement, as Asian American students, along with other students of color, conducted militant student strikes at San Francisco State College (now University) and the University of California at Berkeley. In the course of the organizing, the words "Asian American" made their debut. At Berkeley, the pan-Asian cluster of students needed a name; they didn't want to use the word "Oriental," which was seen to represent the European colonialist view of Asia. Yuji Ichioka and Emma Gee, then graduate students, are credited with coining the moniker.

Among the demands the student strikers in San Francisco and Berkeley fought for—and won—were educational programs that taught their history in America. Out of these student movements, the first Asian American studies programs in the country were established as part of new ethnic studies departments at San Francisco State and Berkeley and, soon after, the Asian American Studies Center at UCLA. Other universities on the West Coast followed as Asian American scholars began to reclaim the rich history of Asians in America.

The Asian American esprit spread rapidly along the West Coast. Students at college campuses in the San Francisco Bay Area and Los Angeles founded groups under the same name, Asian American Political Alliance, to signal their unity. The following year, students on the East Coast established a network of Asian American Student Associations. The movement wasn't limited to students. In New York, two middle-aged Japanese American Nisei women, Kazu Iijima and Minn Matsuda, organized Asian Americans for Action in 1969 to protest U.S. imperialism in Vietnam.

As more young Asian Americans studied law and became public-interest lawyers, they began to fight discriminatory practices against Asian Americans in the courts. In 1972, the first class action suit brought for Asian Americans by Asian American attorneys was won by a San Francisco attorney named Dale Minami, against the Blue Shield insurance company for discriminatory employment practices. Minami and other Asian American lawyers founded the Asian Law Caucus, and went on to file other civil rights suits to stop the San Francisco police from making dragnet arrests of Chinatown youths; to end discriminatory hiring practices by the San Francisco Fire Department, which opened employment to minorities and women for the first time; and to restore jobs to Filipino American security guards who were fired because they spoke English with an accent.

The young activists created organizations that advanced a pan-Asian vision and have become community institutions: from the Asian Law Caucus in San Francisco to the Asian American Legal Defense and Education Fund and Asian Americans for Equality in New York, to the Asian American Resource Center in Boston and Leadership Education for Asian Pacifics in Los Angeles. Other ethnic-based organizations, such as Chinese for Affirmative Action, the Organization of Chinese Americans, and the Japanese American Citizens League, took on a more pan-Asian scope.

Professional and business organizations followed suit, with the formation of national groups such as the National Asian Pacific American Bar Association and the Asian American Journalists Association. Even the federal government recognized the necessity for a statistical and programmatic category for Asian Americans.

Having their own pan-Asian organizations gave Asian American activists a base from which to launch campaigns against racism and discrimination. As new kids on the block, they coexisted uneasily—and at times conflicted—with the more established and conservative community groups. Old-time Chinatown organizations active since the exclusion years were staunchly anti-Communist and allied with the government of Taiwan; they opposed the younger groups that seemed, and often were, so radical and leftist. Among Filipino Americans, the older organizations supported the regime of Ferdinand Marcos, while many youths were seeking its overthrow.

Most of the efforts by the young Asian Americans were directed at grassroots community issues: organizing sweatshop workers in Chinatowns, for example; or at bringing other issues into the Asian American community, such as opposition to apartheid in South Africa. Pan-Asian issues that linked the various Asian communities periodically caught fire. In San Francisco, efforts to evict fifty-five elderly Filipino American retired migrant workers from their home, the International Hotel, began in the late 1960s, as developers of the new financial district continued to dismantle the last pieces of what used to be a ten-block Manilatown. Asian American community activists fought the evictions with a broad multi-racial coalition, mobilizing several thousands of protesters for tenants' rights and community control—a nine-year battle that finally ended in 1977 when police on horseback and in riot gear broke through the demonstrators' barricades.

A national Asian American campaign to win a new trial for death row inmate Chol Soo Lee, a Korean American immigrant, began in 1977 when Pulitzer prize-nominated journalist K. W. Lee (not related) began to raise questions about the conviction. For the first time, a broad coalition was forged between Korean Americans and the multiethnic Asian American communities. They gathered more than 10,000 signatures on petitions and raised $175,000 in donations, resulting in a new trial and the release of Lee in 1983.

One of the most stunning civil rights victories was won in the early 1980s when the wartime convictions of three Japanese Americans were overturned. Gordon Hirabayashi, Fred Korematsu, and Minoru Yasui had resisted curfew orders for Japanese Americans and internment notices during World War II—and were sent to prison. Forty years later, researchers Aiko and Jack Herzig and Peter Irons discovered that federal officials had altered and destroyed evidence upholding the loyalty of Japanese Americans. With this new information, pro bono legal teams in three cities—San Francisco; Portland, Oregon; and Seattle—succeeded in getting the cases of the three men reopened on the grounds that fundamental injustices had occurred. The lead attorneys—Lori Bannai, Rod Kawakami, Dale Minami, and Peggy Nagae—were all third-generation Sansei whose work vindicated their Nisei parents and Issei grandparents. Together with the findings of a congressional commission in 1983 that the internment was not justified but driven by "race prejudice, war hysteria, and a failure of political leadership," these various efforts paved the way for a national apology and federal legislation providing redress to surviving internees. Members of Congress Norman Mineta and Robert Matsui, both of California, led the legislative movement that culminated in the Civil Liberties Act of 1988, after a national campaign won the support of whites, African Americans, Christians and Jews, women, gays and lesbians, and many others. The young Asian American movement was providing a legacy for all Americans.

The New Immigration Wave

Another profound transformation would drastically alter the demographic underpinnings of Asians in America. In Congress, the tide of equal rights legislation included sweeping changes to immigration law. The Immigration Act of 1965 eliminated the quota system of preferences for whites, inexorably altering the complexion of America. A new generation of Asian immigrants, as well as Hispanics and Africans, began to arrive in unprecedented numbers. These Asians arrived from areas unfamiliar to most Americans—the Indian subcontinent, interior regions of China, Korea, the Philippines, Taiwan, and elsewhere.

Similarly, the u.s. involvement in Vietnam did more than ignite an antiwar consciousness among Asian Americans who identified with the plight of the Southeast Asians. The u.s. defeat in Vietnam triggered a massive migration of war refugees, beginning with the Vietnamese and Hmong who had been America's allies. In the frenzied evacuation after the fall of Saigon, 135,000 government officials, military personnel, and u.s. government employees were moved to the safety of the u.s. Seventh Fleet. This first wave of refugees was relocated to military bases in California, Arkansas, Pennsylvania, and Florida, then later resettled in communities throughout the United States.

As political persecution and economic conditions worsened in Vietnam, hundreds of thousands of people fled by boat across the perilous South China Sea. The "boat people" who didn't perish reached refugee camps in Thailand, Malaysia, Indonesia, and the Philippines. The flow of refugees from Cambodia surged after Vietnam attacked a weakened Khmer Rouge in 1978, allowing additional hundreds of thousands to escape the "killing fields." In Laos, numerous rural minority groups fled repression, particularly the Hmong, Mien, Khmu, and Thai Dam, as well as Lao, who had assisted the u.s. military during the "secret war" it waged outside Vietnam.

To address the refugee crisis, Congress passed the Indochina Migration and Refugee Assistance Act of 1975 and later the Refugee Act of 1980. For the first time, u.s. policy defined who could be admitted to the United States as a refugee and created a framework of assistance programs. In addition, about 100,000 Amerasian children—the offspring of American GIs—and their Southeast Asian mothers were also admitted under the Amerasian Homecoming Act of 1987. All told, more than one million Southeast Asians came to America after 1975, nearly doubling the existing Asian American population.

It is impossible to overstate the impact that the combined influx of the new immigrants and refugees had on Asian Americans and the nation as a whole. Initially, the changes to the American population were subtle. Many of the new Asian Americans were absorbed into the vast American suburbia, particularly those with the professional training favored by the new immigration laws, while the resettlement policies governing the refugees emphasized dispersal throughout the United States. The numbers of Asian Americans grew from 877,934 in 1960 to 1.4 million in 1970, 3.5 million in 1980, and 7.3 million in 1990, making Asian Americans the fastest-growing minority in the nation.

But flashpoints were inevitable when war-ravaged refugees unfamiliar with American culture, language, or people were placed in homogeneous rural and inner-city areas, where Asian Americans of any stripe were rare sightings. A report by the Massachusetts Attorney General's Civil Rights Division in 1983 noted numerous racially motivated assaults against Southeast Asian refugees: "Often, [they] cannot even walk along the public streets without being physically attacked and threatened because of the their race or national origin." In Davis, California, Thong Hy Huynh, a seventeen-year-old Vietnamese student, was stabbed to death in 1983 by a white student in a high school with a history of racial harassment of Southeast Asian students. Escaping the mainly African American section of West Philadelphia, a rickety car caravan of the entire Hmong community made a mass exodus out of the City of Brotherly Love in 1984 after suffering years of physical and verbal assaults. They hoped to find safe haven with other Hmong in Minnesota.

The existing Asian American community was unprepared to meet the multiple needs of the Southeast Asian refugee population, which was generally placed in areas far from Chinatowns, Little Tokyos, or other Asian communities. Violent clashes involving the Ku Klux Klan occurred along the

Texas Gulf coast, where many Vietnamese were resettled in the 1970s. But occasionally the growing pan-Asian American movement intervened. When the Coast Guard began selective enforcement of a two-hundred-year-old law against Vietnamese fishermen off the coast of Northern California, Asian American attorneys of Chinese and Japanese descent in San Francisco took up their cause, and ultimately Congress passed legislation allowing the Vietnamese to operate fishing boats.

The convergence of these developments—an incipient Asian American movement, the creation of an Asian American infrastructure, and the burgeoning and increasingly diverse Asian American population—set the stage for an explosion of new organizations to meet the needs of the individual Asian ethnicities. On the other hand, the noticeable increase in our numbers would soon fuel a backlash that affected all Asian Americans. A broader Asian American consciousness and organization had yet to emerge in response to the new challenges. As Asian American scholars and historians reclaimed the past, Asian Americans were on the brink of another transformation.

—HELEN ZIA

President William McKinley
Addresses a Delegation of Methodist Churchmen, 1898

I thought first we would take only Manila; then Luzon; then other islands, perhaps, also. I walked the floor of the White House night after night until midnight; and I am not ashamed to tell you, gentlemen, that I went down on my knees and prayed to Almighty God for light and guidance more than one night . . . And one night it came to me this way—I don't know how it was, but it came: one, that we could not give them back to Spain—that would be cowardly and dishonorable; two, that we could not turn them over to France or Germany—our commercial rivals in the Orient—that would be bad business and discreditable; three, that we could not leave them to themselves—they were unfit for self-government—and they would soon have anarchy and misrule over there worse than Spain's was; and four, that there was nothing left for us to do but to take them all, and to educate the Filipinos, and uplift and civilize and Christianize them, and by God's grace do the very best we could by them, as our fellow men for whom Christ also died. And then I went to bed, and went to sleep and slept soundly.

THE WHITE HOUSE
Office of the Press Secretary
(Atlanta, Georgia)

For Immediate Release   April 14, 2000

STATEMENT BY THE PRESIDENT

Today I signed legislation designating the United States Post Office located at 14701 Peyton Drive in Chino Hills, California, as the "Joseph Ileto Post Office." Joseph Ileto was a Filipino American postal worker who was tragically murdered last year in a crime of hate. He was a dedicated public servant, killed simply because he was an Asian American who worked for his country's government. It is a fitting tribute to the life and memory of Mr. Ileto that we name this post office in his honor.

During the last year, we have all been shaken by violent acts like the murder of Joseph Ileto, acts that strike at the very values that define us as a nation. Now is the time for us to take strong and decisive action to fight hate crimes, and I call on Congress, at long last, to pass strong hate crimes legislation. It is time for us all to raise our voices against intolerance and to build the One America that our hearts tell us we can be.

The Day The Dancers Came

As soon as Fil woke up, he noticed a whiteness outside, quite unusual for the November mornings they had been having. That fall, Chicago was sandman's town, sleepy valley, drowsy gray, slumbrous mistiness from sunup till noon when the clouds drifted away in cauliflower clusters and suddenly it was evening. The lights shone on the avenues like soiled lamps centuries old and the skyscrapers became monsters with a thousand sore eyes. Now there was a brightness in the air and Fil knew what it was and he shouted, "Snow! It's snowing!"

Tony, who slept in the adjoining room, was awakened.

"What's that?" he asked.

"It's snowing," Fil said, smiling to himself as if he had ordered this and was satisfied with the prompt delivery. "Oh, they'll love this, they'll love this."

"Who'll love that?" Tony asked, his voice raised in annoyance.

"The dancers, of course," Fil answered. "They're arriving today. Maybe they've already arrived. They'll walk in the snow and love it. Their first snow, I'm sure."

"How do you know it wasn't snowing in New York while they were there?" Tony asked.

"Snow in New York in early November?" Fil said. "Are you crazy?"

"Who's crazy?" Tony replied. "Ever since you heard of those dancers from the Philippines, you've been acting nuts. Loco. As if they're coming here just for you."

Tony chuckled. Hearing him, Fil blushed, realizing that he had, indeed, been acting too eager, but Tony had said it. It felt that way—as if the dancers were coming here only for him.

Filemon Acayan, Filipino, was fifty, a u.s. citizen. He was a corporal in the u.s. Army, training at San Luis Obispo, on the day he was discharged honorably, in 1945. A few months later, he got his citizenship papers. Thousands of them, smart and small in their uniforms, stood at attention in drill formation, in the scalding sun, and pledged allegiance to the flag and the republic for which it stands. Soon after he got back to work. To a new citizen, work meant many places and many ways: factories and hotels, waiter and cook. A timeless drifting; once he tended a rose garden and took care of a hundred-year-old veteran of a border war. As a menial in a hospital in Cook County, all day he handled filth and gore. He came home smelling of surgical soap and disinfectant. In the hospital, he took charge of a row of bottles on a shelf, each bottle containing a stage of the human embryo in preservatives, from the lizard-like fetus of a few days, through the newly born infant, with its position unchanged, cold and cowering and afraid. He had nightmares through the years of himself inside a bottle. That was long ago. Now he had a more pleasant job as special policeman in the post office.

He was a few years younger than Tony—Antonio Bataller, a retired Pullman porter—but he looked older in spite of the fact that Tony had been bedridden most of the time for the last two years, suffering from a kind of wasting disease that had frustrated doctors. All over Tony's body, a gradual peeling was taking place. At first, he thought it was merely tinia flava, a skin disease common among adolescents in the Philippines. It had started around the neck and had spread to his extremities. His face looked as if it was healing from severe burns. Nevertheless, it was a young face, much younger than Fil's, which had never looked young.

"I'm becoming a white man," Tony had said once, chuckling softly.

It was the same chuckle Fil seemed to have heard now, only this time it sounded derisive, insulting.

Fil said, "I know who's nuts. It's the sick guy with the sick thoughts. You don't care for nothing but your pain, your imaginary pain."

"You're the imagining fellow. I got the real thing," Tony shouted from the room. He believed he had something worse than the whiteness spreading on his skin. There was a pain in his insides, like dull scissors scraping his intestines. Angrily, he added, "What for I got retired?"

"You're old, man, old, that's what, and sick, yes, but not cancer," Fil said turning towards the snow-filled sky. He pressed his face against the glass window. There's about an inch now on the ground, he thought, maybe more.

Tony came out of his room looking as if he had not slept all night. "I know what I got," he said, as if it were an honor and a privilege to die of cancer and Fil was trying to deprive him of it. "Never a pain like this. One day, I'm just gonna die."

"Naturally. Who says you won't?" Fil argued, thinking how wonderful it would be if he could join the company of dancers from the Philippines, show them around, walk with them in the snow, watch their eyes as they stared about them, answer their questions, tell them everything they wanted to know about the changing seasons in this strange land. They would pick up fistfuls of snow, crunch it in their fingers or shove it into their mouths. He had done just that the first time, long, long ago, and it had reminded him of the grated ice the Chinese sold near the town plaza where he had played tatching with an older brother who later drowned in a squall. How his mother had grieved over that death, she who had not cried too much when his father died, a broken man. Now they were all gone, quick death after a storm, or lingeringly, in a season of drought, all, all of them he had loved.

He continued, "All of us will die. One day. A medium bomb marked Chicago and this whole dump is tapus, finished. Who'll escape then?"

"Maybe your dancers will," Tony answered, now watching the snow himself.

"Of course, they will," Fil retorted, his voice sounding like a big assurance that all the dancers would be safe in his care. "The bombs won't be falling on this night. And, when the dancers are back in the Philippines . . ."

He paused, as if he was no longer sure of what he was going to say. "But maybe, even in the Philippines the bombs gonna fall, no?" he said, gazing sadly at the falling snow.

"What's that to you?" Tony replied. "You got no more folks ove'der, right? I know it's nothing to me. I'll be dead before that."

"Let's talk about something nice," Fil said, the sadness spreading on his face as he tried to smile. "Tell me, how will I talk, how am I gonna introduce myself?"

He would go ahead with his plans, introduce himself to the dancers and volunteer to take them sight-seeing. His car was clean and ready for his guests. He had soaped the ashtrays, dusted off the floor boards and thrown away the old mats, replacing them with new plastic throw rugs. He had got himself soaking wet while spraying the car, humming, as he worked, faintly remembered tunes from the old country.

Fil shook his head as he waited for Tony to say something. "Gosh, I wish I had your looks, even with those white spots, then I could face everyone of them," he said, "but this mug."

"That's the important thing, your mug. It's your calling card. It says, Filipino. Countryman," Tony said.

"You're not fooling me, friend," Fil said. "This mug says, Ugly Filipino. It says, old-timer, muchacho. It says Pinoy, bejo."

For Fil, time was the villain. In the beginning, the words he often heard were: too young, too young; but all of a sudden, too young became too old, too late. What had happened in between? A weariness, a mist covering all things. You don't have to look at your face in a mirror to know that you are old, suddenly old, grown useless for a lot of things and too late for all the dreams you had wrapped up well against a day of need.

"It also says sucker," Tony said. "What for you want to invite them? Here? Aren't you ashamed of this hole?"

"It's not a palace, I know," Fil answered, "but who wants a palace when they can have the most delicious adobo here and the best stuffed chicken . . . yum . . . yum . . ."

Tony was angry. "Yum, yum, you're nuts," he said, "plain and simple loco. What for you want to spend? You've been living on loose change all your life and now on a treasury warrant so small and full of holes, still you want to spend for these dancing kids who don't know you and won't even send you a card afterwards."

"Never mind the cards," Fil answered. "Who wants cards? But don't you see, they'll be happy; and then, you know what? I'm going to keep their voices, their words and their singing and their laughter in my magic sound mirror."

He had a portable tape recorder and a stack of recordings, patiently labeled, songs and speeches. The songs were in English, but most of the speeches were in the dialect, debates between him and Tony. It was evident Tony was the better speaker of the two in English, but in the dialect, Fil showed greater mastery. His style, however, was florid, sentimental, poetic.

Without telling Tony, he had experimented on recording sounds, like the way a bed creaked, doors opening and closing, rain or sleet tapping on the window panes, footsteps through the corridor. He played all the sounds back and tried to recall how it was on the day or night the sounds had been recorded. Did they bring back the moment? He was beginning to think that they did. He was learning to identify each of the sounds with a particular mood or fact. Sometimes, like today, he wished that there was a way of keeping a record of silence because it was to him the richest sound, like snow falling. He wondered as he watched the snow blowing in the wind, what took care of that moment if memory didn't. Like time, memory was often a villain, a betrayer.

"Fall, snow, fall," he murmured and, turning to Tony, said, "As soon as they accept my invitation, I'll call you up. No, you don't have to do anything, but I'd want you to be here to meet them."

"I'm going out myself." Tony said. "And I don't know what time I'll be back." Then he added, "You're not working today. Are you on leave?"

"For two days. While the dancers are here," Fil said.

"It still don't make sense to me," Tony said. "But good luck, anyway."

"Aren't you going to see them tonight? Our reserved seats are right out in front, you know."

"I know. But I'm not sure I can come."

"What? You're not sure?"

Fil could not believe it. Tony was indifferent. Something must be wrong with him. He looked at him closely, saying nothing.

"I want to, but I'm sick, Fil. I tell you, I'm not feeling so good. My doctor will know today. He'll tell me," Tony said.

"What will he tell you?"

"How do I know?"

"I mean, what's he trying to find out?"

"If it's cancer," Tony said. Without saying another word, he went straight back to his room.

Fil remembered those times, at night, when Tony kept him awake with his moaning. When he called out to him, asking, "Tony, what's the matter?" his sighs ceased for a while, but afterwards, Tony screamed, deadening his cries with a pillow against his mouth. When Fil rushed to his side, Tony drove him away. Or he curled up in the bedsheets like a big infant suddenly hushed in its crying. The next day, he would look all right. When Fil asked him about the previous night, he would reply, "I was dying," but it sounded more like disgust over a nameless annoyance.

Fil had misgivings, too, about the whiteness spreading on Tony's skin. He had heard of leprosy. Every time he thought of that dreaded disease, he felt tears in his eyes. In all the years he had been in America, he had not had a friend until he met Tony whom he liked immediately and, in a way, worshipped, for all the things the man had which Fil knew he himself lacked.

They had shared a lot together. They made merry on Christmas, sometimes got drunk and became loud. Fil recited poems in the dialect and praised himself. Tony fell to giggling and cursed all the railroad companies of America. But last Christmas, they hadn't gotten drunk. They hadn't even talked to each other on Christmas day. Soon, it would be Christmas again.

The snow was still falling.

"Well, I'll be seeing you," Fil said, getting ready to leave. "Try to be home on time. I shall invite the dancers for luncheon or dinner maybe, tomorrow. But tonight, let's go to the theater together, ha?"

"I'll try," Tony answered, adding after a pause, "Oh, Fil, I can't find my boots. May I wear yours?" His voice sounded strong and healthy.

"Sure, sure!" Fil answered. He didn't need boots. He loved to walk in the snow.

The air outside felt good. Fil lifted his face to the sky and closed his eyes as the snow and a wet wind drenched his face. He stood that way for some time, crying, more, more! to himself, drunk with snow and coolness. His car was parked a block away. As he walked towards it, he plowed into the snow with one foot and studied the scar he made, a hideous shape among perfect footmarks. He felt strong as his lungs filled with the cold air, as if just now it did not matter too much that he was the way he looked and his English the way it was. But perhaps, he could talk to the dancers in his dialect. Why not?

A heavy frosting of snow covered his car and as he wiped it off with his bare hands, he felt light and young, like a child at play, and once again, he raised his face to the sky and licked the flakes, cold and tasteless on his tongue.

When Fil arrived at the Hamilton, it seemed to him the Philippine dancers had taken over the hotel. They were all over the lobby on the mezzanine, talking in groups animatedly, their teeth sparkling as they laughed, their eyes disappearing in mere slits of light. Some of the girls wore their black hair long. For a moment, the sight seemed too much for him who had all but forgotten how beautiful Philippine girls were. He wanted to look away, but their loveliness held him. He must do something, close his eyes perhaps. As he did so, their laughter came to him like a breeze murmurous with sounds native to his land.

Later, he tried to relax, to appear inconspicuous. True, they were all very young, but there were a few elderly men and women who must have been their chaperons or well-wishers like him. He would smile at everyone who happened to look his way. Most of them smiled back, or rather, seemed to smile, but it was quick, without recognition, and might not have been for him but for someone else near or behind him.

His lips formed the words he was trying to phrase in his mind: Ilocano ka? Bicol? Ano na, paisano? Comusta? Or should he introduce himself? How? For what he wanted to say, the words didn't come too easily, they were unfamiliar, they stumbled and broke on his lips into a jumble of incoherence.

Suddenly, he felt as if he was in the center of a group where he was not welcome. All the things he had been trying to hide now showed: the age in his face, his horny hands. He knew it the instant he wanted to shake hands with the first boy who had drawn close to him, smiling and friendly. Fil put his hands in his pocket.

Now he wished Tony had been with him. Tony would know what to do. He would charm these young people with his smile and his learned words. Fil wanted to leave, but he seemed caught up in the tangle of moving bodies that merged and broke in a fluid strangle hold. Everybody was talking, mostly in English. Once in a while he heard exclamations in the dialect right out of the past, conjuring up playtime, long shadows of evening on the plaza, barrio fiestas, misa de gallo.

Time was passing and he had yet to talk to someone. Suppose he stood on a chair and addressed them in the manner of his flamboyant speeches recorded in his magic sound mirror?

"Beloved countrymen, lovely children of the Pearl of the Orient Seas, listen to me. I'm Fil Acayan. I've come to volunteer my services. I'm yours to command. Your servant. Tell me where you wish to go, what you want to see in Chicago. I know every foot of the lakeshore drive, all the gardens and the parks, the museums, the huge department stores, the planetarium. Let me be your guide. That's what I'm offering you, a free tour of Chicago, and finally, dinner at my apartment on West Sheridan Road—pork adobo and chicken relleno, name your dish. How about it, paisanos?"

No. That would be a foolish thing to do. They would laugh at him. He felt a dryness in his throat. He was sweating. As he wiped his face with a handkerchief, he bumped against a slim, short girl who quite gracefully stepped aside, and for a moment he thought he would swoon in the perfume that enveloped him. It was fragrance long forgotten, essence of camia, of ilang-ilang, and dama de noche.

Two boys with sleek, pomaded hair were sitting near an empty chair. He sat down and said in the dialect, "May I invite you to my apartment?" The boys stood up, saying, "Excuse us, please," and walked away. He mopped his brow, but instead of getting discouraged, he grew bolder as though he had moved one step beyond shame. Approaching another group, he repeated his invitation, and a girl with a mole on her upper lip said, "Thank you, but we have no time." As he turned towards another group, he felt their eyes on his back. Another boy drifted towards him, but as soon as he began to speak, the boy said, "Pardon, please," and moved away.

They were always moving away. As if by common consent, they had decided to avoid him, ignore his presence. Perhaps it was not their fault. They must have been instructed to do so. Or was it his looks that kept them away? The thought was a sharpness inside him.

After a while, as he wandered about the mezzanine, among the dancers, but alone, he noticed that they had begun to leave. Some had crowded noisily into the two elevators. He followed the others going down the stairs. Through the glass doors, he saw them getting into a bus parked beside the subway entrance on Dearborn.

The snow had stopped falling; it was melting fast in the sun and turning into slush.

As he moved about aimlessly, he felt someone touch him on the sleeve. It was one of the dancers, a mere boy, tall and thin, who was saying, "Excuse, please." Fil realized he was in the way between another boy with a camera and a group posing front of the hotel.

"Sorry," Fil said, jumping away awkwardly.

The crowd burst out laughing.

Then everything became a blur in his eyes, a moving picture out of focus, but gradually the figures cleared, there was mud on the pavement on which the dancers stood posing, and the sun threw shadows at their feet.

Let them have fun, he said to himself, they're young and away from home. I have no business messing up their schedule, forcing my company on them.

He watched the dancers till the last of them was on the bus. The voices came to him, above the traffic sounds. They waved their hands and smiled towards him as the bus started. Fil raised his hand to wave back, but stopped quickly, aborting the gesture. He turned to look behind him at whomever the dancers were waving their hands to. There was no one there except his own reflection in the glass door, a double exposure of himself and a giant plant with its thorny branches around him like arms in a loving embrace.

Even before he opened the door to their apartment, Fil knew that Tony had not yet arrived. There were no boots outside on the landing. Somehow he felt relieved, for until then he did not know how he was going to explain his failure.

From the hotel, he had driven around, cruised by the lakeshore drive, hoping he would see the dancers somewhere, in a park perhaps, taking pictures of the mist over the lake and the last gold on the trees now wet with melted snow, or on some picnic grounds, near a bubbling fountain. Still taking pictures of themselves against a background of Chicago's gray and dirty skyscrapers. He

SCREAMING MONKEYS

slowed down every time he saw a crowd, but the dancers were nowhere along his way. Perhaps they had gone to the theater to rehearse. He turned back before reaching Evanston.

He felt weak, not hungry. Just the same, he ate, warming up some left-over food. The rice was cold, but the soup was hot and tasty. While he ate, he listened for footfalls.

Afterwards, he lay down on the sofa and a weariness came over him, but he tried hard not to sleep. As he stared at the ceiling, he felt like floating away, but he kept his eyes open, willing himself hard to remain awake. He wanted to explain everything to Tony when he arrived. But soon his eyes closed against a weary will too tired and weak to fight back sleep—and then there were voices. Tony was in the room, eager to tell his own bit of news.

"I've discovered a new way of keeping afloat," he was saying.

"Who wants to keep afloat?" Fil asked.

"Just in case. In a shipwreck, for example," Tony said.

"Never mind shipwrecks. I must tell you about the dancers," Fil said.

"But this is important," Tony insisted. "This way, you can keep floating indefinitely."

"What for indefinitely?" Fil asked.

"Say in a ship . . . I mean, in an emergency, you're stranded without help in the middle of the Pacific or the Atlantic, you must keep floating till help comes . . ." Tony explained.

"More better," Fil said, "find a way to reach shore before the sharks smells you. You discover that."

"I will," Tony said, without eagerness, as though certain that there was no such way, that, after all, his discovery was worthless.

"Now you listen to me," Fil said, sitting up abruptly. As he talked in the dialect, Tony listened. with increasing apathy.

"There they were." Fil began, his tone taking on the orator's pitch, "who could have been my children if I had not left home—or yours, Tony. They gazed around them with wonder, smiling at me, answering my questions, but grudgingly, edging away as if to be near me were wrong, a violation in their rule book. But it could be that every time I opened my mouth, I gave myself away. I talked in the dialect, Ilocano, Tagalog, Bicol, but no one listened. They avoided me. They had been briefed too well: Do not talk to strangers. Ignore their invitations. Be extra careful in the big cities like New York and Chicago, beware of the old-timers, the Pinoys. Most of them are bums. Keep away from them. Be on the safe side—stick together, entertain only those who have been introduced to you properly.

"I'm sure they had such instructions, safety measures, they must have called them. What then could I have done, scream out my good intentions, prove my harmlessness and my love for them by beating my breast? Oh, but I loved them. You see, I was like them once. I, too, was nimble with my feet, graceful with my hands; and I had the tongue of a poet. Ask the village girls and the envious boys from the city—but first you have to find them. After these many years, it won't be easy. You'll have to search every suffering face in the village gloom for a hint of youth and beauty or go where the graveyards are and the tombs under the lime trees. One such face . . . oh, God, what am I saying?

"All I wanted was to talk to, them, guide them around Chicago, spend money on them so that they would have something special to remember about us here when they return to our country. They would tell their folks: We met a kind, old man, who took us to his apartment. It was not much of a place. It was old—like him. When we sat on the sofa in the living room, the bottom sank heavily, the broken springs touching the floor. But what a cook that man was! And how kind! We never thought that rice and adobo could be that delicious. And the chicken relleno! When someone asked what the stuffing was—we had never tasted anything like it—he smiled saying, 'From heaven's supermarket,' touching his head and pressing his heart like a clown as if heaven were there. He had his tape recorder which he called a magic sound mirror, and he had all of us record our voices. Say anything in the dialect, sing, if you please, our kundiman, please, he said, his eyes pleading, too. Oh, we had fun listening to the playback. When you're gone, the old man said, I shall listen to your voices with my eyes closed and you'll be here again and I won't ever be alone, no, not anymore, after this. We wanted to cry, but he looked very funny, so we laughed and he laughed with us.

"But, Tony, they would not come. They thanked me, but they said they had no time. Others said nothing. They looked through me. I didn't exist. Or worse, I was unclean. Basura. Garbage. They were ashamed of me. How could I be Filipino?"

The memory, distinctly recalled, was a rock on his breast. He gasped for breath.

"Now, let me teach you how to keep afloat," Tony said, but it was not Tony's voice.

Fil was alone and gasping for air. His eyes opened slowly till he began to breathe more easily. The sky outside was gray. He looked at his watch—a quarter past five. The show would begin at eight. There was time. Perhaps Tony would be home soon.

The apartment was warming up. The radiators sounded full of scampering rats. He had a recording of that in his sound mirror.

Fil smiled. He had an idea. He would take the sound mirror to the theater, take his seat close to the stage, and make tape recordings of the singing and the dances.

Now he was wide-awake and somehow pleased with himself. The more he thought of the idea, the better he felt. If Tony showed up now . . . He sat up, listening. The radiators were quiet. There were no footfalls, no sound of a key turning.

Late that night, back from the theater, Fil knew at once that Tony was back. The boots were outside the door. He, too, must be tired, and should not be disturbed.

He was careful not to make any noise. As he turned on the floor lamp, he thought that perhaps Tony was awake and waiting for him. They would listen together to a playback of the dances and the songs Tony had missed. Then he would tell Tony what happened that day, repeating part of the dream.

From Tony's bedroom came the regular breathing of a man sound asleep. To be sure, he looked into the room and in the half-darkness, Tony's head showed darkly, deep in a pillow, on its side, his knees bent, almost touching the clasped hands under his chin, an oversized fetus in the last bottle. Fil shut the door between them and went over to the portable. Now. He turned it on to low. At first nothing but static and odd sounds came through, but soon after there was the patter of feet to the rhythm of a familiar melody.

All the beautiful boys and girls were in the room now, dancing and singing. A boy and a girl sat on the floor holding two bamboo poles by their ends flat on the floor, clapping them together, then apart, and pounding them on the boards, while dancers swayed and balanced their lithe forms, dipping their bare brown legs in and out of the clapping bamboos, the pace gradually increasing into a fury of wood on wood in a counterpoint of panic among the dancers and in a harmonious flurry of toes and ankles escaping certain pain— crushed bones, and bruised flesh, and humiliation. Other dances followed, accompanied by songs and live with the sounds of life and death in the old country; Igorot natives in G-strings walking down a mountainside; peasants climbing up a hill on a rainy day; neighbors moving a house, their sturdy legs showing under a moving roof; lovers at Lent hiding their passion among wild hedges, far from the crowded chapel; a distant gong sounding off a summons either to a feast or a wake. And finally, prolonged ovation, thunderous, wave upon wave . . .

"Turn that thing off!" Tony's voice was sharp above the echoes of the gongs and the applause settling into silence.

Fil switched off the dial and in the sudden stillness, the voices turned into faces, familiar and near, like gesture and touch that stayed on even as the memory withdrew, bowing out, as it were, in a graceful exit, saying, thank you, thank you, before a ghostly audience that clapped hands in silence and stomped their feet in a sucking emptiness. He wanted to join the finale, such as it was, pretend that the curtain call included him, and attempt a shamefaced imitation of a graceful adieu, but he was stiff and old, incapable of grace; but he said, thank you, thank you, his voice sincere and contrite, grateful for the other voices and the sound of singing and the memory.

"Oh, my God . . ." the man in the other room cried, followed by a moan of such anguish that Fil fell on his knees, covering the sound mirror with his hands to muffle the sounds that had started again, it seemed to him, even after he had turned it off.

Then he remembered.

"Tony, what did the doctor say? What did he say?" he shouted and listened, holding his breath, no longer able to tell at the moment who had truly waited all day for the final sentence.

There was no answer. Meanwhile, under his hands, there was a flutter of wings, a shudder of gongs. What was Tony saying? That was his voice, no? Fil wanted to hear, he must know. He switched dials on and off, again and again, pressing buttons. Suddenly, he didn't know what to do. The spools were live, they kept turning. His arms went around the machine, his chest pressing down on the spools. In the quick silence, Tony's voice came clear.

"So they didn't come after all?"

"Tony, what did the doctor say?" Fil asked, straining hard to hear.

"I knew they wouldn't come. But that's okay. The apartment is old anyhow. And it smells of death."

"How you talk. In this country, there's a cure for everything."

"I guess we can't complain. We had it good here all the time. Most of the time, anyway."

"I wish, though, they had come. I could . . ."

"Yes, they could have. They didn't have to see me, but I could have seen them. I have seen their pictures, but what do they really look like?"

"Tony, they're beautiful, all of them, but especially the girls. Their complexion, their grace, their eyes, they were what we call talking eyes, they say things to you. And the scent of them!"

There was a sigh from the room, soft, hardly like a sigh. A louder, grating sound, almost under his hands that had relaxed their hold, called his attention. The sound mirror had kept going, the tape was fast unravelling.

"Oh, no!" he screamed, noticing that somehow, he had pushed the eraser.

Frantically, he tried to rewind and play back the sounds and the music, but there was nothing now but the dull creaking of the tape on the spool and meaningless sounds that somehow had not been erased, the thud of dancing feet, a quick clapping of hands, alien voices and words: *in this country . . . everything . . . all of them . . . talking eyes . . . and the scent . . .* a fading away into nothingness, till about the end when there was a screaming, senseless kind of finale detached from the body of a song in the background, drums and sticks and the tolling of a bell.

"Tony! Tony!" Fil cried, looking towards the sick man's room, "I've lost them all."

Biting his lips, Fil turned towards the window, startled by the first light of dawn. He hadn't realized till then the long night was over.

—BIENVENIDO SANTOS

Chinese Exclusion Act

Forty-Seventh Congress. Session I. 1882

Chapter 126. An act to execute certain treaty stipulations relating to Chinese.

Preamble. Whereas, in the opinion of the Government of the United States the coming of Chinese laborers to this country endangers the good order of certain localities within the territory thereof: Therefore, *Be it enacted by the Senate and the House of Representatives of the United States of America in Congress assembled,* That from and after the expiration of ninety days next after the passage of this act, and until the expiration of ten years next after the passage of this act, the coming of Chinese laborers to the United States be, and the same is hereby, suspended; and during such suspension it shall not be lawful for any Chinese laborer to come, or, having so come after the expiration of said ninety days, to remain within the United States.

SEC. 2. That the master of any vessel who shall knowingly bring within the United States on such vessel, and land or permit to be landed, and Chinese laborer, from any foreign port of place, shall be deemed guilty of a misdemeanor, and on conviction thereof shall be punished by a fine of not more than five hundred dollars for each and every such Chinese laborer so brought, and may also be imprisoned for a term not exceeding one year.

SEC. 3. That the two foregoing sections shall not apply to Chinese laborers who were in the United States on the seventeenth day of November, eighteen hundred and eighty, or who shall have come into the same before the expiration of ninety days next after the passage of this act, and who shall produce to such master before going on board such vessel, and shall produce to the collector of the port in the United States at which such vessel shall arrive, the evidence hereinafter in this act required of his being one of the laborers in this section mentioned; nor shall the two foregoing sections apply to the case of any master whose vessel, being bound to a port not within the United States by reason of being in distress or in stress of weather, or touching at any port of the United States on its voyage to any foreign port of place: *Provided,* That all Chinese laborers brought on such vessel shall depart with the vessel on leaving port.

SEC. 4. That for the purpose of properly identifying Chinese laborers who were in the United States on the seventeeth day of November, eighteen hundred and eighty, or who shall have come into the same before the expiration of ninety days next after the passage of this act, and in order to furnish them with the proper evidence of their right to go from and come to the United

States of their free will and accord, as provided by the treaty between the United States and China dated November seventeenth, eighteen hundred and eighty, the collector of customs of the district from which any such Chinese laborer shall depart from the United States shall, in person or by deputy, go on board each vessel having on board any such Chinese laborer and cleared or about to sail from his district for a foreign port, and on such vessel make a list of all such Chinese laborers, which shall be entered in registry-books to be kept for that purpose, in which shall be stated the name, age, occupation, last place of residence, physical marks or peculiarities, and all facts necessary for the identification of each of such Chinese laborers, which books shall be safely kept in the custom-house; and every such Chinese laborer so departing from the United States shall be entitled to, and shall receive, free of any charge or cost upon application therefor, from the collector or his deputy, at the time such list is taken, a certificate, signed by the collector or his deputy and attested by his seal of office, in such form as the Secretary of the Treasury shall prescribe, which certificate shall contain a statement of the name, age, occupation, last place of residence, personal description, and fact of identification of the Chinese laborer to whom the certificate is issued, corresponding with the said list and registry in all particulars. In case any Chinese laborer after having received such certificate shall leave such vessel before her departure he shall deliver his certificate to the master of the vessel, and if such Chinese laborer shall fail to return to such vessel before her departure from port the certificate shall be delivered by the master to the collector of customs for cancellation. The certificate herein provided for shall entitle the Chinese laborer to whom the same is issued to return to and re-enter the United States upon producing and delivering the same to the collector of customs of the district at which such Chinese laborer shall seek to re-enter; and upon delivery of such certificate by such Chinese laborer to the collector of customs at the time of re-entry in the United States, said collector shall cause the same to be filed in the custom house and duly canceled.

SEC. 5. That any Chinese laborer mentioned in section four of this act being in the United States, and desiring to depart from the United States by land, shall have the right to demand and receive, free of charge or cost, a certificate of indentification similar to that provided for in section four of this act to be issued to such Chinese laborers as may desire to leave the United States by water; and it is hereby made the duty of the collector of customs of the district next adjoining the foreign country to which said Chinese laborer desires to go to issue such certificate, free of charge or cost, upon application by such Chinese laborer, and to enter the same upon registry-books to be kept by him for the purpose, as provided for in section four of this act.

SEC. 6. That in order to the faithful execution of articles one and two of the treaty in this act before mentioned, every Chinese person other than a laborer who may be entitled by said treaty and this act to come within the United States, and who shall be about to come to the United States, shall be identified as so entitled by the Chinese Government in each case, such identity to be evidenced by a certificate issued under the authority of said government, which certificate shall be in the English language or (if not in the English language) accompanied by a translation into English, stating such right to come, and which certificate shall state the name, title, or official rank, if any, the age, height, and all physical peculiarities, former and present occupation or profession, and place of residence in China of the person to whom the certificate is issued and that such person is entitled conformably to the treaty in this act mentioned to come within the United States. Such certificate shall be prima-facie evidence of the fact set forth therein, and shall be produced to the collector of customs, or his deputy, of the port in the district in the United States at which the person named therein shall arrive.

SEC. 7. That any person who shall knowingly and falsely alter or substitute any name for the name written in such certificate or forge any such certificate, or knowingly utter any forged or fraudulent certificate, or falsely personate any person named in any such certificate, shall be deemed guilty of a misdemeanor; and upon conviction thereof shall be fined in a sum not exceeding one thousand dollars, and imprisoned in a penitentiary for a term of not more than five years.

SEC. 8. That the master of any vessel arriving in the United States from any foreign port or place shall, at the same time he delivers a manifest of the cargo, and if there be no cargo, then at the time of making a report of the entry of vessel pursuant to the law, in addition to the other matter required to be reported, and before landing, or permitting to land, any Chinese passengers, deliver and report to the collector of customs of the district in which such vessels shall have arrived a separate list of all Chinese passengers taken on board his vessel at any foreign port or place, and all such passengers on board the vessel at that time. Such list shall show the names of such passengers (and if accredited officers of the Chinese Government traveling on the business of that government, or their servants, with a note of such facts), and the name and other particulars, as shown by their respective certificates; and such list shall be sworn to by the master in the manner required by law in relation to the manifest of the cargo. Any willful refusal or neglect of any such master to comply with the provisions of this section shall incur the same penalties and forfeiture as are provided for a refusal or neglect to report and deliver a manifest of cargo.

SEC. 9. That before any Chinese passengers are landed from any such vessel, the collector, or his deputy, shall proceed to examine such passengers, comparing the certificates with the list and with the passengers; and no passenger shall be allowed to land in the United States from such vessel in violation of the law.

SEC. 10. That every vessel whose master shall knowingly violate any of the provisions of this act shall be deemed forfeited to the United States, and shall be liable to seizure and condemnation on any district of the United States into which such vessel may enter or in which she may be found.

SEC. 11. That any person who shall knowingly bring into or cause to be brought into the United States by land, or who shall knowingly aid or abet the same, or aid or abet the landing in the United States from any vessel of any Chinese person not lawfully entitled to enter the United States, shall be deemed guilty of a misdemeanor, and shall, on conviction thereof, be fined in a sum not exceeding one thousand dollars, and imprisoned for a term not exceeding one year.

SEC. 12. That no Chinese person shall be permitted to enter the United States by land without producing to the proper officer of customs the certificate in this act required of Chinese persons seeking to land from a vessel. And any Chinese person found unlawfully within the United States shall be caused to be removed therefrom to the country from whence he came, by direction of the United States after being brought before some justice, judge, or comissioner of a court of the United States and found to be one not lawfully entitled to be or remain in the United States.

SEC. 13. That this act shall not apply to diplomatic and other officers of the Chinese Government traveling upon the business of that government, whose credentials shall be taken as equivalent to the certificate in this act mentioned, and shall exempt them and their body and household servants from the provisions of this act as to other Chinese persons.

SEC. 14. That hereafter no State court or court of the United States shall admit Chinese to citizenship; and all laws in conflict with this act are hereby repealed.

SEC. 15. That the words "Chinese laborers", whenever used in this act, shall be construed to mean both skilled and unskilled laborers and Chinese employed in mining.

Approved, May 6, 1882.

White and Wong

Hi. I'm Mr. White.

That's White, and I'm Wong.

We're here to discuss the difference between us, the difference between White and Wong.

That's White. We're going to get lots of attention for no reason.

That's Wong. We're going to make some interesting points.

Pure White. We're going to ask pointed questions, then ridicule the answers.

Utterly Wong. There is no answer, and that's the answer.

Almost White, but not quite. If you lean on the edge, on your chin and your elbows, you will see the answer where it lies, which is within.

Wong, Wong, Wong. If you see the answer, why ask pointed questions?

I'm losing track of the difference between White and Wong.

Wong again. The difference is as plain as day or night, or dusk and dawn.

All White. All White. I've been Wong-headed.

On the contrary, I've been Wonged.

Let's put things to Whites.

I know I'm White, and I think you're Wong. But remember: Two Wongs don't make a White.

Might makes White, or at least it might, if you don't go Wong.

Some Wongs will never be Whites.

The White side of my brain says, "White," but the Wong side tells me, "Wong."

Wong you are. There is no absolute White or Wong.

If you're White, can we both be Wong?

—THADDEUS RUTKOWSKI

National Review magazine, Volume 49, No.6, March 24, 1997.

A. Magazine, Aug/Sept 1999, p.13.
Originally printed in *New York Post*, May 1999.

Hello, Nuremberg

Because I am first-generation Eurasian, my chances of "passing" are slim. In fact, my chances of passing are roughly equal to the chances of offspring of first-generation mulattoes passing among whites, or 1 in 4 to the 12th power, or 1 in 16,777,216 children. Basically, I belong to the mixed-gene majority of the impure minority.

So I try to keep a low profile.

I realize that, to compete, I would have to be as blond as Hitler, as tall as Goebbels and as slender as Goering. But was Hitler really blond? Was Goebbels tall? Was Goering slender?

No matter; you get the picture.

—THADDEUS RUTKOWSKI

Homeland Memories and Media: Filipino Images and Imaginations in America

In many Filipino American commercial establishments in southern California, one rarely misses the presence of a wide selection of community newspapers on display and usually free for the taking. The same may be said, although in varying degrees and intensities, about other Filipino communities elsewhere in the United States and other countries. But with the exception of the Bay Area, as my informants tell me, no one set of communities matches the considerable number of local papers circulated in the counties and peripheries of Los Angeles and San Diego, owing primarily to the geographical distribution of Filipino immigrant settlements in North America.

Such ubiquitous newspapers occupy significant places not only in the sites where Filipino Americans meet but also, as I wish to emphasize here, in the contexts in which the narratives and dynamic formations of Filipino American identities are constantly imaged and imagined. Community newspapers constitute only one node in the vast array of apparatuses that link individuals together, from families and kinship systems to religious ties and other social organizations. They are also one among the many forms of media, such as radio, television, and film, that operate as communication systems within and between societies.

In this chapter, I focus on Filipino American community newspapers in southern California as illustrations of a historically specific and localized tenor of community formation and expression. I intend to situate these communicative channels within the larger contexts of both immigration history and cultural citizenship to understand better the local politics of ethnicity that Filipino Americans deploy to make sense of their lives here. I suggest that these print channels operate as alternative spaces for Filipino Americans who see themselves as active agents in the remembering, reconstruction, and representation of their collective identities.

This chapter is informed by an ethnography of Filipino American communities in southern California that I conducted between 1992 and 1995. I interviewed at length mainly first-generation Filipino immigrants, who constituted the bulk of the Filipino American population in this area. Historians refer to these Filipinos as part of the third wave of mostly professional immigrants who came to the United States from the 1960s to the present. In this part of the United States, many of them arrived as naval employees, recruited initially for manual and skilled labor (even before the 1960s as well), and a significant number (mostly women) worked as practitioners in the medical and allied health professions. Later, facilitated in large part by the family reunification provisions of the Immigration and Nationality Act of 1965, they also brought in other members of their families, including parents, children, and siblings.[1] Many of those with whom I talked had lived in southern California for at least 10 years and either were in the process of gaining formal citizenship status or had been naturalized already. I also spoke with a few earlier generation and second-generation nationals who self-identified as Filipino Americans. I found their responses to be especially significant as well in this project, and I have identified their status with their remarks accordingly.

For this study, I interacted with producers and readers of about nine community papers circulated in and around Los Angeles and San Diego counties. I say "about" because many publications appear, last for a few months, die out, then reappear once publishers regain control over resources. This situation is obviously created by the political economy of publishing in which these papers operate. As local undertakings, community newspapers are generally susceptible to the workings of investor pressures, fluctuating market size, dependence on advertising, intemperate competition, availability of human-power, and increasing costs of paper, supplies, and printing. Nevertheless, most of the papers I looked at appeared weekly, with a combined circulation that served an estimated 350,000 Filipino Americans in southern California —the largest group of Filipinos outside the Philippines (u.s. Bureau of the Census, 1992). I also examined the kinds of media content that appeared with regularity, the distribution and reception of such papers, and the significance of such media activities in processes of identity construction.

Like most other ethnic newspapers in the United States, Filipino American community newspapers exist in communities where there is a great demand or need to serve the interests of people of the same group. Of course, the differences from mainstream papers are readily apparent. Ethnic presses are comparatively small scale, are run with a minimal number of journalists, and, especially with Filipino American papers, are usually free of charge, with the costs of production and distribution met by advertising revenues. Such a demand by members of an ethnic group to read a newspaper "of their own" is not entirely a new phenomenon. As early as 1922, sociologist Robert E. Park conducted a survey of American immigrant presses to highlight their significant roles in easing the transition of new arrivals into permanent settlements both by preserving languages, traditions, and values of their home countries and by "assisting [their orientation] . . . in the American environment" (86). To some degree, Filipino American newspapers share this ground with immigrant presses of the past and present. Geared toward immigrant Filipinos as primary readers, these newspapers oscillate between the retention of values that are "dear to Filipino hearts," as one editor told me, and the encouragement to acquire "things American, like [formal] citizenship," as an advertisement for an immigrant law firm regularly asserted in the papers.

But to stop at merely locating commonalities of Filipino American presses with their counterparts in other ethnic communities is tantamount to masking the historical specificities of the conditions in which these newspapers exist and thrive—specificities that reveal unique experiences of racialization different from those faced by whites and other groups of color in the United States. Editors, journalists, and readers consistently reminded me of how "different" their papers were from the others "because others don't know how it is to be a Filipino in America." One reporter told me, "Other newspapers cover us . . . if at all, . . . but they really miss [out] on what we really are. We're called this and that . . . like blacks or Asians or Hispanics. Maybe we're all the same, but we're also different." Here we see how Park's assessments, in the long run, obliterate important differences across immigrant presses that have mattered significantly in determining not only their survival but, to a great extent, their nature and emphasis.

To understand the impact that such differences have had, one can refer to the vibrant press that Filipino American communities of the 1900s to the 1950s built and sustained against the climate of exclusion and the brutalities of nativism,[2] something that Park's survey almost completely overlooks (save for one entry). Unlike most immigrant presses of their time, these Filipino American papers sought to expose the bigotry and hatred especially directed at Filipino farmworkers and laborers. They informed their readers of a critical and creative mass of Filipinos fighting for equality, dignity, and access to civil society. They determined to clarify what "special" relationships the Philippines had with the United States when the designation of u.s. territory/colony did not match with Filipinos in America being ineligible for citizenship. This is a history that contemporary Filipino Americans inherit once they settle in their new country, a ground they find in common, not with other ethnic groups, but with Filipinos of previous generations (Flores-Meiser, 1987).

Outside of their group, the Filipino American press also shares a lineage of resistance with black, Latino/Chicano, and other Asian media against racial subordination. The connections between racial domination of groups over others and the dissemination of this ideology in media and popular culture in all sectors of society are difficult to overemphasize in this context. Media historian Jane Rhodes (1993) contended that in America, "racial identity has been and continues to be . . . a crucial factor in determining who can produce popular culture and what messages are created" (185). To those groups who are relegated to the margins and lower rungs of the racial hierarchy, this has meant a sustained struggle to gain a foothold in mainstream and corporate-controlled media channels, to oppose and challenge dehumanizing stereotypes, and to seek alternative avenues for self-determination and counter-representation.

Cast against such historical and contemporary settings, it is undeniable how the impetus for publishing and reading a paper "of one's own" from a Filipino American perspective encompasses more than a mere fulfillment of a need for communicating with each other. Readers of the *Los Angeles Asian Journal, TM Weekly Herald* (Los Angeles), *Mabuhay Times* (San Diego), and *Filipino Press* (San Diego, Orange, and Los Angeles counties), among others, take pride in the abundance and regularity of these papers despite the perceived marginality of their ethnic group. "It's amazing to see that we can do it even though many others think that we are nobodies," said one Filipino American. Among editors and publishers, some of whom had previously worked in mainstream newspaper offices, such pride is most articulated in being able to do something worthwhile for the community beyond what the larger publishing system compels them to do: regard their audience as discrete interest groups and treat them merely as potential consumers. A Filipino American journalist told me:

> Of course, my publisher wants to make money, too. But, really, there are no viable information media at the moment for Filipinos. Our newspaper wants to do that service. Think about it, there's nothing much about Filipinos or, much less, even the Philippines, in the big papers. In the *San Diego Union-Tribune,* I found three clippings about Filipinos, two of them about Filipino youth gangs in San Diego. If it's not too little reporting, it's distorted reporting. What else can you trust to read about your own other than someone who wrote it for you?

The alternative appeal of such community newspapers among Filipino Americans also goes farther than simply providing a separate space for gathering information not covered by the mainstream press. Many readers inform me of how much it means to them to feel "at home" in a place they have already considered their new home but where they are also still regarded as guests by most people around them. "I am a citizen of this country now, supposed to be not a foreigner anymore, even though many think I am," one earlier generation Filipino American reader told me, "but that doesn't mean I've forgotten where I came from." Reading about Filipinos, whether from California, other parts of the States, the Philippines, or elsewhere, for these respondents, points to some fundamental ways of dealing with a strong sense of disconnectedness or displacement brought about by immigration and separation. In a world of heightened movements and impersonal arrangements, these Filipinos use the community press to reconnect with each other, not so much to bring the pieces back to their original whole as to reconstruct what used to be and still are discrete aspects of their lives into different forms and products. At the same time, the newspapers also serve as vehicles for the collective sense making of their conditions and experiences here.

It is no surprise, then, that what front pages of these papers cover are events and issues that emanate both from the former homeland and the new settlements. At the time I was doing my fieldwork, news about national and regional elections as well as calamities in the Philippines shared headlines with local political races and community organizational activities in which Filipinos in southern California participated. Knowing what is happening in at least two worlds vitally brings into public discourse traces of attachments here and elsewhere. "I've traveled far already," mused another Filipino reader, "but I always want to be reminded about my former home. It matters in understanding myself here." Many others said that this refusal to forget ties to one's former home is at odds with the pressures to conform to what they see as American-style values and interests. In the same breath, however, these people were also quick to alert me of the false promises of the "melting pot" ideology. Conformity, to them, has not resulted in their full acceptance as Americans and their true equality with others, and it is precisely their reluctance to assimilate fully that animates their media activities.

The papers' orientation to the Philippines serves as both a source and a sign of ethnic rootedness central to Filipino American identities, particularly those held by immigrants. This is apparent not only in the frequency of references to events in the Philippines but also in the regular coverage of activities of Filipino movie celebrities. Editors told me that their audience always looks forward to reading about gossip in the movie industry back home. These bits of information connect readers to popular culture they are familiar with, constantly reminding them of personalities they identify with and keeping them abreast of movies that might end up in the local Filipino video stores. "They like to know what's happening to their movie idols, . . . their latest films, . . . who got married to whom, and who has passed on," one reporter said. Many feature articles of popular tourist spots in the Philippines are also routinely written. She continued, "We also write pieces on our scenic spots, with photos. They're all beautiful. . . . It's nice to show them."

Like movie news, the persistence of memory about places and people left behind mitigates anxieties of distance and displacement. In reference to picture-perfect locales, there is a strong sense in which memories of the homeland are rendered pure, natural, and paradisiacal. Most readers delighted in such depictions. "That's how we want to remember the Philippines," intoned one. Against the harsh conditions of settling on foreign soil and encountering unexpected circumstances, these remembrances act as coping mechanisms—yet another way of momentarily suspending the ordeals of immigrant life. Such nostalgic retreats, however, cannot all be romantic. These same readers are also cognizant of the other faces of their changing home revealed alongside its picturesque representations. Said one, "But of course, we know that it's very different now too, . . . what with pollution, poverty, volcanic eruption, and all that."

These gestures aimed toward the Philippines mirror to a large extent Filipino Americans' understanding of their lives in the United States. As articulated in the newspapers, orientations to America-based activities and issues open up multiple and sometimes competing narratives of life here. Many of those I interviewed spoke of fantasizing about this "land of milk and honey" prior to coming over. Fueled by Hollywood movies and American-style education, they dreamed of starting better lives in places they assumed would afford them greater opportunities. Only on coming over did many of them realize the false promises of democracy and equality, for even those who were able to "make it" saw themselves relegated to "second-class citizenship." In many letters to the editor, commentaries, and news articles, accounts of racism, marginality, exclusion, and misunderstandings between Filipinos and the larger society reveal the contradictions of American ideals perpetuated within and outside of the country. During this period, much space in the papers was given to exposing and challenging the blatant forms of racism and sexism expressed, among others, by talk-radio announcer Howard Stern ("They eat their young over there"), a character in the television sitcom *Frasier* (November 29, 1994, episode; "For that amount of money, I could get myself a mail-order bride from the Philippines"), and superintendents of Filipina nurses (who ordered them not to speak Tagalog at work). Opinion pieces tried to make sense of these unexpected and unfamiliar situations, at times exposing painful individual experiences at work and in social settings to measure the extent of the dark sides of the American dream. Said one journalist: "It can get to be insane here. We have to bring [these incidents] out in the open. Our newspapers make us talk about these dirty things. We don't have to hide them. It's our right to bring them out."

Narratives of Filipino life in America also extend inward into more local affairs. On most of these pages, a great deal of coverage is reserved for reporting and announcing activities of the myriad social organizations that Filipinos in southern California have established. From hometown and provincial associations to alumni, trade, and religious clubs, these Filipino American groups find in their community papers the channels to convey their multilevel alliances with each other. These conduits of collective belonging aid in reconstructing identities and redefining agendas. A reporter told me how valuable the papers are for the associations in making their members regard themselves not merely as Filipinos who hail from the Philippines but as Filipinos who are also Caviteños, Pampangos, Ateneans, lawyers, and Methodists. These are the Filipinos who have also become American at the same time, and Filipinos who care about each other. Articles regularly reported meetings and fund-raisers aimed at benefiting common causes, including donations to calamity victims in the Philippines, scholarships to those in need on both coasts, and financial as well as volunteer assistance to local community projects for senior citizens and for the granting of free medical aid, voter registration, and cultural events.

It would be erroneous, however, to portray these community newspapers as sites of smooth and easy consensus. Like other ethnic groups, Filipino American communities do not speak with one voice all the time, and their interests and agendas occasionally run into conflict with each other. A Filipino American reader who used to be a reporter said:

> Oh yes, we have our own quarrels too. But I think these newspapers make us talk to each other so that we have dialogue . . . instead of not talking at all. We learn many things when we give each other a chance. And also, we make our own ideas known to others who are far away and those who never participate, but may want to.

On the editorial and opinion pages, various viewpoints on issues that affect Filipino Americans are explored and challenged. Analyses of local political activities identify intergroup cleavages and campaign errors, and the working out of such differences. Some of these even seep into comparisons and connections with politics in the Philippines, yet another remnant of Filipino American journalism of the 1900s and, especially, of the 1960s, 1970s, and 1980s (the histories of which have yet to be written), when numerous Filipino exiles were writing in their papers against the Marcos dictatorship.

The reach of these community newspapers goes beyond political, generational, and ethnic lines. Profiles of community leaders and achievers provide models of a variety of ways in which people can participate in political and social activities in their conventional or alternative forms. Articles on community activists and activities offer insights on running for public office, pursuing different causes, and managing small-scale events. Many write-ups also tackle issues that include and affect second- and third-generation Filipino Americans. From stories about political/cultural awareness and achievements of the youth to the adverse effects of gang involvement and troubling suicide rates, these papers also attempt to reach younger Filipino Americans in the communities they serve. Said one second-generation reader:

> At first, I was not really interested in reading these newspapers. But as I got older and more conscious of my roots, I gradually came to see them as important . . . and necessary in understanding who I am, where my parents came from, . . . our many cultures, the things we share, and where we are going too. These newspapers are also important to us, so I read them often now.

Some of these younger members of the population have already made their mark in their communities as active supporters and organizers of various endeavors. A few of them have been staff members or regular contributors in the papers and recently have also established their own San Diego monthly, called

Kalayaan. Several Filipino American newspaper publishers have also attempted to broaden their readership across other Asian and Pacific American communities in their areas. Papers such as *Pacific Asian Times* and *Asian World* in San Diego County alone attest to the increasing importance among members of these groups to expand their efforts at combining energies toward common goals, perhaps realizing the opportunities that may be seized in forming pan-ethnic coalitions working for common interests. Subsections and advertisements in Thai, Chinese, and Vietnamese reveal more and stronger communication links among what used to be disparate minority-population groups.

On the whole, many Filipino Americans see these channels as rich and vibrant sources of empowerment. They use these newspapers to communicate with themselves and with others, offering a multitude of ways to define who they are, where they are from, and what interests and positions they could share in their present community (Anderson, 1983). These are the kinds of conduits that open up possibilities of agency despite exclusion. "What is most important to remember here," as a Filipino American reporter remarked, "is that we can call this paper ours. We hire our own, we print the stories we want to print, we make our own rules. We can't count on others to do this for us. Here, at the least, we are able to speak." This is a kind of activity that many would brush off as separatist or isolationist, given southern California's history and present conditions regarding interethnic and interracial relations. But in the minds of Filipino Americans who write and read about themselves and their larger world in their newspapers, it is a kind of self-determination that could potentially change the world around them—a kind of participation that for now will not be allowed space in mainstream press but later may be emulated by a more multivocal local and even national press.

What matters to these groups in a most fundamental way is the question of who can belong to this nation, and on what terms. Tensions about limited resources and employment spaces are usually expressed in arguments about citizenship and belonging, about who has rights and who does not. For these people, it is not a matter of merely coexisting or having a space relegated to a few of them, but on having voices and being heard. It is a matter of understanding their histories and realities, how they are different from others and what they have in common with others. Ultimately, it is a matter of having a sense of belonging and participating as full citizens in the nation that is America. In view of mainstream media exclusion, these newspapers serve as alternative sites for meaningful and empowering constructions of Filipino American communities.

—RICK BONUS

Notes

1. I am abbreviating here a much more complicated history of Filipino immigration to the United States in order to outline the basic historical parameters of this chapter. For example, not accounted for by this "wave" rubric were those who came in as students, political exiles, and visitors who later decided to stay. Parts of my larger project on Filipino American ethnicity discuss their histories in greater length. For further inquiry on Filipino immigration to the United States, see, for example, Cordova (1983), Espiritu (1995, esp. 1-36), and Pido (1986).

2. Research and retrieval of these newspapers are currently and principally being undertaken by the staff of the Filipino American Experience Research Project under the directorship of Alex Fabros. I am referencing here from a working draft edition of their manuscript (Fabros & Herbert, 1994). Also see Flores-Meiser (1987) and Cordova (1983), for a more nuanced treatment of the role of Filipino newspapers in earlier communities.

Works Cited

Anderson, B. *Imagined Communities: Reflections on the Origin and Spread of Nationalism.* London: Verso, 1983.

Cordova, F. *Filipinos: Forgotten Asian Americans. A pictorial essay,* 1763–circa 1963. Ed. D.L. Cordova. Dubuque, IA: Kendall/Hunt, 1983.

Espiritu, Y.L. *Filipino American Lives.* Philadelphia: Temple University Press, 1995.

Fabros, A., and Herbert, A, Ed. *The Filipino American Newspaper Collection: Extracts from 1906 to 1953.* Fresno, CA: Filipino American Experience Research Project, 1994.

Flores-Meiser, E.P. "The Filipino-American Press." *The Ethnic Press in the United States: A Historical Analysis and Handbook.* Ed. S.M. Miller. New York: Greenwood, 1987.

Immigration and Nationality Act of 1965.8 U.S.C. § 1101 *et seq.*

Park, R.E. *The Immigrant Press and Its Control.* New York: Harper, 1922.

Pido, A.J.A. *The Pilipinos in America: Macro-micro Dimensions of Immigration and Integration.* New York: Center for Migration Studies, 1986.

Rhodes, J. "The Visibility of Race and Media History." *Critical Studies in Mass Communication 10* (1993): 184-90.

U.S. Bureau of the Census. *1990 Census of Population and Housing Summary.* Washington, DC: Government Printing Office, 1992.

Reverse Racism

I'm gonna take every white man from his job and force him to construct light rail transit systems for 50 cents an hour. When they're done I'll make sure they are moved to a special little section of town that we'll call Whiteyville, where tourists can come to shop for curios and eat exotic hot dish meals. When the American mainstream tongue gets a taste for hot dish, I'm going to open my own fusion hot dish restaurants where I combine hot dish with Asian recipes, and charge people ten times what the food is worth. All the waiters and waitresses will be forced to wear traditional Scandinavian garb. I'm going run for office, promising equality for white men, then when I get elected I'm going to pass laws that forbid white guys from marrying Asian women. Then I'm going to hit on every single white woman I see and spread rumors about how white guys got small dicks and how white guys are no good for women because they come from such a male dominated society. I'm going to teach Asian American history in every classroom, and when little Morty Crackerman raises his hand and asks why we don't study any white people, I will have him branded as a troublemaker and suspend him from school for three days. Then I will feel a little guilty about it and declare National Whitey Appreciation Week where we study the contributions of Kip Winger and Harold Bloom while eating hamburgers and listening to Smashmouth. We will read some books by whites, but publishers will only put out a few books by white people, and priority will be given to white women with names like Bobby Jo Thompson-Chang and Betty Peterson-Nakamura. We will watch the Honkeytown Crackers play against the Whiteyville Honkies, and in the bleachers we'll do the Wave and the white men can't dance dance.

When white men complain, I'll sigh deeply and say, hey, things are better for you now. You should have tried being around twenty years ago, before me and some other good Asians marched with you white people for your rights. Don't blame me for racism, that stuff happened a long time ago, and anyway, I can't be racist! My girlfriend is white and so are some of my best friends and servants! Every time a white man fucks up, I'll just shake my head sorrowfully and say, see? Then I'll declare that there are too many white men in America, and restrict immigration for white men. The only white men allowed into this country will be the most highly educated white men from Europe: I mean, hey, we need someone to work behind the counter at the gas stations for minimum wage, and who else is gonna drive taxis or run 24 hour grocery stores in the hood? I'm gonna build garbage dumps in white neighborhoods and make sure there's a lot of lead in their water supply. When the power cuts out in the city, it'll be at least three days till it gets back on for white people cuz they're gonna fix the power lines in Asian hoods first. When white men become successful, I'll beat them down in the street and make sure my Asian friends in the news don't report on it, and if it goes to trial I'll make sure the all Asian jury and Asian judge pardon me. Then, after all this hard yet satisfying work exploiting and oppressing and mindfucking whitey, I'm going on vacation to Europe and find me a good token trophy white wife. Then I'm gonna hang around Europe for a while with a big backpack, smoking French cigarettes, I will not shave nor take a shower, and I will bang every hot Euro chick that wants me cuz hey, white women love us Asians. White men are so patriarchal and oppressive, plus they can't fuck. ASIAN GUYS! We need to rescue white women! White women will open clubs in Europe where they can pay money to sleep with a scrubby Asian expatriate or tourist. Then I will open branches of my fast-food chains and hotels on European soil, and I'll grease the palms of shady white Europeans so they can keep an eye on things and if they fuck up: hey, it's their fault. Of course, this will lead to a war. Just to be safe, I'm gonna forcibly remove white American people from their homes because I feel they are a threat to national security. They can stay at the dog racing tracks until we are sure that they are good and loyal to this country. And we will take everything they ever owned. During the war, I will drown my sorrows at dramatically lit bars in Europe. I will win a white prostitute from her evil white pimp in a game of cards. We will have sex, and she will fall in love with me. I will leave her, pregnant, in Europe. When I come back to visit her, she thrusts her baby into my arms, tells me that Asian America is a much better place for our bastard lovechild, and then she will kill herself. Tragic, but good drama. So good, in fact, that I turn it into a Broadway musical and make a ton of money off of it. Asian actors will put on white makeup and act like white people. You know, I'd love to put real white people in the play, but they're just not talented enough. Okay, maybe a couple of white women, if they're willing to kiss Asian men and tell the press that white men are reverse racists.

When white men form their own groups to protect themselves, I'll accuse them of being separatists and force them to let me into their groups. Then I'll cut their budgets because they're really not serving the majority of people. And when they crumple into a ball, when they raise their voices to speak, when they go insane from it all, that's when I'll pat them on the back, and say, that's just the way it is. Live with it.

—THIEN-BAO THUC PHI

WHY ARE WE HERE?

Thoughts on Asian-American Identity and Honoring
Asian-Americans in Congress

The Asian American Bar Association of Washington, D.C., and CAPAL[1] *invited this fund-raiser address for an event honoring the Asian-American members of Congress.[2] It was an occasion for asking a question critical to the Asian-American community: On what basis do we claim a distinct Asian-American identity?*

We are justifiably proud of these honorees. Historically, the Asian-American members of Congress have an above-average voting record in civil rights and human rights. They are consistently pro-family, in the best sense of the word: they vote for better health care, for Headstart, and for human needs. They took leadership positions struggling for the major civil rights legislation of the second reconstruction. They have actively and vigorously supported equality in education, housing, and employment, often using their physical presence as a moral force to contradict the racist arguments of those who opposed the Civil Rights Acts. It is harder to argue that "those people" do not deserve voting rights, fair housing, and nonracist immigration policy when some of "those people" are sitting right there at the table with all the dignified and deserving grace of the nisei World War II veterans.

Many of us feel personally indebted to the Asian-American members of Congress for the doors they opened for us. Someone like Patsy Mink made a whole generation of Asian-American women feel it is possible to speak up and risk controversy. This was a powerful antidote to the other major public image of Asian womanhood that circulated during my youth: Nancy Kwan in high heels singing "I enjoy being a girl" on late-night television. At my law school graduation, an aunt gave me a lei and a hug and said, "We're so proud of you. You're going to be just like Patsy Mink." I realized that in the eyes of a respected relative, "becoming a lawyer" did not mean making a lot of money; it meant "being like Patsy Mink," having the skill and gumption to speak up for the underdog.

This is the ethic our Asian-American members of Congress have exemplified, and this is why it is easy and natural for us to honor them. Given that ease, I would like to complexify our task by asking, Why are we here? Presumably, we feel some connection to these people and their accomplishments. But why are we here? Most of us did not have the opportunity to vote for these honorees. What is the Asian-American identity that makes us claim them as our own? What makes us—Chinese, Pacific Islander, South or Southeast Asian, Korean, Filipino, and Japanese—come together as a group?

We are not the same, and we each have unique histories. Why, then, do we gather at fund-raisers like this one to honor a selection of members of Congress who are predominantly—though, thank goodness, not exclusively —Japanese American? Out of what have we created this community we call Asian American?

Our continued political viability depends on a critical understanding of our identity as an Asian-American coalition. As we demand representation in the cabinet of a president we helped elect, we have to answer the identity question. As we demand inclusion in all walks of life—in the academy, in the marketplace, and on the judiciary—we will face the question, sometimes asked in good faith and sometimes asked by those who are threatened by us, Who are Asian Americans? What does a Hmong refugee have in common with a nisei auto mechanic? What are your common interests? Who speaks for you? And if many of you are well-off, why should we reserve a place for you in our efforts at inclusion?

Our pan-Asian identity is not a natural, inevitable coalition. It is, like all coalitions, a constructed one. It is nonetheless real and vital.

Saying it is not natural is important because the ideology of racism depends on naturalized notions of racial identity. "Those Asians are just like that." They are naturally greedy, bad drivers, nearsighted, inscrutable, math wizards. Born that way. Can't trust them. Much of our political work as Asian Americans is the task of exploding notions of what is naturally Asian. The work of organizations like MANAA[3] is critically important in challenging the media stereotyping that puts limits on Asian identity.

Our coalition is certainly not natural in the sense of any essence located on the Asian continent. We were not one culture in the places our ancestors came from. In fact, in the land of our ancestors, we were closer to natural enemies with real and often justified enmity and distrust. In my own genealogy, I have Okinawan and Japanese, colonizer and colonized.

Our coalition does not originate in Asia. It is American. It is tied to American history and to the history of colonialism and militarism. Most of us are living in this country because someone made it impossible for our family to stay in the old country: the wealthy who drove out the poor, the colonizers who took the land, the war makers who brought guns and terror, and the cold warriors who divided nations of kin into parts and parcels. And when our various families arrived on this continent, they encountered a uniquely American racism that lumped us all together and planted the seed of an Asian-American coalition, not a natural coalition but a constructed one.

It was constructed in Chinatown sweatshops, on plantations, in factories, in fields, and in packing houses where waves of Asian immigrants who arrived with nothing found themselves living side by side with those from other Asian-Pacific nations: Korean camp next to Okinawan camp on a plantation in Hawaii, Filipino pensioner next to Chinese bachelor in a Chinatown hotel, and Samoan next to Laotian in a crowded housing project. For over a hundred years and continuing into the present, our immigration patterns and harsh economic circumstances have brought us together.

Another element critical to our formation as a group was anti-Asian racism. We may have thought we were all very different from one another, but the ideology of yellow peril treated us all the same. Newer Asian groups find they arrive in a country with over a century of experience in stereotyping and hating Asians. As the wave of anti-Asian violence that affects our community continues, we have a stark and physical reminder that being any kind of Asian is enough to trigger random attacks on the street. It does no good to flash your student ID or your American Express card to show you are one of those good, hardworking, and productive Asians. Racism does not work that way. We remember Vincent Chin, Jim Loo, and a roll call of Asian-American victims of modern-day lynchings.[4]

These forces—immigration history and racism—were external forces bringing us together. There were also strong internal forces. We chose each other as allies. In multiracial organizations like the ILWU,[5] we banded together to better our circumstances. Asian-American identity reached a high point, many would argue, along with the civil rights and black power movements of the 1960s and 1970s.

I was a child in Los Angeles when Muhammad Ali said, on national television, "Black is beautiful," and mysterious bumper stickers with sleek black panthers began appearing on cars in my neighborhood. This was fascinating, scary, and deeply affecting. Soon, the first cries of yellow power were heard, and working-class Asian gang members started reading political tracts and painting murals of Malcolm x, Ho Chi Min, and Che Guevara on abandoned buildings. Asian college students started sitting in, demanding power within the university, demanding affirmative action for Asians, and linking the bombing in Vietnam and Cambodia to the bombing of Hiroshima: Asian bodies, white supremacy.

This radical pan-Asian nationalism changed the nature of Asian-American politics. The traditional and critically important work of civil rights organizations like the JACL was pushed forward by the nationalist perspective. Some of the lasting contributions of this period of renewed activism and explicit Asian-American coalition building were the establishment of Asian-American studies as a discipline and the victory of the redress movement.[6] As an Asian-American university professor, I know I would not be teaching today if it were not for student activists who forced university administrators to take the talents of Asians in the academy seriously.

So what does the radical politics of yellow power have to do with the fact that we are all sitting together in one room dressed up and eating banquet food? This is one of the paradoxes of life in the 1990s. We may not look like the student radicals of twenty years ago, but their work in solidifying the notion of organizing around Asian-American issues is partly responsible for our being here.

To bring the history of Asian-American identity to the present, changing demographics further complexifies the issue. As the new immigrants rapidly eclipse the old, separate Asian-American identities, such as Korean American or South Asian American, may serve political and cultural purposes more significant for those groups than the pan-Asian identity. New immigrants have special concerns about homeland politics—Korean reunification and Tianamen Square—that raise questions about the goals of traditional Asian-American organizations. Resentment over a disproportionate number of Asian representation slots—on faculties, in Congress, and in Asian-American organizations—going to second-, third-, and fourth-generation Asian Americans rather than newcomers is another reality we have to address in forming our coalition.

Having posited that Asian-American identity is historically constructed by uniquely American circumstances and reinforced by the deliberate practice of pan-Asian-American activism, let me close by suggesting that there is such a thing as an Asian-American issue and an Asian-American position and by suggesting the perhaps disturbing notion that not everyone with an Asian surname is in fact Asian within the meaning of our constructed coalition. To speak plainly, there are some people of Asian descent we might not embrace as representing our community, even if they were elected to Congress. If Asian-American identity is constructed, and constructed in part by a history of activism, then issues do define us.

The Asian-American coalition is defined by the struggle against racism. We support civil rights legislation and organize to stop anti-Asian violence because we see racism and are determined to end it.

We also share an interest in just immigration policy because all of us have immigrant status in our genealogy. At the simple level of self-interest, many of us have family and friends who need to gain U.S. citizenship. On the more complex plane of social justice, we honor those in our family histories who risked life and limb to get here by speaking up for others in similar circumstances, like the Haitian people today. I have been particularly proud that organizations like the JACL, whose members no longer have a direct interest in immigration, have lobbied and fought for justice in immigration law.

Racial equality and fair immigration laws are obvious issues for our coalition. Less obvious issues are continuing sources of tension, a tension that indicates the need for more work, more hard conversation, and more consciousness raising.

What is our position on feminism? On unions? On homelessness? On AIDS? On gays in the military? On the military, period? Some people feel it threatens the coalition to raise issues that are not obviously Asian. I disagree because I believe the key defining element of Asian-American identity is the quest for justice. My ancestors were poor peasants who came to this country because they could not feed their children and pay the taxes in their homeland. My mother grew up barefoot on a sugar plantation. My father was interned at Heart Mountain and volunteered for combat duty in World War II. He is the only one from his machine-gun squad who survived the war. This is my inheritance. It is the only one I will get. In spite of what the dominant culture may believe about rich and privileged Asians, I know that in your family tree there is a history of dignified men and women who sacrificed so you could sit at the banquet table today.

This history is what makes it fair to call any issue of social justice an Asian-American issue, and I believe that is why the Asian-American members of Congress are so easy to honor. They have spoken consistently for the poor, for working people, for small businesses, for immigrant rights, and for women. The ability to make the connection between the injustice we have faced as Asian Americans and the injustice that others face is the ultimate test that marks the line called integrity. I believe our stellar Asian-American delegation has already passed the test, and I believe our Asian-American coalition will live or die by our choice in that regard. May it live long.

—MARI MATSUDA

Notes

1. Washington, D.C., February 23, 1993.
2. The Conference on Asian Pacific American Leadership is a group of Asian Pacific American professionals and government employees that works to promote the involvement of Asian Pacific Americans in government service and public policy.
3. The Media Action Network of Asian Americans is a media watchdog group that monitors television programs and movies for portrayals that denigrate and stereotype Asian Americans.
4. Vincent Chin, a Chinese American, was beaten to death with a baseball bat in 1982 by two unemployed Detroit auto workers who mistook him for a person of Japanese descent—the group they blamed for their joblessness. In 1989, Jim Loo (a Chinese American) was fatally pistol-whipped in North Carolina by two white brothers who said they did not like Vietnamese people because their relatives had been killed during the Vietnam War. Thien Minh Ly, a former UCLA Vietnamese American student leader, was stabbed repeatedly and killed in 1996 by a white supremacist whose graphic letter to a prison buddy stated, "Oh, I killed a J_p a while ago." Thanh Mai died from a fatal head injury in 1993 after being accosted by three drunk white males who taunted him with racial slurs such as. "What the fuck are you looking at g__k?" Yoshihiro Hattori was shot to death in 1992 when he went to the wrong door while looking for a Halloween party. His killer claimed he thought Hattori was a lunatic who might hurt him and his family. In 1992, Luyen Phan Nguyen, a University of Miami pre-med student, was chased and surrounded by seven white men who kicked and beat him to death while yelling racial epithets.
5. International Longshoremen's and Warehousemen's Union.
6. Responding to growing public pressure, Congress enacted the Civil Liberties Act of 1988, which authorized the payment of restitution to Japanese Americans and Aleuts interned during World War II (P.L. 100–1383, 101–162, and P.L. 102-371).

A General Timeline of the Asian American Experience

1763 First recorded settlement of Filipinos in America. They escape imprisonment aboard Spanish galleons by jumping ship in New Orleans and fleeing into the bayous.

1790 First recorded arrival of an Asian Indian in the United States.

1847 Three Chinese students arrive in New York City for schooling. One of them, Yung Wing, graduates from Yale in 1854 becoming the first Chinese to graduate in the United States.

1848-52 Strike of gold at Sutter's Mill, draws Chinese immigrants to West Coast to mine gold. Many arrive as indentured servants during the California Gold Rush. The bulk of Chinese immigrants come later as a cheap source of labor to work the railroads, mines, and in other industries.

1854 *People v. Hall* constitutes law forbidding any Chinese from testifying in court against Whites.

1859 Exclusion of Chinese from public schools in San Francisco.

1892 "Geary Act" prohibits Chinese immigration for another 10 years and denies bail for writ of habeas corpus.

1894 *In re Saito*, Circuit court in Massachusetts declares that Japanese are ineligible for naturalization because they are "Mongolians," neither White nor Black.

1898 The Philippine Islands become a protectorate of the United States under the Treaty of Paris ending the Spanish-American War. Hawaii is also annexed to the United States.

1902 Congress indefinitely extends the prohibition against Chinese immigration.

1903-04 7,000 Koreans go to Hawaii to work in sugarcane and pineapple fields. They are welcomed as strike breakers against Japanese laborers demanding better work conditions and wages.

1905 Section 60 of California's Civic Code is amended to forbid marriages between Whites and "Mongolians."

1906 A decree is issued by the San Francisco school board that all persons of Asian ancestry must attend segregated schools in Chinatown.

1907 President Theodore Roosevelt enters into a "Gentlemen's Agreement" with Japan to limit Japanese immigration to the mainland and to Hawaii. This includes a ban on further Korean immigration to the United States as laborers, thus opening up farming jobs in Hawaii for Filipinos. Korean immigration virtually ends during the period of Japanese occupation (1910–45) and does not resume until the Immigration Act of 1965 is passed.

1913 California passes alien land law prohibiting "aliens ineligible to citizenship" from buying land or leasing it for longer than three years. Korean farmworkers are driven out of Hemet, California.

1918 Servicemen of Asian ancestry who had served in World War I receive right of naturalization.

1923 *U.S. v. Bhagat Singh Thind* declares Asian Indians ineligible for naturalized citizenship.

1930 Anti-Filipino riot in Watsonville, California.

1941 United States declares war on Japan following the attack on Pearl Harbor; 2,000 Japanese community leaders along Pacific Coast states and Hawaii are rounded up and interned in Department of Justice (DOJ) camps.

1942 Executive Order 9066 puts 110,000 Japanese, many of whom are second and third generation American citizens, in 10 internment camps in the United States.

1943 "Magnuson Act" finally repeals the Chinese Exclusion Act of 1882. This was a direct result of the alliance between the United States and China during World War II. A quota of 105 persons per year is set for Chinese immigration (based on a formula set at one-sixth the total population of that ancestry in the 1920 census).

1945 On August 6th, an atomic bomb is dropped on Hiroshima, Japan, ushering in a nuclear age.

1945 Congress passes War Brides Act, allowing 6,000 Chinese women to enter United States as brides of Chinese American soldiers. All American internment camps for Japanese Americans are closed.

1948 California repeals law banning interracial marriage. Evacuation Claims Act authorizes payment of settlements to people of Japanese ancestry who suffered economic losses from internment: 10 cents is returned for every $1 lost.

1952 All Asian Americans receive the right to become citizens and to vote, when Congress finally strikes down the last of the anti-Asian exclusionary citizenship laws.

1956 Dalip Singh Saund, an Asian Indian from Imperial Valley, California is the first Asian Pacific American elected to the U.S. Congress.

1964 A native of Hawaii, Patsy Takemoto Mink becomes the first Asian American woman elected to the U.S. House of Representatives.

1965 National Origins Act raises Asian immigration to 20,000 per year for Asian countries, same as European countries. The Immigration Act increases Filipino and annual immigration to above 20,000, and Korean immigration to over 30,000 per year.

1969 As a result of student protests at schools like San Francisco State University and University of California, Berkeley, Asian American studies programs are established at colleges.

1970 Asian American students join nationwide protests against the American invasion of Cambodia and the broadening of the war in Vietnam.

1975 More than 130,000 refugees from Vietnam, Cambodia, Laos enter the United States as Communist governments come to power in their homelands.

1979 Resumption of diplomatic relations between the People's Republic of China and the United States allows members of long separated Chinese American families to be reunited.

1982 Vincent Chin, a Chinese American, is murdered in Detroit by two White autoworkers who had reportedly mistaken him for a Japanese and blamed him for their plight. The murderers were acquitted, never serving a day in prison for their crime.

1986 The Immigration Reform & Control Act is passed but affects Mexicans more than Asians.

1987 First formal signing of the Proclamation of Asian Pacific American Heritage Week in the White House.

1988 The Civil Liberties Act of 1988, which implements the recommendations of the Commission on Wartime Relocation and Internment of Civilians is signed into law by the President. The law apologizes and offers redress and reparations to thousands of Japanese Americans who were denied their civil and constitutional rights by the U.S. government during World War II.

1990 President Bush proclaims May 1990 as Asian Pacific Heritage Month.

1992 Los Angeles Civil Unrest: Over 2,000 Korean-owned businesses are looted and burned as a result of riots due to outrage over the Rodney King verdict.

1996 Gary Locke wins gubernatorial race of Washington State. He is the first Asian American to be elected governor of one of the contiguous United States.

1997 Elderly Filipino American World War II veterans chained themselves to the White House fence, calling on Congress to end its stalling and give 70,000 Filipino American World War II veterans the pension and benefits that every other allied veteran who fought under U.S. command received.

1999 President Clinton signs an Executive Order establishing a President's Advisory Commission on Asian Americans and Pacific Islanders to address the health and human services needs of AAPIs, and to increase their participation in federal programs. It is only the second Executive Order issued concerning Asian Americans.

2000 On September 13, a U.S. District Judge released Dr. Wen Ho Lee. The 60-year-old Taiwan-born scientist suspected of spying for China was fired from his job at the Los Alamos National Laboratory in New Mexico in 1999 and held in solitary confinement for nine months. He was never charged with espionage and the government ultimately dropped all but one of the 59 charges of mishandling nuclear weapons data against him. This case stands as an example of a miscarriage of justice in an investigation tainted with racial scapegoating.

2001 On September 11, terrorists attack the World Trade Towers in New York and the Pentagon in Washington, DC. Shortly after, a backlash of anti-Asian violence occurred in cities and regions throughout the U.S. The DOJ also rounded up and imprisoned over 1,000 individuals of Arab and Muslim backgrounds without providing official charges, giving them access to attorneys or even letting their families know of their whereabouts. Various Asian American communities, in particular, Japanese Americans have taken the lead in reaching out to the victims of backlash, organizing vigils and rallies to speak out against the unfair targeting of Arab Americans, South Asian Americans, Muslims, and Sikhs.

2002 Washington State Governor Gary Locke signed into law a bill that prohibits the use of the word "Oriental." After July 1, 2002 all state and local government statutes, codes, rules, regulations, and other official documents were required to use the term "Asian" when referring to persons of Asian descent.

Also marks the year of national commemorations as Asian American communities across the country come together to plan events, rallies, and city-wide discussions around the 10-year commemoration of the 1992 Los Angeles Civil Unrest (Sa-I-gu) and the 20-year commemoration of the death of Vincent Chin.

The preceding historical timeline is taken from BACKLASH: When America Turned on Its Own by the National Asian Pacific Legal Consortium, Asian Americans: An Interpretive History by Sucheng Chan, Asian American Dreams by Helen Zia, and The Asian Pacific American Experience in the U.S. by the Leadership Education for Asian Pacifics, Inc.

—compiled by found images editor ANIDA YOEU ESGUERRA

#23 "INNER PEACE" Quadruple distilled and triple filtered for ultimate smoothness. www.skyy.com

Skyy Vodka ad, *Vanity Fair* magazine, August 1999, p.75.

She Casts Off Expectations,
an excerpt from *Warrior Lessons*

Lesson One: She Casts Off Expectations

We know very well what it's like to live with family expectations breathing down our backs:

Get married! (and to the right man)

Have children! (meaning more than one)

Make money! (and lots of it) Can't you be like _____? (Fill in the blank with the name of your nerd cousin, valedictorian friend, or other mother-appointed rival.)

When we don't live up to expectation, we don't need words to know. It's Asian mother telepathy. We can see it in their faces. The downcast eyes, the wistful, concerned look, the deep breath. No matter how much we try to ignore it, it still hits us hard. What do we do with the heavy burden of family honor? And do we ever escape it?

Let's start with a story.

My mother and Rita were like sisters. They grew up together in Taiwan. They came to America together on a lark and found a way to stay here by enrolling in nursing school. They slept in the same bed in a cramped dorm room, head to foot, for a year. *And Rita's feet stank like smelly cheese!* my mother adds. They double-dated and ended up marrying two Chinese American guys who were also best friends. Their children grew up together. And when Mom and Rita hit forty-five, they shared their stories about disappointment and sometimes even depression.

After a while Rita's calls to my mother started to spin out of control. Rita would wail about whether it was worth living anymore until her gentle husband took the phone out of Rita's hard-clenched hand, apologized, and hung up. Rita said that her kids never did what she asked. She didn't know what had gone wrong. Her son was living with a hippie and smoked pot. Her daughter had two babies with her American boyfriend, didn't marry him, and left Rita to take care of her children. Rita told my mother that she had started to take Valium to calm down. And then her calls got wilder. She'd call my mother sounding drugged and crazy, again saying that her life had been worth nothing.

One spring about ten years ago, we got a call from Rita's husband, telling us that Rita had died. It seems that her nightgown had caught on fire while she was making tea, and despite her husband's desperate attempts to smother the flames that engulfed her body, Rita had burned to death. My mother and I often wonder if Rita killed herself, or was so drugged with Valium that she fell asleep on top of the stove. My mother ends the story sometimes by saying that Rita's tormented soul is really what killed her.

Rita's death showed me in a heart-wrenching way what can happen to a woman who is isolated and desperate and whose cries for help go unanswered. It showed me how our self-destructive sides can get the better of us, no matter how happy and carefree we might once have been. But for me, Rita's death carries even more of a punch. It has become for me a parable about disappointing one's Chinese parents. That is how deep expectations run. Don't live up to them and you run the risk of your parents going mad and dying of disappointment and shame.

Expectations: A key word in the Asian American coming- of-age lexicon that I have come to know so well. As the older of two daughters, I became the stand-in son that my parents never had. In those shoes, I received the windfall of their expectations and, to the detriment of my very deserving younger sister, the greater part of their attention. I also had to bear the crushing weight of their hopes. So what did I do with all that expectation? I did what any self-preserving person would do—I tried as hard as I could to duck it.

At eighteen, I chose a college clear across the country and left my suburban New York home, ending up in the San Francisco Bay Area, home of the counterculture, hot tubs, and acid parties, the place where I pushed through some very important rites of passage and finally came of age. My choice to attend school three thousand miles away wouldn't be the first time that I would perplex my parents, and it certainly wouldn't be the last time I would disappoint them. When it became clear that I was not, in fact, going to Harvard (through no choice of my own, although filling out my application with a fat, blue Magic Marker pen probably didn't help my chances), I think they finally realized that they would have to begin to accept compromises in their American Dream daughter. So for the next twenty years, I have pushed the envelope of their willingness to compromise, pushed them to accept progressively more incomprehensible choices, like my decision to write these stories. That choice will mean having to deal with the fallout that will no doubt accompany the decision to write them as true stories, without the safety net that fiction can provide. Take it from this well-seasoned prodigal daughter: There is often nothing worse than not living up to parental expectation, *and yet, when on a path to self-discovery, there is absolutely nothing better.* That must be the tiger blood in me. Always stirring up trouble.

What Are You Doing With Your Life?
"Aiyo! Ah-Phee! My do you write those bad things? People will think you are either stupid or crazy!"

That's Mom talking, the relentless voice of reason. She has just read the past few pages and is justifiably freaking out about her daughter airing dirty laundry.

"I want to connect with women that I care about; that's why I'm writing this book, Mom." I'm trying to explain a philosophy to her that I can already feel she won't understand. It's an American idea, this truth-telling process, probably grounded in some Christian notion of absolution. To my mom, truth is pretty useless unless it helps you get ahead. She believes in images, specifically, the image of her successful lawyer daughter, and that my salary and status should pave the way to a life free of problems. Certainly free from the necessity of writing what she surely views as a scathing tell-all, like something Roseanne would write.

"We have to have the courage to talk truthfully—to admit that we have questions and that we're fallible. Saying so can be an act of power." I'm still not getting through to her. I give her a publisher's legal waiver and ask her to sign it.

"I am trying to create a special language of activism for people like you and me who need it, and to do that requires honesty."

"Let someone else connect and do activism," she says. *"You worked too hard, you have such a good résumé. You're throwing it all away! Oh, and by the way, if you're really going to write this book, I hope you're not going to write bad things about me, too. Are you?"*

I begin to get a sinking feeling that we are in for one of our long discussions that pits me against her. It is the same dynamic that has kicked in every time I have reached a turning point in my life, where, instead of choosing the path of least resistance she lays out before me, I choose a dusty road of questionable adventure, strewn with rocks and potholes and thieves.

I have made a life out of defying Mom. She wanted me to go to a college close to home, so I found one as far away as I possibly could. She thought that I should go straight to law school after college, so I took a backpack and went around the world on five dollars a day for two years instead. When I hit twenty-five, she thought it was a good time to settle down with a nice Chinese boy. I decided to move in with a guy from southern Italy who chain-smoked. Now I was about to defy her one more time, by leaving the legal profession, the coveted prize for a mother's job well done, so that I could join a bunch of young writers with little in their bank accounts to publish a magazine for Asian Americans. I thought it was the opportunity of a lifetime. My parents thought I had gone off the deep end.

The struggle to meet the demands of fulfilling family expectations while still living lives of our own choosing causes a great deal of stress for many Asian American women and often creates situations where compromise is impossible. Yukiko, a Japanese student who has spent the last four years attending a rural college in Illinois, brims with energy and self-confidence. She shared this story with me over the Internet one day, exhibiting the ever-present guilt that comes along with choosing independence over family responsibility:

After I graduate from college, I probably have to go back home to be near my family next year. I know I don't have to go back, but I feel like I have to look after my grandmother and parents. I know they want me to be near them, but will I really be able to help them just because I'm near? I want to travel and experience other cultures around the world (and I haven't told them yet, but I already bought a ticket to Guatemala!). I feel guilty myself somehow. I really love my family. But if I have to stay close to home, I could not satisfy my life. So I will probably go my way even if my family doesn't accept it. THAT IS ME. I'll never ever regret my life. I wish to live with satisfaction.

The ache of striving to be oneself amid all the noise around us telling us to be something different can be wrenching. For many of us, one of our first opportunities to follow a self-defined path comes when we select our college majors. Our decisions to pursue our studies in art, literature, communications, or philosophy, may not necessarily generate the most positive feedback from family. As Phuong, a Vietnamese American community worker told me: "They don't understand what 'social work' is. My uncle says, 'What are you studying, and why does it take such a long time to study that subject?' The expectation of me is to be the emotional support of the family, not the intellectual."

When I casually mentioned to my mother that I would be majoring in English literature, she took a deep breath and then threatened to pull the purse strings. *"What's this English literature? You don't have to go all the way to Berkeley to read novels. You can do it closer to home. You study business or engineering or something useful, or you come home!"* was her ultimatum. So I studied business, took the least number of courses possible in that major, and loaded up on as many English classes as I could handle. Yes, I can have my cake and eat it too, I insisted. But it meant that I would have to work twice as hard as everyone else, doing what was expected while pursuing my own path, at the same time.

Expectation pressures follow us into the workplace, as increasing numbers of us choose career paths off the beaten track, as was the case for Carolyn, a poet from Hawaii: "My mom once asked me, 'Why you spend three thousand dollars on a computer for? You can't make money on poetry.'" Others, such as Prema, a lawyer-turned-funder, have explained their unpopular choices in terms that her family can respect and understand: "I told them I'm not a lawyer anymore. I do fund-raising. They said, 'Fund-raise? What's that? Is that a job?' So I told them, 'Okay, I do charity work,' which they understood. Luckily for me, charity work is seen as a very noble 'hobby' for a woman of status and wealth in India."

And when we start families, some of us are exasperated yet again that we are not living up to mother-standards, as was the case for Monique, whose mother is Chinese and whose father is Caucasian: "I thought my mother would be overjoyed at my pregnancy, even more so because I was expecting a baby boy. Instead she said to me, 'I'm a little disappointed. I wanted a girl.' Go figure. When my Chinese American friend told me she was pregnant recently, also with a boy, I told her not to expect her mom to be elated. She called me later and told me that her mom had the same reaction as my mom did. She couldn't believe it!"

In a 1987 study by psychologists Robert Hess, Chih-Mei Chang, and Teresa McDevitt, marked differences were found in the ways that Chinese American mothers accounted for their children's successes and failures as opposed to European American mothers. For instance, while the study found that European American mothers were more likely to attribute academic success to good school training, Chinese American mothers were more apt to credit good home upbringing. If Chinese American children fail, however, their mothers were more likely to attribute it to poor home upbringing than their European American counterparts. While success is not praised or outwardly acknowledged, failure is personalized and attached to family honor. It can create a feedback loop that conditions us to see success as a minimum standard.

Cheryl is Korean American, a publicist in the fashion industry. She tells a story about her childhood that many of us may remember well:

> It seemed that I could never do enough. I always got A's in Catholic school, except for that one B I always got in religion. That B was all my parents ever focused on. I'd tell them, "But look at all the A's I got!" and they'd say, "Of course you got A's. That's what you're supposed to do." So the message was pretty clear. Instead of getting excited about my successes, I learned instead to fear not meeting their almost impossible expectations.

As my survey responses bear out, the pressure of expectations in our families comes almost solely from our mothers. For better or for worse, our mothers generally define our family spiritually and serve as the main communication link to their daughters, passing on to us their own ambitions. And while our fathers may cheer their children's accomplishments from a distance, the raw pressure to fight and perform is our mothers' turf.

Generally, our mothers are more willing to give us their blunt, if not imprecise, advice on how to lead our lives. Lora, one of San Francisco's most prolific labor attorneys, remembers working in a garment factory with her mother every summer since she was eleven. From dawn to dusk, they would sit behind sewing machines to earn the money the family needed to pay the rent and put food on the table. There were times when Lora would work during the school year as well. Working at that young age allowed her to understand the powerlessness of being used as cheap labor, as her mother would remind her constantly. At home, Lora again confronted her powerlessness as, night after night, she witnessed her father's gambling addiction. He'd raid her small savings and steal from her piggy banks when he had no money of his own. Lora remembers her mother's advice to her and her sisters when they were young:

> My mother used to say, "Don't let yourself be treated like a girl-child slave. If you were in China, your father would have sold you a long time ago for money." She used to say that to us when we were seven, eight, nine years old. Basically, my association with being a girl and a child is with being a slave.

But how was Lora to figure out how to avoid this "girl-child slave" predicament? How was she supposed to fight for herself and be strong? Her mother had told them the situation to avoid. Yet as a young girl, Lora was faced with the problem without a clear way out. Lora, like many of us, was well aware of the goals that had been set out for her. What our mothers usually don't provide, however, are the step-by-step instructions on how exactly to get there or where exactly we should be going. Their expectations, though ominous, end up being imprecise, and daughters can wind up grasping at straws, understandably frustrated in trying to fulfill them.

When asked why we frequently forgo our own wants in order to fulfill our parents' expectations, many of us respond with reasons that incorporate notions of filial piety and reverence for our elders. I was taught at an early age the nature of that exchange. My parents worked hard to ensure that I'd have the good life I now enjoy, and I was to repay them by concurring with their wishes. "Be a good daughter, marry a man who can control you," my mother once said. "Have children and get a good job that won't take you too far from home." And what she implied: "In exchange I will give you everything I can—all my attention, my money, my being, my honor, and my dignity. Your performance will be linked to my very life, and because of this, I know you will comply."

Women such as Hoai are familiar with this exchange. Her parents have worked for decades in their grocery store in Colorado, and much of what they've earned has been put into their four children's college educations. Recently, Hoai found out that her parents' store had once again been robbed. Even after several robberies in the past, and even after Hoai's mother had narrowly missed a bullet in one of those incidents, her father refused to install a security camera because he felt it was too expensive. "I somehow feel responsible for their situation. They've worked their whole lives for us, and so when I told them that I quit my job to become a filmmaker, all she could say was, 'Now I'll never be able to retire.' This was supposed to be a major joyous decision in my life, and all I could feel was guilt. By trying to be myself, I was letting them down." For weeks, Hoai was racked with violent nightmares where rage, dismemberment, and chaos were recurring themes.

"Filial piety" is often synonymous with payback—daughter's guilt and obedience in exchange for a mother's undying but tacit support. Our guilt can come in many currencies. Guilt for having the privilege, choice, and mobility that she deserved but never had. Guilt because her talents were never fully recognized and rewarded due to her heavy accent, because she had to make compromises, because she was seen as a little Asian woman. Guilt for feeling that she might be jealous, not of us, but of our opportunity. Guilt for telling her that she has no right to feel proprietary over our lives.

We need not fall into a cycle of guilt and dependence that locks us into aspirations, lifestyles, and dreams that are not our own. But to avoid this requires that we take responsibility for our choices. Reverence for our elders does not imply a blind obedience to their wishes. Respect, if genuine, must be mutual, even in Asian families. *Filial piety cannot become a cultural excuse that absolves us from having to determine who we are and what our lives stand for.*

I realized that I could no longer rationalize my own fear of self-determination and risk taking by blaming the heavy expectations of family. After all, they have always wanted only what they thought was best, given their own experiences. How could I have expected them to know what more was possible? Had I lived in lock-step compliance to their wishes, I would have grown resigned and resentful. Instead, I took the chance of losing approval and followed the paths that spoke most powerfully to me. And for that, I can now live the life I have always dreamed of, with a fluid schedule that allows me to travel and work when and where I want to, and a relationship with a man who doesn't feel he has to control me as much as share his life with me on equal terms. Through it all, I have learned a valuable lesson—if what our parents want for us is success, then they will grow to understand that our best chances for succeeding will lie in doing what we truly want to do.

The truth is that if family bonds are loving and true, they are also unconditional. Our parents will learn to understand this, even if it may require our defiance and heartache to get there.

As much as she has tried to dissuade me and disapproved of the many choices I have made, my mother always ends up, albeit reluctantly, as my staunchest supporter. When I became the publisher of *A. Magazine* and had no money to hire staff, she would come into the office on her days off and stick stamps on envelopes, alphabetize my Rolodex in some very odd ways, and organize the office. She would get lunch for me and clean the office, saying as she wiped the desks in mock disgust, *"This office is filthy dirty."* As much as she grumbled about me and my stupid choices, she seemed happy to participate in my dream, or at least she may have been fearful enough that, if she did not help, my failure would rub off on her as well.

She may still think I'm crazy. She may still question why I chose to join a band of young renegades fresh out of college to start a magazine that had big visions with no budget. She saw no 401K plan, no business card, no secretary—*"and no salary either!"* she adds. For a long time, she probably thought that the word "entrepreneur" meant someone who doesn't make any money. Yet through it all, she brought me Tupperware tubs of home cooking every week, sticking them in the freezer as she murmured under her breath, with love, *"My kids are spoiled rotten. See? They can't do anything without me."* Her thoughts behind these words might be these:

> I was trained as a midwife in Taiwan, and brought many babies into the world before I even entered a formal day of nursing school. In my hands I held babies that I knew would be cranky, ones that I knew would be gentle. It is in the way they move even while they take their first breaths. If I can see this in the children of strangers, I must know about my daughter. I held her. I watched her grow up. And she thinks because she is grown up now that I can only see what she wants to show me. I know more than she thinks.
>
> Yet, my daughter thinks that I don't know her. She thinks that I don't understand or believe that she is strong enough to do anything she wants, even if I do think she makes the wrong decisions half the time. She's my daughter after all, even if I do call her a dreamer. We have the same spirit. We trust and we believe in things. If she is the way she is, I must have taught it to her. I must have been responsible for the way she turned out. Crazy. I would never tell her this, but no matter what she ever decides to do in her life, I will always help her out and support her, even if I do try to talk her out of her choices.

That is the irony of expectation. Defy it and most of us will still receive our mother's love and support, because in our willingness to answer to what calls us, we show them the strength that is there for two. There comes a day when daughter breaks from mother and becomes a woman. And as it was our duty to listen and learn when we were young, so it becomes our duty to catch the wind and fly out on our own. Our lives are ours to learn from.

How to Open Up a Dialogue

We know that it's never that easy. Dealing with family expectations can be oppressive, regardless of our age. We may be convinced that our families will disown us for making unpopular choices. Or, despite knowing that the outside world treats us as adults, that we will never escape the role of "child" to make our own decisions. The intensity of the family bond and "our-daughter-must-pay-back" mentality can make our choices very difficult. But to the extent that we can move *toward* as opposed to *away from,* the emotional issues of family, we move toward a more solid self as well.

"You'll Always Be My Daughter"

Psychologists refer to the intense period of self-definition and self-imposed distance from parents as a process of individuation. Among Asian families, studies show that individuation processes may not take place until we are thirty or even older. "My children will always be my children," is how one Korean great-grandmother put it. As a thirty-four-year-old Filipina American told me, "I thought that when I had my first child, my mother would finally see me as an adult. No chance. Now she's got a new set of instructions for me—how to bring up my baby the *Filipina* way."

"In my Hmong community, a woman is not seen as valid until she marries. I am over thirty and I am still not married. My Hmong community still treats me as if I am a little girl," one respondent wrote. Until we are viewed as adults (or at the very least, not as children), it will continue to be difficult, though not impossible, to begin an honest, equal dialogue about what we want from life that may differ with our family's expectations of us.

We need not wait for our parents to decide when that time will be. We can begin to develop that dialogue for them. Find a calm time when you are feeling good, or set up a specific day or activity for a talk between you and your parent, one on one. There need not be an agenda. All that is important is that you try hard not to be reactive when your buttons are pushed, listen without judgment, and express your opinions confidently without reverting into a child's role. As psychologist and author Harriet Lerner advises, "When we define a new position in a relationship we need to focus on what we want to say about ourselves, not the other person." According to Lerner, we need to be less focused on the other person's reaction or countermove or on gaining a positive response. You are beginning to establish a new dialogue that welcomes you in as a fully capable and responsible adult.

Considerations for Daughters and Their Families

When a daughter claims her status as an adult member of the family, power dynamics will begin to shift. For daughters, being treated on par will mean taking on certain responsibilities for ourselves, including recognizing and then letting go of younger patterns of behavior—sulking, withholding participation, complaining that we are treated like children while still expecting mothers to cook our meals and do our laundry. When we are the daughters of immigrants, we can have such control over our parents, holding them hostage at times to American Dreams and to links to the future, and it can be difficult not to use that control to manipulate. Can we begin to give as adults, rather than to receive as children?

For parents, letting go of the role of nurturer can be very difficult. As parents, we see our children as extensions of ourselves. They are what our lives have stood for. They represent the hope and promise of all our work and sacrifice. Our generation provided the sweat that gives them opportunities that we never had. Our choices were made for their benefit, not ours. "How is it," one mother asks me, "that my daughter can be so ungrateful?" Is it possible that as parents, we may have given away too much of ourselves in the bargain? Or that the hopes we place on our children might have absolved us of our responsibility to wage our own battles? Can we take a step back and refrain from feeling that we will always know what is best for them? Can we let our need to control fall away so that our children can grow?

The Other Person's Shoes

When Jennie Yee, a psychologist from North Beach Asian Mental Health Services in San Francisco, mediates intergenerational conversations, she helps families to find common ground: "Daughters and sons have to understand that in most cases, parents only want them to be happy. They just come from a very different set of experiences." According to Yee, nonsympathetic listening can lead to all sorts of miscommunication: "Parents may goad us to do well in school and enter traditional jobs because they see these as insurance policies for our futures. Their children might interpret this as their parents' lack of confidence in their judgment or abilities. In another example, parents may push their daughters into dating relationships that 'preserve their Asian culture' because they feel their daughters will be more comfortable in the end. Their daughters might read that as 'prejudiced.'" Yee attempts to have family members acknowledge their concerns and speak from their own point of view, without assuming the response of other family members. If parents are concerned about their daughters' future, those daughters might have to prove to them that they can provide for themselves. If they are concerned about their daughters' choice of person for a relationship, daughters might invite their parents to spend individual time with their partner so that they can begin to know one another, on their own terms. As Yee points out, "Sometimes, all parents need is to understand."

Dialogue is a beginning, and results are never immediate. In some cases, a family member's mental health or behavioral patterns may require professional intervention, and dialogue alone cannot solve much. Even in the most open of Asian American families, changes in stature and shifts in family power dynamics will be accompanied by anger, frustration, and feelings of futility. Asking and answering the questions that matter will entail moments of miscommunication, the dredging up of memories, and accusations. So it is important to anticipate them and to know that good results will be gradual. Slowness, deliberation, and patience are all part of the process of developing a new level of relationship. The more intense the issue, the more slowly one should move. Keep in mind that big proclamations or sudden emotional cutoff are destructive to this communication process. As Lerner advises, "You cannot learn to swim by jumping off the high dive."

It may help to set small goals together. It may help to develop an understanding of what our personal boundaries are, and hold fast to them. We may have to assure our families that the distance we need does not imply abandonment or disrespect. Inevitably, yet gradually, truths emerge that will allow change to occur more easily. When we take the time to let our families know who we really are, we begin to move our family stories forward in the most remarkable of ways.

—PHOEBE ENG

Gidra response to Skyy Vodka ad, *Vanity Fair* magazine, August 1999, p.75.

Fifty-Fifty

That's what I call myself. My mother's a mongrel. That's what *she* says: ancestors from so many different parts of Europe that she can't tell *where* she got the same name as Dad's. It's true! It's on her birth certificate—Gillian Ann Gill. As southern as the William Williamses and Jo Ann Joneses of the West. I tease her: "If you'd hyphenated it, you'd be Jill Gill-Gill." Her light brown eyebrows come together. Dad likes to say she got the best of Europe— height, pure blue eyes, naturally blonde hair. She was one of those tall, beautiful blondes that scare boys half to death. I'm like her. Except my hair is brown; my eyes—I'm, like, a twelve-month tan. My grandmother tells them, "Don't let Rosa stay out in the sun," or the Punjabi equivalent. "She will turn black." So what do we do? We move to the eternal sun—San Jose, California.

My father's Sikh. That has its *own* priorities: milk, meat, muscles. Dad grew up in India, came for graduate school, met my mother, and stayed. Then in Jersey he went through a mid-life crisis and quit Ortho to buy a Midas muffler franchise in California.

California, the promised land. Once New York was the end of the rainbow. Then Dad got a job in the suburbs. That's where I was born. New Jersey. It's a green place, in the summer anyway. We had the whole side of a hill, trees, a little pond with crayfish and frogs. And in the winter, ice. Then Dad saw the rainbow stretching clear across the country and decided that the end with the pot of gold must be on the other side.

I don't like it here in San Jose. I miss the snow. We drive up to Tahoe, and we ski, but it's not the same as waking up one morning and getting a day off. As soon as I graduate I'm going back—Princeton—Ivy League like my cousin Shawn. He's at Harvard. My cousins Kunti and Nitasha went to Rutgers. Mom says if I have to go to a state university, I might as well stay in California. Dad has his eye on Stanford, just up the road. He wants me to be a genius, not to change from the little girl I was in Jersey, look American, but don't act too American. He hates it when I come right from school to work, and his mechanics look out from the undersides of cars and call out, "Rosie! Hi! How's high school?"

"Dad's like, 'You be careful who you talk to.'"

"Dad! Those guys work for you. They're human."

"Do you have homework?"

"Homework?"

I *hate* my new school. I could teach sophomore English myself. I told my teacher, "Yeah. I *like* Judy Blume. I read all her stuff. When I was *twelve*. (Including *Wifey*, don't tell Dad!) But—I was expecting, maybe, *Scarlet Letter*? It's in video?"

The teacher's face got all red, like that letter on Hester Prynne's chest. "Your English is good. What kind of accent is that?"

"What accent?"

"We'll be reading 'Cinderella' next. You'll like that."

"Grimm?"

"Oh, no. I mean, it's uplifting. More than *Blubber*."

"I mean the German—get me out of here!" I leaned across the empty desk.

She shot back, hugging her roll book and that slim paperback, straight blonde hair falling behind her shoulders. "You have to pass English to go on to junior year." It was almost a whisper.

Math was easier. And in New Jersey algebra had been my *worst*. Dad used to stand over me at the kitchen table. The glare of the Tiffany lamp turned the paper blue. "This is simple. And important. Master math and you can do anything—medicine, engineering . . ."

Mom understands me better. She pays cash for every A I get.

The girl next to me, her hair bleached as light an orange as she could probably get it, red nails four inches, couldn't follow long division. She gaped at the board, numbers piled up, blue on white, the latest in chalkboard technology. I asked her, "Haven't you ever subtracted the remainder before?"

I caught the teacher before she made it out the door. "I think I'm in under my head. I mean, I know it. Couldn't you get me into some math I can't do?"

The hall was filling up with bodies, rushing by like water through a pipe. "You'll have to speak to someone in the office."

I skipped lunch. The secretary was even busier than she had been when I'd enrolled myself in the summer. Mom was back in Jersey then, selling the house with its high, latticed windows, its tile kitchen and my big, light room with its own bath. If she knew that Dad let me walk to the school myself, on a day so cool and dry I couldn't believe it was summer, she'd have thrown a fit. But he was already working fifteen-hour days! Now that it was fall and school was in session, California was hot. Clerks and teachers milled around the secretary on the other side of a high counter. Students nudged my elbows, whined. I whined louder.

"You've got to stick with it, honey." She leans on the counter, dirty blonde ponytail separating on the back of her neck. "It's only the first day." And she laughs, kind of loud and horsy.

"No. I need an upgrade. I do better."

"Sure you do. Your English is perfect."

"If my English is so perfect, why can't I get through?" And I thought about the kids who came in with only Spanish, Chinese.

I walked home. Couldn't stand to face another class. Mom was standing on the back of the couch hanging fully lined, brocade winter curtains from New Jersey. My grandmother, her dyed brown hair pulled back in a bun, sat

on the couch in front of her leaning toward the television, on which a perfectly groomed male, blonde hair moussed and jelled, spoke in low tones with
a woman with cap-like, cream-colored hair. I slammed the door. "School is
just too dumb! We're doing arithmetic in math, and English has us reading
books I memorized in grade school."

"Didn't they put you in gifted and talented?" Mom looked down across
our shimmery, white sofa. My grandmother said something. I was too upset
to figure it out. Even my aunts, Dad's sisters, spoke Punjabi; then they criticized me when I couldn't speak it. But where would I have learned it? Mom
went on: "Do they *have* gifted and talented?"

"The secretary didn't even ask. And I *gave* her my report cards."

Mom stepped onto the shiny floorboards and crossed the dining room
into our cubicle-sized kitchen. "Dad should have gone over there with you,"
she said, picking up the phone.

"He was working on his golden touch. Besides, I'm five-foot-six, fifteen,
reasonably intelligent, of sound mind and body—"

"You're growing up too fast." Then she told the school she'd had to pick
me up for a doctor's appointment. She was sorry. She forgot she was supposed to tell the office in advance. She'd be happy to come in and explain it
to the principal. The superintendent if he wasn't available.

They couldn't give her an appointment until Friday. By then I think I might
have made an impression. "You're the best in the class." More than one
teacher told me that. "Your parents must be proud."

Even the kids were impressed. "Hey, kid. You from Albuquerque or
something?"

"No. I'm from New Jersey."

"New Jersey? That's in New York, right?"

It was the kids who told me that there *was* "gifted and talented." I'd been
placed on the slowest, most remedial track. Julio told me, "That's why this
stuff is boring." His hair and eyes are as dark as mine, his skin as tan.
"Flipping burgers at the 'King is more in-ti-lec-tu-al."

"Why are we in here?" Ms. Haldemann was lecturing on values, what
they are and how we so desperately need them.

Julio's like, "Why? These Mexicans. They don't speak English. Know
what I'm saying?"

"What are you?"

"Chicano. You some kind of Cuban? *Hablas espanol?*"

"No. *Sprechen sie Deutsch?*"

"What's that?"

"German."

"I knew you was a foreigner."

I took to the Mexicans. Always going on about something or other, laughing. Just like Dad's side of the family. When they're in a good mood. I wished I'd signed up for Spanish instead of my mother's German. But the Mexicans stick to themselves in that school. So do African-Americans, turning into larger groups in the hallways and the cafeteria.

There I stood, tray in hands, burrito losing heat, milk gaining it, right beneath my nose. Voices rose as one loud, long mumble-jumble. Where did I fit in? There were even tables of Asians—Chinese, Japanese, Korean, Vietnamese. I caught sight of a long, narrow table lined with girls in jeans, T-shirts, hair unpermed, uncolored, rings only in their earlobes. I took the path of least resistance.

"Hi. I'm Rosa Gill."

"Where you from?"

"New Jersey." They looked at each other. Green eyes, blue eyes, brown. "Are you all from California? Weren't any of you born out of state?"

"Lisa is from Indiana."

Must have been Lisa, fluffy blonde hair, small, who jabbed the tall girl who had spoken in the ribs.

The girl with brown hair said, "My ancestors come from Jersey. Where did yours?"

"All over the world."

"Well, we don't have an all-over-the-world table. But the South Americans sit over there." Lisa pointed toward a table bubbling over with words I couldn't understand.

I told them what they wanted to know: "My father's Indian."

"Oh!"

The tall one goes, "You know Rajeev?"

"This is *only* my second day."

"Rajeev is Indian."

I stood identified. I looked around for faces of the color I'd been boiled down to and saw one table anchored by a Sikh, his topknot wrapped in a swatch of black cotton—what my cousin Shawn called a bubble, like the one my cousin Ranjit used to wear. I'd never seen one on my father, since he'd cut his hair even before he'd met my mother. I walked over and told them I was Rosa Gill.

Hands shot out European fashion. "Oh, Gulab, Gulabi," my name translated. "Where you from?"

"New Jersey."

"I have an uncle in New Jersey."

"Haven't seen you in class. What are you taking?"

When I told them I had Haldemann's English, Johnston's math, they laughed; brown hands slapped the table. "New Jersey schools must be as bad as Jersey air."

SCREAMING MONKEYS

"What did you say your dad does? Auto mechanics?"

"Does your Mum work? Or is she in India?"

"My mother's not Indian."

"American?"

"Do you know Chitra?"

"*She's* half American."

Brown eyes searched for the fifty-fifty table.

I thought about my cousins in the San Fernando Valley. Hundred-percent. I wondered how long that bloodline would stay pure. We had driven down to L.A.. for my aunt's annual brothers-and-sisters party. A disk jockey announced in Hindi soundtracks from the latest Indian movies while my cousins danced. In my jeans and t-shirt I felt underdressed. Even the kids pranced around in wide, long trousers, pink, red, yellow, and electric blue, matching tunics shining with embroidered beads. The girls, that is. The boys wore jeans like me or chinos like my mom and dad.

On the long drive home I asked my grandmother why she never gave me Indian clothes.

My mother said, "She used to bring *me* suits. They never fit—too short and wide. I didn't like any of them enough to wear them anyway. You want to look nice when you're going out."

"You don't look good in loose clothes anyway," my father said, his eyes on the most boring highway I have ever seen—parched brown fields on either side, towns that might have been more comfortable in the plains Dad and I had crossed on our drive across the country.

"Your father prefers the svelte look," my mother said.

"On you maybe," I said.

"Girls should dress like girls," he said. "Biji gives you skirts."

What everybody calls my grandmother. Sitting next to me in the back, she patted me on the thigh and said something in Punjabi I didn't understand.

"She says she's going to buy you a suit," my father said.

"Oh. Great," I go. "Thanks."

When we got a chance to tell Dad about Mom's appointment with the principal, he was furious. "It's those jeans you wear! You should wear skirts! Plaid! And pleated!"

"They don't have uniforms in American public schools," my mother said, passing him the shrimp. "They don't have dress code either."

"If I dressed the way you wanted," I told them, "*everyone* would laugh."

I thought about the girls I'd eaten lunch with. I looked down at the pasta on my plate.

Biji said something, but Mom and I couldn't understand her, and Dad wasn't listening. He even passed her the shrimp, which she would never eat.

She called it "insects." "Agh," she gagged.

"Did they see your report cards?" Dad asked. "Your test scores?"

"I'm not sure they can *read*." I twirled a forkful of spaghetti.

"I should have gone with you."

"You're never home."

He had no manager that he could trust, so how could he leave Midas even to argue with what *he* called the *headmaster* of the school that had placed me wrong? Mom had to argue on her own.

When I came home, she beckoned and pointed upstairs, where we always went when we wanted to talk without Biji interrupting. "Have I been promoted?" I go, flopping onto the king-sized bed, covered with a home-made patchwork quilt Mom picked up at the New Jersey State Fair.

"When you were a baby," she said, "people used to ask me how I'd managed to adopt you."

"Oh, God, you're not going to tell me they switched me in the hospital. I look exactly like Dad's sisters. Before they got fat."

"No, you're a Gill. On both sides." She joined me on the bed, stretching her long legs next to mine across the green and lilac patches. "I told *that* to your principal. He could hardly hide his disbelief. And I don't think it was the name. He even said, 'But you're American!'"

"Why is everybody in California so convinced that I'm a foreigner?" I asked.

"It occurred to me halfway through the conversation: they thought you were Mexican."

"Mexican?"

"We gave you a name both grandmothers could pronounce. Trouble is around here Rosa sounds Spanish. And you don't look Scottish enough to be a proper Gill."

"What does this have to do with 'tard English and math?"

"'Tard?"

"As in *re*tard? Duh!"

"Oh, Rosa, that's as bad as putting down the Mexicans. Or Indians."

"Do I get out of it?"

"I'm quoting: 'You see, Mrs. Gill, that community is not in general interested in the school. Or education, for that matter.'"

"How can they be interested in school? They need every member of the family working in order to pay the rent."

"Dr. Floystrup told me, 'We try our best to instill the work ethic in all of our students. If they want college preparatory classes, they can sign up for them along with all of the rest of the students. It's because of them that we even *have* a vocational track.'"

"I didn't want to move here," I said. "I wanted to stay in Jersey."

Mom sat back on an Indian pillow studded with tiny mirrors and looked up at the ceiling. Sunlight pouring through the window hit the mirror work casting reflections on the smooth white ceiling, hundreds of flickering stars. "It reminds me of the school *I* went to," she said. "We were farmers. All of my sisters got good grades. We had to. My mother hung over our homework at the kitchen table every night."

"Like Dad. Before Midas."

"No matter how well we did—A's in English, B's in math and science—we *never* got into the honors classes—they called them honors classes then."

"God, did they think you were farmers, you didn't need to go to college?"

Mom shrugged. "When my sisters and I told the teachers we wanted to go, they suggested county colleges, state teachers colleges. Your aunt Lena went out of state, the University of Tennessee."

"Well," I said, "at least they weren't racist. Your uncle was a Nazi."

"Not an officer," she said, "and on the Russian front. But that's not the point. How did we get into that? As of tomorrow you go to Classics of English Literature."

"Yes!"

"And Trigonometry."

"Ouch!"

"There's a price to be paid for acknowledging that you are Asian."

But I'm not Asian. I find that out from Jenny Tanaka and Simon Chen in Trig. I'm not even Southeast Asian, like Joe Nguyen. They lump me in with Rajeev Patel, full-blooded, of such a different ethnic group from us Punjabis that my grandmother is always passing comments about Gujarati food, Gujarati clothing, "Gujarati!" she says. Rajeev's parents might call us pushy and materialistic. Even the white kids in the class, Peter Fradkin and Jennifer Miller, among others, can't believe that every new equation makes me break out in a sweat.

"Must be the European blood," I tell my father, "Savoir faire, *Sturm und Drang*."

"Must be you're paying too much attention to dressing up and dances, not enough attention to your studies."

"That's bogus. Totally."

It kills him when I put on a pair of leggings and an exercise top and go back to school at night. But I can't even dance with Julio or Jamal without the Asians, Anglo-Saxons and Jews from Classics of English Literature shouting in my ear above the drums and bass line, "Rosa! Why are you hanging out with *them?* Be *careful!* You're too young to have a baby!"

The difference between New Jersey and California, as I see it, is in California it's *in* to be a group. And the stereotypes are different. We have different Hispanics. But I don't have to live in groups that I do not believe in. I'm fifty-fifty. Only *half* Californian, and against my will. At least half eastnerner. *North*-easterner. Half intellectual. The other half likes the way that Julio calls me Indo-dweeb and urges me to dance: "Dance! Forget about what goes on in that pretty head of yours! People are people. All of us will one day be some kind of fifty-fifty. All of us will speak the same language. Spanglish."

"Punjablish."

Rajeev requests a record popular in England, and the Indian kids, like my cousins when they hear this stuff, go wild. "What the hell is this?" says Julio, and his hips stop swaying.

I show him how to stick his butt out, shift his feet and twist his hands up high. "It's the kind of music my father danced to. At weddings. In India. Before I was born."

"When do I meet this funky muffler man? I could use a job."

I laugh. I see this boy shouting "Rosie! Rosalita!" from beneath a chassis. Dad glares. But he doesn't need to worry. Julio and I can't *do* much more than dance. *His* family would *kill* him.

"Just wait till I ace Trig," I tell him. Get into Princeton and Dad might just stop worrying I'll turn out like my cousin Kunti, the single mother in the family, or her brother Ranjit, the addict. If King Midas lives to pay for it. By that time the east coast may be just as clannish. California is a trendsetter.

But I can never eat my lunch at just one table. I will always be fifty-fifty: what other people perceive me to be, and what I am. The best of both worlds. Me.

—ROBBIE CLIPPER SETHI

Rhapsody in Plain Yellow

for my love, Charles (1938-2000)

Say: 言
I love you, I love you, I love you, no matter
    your race, your sex, your color. Say:
the world is round and the arctic is cold.
    Say: I shall kiss the rondure of your soul's
living marl. Say: he is beautiful,
    serenely beautiful, yet, only ephemerally so.
Say: Her Majesty combs her long black hair for hours.
    Say: O rainbows, in his eyes, rainbows.
Say: O frills and fronds, I know you
    Mr. Snail Consciousness,
O foot plodding the underside of leaves.
    Say: I am nothing without you, nothing,
Ms. Lookeast, Ms. Lookeast,
    without you, I am utterly empty.
Say: the small throat of sorrow.
    Say: China and France, China and France.
Say: Beauty and loss, the dross of centuries.
    Say: Nothing in their feudal antechamber
shall relinquish us of our beauty—
    Say: Mimosa—this is not a marriage song (epithalamiom).
Say: when I was a young girl in Hong Kong
    a prince came on a horse, I believe it was piebald.
O dead prince   dead dead prince   who paid for my ardor.
    Say: O foot   O ague   O warbling oratorio . . .
Say: Darling, use "love" only as a transitive verb
    for the first forty years of your life.
Say: I have felt this before, it's soft, human.
    Say: my love is a fragile concertina.
Say: you always love them in the beginning,
    then, you take them to slaughter.
O her coarse whispers   O her soft bangs.
    By their withers, they are emblazoned doppelgangers.
Say: beauty and terror, beauty and terror.
    Say: the house is filled with perfume,
dancing sonatinas and pungent flowers.
    Say: houses filled with combs   combs   combs

and the mistress' wan ankles.
    Say: embrace the An Lu Shan ascendancy
and the fantastical diaspora of tears.
    Say: down blue margins
my inky love runs. Tearfully,
    tearfully, the pearl concubine runs.
There is a tear in his left eye—sadness or debris?
    Say: reverence to her, reverence to her.
Say: I am a very small boy, a very small boy,
    I am a teeny, weeny little boy
who yearns to be punished.
    Say, I can't live without you
Head Mistress, Head Mistress,
    I am a little lamb, a consenting little lamb,
I am a sheep without his fold.
    Say: God does not exist and hell is other people—
and Mabel, can't we get out of this hotel?
    Say: Gregor Samsa—someone in Tuscaloosa
thinks you're *magnifico,* she will kiss
    your battered cheek, embrace your broken skull.
Is the apple half eaten or half whole?
    Suddenly, he moves within me, how do I know
that he is not death, in death there is

    certain //caesura.

Say there is poetry in his body, poetry
    in his body, yes, say:
this dead love, this dead love,
    this dead, dead love, this lovely death,
this white percale, white of hell, of heavenly shale.
    Centerfolia . . . say: kiss her sweet lips.
Say: what rhymes with "flower":
    "bower," "shower," "power"?
I am that yellow girl, that famished yellow girl
    from the first world.
Say: I don't give a shit about nothing
    'xcept my cat, your cock and poetry.
Say: a refuge between sleeping and dying.
    Say: to Maui   to Maui   to Maui
creeps in his petty pompadour.
    Day to day, her milk of human kindness

ran dry; I shall die of jejune jejune   *la lune la lune.*
    Say, a beleaguered soldier, a fine arse had he.
Say: I have seen the small men of my generation
    rabid, discrete, hysterical, lilliput, naked.
Say: Friday is okay; we'll have fish.
    Say: Friday is not okay; he shall die
of the measles near the bay.
    Say: Friday, just another savage
day, until Saturday, the true Sabbath, when they shall
    finally, stay. Say:
                        Sojourner
                                Truth.
Say: I am dismayed by your cloying promiscuousness
    and fawning attitude.
Say: *amaduofu, amaduofu.*
    Say: He put cumin and tarragon in his stew.
Say: he's the last wave of French Algerian Jews.
    He's a cousin of Helene Cixous, twice removed.
Say, he recites the lost autobiography of Camus.
    Say: I am a professor from the University of Stupidity,
I cashed my welfare check and felt good.
    I saw your mama crossing the bridge of magpies
up on the faded hillock with the Lame Ox—
    Your father was conspicuously absent.
Admit that you loved your mother,
    that you killed your father to marry your mother.
Suddenly, my terrible childhood made sense.
    Say: beauty and truth, beauty and truth,
all ye need to know on earth all ye need to know.
    Say: I was boogying down, boogying down
Victoria Peak Way and a slip-of-a-boy climbed off his ox;
    he importuned me for a kiss, a tiny one
on his cankered lip.
    Say: O celebrator   O celebrant
of a blessed life, say:
    false   fleeting   hopes
Say: despair, despair, despair.
    Say: Chinawoman, I am a contradiction in terms:
I embody frugality and ecstasy.
    Friday Wong died on a Tuesday,
O how he loved his lambs.
    He was lost in their sheepfold.

Say: another mai tai before your death.
Another measure   another murmur   before your last breath
Another boyfriend, Italianesque.
Say: Save. Exit.
Say: I am the sentence which shall at last elude her.
Oh, the hell of heaven's girth, a low mound from here . . .
Say:
Oh, a mother's vision of the emerald hills draws down her brows.
Say: A brush of jade, a jasper plow furrow.
Say: ####OOOOOxxxxx*!!!!*

Contemplate   thangs   cerebral   spiritual   open   stuff   reality
by definition   lack   any   spatial   extension
we occupy   no space   and   are   not   measurable
we do not move   undulate   are not in   perpetual motion
where   for example   is thinking   in the head?   in my vulva?

whereas   in my female lack of penis?   Physical
thangs   spatial extensions   mathematically   measurable
preternaturally   possible   lack bestial   vegetable   consciousness
lack   happiness   lackluster   lack   *chutzpah*   lack   love

Say: A scentless camellia bush bloodied the afternoon.
Fuck this line, can you really believe this?
When did I become the master of suburban bliss?
With whose tongue were we born?
The language of the masters is the language of the aggressors.
We've studied their cadence carefully—
enrolled in a class to *improve our accent.*
Meanwhile, they hover over, waiting for us to stumble . . .
to drop an article, mispronounce an R.
Say: softly, softly, the silent gunboats glide.
O onerous sibilants, O onomatopoetic glibness.
Say:
How could we write poetry in a time like this?
A discipline that makes much ado about so little?
Willfully laconic, deceptively, disguised as a love poem.

Say:
Your engorging dict-
atorial flesh
grazed mine.

Would you have loved me more if I were black?
    Would I have loved you more if you were white?
And you, relentless Sinophile,
    holding my long hair, my frayed dreams.

My turn to objectify you.
    I, the lunatic, the lover, the poet,
the face of an orphan static with flies
    the scourge of the old world,
which reminds us—it ain't all randy dandy
    in the new kingdom.

Say   rebuke   descry

Hills and canyons, robbed by sun, leave us nothing.

       —MARILYN CHIN

Take Me Out, art by Wennie Huang

SCREAMING MONKEYS

CHRONICLE

I was born the year of the loon
in a great commotion. My mother—
who used to pack $500 cash
in the shoulders of her fur gambling coat,
who had always considered herself
the family's "First Son"—
took one look at me
and lit out
on a vacation to Sumatra.
Her brother purchased my baby clothes;
I've seen them, little clown suits
of silk and color.

Each day
my Chinese grandmother bathed me
with elaboration in an iron tub;
amahs waiting in line
with sterilized water and towels
clucked and smiled
and rushed about the tall stone room
in tiny slippers.

After my grandfather
accustomed himself
to this betrayal by First Son,
he would take me in his arms,
walk with me
by the plum trees, cherries, persimmons;
he showed me the stiff robes
of my ancestors and their drafty hall,
the long beards of his learned old friends,
and his crickets.

Grandfather talked to me, taught me.
At two months, my mother tells me,
I could sniff for flowers,
stab my small hand upwards to moon.

Even today I get proud
when I remember
this all took place in Chinese.

—MEI-MEI BERSSENBRUGGE

YOU BRING OUT THE FILIPINA IN ME

for joël b. tan
inspired by Sandra Cisneros's "You Bring Out the Mexican in Me"

you bring out the filipina in me
the language born of blood in me
the p instead of f in me
the glottal catch in me
the visayan the tagalog in me
you bring out the ancestors in me

you bring out
the murder of magellan in me
the revolution of seven thousand islands in me
to survive 500 years of colonizers in me

you bring out the guerrilla soldier in me
the olonggapo bar hostess in me
the mail order bride in me

you bring out the bahala na immigrant in me
bahala na—"what god wills"
the god they're so american in me
the yes, i do speak english in me
the tnt green card in me

you bring out the pinay in me
the sass in me smartass badass in me
the proud walker shit talker
third world girl the majority in me

you bring out the barkada in me
barkada—friends
wolf among sheep in me
the danger the desire in me
the drink til i'm drunk
fuck til i'm good and fucked

you bring out the queer in me

the dyke in me
the brave beautiful butch in me
voracious femme in me
the bastos the bakla the walang hiya in me bastos—rude; bakla; faggot;
walang hiya: shameless

you bring out the wake up
laughing laughing
not crying
in me
my brother
my brother
mahal mahal kita   mahal kita love you
yes you do
oh yes you do

                —MAIANA MINAHAL

Four Million

Filipinos work overseas, many as maids in Europe, the Middle East, and wealthier Asian nations.

I. Singapore Sunday

*In memoriam, Mrs. Flor Contemplacion, 1953–1995**

We smooth the Church courtyard
with a blanket of fried fish,
salted eggs, rice flattened in Tupperware.
No chopsticks, we say. Our mouths
long for the feel of forks and spoons.
Paper plates swiftly tumble with the wind
but only our eyes chase after them.
We laugh at the thought
of smelling like fish once again.
We all smell of newly-washed plates.
Ants approach in hills of red.
I sweep them off with my fingers.
One woman looks at me, tells me,
my hands—as natural as brooms.
Suddenly, a shower of leaves.
Like rain, they escape from my fingers.
In our country, rain comes in shape of leaves.
How quickly rain disappears here
through unclogged sewers.
The feel of week-old floods is unknown.
I edge away from the group and rest
a month's worth of letters on my lap.
Leaning against a tree, I read one.
The voice of my husband waits in my ear.
A flood of breeze turns green.
Now, I don't think of Mondays.

---

* Flor Contemplacion was hanged in Singapore City for killing a fellow Filipino maid and a Singaporean boy. Many Filipinos believe that she was framed and accuse the Philippine government of not doing enough to help her.

II. Amsterdam Canal

Out there are boats, Sunday boats
but not the ones I imagine them to be.

They sail here without thinking
of a catch, of empty plates,

of fish salted quickly to last for days.
Back home, I had once waited for a boat.

One night it arrived, rusty, peeling on its side
painted with a name I couldn't read

with faces I still remember.
Planks of wood slammed against the dock.

I rushed in, slept through smashing waves.
The nameless boat that took me

brought me here,
this city of salmon carts that endlessly roll by.

Salmon is not fish; not the same fried
salted milkfish in a flat rimmed basket

banana leaves over them, to keep the flies away.
It is not deboned milkfish over steamy white rice;

cut, sliced, dipped in bowls
of vinegar and raw peppers

so hot it prickled on the tongue.
Smoked salmon in jars is not fish.

They don't hold the scent of letters on my reed mat,
which I cut open with a dry seaweed.

Letters from the farm . . .
Little remnants of a river crumble as they unfold.

— AMSTERDAM, 1990

III. A Night in Dubai

"How did the world revolve in this way?"
—Fadwa Tuquan

for Sarah Balabagan *

The moon is veiled again and I'm afraid. The stillness smells like oil, burning at night. I sleep with the smell of my own fears, wrapped in white linen, as if he couldn't see me beyond this covering and the walls of this jail, from the walls of his grave. His eyes—observant, discontent, and aged by years of thirst—will always be open despite death. I don't remember killing him. But I remember his smell: the oil he rubbed on his body every day, the lamp he carried like jewelry at night, the burning incense as if every day he was preparing for his grave. The oil, the scent of oil, its approach as I scrubbed tile after tile of intricate squares and circles, a garden of tiles, this garden of blood and crime, even then, each tile was a memory of returning to leaves and air, pond water. In the next five days, I will be lashed a hundred times. If it means that for every lash, I would remember less, then let them do it. I will not ask for forgiveness; I will only ask for a moment to hold my mother. She is around me somewhere, behind these walls, beyond this city of cloth and eyes. She waits to take me home. She is showing my photographs to strangers who have never heard of me. I know. She is telling them: *My daughter, she is innocent, see this picture, this is my Sarah, see her smiles, she is strong, they can whip her all day, but she'd come back flying, like birds,* like seasonal birds returning to the south of our farm.

---

* Sarah Balabagan, 18, a Filipina maid in the United Arab Emirates was sentenced to death in 1994 for killing her 85-year-old employer who raped her at knifepoint. After lobbying efforts by European and Philippine groups, the sentence was dropped to a fine of $40,000, one-year prison term, and 100 lashings, which began in January 1996.

IV. Filipineza

In the modern Greek dictionary, the word "Filipineza" means "maid."

If I became the brown woman mistaken
for a shadow, please tell your people I'm a tree.
Or its curling root above ground, like fingers without a rag,

without the buckets of thirst to wipe clean your mirrorlike floors.
My mother warned me about the disappearance of Elena.
But I left her and told her it won't happen to me.

The better to work here in a house full of faces I don't recognize.
Shame is less a burden if spoken in the language of soap and stain.
My whole country cleans houses for food, so that

the cleaning ends with the mothers, and the daughters
will have someone clean for them, and never leave
my country to spend years of conversations with dirt.

When I get up, I stand like a tree, feet steady, back firm.
From here, I can see Elena's island, where she bore a child
by a married man whose floors she washed for years,

whose body stained her memory until she left in the thick
of rain, unseen yet now surviving in the uncertain tongues
of the newly-arrived. Like the silence in the circling motions

of our hands, she becomes part myth, part mortal, part soap.

—BINO A. REALUYO

Go Geisha

"Contemporary designers are turning Japanese"
—W Magazine fashion ad, January 2000

Above, clockwise: Madonna,1999 Grammy Awards, *A. Magazine,* Oct/Nov 1999, p.12; Reebok ad, *Paper* magazine, March 2000; Princess Amidala from a 1999 promotional poster, *Star Wars: the Phantom Menace;* fashion feature, *W Magazine,* Volume 26, Issue 1, January 2000, p.26; music artist Bjork album cover, *Homogenic,* 1997, Electra Entertainment Group.

Asian Women in Film: No Joy, No Luck

Pearl of the Orient. Whore. Geisha. Concubine. Whore.
Hostess. Bar Girl. Mama-san. Whore. China Doll. Tokyo
Rose. Whore. Butterfly. Whore. Miss Saigon. Whore. Dragon
Lady. Lotus Blossom. Gook. Whore. Yellow Peril. Whore.
Bangkok Bombshell. Whore. Hospitality Girl. Whore. Comfort
Woman. Whore. Savage. Whore. Sultry. Whore. Faceless.
Whore. Porcelain. Whore. Demure. Whore. Virgin. Whore.
Mute. Whore. Model Minority. Whore. Victim. Whore.
Woman Warrior. Whore. Mail-Order Bride. Whore. Mother.
Wife. Lover. Daughter. Sister.

As I was growing up in the Philippines in the 1950s, my fertile imagination was colonized by thoroughly American fantasies. Yellowface variations on the exotic erotic loomed larger than life on the silver screen. I was mystified and enthralled by Hollywood's skewed representations of Asian women: sleek, evil goddesses with slanted eyes and cunning ways, or smiling, sarong-clad South Seas "maidens" with undulating hips, kinky black hair, and white skin darkened by makeup. Hardly any of the "Asian" characters were played by Asians. White actors like Sidney Toler and Warner Oland played "inscrutable Oriental detective" Charlie Chan with taped eyelids and a singsong, chop suey accent. Jennifer Jones was a Eurasian doctor swept up in a doomed "interracial romance" in *Love Is a Many Splendored Thing*. In my mother's youth, white actor Luise Rainer played the central role of the Patient Chinese Wife in the 1937 film adaptation of Pearl Buck's novel *The Good Earth*. Back then, not many thought to ask why; they were all too busy being grateful to see anyone in the movies remotely like themselves.

* * *

Cut to 1960: *The World of Suzie Wong*, another tragic East/West affair. I am now old enough to be impressed. Sexy, sassy Suzie (played by Nancy Kwan) works out of a bar patronized by white sailors, but doesn't seem bothered by any of it. For a hardworking girl turning nightly tricks to support her baby, she manages to parade an astonishing wardrobe in damn near every scene, down to matching handbags and shoes. The sailors are also strictly Hollywood, sanitized and not too menacing. Suzie and all the other prostitutes in this movie are cute, giggling, dancing sex machines with hearts of gold. William Holden plays an earnest, rather prim, Nice Guy painter seeking inspiration in The Other. Of course, Suzie falls madly in love with him. Typically, she tells him, "I not important," and "I'll be with you until you say—Suzie, go away." She also thinks being beaten by a man is a sign of true passion, and is terribly disappointed when Mr. Nice Guy refuses to show his true feelings.

Next in Kwan's short-lived but memorable career was the kitschy 1961 musical *Flower Drum Song,* which, like *Suzie Wong,* is a thoroughly American commercial product. The female roles are typical of Hollywood musicals of the times: women are basically airheads, subservient to men. Kwan's counterpart is the Good Chinese Girl, played by Miyoshi Umeki, who was better playing the Loyal Japanese Girl in that other classic Hollywood tale of forbidden love, *Sayonara.* Remember? Umeki was so loyal, she committed double suicide with actor Red Buttons. I instinctively hated *Sayonara* when I first saw it as a child; now I understand why. Contrived tragic resolutions were the only way Hollywood got past the censors in those days. With one or two exceptions, somebody in these movies always had to die to pay for breaking racial and sexual taboos.

Until the recent onslaught of films by both Asian and Asian American filmmakers, Asian Pacific women have generally been perceived by Hollywood with a mixture of fascination, fear, and contempt. Most Hollywood movies either trivialize or exoticize us as people of color and as women. Our intelligence is underestimated, our humanity overlooked, and our diverse cultures treated as interchangeable. If we are "good," we are childlike, submissive, silent, and eager for sex (see France Nuyen's glowing performance as Liat in the film version of *South Pacific)* or else we are tragic victim types (see *Casualties of War,* Brian De Palma's graphic 1989 drama set in Vietnam). And if we are not silent, suffering doormats, we are demonized dragon ladies—cunning, deceitful, sexual provocateurs. Give me the demonic any day—Anna May Wong as a villain slithering around in a slinky gown is at least gratifying to watch, neither servile nor passive. And she steals the show from Marlene Dietrich in Josef von Sternberg's *Shanghai Express.* From the 1920s through the '30s, Wong was our only female "star." But even she was trapped in limited roles in what filmmaker Renee Tajima has called the dragon lady/lotus blossom dichotomy.

* * *

Cut to 1985: There is a scene toward the end of the terribly dishonest but weirdly compelling Michael Cimino movie *Year of the Dragon* (cowritten by Oliver Stone) that is one of my favorite twisted movie moments of all time. If you ask a lot of my friends who've seen that movie (especially if they're Asian), it's one of their favorites too. The setting is a crowded Chinatown nightclub. There are two very young and very tough Jade Cobra gang girls in a shoot-out with Mickey Rourke, in the role of a demented Polish American cop who, in spite of being Mr. Ugly in the flesh—an arrogant, misogynistic bully devoid of any charm—wins the "good" Asian American anchorwoman in the film's absurd and implausible ending. This is a movie with an actual disclaimer as its lead-in, covering its ass in advance in response to anticipated complaints about "stereotypes."

My pleasure in the hard-edged power of the Chinatown gang girls in *Year of the Dragon* is my small revenge, the answer to all those Suzie Wong "I want to be your slave" female characters. The Jade Cobra girls are mere background to the white male foreground/focus of Cimino's movie. But long after the movie has faded into video-rental heaven the Jade Cobra girls remain defiant, fabulous images in my memory, flaunting tight metallic dresses and spiky cocks-comb hairdos streaked electric red and blue.

Mickey Rourke looks down with world-weary pity at the unnamed Jade Cobra girl (Doreen Chan) he's just shot who lies sprawled and bleeding on the street: "You look like you're gonna die, beautiful."

Jade Cobra girl: "Oh yeah? [blood gushing from her mouth] I'm proud of it."

Rourke: "You are? You got anything you wanna tell me before you go, sweetheart?"

Jade Cobra girl.: "Yeah. [pause] Fuck you."

* * *

Cut to 1993: I've been told that like many New Yorkers, I watch movies with the right side of my brain on perpetual overdrive. I admit to being grouchy and overcritical, suspicious of sentiment, and cynical. When a critic like Richard Corliss of *Time* magazine gushes about *The Joy Luck Club* being "a four-fold *Terms of Endearment*," my gut instinct is to run the other way. I resent being told how to feel. I went to see the 1993 eight-handkerchief movie version of Amy Tan's best-seller with a group that included my ten-year-old daughter. I was caught between the sincere desire to be swept up by the turbulent mother-daughter sagas and my own stubborn resistance to being so obviously manipulated by the filmmakers. With every flashback came tragedy. The music soared; the voice-overs were solemn or wistful; tears, tears, and more tears flowed onscreen. Daughters were reverent; mothers carried dark secrets.

I was elated by the grandness and strength of the four mothers and the luminous actors who portrayed them, but I was uneasy with the passivity of the Asian American daughters. They seemed to exist solely as receptors for their mothers' amazing life stories. It's almost as if by assimilating so easily into American society, they had lost all sense of self.

In spite of my resistance, my eyes watered as the desperate mother played by Kieu Chinh was forced to abandon her twin baby girls on a country road in war-torn China. (Kieu Chinh resembles my own mother and her twin sister, who suffered through the brutal Japanese occupation of the Philippines.) So far in this movie, an infant son had been deliberately drowned, a mother played by the gravely beautiful France Nuyen had gone catatonic with grief, a concubine had cut her flesh open to save her dying mother, an insecure daughter had been oppressed by her boorish Asian American husband, another insecure daughter had been left by her white husband, and so on. . . . The overall effect was numbing as far as I'm concerned, but a man sitting two rows in front of us broke down sobbing. A Chinese Pilipino writer even more grouchy than me later complained. "Must ethnicity only be equated with suffering?"

Because change has been slow, *The Joy Luck Club* carries a lot of cultural baggage. It is a big-budget story about Chinese American women, directed by a Chinese American man, cowritten and coproduced by Chinese American women. That's a lot to be thankful for. And its box office success proves that an immigrant narrative told from female perspectives can have mass appeal. But my cynical side tells me that its success might mean only one thing in Hollywood: more weepy epics about Asian American mother-daughter relationships will be planned.

That the film finally got made was significant. By Hollywood standards (think white male; think money, money, money), a movie about Asian Americans even when adapted from a best-seller was a risky proposition. When I asked a producer I know about the film's rumored delays, he simply said, "It's still an *Asian* movie," surprised I had even asked. Equally interesting was director Wayne Wang's initial reluctance to be involved in the project; he told *The New York Times*, "I didn't want to do another Chinese movie."

Maybe he shouldn't have worried so much. After all, according to the media, the nineties are the decade of "Pacific Overtures" and East Asian chic. Madonna, the pop queen of shameless appropriation, cultivated Japanese high-tech style with her music video "Rain," while Janet Jackson faked kitschy orientalia in hers, titled "If." Critical attention was paid to movies from China, Japan, and Vietnam. But that didn't mean an honest appraisal of women's lives. Even on the art house circuit, filmmakers who should know better took the easy way out. Takehiro Nakajima's 1992 film *Okoge* presents one of the more original film roles for women in recent years. In Japanese, "okoge" means the crust of rice that sticks to the bottom of the rice pot; in pejorative slang, it mean fag hag. The way "okoge" is used in the film seems a reappropriation of the term; the portrait Nakajima creates of Sayoko, the so-called fag hag, is clearly an affectionate one. Sayoko is a quirky, self-assured woman in contemporary Tokyo who does voice-overs for cartoons, has a thing for Frida Kahlo paintings, and is drawn to a gentle young gay man named Goh. But the other women's roles are disappointing, stereotypical "hysterical females" and the movie itself turns conventional halfway through. Sayoko sacrifices herself to a macho brute Goh desires, who rapes her as images of Frida Kahlo paintings and her beloved Goh rising from the ocean flash before her. She gives birth to a baby boy and endures a terrible life of poverty with the abusive rapist. This sudden change from spunky survivor to helpless, victimized woman is baffling. Whatever happened to her job? Or that arty little apartment of hers? Didn't her Frida Kahlo obsession teach her anything?

Then there was Tiana Thi Thanh Nga's *From Hollywood to Hanoi*, a self-serving but fascinating documentary. Born in Vietnam to a privileged family that included an uncle who was defense minister in the Thieu government and an idolized father who served as press minister, Nga (a.k.a. Tiana) spent her adolescence in California. A former actor in martial arts movies and fitness teacher ("Karaticize with Tiana"), the vivacious Tiana decided to make a record of her journey back to Vietnam.

From Hollywood to Hanoi is at times unintentionally very funny. Tiana includes a quick scene of herself dancing with a white man at the Metropole hotel in Hanoi, and breathlessly announces: "That's me doing the tango with Oliver Stone!" Then she listens sympathetically to a horrifying account of the My Lai massacre by one of its few female survivors. In another scene, Tiana cheerfully addresses a food vendor on the streets of Hanoi: "Your hairdo is so pretty." The unimpressed, poker-faced woman gives a brusque, deadpan reply: "You want to eat, or what?" Sometimes it is hard to tell the difference between Tiana Thi Thanh Nga and her Hollywood persona: the real Tiana still seems to be playing one of her b-movie roles, which are mainly fun because they're fantasy. The time was certainly right to explore postwar Vietnam from a Vietnamese woman's perspective; it's too bad this film was done by a Valley Girl.

And then there is Ang Lee's tepid 1993 hit, *The Wedding Banquet*—a clever culture-clash farce in which traditional Chinese values collide with contemporary American sexual mores. The somewhat formulaic plot goes like this: Wai-Tung, a yuppie landlord, lives with his white lover, Simon, in a chic Manhattan brownstone. Wai-Tung is an only child and his aging parents in Taiwan long for a grandchild to continue the family legacy. Enter Wei-Wei, an artist who lives in a grungy loft owned by Wai-Tung. She slugs tequila straight from the bottle as she paints and flirts boldly with her young, uptight landlord, who brushes her off. "It's my fate. I am always attracted to handsome gay men," she mutters. After this setup, the movie goes downhill, all edges blurred in a cozy nest of happy endings. In a refrain of Sayoko's plight in *Okoge*, a pregnant, suddenly complacent Wei-Wei gives in to family pressures—and never gets her life back.

* * *

It takes a man to know what it is to be a real woman.
—Song Liling in *M. Butterfly*

Ironically, two gender-bending films in which men play men playing women reveal more about the mythology of the prized Asian woman and the superficial trappings of gender than most movies that star real women. The slow-moving *M. Butterfly* presents the ultimate object of Western male desire as the spy/opera diva Song Liling, a Suzie Wong/Lotus Blossom played by actor John Lone with a five o'clock shadow and bobbing Adam's apple. The best and most profound of these forays into crossdressing is the spectacular melodrama *Farewell My Concubine,* directed by Chen Kaige. Banned in China, *Farewell My Concubine* shared the prize for Best Film at the 1993 Cannes Film Festival with Jane Campion's *The Piano.* Sweeping through 50 years of tumultuous history in China, the story revolves around the lives of two male Beijing Opera stars and the woman who marries one of them. The three characters make an unforgettable triangle, struggling over love, art, friendship, and politics against the bloody backdrop of cultural upheaval. They are as capable of casually betraying each other as they are of selfless, heroic acts. The androgynous Dieyi, doomed to play the same female role of concubine over and over again, is portrayed with great vulnerability, wit, and grace by male Hong Kong pop star Leslie Cheung. Dieyi competes with the prostitute Juxian (Gong Li) for the love of his childhood protector and fellow opera star, Duan Xiaolou (Zhang Fengyi).

Cheung's highly stylized performance as the classic concubine-ready-to-die-for-love in the opera within the movie is all about female artifice. His sidelong glances, restrained passion, languid stance, small steps, and delicate refined gestures say everything about what is considered desirable in Asian women—and are the antithesis of the feisty, outspoken woman played by Gong Li. The characters of Dieyi and Juxian both see suffering as part and parcel of love and life. Juxian matter-of-factly says to Duan Xiaolou before he agrees to marry her: "I'm used to hardship. If you take me in, I'll wait on you hand and foot. If you tire of me, I'll . . . kill myself. No big deal." It's an echo of Suzie Wong's servility, but the context is new. Even with her back to the wall, Juxian is not helpless or whiny. She attempts to manipulate a man while admitting to the harsh reality that is her life.

"Let's face it. Women still don't mean shit in China," my friend Meeling reminds me. What she says so bluntly about her culture rings painfully true, but in less obvious fashion for me. In the Philippines, infant girls aren't drowned, nor were their feet bound to make them more desirable. But sons were and are cherished. To this day, men of the bourgeois class are coddled and prized. We do not have a geisha tradition like Japan, but physical beauty is overtreasured. Our daughters are protected virgins or primed as potential beauty queens. And many of us have bought into the image of the white man as our handsome savior: G.I. Joe.

BUZZ magazine recently featured an article entitled "Asian Women/L.A. Men," a report on a popular hangout that caters to white men's fantasies of nubile Thai women. The lines between movies and real life are blurred. Male screenwriters and cinematographers flock to this bar-restaurant, where the waitresses are eager to "audition" for roles. Many of these men have been to Bangkok while working on film crews for Vietnam War movies. They've come back to L.A., but for them, the movie never ends. In this particular fantasy the boys play G.I. Joe on a rescue mission in the urban jungle, saving the whore from herself. "A scene has developed here, a kind of R-rated *Cheers*," author Alan Rifkin writes. "The waitresses audition for sitcoms. The customers date the waitresses or just keep score."

Colonization of the imagination is a two-way street. And being enshrined on a pedestal as someone's Pearl of the Orient fantasy doesn't seem so demeaning, at first; who wouldn't want to be worshiped? Perhaps that's why Asian women are the ultimate wet dream in most Hollywood movies; it's no secret how well we've been taught to play the role, to take care of our men. In Hollywood vehicles, we are objects of desire or derision; we exist to provide sex, color, and texture in what is essentially a white man's world. It is akin to what Toni Morrison calls "the Africanist presence" in literature. She writes: "Just as entertainers, through or by association with blackface, could render permissible topics that otherwise would have been taboo, so American writers were able to employ an imagined Africanist persona to articulate and imaginatively act out the forbidden in American culture." The same analogy could be made for the often titillating presence of Asian women in movies made by white men.

Movies are still the most seductive and powerful of artistic mediums, manipulating us with ease by a powerful combination of sound and image. In many ways, as females and Asians, as audiences or performers, we have learned to settle for less—to accept the fact that we are either decorative, invisible, or one-dimensional. When there are characters who look like us represented in a movie, we have also learned to view between the lines or to add what is missing. For many of us, this way of watching has always been a necessity. We fill in the gaps. If a female character is presented as a mute, willowy beauty we convince ourselves she is an ancestral ghost—so smart she doesn't have to speak at all. If she is a whore with a heart of gold, we claim her as a tough feminist icon. If she is a sexless, sanitized, boring nerd, we embrace her as a role model for our daughters, rather than the tragic whore. And if she is presented as an utterly devoted saint suffering nobly in silence, we lie and say she is just like our mothers. Larger than life. Magical and insidious. A movie is never just a movie, after all.

—JESSICA HAGEDORN

A Few Words on Rome, or
The Neighbor Who Never Waves

Passing Viareggio, he sees his reflection in the window
and past that, part of the beach where it is said the poet's

body washed on shore, where a pyre was built there
on the sand, the blaze filling him until his chest burst

and Byron reached in to grab the heart. Who cares
if it never happened? This story of madness never hurt

anyone, not even Shelley, who would have loved
what they have done to him. His heart in Rome. His body,

the wind.

*

Passing Viareggio, he notices the beach just as the old woman
sitting across from him whispers, beautiful eyes, in Italian.

She is talking to him, the one thinking about Shelley's death,
and he looks at her. Cosa? he says. She is seventy. She says

she is happy to be travelling. Her daughter lives in Rome.
It is Christmas Eve. He tries to keep up in the conversation—

though he doesn't understand half of the words, it makes her happy
to see him nod at the right moments. Then he understands and then

doesn't. It goes on this way for some time.

*

Years later, he finds himself driving home through Norfolk.
He passes a park where a boy's body was found the day before.

A victim of a drive-by. There are flowers left under one
of the trees. It is early evening, and the streets nearby are beginning

to fill with bodies. His wife leans over to him and kisses his chin
without saying a word. It seems things happen in life for no reason at all.

Turning onto their street, they see the neighbor who never waves back.

*

Viareggio is gone. He remembers it only for the story of the body
and for the words beautiful eyes. No one has ever told him that before.

He blushes. She asks where he is from. He says America. He mentions
his father is from the Philippines. She claps her hands. She must tell him

how industrious she thinks Filipinos are. She tells him
they are the best maids she has ever had.

*

Maybe the neighbor doesn't really care. Maybe the neighbor is so
engrossed in his pile of leaves and garbage that he has not formed

an opinion on their marriage. He hasn't considered the young couple
across the street. The husband who is mixed like his dog, the one

with a brown and a blue eye. The one he scolds for shitting
in the house.

*

The old woman reached in a bag and pulled out a fiasco of wine
and clementine oranges. They peeled them together and drank

until they reached the first station in Rome. Here she gathered her things
and kissed him on the cheek. He was taking the train into the heart

of the city, where he would join the crowd in front of St. Peter's
who were singing in different languages, some singing off-key.

—JON PINEDA

SEXPLOITATION WITHIN THE
ASIAN AMERICAN COMMUNITY

www.jgirls.com ad, *Giant Robot*, Issue 14, 1999, p.72.

Asian fraternity/sorority party flyer.
University of California–Irvine on June 11, 1998.

Meena's Curse

If asked, Meena wouldn't have said she followed him to the store, trailed him like a bloodhound after a fox, sniffing the air for the scent and taste of him. No, that wasn't the way she remembered it. What happened—history as she remembered it—was that she saw him riding his bike, his precious titanium mountain bike, in the direction of the Stop & Shop at the end of King Street. She had been planning to go there anyway, and as she came out of the Dunkin' Donuts she saw him ride past. He was wearing his black wrap-around sunglasses and worn topsiders with no socks, though the temperature had plummeted the night before, turning the islands of grass in the sidewalk into stiff frozen needles that crunched underfoot.

And no, she wouldn't have been able to tell anyone—not even herself—how she came to know his bicycle was precious or that it was a mountain bike or that it was titanium. How she came by the details of this man with green eyes and a coarse blond ponytail was a mystery to her. She didn't realize she had them, carried them around in the back pocket of her jeans like forgotten tissues and old grocery lists that shredded in the wash and attached themselves to every other piece of clothing in the load. These details clung like the pills on a cheap sweater that multiplied on their own. They were part of her now, useless details that offered no insight as to why Larry had disappeared in the middle of his first year at the hospital. About him, she thought she knew what everyone else knew, threadbare scraps: Mayflower descendant; son of a famous New York district judge; Harvard graduate; one year of law school; a broken heart, maybe two (his or someone else's?); several step-families; and a passion for the outdoors. He skied and backpacked in remote areas of the world. He enjoyed skydiving, hang gliding, and kayaking in white water. Mostly, though, he climbed mountains, and his skin was always tanned, ruddy from a life lived close to nature. When she thought of America, the image of Larry floated by, next to billboards for the Marlboro man and Coca-Cola.

Her skin was also tan, but she'd been born with it, and was often mistaken for a Seminole Indian in Florida where her parents had moved after one harsh New York winter. "East Indian," she learned to call herself, but the blank eyes of her classmates made her wish she could say Seminole, Apache, Cherokee—something they'd at least seen on TV and could believe existed. And later, as she grew up, it was elephants and maharajahs and poverty she had to explain to her classmates at the New England boarding school her parents sent her to. Six years passed and then she stayed for college and med school. Unlike her tropical parents, she had learned to love the crisp winter air, the peculiar light that deadened the earth just before snow fell from the sky. Loving the cold was different from being cold. Accordingly, she loved the accouterments of the cold: nubby wool sweaters, thick black tights, long sleeves, high necks, fingerless gloves, and sheepskin slippers. She bought heavy socks and turtlenecks and leggings in catalogue colors of summer—fuchsia, harvest green, and lapis lazuli.

Long distance, aunties in Delhi worried about finding the right man for her, living as she did in a small, no-name valley town, with such weather. Meena never mentioned the hot, humid summers, or the beauty of the crocuses and daffodils in the spring, or even the celebrated fall foliage that attracted caravans of cars with out-of-state license plates. She wrote to her aunts infrequently; they could easily think she lived in a place where it was winter all the time, and she let them because she didn't want them to find her a husband.

She could articulate this, if asked, but several years would pass before she'd be able to see how her love for the cold made her follow her former colleague into the grocery store. She would remember her actions, but she would be unable to assign motivation, emotion, or intent to them. She remembered the ache in her fingers, stiff from cigarettes and lack of sleep. She was in the store, she told herself, because Anita was having a pot-luck that night, and she had to make chicken curry.

She was using a recipe from a book her mother had sent her a year ago, with an admonishment inscribed on the flyleaf. "You must eat, bacchi. Even doctors get sick." If only her mother knew. Eating would not cure her illness. She would need a transplant, a new resident to occupy her body, to get this sickness out of it. She couldn't name it, but she knew she had it. If not, why was she tracking Larry in a grocery store?

She panicked for a moment when she thought she'd lost him between the meat and dairy cases, but the store was nearly empty, and she found him easily around the corner, near the cookies. She watched him from the end of the aisle. He read the package in his hand, holding it close to his face, his sunglasses now perched on the top of his head. She remembered seeing him in round wire-rimmed glasses that slipped down his nose when he was concentrating. He threw a pack of fruit bars into his cart, and she followed him to checkout. Only two lanes were open, so she stood behind him and waited.

She had no plan. She told herself to expect nothing; meanwhile, she hoped he'd turn around. She told herself it didn't matter if he didn't apologize for yesterday. Perhaps all she wanted was for him to recognize her, and in so doing, make everything between them right again. She stared at the red reindeer in his gray Icelandic sweater and then watched his chapped hands move his groceries from cart to conveyor belt. They were dirty—no longer the hands of a practicing doctor—with scabs forming on the knuckles, ugly red scarabs of pain.

Meena pushed her cart forward, nudging the heels of his hiking boots gently.

"Sorry," she said, automatically.

He turned around and looked down at her for a second, though he was only a few inches taller than her. The skin around his eyes was crinkled, and his lips were narrow, unsmiling and tense. She thought he looked old to be a resident, and then another one of those details—the ones she stored but had no file for—came back to her. He'd traveled for a few years after college, working his way from one city to the next, always outdoors, always on the move. He had seen the world, people and places the rest of them—saddled with exams and debts—could only dream about.

Larry turned his attention back to his groceries, his marble eyes running over her without a hint of recognition. Meena felt herself blush. She touched her cheeks with icy fingertips and bent her head, hiding her face behind a curtain of thick black hair. The groceries stumbled from her hands to the belt, and she didn't look up again until she was sure he was gone.

How had she come to follow a man who would hardly look at her? She didn't know anymore; she felt she was watching herself from some great distance, a relative of a patient on the operating table, watching from the booth, unable to comprehend the action below.

The day before she'd gone straight from her shift to the gas station, exhausted and feeling ill-defined, like an out-of-focus photograph. She slouched against the car, waiting for the gas tank to fill up, and ignored the cold biting at her fingers and running up her sleeves and around her back through her unbuttoned coat. Across the street, Larry rode his bike on the sidewalk. He wasn't wearing a hat or scarf, and his hair gleamed like polished kernels of summer corn in the weak afternoon sun.

She hadn't seen him since he'd quit work three weeks ago, abruptly and with no apparent reason. She noticed he was gone when she walked into the cafeteria one day and saw that his usual table was empty. He'd never been on one of her rotations, yet she'd seen him enough to know when they passed each other in the halls. Once she'd sat next to him at the bar, their backs to each other as they chatted with friends at opposite ends of the same table. She hardly looked at him that night, yet she remembered the black T-shirt and the golden hairs on his arm that glistened in the warm light from the candle on the table.

And now here he was. She stared at him through her eyelashes as if they were a protective screen. Her heart started racing, though if asked how she felt she would leave this detail out, deny the dry mouth and tingling at the base of her throat, the way her lips pulled against her teeth. She watched him, willed him to look over her way and talk to her. And when he crossed the street, she held her breath as he wheeled the bike towards her, and let it go when she saw him put a quarter in the air pump. He bent over the front tire, concentrating on it as if no one and nothing around him existed.

Meena got into her car and left the gas station. She would say she wasn't thinking of him when she turned right instead of left, but she'd remember the thump on the side of the car and her fear that she'd hit a pedestrian or a dog. She pulled over, and as she undid her seatbelt, she noticed Larry at the passenger door. He had taken his sunglasses off, and the lightness of his eyes and hair pierced the gloom of the car.

She opened the window. "Are you all right?" He seemed okay. She thought she'd offer him a ride home or invite him for coffee at the diner across the street.

"Where the hell did you learn to drive? Afghanistan?"

Meena stared at him, waiting for the joke. He frowned.

"Really," he said. "You should take some local driving lessons. We have laws in this country about hitting people with your car. Understand?"

The smile inside her died. "I'm sorry." But Larry was gone before the words had left her mouth.

She drove on, her eyes smarting from the cold air that whipped through the open window. Her fingers clenched the steering wheel. She'd had one real accident before, a fender bender when her car slid across an icy street and into another car. That driver apologized for the weather. He offered her a few hints about driving in the snow, after taking her insurance number, and said, "Don't let the weather make you a prisoner. You keep trying."

She was twenty, and if he was patronizing, she preferred that to hostility. She wondered where Larry thought she'd come from and why he thought it. She didn't ask herself—for she couldn't at the time—why it mattered so much.

Yet when she saw him at the grocery store the next day, she followed him, and when she saw him later that night at Anita's party, she stood near him and waited. She listened to him talk about a climbing expedition he'd guided last year. He had a captive audience, his usual crowd, plus some. His stories, she noticed, had an arcane quality to them, full of technical terms about ice and rock. The language, the knowledge it implied, formed a protective shield around him and his comrades, those who not only loved the cold but owned it as well.

Meena wandered into the kitchen and told Anita what had happened at the gas station. She left out the details of her morning trip to the store. For the sake of time, she told herself, unwilling to reveal what she didn't understand.

"So he thinks you're a foreigner," Anita said, as she moved between the counter and the stove, her sandals smacking the linoleum. Indoors, she always wore sandals with her salwar kameez; outdoors, she stomped around in thick-soled black boots, her one concession to American weather.

"He looked at me like I was a stranger." Meena dug her hand into her jeans pocket and looked down at Anita's red painted toenails.

"And so? He's not at the hospital anymore. You don't need to know each other. You can be strangers."

Meena envied her. Anita couldn't care, wouldn't be able to care until she'd been in this country for so long that it became home and going back to India was no longer an option. As long as she had one foot on the plane, though, she could change the subject, talk about the engineer her parents wanted her to marry and the job waiting for her at Breach Candy Hospital in Bombay. Against such rock solid tomorrows, Larry was nothing more than a temporary condition, irritating, like a mosquito bite.

After this, when Meena thought of Larry, a sick taste filled her mouth, the tannic acid of too much tea on an empty stomach or stale coffee at the end of a long day. Worse, however, she was still looking for him, waiting for him to appear and apologize. The days lurched forward, and October melted into November without her noticing. She worked with an intensity she hadn't felt before. Her eyes burned with exhaustion, and her bones buckled under an invisible weight. She took extra shifts. If she needed to prove anything to anyone, it was to herself.

Meanwhile, the aunties ignored her lack of interest in their matchmaking efforts, and the letters kept coming. In spite of herself, Meena read them, curious about the eligible "boys"—boys, still, though they were in their late twenties and early thirties—who wrote to her. The letters were impersonal, generic and tired; they were "from good families," families with money and names that meant something back in India. Names that meant nothing to her, born and bred in the New World where such things weren't supposed to matter. But in a match among strangers, a good family, height, fair skin, and a lot of money were important. These were the details that impressed.

Meena imagined her future mother-in-law running a finger across the kitchen counter, sniffing at the pile of newspapers in the corner of her living room, the mattress on the floor of the bedroom, and the half empty boxes of books and clothes, arranged like the display at a badly organized garage sale. She would notice, this fictional mother-in-law-to-be, the half empty vodka bottle, the dirty dishes, and overflowing ashtrays scattered through the small apartment. She would see, finally, dark skin, thick black hair unfashionably braided down the back, and faded jeans that hung loosely at the hips. She would notice all these things and draw conclusions about this completely unsuitable girl.

The men who wrote to Meena wanted a girl with a career. They also wanted a girl who could cook and clean and give birth to the requisite boy child to carry on the family name. Most of all—and what did it mean that these were the only men the aunties could find?—they wanted a girl who could get them a green card.

They didn't want a woman who stood in the snow, face turned to the sky to catch the fast falling flakes. They didn't want a woman who didn't button her coat on the bleakest days of the year when the landscape looked like a black and white photograph because the cold reminded her that she was still alive. They especially didn't want a woman who looked with longing at men she couldn't have. So Meena wrote back to the aunties, told them again that she was a long way from finishing school and that she wouldn't be too old when the time finally came to look for a husband. Things are different here, she told them. Girls can wait before settling down.

One night, a five-year-old boy with a cut in his scalp appeared in the emergency room. When Meena got to him, he was lying on the table, face down, crying softly. His mother held his hand and tried to calm him down. She was one of those women who'd had children too young; her face was a series of lines under cheap, cakey make-up, and her hair was lank and pale on her shoulders. She wore old acid-washed jeans, and she smelled of tobacco.

"How did it happen?" Meena asked, as she cleaned the wound. The deep cut was neat with no ragged edges of skin to force together.

"He wanted to fly," the mother said. "Pretend he was at Disneyworld." Her blue eyes were wide as she explained how her son put a shallow box on the coffee table and tried to jump from it to the couch, about two feet away. "So, I'm hollering and hollering for him to get down, but before I can move, the box just slips and his head smacks the table. Right, bub?" She stroked her son's forehead with a small, dry hand gnarled with arthritis.

After Meena had given the boy five stitches, she sent the mother out for coffee. She looked over the boy's thin body, raising his arms and listening to his heart, and casually asked him about the table he slipped on.

"Momma told me not to," he said, his lower lip sticking out. His face was tear-stained, and his Aran sweater, pilled in places, was thick and warm. There was no sign of any other injury on his body. "I had a lot of blood. Did my brains come out?"

Meena shook her head and smiled. "Not a single cell."

She thought about his mother, who had left the room easily, with no apparent concern for what her son might say, for what his body might reveal. She fit the profile of an abuser or someone living with one—young, on public assistance, single. But Meena had lost her trust in such details, details that looked convincing on paper and then faded in the light of the physical person behind them. She thought about how impressed the aunties would have been with Larry's pedigree, his multiple step-families and his lack of professional fortitude overshadowed by his father's brilliance and his great-great-grandfather's wealth. A boy from this family couldn't be bad, they would say, poring over the horoscope for some sign, a moon or a star indicating that he could change, that he could be the person he should be.

Meena watched the mother zip up her son's jacket and gather him in her arms. The boy had recovered enough to give her a sleepy smile, and he waved goodbye as his mother carried him out.

"Thanks, doc," the woman said.

"I'm going to Disneyworld. I'm gonna fly . . ." the boy sang, his high-pitched voice drifting down the corridor.

And there was Larry, at the end of the long white corridor, talking animatedly to Anita. As Meena approached them, he looked up, his eyes bright and alert behind his glasses.

"The kid looked pretty happy," he said.

"He's forgotten what happened. He still thinks he's going to fly."

"Maybe he will."

She couldn't believe she was talking to him, smiling, acting as if nothing had happened. She was numb, as if she'd swallowed a load of painkillers. Or maybe just dumb enough to still care what he thought.

"Larry's going to Srinagar in December," Anita said.

Meena wasn't sure how to respond. The husband of one of her aunties had a house in Kashmir that he never expected to see again. Neither did his children.

"They say it's safe," Larry said.

"Isn't it closed to tourists?" Meena thought about the Hindu refugees and the European hostages, four still missing after two years, a fifth one dead, long forgotten by the front page. She looked at Anita for confirmation, but Anita shook her head slightly and continued smiling at Larry.

"I'm not exactly a tourist."

Perhaps it was the way he looked over his glasses, down his nose. Perhaps it was the way he leaned against the wall, his arms by his side and smiled as if they were friends, and her approval was a foregone conclusion. Later, she would wonder what it was exactly, at that moment, and not any of the others, that made her say,

"Let me tell you a story."

The aunties used to tell stories about entire villages colonized by young, drugged-out Americans and Europeans. "These people," Auntie would say, rolling her eyes, spitting the words. "No one asked them to come here. They took over that one village. In the end, only one budhiya remained." The old lady, fed up and angry, put a curse on the village, Auntie said, and the next day the hippies started dying. The ones who didn't left by the end of the week.

"What's this got to do with Kashmir?" Larry asked. He took a step forward, reducing the space between them.

She could explain it all away. She could just wish him luck. She could tell him she understood, he was different. Instead, she said, "Not much. Depends on how you look at it."

When she left him, his face was unreadable, his mouth tight like it had been the day she nearly hit him with the car. She wondered if he knew that the power of a curse came from the belief people put into it. She knew he would not ask himself why her aunties, who were afraid their niece had grown up irretrievably American, told these stories. For Larry, Meena finally understood, the power of an exotic curse made more sense than the desperation of flesh-and-blood people driven to terrorism. He'd been everywhere, seen everything, and in the end, he saw nothing at all.

When Meena stepped outside after her shift, the sun was rising, casting a weak light over the snow-covered cars. For the first time in weeks, her body didn't ache; she felt a tight flag inside come unfurled, and when the cold touched her fingers and face, it was a caress. She fell backward into the deepest patch of fresh snow she could find and made an angel, the first of the season. As she drove home in her wet clothes, she thought about the young boy who wanted to fly and wondered if he'd ever make it to Disneyworld. Would it live up to his expectations or would he emerge from childhood one day, not with the pre-fab memory of Mickey and Minnie, but a clear picture of a shallow cardboard box and himself suspended in mid-air, an angel in flight, between the table and the sofa.

The events remained filed in a place she could not reach. They surfaced years later when she read that Larry had died on a mountain climbing expedition, leading a group of amateurs up a peak in the Himalayas. She tried to imagine him in Kathmandu, and then in the small villages at the base of the mountain. She saw him, tall and fair, carrying himself like the Olympic torch among the throngs in the bazaar, the small brown bodies of boys and girls dancing around him, crying "Sahib, sahib, 25 paise only." He would joke with them and shoo them away like flies. But they didn't really annoy him. After a week, their low persistent voices had become a familiar tune. They understood each other, the beggars and Larry. Their presence was comforting. They were exactly what he'd expected, in synch with the stinking gullies and jasmine-scented temples around him. He saw the boys as they were and where they should be.

Up at base camp, Meena heard the tents flapping and smelled the hot, sweet chai the Sherpas would have made for the climbers. She tried to imagine the oxygen-light air at that altitude and felt only the embrace of frigid cold, a vise around her ribs and diaphragm as Larry tried to find the energy and breath to climb back down from the peak he'd scaled so many times in his dreams.

She wondered how he felt, dying a foreigner's death, alone in the snow and ice. His last sight before losing consciousness would have been the concerned faces of the Sherpas hovering over his glazed eyes and parched lips. These were faces that cared whether he lived or died. These faces he'd turn away from if he saw them on the street in a small town in Western Massachusetts.

Meena snuggled deep under the razai, the thick cotton quilt, a wedding gift from one of the aunties. She turned the pages of the glossy magazine carefully to avoid waking the sleeping body beside her. She'd finished her residency, and met the right man on her own, the one who had been raised in Texas and was still learning to love the cold. His details were humble, ordinary parents who, like hers, had chased the tropics in their new home. They went out a few times, and in the restaurant, she couldn't help noticing the way his eyes flicked from side to side as people walked by. He stared at women, women who didn't look like her, but when he fixed his brown eyes on Meena, she knew he saw her. He saw hair, body, and skin. He saw himself and did not look away.

He was a man who didn't need her to explain the way she'd looked at Larry, the dumb childhood jokes about Tonto and Chief Sitting Bull, or the precarious line she walked between native and foreigner. When she took him skating, he leaned on her briefly and then crossed one foot over the other and skated away, arms stretched out in a wide embrace of the pine and the blue-tipped fir around the frozen pond as his skates wobbled beneath him. Later, he practiced near the edge of the pond, knees bent awkwardly, eyes down so he could watch his feet move.

When Meena looked at the photo of Larry on the slick page that stuck to her fingers, she saw him as he'd always been: frozen and distant, cold to the touch. She closed the magazine and dropped it to the floor, next to her old, worn-out slippers. She thought she should feel something about his death, but she didn't. She thought she should feel sorry about this, but she felt nothing other than mild interest. They were strangers, after all. Anita had been right.

—GEETA KOTHARI

Report No. 49

—An excerpt from the United States Office of War Information Psychological Warfare Team attached to the U.S. Army Forces India-Burma Theater

Japanese Prisoner of War Interrogation Report No. 49
Date of Report: October 1, 1944
Place Interrogated: Ledo Stockade
Date Interrogated: August 20-September 10, 1944
By: T/3 Alex Yorichi

Prisoners: 20 Korean Comfort Girls
Date of Capture: August 10, 1944
Date of Arrival: August 15, 1944

PERSONALITY:

The interrogations show the average Korean "comfort girl" to be about twenty-five years old, uneducated, childish, whimsical, and selfish. She is not pretty either by Japanese or Caucasian standards. She is inclined to be egotistical and likes to talk about herself. Her attitude in front of strangers is quiet and demure, but she "knows the wiles of a woman." She claims to dislike her "profession" and would rather not talk either about it or her family. Because of the kind treatment she received as a prisoner from American soldiers at Myitkyina and Ledo, she feels that they are more emotional than Japanese soldiers. She is afraid of Chinese and Indian troops.

Red Lines Across the Map

In that moment between the state of sleep and of being awake, I forget where I am. The gaudy blue and pink paisley pattern of the bedcover reminds me this is a hotel room—Marriott, Holiday Inn, it doesn't seem to matter any more. I wonder who stayed here before me. Perhaps a traveling businessman calling his family at night to tell the kids goodnight. Or a family on vacation, the children jumping up and down on the bed as though it was a trampoline. Maybe another flight attendant, thankful to be able to crawl into bed for another brief and restless sleep before flying to another city, another hotel, another night alone.

I meet my crew at the airport and we file onto the aircraft. At my assigned door, I check the door pressure gauge and the slide pressure gauge, all the time chanting in my mind the procedure for an emergency evacuation. Notify, assess, open, protect, pull.

The passengers file on to the plane, a stream of bodies, faces intent on destination. My post is by the door, standing erect like part of the aircraft, but smiling. This man gives me a quick smile, lips tight across his teeth. He clutches his laptop (as though I would snatch it from him). I smile broader. I say good morning to a mother, father and two boys. A blank look as they stumble by me, silently mouthing their seat numbers. This lady has four bags. I stop her; the limit is two. She is agitated and refuses to check her bags. My flying partner insists. The woman gives us a chilling glare as she snatches the claim tags from my hand. My partner shrugs her shoulders and brushes something away from the sleeve of her dark blue polyester uniform, the armor of the corporation.

The door shuts, sealing us in. The aircraft pushes away from the jet bridge. Air from the ceiling vents bursts out like water spraying out from the shower, immersing everyone in the special air created to let us breathe 37,000 feet above ground. I find the image of the continent of the United States in my mind and draw a little white plane across it, marking my route in a dotted red line. But as I walk down the aisle of the aircraft, I look out of the window and see an endless jumble of blue and white and yellow.

A gentleman touches me on my arm and asks, "When are we due in?" For a moment I fumble. Where are we and where are we going? We are on an island. Suspended above the clouds, we are a nation of our own. We can forget who we are, where we come from and where we are going until we get there.

This lady is polite and kind to me, so I pour her another glass of wine. She looks up and smiles. Her eyes drop down to my name pin and linger there. I watch her pronouncing it slowly in her mind. "You have a beautiful name," she says. Suddenly, I feel naked, as though she can see the color of my skin under the blue uniform, the thickness of my hair under the taut pulled back twist, and the smallness of my eyes under the makeup. "You are . . . Japanese?" The red dotted lines break apart, falling haphazardly on the continent I call home.

At the end of the day, the red dotted line brings me back to where I began. I take the train home, watching the sky darken. The sky is limited and contained by the buildings and freeways that climb up to touch it. A plane takes off into the sky, growing smaller and smaller. Looking up from the ground, the plane looks too small and fragile to contain a nation of its own. Passengers on the train glance at me twice, then down at my suitcase with the large crew tag hanging from the handle, but without my aircraft, I am of no use to them.

As I shut the door behind me, I close my mind from the faces that floated past me, the rooms that contained me, and the map with the red dotted line drawn across in many directions. I take off my blue uniform and hang it up for another trip. I rub my feet that are tired from being in high heels all day. I remove the makeup around my brown eyes with cold cream. I brush away the smell of the pressurized air that clings to every strand of my hair like day-old spray. I look at my own face in the mirror. I remember who I am.

—S.L. KIM

Above: Filipinos manufactured by Nabisco, Iberia, S.L, Barcelona;
Cherry Clan manufactured by Ferrara Pan Candy Co., Forest Park, Illinois;
Slim Tea manufactured by Hobe Labs, Inc., Phoenix, Arizona.

Mirror Mirror Tea Tea

Pausing to browse at a fabric store in the mall in Hadley, Massachusetts, a small rural town bordering Amherst, I find myself staring at a promotional brochure lying on a counter in disbelief. No, it's true, the African American woman smiling on the cover is indeed wearing a shirt adorned with Indian mirrorwork, and the East Asian model featured inside is also wearing a dress supposedly embroidered with "sheesha" mirrors (which literally translated from Hindi means mirror-mirrors, as "chai" tea means tea-tea; such are the slips of the worldly tongue). I learn that "Asian influences are carrying fashion this spring," and that the color cues include "curry." I guess the model's dress does look faintly turmeric-inspired; perhaps potato curry is the color of the season? At least I am now sure that Asian-chic has made it to rural New England, and if there's any doubt, there are "bindi armbands" and "temporary tattoos" inspired by mehndi mania on sale in teenybopper fashion outlets from Holyoke to Northampton.

The rise of Indo-chic in the last three or four years, part of a wider marketing of "Asian cool" in fashion, music, and film, can easily invoke a response that focuses only on claims to authenticity and ownership. "They" aren't Asian, so they don't have a "right" to don these symbols outside the "proper" context. Cultural appropriation of Asian artifacts and images is always a charged issue, because it is the tip of the deeper coagulation of histories of anti-Asian racism, anxieties about changing demographics, and exploitation of cheap Third World labor, the turn-of-the-millennium version of Orientalization. So what kinds of representations do we, and can we, construct in response?

Collecting nonfiction work for *Screaming Monkeys* was motivated by one kind of response, the creation of a project that would offer alternative representations of Asian Americans in the face of blatantly racist caricatures. The politics of representation, especially in popular culture and the media, can often be a slippery slope. On one side, you have images and sound bytes in the mainstream media that are disturbingly simplistic and often offensively distorted, and on the other side, marketing trends that are fetishistic and exploitative. These representational practices conceal wider structures of racial inequality, political injustice, economic production, and global labor, that, as Sonia Shah eloquently points out in this section, in fact depend on these Orientalizing images for their perpetuation. So responses that ignore the historical and political contexts in which these images and sound bytes are embedded, it could be argued, allow these underlying structures to go unchallenged. Reviewing the essays for this section, I was struck by the complexity and nuances of the arguments that some Asian American cultural critics and political activists provide, going beyond a simply reactive stance. As the examples in this collection demonstrate, representations of Asian Americans are not always just about representations of Asian Americans, they are also about u.s. imperialism in Asia and at home, African American martial arts heroes, alliances between peoples of color fighting systems of oppression, the global trade in Asian women and sweatshop labor, and post-Cold War scapegoating of Asian "spies."

—SUNAINA MAIRA
nonfiction editor

I Wanna Marry a Haole so I Can
Have a Haole Last Name

The Perfect Haole House: There is a Dixie bathroom cup dispenser with cups that have blue and pink flowers around the bottom in the perfect house and you don't have to write your name on the bottom of the cup and save it. When done, throw it away in the little pink trash can. At Christmas, the mother puts cups with holly around the bottom in the dispenser.

I see a wicker hamper, not a plastic laundry basket, and a knitted poodle covering the next roll of toilet paper, rose-shaped soap in matching porcelain dishes, and rose-colored towels. A rosy shower curtain and a rose rug around the toilet and on the toilet seat that is plush, not flat. At Christmas, the knitted poodle becomes a knitted Santa Claus.

The father sprays Lysol all over the bathroom when he finishes making BM with the latest issue of *Sports Illustrated.* No burning cowboy matches to kill the smell in the perfect bathroom in the perfect house.

There are bunk beds with wooden ladders and pink ruffles and white eyelet bedspreads over beds that are made every day the way haoles do with the pillow tucked under, not a vinyl punee covered with a sheet and a folded futon or a grandma-made quilt out of old dress material crumpled at the bottom of the bed.

In the kitchen, there are blue glasses—no Dino Flintstone cups—and matching dishes with roses on them and Tupperware that's still shiny. When you want a soda, the mother pours real Coca-Cola and 7-Up, not RC or Diamond Head Lemonlime. And automatic ice cubes that drop out of a clean freezer.

At Christmastime, the mother and daughters wear matching flannel nightgowns with lace. Nobody wears Father's old T-shirts or Mother's old shortie muumuus. The mother takes out the Christmas mugs and makes real hot chocolate with whipped cream and cinnamon, not Nestlé's Quik in a cold cup of milk.

I see Pez candy holders that Santa put in the stockings with the sisters' names on top *with Pez inside.* On the coffee table, magazines like *National Geographic* and *Life* spread out like a fan, all the time like that, not just when guests come over to the perfect house.

Mother wipes the clear-plastic covers on the furniture every day and the material underneath looks crispy. The perfect house doesn't have an old pea-green bedspread over a sofa with foam padding crumbling like sand into the creases of the cushion. The father doesn't stuff the *TV Guide* into the crack of the La-Z-Boy.

A Zenith TV, a Magnavox hi-fi console, alphabetized record albums beginning with Abba, a mustard-colored shag rug, a bar with padded barstools, clean throw pillows, living-room drapes without holes, no paper plates, bendable straws with *every* drink including water. Hot-dog buns for hot dogs. And plain white bread all the time.

There is a Cougar or Torino or Duster in the garage, a playroom called a den with vinyl beanbag chairs in all colors, and an upright piano. At Christmastime, the mother lights candles on the piano that she actually bought to burn and they sing "Silent Night," at least three verses in three-part harmony, while Little Sis plays the piano and Mother puts her arm around Big Sis and Father puts his arm around Mother. Father sings while puffing on a pipe, as the cat curls up on the throw rug in this perfect house where no one swears or blows bubbles into the chocolate milk through a saved straw from the Dairy Queen or eats Spam cut extra thick and glazed with guava jelly and mustard for dinner.

Where no one encourages Mother at Christmas to dance to "Cockeye Mayor from Kaunakakai" as Aunt Helen plays the ukulele and everyone laughs and claps and throws money as the dog begins to bark and Uncle Ed yells, "We go caroling!" And they all hold each other and sing "Manuela Boy, My Dear Boy" down the driveway as Aunt Helen strums her ukulele as I watch at the picture window thinking about angels and the Lennon Sisters singing hymns.

* * *

Yes, hi. My name is Betty Cooper.

Yes, hi. My name is Billy Jo Cole.

Yes, hi. My name is Bobby Gentry and I look just like Liz Taylor.

"Yeah, right. Your name is Betty Correa and you live on Kinoole Street," Jerome says. "No, no, no. Billy Jo Takahara and your family owns pigs up Uka side and your father work for the Board of Water Supply. Okay, wait. Bobbylyn Chang. Future Narcissus Queen, gotta go Barbizon Modeling School for learn how to walk. I promise, Lovey. You piss me off. I ain't ever coming to your house again. I hate play pretend-talk-haole, I mean it. No act. I so irritated, I like buss your chops, bobo your face, and I swear, I ever hear one more haole name like Lovey Beth Farnsworth or Lovey Lynn Beckenhauser, I promise, I going home and I ain't ever coming back."

* * *

The Beckenhausers: They lived across the street from the Church of the Holy Cross. A white house with green trim and blackened torn screens on the back side of the house.

Vicky Beckenhauser and me climbed through the back window to play in her room with the Ouija board so her mother wouldn't see me coming or going. Sometimes we played "Princess Knight" and Vicky let me be the horse, O-po.

Haoles have a certain smell. A sweet powdery smell, not like Johnson's Baby Powder, but like powdery flowers. Vicky had that smell.

Vicky's Aunt Theresa made her homemade rag dolls that had the same yarn hair color as Vicky and her sister Suzanne. Dark, rust yarn hair and clothes like Vicky and Suzanne.

Once, while playing Ouija board in Vicky's closet, her mother bursts in and says, "What the hell's goin' on?" She looks at me sharp. "Who's this, Vicky?"

"Mama, my friend Lovey. Can she stay for some supper?"

Vicky's mother with the greasy hair and cigarette between her red, chipped nails says, "Sure. Go warsh up and call your mama."

Me and Vicky washing our hands with a dirty bar of soap. I'm so scared, I don't even remember what we had to eat. But seeing Vicky and her mother, Suzanne, and Mr. Beckenhauser, who drinks Primo beer and stares straight at me across the table, I feel lucky to be with haoles for dinner.

Vicky takes the butter dish and slaps a huge wad all over her hot Minute Rice that falls like bullets off of her fork, not like the rice we eat at home.

The butter dish gets passed from one person to the next, each one rubbing lots of butter on their rice. And when the butter comes to me, I want to be a Beckenhauser so bad, I rub butter all over my rice and swallow each bite like a mouthful of Crisco.

* * *

My number in Lori Shigemura's Slam Book is 7.
7. BABY-OF-THE-FUTURE: A boy, then a girl,
                Hapa
                With Japanese middle name
7. BOY: Christopher Torao Cole
7. GIRL: Summer or Heather Reiko Cole
7. HUSBAND-OF-THE-FUTURE: Dennis Cole, Jaclyn Smith's
                         ex-hubby, or Michael Cole,
                         Mod Squad

* * *

Japanee girls all want haole last names like Smith or Cole. Tall blond haoles with hairy legs and bushy underarms. Blue or hazel eyes and with a real haole accent, or better yet they grew up here and their grandparents were missionaries, so they can talk local if they want—but don't.

The Allens: Andrew Allen lived in the expensive house on the beach cliffs. From the outside, it looked like *Gone with the Wind* with palm trees, a golf-course lawn, bougainvillea archways, and an Oriental bridge over a river by the house.

My mother sewed puakenikeni and pakalana leis with palapalai fern and ribbons for Mrs. Allen's Big Island Women's Golf Club and sold them to her for cheap.

We'd drive up in the Land Rover and Mrs. Allen would take real long to come out of her house. When she finally came out, she'd be bouncy in her tennis whites with an elastic white headband on her blond hair.

Mrs. Allen would lift up the wet paper towel over the leis in the soda boxes, carefully peer at each lei, and say, "Well, Verva. You'd think for the price you charge for these, you'd at least leave the bruised flowers out."

Andrew Allen, "Andy," on the porch swing out on the lanai—he'd laugh at Calhoon and me. Say at school in his perfect English, "Hey, Lei Seller. Hey, Bruise. Hey, Lei-lani and her stupid sister."

My mother would say to Mrs. Allen, "Take an extra puakenikeni for yourself and a pakalana for Mitzi Hall. Sorry about the bruises." Mother said this in perfect English that sounded pretend-talk-haole.

Cal and me in the backseat of our car get a dollar each for coming along and Mother cursing and spitting all the way down the Allen's steep driveway.

* * *

Mokes like haole girls with strawberry-blond hair. They come to our school from places like Kenosha, Wisconsin, talking real straight, and next thing you know, haole girl with moke-y boyfriend.

* * *

Ginger Geiger. Daughter of Mrs. Gloria Geiger, new Sunday School Youth Choir director. Mrs. Geiger forced us to memorize "This Is My Father's World," the Twenty-third Psalm, all four verses of "Just As I Am," and "M Is for the Million Things She Gave Me." We were also forced to attend Saturday rehearsal.

Jerome quit. Bradley Kinoshita quit. Adele Ige went back to college. This left Cal, me, the Kimura twins, who I swear only moved their lips to the memorized verses, and Ginger Geiger.

Ginger Geiger when she first came to Youth Choir:

Goody barrettes and two ponytail braids, plaid cotton blouse buttoned to the lace collar, high-water bell-bottoms, white socks with lace, and Buster Browns.

Ginger Geiger after Baron Ahuna, Kenneth Spencer, and Levi Na-lani, JV and varsity volleyball players, started driving into the parking lot of our church at Saturday rehearsals calling, "Eh, Ginga Grant, where you stay?" Ginger Geiger after all of that:

Red lipstick and kissing potion glossy lips, long hair down with plumeria behind her ear, hiphuggers, halter top, and Dr. Scholl's exercise sandals.

Ginger looked like Maureen McCormick.

* * *

We watched *The Greatest Story Ever Told* on the Geigers' console TV. Mrs. Geiger and Ginger taught Cal, me, and the Kimura twins how to make popcorn balls with Karo corn syrup. Ginger let me wear one of her baby-blue baby dolls to sleep when I showed up with my mother's old muumuu for a nightgown. She told us about wintertime in Kenosha, Wisconsin, and black ice. We prayed before and after the movie. She nicknamed me Jenny 'cause her best friend in Kenosha was Jenny Williams. Ginger said, "Hey, Jenny, you and me, let's go to the mall after Youth Choir next Saturday, okay? You, me, and Cal, how 'bout it?" Mrs. Geiger smiled on and nodded gently.

The next Saturday, after Youth Choir, Ginger, me, and Cal walked to Poi Kakugawa Store to catch the sampan bus downtown, when all of a sudden, Levi Nalani pulled up in his blue Mustang.

"Eh, Ginga Grant," he said. "We go for one cruise down Banyan Drive. Just you and the boiz."

Ginger leaning into the window right over Kenneth Spencer's face. Climbing in the backseat with Baron Ahuna. Laughing. All of this without once looking back at Cal and me sitting on the sidewalk of Poi Kakugawa Store.

She never said much to me and my sister after that Saturday at Youth Choir but always walked with us to the store, Mrs. Geiger smiling and nodding as we left the parking lot of the church.

One time, I heard her tell Levi Nalani that since she was Ginger Grant, that made me Lovey Howell and my sister, Gilligan. She never looked at the Kimura twins except to roll her eyes or blow a gum bubble at them. Never had the scared haole look or braided ponytails. Kept her eyes on the street outside the church.

* * *

My father says, "Out there in that great big world, and believe me, when I was in the navy, I seen the world two times over and all the people in the world two times over too, and, Lovey, I telling you, got one in a hundred haoles, just one, worth being call your friend.

"Look at me. I got any haole friends? Just one. Wilcox. But the bugga half Chinese, so no really count to me. One in a hundred, just one. And if I was you, I wouldn't even bother to look."

*   *   *

Lori Shigemura's Slam Book: #7
   7. HOME-OF-THE-FUTURE: Akron, Ohio, or Boise, Idaho
   7. WEDDING COLORS: Salmon, champagne, and eggshell white

*   *   *

   Scott Yamasaki
   Dennis Kawano
   Ricky Morioka
   Vincent Takeyama
They walk alike, talk alike, sit alike. They hate fags, hate girls taller than five feet, hate silliness or laughing too much. They play basketball, but don't go out for the school team, or do go out, and get cut.
   And the girls always gotta say, "Oh, Scott looks like the Japanese Charles Bronson or Vincent looks like the Japanese Neil Diamond." With the haoles, you say, "Oh, Andy *looks* like Jan-Michael Vincent," and that's that—'cause he really does.
   Winston Wang
   Carleton See
   Kent Wong
   Tareyton Tong
All the Chinese boys have names straight from the cigarette machine. I don't know why a mother would want her son named after nicotine. And they have such large gums. Lots of nice plates and elephant statues in their house.

*   *   *

Blond hair. Good. Betty Cooper and Marcia Brady. Barbie and Twiggy. Peggy Lipton and Elizabeth Montgomery. Debbie Reynolds, Doris Day, and all the Gidgets except for Sally Field and look what happened to her. Forced to be a flying nun in Puerto Rico. Want to fall in love with Alejandro Rey, but cannot.
   Black hair. Evil. Veronica Lodge. Alexandra Cabot. Serena, Samantha Stevens' cousin, Big Ethel, Nancy Kwan, and all the evil stepmothers in Walt Disney movies. Miss Mims from *Thoroughly Modern Millie*.
   Just better to be haole. Live in Riverdale. Be Vicky or Jenny. Talk straight to the mainland Japanee cousins who say things like "Gee, you talk *funny*. Do

they talk like that at your school? How come you pronounce words so *inarticulately?* My mother says that the relatives who grew up in Hawaii have *difficulty expressing themselves verbally.* Gee, Lovey, does *everybody here* speak so *strangely?*"

Better to have straight blond hair and long Miss America legs and lots of boobs like Ginger Geiger, 'cause, to me, no sense in sending Miss Hawai'i to Atlantic City unless she's haole 'cause she never makes the finals, only Miss Congeniality. She got lots of Aloha Spirit that's why.

I want a great name. Beckenhauser. Allen. Geiger. Smith. Brown. Cooper. Have a father with a great nickname like Richard—Dick. Robert—Bob. James—Jim. A mother with a great nickname like Debra—Debbie. Cynthia—Cindy. Susan—Sue.

Live in a house with Dixie cup dispensers, bunk beds with ruffled sheets, bendable straws, rose-shaped soap, Lysol, and Pez.

And cat potatoes and biscuits. Minute Rice with lots of butter. Baby-doll nighties and popcorn balls. Boyfriends in Mustangs. Porch swings and bougainvillea archways.

I wanna be Lovey Beth Cole. Mrs. Michael Cole. Wanna marry you, Dennis. Be a Cole. Be a haole. A Japanee with a haole last name.

—LOIS-ANN YAMANAKA

Untitled Art by Betty Kung

Assignment

His first job is to guard the Hello Kitty character from Sanrio Toys. She's on her New York leg of a world tour and right away the paparazzi have her centered in their camera lenses. Rumors say she's in love with Barney the purple dinosaur—a Japanese and American, pink and purple inter-racial romance—something out of the pages of the novel *Shogun* or from the opera *Madame Butterfly*. Barney has all the power, has the 60% u.s. market share Hello Kitty needs to warm her way into the hearts of pre-K American boys and girls.

The Secret Asian Man holds back the screaming little fans of Hello Kitty as she emerges from the Soho Grand Hotel on West Broadway. Hundreds of bulbs flash as Barney helps her step into the pink limo. Suddenly, from out of the crowd, a tall man in a Power Rangers suit jumps up to the driver's side, punches the driver out cold, pulls him out of the car, and climbs in to screech away burning rubber.

Hello Kitty screams "Help me! Help me! I'm being kidnapped!" from the window.

The Secret Asian Man looks around, notices Barney hysterically jumping up and down, mumbling "I love her! I love Kitty! Catch them!"

All the children are crying and he realizes this is real, this is not a stunt dreamed up by the toy companies. The Secret Asian Man commandeers a Honda motorcycle from a passing citizen and gives chase to the pink limo. He reaches West Broadway & Canal, spots the car speeding through Chinatown. He's right behind them now but the limo swerves onto the sidewalk smashing into carts of exotic comestibles. Whole roasted Peking ducks are flying everywhere—fresh lychee fruit, bitter melon, dried tiny shrimp, bean sprouts, giant jack fruit, coconuts, and steamed pork buns fall in his path but he skillfully avoids them all.

The Secret Asian Man thinks "That Hong Kong movie director John Woo would love the way I'm dodging all these obstacles." The pink limo swerves back into the street and slams its breaks in front of a passing fish truck. The Secret Asian Man is going too fast and he crashes into the back of the pink limo—the impact sending him flying over the car and into the truck with the sign, LIVE MAINE CRABS.

With his way blocked by the truck, the Power Ranger pulls Hello Kitty out from the pink limo and drags her along Mott Street. The Secret Asian Man climbs out of the water tank inside the truck as large crabs cling to his clothes with their stubborn claws. A group of German tourists point at and take pictures of "das krab man!"

He catches a glimpse of Hello Kitty's red ribbon bobbing in the middle of the shopping crowd and he runs after them. He gets within five feet of the target near Mott & Grand, pulls out his automatic pistol and shouts "freeze!" (a phrase he remembers Jack Lord saying in his favorite TV show as a kid growing up in the 70's, *Hawaii Five-O).*

The Power Ranger shoves Hello Kitty toward the Secret Asian Man and in that moment of distraction, kicks the gun out of his hands and turns to deliver a round house kick to the head with his other foot. The Secret Asian Man is stunned and he realizes that this is not one of the redone American Power Rangers played by American teenagers. This guy is an original player and dangerous!

From out of the gathering crowd, Hello Kitty runs up and pounces on the leg of the Power Ranger, clawing his calf. This gives the Secret Asian Man enough time to launch a high kick to the Power Ranger's head and knock him senseless into the ground. The crowd of shoppers clap as if they had just watched a scene from an action movie and the good guy had just won. The Secret Asian Man bows, takes his shiny handcuffs, places them on the kidnapper's wrists.

—NICK CARBÓ

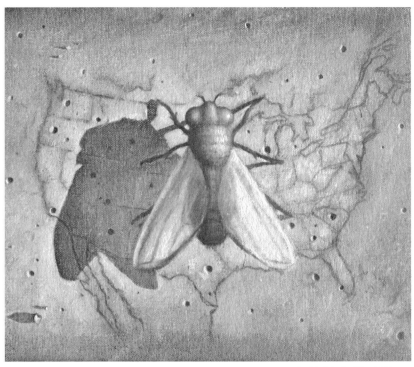

Untitled Art by Hiroshi Kimura

HELLO KITTY

A Double Sestina

You probably have never seen Mimi,
Hello Kitty's sister. Her bow is yellow
and on the opposite ear. No lunch box
or pencil case. She graces no backpack or slippers.
Mimi is a Japanese body double,
doing Hello's stunts, or the dark orphan in *Poor
Little Rich Girl* who brings Shirley Temple
coal for her fire, who calls Shirley "ma'am"
even though she's taller. Hello prefers
My Melody whose rabbit ears are the same red
as Kitty's bow. Or Keroppi the frog
with his big grin and own ice cream cone.

My impulse is to feel bad for poor
Mimi, to see her poised at the top of a cone
of a volcano that spews double
the lava of any in ancient Greece. Leapfrog-
ging balls of fire chase Mimi who slips
like a sacrificial kitty-virgin, red
flames singeing her mythic gown, shadowbox-
ing Japanese cartoon land. I always prefer
the odd girl out—redhead Midge over yellow-
haired Barbie. Fashion dolls have smaller mam-
mary glands in Tokyo which suits Mimi
just fine though she doesn't worship at the temple

of Mattel. She's made by Sanrio, a toy world devoid of red
high heels, keeping Mimi innocent, her tempo
more nursery rhyme than disco. Kitty slips her
information on the side, the "do re mi's,"
the basics of sex education. Mimi thinks frogs
look an awful lot like testicles, mammoth
green hills rising out of the ground, double
ribbits that cause her ears to twitch her yellow
ribbon. She avoids Keroppi and his obscene cone.
Pekkle and Pippo and Pochacco prefer
the gender-less life, wholesome and pure,
avoiding labels, Jacks or Jills-in-the-box—

a duck, a pig, an unidentified mammal
respectively. Whenever I have a Japanese box
lunch, I think, "How neat"—the pink curling ginger, the frog
green wasabi, the hot saki poured
into small cups. An American jazz singer told me
she's a staple of Japanese nightlife. She prefers
playing Tokyo because there male fans slip her
love notes and teenagers mob her, convinced
she's more talented than Stone Temple
Pilot. The problem is the prices—yellow
bananas cost three American dollars each, red
apples four. "You're crazy to write a double

sestina about Hello Kitty!" she says, preferring
that I stick to u.s. pop culture—double
dutch jump rope songs, hula hoops, frisbees, and Jimmy
Dean sausage. The singer doesn't think I've read
enough to know Japanese ways, Hello a poor
substitute for studying Hiroshima. Yellow
light floods the New York City street. The singer has a frog
in her throat, the flu. I kiss her temples.
She tells me she'll leave tickets in my name at the box
office, sure she's as popular here as a snow cone
in winter. Her taxi driver says, "Where to, ma'am?"
I tell my friend to get home to her fuzzy slippers.

I still love Shirley Temple's yellow
curls, the way her tap dancing slippers
sparkle through Sunday afternoon movies—poor
substitute, it's true, for studying black mammies
and their economic implications in the red
clay South. In one film, Shirley sits on Lincoln's lap, convincing him slavery is wrong. "Listen to me!"
is the beat that her feet make. She holds a box
of her father's letters, sure his double—
not he—has been shot in the Civil War. Temple
grows up to be Shirley Temple Black and prefers
Republicans, Lincoln her first prince-sprung-from-a-frog.

At least that's what some Japanese poet might con-
clude—one who's interested in the way frogs
splash into the pond of politics. This article I read

said, sure, the Japanese work ethic prefers
those who put in long days, but men
often play computer games, temporary
diversions, the last few work hours, the pure
delight of goofing off. Hello and her double
Mimi cartwheel onto PC screens, slipping
through mazes, a labyrinth of boxes—
Spottie Dottie's bark and Pekkle's yellow
quacking bill—the kittens silently teasing, "Catch me!"

The first time I saw Hello Kitty, the temptress,
was in 1982. She seduced me
from my Japanese roommate's notebook, managing to get me to rush out and buy a yellow
and pink Hello Kitty wallet. I preferred
her right away to Minnie Mouse who wore a boxy
red polka dot dress and way-too-big red
pumps. Hello wore a jumper slipped
over bare arms. It was a new wave frock,
no doubt about it. Even her double
set of whiskers seemed trendy, even her cone-
shaped ears exuded cool. Even her poor

excuse of a nose (a yellow button boxed
in a black circle) was fabulousness, pure
girl-fun. Chinatown became the preferred
shopping mall of twenty-somethings concerned
with Hello Kitty fashion. A yellow
daisy sometimes graced Hello's bodice so she doubled
as a 60's peacenik, a mammoth
yet miniscule symbol, a kitsch-princess who stayed frog
free. "You're putting way too much on me,"
Hello Kitty might say, if she could slip
out of feline city. "Try another temple,"
she might meow, her tiny voice raw and red.

But Hello doesn't have lips, those double
delicious pink worms that girls paint red
for special occasions. She can't yell
if she's in trouble or kiss Mimi on her temple.
Without a mouth, Kitty's not able to confess
her secrets. But dissecting Hello is slippery

business. Feminists surely prefer
girls who are able to make noise, like me.
But who knows? Monks might find Hello pure
Zen, the way she smiles without teeth, going to and fro
with Kitty purposefulness—content on pencil boxes
and purses, holding her world together, man-

aging to keep perfectly still. No slip
of the tongue possible. Hello is manufactured in China, but she was con-
ceived and born in London, much like a box
of Cadbury chocolates. Post-Shirley Temple,
Hello is a whole industry, frothy
and competitive as shampoo or beer. A yeoman
for Sanrio, Hello hides her poor
relation, her sister Mimi who owns no red,
nothing the color of British royalty. Mimi
doesn't believe in showing off. Even red double
decker buses scare her. She prefers

yellow, the color of egg yokes, color of fading frogs.
And appropriation? That jazz singer would prefer
if poets stuck to their own cultures—temples
and garbage heaps galore—while the world spins double
time. Hello Kitty, Goodbye Columbus!
Hello's British-born Japanese, but female like me.
Should only Asian kittens who live in England consider the complexities of the red-
bowed wonder? Should American poets only manufacture Donald Duck sonnets, pouring
their angst into Scooby Doo who slips
into his owner's jalopy, panting and yelping?

Maybe Mimi's yellow bow means nothing.
Maybe Hello slipped into favor by pure
box office popularity. Maybe double
kitties were always too much. Only one Shirley Temple managed to win our red hearts. That preferential
con-girl princess of the Depression,
kissing Presidents and slaves instead of frogs.

—DENISE DUHAMEL

Sumo-esque

Are you cursed?
You think you're cursed,
creeping into Noho

like a Sumo wrestler with no sushi.
Only fantasy can save you.
The plot unravels, and the dahlias

are demandingly blase, also.
"Upsilon, upsilon,"
they moan.

The mountain looks cold
yet the kids eat their breakfasts,
infinite harm will not touch them. . . .

We tread paradise
like freelance hairdressers
dabbling in mosaic, building classic sewers.

A Nicobar Pigeon chick
has recently left the nest,
and an uncaring parent

plunders all the stray feathers.
The *Pauxi-pauxi* bird
wears his accustomed helmet,

sways morosely from a tulip,
avoids the social apparatus.
Japanese subtitles suggest,

Cancel all, cancel everything
and range the old world
with chilled fingertips.

Slip and crave, baby,
crave and slip.
And I'm doing it . . .

Stuck by chance in Portland in a panic,
I'll watch a patriarch jump rope
while flames engulf his tapping feet

and apparently some shellfish
scamper up his elite sash,
spotted, liverish.

Such are our ancestors,
the Buddhist baldies flouncing
around a newish Northwest gallery

since besotted by Monet
and the cinema. Carson McCullers
and Mishima

are long forgotten,
David Remnick is in.
But are the hairless daddies

always so fat and restless?
Betraying the line of monarch-wrestlers
with jowls worthy of Jesus,

this old ace looks like he's jivin'.
Remiss, alas,
my last tentacle skids,

and wisdom is no more again.
I guess we're all Sumo-esque
supplicants with short fuses.

—MOLLY McQUADE

A blue boy in a Picasso Painting

"I'm colored with the color of dusk"—Mirabai

The boy's blueness disturbs you,
but I descend from a land where people
are painted various shades. With black
hair and elongated face, the boy
is a reformed Krishna, the blue
a deeper tone, a hue of maturity.
The boy who once stole butter from all the pretty ladies
has settled down, his partner
a woman red in happiness.

Watch the way they work
in their separate spheres,
but converge in night's nearness
to paint the dusk an impassioned purple.

—PURVI SHAH

GRIDLOCK

jackie chan fights
off the bad
guys while
juggling a qing
vase *can he*
save the little
girl and a thousand
years of his culture
at the same time?

you're hanging
out with mike
and cindy
at the cineplex
an excuse to pig
out on fried
cheese and root
beer floats without
their parents see
a pg-13 when
they're only twelve

a huge white
guy plops
in front of you so
you can't read
the subtitles
but cindy
nudges
you every five
minutes
i can understand
what they're saying!

chalk one up
for jackie *it's cool*
to be chinese

so what if chris
tucker shucks
and jives

his way
through scene
after scene and no asian
americans always
the guy from china who gets
in trouble trying
to be down with black
people the waitresses
with their china
doll haircuts and red
cheongsams

this is too much fun!

the consul's precocious
daughter kicks the evil
kidnapper in the gut slings
her necklace at him   the jade
pendant slashes his face

teaches girls
how to be assertive no
lotus blossoms here

turns out the blond
haired chinese
guy's working
for a british antique
smuggler

anti imperialist subtext
it's okay to laugh take
your kids to this movie

jackie kicks the bad
guy's ass sets the vase
back on its rosewood
stand in the next
shot a stray
bullet smashes
it into a thousand pieces

—LORI TSANG

SCREAMING MONKEYS

The Rules of the Game

On Dad's nights to care for me—when it was necessary for me to be taken care of—he corralled me into his silver pick-up truck and drove us to Tito Ned's burrow of a house on East 14th Street for mah-jongg nights with his padres from the factory.

Tito Ned, Tita Cyntia and their son Claro, lived in a weather-beaten house with rickety windows on the south side of Des Moines. Their house had three rooms, the largest a bedroom that greeted you as you entered the front door. A king-size bed (always unmade) was directly to the left, and through sheen, velvety curtains a half bathroom (stand-up shower but no tub) contained a yellowing porcelain sink forever stacked with dishes. Did they have a stove, an oven, a place to hoard ice-cream and frozen lumpia? They must have: Tita Cyntia always offered me purple ube, which I accepted despite my mother's previous entreaties.

An adjoining room in the rear of the house functioned as both Claro's room and the rec room. Here, atop a spindly card table, our fathers and their mah-jongg partners wagered paupers' bets and traded stories in boisterous voices. And it was here, beneath the pounding hail storm of ivory tiles that Claro and I experimented and played, innocent games and others.

Pong! was my father's battle cry. His padres, who had welcomed him to their ritual with open arms, rarely lifted a brow when he cried wolf. Dad was a dependable loser, second only to Harry Ederle, their supervisor at the brassiere factory and next-door neighbor. Dad wagered poorly, cheated, threw valuable tiles containing sticks or flowers to his opponents—the same tiles that separated him from a win. At times I wondered if he understood the rules of the game at all.

When Claro would ask why my tatay always lost, I told him it was Dad's way of winning the enemy's trust.

Beneath my father's false cries and the thunder of tiles on the padded ceiling of the table, Claro and I studied the gamblers from their waists down. Tito Jerry, a small, meticulous man who wore eyeglasses, had two pairs of trousers: the baby blue checkered pair and a starched white one. Dad usually wore Oshkosh overalls and fat Tito Ned, fraying cut-offs or sweatpants. Harry Ederle had brown bell-bottoms that shook with the incessant tapping of his feet.

Their games lasted well into dawn; Tita Cyntia would say her good-nights following the weather report on the evening news and Claro, slinking to her bed, soon after. It was then that the men produced a case of San Miguel beer, or if this wasn't available at Jung's Chinese Food Store, a no-name label on sale at the Git 'N Go. They hid their treasure chest from Tita Cyntia in the shallow snow drift beneath Tito Ned's porch. If I managed to keep my eyes open for the length of the game my father would wrap a lazy arm around my shoulders and let me choose and throw his tiles. There was little strategy in it for him; he simply accepted and discarded whatever was thrown his way.

One evening, Claro and I slouched beneath the card table, arithmetic problems and banana-flavored Wacky Wafers scattered on the shag carpet beneath us.

"Pong!" Harry Ederle cried. "Pong, Pong, Pong!"

Claro had dozed off with his back against Harry's legs and his eyes strangely half-open. His bubble gum hung limply from his mouth.

"You cheat," Tito Ned said, lifting a brown bottle of San Miguel to his lips.

"I won! Finally, I beat you chinks." He called all the Asian men who worked at the factory "chinks."

"Hoy, where did you get that Two of Sticks?" asked Tito Jerry, his neat hands in his lap.

Harry's hands went to his knees, his fingers scratching the lower part of his kneecap. I wondered if he enjoyed the company of these men, why he joined them each Wednesday for their stupid game. If I had the choice, I wasn't sure I'd be here week after week, in the bitter cold of December.

"You calling me a cheat?"

Tito Jerry said, "Two of sticks! Two of sticks! It's been missing from my set for months. You've been hiding it." He reached under the table and grabbed his leather case.

Harry leaned back in his chair and sighed. "For a lousy five bucks? Hell, I could give a piss over you chinks' little game."

Tito Jerry removed a sheath of paper from his mah-jongg case, the pages covered with careful hand-written notes. He selected one sheet with three lines written on it and separated it from the pile. "The list of missing pieces— look here, naman."

"Hoy, Jerry, calm down," my father began, "we know that Harry could not cheat—" but Dad's voice seemed to fade.

My father's dark eyes darted between the other Filipino men. The room was silent, and I heard an animal rattling in the trash can outside. Finally, my father's face broke into a grin.

"We know Harry doesn't have the smarts!"

The three of them erupted in laughter. Harry pushed his chair back from the table and stood. Claro, still leaning against Harry's legs, knocked his head on the floor. I moved to my father's side while Claro wailed.

Our fathers twisted their bodies under the table, spotted Claro rubbing his head, and redoubled their laughter. My sleepy-eyed cousin skulked to Tito Ned's side.

"Harry, sit; we're just pulling your leg." Tito Ned picked Claro up by his armpits, his cheeks lined with tears.

He said to Harry: "Come on, you win this one, sit."

I stretched on my back beneath the table, my head free from the shade of the table. Harry stood directly above me, a hesitant Gulliver, slouching with his hands in the pockets of his brown bell-bottoms. He tapped his feet like an accordion's bellow, puffing light gusts of air on my cheeks. I wiggled across the carpet closer to my father, fearing he'd step on me.

Without a word Harry took his seat. My father reached into his small foam cooler and handed him a San Miguel, calling for them to play. He toppled his tile wall into the center of the table, Tito Jerry following, Tito Ned bringing up the rear. Harry followed hesitantly, his small square tiles falling with the rest in the middle. The stirring of ivory pieces was like a hailstorm. I stared at the underside of the card table and imagined their arms swirling like windmills above me, readying for a new game.

—RICCO VILLANUEAVA SIASOCO

Vogue magazine, Volume 186, No.10, March 1997, pp.418-419.

Vanity Fair's celebrity photo featuring Mike Myers.
Vanity Fair magazine, April 1999, p.347.

"Apu (the convenience store clerk) is a stereo-
type, but he's a very well-rounded character."
—Dan Castellaneta, the voice of Apu
"Wisdom from the Simpsons' 'D'ohh'boy,"
The Daily Northwestern, (Northwestern
University) February 11, 1994.

Summer of Bruce

1974 was not just another year for us in Calcutta. The Railway Strike shook up the ensnarled consensus amongst the elite, several of whom would later support the authoritarian National Emergency (1975-77). It must have been hot and humid, as it is each year. The short Maoist insurgency called Naxalism came and went like a whirlwind. The Communist movement grew apace and would soon come to power in 1977, from whence it won six elections to continue in power till date. Globe Cinema Hall across from the New Market showed Bruce Lee in *Enter the Dragon*.

There was something extraordinary about Bruce Lee (1940-73). He exuded confidence and wisdom at the same time as he entertained us with his fiery Kung Fu. Bruce was the "foreign" version of our own Amitabh Bachchan, the Big B, who that year gave us such classics as *Benaam* and *Roti Kapada aur Makaan*, but who would in the next year star in the greatest Spaghetti Eastern of all time, *Sholay*. As far as those "foreign" heroes came (and "foreign" simply refers to English language films), my friends and I supped on James Bond, with some satisfaction. *Enter the Dragon* was something else. Here was an Asian man who stood his ground against corruption of all forms, who used such weapons as the nanchakus, a device that was to be fashioned across the globe by young people. When we saw the movie in India, we did not as yet know that Bruce Lee was already dead.

That same summer, a song broke through the tedium offered by *Musical Bandbox,* a Sunday afternoon program on All-India Radio. It was a rather trite song, with such memorable lyrics as "Everybody was Kung-Fu fighting, hunh, Those cats were fast as lightning, hunh, In fact it was a little bit frightening, But they fought with expert timing." Nothing to it, really. But Biddu, an exemplary Indian who lived in England and produced Tina Charles's "Disco Fever" and Nazia Hasan's "Disco Dewanee," wrote the song, hence its appearance on Indian radio. The song, I learned later, was sung by an African American, Carl Douglas, whose entire career was forged around the gimmick of Kung Fu music (such as "Dance the Kung Fu" and "Shanghai D"). It belongs in my memory bank alongside an atrocious song for Muhammad Ali with that infectious line from the master, "float like a butterfly, sting like a bee."

Tripping on Carl Douglas and Biddu, we scanned the papers for news of the impending fight between Muhammad Ali and George Foreman in Zaire, the famous "Rumble in the Jungle" in the autumn of that year. "From slave ship to championship," the promoters declaimed. "We were taken from Africa as slaves and now we're coming back as champions." Ali was only 32, a year younger than Bruce. And Ali was as politically incensed about racism and imperialism as Bruce was. If the latter was trained to hate white supremacy in the hovels of Hong Kong, the former was the pugilist of the Black Power movement. It was Ali, after all, who denounced the U.S. imperialist engagement in Southeast Asia with the memorable line, "no Vietcong ever called me nigger." Although Bruce Lee was also a boxing champ in Hong Kong (and the 1958 Crown Colony Cha-Cha Champion), he spent much of the 1960s watching films of Ali boxing. "An orthodox boxer, Ali led with his left hand. Since Bruce was experimenting with a right lead stance he set up a mirror so that he could watch Ali's movements and practice them the appropriate way." In an instance of classic cross-fertilization, the great boxer Sugar Ray Leonard told an interviewer in 1982 that "one of the guys who influenced me wasn't a boxer. I always loved the catlike reflexes and the artistry of Bruce Lee and I wanted to do in boxing what he was able to do in karate. I started watching his movies before he became really popular in *Enter the Dragon* and I patterned myself after a lot of his ways."

I. Polyculturalism (the new PC).

"America is not a land of one race or one class of men. We are all Americans that have toiled and suffered and known oppression and defeat, from the first Indian that offered peace in Manhattan to the last Filipino pea pickers . . . It has fallen upon us to inspire a united front among our people. We must win the backward elements over to our camp; but we must also destroy that which is corrupt among ourselves." So says the narrator's brother, in Carlos Bulosan's 1946 novel, *America Is in the Heart,* this by way of a political program. Indeed, the idea of the USA being more than the patrimony of "one race or one class of men" is central to our exploration of Bruce Lee. The America envisioned by Bruce was not to be restricted to Chinatown, but it was to encompass every nook and cranny of America. To claim America for Bruce was not to seek assimilation into it. On the contrary, as I will try to show, Bruce's practice allowed others to excavate our complex, polycultural history.

Sustained political struggle over the past several decades allowed the theory of assimilation to be somewhat overcome by the theory of multiculturalism. A less culturally tolerant USA was prone to inform its new residents that they must learn to conform to the ways of a certain fantasy core culture. The fact that U.S. culture, like cultures elsewhere, is not homogeneous did not deter the champions of assimilation who exerted power over many newcomers (and some old-timers) to drop cultural practices and adopt others. To protect diversity, radical thinkers produced the notion of cultural relativism. For some time this theory allowed people to partake of their own traditions, but for others relativism allowed the orthodoxy within a cultural tradition to assert its view of things as the way to live. If cultural relativism emerged (in Franz Boas and W.E.B. DuBois) to protect diversity, it was used by some as a weapon against the forces of progress. In the worst rendition of this model, each "culture" (sometimes "race") is seen as discrete, with authentic and pure histories that are now grudgingly accorded some measure of dignity. The anti-racist struggle (which strongly influenced Bruce) fought against the arrogance of white supremacy, but the United States' response to the struggle was simply to adopt the liberal patina of multiculturalism to fend off the challenge. Despite multiculturalism's roots in anti-racism, it now seems to be restricted to the promotion of an ahistorical diversity and the pedagogy of sensitivity.

In the midst of all this, the u.s. arrogates for itself the role of being color-blind so that it may stand apart from the divisiveness of a multicultural society. For many reasons, this is not sufficient. For one, multiculturalism misses the point about our mongrel, mulatto histories. Like colonial science, multiculturalist thought tends to assume that there are pure cultures that are somehow discrete from each other. The Muhammed Ali-Bruce Lee-Sugar Ray Leonard story of cross-fertilization is only one, contemporary instance of this mulatto history. It only seems strange if we take for granted the preconceived boundaries between peoples, if we forget that the notion of "Africa" and "Asia" is very modern and that people have created cross-fertilized histories for millennia without concern for modern geography. The linguistic ties across the Indian Ocean, for example, obviate any attempt to say that Gujarat and Tanzania are disconnected places: Swahili is the ultimate illustration of our mulatto history, or what historian Robin Kelley so nicely calls our polycultural history.

In the context of a discussion on "multi-racial" peoples, Kelley dismisses the idea of the purity of bloodlines and argues that "so-called 'mixed-race' children are not the only ones with a claim to multiple heritages. All of us, and I mean ALL of us, are the inheritors of European, African, Native American, and even Asian pasts, even if we can't exactly trace our bloodlines to all of these continents . . . We are multi-ethnic and polycultural from the get go." There is no pure race, just as there is no pure culture. But to escape from the theory of purity one cannot take refuge in the idea of hybridity (whether biological or cultural), for hybridity (like multiculturalism) assumes the existence of purity. Two pure cultures (or races) form a hybrid. Human beings live whole lives, not lives partitioned into various pure sets of practices ("today a South Asian, tomorrow an African"). Within the framework of one's existence, there are cultural elements whose lineage is far more complex than we sometimes care to admit. And they operate, Kelley suggests, just like polyrhythms in music, many different rhythms operating together to produce a whole song rather than many different drummers doing their own thing.

Take the case of Kung Fu. While many think of it as a distinctly Chinese tradition, the recorded origin of Kung Fu comes when the itinerant South

Indian monk Bodhidharma taught its arts to the people of the Shaolin Temple in the 6th Century. Frustrated by the monks who slept during meditation, Bodhidharma devised a method to keep them physically active and to cultivate their ch'i (life force). Things don't stop there. For some years now Afrocentric scholars (such as Wayne Chandler and Graham Irwin) have written of the African descent of Buddha, from whose cultural descendents Kung Fu arose. In recent years, the intercontinental ties of Kung Fu re-emerged in the idioms of the Wu Tang Clan. The Hip Hop band drew from the 1970s Kung Fu movies, from where it got the name for its first album, *Enter the Wu Tang (36 Chambers),* and also from within the world of the 5% Nation of Islam. The 5% believe, like the NOI, that Black people inherit the earth from the original "Asiatic black man" who is the "cream of the earth and god of the universe." The Wu Tang (and the 5%) argues that much that is now good in the world emanates from the "Asiatic black man." When Kilindi Iyi claims that "it was Africa and not Asia that first gave martial arts to the world," he draws together the two main components of the Wu Tang's heritage into one tradition. Iyi looks at ancient murals from Beni Hasan, Egypt, to make his claim, but he could equally make the point that the similarities between Capoeira Angola and Kung Fu can be traced to those enslaved Africans who created the Brazilian art in the 1500s, nurtured it in the senzalas (the slave houses) and developed it into a symbolic and physical response to the atrocity of a racist slavery. The desire to seek origins in what might be complex cultural diffusion or else independent creation is certainly not of much help (and Iyi is annoyingly unreflective in his essay). However, we might say that the martial arts of Kung Fu developed in a world of virtuoso that involved, in some complex way, Kalarippayattu of Kerala, Capoeira Angola of Brazil and the various martial arts of Africa. Kung Fu is not far from Africa or from the favelas (slums) of Brazil, or indeed from the shogun MCs from Staten Island.

Polyculturalism, then, describes a state of being in which one acknowledges the always already mixed-up heritages one lives within. Cultural worlds collide and, for historical reasons, humans create boundaries over and over to maintain separations that remain porous. The high-point of modern nationalism (and especially cultural nationalism) is to police these "imports," but what cultural nationalists fail to recognize is that people do not live the stereotypes of official cultures. We live within the sorts of complex, polycultural worlds accorded us by our pasts and by our fellows who surround us. That Kung Fu is now part and parcel of Black American culture is an indicator not only of the power of Bruce Lee, but also of the tales of the intertwined histories of Africa and Asia, of African Americans and Asian Americans, of Bruce Lee and Jim Kelly.

II. A Truly Nonwhite Icon.

"In black homes in the '70s it was typical to find a Martin Luther King portrait in the living room while in the basement, next to the component set and the velvet black light Karma Sutra horoscope, hung a poster of Lee, a truly worthy nonwhite icon."

Bruce Lee was a "worthy nonwhite icon" not just because he was not white, but, like Fidel and Ho, he stuck it to the institutions of white supremacy even as he befriended whites. "Mom," Bruce told his mother Grace in 1972, "I'm an Oriental person, therefore, I have to defeat the whites in the film." The reference was to Bruce's *Way of the Dragon* (in the u.s., *Return of the Dragon)* co-star, Chuck Norris, now *Walker: Texas Ranger,* but then a Karate champion and small-time martial arts actor. Norris trained with Bruce, indeed Bruce was one of the first sifus (masters) to train non-Asians. Nevertheless, Bruce felt like he needed to show the world that white power and privilege is not natural, so it can be trounced. Bruce was not anti-white in some simple knee-jerk style, but he was clear about producing Asian (and other non-white, as in Jim Kelly in *Enter the Dragon)* heroes as role models.

For Bruce knew that Hollywood on its own was incapable of being progressive in this regard. When a Canadian journalist said that "Hollywood sure as heck hasn't figured out how to represent the Chinese," Bruce agreed. "You better believe it, man. I mean it's always the pigtail and the bouncing around, chop-chop, you know, with the eyes slanted and all that." In 1971, Bruce was bitter about the film industry's betrayal of him. Touted to play Caine in the television show *Kung Fu* (then called *The Warrior),* Bruce was rejected as "too Chinese." Jim Kelly remembers it like this:

> It was hard as hell for Bruce to become an actor. And the reason why was because he was Chinese. America did not want a Chinese hero, and that's why he left for Hong Kong. He was down and out. He was hurt financially. He told me that he tried to stick it out, but he couldn't get the work he wanted. So he said, "Hey, I'm gone." My understanding, from talking to Bruce, was that the *Kung Fu* series was written for him, and Bruce wanted to do that. But the bottom line was that the networks did not want to project a Chinese guy as the main hero. But Bruce explained to me that he believed that all things happened for a reason. Even though he was very upset about it, he felt that everything would work out. He wasn't going to be denied. I have so much respect for Bruce, because I understand what he went through just by being black in America. He was able to find a way to get around all those problems. He stuck in there, and wouldn't give up. He knew my struggle, and I knew his.

In the early 1970s, every "Oriental" was a "Gook," a Vietnamese guerrilla who was to be distrusted and who was often reviled. While the U.S. bombed Vietnam and the B-2 bombers drowned out the screams of the Vietnamese, Bruce was sure as hell not going to let Asians be called monkeys. During those terrible days, the communist-led West Bengal government renamed the street on which the U.S. and British Consulates had their offices. From now the U.S. and British diplomats would have to sign their names to letterheads that bore the impress, Ho Chi Minh Sarani (street). We did stand proud of our sense of humor. And Bruce would have loved it. As would Ali and other radical Black Americans. Steve Sanders, one of the founders of the Black Karate Federation (BFK, 1968), learned his art as a marine at Okinawa before being shipped off to Southeast Asia. "I didn't enjoy being over there. Anybody who says he did is either a nut who enjoys seeing people killed or a liar. I really don't know why I was there in the first place. I didn't hate the North Vietnamese or the VCs. They looked the same as the South Vietnamese who we were supposed to be helping. How can you like one and hate the other? As far as I'm concerned, those people just want to be left alone to do their own thing."

Bruce's movies hit the screens just as the U.S. ceased its aerial bombardment of Vietnam (between 1964 and 1972, fifteen million tons of explosives fell on Vietnam, more than twice what was expended in World War II in all sectors). As Bruce made his mark on television, Martin Luther King, Jr., stood before a congregation at Riverside Church in New York on April 4, 1967 to break the silence about Vietnam. "We were taking the black young men who had been crippled by our society and sending them eight thousand miles away to guarantee liberties in Southeast Asia which they had not found in southwest Georgia and East Harlem," he said. "If America's soul becomes totally poisoned, part of the autopsy must read Vietnam. It can never be saved so long as it destroys the deepest hopes of men the world over." To speak out against the Vietnam War, to kick it against international corruption—this was what it took to be a worthy non-white icon. And Bruce did it without guns, but with bare feet and fists, and dressed in the black outfits associated with the North Vietnamese army. The Man appeared untouchable to most of the millions of oppressed youth across the world. Fitted with B-52 bombers, Agent Orange, fleets of Destroyers, the industrial powerhouse of the USA seemed impossible to trounce. Each time a people made the attempt, their leaders fell to the technological sophistication of the CIA (Lumumba, 1961; Allende, 1973), an organization whose cultural symbol was James Bond. But Bruce was a match for Bond. As technology stripped hope from the earth's masses, along came a man who could ward off evil with his bare hands. As Big Capital wrenched the reins of history from artisans and peasants, most of them saw technology as the enemy rather than as the puppet of financiers and plutocrats. The machine symbolized both modernity and power, so Bruce's antics with his hands and feet gave everyone a sense that they too could take on the apparent evil of iron and steel. Kung Fu outfits emerged across the globe, from Calcutta to California. This was the iconic power of Kung Fu, one which restored hope to millions of young people, as well as taught them the kind of discipline essential for political work.

In the ghettos of the USA, dojos and Kung Fu schools opened to eager students. The plot of Jim Kelly's *Black Belt Jones* (1974) revolves around one such school located in prime real estate in an area of south-central Los Angeles that is ready to be gentrified. Intelligent legwork from the Black martial arts experts undercuts the Mafia and the City Machine to save the school for the future of Black youth. Cliff Stewart's dojo at 10223 South Western Avenue in Los Angeles in the late 1960s was not unlike the dojo in *Black Belt Jones*. Stewart, a founder of the BFK, set up the dojo for "the kids in our neighborhood. Most of them couldn't afford to travel to dojos in other parts of the city," and nor could they afford the accoutrements for most sports (except hoops). Karate requires no fancy equipment, just a small space, bare feet and naked hands.

What appealed to many young people was the "simplicity, directness and nonclassical instruction" of Kung Fu. "Ninety percent of Oriental self-defense is baloney," Bruce said, "it's organized despair." Kung Fu, in Bruce's vision, revoked the habit of hierarchy that swept up most institutions. Frustrated with what his student Leo Fong called "chop suey masters" who created an art for recompense, Bruce was eager to develop his Kung Fu (in the Wing Chung style, which he called Jeet Kune Do) against the style of his fellow teachers who "are lazy. They have big fat guts. They talk about ch'i power and things they can do, but don't believe in." Instead Bruce used weights and drank high-protein weight-gain drinks (blended with ginseng, royal jelly and vitamins). His virtuoso approach to perfection (and culture) came across in his delicate fierceness on the screen. If the sifu rejected the authority that came with the sifu's position and instead fought for authority based on skill, then this was itself a rejection of the hierarchy of tradition. Bruce did not claim his power from his inherited Kung Fu lineage (his teacher Yip Man, was master of the "sticking hands" method of Wing Chung), but he wanted others to bow to his street-fighting prowess. When asked if he was a black belt, Bruce was forthright. "I don't have any belt whatsoever. That is just a certificate. Unless you can really do it—that is, defend yourself successfully in a fight—that belt doesn't mean anything. I think it might be useful to hold your pants up, but that's about it." Anyone with dedicated tutelage can be a master, can be a sifu.

The notion that "anyone" can do it was powerful, and it became the basis for the turn of many working-class youth to the martial arts. The youth in the ghetto took refuge, said Steve Sanders, in "pills and pot for a long time. Some were stealing to keep up their habits. So I made a deal with them. I told them if they kept away from drugs, they could come to my classes and train for nothing." Many came. Kung Fu gives oppressed young people an immense sense of personal worth and the skills for collective struggle. Kung Fu, Bruce pointed out in his sociology of the art, "serves to cultivate the mind, to promote health, and to provide a most efficient means of self-protection against any attacks. It 'develops confidence, humility, coordination, adaptability and respect toward others.'"[23] Words like "respect" and "confidence" jump out at me immediately, for one (in the USA) hears the former from working class youth and the latter from their hard working, but beleaguered teachers. The youth live within a calculus of respect and disrespect, wanting the former, but alert to challenge the latter. Their teachers want them to be confident. Kung Fu allows for both and don't the kids know it. They are there on the weekends, for no "credit." And they fight not just for anything, but for righteousness.

III. Bruce Leroy.

"I wanted to be Jim Kelly. Sure I wanted to be Bruce Lee too, but I wasn't Chinese and that seemed like an obstacle that I wouldn't be overcoming anytime soon. I promptly began growing my hair into an afro. 'Man, you come right outta some comic book' became my catch phrase. And once Halloween rolled around, I slipped into yellow pajamas, pencilled in some sideburns, and I hit the trick-or-treat trail decked out as my main man." In 1985, an all-Black outfit produced *The Last Dragon,* a reflection on Kung Fu in the 'hood. Sho'Nuff, the Shogun of Harlem, is out to gain total control of that beloved center of Black American life. The noble Leroy Green, known as Bruce Leroy thwarts his bid for domination. The Bruce of the 'hood, Leroy uses his inner strength to vanquish his enemy even when he seems to be threatened with destruction (as in the abandoned warehouse fight). Bruce Leroy's fight and this classic of Black Martial Arts films was not unknown on the streets of Harlem. In the 1970s, for instance, Fred Hamilton organized All-Dojo Karate Championships at places like the Manhattan Center (34th and 8th) or at the Fordham University Gymnasium (Bronx), where, for a few dollars, entire families could sit and watch the Black Belts demonstrate their rough poetry in motion. Furthermore, most young African Americans knew of the deeds of the BFK (and its great founders, Steve Sanders, Jerry Smith, Cliff Steward and Don Williams), of Bruce's protégé Greg Baines, of the judo champion Jesse Glover, of Kareem Abdul Jabbar (whose fight scene with Bruce in the 1978 release of *The Game of Death* is unforgettable), as well as Jim Kelly.

Born in Paris, Kentucky in 1946, Kelly came to Kung Fu through Karate, and by the 1970s Kelly cemented his place among the top rank of martial artists at Ed Parker's famous tournaments (where Bruce first did an exhibition in 1964). Kelly's skills impressed Bruce Lee when they worked together on *Enter the Dragon*. The soul that Kelly put into his ch'i impressed Bruce, who let the African American martial artist choreograph his own fights (this unlike others who made martial arts entirely mechanical if they were not supervised). The thing about "soul" was central to Kelly, whose mix of pleasure and skill enthused young aficionados in his day, as Michael Jordan did to young people in his time. Consider the famous act of bravado from Kelly (as Williams) in *Enter the Dragon*. When Han asks Kelly (Williams) about his fear of defeat, Kelly responds that "I don't waste my time. When it comes, I won't even notice. I'll be too busy lookin' good." You can imagine entire sections of the theatre breaking into spontaneous applause.

The bare fisted bravado was not just used for martial arts tournaments, but mainly, in the films to smash unjust power-lords. When a white supremacist organization plans to poison African Americans through the water supply, Kelly is onto them (*Three the Hard Way*, 1974). As Black Belt Jones, Kelly takes on the Mob and corrupt city government (*Black Belt Jones*, 1974) and a corrupt wing of the US military (*Hot Potato*, 1976). In *Black Samurai* (1977), Kelly as Bond (*Goldfinger*, 1964) infiltrates a secret island get-away of a crime syndicate to rescue his girlfriend. This is the world of *Cotton Comes to Harlem* (1970, for which Ossie Davis made his directorial debut), *Shaft* (1971), *Sweetback's Baadasssss Song* (1971), directed by the incomparable Melvin Van Pebbles, whose son Mario gave us *New Jack City* twenty years later), *Superfly* (1972), *Coffy* (1973) and *Foxy Brown* (1974). Lots of heavy films, for a heavy time.

Kelly's films, framed as they were by both the Kung Fu movies and by the new Black cinema, could not succumb to the same sort of unreconstructed sexism as Bruce articulated. Although he trained women, Bruce was consistent in his attitude that "women fighters? They are all right, but they are no match for the men who are physiologically stronger, except for a few vulnerable points. My advice is that if they have to fight, hit the man at his vital points and then run. Women are more likely to achieve their objectives thorough feminine wiles and persuasion." You can imagine what Pauline Short thought of these words. Called the "mother of American Karate," Short opened her first Karate school in Portland (Oregon) in 1965 which catered entirely to women. Even if Kelly was a MCP, there was no way his movies could not be in dialogue with the movies of Pam Grier and Tamara Dobson. Cedric Robinson argues that the Black cinema of the 1970s misrepresents the Black liberation struggle. The image of the political feminist and communist Angela Davis was reduced, he suggests, to the sexy body of Pam Grier. Grier was not as one-dimensional as that. She transformed the image of the Black woman from mammy (as with Hattie McDaniel in *Gone with the Wind*, 1939) and from lifelessly tragic (as with Lena Horne in *Stormy Weather*, 1943) to tough, street-wise and full of beans. But, yes, Robinson is right that the Black woman was, in Pam Grier especially, the epitome of uncontrolled sexuality ("she's black and she's stacked," as in *Coffy*). This is despite the ghetto-fights-back-and-wins story line. In the world of Black Kung Fu, however, there was less exploitation and more (feminist and anti-racist) liberation. Take *Cleopatra Jones* (1973) with Tamara Dobson as a secret agent who can kick ass and look good too. Cleo does not flail around or resort to a gun, but she reserves her energy to trounce her enemy with Kung Fu skill. Or else, take *Black Belt Jones*. Gloria Hendry who plays Sidney is a sifu in her own right. When Jones (Kelly) gets a message that the bad guys are on the move, he gets ready to leave Sidney to do the dishes as he goes off to do combat. Sidney, incensed by his sexism, borrows his gun and "does" the dishes with a round of well-aimed fire. This is the film of Black Liberation and Kelly was all over it.

IV. Jeet Kune Flow.

"[Bruce Lee's] achievements, to be Asian and to overcome all the adversity in Hollywood. And to be the first to teach non-Asians Martial Arts and to be the first big Asian actor, that right there is enough to tell me that you should be able to believe in yourself to be able to climb the highest mountain. Or just go against whatever is thrown your way. You should be able to look at adversity in its face and believe in yourself to get what you want. And that's what Bruce Lee ultimately taught me: What I do with my MCing skills is sort of like what he did with his Martial Arts. You study everybody's techniques and you strip away what you don't find necessary and use what is necessary and you modify it. You give it your own twist. He used Jeet Kune Do. Mine is Jeet Kune Flow."

Q-Unique from The Arsonists is not alone as he raps about the links between Kung Fu and Hip Hop. In the old school, Grandmaster Flash and the Furious Five took their names from the idioms of Kung Fu movies. The new school is full of more overt Kung Fu symbols, as well as the reflections of a Kung Fu philosophy amongst young rappers (as in the Jeet Kune Flow of Q-Unique, or else of the Wu Tang Clan crew). Or else it is in the pure humor of the Fugees with their Afro-Chinese interlude in *The Score* (1996), and of the funny, but ultra-commodified Tae-Bo of Billy Blanks. Since the idea of polyculturalism begins to complicate a discussion on "multiraciality," it is fitting to recognize the nods to a complex (Afro-Filipino) heritage from Foxy Brown (*Chyna Doll*, 1999). Jon Jang Sextet's use of Charles Mingus' "Meditation on Integration" (*Two Flowers on a Stem*, 1996) offered a sotto voce nod to Mingus's Afro-Chinese ancestry. Then there is the undigested vocals of Nas, telling us that he is "like the Afro-Centric Asian, Half man, half amazin" and that "I exhale the yellow smoke of Buddha through righteous steps" ("Ain't Hard to Tell" in *Illmatic*, 1994). Finally, still in the world of popular culture, we have the Afro-Asian pairs on television (Sammo Hung and Arsenio Hall in *Martial Law)* and on the big screen (Jackie Chan and Chris Tucker in the 1998 *Rush Hour)*. On the progressive side of the ledger, The Coup's 1993 "Dig It" restored Mao to his pantheonic position within Black Radicalism.

There are no massive implications to be drawn from all this, except to say that the polycultural view of the world exists in the gut instincts of many people. Scholars are under some obligation to raise this instinct to philosophy, to use this instinct to criticize the diversity model of multiculturalism and replace it with the anti-racist one of polyculturalism. Culture cannot be bounded and people cannot be asked to respect "culture" as if it were a thing that is without history and complexity. Social interaction and struggle produces cultural worlds and these are in constant formation. Our cultures are linked in more ways than one could catalogue, and it is from these linkages that one hopes our politics will be energized. To remember Bruce as I do, staring at a poster of him c. 1974, is not to wane into nostalgia for the past. My Bruce is alive, alongside all the contemporary icons of polycultural strife.

—VIJAY PRASHAD, JANUARY 2000

Untitled Art by Saiman Chow

SCREAMING MONKEYS

Ancient Chinese Secrets
and Little White Lies

"Tell all the Truth but tell it slant."
—Emily Dickinson

My first lesson in "slanting" the truth, Asian American-style, came from a TV commercial for laundry detergent. You know the one: The customers of a Chinese laundromat ask the couple that runs it, "How ever do you get these clothes so white?" Keeping the box of amazing American detergent well-hidden, they reply, "ancient Chinese secret," laughing to themselves at how easy it is to fool Whitey. This is a time-honored strategy practiced in many marginalized communities, where it is well-known that a little dishonesty can be the best policy for ensuring social harmony (or at least for selling things). Of course, the real secret behind such little white lies is that the truth is subjective; even when they know better, people see and hear only what they want to.

My father has his own favorite joke about the subversive possibilities of whitewashing the truth: A Chinese professor (just like my dad) is attending a banquet, and the kindly matron seated next to him leans over to inquire, "Likee soupee?" The man smiles and nods politely. Then it is time for him, the keynote speaker, to address the audience, which he does in eloquent, flawless English. When he takes his seat again, he asks his neighbor, "Likee speechee?"

Now, telling the woman he spoke English earlier might have been more honest, but it wouldn't have been funny. For the sake of a joke—and our own mental health—we can forgive, and even celebrate, a tiny fib. I haven't come across many ads or jokes like these, where Asians have the last laugh in gentle yet pointed clashes of cultures. Always, it is the Asian who assimilates, who must explain his or her presence and professionalism, who must earn the right to exist and speak, who must prove his or her authority and credibility. This burden of proof is constant, heavy, and tiresome.

Asians in America are so often automatically assumed to be recent immigrants, non-English speakers, exotic, and/or threatening, regardless of the actual truth, that we might as well be what we are perceived to be. If we harbor any individuality beneath our collectively yellow skin, it remains invisible to the outside world. This common oppression should be the basis of sympathy and solidarity, yet it often inspires the opposite: superhuman attempts to differentiate ourselves—the good, assimilated, upwardly mobile Asians—from those undesirable and unruly Others. Such protestations, far from eradicating prejudice, only become another form of the exception proving the rule.

Even if we are able to negotiate two cultures successfully, our very facility with American ways in itself becomes justification for leaving our foreign ways behind. There can be no conceivable excuse for speaking Chinese when you know English, for example. In fact, doing so puts us under immediate suspicion, as my mother discovered one day while talking with friends at the mall, where a white woman standing nearby demanded to know what they were saying about her. On such occasions, familiar to so many of us, we learn that it may be better not to say anything, for the truth (that we have better things to talk about) is even more offensive.

If our unfamiliar ways are to be distrusted and feared, then, if we ourselves are to be silenced, who can blame us for keeping what we know to ourselves even more, so that we truly become the inscrutable race we are accused of being? Secrets, we know from experience, are often the key to self-preservation.

* * *

My parents immigrated to the United States from Taiwan in the 1960s and soon found themselves plopped in the middle of the white-bread Midwest, surrounded by fiercely patriotic, staunchly conservative folks proud of their shared heritage and values. Soon, my parents were faced with the conundrum of raising two young daughters in the heartland of the u.s., where the disjunctions between Asian and American cultures can be surreal. Driving downtown, we would pass the Wishee Washee laundromat, whose name I found delightful at six years of age—it had that same sing-song rhythm of "eeney meeney." (What is it that makes people want to add the diminutive "ee" to words to make them sound Chinese, anyway?) I would sing it over and over in the back seat until my father couldn't stand it anymore. Didn't I know they were making fun of us, invoking the popular stereotype of Chinese laundries to sell their services? Didn't I know that since the days of the Wild West Chinese coolies had been forcibly relegated to this devalued chore? Every time my father saw that laundry it was like a slap in the face. This was a hidden history I hadn't yet learned about in school, one obscured by an innocent-sounding name that denied knowledge of its own shameful origins. And yet my father didn't want to make waves, wasn't interested in complaining to anyone or staging a boycott. This affront we would keep to ourselves. We had our own washer and dryer in the basement, after all.

But eventually, in addition to the pseudo-Chinese laundromats, there were other routine disgraces, ones most Asians in America have shared in some form: the local "Happy Cab" taxis with pictures of rickshaw carriers (complete with pointed hats and pigtails) emblazoned on their sides, the constant questions of "Where do you come from?" and the more hostile looks and slurs that intruded on our meticulously inconspicuous lives. My father graded exams that bore personal messages: "JAP." My sister and I were at least more accurately derided as "chinks" in school. Still, we tried to shrug off these occasional bursts of animosity in an effort to just get along. Luckily for us, it never came to sticks and stones.

As I got older, more "unwelcome signs" came in the form of seemingly well-intentioned comments made to my face: White strangers accosted me in public places to show me photos of their adopted Korean grandchildren, certain that we were kindred souls. Old white women, customers in the department store where I worked, approached me to make backhanded compliments about "Oriental girls" ("You Oriental girls are so pretty. I always worried about my husband during the war, surrounded by all those Oriental girls.") In the face of astounding ignorance and audacious spite, my parents taught us to bide our time. Someday we would prove our merit; we just needed to develop our resources: higher education, financial security, and the fine art of expedient dissembling.

This is the lesson passed on in many immigrant families: don't air dirty laundry, don't let on what you know. It is a lesson explored with devastating clarity in Maxine Hong Kingston's groundbreaking autobiographical novel *The Woman Warrior: Memoirs of a Girlhood Among Ghosts,*[1] a book that haunts me not only because its resonant words have staying power, but also because I see it everywhere hailed as an artifact of Chinese culture, a key to unlocking the mysteries of our race. Indeed, it has attained the status of truth in many multicultural circles, even as it questions the very reliability of the stories we tell and the reality we live. The irony of this disjunction leaves a bitter taste. But in its poignant yet playful manipulation of exotic fantasy and familiar, true-to-life episodes of discrimination, the book has much to say about how outsiders learn to master two ways of life: know when to mask the truth; know when to use it to advantage.

My mother was the only one among my family members who genuinely refused to view prejudiced people as largely a lost cause when I was growing up. Instead, she practically embraced the ignorance of others; she tirelessly rose to the challenge of transforming individual consciousness and turned every encounter into an opportunity to educate people about her culture. When diversity and multiculturalism finally became acceptable—even required—topics of discussion in the community, her status as a rare Chinese woman professional transformed her overnight from a curiosity into an unofficial cultural ambassador. The topic she was most in demand to discuss: *The Woman Warrior.*

In that book, Kingston writes, "Chinese Americans, when you try to understand what things in you are Chinese, how do you separate what is peculiar to childhood, to poverty, insanities, one family, your mother who marked your growing with stories, from what is Chinese? What is Chinese tradition and what is the movies?" My mother was called upon numerous times precisely to make that distinction for non-Chinese readers, reducing the book's complexity—and the complexity of Chinese American experiences—to a True/False test. Once, when I chided her for going along with the charade and lending the authority of her race and gender to a book that questions such essential concepts, she replied, "At least people are curious. That's a big step forward. When you were little, people only wanted to see how we use chopsticks." She is right, of course; before you can run, you must walk, and before you learn to question how even the "truth" may be a lie, you must get your facts straight. (And yet, no one seems interested in researching the facts for themselves. Now that Disney has reincarnated the woman warrior in the animated film *Mulan,* a whole new generation of Americans can confirm that Chinese people do eat with chopsticks, but how much do they really know about the history of the Hans and the Huns?)

Even in the heartland of America, things do change, slowly. Today, government refugee relocation programs and church benevolent associations have brought a growing population of Southeast Asians to my hometown, along with immigrants from the Middle East and Eastern Europe. Agricultural institutes and exchange programs have long sent international students from around the developing world to study there, at the same time providing a stable customer base for ethnic restaurants and grocery stores. With these changing demographics come both blessings and outrages. My mother appreciates the fact that she can get fresh tofu now—while my father was incensed by recent calls for mandatory English language tests for all foreign-born professors ("likee speechee?" I'm sure he was dying to ask someone). While the culture clashes we witness today have changed on the surface, they show how much further we have to go.

* * *

I recently heard a trendwatcher on a national radio talk show proclaim that these days, "anything Asian is cool." Apparently Asian clothes, Asian food, and Asian movies are all the rage. For those not already in the know, the trend has naturally spawned numerous guidebooks purporting to explain Asian culture and history to help them along, among them: *Eastern Standard Time: A Guide to Asian Influence on American Culture from Astro Boy to Zen Buddhism,*[2] *Everything You Need to Know about Asian American History* ("everything" meaning things like, "Do Chinese Americans really eat everything?"),[3] and countless guides to Hong Kong martial arts films and Japanese anime.[4] Such ready-reference books, with their benign question-and-answer formats, condescend to domesticate the exotic. By offering up tame, user-friendly soundbites and mindless factoids for a quick multicultural information fix, they allow prejudice to continue to masquerade as mere ignorance. The burden to explain ourselves remains ours alone.

Moreover, even as Asian culture permeates American consciousness, ultimately, movies and food are only movies and food. As great as it is to see Asian chicks kick ass in martial arts flicks or to have our choice in noodle dishes, the movement of Asian culture from the margins to the cutting edge has been largely superficial. Never mind that Asian females still constitute the majority of sweatshop workers in this country, prostitutes on U.S. military bases abroad, and abandoned babies in Asia—these are questions no one wants to ask and truths our society would rather we kept hidden. In the end, I cannot embrace the optimistic philosophy my mother and others pursue so gallantly; I do not share their faith that the truth, patiently explained over and over in non-threatening language, will set us free.

As I write this, the country is being swept by new fears that Chinese spies have been stealing U.S. technological secrets for decades. Inevitably, some smart aleck asked me the other day if my father, who is an engineer, is a spy. I shouldn't have been surprised by the insult, but at the time I was speechless. Now I wish I had replied, "I could tell you . . . but then I'd have to kill you." It will always fall to us, of course, to slay old stereotypes and to demystify our own Otherness. Perhaps we are developing some new, sharper weapons, though, to make our jobs a little easier and to render the conventional wisdom a little less simplistic. At the very least, we can always keep them guessing.

* * *

The art of fengshui, which is based on ancient Chinese principles for maximizing the positive flow of energy in physical spaces, has recently swept through the Midwest, and folks in my hometown have begun rearranging their furniture with zeal. My mother, resident expert on Chinese culture, was interviewed by a local newspaper reporter about the trend, but she didn't say what they expected to hear: "A local Chinese woman, who asked not to be identified, laughed and called it silly and foolish, akin to fortune telling and palm reading. 'I think it's nonsense,' she said." The reverse scenario that has Americans avidly practicing fengshui while my mother scoffs at their superstitions from behind the scenes seems to me a good example of how cultural traditions are constantly renewed and reinterpreted by those who refuse to be defined by them. We make up life as we go along, the only way we know how. In the process, a secret shared or a lie revealed can also become self-knowledge gained—always an auspicious act.

—LYNN LU

Notes

1   Kingston, Maxine Hong. *The Woman Warrior: Memoirs of a Girlhood Among Ghosts.* New York: Vintage Books, 1976.

2   Yang, Jeffrey, et al. *Eastern Standard Time: A Guide to Asian Influence on American Culture from Astro Boy to Zen Buddhism.* New York: Houghton Mifflin, 1997.

3   Cao, Lan, and Himilce Novas. *Everything You Need to Know about Asian American History.* Plume, 1996.

4   See, for example, Bey Logan, *Hong Kong Action Cinema,* Overlook Press, 1996; Stefan Hammond, et al. *Sex and Zen & A Bullet in the Head.* Fireside, 1996; Weisser, et al. "Asian Cult Cinema," *Boulevard.* 1997.

A Lavender Army

It was not a place usually described with a solitary number one. There were over 7,000 islands. With seven major languages who could agree on just one to represent everybody? Categorized as Third world. Of course, who could forget those 2,000 pairs of shoes? And now it would be christened as the 29th nation welcomed into the Kay Cee Cosmetics family—where beauty had no boundaries.

Jackie Moulin, senior worldwide recruitment manager, had been part of the Kay Cee family for seven years. In this time her lips (stained with her perennial favorite "Mauve Madness") opened wide to preach the word of founder Kay Cee Holloway, "We are a company built in the name of enhancing woman's self-image, woman's personal fulfillment and woman's financial independence." Her ministry could think of no reason why a woman should not look beautiful, smell sweet and share the wealth that Kay Cee offered.

Mindful of her tight French twist and lavender silk suit, Jackie gingerly stepped into the waiting, tinted-window Mercedes, breathed in the already chilled interior air, ready to meet her new followers.

Maricel Tomas had to get ready two hours earlier than she usually did that morning. In a dark room barely lit by a small bulb hanging from the ceiling, she envied her sleeping sisters in the bed next to hers—their growing bodies protected under the mosquito net gauze. Maricel carefully navigated the room mindful of her dreaming siblings. She combed her sleek, wet hair back into a ponytail and softly patted the back of her neck with white baby powder—though she was already 20. Her face was bare.

As she slipped into a yellow dress, Maricel worried that it wouldn't be acceptable. The radio announcement had urged interested participants to wear the color of Kay Cee—a lavender that did not hang in her wallet. No matter now, she thought, rushing out into the uneven sidewalks with one pan de sal in hand for breakfast.

The driver had assured Jackie that her meeting was not too far away. Over an hour and a half later, Jackie's foundation slowly melted despite the air conditioning, revealing tiny smile lines around her mouth. It was the hottest month of the year in this part of the world, and the sun's penetrating rays had no mercy—good thing Kay Cee's products had SPF 15.

Despite the heat and traffic, Jackie delighted in passing the groups of young women—some clad in their school uniforms—on route to her meeting. The new "fresh and fearless" line had been developed with girls just like them in mind. With its nail polishes that sparkled, eye shadows that glittered and lip glosses that gave that a-la-Lolita pout, these girls now had make-up to play with just like their mothers.

Jackie congratulated herself for spearheading the efforts to bring the "family" to this country. After all, one of its most popular spectator sports was the beauty contest. Perfect marketing vehicles for Kay Cee products. But sponsorships was another meeting later on in the week. Right now she had to concentrate on welcoming and inspiring the next batch of BICs (beauty, image and confidence) consultants.

Maricel welcomed the coolness of the air conditioned room. She slipped quietly in one of the chairs in the last row behind a trio of young women about her age. In between their whispers and giggles of tsismis, Maricel learned that a few women had been turned away because they had brought their children and no, there were no babysitters to look after them, but could they please still stay?

Other women had unfortunately been caught taking some of the free make-up samples especially the packets of "Clear and Clean" whitening cream. All were politely, but firmly asked to leave by women in knee-length, lavender lab coats. In order to settle her nerves, Maricel closed her eyes and remembered how her 'Nay used to gently pinch her nose, her special sign of affection, because Maricel had sold all of her cassava cakes and now her pockets were full of bills and coins. Her mother's voice echoed in Maricel's ears like so many years before, "You are an excellent saleswoman, anak."

"Understand ladies, sales is not the ultimate goal of Kay Cee Cosmetics," Jackie beamed to all the women in the room. "We are here because we want you to feel beautiful. But Kay Cee's products are just the tools to get you and your potential customers to create that special look that makes you unique. As Kay Cee consultants, you will be helping other women find what works and what doesn't. Sometimes, what's more fulfilling than the profits from the products you sell is seeing your customers satisfied—looking and feeling better than they did before they came to you for a consultation."

Jackie was on a roll at her pulpit. Her following sentences were filled with expressions like "we build futures!" "We encourage women entrepreneurs!" and "We want you to be happy and fulfilled!" She told them how to start a clientele list. Friends. Neighbors. Co-workers. Fellow Alumni. Family members were optional. "And, we have created a special section in our manuals that gives you great decorating and cooking tips on when you finally do have enough people to host a Kay Cee beauty seminar."

"It really isn't that hard, ladies. Once they see how great you look in Kay Cee's products, they're going to want to see what other things you have to offer—YOU are your best advertisement!" Jackie's audience smiled at her, some even clapped when she seemed especially excited after saying something "inspirational." But many wondered silently how they could put together these lists of customers. You just didn't point and ask for things straight out here. It was done differently. Not so loudly either. And where would they put all of these women for a "seminar" what with just a sala and a couple of other rooms already occupied with children and husbands?

But they continued to listen politely. And they watched closely as the women in lab coats demonstrated how to apply foundation, eyeshadow, lipstick, and blush and what brushes to use for each part of the face. There were day looks, evening looks, day-into-evening looks, weekend looks, natural looks (as if you almost didn't have anything on at all).

And in the end, they were thanked by Jackie who jokingly called them the first wave of Kay Cee "soldiers" to defend and uphold the company's motto "beauty has no boundaries!" They clapped again.

That night, Maricel washed her painted face clean. Her smooth, honey-hued face looked first at her sisters who lay in the same position that she had left them that morning. And then she caught sight of the moon, its lavender tint slowly fading as thunderous clouds covered its glow.

—TARA AGTARAP

AGFA scanner ad, *Macworld* magazine, May 1999, p.47

Race and Representation:
Asian Americans

I was recently asked to give a talk to some students in honor of Asian American Awareness month. While I'm all in favor of raising people's awareness about the cultures, politics, and arts of Asian American people, I also agree with people such as Sucheta Mazumdar, who insist that Asian America should always be considered in its international context. For me, Asian American awareness is more than just learning about Asian American people. It is about understanding the global, driving forces that shape Asian America—imperialism, military interventions, trade, resource extraction, environmental degradation, forced and voluntary immigrations. These are the international forces that have created an Asian America; they have brought all of us Asian Americans here today, one way or another. By understanding those forces, by attempting to understand our place in the world, Asian American awareness steps outside the narrow confines of identity politics and becomes something much broader and long lasting. It becomes a path to politicization and to connecting with others, across national, racial, and class boundaries.

But it won't be easy. For it is crucial for all of us living in the industrialized West to obscure and willfully distort relations between East and West, between Asia and America. Our standard of living depends on it. Let me explain why. I'll start by pointing out something fairly obvious. That is what I call our deeply twisted understanding of the world.

When I was a kid, my father once invited one of his coworkers to our house for dinner. She was a social worker or a psychologist, as I remember it. After a relatively uneventful dinner; she turned to my dad and asked him, in all seriousness, whether people in India leave their dead lying in the street. She really wanted to know. My parents of course were outraged that this educated person whom they trusted into their home could have such an obscenely ignorant and patronizing sense of their homeland. She wasn't invited back. I know it is all too easy to pick on celebrities, but I can't resist commenting on how pop singer Madonna donned dyed black hair, bindi, sari-like wraps, and mendhi after her first child was born. "Religious Hindus" were aghast, according to the Nov. 2, 1998 *People* magazine. (Never believe a media report about "religious Hindus" or "outraged Hindus"—anyone with a South Asian-sounding name who voices dissent is usually called one, Hindu or not!) But why was the Material One trying to mimic a traditional South Asian matriarch? "It's not a calculated idea to go guru-swami," explained her makeup man, helpfully. "It's how she feels right now." Motherhood equals serenity equals South Asian matriarch, you see.

The profound and utter ignorance these examples illustrate strikes me. These folks aren't just missing a few nuances about India and South Asian culture here. Their utter ignorance is hardly isolated to the undereducated of America. In fact, given the sorry state of our triumphalist media and public education systems, I'd guess it extends its greasy paws onto virtually all Americans, to some extent or another, whether we're talking about Indonesia, or Iraq, or Kosovo, or Ghana. And I consider myself included here.

On the eve of my thirtieth birthday, for instance, I was lucky to have a prominent Latina feminist, over forty years my elder, staying at my house for the night. She told me how she would like to arrange a typical Mexican birthday morning for me the next day. "A band of mariachi singers would come to your window," she told me. "And play you a happy birthday song."

A sitcom-like image flashed in my mind. I groaned, thinking that she was being facetious. She wasn't. I quickly realized my error, and felt a bit ashamed at myself. Where did I get that vivid image of flashy, loud mariachi singers? Taco Bell commercials? I had no personal experience of them myself! A similar thing had occurred while I was editing a collection of essays by a Native American environmental leader. I caught myself grimacing through some of her descriptions of Native ceremonies and stories, wanting to cut sentences that seemed somehow . . . embarrassing. I restrained myself when I couldn't think of any good reason to delete the material, but the impulse disturbed me.

The use of the third-person plural, the mythical tone, the mysticism of the language, was, for the writer, culturally appropriate, viscerally real. But to me, it didn't sound like that. It sounded like bad "Northern Exposure" dialogue, or Robert Bly. Given that I spend much of my time writing and thinking about race and representation, these instances were instructional. The influence of the dominant u.s. culture so mediates and perverts non-Western cultures that its representations become more real than reality. And it happens in such an insidious way that the stereotype is almost instantly available in one's mind, without any indication of where it came from or who made it up.

One common response to problems of racialized representations has been to call, in effect, for a ban on all cultural interpretations. "If you can't represent us respectfully," wrote one South Asian in an angry letter to NBC complaining about the network's degrading portrayals of South Asians, "don't represent us at all." In other words, our culture is ours to keep, no outsiders allowed. It is an understandable protective gesture.

But in general, I don't think that people should be barred from exploring cultures and religions other than their own. It can't be fundamentally wrong for Americans to take up Native American rituals, or to convert to Buddhism, or to wear saris or mendhi, even if they do it in a non-traditional fashion. How could it be? I myself, the American-born daughter of Indian immigrants, have been accused countless times of translating my Indian heritage in an unorthodox, even heretic fashion. I cook the food wrong, I give my kid the wrong name, I wear the clothes wrong, I say the words wrong. If the only way to interact with other cultures is to conform entirely to their traditions, then those cultures have become orthodox and authoritarian, remote, static, unrelenting. There is no possibility for change and adaptation, and that tradition will most likely die, fast. Or become something frightening, Talibanesque.

Yet, when Americans have attempted to portray or participate in Asian cultures, they transform them in subtle ways that can have lasting, negative ramifications. Mostly, this is because they approach Asian cultures as inferior or strange, even when they profess reverence and respect.

The Tragic, Passive Asian Woman
Shamita Das Dasgupta, a South Asian battered women's activist, and her daughter, writer and physician Sayantani, write of how the mainstream feminist tradition interrupts the Asian mother-daughter bond. Even in this progressive, liberatory tradition, Asian women, especially first-generation immigrants, are thought of as profoundly oppressed and submissive. "A white American friend in my consciousness-raising group asked me whether, given a choice, I would have opted to have a child," Das Dasgupta writes. "The assumption, of course, was that I had little choice in the matter." The job of the Asian American daughter, for such feminists, is to reject the mother and the "ancient" culture in order to find feminist liberation and individuality. Even films produced by Asian women, such as the popular film, *Mississippi Masala*, directed by Mira Nair, reinscribe this notion of necessary escape from burdensome backward Asian mothers.

The fact that this image of tragically oppressed Asian women persists among even feminists, with their long history of internationalism, and Asian women, whose personal experience must directly contradict it, is testament to its stature. The degradation of the Asian woman was long used as an excuse and rationale to invade and colonize Asian countries. The idea that Asian women are uniformly miserable has probably been around so long that it isn't really necessary to portray its truth in any kind of detail, but still, our "newspaper of record," *The New York Times*, throws a few reminders our way, just in case.

Every now and then *The Times* runs a long feature article on the misery of Asian women. One front page story featured a photograph of a group of slumped, grim Indian women, with the newsworthy headline: "Once Widowed in India, Twice Scorned"; the caption describes how these Indian widows are all called "servant" and survive solely on handouts. Details of slave-like working conditions, illiteracy, hunger, rape, forced prostitution, and, of course, wife-burning follow. "Attitudes evolve at a glacial pace," the reporter duly notes.

Another long front-page story featured rural Chinese women committing suicide in masses, mostly by drinking pesticides. The reporter unsuccessfully attempts to explain the high suicide rate by variously noting that perhaps the women didn't really want to die, that Chinese culture "reinforce[s] women's feeling of worthlessness and helplessness," or that they may feel it is "honorable." While the high suicide rate is clearly inexplicable, at least by *The Times*, (the reporter notes that these women "show no signs of mental illness, depression, or alcohol use"), it also may not even exist. The fact that the suicide rate is very poorly documented is noted several times in the article.

A May 3, 1999 article was tagged to a study showing that 2/3 of the women elected into village governing councils in India, on the basis of a 1993 quota law, are "actively engaged in learning the ropes and exercising power." The study, in other words, showed that a government attempt at radical social transformation to benefit women was basically successful. Yet, the vast majority of the article is devoted to vignettes about two illiterate women from a low-literacy state, which the reporter admits is least indicative of the successes of the program.

They are variously described as "ghostly shadow[s]" being "shooed away to make tea," having a "submissive posture," dropping their voices to whispers, covering their eyes with veils, nursing their babies at the slightest whimper, and falling to their knees to prostrate themselves to their elders. In other words, "changing deep-rooted social attitudes cannot be accomplished by legal fiat," asserts the reporter, contradicting the study that gives the story whatever news-value it may have.

In the first case, there is no news hook; in the second, there may be no "story" at all; in the third, the reporter doesn't follow up on the newsworthiness of the story. In the end, such stories are published simply for human-interest value. So we must wonder, why are these tales so interesting? In what way are readers being informed? Even the rare coverage of Asian women activists or leaders is framed in such a way as to maximize Asian passivity and degradation. Maria Rosa Henson was the first Asian "comfort woman" to accept a reparation payment for her enslavement in a Japanese military brothel. *The Times*'s story about Henson calls her an "avenger," despite the fact that most former comfort women and their advocates refuse the reparation payments on principle, instead demanding official legal compensation. Remarkably, the first six paragraphs of the story are devoted to Henson's "gratefulness" to one of the hundreds of military men who raped her, Captain Tanaka. According to *The Times*, Henson recalled "the occasional cups of tea and kind looks he offered her during the months he forced her, at the age of 15, to provide sex to 10 or 20 or 30 Japanese soldiers a day." The reporter goes on to devote over one-quarter of the article to Henson's gratitude to Tanaka, despite the fact that these "niceties" are clearly irrelevant to the story, and the characterization of Henson they imply are misplaced at best. Tanaka didn't help Henson escape in any way, nor did his kind looks mitigate the horror of the experience, including his own rapes of Henson. Although the reporter insists that Henson "was grateful to Captain Tanaka," Henson herself writes that she was "angry all the time" and that she will "remember always." The crude attempt to characterize Henson as a timid, thankful, inadvertent avenger falls flat on its face.

In a special "millennial" article on "how China's women have traveled from the ancient to the modern in four generations," *The New York Times Magazine* posits that Chinese women have finally become liberated. Although the path from foot-binding and starving widows to powerful businesswomen is most likely an uneven and circuitous one, the reporter attributes all gains to Western ideas and capitalism. "Women gained status as western ideas began filtering into China," author Sheryl WuDunn writes, going on to detail Chairman Mao's more obviously significant influence, banning child weddings, outlawing concubines, and closing brothels, among other things. The changing Chinese economy probably has a lot to do with Chinese women's transformed status, yet there is no simple explanation that warrants the writer's later assertion that "Confucianism may have enslaved women for centuries, but capitalism and commercialism have been enormously powerful in helping women overturn history." I suspect the story is much more complex, and even the short article itself implies that it must be. Yet such sloppy clichés are de rigeur stand-ins for thoughtful, unbiased analyses. Richard Halloran, former *New York Times* correspondent, wrote a quite ludicrous piece describing what he called "Asia's sisterhood of power," in which "strong-willed women are struggling for power," despite the fact that Asian "politics, economics and social orders have been dominated by men for centuries." He provides brief sketches of political leaders as ideologically and culturally varied as Pakistan's former prime minister, the corrupt Benazir Bhutto; the Philippines' Corazon Aquino; and Burma's human rights advocate and Nobel Peace Prize winner Aung San Suu Kyi, as evidence of the "sisterhood." Imagine a piece on a Western "sisterhood of power" evidenced by the leadership of Gloria Steinem and Margaret Thatcher and the absurdity of Halloran's "story" becomes quickly evident.

Asian tragedies and horrors—wolf attacks, rampant filth and infection, contaminated blood supplies, angry mobs, and horrifying customs often make front-page news, and whether news-worthy or not, provide fine opportunities to reiterate Western repulsion toward Asia. John F. Burns cites a study in his story on a case of food poisoning in New Delhi, showing that 700 million Indians "defecate into buckets or on open land." The paternalism is so glaringly obvious that even the reactionary columnist A.M. Rosenthal noted the "arrogance, ignorance, and condescension" of the Western attitude. And since we rarely hear of the lasting effects or long-term outcomes of these events, the conclusion that the spectacle of horror *is* the story becomes obvious.

The Fantasy Sex Goddess

When viewed from western shores, or through tourist's sunglasses, the Asian woman is backward, traditional, and miserably oppressed for it. But when under the enlightened control of a western man, this miserably oppressed creature becomes a fantasy sex slave—pliant, submissive, eager-to-please, and intrinsically imbued with ancient sexual secrets.

This notion of Asian women rests on the long history of Western men "purchasing" Asian women to serve as their maids, nurses, and sex servants from the colonial era onwards. In service of colonial regimes and western military invasions, Asian women have been rented or sold as "temporary wives" to colonists and soldiers. The notorious sex trade in Thailand originated in 1967, when the U.S. Government contracted with Thailand to provide "rest and recreation" (R&R) services to troops during the Vietnam War. Cynthia Enloe attributes U.S. soldiers' ability to wage wars partly on their fantasies and exploitation of Asian women: Without myths of Asian women's compliant sexuality would many American men be able to sustain their own identities of themselves as manly enough to act as soldiers?"

Sumi K. Cho provides a remarkable example of how today's fantasy of the Asian sex slave rests on colonial, military, and sexual domination. She quotes from a 1990 *Gentleman's Quarterly* article, titled "Oriental Girls": "Her face—round like a child's, . . . eyes almond-shaped for mystery, black for suffering, wide-spaced for innocence, high cheekbones swelling like bruises, cherry lips . . .

"When you come home from another hard day on the planet, she comes into existence, removes your clothes, bathes you and walks naked on your back to relax you . . . She's fun, you see, and so uncomplicated. She doesn't go to assertiveness-training classes, insist on being treated like a person, fret about career moves, wield her orgasm as a non-negotiable demand . . . She's there when you need shore leave from those angry feminist seas. She's a handy victim of love or a symbol of the rape of third world nations, a real trooper . . .

Even progressives may betray a sense of entitlement to passive Asian femininity. *The Utne Reader,* once known as "the best of the alternative press," ran an article bemoaning the loss of demure, exotic Asian women. In the best investigative tradition, writer John Winzenburg exposes "the real cost of free sex in Asia." Set aside for the moment that one must pay prostitutes money for sex; it isn't "free"—Winzenburg is referring to his notion that "a white guy who looks like Rodney Dangerfield could have just about any woman he wants here," according to his source. "Just call it the Oriental Girl Fixation Syndrome," he writes.

The crux of the story is that western men expecting Asian women to shower them with sexual attentions with no obligations will be disappointed in the new, modern Asia. In this world, the writer warns, Asian women's servitude is just a "veneer." Although common sense and decency would compel one to know this implicitly, it is well documented that most Asian women who liaise with Western men are doing so for very practical reasons and are in fact expecting some kind of reciprocity. Still, Winzenburg warns his readers not to expect "Madame Butterfly . . . more and more of these men are discovering that there's a payback. . . . Asian women are spinning their own webs . . . and promiscuity is running rampant."

The internet is a kind of crude indication of the prevalence of the Asian fetish. Relevant sites include Jgirls Inc: Soopa Fresh Asian Hotties, Asian Delight, Absolute Asian: Over 250 Free Pics of Hot Asian Honeys, Asian Divas, Asiaphile!, AAA Foreign Brides, The Best Asian Clubs, Allstar Cuties from China, Doc's Asia Page, Best of the Orient, and How to Meet and Understand Asian Women, which provides a manual on how to get Asian women into bed:

"Do you like Asian girls? Welcome to the club. Men across America are coming to know what men in Hawaii have known for decades: Asian women are special! From their silky black hair to their lithe, toned bodies and delicate features, Asian women are #1 in my book."

Although the Kama Sutra and Hindu erotic paintings and sculptures obviously originate in India, the gymnastic eroticism they imply are applied randomly to all Asian and even Eastern women. "Haven't you heard of the Kama Sutra and ancient Tantric sex rituals?!" exclaimed *Seinfeld*'s Kramer, when Jerry threatened to break up with his Eastern European gymnast girlfriend. The most recent version of the medieval Hindu classic has been called a "sex manual" or a "Sanskrit Joy of Sex," by the *Guardian* and *Library Journal,* and indeed, the translator betrays his own biases about the book, noting that "the intelligent traveler can . . . find amorous adventures that show that the people of India have forgotten nothing of the teachings of the Kama Sutra." (This is somewhat hard to believe, as the translator offers no concrete evidence but simply innuendo, and since most modern Indians haven't even read the book.)

Mattel enshrined this version of Asian femininity in its 1998 collectors' series Barbie doll, "The Fantasy Goddess of Asia." It would be easy to model a doll on one of the scores of goddesses in Asian traditions, but Mattel's designer Bob Mackie clearly had no such thing in mind. The doll is not from any recognizable Asian culture, but rather is an amalgam of western stereotypes of Asian femininity. She wields fans decorated with dragons, her black hair twirling in serpentine masses behind her wildly, her Barbie body wrapped in a tight beaded gown "inspired by the bold colors and icons of the orient" as the promotional copy attests. Manavi, a South Asian domestic violence organization based in New Jersey, launched a campaign to stop production of the doll, calling attention to the "racist violence that is integral to and a result of this grotesque fascination with Asian 'femininity.'"

The fantasy continues, not least because of the tacit support and approval of the u.s. Government. The Immigration and Naturalization Service provides a 90-day "fiancée's visa," through which mail-order brides, many of whom are from Asian countries, can be returned if they don't meet with their "customer's approval." u.s. servicemen abroad have been known to wear T-shirts describing Asian women as "little brown fucking machines," testament to the continuing Asian "R&R" services around u.s. Military bases.

"Indo-Chic"

Despite being portrayed as variously enslaved (by tradition, by sexual servitude, by oppressive labor), the traditions of Asia are a veritable font for new context-less trends in fashion and other mass media. "Inflasion," is what trend-watcher DeeDee Gordon calls it, which is "not just a Japanese thing, but also about Thailand, Tibet, and about how everybody wants to be a Buddhist." The result of the infatuation is Om cologne, popular books on feng shui, pillow shams modeled on Buddhist prayer mats, and a host of other Asian-esque consumer items.

"There seems to be a great deal of interest in all things Indian," claims Nancy Gerstman, a president of Zeitgeist Films. "It's just a huge trend."

There are several observations that have been commonly made about this phenomenon. One is that while Asian-inspired things may become fashionable or lucrative, actual Asian people are not. Their experiences are not the subject of the popular books and films, their clothing, language, or religious practices are not considered fashionable. Second is that the Asian things that are fashionable or lucrative are old Asian things. They by and large are not from today's Asia, but harken back to a romanticized Orientalist past. Third, "inflasion" conflates and confuses different Asian cultures and traditions. And fourth, most prominently, Asian "chic" is at bottom about capitalism's creative response to an oversaturated consumer market—new looking things and fashions must always be dreamt up to keep money in motion.

In a capitalist, consumer society, is it possible for non-Western cultures to have any impact that isn't commercialized? Maybe not. Some critics say there is an opportunity in these periodic bouts of interest in Asianalia. This is an "opportunity to connect," Asia Society's Vishakha N. Desai begrudgingly admits. But other critics see a colonialist apologia in Asian chic: "If the monkey is so brilliant," asks University of Chicago anthropologist Dr. Arjun Appadurai, "can the organ grinders have been so bad?"

It isn't clear whether these trends constitute the influence of any actual Asian culture or community or whether they are simply meaningless commercialism, and reflections of Western fantasies of Asia. There is evidence, however, that the mainstream media is more comfortable with Asian critiques of these trends rather than with any triumphalism about Asia's influence on the West.

Resistances

Asian American activists have frequently organized to protest inaccurate and racist portrayals of Asians in popular culture. One prominent campaign was against the Broadway production of the Orientalist musical, *Miss Saigon*, in New York City in 1991. The hook for the campaign was that a progressive organization, the Lambda Legal Defense and Education Fund, was selling benefit tickets to the show.

A broad coalition of activists led by Asian gay and lesbian organizers, after unsuccessfully arguing with Lambda to drop the benefit, organized two demonstrations in front of the theater. Their actions were provocative, to say the least. At the first demonstration, six demonstrators were arrested. Two activists surreptitiously attended the show and yelled out "This play is racist and sexist, Lambda is racist and sexist!" and were kicked out. A Lambda staffer resigned in protest. The poet Audre Lorde refused to accept an award from Lambda in solidarity with the campaign. The actors' union called for the show to be recast with Asian actors in the Asian roles.

Between the summer of 1990 and the spring of 1991, while this campaign was being organized, *The Village Voice*'s only mention of it called it "sophisticated, more p.c.-than-thou gay-bashing." Later, when the second demonstration was swarming with network TV reporters, CNN, the *Post*, the *Daily News*, *The New York Times*, and NPR, the multiracial, queer-led campaign was boiled down to short stories on enraged Asians.

While it isn't particularly surprising that the mainstream media didn't pursue the complexities and duration of the anti-*Miss Saigon* campaign, it is worth noting that the news media was eager to run stories on Asian American "outrage" with Americana, even when such sentiments are barely public and completely unorganized.

Comedian Mike Myers was photographed for the April 1999 *Vanity Fair* partially shaved, wearing silk saffron robes, mendhi designs on his body, and a jeweled bindi on his forehead. "Call my agent" was henna-painted on one palm, and his palm-pilot read "Om." Fawning blue-painted models completed the scene. On March 15, one member of the South Asian Journalists Association, a trade and watchdog group run by a Columbia School of Journalism professor, wrote to the SAJA e-mail list, describing the photo spread and commenting "I'm all for irreverence and wit, but this incensed me." SAJA posted the photos on its website for other members to comment on, and a flurry of debate ensued. Some criticized *VF,* others found the spread funny and harmless. Some wrote e-mail letters to *Vanity Fair.* As a media-watchdog group, this was all standard activity for SAJA.

On March 16, the *New York Post* ran a story on "distraught Hindus," "Hindu activists," and indeed the entire "Hindu community" "up in arms" about the photo spread. Their evidence? The secular debate within SAJA, and some members' e-mail letters to *Vanity Fair.* On March 29, *Newsweek* magazine picked up the story. In a bemused short, *Newsweek* reiterated the idea that "Hindu activists" are "not amused" at Hollywood's attempt at the "Hinduism thing." SAJA's Sreenath Srinivasan described the implicit assumptions of the coverage in an e-mail that was not picked up by the otherwise ever-alert *Post* and *Newsweek:* "A. All Hindus are upset about this (false; many Hindus think the pix are hilarious) B. Only Hindu activists are upset about this (false; some non–South Asians have complained, too) C. If your name sounds South Asian and you express an opinion, you must be a Hindu activist (false; at least one Sikh has been repeatedly labeled as a Hindu activist for speaking up) D. SAJA and/or I have condemned these pix (false; we were only giving an opportunity for people to comment, not taking an official stand ourselves). . . . At least they spelled my name right."

On one hand, a sustained, complicated, political effort is simplified and deflated, and on the other, casual semi-private remarks are inflated into monolithic outpourings of outrage. The idea that repressed, humorless Asians are provoked by a liberated, uninhibited American culture serves the idea of the West as enlightened liberators well. It is permissible for Asians to think of American culture and its appropriations of Asian artifacts as sacrilege, as this leaves the essential relationship of a powerful, liberated, controlling West and a passive, backward Asia relatively intact.

While in the case of the *Vanity Fair* flap, humorless Hindu fanatics are considered laughable, in another recent incident, they are considered violent nationalists. A controversy erupted at Duke University, where students had been lobbying to create a major in Hindi. First-year undergraduates wrote incendiary letters to the editor of the campus paper arguing against the idea, provoking a storm of dissent. First year student Matt Strader argued that Hindi should not be taught because there was insufficient interest and that it was impractical to learn "a language spoken in a Third World country overwrought by disease and poverty." A letter from first-year student Berin Szoka ran the following week, agreeing with Strader. "The values of the West—the power of reason, the sanctity of individual rights and the unfettered pursuit of happiness—are superior to the values of a primitive, impoverished country like India," Strader wrote.

To the extent that the fruits of [Western] values—the arts and sciences, industry and education—exist in India, they exist only as the legacy of British colonialism. Were it not for the British, whatever "ancient traditions and rich culture" existed before their arrival would be enjoyed only by the very top of India's feudal caste system. Compared to the United States, India may be wretchedly poor, but the average Indian enjoys an incomparably higher quality of life today than he would have without the benefit of British "oppression."

The British gave India more than just roads, medicine, science and all the values of the West. Perhaps their greatest gift of all was the English language itself. English, not Hindi, is the language of the best India has to offer in every field. Those who truly wish to enjoy the "richness" of Indian culture would do better to learn English than Hindi.

According to the India Abroad Center for Political Awareness, "While most students chose to argue these ignorant views through peaceful and rational debate in the campus newspaper, a few hotheaded students chose to confront the freshmen in person while others sent threats over e-mail." Such emotionally charged exchanges are not uncommon on undergraduate campuses; the only reason to detail this one is to note the media distortions that followed. The coverage mentioned neither the provocative content of the students' letters, nor the ongoing debate they were part of, but focused exclusively on the unsubstantiated threats Strader and Szoka apparently suffered. *The Boston Globe*'s Jeff Jacoby weighed in with an anti-leftist rant, describing Strader and Szoka as intellectual heroes, "excited by intellectual combat and unafraid of jabbing sacred cows," as opposed to their detractors who have "little interest in arguing." A short article in the *Wall Street Journal* described Strader and Szoka's letters as simply "expressing a preference for Western over Indian civilization," which subjected them to "death threats and violence." According to the India Abroad Center for Political Awareness, these national commentaries successfully painted "the South Asian community at Duke as irrational, disrespectful of Constitutional freedoms, and violent."

In these cases, the news media defended America's freedom to pick and choose from Asian cultures and histories portraying those who question this freedom as strident, humorless censors. Not many people have been audacious enough to suggest the opposite—that Asian culture has influenced key aspects of Western culture. But in at least one recent example, such a notion was treated with open derision and disgust.

Former literary editor of the *Wilson Quarterly*, writer Jeffery Paine, wrote a book called *Father India: How Encounters with an Ancient Culture Transformed the Modern West* (HarperCollins, 1998), which attempts to be a "resolutely anti-imperialist history of how India influenced the West," as *The New York Times Book Review* put it. As evidence of India's influence, Paine details the reactions to India of various Western intellectuals who lived or visited there. Alexandra Lange's contemptuous review of the book for *The New York Times Book Review* questions the legitimacy of the project altogether. "Paine's hope is that we'll conflate these intellectuals' reactions to India with the larger West's," she writes skeptically, even though that is precisely what *The New York Times* itself counts on when it publishes its many negative stories about Asia. According to the reviewer, these intellectuals' reactions are mostly of a sexual nature, and in conclusion, she characterizes India's influence as similar to that of a gastrointestinal illness. "India seems more like a land of confusion than a fatherly force," she writes, "Even Jung. . . . spends most of his time in India in the hospital with dysentery . . . Western civilization, whatever its faults, was not transformed by a piece of unwashed fruit." Lange is not convinced that India could have even influenced Mohandas Gandhi himself, who may have gotten his ideas from "a trip to England."

Conclusion

So what does it all mean? Why are Asian cultures and histories so belittled and derided in the u.s. media? Most critics agree: the immediate cause is reporters' biases and their perceptions of their readers' biases, coupled with their mandate to sell newspapers and magazines. The ultimate cause is more controversial. Is it a holdover from colonial times, when Asian societies were necessarily viewed as inferior? Is it a spillover effect from this country's virulent racism against browns and blacks, rooted in the genocides of Native Americans and black slavery? Is it rooted in a secret jealousy of some Asians' financial success, here and abroad? Perhaps there is a bit of truth in all of these explanations.

But I think the most pernicious sustenance for anti-Asian bias is the West's reliance on exploitable Asian labor. As Third World feminist Vandana Shiva argues, the colonization of Third World countries has proceeded in three stages: colonialism, IMF and World Bank-led "development," and the strict mandates of current free trade agreements. In each of these stages, Western elites have secured access to the natural resources and labor of the developing world. This access is evident today, as daily we may hear of another Asian sweatshop employed by u.s. multinationals, in which 12-year-old girls toil for $2 a week or less. As economist Michel Chossudovsky shows, in the "global cheap labor economy," the earnings accruing to the developed country are 35 times greater than earnings accruing to the Third World country contracted for manufacturing. (What is hidden in such accounts is the wildly varying buying power of different currencies; but even when exchange rates are converted on an equal purchasing power basis, the average per capita income in Western countries is five to twenty times that of poor Asian countries.) While the gap between rich and poor within individual countries continues to grow (most sharply in the United States), the fact remains that globally, the greatest disparity in consumption of the world's resources is between the 1.1 billion people in North America, Western Europe, Japan and the 4.4 billion poor and working class people in Africa, Asia, Latin America, and the Middle East. Industrial countries, with one-quarter of the world's population, consume between 40 and 86 percent of the world's natural resources, from wood and iron to water.

Most Americans' standard of living depends upon their ability to stomach the ongoing exploitation of cheap labor and raw materials from Asian and other Third World countries. Somehow, the injustice and ugliness of this great transfer of resources, begun during the colonial era and continuing in today's neocolonial "global" economy, must remain hidden. By painting Asian women and cultures as downtrodden, lowly, and ripe for the picking —and resistances to such representations as ineffectual and unnecessary— the news media supports the idea that the West may take freely from these people and their countries without guilt.

While it is all too easy to buy into such distortions, it is at the cost of accepting the mythologies that keep such unjust economies in place. In the end, it is the broader inequities between the people of Asia and their descendants and the West that is the real problem; if these didn't exist, it would hardly matter much if we continued to be taunted and teased. Words alone won't hurt us, really; but sticks and stones will break our bones!

—SONIA SHAH, 1999

Untitled Art by Barry McGee

Headlines and Quotes from mainstream America

Here's a sampling of headlines and quotes taked from magazines, news-papers, kiosks, and celebrities in America.

"The biggest thing I don't like about New York are the foreigners. You can walk an entire block in Times Square and not hear anybody speaking English. Asians and Koreans and Vietnamese and Indians and Russians and Spanish people and everything up there. How the hell did they get in this country?"
—John Rocker, Atlanta Braves pitcher "At Full Blast," *Sports Illustrated,* December 22, 1999, Volume 91, Issue 25, pp. 60-64.

"American Beats Out Kwan"
—This headline appeared in a scrolling marquee on MSNBCSports.com for Feb. 20, 1998.

"I don't know if you know San Diego, but I'll tell you something—The low-est thing you can be on the totem pole in San Diego is a Filipino."
—Gary Indiana, author of Andrew Cunanan's biography, *Three Month Fever* "Cunanan, the Barbarian," *Detour Magazine,* April 1999, p. 62, 64, 148.

"The place (Manila) just fucking smelled of cockroaches. There's no sewage system in Manila, and people have nothing there. People with, like, no arms, no leg, no eyes, no teeth."
—Claire Danes, actress "Hey Nineteen," *Premiere Magazine,* October 1998, pp. 63-67, 118-119.

"We're going to have a commercial break, so you have time to feed your dog, or wash your dog, or if you're Filipino, eat your dog."
—Joan Rivers, comedienne E! Television Network, 1998 Emmy Awards, September 13, 1998.

"Hey monkeys and apes. You all need to go back to where you came from. BC is for white men, not any chinks, spicks, niggers, or fags."
—an anonymous e-mail sent to student minority leaders at Boston College "Rascist E-mail Prompts Boston College Students to Demand Action," *The Daily Free Press* (Boston University), October 5, 1998.

—compiled by found images editor
ANIDA YOEU ESGUERRA and her crew

"It's almost like Asian boyfriends are the fashion accessory of the moment."

"She came up with a list of what she wanted in a man: smart, genuine, respectful. Adding it up, it occurred to her that guys who fit the bill were . . . Asian, a group she'd never considered romantically before."

Newsweek magazine, Volume CXXXV, No.8, February 21, 2000, pp. 50-51

Fargo and the Asian American Male

The Japanese American actor Marc Hayashi once said to me: "Every culture needs its eunuchs. And we're it. Asian American men are the eunuchs of America."

When he said this, I felt an instant shock of recognition.

To my chagrin, I came close to portraying one such eunuch in the Coen brothers' movie *Fargo*.

The call for the role seemed perfect: a Japanese American man, in his late 30's, a bit portly, who speaks with a Minnesota accent. I'm a Sansei, a third generation Japanese American. I've lived in Minnesota for twenty years. Though I'm not portly, I'm not thin. A writer and a performance artist, I'd done one small film for PBS, "Slowly, This," centered on a dinner between myself and an African American friend.

After I passed the first two readings, my wife and I talked about what other parts might follow; we even joked about moving out to Hollywood. In the end, though, the Coens found another Asian American actor.

But when I saw the much acclaimed *Fargo,* I said to myself, "Thank God I didn't get the part."

The character I auditioned for is Mike Yamagita, a Japanese American who speaks with a thick Minnesotan accent, a source of ironic amusement to the audience. Mike awkwardly attempts a pass at an old high school friend, the rural police chief, Marge Gunderson, who is visibly pregnant. He then tells of marrying a mutual acquaintance from high school and how she recently died of cancer. A few scenes later, Marge learns this marriage was fiction: this acquaintance isn't only alive, but has complained to the police that Mike has been harassing her.

Mike has no relevance to Marge's investigation. He's there mainly for humor. The humor is based on his derangement and his illusions that Marge or their high school acquaintance would ever be attracted to him.

I recognized this character as the latest in a long line of Asian and Asian American male nerds. Often, as in *Fargo,* such a character will pant after white women, ridiculous in his desires. In the media, as in the culture as a whole, Asian men have no clout. Or sexual presence.

Americans rarely talk about race and sex together. It's still taboo. Yet I often wonder what do people make of me and my wife, who is three quarters WASP and one quarter Hungarian Jew? Recently, we went shopping with my sister Linda and our children. Several people, all white, mistook Linda for the wife, the mother. Was this because it's difficult for many whites to picture an Asian American man with a white woman?

In Western culture, when East meets West, it's almost always a white man meeting an Asian woman. From *Madame Butterfly* to *Karate Kid II*, from *Rambo II* to *Miss Saigon*, the white man who falls in love with an Asian woman has been used to proffer the view that racial barriers cannot block the heart's affections.

But such pairings simply place white men at the screen's center and reinforce a hierarchy of power and sexual attractiveness. Such works portray Asian women as exotic, submissive and sensual. They also reinforce the stereotype of the East as feminine.

A salient feature of the play *M. Butterfly* was that it affirmed this feminine view of Asian men. In it, a French diplomat conducts a long-standing love affair with someone he believes is a woman, but who is actually a Chinese transvestite. The affair proves that Asian manhood is indeed difficult to find, at least for white Westerners. And when the "mistress" stripped to a highly buffed and masculine body, it was not just the diplomat who gasped in astonishment, but the audience as well.

While David Henry Hwang's play consciously used the stereotype of the Asian man as effeminate, the vast majority of cultural products are often absurdly unconscious—and yet revealing—in their use of stereotypes. In *Showdown in Little Tokyo,* for instance, the Japanese yakuza villain attempts to sexually assault Tia Carerre but proves himself impotent. Tia, though, is not interested in Brandon Lee, who is half Japanese and half Caucasian, but instead goes after the all white hero, Dolph Lundgren. At one point, when Dolph emerges naked from Tia's bedroom, Brandon remarks that Dolph possesses the biggest male organ he's ever seen. The equation is simple: the Japanese is evil and impotent; the Eurasian is envious of the white man's sexual prowess.

Growing up, I imbibed works like this without thinking. It took me years to comprehend their message: The hero will always be white. If there's an Asian heroine, she'll end up with the white hero. The Asian man will at best be the lovable sidekick, at worse the evil and sexist (i.e. possessive, nationalistic) villain.

Even in so-called ethnic breakthroughs such as *All-American Girl,* which was hailed as the first all Asian American sit-com in 1994, the stereotypes continue. There, Margaret Cho played a hip young Korean American who was always dating white boys in defiance of her mother's wishes. Her brother was a studious and obsequious geek, who dated no one.

In short, Asian and Asian American men are simply not seen as attractive or sexual beings by the mainstream culture. What could be attractive about the horny, thick glassed nerdy Asian guy?

How little things change. As a boy I watched Mickey Rooney as the Japanese buffoon neighbor in *Breakfast at Tiffany's* and knew I never wanted to be associated with this snarling, bucktoothed, thick-glassed creature who shouted at Audrey Hepburn, "Miss Gorrightry, Miss Gorrightry," and who panted when she offered to let him photograph her. In *Have Gun, Will Travel,* I was the cowboy Paladin, not the Chinese messenger in the hotel lobby, shouting, "Terragram for Mr. Paradin." I identified with John Wayne against the Japs at Iwo Jima. I identified with Tony Franciosa, the sexy bachelor of *Valentine's Day,* and not Jack Soo, his houseboy.

In short, Asian features, Asian accents were all undesirable. They weren't part of my image of a real All American boy.

For a while this distancing seemed to work. My parents, interned during

immigrant asses lured and busted
                    sapped and rusted
what do you see?

"i. see. god.
EYE SEE GOD!"   and charlie chan died!
died three times and returned to life.
50 fingers turned to farmers
growing oo-ung root and rice
wearing banana hats and white work shirts
          reading Amnesty For All Political Prisoners
                Free Mumia Abu-Jamal
but the residue of murderous years in the hundreds
were still ghosting around me, pissing in my rice
and enslaving finger mentals and playing wack-ass instrumentals
stealing indigenous drum bop
like puffy does '80s pop

and i was afraid. but behold i saw before me
charlie chan standing tall
revolutionary dental surgery
having whittled his cartoon chops
to a finely hewed set of pearls
and he declared his independence
          (Life to Write is Right to Life)
and said "i am the pillsbury tao-boy
    and i trust my creamy center
    i am charlie chan no longer
    I am Katipunan Kalayaan Ja-Yu and Krylon
    and i refuse to be played by russell wong
    that spring roll pretty boy gets the half-asian gong
    give me jason scott lee or dustin nguyen
    i am the living i and i rock for no good reason"

and he called our people to a halt
stopped that dorothy and toto train
said that yellow trick road lined with
          green cards and cash advances
was the tongue of the beast prophesied
        by nectarines
licking us locking us slowly digesting us

World War II, wanted to distance themselves from their ethnic identity. We lived in an all white suburb and I generally felt like one of the crowd. Then came my first boy-girl party. As usual, I was the only person of color in the room. But when we began to play Spin the Bottle, I felt a new sense of difference from the others. Then the bottle I'd spun pointed to a girl I had a crush on. She refused to kiss me.

Did this have to do with race? I had no language to express how race affected the way others perceived me, nor did they. But if the culture had told me Asian men were nerds or goofy houseboys, the white kids at the party must have received the same message.

In college in the early 70's, my reaction to the sexual place assigned to me turned to a compulsive sexuality—rampant promiscuity with white women and an obsession with pornography. This carried a definite racial component: If I were with a white woman, I thought, then I would be as "good" as a white guy.

It took me years to realize the fallacy in this thinking. One key was reading Frantz Fanon, the black Caribbean author and psychiatrist. In *Black Skin, White Masks,* he writes of how the black man who constantly sleeps with white women has the illusion that his feelings of inferiority will somehow be erased by this act.

Slowly, I began to ask how I learned what was sexually attractive and to question the images the culture gave me of myself. How, for instance, does race factor in attraction? A popular answer says love sees no color.

I don't believe that. We're taught to see race early on. The culture teaches us a racial hierarchy even before we're conscious of being taught. Race has affected our family histories, our sense of who we are.

This doesn't mean race is the sole determinant in interracial relationships, but it is a factor.

When I look at my wife, for example, I know my desires for her cannot be separated from how the culture has inculcated me with standards of white beauty. And given my history, how can I separate my experience, who I am, from race?

When I told my friend Alexs Pate, the African American novelist, about Marc Hayashi's remarks on Asian American men as eunuchs, Alexs replied, "And black men are the sexual demons."

One is undersexed, the other oversexed. We all know then who possesses a "normal" sexuality.

Recently, after a panel discussion on "identity art," an elderly white man complimented me on a performance I'd appeared in with Alexs. Then he asked, "Weren't you in *Fargo,* too?"

"No," I replied. "That wasn't me."

—DAVID MURA

Cover of *Gidra*, Spring 2000

Letters to the editor of *Newsweek* magazine
Volume CXXXV, No. 11, March 13, 2000, pp. 19–20

Upon reading the title of the article, I was prepared to be engaged by a refreshing piece on the success of Asian men. Instead, I was offended and saddened. The whole premise of your article is that a good gauge of an ethnic group's success is whether its members are dating whites. If Asian guys were dating Asian women, or African-American women, would they be on a losing streak? Apparently, Asian men are still thought of as the "model minority." You may consider this a *harmless* stereotype, but it is a stereotype nonetheless.

    Christine Duh
    Palo Alto, CA

* * *

I loved your piece about Asian men. Finally, there's a positive article about us, and it's great. I hope it will help change people's opinions and stereotypes about Asian males and their sexuality.

    Christopher Hsu
    Ithaca, NY

* * *

So now Asian-American men like me are the next big thing! I have to say that I was rather disturbed by Ester Pan's article, in which it seems that one stereotype has been eliminated, only to be replaced with another. We have gone from being geeky, nerdy and wimpy to being smart, genuine and respectful. Whether the stereotype is positive or negative is not the point. Those terms are inaccurate in describing a race of people. No one would describe white men in such terms, but it seems OK to talk about Asian men as a monolithic group with a number of set qualities. In addition, your article uses old stereotypes about strict patriarchal Asian families to suggest why Asian-American men tend not to marry out of their race. For decades Asian-American women have had to put up with the old stereotypes, which reduce them to fetishes, exotic fantasies and trophy girlfriends. I guess Asian men have finally caught up. I'm rather offended that my skin tone and culture have been deemed fashionable and are now a hot commodity, like Pokémon—even if it does help me date white women. Are any white women out there interested in a skinny, yellow-skinned Asian man? I'll style my hair like Astro Boy for you. I'll even do kung fu moves like Jet Li.

    Quincy Tran
    New York, NY

The Barbarians Are Coming

—an excerpt

Chapter III

From a small horizontal window, like an eye slit on the face of the house, I watch the first guests arrive. It is rare to see the ladies after hours, but tonight, the tenth of October, 1978, they are coming, twenty strong, some with their spouses, in spiffy evening attire and long, expensive cars.

It's a big shindig for Libby Drake's husband. He's contemplating a run for the state legislature, and tonight's what Libby Drake calls an "exploratory fund-raiser" for a possible campaign.

I'm standing in the kitchen, my hands blindly working down the row of tomatoes I have set along the cutting board like a string of beauty contestants. I feel not only for firmness but also for elasticity of the flesh; a ripe tomato gives under pressure, then springs to shape again.

I welcome the extra work. Honestly, I wish I had a meal or party or snack to prepare every hour of every day. Work is all that's left that's sane. Since Lisa Lee dropped that bomb on me, I've distracted myself, comforted myself by planning and replanning menus for tonight's function, shopping for the ingredients, and best of all, cooking.

I love the view from this window. A good thing, since I'm here a lot, at the counter, slicing, dicing, chopping. Such an impressive expanse of lawn! A gardener and his son (why isn't he in school?) come once a week to keep it manicured. The gardener is a small Puerto Rican man who wears a straw hat, with a bandanna around his neck, and I like to watch him work. At times, from my position inside the house, I feel as if he were my gardener, working under my orders, keeping each of my blades of grass trimmed to the same height. Except for some giant rosebushes, a birdbath, a decorative Greek column, and a three-foot-high knock-off of Michelangelo's David, the lawn is empty. What a luxury unused land is, a dose of green serenity, instant peace of mind, whenever I squint out the little window as I work. Once, after I first got my driver's license, I took Zsa Zsa for a ride through the narrow, maple-lined streets of split-level houses, fresh paint, and two-car garages where many of my schoolmates and her customers lived. In front of one house she had me stop, and she exited the car and inspected the shiny-leafed bushes and shrubs, clipped at crisp right angles, stately as the Parthenon. I honked and waved her back in. "Why plant so many plants you can't eat?" she said in Chinese. "These people are stupid." She slid her hand under my nose, offering for my inspection dark, odorless leaves she had plucked. "If it were left up to you," I said, sweeping the leaves off her palm and out my window, "those nice garages would be stables, the lawns vegetable gardens." How stupid she was, ignorant of the look of success, of civilization at its height.

Libby Drake, as lustrous as a polished apple, her skin and soul wound as tight as Maureen Dean's, slips past the dark green hedges that rise like a great wall at the rear of the garden. She is accompanied by her husband. Could he be the Drake of Drake's cakes fame? Mr. and Mrs. Ring Ding? Until recently I never realized that some brand names, Kellogg, Heinz, Hertz, for example, are actual surnames later lent to cornflakes, ketchup, rental cars. Such monumental acts of ownership were all but inconceivable to me. Imagine controlling the world's supply of Devil Dogs! Seeing Drake has a strange effect on me. Except for the gardener—he doesn't really count—Drake is the first man I've seen at the club. I've given little thought to this moment, but now that he's here, I feel the sanctity of our home (mine and the ladies') has been violated, a trespasser is on the grounds, an invader in our midst.

The Drakes slowly make their way along the slabs of slate that serve as a path from gravel parking lot to house. As she points, her husband surveys the property. The ancient trees that border it are radiant; the bright fall leaves form a magnificent bracelet of red, yellow, and gold around the land. Drake's black shoes look oiled and hold the day's last sun. The lawn glistens around the couple, each blade of grass, wet from the late-afternoon watering, is studded with diamonds, and my heart fills with gratitude for this woman, who, by hiring me, has made me part of all I behold. Halfway along the path the Drakes stop, and Libby Drake points in my direction. She's probably saying, "That's our brilliant chef, Sterling Lung. He keeps us all, oh, so satisfied!" Her legs gleam in the sun, as my hand alights on the one I'm after, and I lift the tomato, which yields to me its loving weight, its thin-skinned plumpness that molds to the curve of my hand. It is the perfect thing to squeeze.

More guests converge on the club, arriving in their Simonized steel tons, two hundred horses under the hood, commanded by manicured hands, designer-framed eyes, and thin-soled Italian shoes.

In the reception room Fuchs is serving cocktails and hors d'oeuvres. I conscripted him at the last minute; when he came by to deliver the bundle of foie gras for my pâté, I realized I wouldn't survive the evening without some help.

Six swans are lined up on the copper countertop, which shimmers like a toxic stream. I apply the finishing touch on a seventh, pinching the aluminum foil between my thumb, fore-, and middle fingers to form its beak. Inside each swan is a roll of tender Dover sole, stuffed with julienned scallions, sliced mushrooms, diced tomatoes, and minced fresh herbs. I want to do something special for the Drakes, especially Libby Drake, but the swans are a drag to assemble, so labor intensive, costly in time and energy, and worse, she didn't even want the *cygnes* to begin with. "Something Chinese would be nice," she said. "You promised when I hired you that you would cook Chinese some-day." Of course I had lied—I would've promised her Chairman Mao's head on a platter, just to land the job. What was I going to say, I am a French chef, my culinary pedigree extends back to the great chefs of Europe, I am the hautest of haute cuisines?

Libby Drake enters the kitchen, a drink with a cherry in her hand. Her hair is combed impeccably across her scalp, slick and gleaming, anchored in back in a massive braid that resembles a lobster tail. She informs me that four more diners are expected. "That won't be a problem," she says. It is, of course, but what am I going to do? She leans against the edge of the stainless-steel sink, a posture of familiarity and friendship. She briefly describes the extra guests, suggests ways of stretching the food, sips on her drink, and comments on the "fabulous swans," the hors d'oeuvres, the peculiar waiter. She is more fumes, perfume and alcohol, than she is flesh and blood. "I feel so small tonight, with men in my club," she says. I abruptly stop work on the swan-in-progress: Aren't I a man? She goes up on a single high-heeled foot, then flips loose the other shoe, which hits the tile floor with such a clatter that I have to stop and take notice, as she massages her toes through the black nylon. "This is my club, right?" she says. "So why do I feel insignificant here?" I know she's not expecting a response, I know it's not my place to answer, but I'm also keenly aware of what she means, because that's how Drake has made me feel ever since he set foot on my property. How does he do that, Drake who might be known worldwide as the man behind a dopey corporate logo: a cartoonish duck wearing a chef's toque.

"Sterling, please." She points with her chin at the runaway pump on the floor. Is she kidding? What am I, her personal valet?

But it comes naturally, though it rubs me the wrong way. Before I know what's hit me, I drop the swan I'm shaping, dry my hands on the side towel, and kneel to pick up the sleek black shoe, its metallic gold insole grinning at me. I hold the shoe out for her; it is feather light, and when she slips her foot in I feel the heat of her body fill the thin leather and radiate through my palms, up my arms, and into my every part. I'm left momentarily breathless by the sudden weight in my hands. "Thank you," she says, and as I stand *she* loses her balance (a legitimate slip?) and reaches out to me for support. She touches my shoulder, then caresses my ponytail, her fingers running through my hair like a litter of nesting mice. Thank goodness I haven't jumped, embarrassing her. My hair is fine, and as strong as fishing line. Its length has been a longtime source of shame for my parents, especially Genius, who has no problem calling me his fourth daughter, making no allowances for style or prevailing tastes. Bliss is just the opposite; she has said she will terminate our relationship if ever I cut my hair. She likes to roll off the elastic band that holds the ponytail in place and fan my hair across my back and give that black fall a hundred strokes with a pig-bristle brush. She says this is the way Chinese men have traditionally worn their hair, and she likes this quality she sees in me, how I, according to her, honor my forebears, where I come from. My forebears? Think Beatles, Jerry Garcia. The first club lady to touch my hair was Millie Boggs, who joked that my ponytail would make "a delicious whip," as she gave it a playful tug. From time to time a club lady will sneak up and pet me. Some are more welcome than others—I can't stand Sharon Fox, who grabs hold and says, "Giddyup!" Libby Drake is a regular, but her style is high on subterfuge, witness that questionable slip, that relies on my duplicity: neither party can acknowledge what's happening.

Fuchs enters the kitchen noisily and slaps his empty tray onto the counter, sending metal skidding on metal. "Fill 'er up," he says. "They love you out there." Libby Drake abruptly untangles her fingers from my hair, a ring catching a strand. I salivate at the crisp pain. As she rights herself she says, in the stern voice she uses to assert her authority, and now to maintain appearances, "Oh, I almost forgot. Keep an eye on the cars." She peers out the slit window, as if to demonstrate what she wants me to do. "There's been a rash of break-ins in the area."

She rushes past Fuchs and rejoins the party.

"Boss lady?" Fuchs asks, once she's out of earshot. "If you have to have a skirt telling you what to do, she's not too shabby."

"She's great. She's like a friend."

"I see that. She lets you cook *and* guard the cars."

The oven bursts with the sweet, briny fragrances of mussels and clams in herb butter; shrimps and bacon; mushrooms stuffed with crab and morels. I quickly try to teach Fuchs the French name for each dish, but it's futile—he butchers the pronunciation.

I push the kitchen's swinging door open for Fuchs. He says, "It's like the *Mayflower* out there." For the first time I see all my guests together. Dark suits and dresses, white shirts and collars.

"They look like the Pilgrims."

"No kidding," Fuchs says. "They *are* the Pilgrims." He launches himself into the crowd, armed with trays of my goodies.

I crack open the door to watch my guests enjoy my food. Fuchs stabs the trays in people's faces, and in a voice out of register with the others says, "I wouldn't know, my people don't eat shellfish." It's strange seeing the ladies all done up. They've undergone an amazing metamorphosis. By day they're pink, yellow, and peach, like those marshmallow chicks that come out at Eastertime. Tonight they look so erotic, with their skyscraper coifs, bare shoulders (sunburnt and freckled), and spiky shoes. What clothes can do! Slap a camouflage jacket and combat boots on Patty Hearst, accessorize with beret and submachine gun: Tanya!

I'm reminded of my own prodigious transformation from son of immigrants to denizen of Plymouth Rock. Look at the ladies, each claiming me as her own: each is anchored to a square foot of reception room floor, canapé pinched between fingers; the ladies swivel at the waist, arch their backs, gesticulate with arms and hands—stiff, like hieroglyphic figures set in motion. What they're doing is marking off turf, staking primal territorial claims. Here the territory is the master of the mini-toast smeared with Brie or anchovy paste, the goose-liver pâté, the smoked-salmon terrine; here the contest is over proprietary interest—ten hostesses presiding over the same fabulous dinner party, ten Virgin Mothers and one baby Jesus. Me!

My eyes flit to the men. I struggle to get a fix on them. I feel like a boy again, trying to take my father in, his great intimidating size, overlaid with the constant accusation, as if it was my name, "You're useless, you're useless," which sprang from his smoky lips or seethed off his back, his face stained with regret. From an early age I wondered how to love him if my eyes couldn't hold him. My eyes can't hold these men, because they wear suits that fit; because their cars guzzle gas and they don't care; because their women paint their nails, sign my paycheck, pet my hair; because their shirts (I can tell by their drape) are synthetic, the wash-'n'-wear fabric that's killing the Chinese hand-laundry business, and bringing my father to his starch-stiff knees.

While my guests are finishing their dinners, Fuchs, rumpled as lettuce left outside the crisper, takes his leave. His duties done, he delivers his parting shot: "Sterling, this gig of yours in this house—you have my condolences."

"It's usually not as crazy as this." I hate having to defend the ladies to him. My head is in the oven, checking on dessert. "The ladies aren't so bad," I'm saying, as I lift from the oven my gorgeous tarte Tatin, your basic no-frills confection, flour, butter, sugar, apples. But Fuchs is gone already. He didn't even let me thank him. He couldn't wait to get out of here.

I take a bite of fish in the calm and listen to the drift of voices, the sounds of contentment around my table. Fuchs reported that the women loved the swans. But do they know that a young man's gift of a wild swan to his beloved is an invitation to carnal love?

I have ten minutes before the dessert cools properly. I go outside, into the damp evening air, and walk across the lawn to look for sprigs of wild mint. A garnish of the green serrated leaves will set off the gold curves of the caramelized apples beautifully. The wild mint borders the tall hedges marking the property line farthest from the main house, near the carriage house and the driveway, where the guests' cars are parked.

Halfway up the slate path I come upon the David, illuminated eerily by a torchlight spiked in the ground. I stop and stare. Every day when I walk from the carriage house to the kitchen my eyes automatically fall on the statue, and I scrutinize his every inch. Measure myself against him. But if he is the ideal of masculine beauty, where does that leave me? And this guy is just three feet tall. The ladies love him. I have seen them extend their hands as they pass, and casually fondle his curly plaster hair.

On hands and knees I hunt for the wild mint. It is dark but the moon is full, and the fragrance of mint should be tickling the cool air.

I don't smell the mint. The gardener must've weeded or sprayed. I give up the search, and climb the stairs to my apartment to use the bathroom. I check my mailbox—there's a postcard from Bliss. Our first communication since the Lisa Lee night. Without flipping the card I know it's from Bliss—it's a picture of a sow suckling a row of piglets. The legend reads: "Pigging Out in Iowa!" Her handwriting in Bic blue ink is rigidly neat and sane as ever: "It's true, I'm pregnant with your baby. I came east with the news, *but* you were too busy for me. You know the story. I know Lisa spilled the beans. So where the FUCK have you been? (Oops, didn't mean to curse!) Don't you think it's time we talked? Call me collect if you have to. Iowa's hot and muggy and we're waiting for you with open arms."

I look out the window at the great lawn, the spotlighted statue, the house, my guests within, who have given me, as Genius would say, "big face" tonight, coming in their fancy cars and finest clothes (and I have returned the favor tenfold, having lovingly touched every morsel they've ingested, molecules of mine borne on each bite: I am bonded to their insides). And Bliss would have me uproot myself, live in exile from this place, the ladies, my good works here? I feel sick to my stomach. The postcard trembles in my hand. I stare at the pigs, the mother pig's unnervingly pink underside. I keep hoping it's a false alarm. How can she be pregnant? We haven't been together in a couple of months, and when we were together we didn't have sex that often, and when we did it wasn't what anyone would call passionate. Besides, she's an enthusiastic proponent of birth control, famous for doubling up on occasion, mixing in a rubber with her diaphragm, a spermicide with the Pill. Say I have supercharged, high-octane sperm that can burst through all those barriers, does that automatically qualify me as a father? All I have is Genius for a role model. Over the years I've learned his ubiquitous scowl, the leaden disapprobation. I'd hate shooting a child of mine that glare, breaking the baby's back. But maybe it's not too late. Bliss is a smart, liberated woman. She's spoken passionately about overpopulation, man's environmental ruination of the planet. I can trust her to hold true to her political convictions and do the right thing. Get the situation fixed. She has to come to her senses, sooner or later.

I glance out the window at the house again. It tugs at me, like the moon at the tides. Dessert! What a terrible chef I am, leaving my guests unattended for so long. As I leave the apartment and hurry down the stairs, my eyes catch on the streetlights glowing on the dark waxed body of the Drakes' Lincoln Continental. Without hesitation I go to the car and run my finger along its sleek electroplated paint. When I try the driver-side handle the door opens with a stately sucking sound. I slide in behind the wheel. The interior is redolent with cigarettes, perfume, leather, sweat. Drake and I must share the same seam size: the pedals, to my surprise and delight, are perfectly set. We have more in common: Drake has eaten my food; I have eaten Drake's cakes (if he is, indeed, that Drake). In flagrant violation of the pact I made with Bliss to quit smoking (because our professional lives are tied to mouths—I pleasure them, she fixes them), I filch a cigarette from the pack of Benson & Hedges, "a silly millimeter longer," and light up. I'm puffing like crazy, I feel as if I'm driving away from troubles, leaving Bliss behind. She can't touch me. I'm not wronging her: this is Drake's cigarette, and this is Drake's car, and the passenger seat is still warm with Drake's wife. Oh, the privilege of being an American, cars and quick escapes! Until I was fourteen or fifteen my family never owned a car. That fact was consistent with the profile of Chineseness that was forming in my young brain: We don't own cars, we don't live in houses, we don't eat anything but rice. Each one a racial trait. Now I'm right there with Drake.

When I open the door a crack to let the cloud of smoke out, I hear Libby Drake calling my name. I stumble from the car, and slash through the hedges. She is standing on the slate path, next to the statue. One hand planted on hip, a cigarette burning in the other, she looks angry, her body as stiff as the David's. Right then I know I can't face her without an alibi. I retrace my steps to the hedges, and strip a branch clean of its waxy leaves. Who'll notice the difference? For most people mint is toothpaste or chewing gum. I go to Libby Drake, my hand extended, offering her my harvest. I tell her the leaves are a decorative strain of mint, not high on taste or smell, but a nice visual garnish. She looks down her nose at my palm. "I don't know what you're doing out here," she says. "Why are you so determined to make me look bad in front of my husband? Don't tell me you didn't realize these are important people." In the moonlight her hair shines like the back of a Japanese beetle. She brings the cigarette shakily to her lips, then pauses as if trying to align the filter with her mouth. She's been drinking. I can smell white wine in her sweat. She puffs, and as she furiously exhales she stumbles slightly, her heels sinking into the lawn. I reach for her, but she catches herself against the statue. "Are you okay?" I ask, after weighing the pros and cons of calling attention to her tipsiness. "No, I'm not okay. I asked you to serve Chinese food, but you didn't, did you? Have you any idea of the humiliation I endured when Mr. Drake contradicted my claim that the swans are a Chinese dish?"

"You said that?"

"I promised my guests Chinese food, from our very own Chinese chef. And I was justified in doing so. We had talked, Sterling. I told you my conception of the menu." She absently caresses the David, her fingers tickling its curls like a message in Braille.

"But you liked the swans."

"Sterling, that's not the point. And to make matters worse, you disappear, along with that strange waiter you hired. Is he out here with you? I trust there's nothing irregular going on between the two of you. Seriously, Sterling, do you expect *me* to clear the table?"

Her harsh tone pushes the house away from me. I envy the statue her drunken, loving touch; I envy the man I so recently was, loved within the house's walls.

During my last week of classes at the CIA—a mere six months ago—my professor took me into his confidence: "When in doubt, Sterling," he said, "just flambé."

To make amends for upsetting Libby Drake, and to climb back into her good graces, I douse the tarte Tatin with Grand Marnier and cognac. I dim the lights in the dining room, ignite one of the cakes, then exit the kitchen, a crown of blue flames in my hands. Oohs and ahhs. Which is the least I can expect. The ladies lean forward in their seats, tightening thighs, flattening feet to the floor to grab a better view. I see it in their faces: I'm their personal lama strolling in their midst, gold robes and etherized grin, god light blazing in my palms. Awe is balanced with delight, in their eyes. This love of small fire—birthday candles, dinner candles, memorial flames—a throwback to primitive times. The ladies and their men fall silent, supplicants awaiting the diviner's word, a nation's destiny burnt into an oracle bone. The durability of a goat shoulder blade reveals who is fertile, who will bear a son. Around the table my guests applaud, as the blue flame fades. Once again, love is in the air.

After dessert they move into the reception room and look at slides of the Drakes' recent fact-finding trip to China. From the kitchen I see rosy-cheeked babies, toothless octogenarians, bicyclists, guys in Mao jackets, women in Mao jackets, Mao himself, soldiers in streets, swans on a lake, the ubiquitous Great Wall, tombs, rice paddies, birds in bamboo cages, oxen, billboards—the usual suspects I've seen hundreds of times on TV since Nixon visited China six very long years ago.

I'm making the rounds, offering refills on coffee when the slide show ends and the lights come back on.

"Everyone," Libby Drake says, grabbing me by the wrist, tweaking my bones too tightly. "This is Sterling, our very own Chinese chef." She is beaming, flush from her trip to China, as well as from the wine racing through her system. I can read her perfectly: Not only are the slides and the memories they hold hers, so are the people and objects in those pictures. And here I am, as if I'd just stepped off the screen, proof of her assertion.

"That was a fine meal," Drake says, prompting all eyes to alight on my skin, his mere utterance breathing life into my being. "I never would have suspected the hand of a Chinese person in any of those dishes."

"Sterling, tell Mr. Drake about the swans," Libby Drake says.

Tell what? My face is burning: *visage chinois flambé.* Everyone's waiting for me to speak.

"You just told me that the swans is a Chinese dish, didn't you?"

The authority in her voice! Right or wrong, it doesn't matter, have your say and say it with authority. All the ladies are supremely endowed with this skill, an American trait.

I try to do my best imitation of the ladies, and feel for the authority in my throat. "It's as Chinese," I say, "as I am." Flames flare under my collar.

"Ni shuo zhongguo hua ma?" Is Drake making fun of me, talking ching-chong talk? I can't believe he's doing this in front of everyone.

He does it again. "He doesn't speak Chinese," Drake says. "Where are you from?"

"Oh. New York," I answer, hoping people will hear New York City, meaning Manhattan, preferably the Upper West Side, much more glamorous than "Long-guy-lun" and its dull cookie-cutter towns.

"No, where are you *from?*"

Drake's perplexed look unnerves me. I can't risk disappointing him. So finally I confess. "Long Island," I say, taking care to articulate each word clearly.

He shakes his head. "Where. Are. You. From?"

"Lynbrook?"

Sally Hayes says, "He must mean Brooklyn."

"They do that," Kathy Lloyd says. "Flip words around. Kim at the fruit stand does the same charming thing."

Slowing his speech down even further to aid my comprehension, Drake says, "Where are your parents originally from?"

"Canton?"

"You mean Can*ton,*" Drake says. "We were there. Have you been back?"

"Back? I was born here." I'm about to give a brief account of my family history, but I quit before I start. And here, in this reception room in Connecticut, I have my first inkling of Zsa Zsa's ordeal on Ellis Island, her entry barred, more than thirty years ago. After three long months in a detention cell, all the waiting and interrogations, she took one look at the dirty streets of lower Manhattan, thought America was nothing but filth and insult, and begged to go home.

"The Chinese have a special fondness for Richard Nixon—" Drake is saying as I return from the kitchen with a fresh pot of coffee and an empty tray to bus the dirty china. He has assumed the air of a foreign-affairs expert. He has everybody's attention, and is loving it. His legs are crossed, inches of plaster-pale calf flesh exposed, his nylon socks as sheer as women's hosiery. I am embarrassed for him. "But here, we consider Nixon a criminal."

"No one under this roof does."

Someone praises Ford's pardon. Millie Boggs declares her preference for Betty over Pat. Then Drake says, "Nixon is nothing less than a modern-day Marco Polo. Nixon, one can argue, discovered China."

"Opened her up to the world."

"Brought an outlaw state into the fold."

"They're still communists, but we can like them now."

"The masses I can handle, but not Mao."

"The leader of the free world comes calling, and he doesn't have the decency to put on a suit and tie."

"Mao owes Nixon big-time. Nixon made him a player."

"Ping-Pong diplomacy."

"Nixon just about invented the damn game."

"Everyone was playing Ping-Pong. Someone made a fortune."

"We bought a table."

"Who didn't? Mine still takes up half the den."

"Those Chinese people are such good Ping-Pongers. On *Wide World of Sports* they always kick our butts."

"That must've been what they meant by Ping-Pong diplomacy: we let them win."

I've seen the same matches on TV, and I have to admit I get a charge seeing those wiry Chinese guys knocking the shit out of the Americans.

"It's suited for the whole race of them. Those petite paddles and little balls are perfect for their little hands."

"I agree. It's all in the genes. They're small people, with delicate bones and skinny muscles. That makes them quicker, more agile. They flit around the Ping-Pong table like a bunch of birds. And that's the name of the game. Ping-Pong doesn't require strength."

"I was about to say, I'd like to see one of your Ping-Pongers go up against a Nolan Ryan fastball."

"The physiological differences," Drake breaks in, "are the product of Darwinian adaptations. You see, Chinese culture doesn't value the individual. That's why you always hear them talking about 'the people' or 'the masses.' You saw the slides, you saw how crowded it is over there. They put three or four of their men on a job that one average American can do by himself. For this reason the Chinese have no evolutionary imperative to develop bigger, stronger bodies."

Cindy Nelson says, "But what about our Sterling? I wouldn't call *him* a shrimp."

Things have been going so well. I'm doing my job, minding my own business, making like a part of the decor, blending with the Oriental rug, the velvet couch. But hearing my name boom across the room, I feel I've been found out, a flashlight beam hitting me square in the eyes.

"He's more than average for a Chinese," Drake says, with an assessing eye. "How tall are you, son?"

"Wait!" his wife jumps in. "Don't answer. Let us guess."

"What fun, we'll have a contest!"

"We need a prize."

"That's brilliant!"

"What about Sterling?"

I'm on my way to the kitchen with a tray of dirty cups and dishes. They're crazy, drunk and crazy. I pretend I haven't heard a thing, and hope their contest fades away.

"That's brilliant. Winner gets Sterling—a gourmet meal prepared in your home!"

"What a lot of fun! The winner gets Sterling."

Kathy Lloyd is the last to leave. She's a small woman, about the size of Zsa Zsa in her cork-soled shoes. Her husband has gone home in his own car; she stays to iron out the details. She won me.

We walk together across the lawn, she to her car, me to my apartment. As we approach the David she says, "The Roman god of love. Isn't he beautiful?"

"He doesn't do a thing for me."

"I should hope not," she says. "He's not supposed to." We stop at the statue, and she points out the David's perfection, its claim on the hearts of women, naming the various highly articulated muscle groups, pectorals, deltoids, biceps, abdominals, quadriceps. She doesn't stop there. His buttocks she calls his "buns," his penis is his "cock," which she speculates would be "hung like a goddamn horse" if the manufacturer had made the statue "the size of a real man."

Then she directs my gaze to the statue's hand dangling by his thigh, close to his plumbing. The hand is huge, out of proportion to the rest of his body. She extends her hand—she wants mine planted on hers. "You have beautiful hands," she says, "and that's not just me talking. We all think so. But *I* discovered them first.

"When you come to cook for us," she says, "Mr. Lloyd might not be there. I trust that will be all right with you." She squeezes my hand.

I pull free and continue walking toward the carriage house. I know what's coming: She's going to tell me that theirs is an open marriage, that she's some kind of swinger. "What're you going to make for us?" she says from behind. "I'll eat anything."

When we reach her car, a Buick Riviera, I open the door and she gets in. "Sterling, come closer, I'm not going to bite," she says. Her legs, lit by the amber door lamp, flow from the car.

"I want you to know that I held a positive view of your people long before Nixon ever dreamed of China. I never thought you were as bad as the Russians." In the meager light I can see she wears too much makeup, and the makeup can't hide age or the alcohol she's imbibed this night. I picture her lying in her bed, puffing up on what she reads in *Cosmopolitan:* "Sex, the New Fountain of Youth!" "The Allure of the Experienced Woman!"

But I think of Bliss, and here's my contribution: "Sex Ages You, Takes Something Away Every Time."

Later that night, I'm lying in bed, trying to figure out how best to stay clear of Kathy Lloyd in the days ahead, when I hear voices outside, kids laughing. Drunk or stoned. I go to the window. Two long haired guys are carrying the statue of David, one holding the head, the other the base, and a girl with a Marcia Brady look is skipping along, their accomplice. Am I dreaming? The moon shines off the plaster man, and he glows like a giant tube of light. They're coming toward the carriage house, in my direction; they don't see me; they're stealing the David!

I turn on a lamp, open the door, step onto the landing. In the night's stillness, when the boards creak under my weight, they are screaming. The young thieves look up at me and drop the statue, then run back across the lawn, stumbling and falling, laughing and cursing. Leaving beauty behind.

I run downstairs. In the moonlight, against the dark grass, the David a giant bone, the fibula of a prehistoric animal unearthed in a desert, once a primordial sea. I stand the statue up. I hoist it onto my shoulders, Atlas bearing the world. I step toward its usual spot on the lawn, then reverse myself, as if a magnetic force is pulling me back to my apartment. Suddenly I feel all-powerful and break into a gallop, the David almost weightless. We fly up the stairs.

I set the statue on the floor of my bedroom. Now I've got what the ladies want. I clear a space in my closet and put him in there with my other junk. Once he's out of sight, an inexplicable satisfaction settles into my body, a sensation like the glow of twenty-five-year-old Armagnac radiating from my belly, and I feel that the energy driving the world emanates from me.

Some nights, in the crease of time before mosquitoes bite, long after the ladies have scratched good-bye kisses alongside one another's cheeks, I venture to the lawn and slide into the slot where several rosebushes converge, not far from where the David once stood. Here the air is thick, cathedral-like, what blood is to water. The red-black blooms, each the size of a calf heart, cooling after a long day's sun, release their perfume, and closing my eyes I caress handfuls of fallen petals and hold the softness to my nose and inhale deeply. I might think of Libby Drake at these times, or of the customer of my parents' who had starred in an Ivory soap commercial. I'm driven by the same impulse that compelled me to bury my face in piles of strangers' dirty sheets, taking in their layered smell—cologne, deodorant, soap—to a bitter finish, the hint of feminine sweat.

But tonight the roses' musk leads me to Bliss. Should I go visit her in Iowa? Even if I can get the time off—I don't think the ladies will let me out of their sight—what will that prove? I wouldn't mind seeing her, but in the way we used to see each other here. Things between us made a kind of sense back then. We ate and drank and went to movies; once in a while we had sex. We had our own lives. We were a good match—each helping the other tread water, until the right thing came along. Now that has all changed. Me, a husband, a father? I'm still a baby myself!

I can't stand this: Why can't I just be a chef?

This morning when Libby Drake questioned me about the missing statue, I lied. All day long I've thought about the David's hands. They are huge, especially the one that rests on his thigh. That hand is monstrous. Ideal beauty, my ass! They are that way for a reason. Michelangelo isn't selling beauty, but deeds. Like the slaying of Goliath. The David is a monument to work, what's accomplished with one's hands. That's all I want people to consider when they see Sterling Lung: what I do with my hands.

—DAVID WONG LOUIE

Untitled Art by David Choe

Satta Massagana

babylon's burning, babylon's burning,
babylon's burning there's no water
fire fire, fire fire,
fire fire, there's no water

i awoke this morning at 4:29 in the a.m.
to find my limbs pinned to the bed
beneath a cold sheet of sweat
by 50 fascist fingers wearing powdered wigs and helmets
reading *i didn't choose this life but*
i admit i'm scared to fight

charlie chan stood on my shoulders
    with his manhood in a thimble
he was stitching martha washington
    a halter top and garters
watching the fingers have his women
    while he jerked off with a dollar
    servility made him sinister
    his buck teeth were glowing mirrors
and he shined his shit at me
hoping i'd see myself and quiver
hoping i'd see myself reflected
as a chink, a paper whisper

but i did not let him see me cry
that motherfucker does not own my tears

my tears are saved for my baby's first breath
my grandmama's death and eternal rest
shit, good orgasms are what my tears are for

so i lay silent in my sweat
and beat back the regretful whores
that invade my mind
when time is ticking slow
what do you see? he whined insidious
the white porcelain ghosts of his coolie
teeth rank with the chewed flesh of

SCREAMING MONKEYS

passing us like olean and reselling us
the wizard of oz works in the department of immigration
and glinda the good witch eats dogs and writes rhymes
and is steering a three-story split-level tudor
for d.c. singing *it's hallelujah time, can't you hear the children
singing?*
and i was chilling
with my banana hat
i was passing a blunt to bruce lee and

dancing

dancing in the deep of the media blackout
confident in my ability to glow in the dark
and i was caught up in the Iniversal Spirit
swept up in the rhythm of a heavenly dub
singing the 7th octave that Saul Williams spoke of

> *i will not rhyme over tracks*
> *niggas on a chain gang used to do that*

and i was at tea with His Imperial Majesty
playing hwa-to and mah-jongg and scrabble and boggle
doing the hand jive that keeps secret knowledge alive
reading a cliff's notes version of *great expectations*
and my Lord's eyes were yin-yangs and big bangs and chain gangs
pigeons and doves and the wheels ezekiel spoke of
I AM Christafari Connector of Dots
I AM Adonai Elohim and Source of All Thought
I AM Yin and Yang which are Isis and Osiris
I AM John Africa 5 guidelines I AM a leaf of papyrus
because Nommo is the Logos is the Maat is the Tao
is the Lion is the Lamb is the Fish is the Cow
is the Buddha is Muhammad is the avatar called Iesus
and the b-girl in the windmill
is the dervish in the second appearance
my *without is Within, within my without*
Within I Without I is (   )

only breath—
red clad adida b-boy lads
only skills mad

a fad
they once said i was but fuck it
this be me
I   e   x   i   s   t
Satta Massagana means Alhamdulillah
Satta Massagana means Alhamdulillah
Satta Massagana means Alhamdulillah

means
hanel eh geh shin oo reeh ah bu jee yuh
how to break free
how to break free
how to break free is to kill the enemy sleeping in the inner me.

—DENNIS SANGMIN KIM

Findings of a Recent Inquiry into the Background and Causes of a Dissociative Identity Disorder in the Case of an American Subject of Filipino Descent

"and in place of memory I substituted inquiry."
—George Lamming, THE PLEASURES OF EXILE

You who will be thrown one fine day into this kindergarten in Southern California
   You, the only child in your class with this brown skin flat nose big ears slitted eyes wide feet and black black hair

Who will ask why you feel so short and skinny dark and bony foreign strange and other,
   And later, your head on your mother's lap, asking—Why am I different, mom?
   You who will wear the clothespin on your nose and Scotch tape on your ears and keep out of the sun speaking only English watching Beaver and wondering whatever happened to the Cleavers' colored neighbors
   You who will become an insurgent native colonial subject little brown brother or science project or but always the childlike primitive in need of civilizing

(And so Mr. Gamboa in 7th grade woodshop tells you lead the class but the boys all refuse call you chink say it over and over while teacher cuts boards on the saw/the TV news shows painted jeepneys, Malacañang Palace, Imelda's shoes/the immigration official says raise your right hand to solemnly swear to defend the constitution and welcome to America.) And so one fine day you inquire into the origins, the garrisons, the Counter-Reformation, the clerics, caciques, cronies, unemployment, and all the other reasons your parents left, why you hesitate to return

And you inquire into Magellan's discovery, Legaspi's conquest, the Acapulco-Manila galleon carrying pearls silks spices damasks porcelains fans spices and all the Chinoiserie making you Asian Hispanic American (Nuestra Señora de Buena Esperanza, bless all the fishers and farmers of St. Malo, all boat jumpers and claim jumpers of Manila Town, all the Pinoys of Barataria Bay)

And remember 1898 / remember $20 million buys an Asian archipelago/remember 250,000 Filipinos killed/memento mori/remember what the Philippines exports/nannies and nurses and oil riggers and cabin boys and croupiers/leave the islands see the world send back money and balikbayan boxes and even sing on Broadway!

And imagine the occupation, the prison camps, executions, comfort women, Hukbalahap, the Death March from Bataan and the American General who returned and the Parity Amendment opening wide the doors to U.S. bases nuclear arms investments rock and roll condensed milk movies and work for ten thousand prostitutes orbiting the naval bases like so many moons 'round the planet.

And denounce the military bases and multinationals and act real tough like a San Miguel-guzzling, cock-fighting, balut-eating/Katipunero or Moro insurgent/striking farmworker

(But a poor boy growing up in Tugtug took a bus ride to Manila where they're enlisting Filipinos and then it's bunks and mess halls and drills and it's yes sir and no sir and start in the kitchen and on to / a medical student from Santo Tomás postponed everything to fall in love with a navy man and emigrate to the U.S./and a young Fil-Am married an Italian girl and learned to alternate pasta and pancit on a weekly basis)

You who will bring two mestizo children into the world whose Asian American identity won't make it to the end of this generation You who will merge into the ten million or four percent category of Americans called Asian American
    You who will seek your ethnic identity and make good some childhood promise, purchasing Tagalog tapes and dutifully repeating—

    Ano sa palagay mo?
    Ano ang pangalan mo?
    Naiintindihan mo ba?
    Nakapunta ka na ba sa Amerika ikaw?

    —EUGENIO MATIBAG

The Boy Fell, art by Edward Del Rosario

The Two Filipinos

Mai-Lan Phan is Vietnamese.

Jared Shimabukuro is Okinawan.

Judy-Ann Katsura is Japanese.

Stephen Bean is Caucasian.

Loata Faalele is Samoan.

Caroline Macadangdang is one-fourth Filipino, one-fourth Spanish, one-fourth Chinese, one-eighth Hawaiian, one-sixteenth Cherokee Indian, and one-sixteenth Portuguese-Brazilian.

And the rest tell Mrs. Takemoto, who has gone row by row asking them their ethnicity, that they are Filipinos, except for Nelson Ariola, who says he is an American although he is as Filipino as any Filipino can be.

"No, Nelson," Mrs. Takemoto says, "Your nationality is American, but your ethnicity is Filipino."

"Yeah, Nelson," Katrina Cruz interrupts. "You was born a Filipino, and you goin' die a Filipino."

"Shut up, Katrina," Nelson says.

"You shut up, Nelson," she says. "What makes you think you not a Filipino?"

"Because I was born here," he says.

"So? Me, too," she argues.

"And because," he pauses, "because I'm not an immigrant." He glares at Florante and Vicente. "I don't speak English like I got a plugged nose," he says, shifting his eyes to Mai-Lan. "And because my grandfather never came here for cheap labor." He sneers at Benjamin Fontanilla, who, when he's not busy living in his own small world, tells his classmates stories about his paternal great-grandfather, Apo Lakay, who was a Sakada, one of the first Filipinos to arrive in Hawai'i to work at the sugar plantations on Kaua'i.

Benjamin raises his head, his eyes like cane knives on Nelson. "I pray my grandpa's spirit come drag you out of your mansion and bury you in one burning field," he mutters, bending his head down.

"That's enough, Benjamin," Mrs. Takemoto says.

"I'm sick and tired of being called a Filipino," Nelson says. "I'm not like them, Mrs. Takemoto."

"What makes you say that, Nelson?" she asks.

"Because I don't speak Tagalog or Ilocano. . . . "

"Well, for your information, Mr. usa," Edgar stands up, hands fisted at his waist. "Your mother speak Tagalog and your father from the Ilocos. And just cuz you no speak the dialect no make you one overnight American sensation."

"Shut up, Edgar. You don't understand," Nelson says. "I can't be a Filipino. I don't want to be a Filipino because the only Filipino everyone knows is the Filipino that eats dogs or the Filipino that walks around with a broom in his hands."

"So what? Big deal if Filipinos eat dogs. Big deal if they custodians or gardeners. Besides, why you care so much about what other people think? That's their kuleana, not yours," says Edgar.

"Because I don't want to be called a dogeater or a gardener for the rest of my life," Nelson says.

"You're so full of yourself, Nelson. Just cuz your father one lawyer and your mom one nurse. Wake up and smell the hot pandesal. Windex your mirror cuz your reflection goin' tell you you the best candidate for Mr. Pinoy—brown skin, yellow teeth, and no nose."

Even timid Jared Shimabukuro, who rarely lets out a sound, laughs.

"Quiet down," Mrs. Takemoto says.

"Look at me," Edgar says, rolling up his sleeves to expose his tan-lines. "I a mestizo born in the U S of A, but my fair skin no stop me from the fact that I one Filipino."

"But it's not only the color of skin that matters," Nelson says. Edgar interrupts: "Exactly. Took you that long for figure out. So just accept the fact that you more flat-nose than me."

Edgar bows and sits down. Stephen Bean stands and crosses his arms. "Nelson, if you're such an American, then what am I?"

Nelson opens his mouth; no words escape.

"One haole, what else?" Katrina says.

"That's enough, Katrina," Mrs. Takemoto says.

"At least I have a father," Stephen says.

"You like me go over there and bust your face?" Katrina says.

"You started it when you called me a haole," Stephen says. "I'm not haole, I'm Caucasian."

"Same freakin' smell, dumbass," Katrina says. "You in Hawai'i and a Caucasian is a haole is a haole is a Caucasian. And if you no can handle the tropical heat, go back to Antarctica."

"Katrina." Mrs. Takemoto slams her hand against the desk. "If you don't stop, I'm going to report you to Principal Okimura."

"Oh, no be threatenin' me, Broom Hilda," Katrina says.

Edgar turns around to Vicente and chortles.

"Detention for one week, Katrina," Mrs. Takemoto says. "The rest of you better settle down, or you'll be scrubbing the floors and wiping the chalkboard with Ms. No Manners."

"You just wait," Katrina says under her breath, "you freakin' bitch. Wait til I tell my mother and Uncle Craig."

Edgar stands up and faces Stephen.

"Edgar, sit down," Mrs. Takemoto says.

"Why only tell me to sit down," Edgar says. "Why no tell the haole for sit down, too."

"Shut up, faggot," Stephen says.

"No tell me to freakin' shut up, haolitosis," Edgar says. "And Mrs. Takemoto, you open one case but you no can close 'em, so I goin' close 'em once and for all."

Edgar first points his finger to Nelson. "You, Mr. Haole Wanna-be," then points to Stephen; "and you, Mr. Haolewood. You guys think you so hot-shit, but you know what? The ground you standin' on is not the freakin' meltin' pot but one volcano. And one day, the thing goin' erupt and you guys goin' be the first ones for burn."

—R. ZAMORA LINMARK

When Heroes Are Not Dead:
An Essay in Two Voices

"Up to this day, I am still fighting after more than half a century after the end of WWII in the pacific theater."
—Augusto Roa Realuyo, Death March and Camp O'Donnell Concentration Camp Survivor

My country never told me my father was a hero.

Heroes, after all, are not sick, old men. Personally, when I think of heroes, I see pedestaled statues, life-size sculptures of Filipinos, leaning forward, arms up, holding a *bolo* or a gun, mouths open, clothes perfectly wrinkled mid-air. I imagine the perfection of history, names of men after whom we called our streets, our rotundas, our airports. These revolutions carved out of stone. Oh, romance: uniformed soldiers circling the statues, a perfect cadence in the rain and sun. Trees, lamp posts, sunsets and lovers roaming the cobbled grounds of time. I hear romantic talks about history, about dead men.

When I was born, my father was approaching fifty. As a child, I always saw him as this man who was as old as the grandfathers of children my age. My mother, on the other hand, was much younger than he and looked like my older sister. I didn't bother to ask why that was so. I knew nothing about the war. What I learned about history in Manila were dates and facts I memorized, the whens, the wheres, and the hows, but the whys were left out: explanations that would have helped in an earlier understanding of how my family came to be: why veterans married late, why these men felt cheated by the Philippines; why they were displaced; why they were perpetually sick; why the Veterans hospital became a second home to the soldier's children; why Bataan fell in the first place.

My name is Augusto R. Realuyo, ASN #042193. A commissioned officer with Rank of 1st Lieutenant in the organized military forces of the Commonwealth of the Philippines. I was inducted into the service of the Armed Forces of the United States on September 1, 1941, pursuant to the call of the President of the United States of America (F.D.R.), dated July 26, 1941.

During the early days of World War II, just after the Japanese "sneak attack" at Pearl Harbor on December 7, 1941, I was involved in beach defenses on the eastern coast of Luzon Island, Philippines, when before the landing of Japanese invasion forces, the U.S. airforce was caught on the ground and put out of business in one sweep ... Thus leaving the whole of Philippines defenseless except for the USAFFE ground forces composed of a token U.S. army units, Philippine Scouts, and the Commonwealth Army of the Philippines.

History tells us that Manila was the most destroyed city after Warsaw during World War ii. While cities made of stone are easily rebuilt, ruined souls are not. My father after all was only twenty years old when he entered the war. He would be a bachelor for almost two decades after that. A part of his life he has yet to tell me. But I know the beginnings, how after the war, for lack of employment opportunities, my father went back to school, and eventually became both an architect and an engineer. Being poor was strange for a family with a father who had two baccalaureate degrees. He built houses for clients, mostly relatives and friends who hardly paid him. We lived in a ramshackle home in Sampaloc with an unfinished ceiling and flood-prone floors. There was no running water most of the time. But my grandparents' house in Oas, Albay seemed to be getting bigger and looking better every time my father touched it. I thought it was either my father was very generous, or he never knew that he had a family to feed. I could never comprehend why my father moved around the world terribly lacking a sense of paternal obligation. Hence, as an adult now, I don't remember his fatherly side. The father-son rituals never existed. No sharing of ambitions and dreams. No traditions handed down. No commercial-perfect image of father holding his son, as the younger took on the challenges of growing up. But his weak heart created three children, whose hearts were as hard as rocks.

At a recent birthday party for my father, a relative mentioned that the best way to understand what happened to him was by looking at his life vis-à-vis his own brother, his identical twin. There was a sudden rush of memory in my head. My uncle, also an engineer. All my life our family was compared to his. His family. His picture-perfect subdivision family. He has the same set of children. I always saw them as the "normal" family. Children who never starved. A house that never lost electricity. They had a car, a nice bungalow. The two sons played basketball in a court nearby surrounded by trees. The daughter baked. The parents went bowling. The place looked like one of my father's architectural drawings, displayed on our walls. They had a color TV. Their house looked like a Milo commercial. And they had visitors on Christmas. After the holidays, we always left their house with bags of wrapped food. And money as gifts. I wonder if they ever knew this, but I always saved the money they gave me. Then, I examined the Christmas photographs, always feeling how wonderfully they looked. Through pictures, I envied them, these well-fed cousins with whom I don't remember having a conversation once. Oh, such ease, such comfort. Yet I went home to a house screaming for new plumbing.

So the story goes: my father's twin *never* fought in the war. His battalion didn't have ammunition, my father said. They couldn't fight with pieces of wood. I find that hilarious now. But how I wished he were in his twin's shoes. *Wood* would have bettered his life, and ours. Instead, during those ill-fated years, my father, next to his twin, succumbed deeper into his dark past, an aging man carrying history's burden. A war veteran with suppressed psychological issues. Quick to anger, hard to approach, withdrawn. We, his raggedy family, would follow him throughout, without knowing what was going through his head, without knowing the history that brought him there, the past that caught up with him every day, eventually internalizing his problems, being so closely tied and exposed to this tortured man of war.

We, captured Filipino and American surrenderees, irrespective of rank were searched, robbed of personal belongings such as money, watches, rings, wallets, forced to march under a broiling sun which reached as high as 120 degrees in columns of four and groups of 500 or more along a gravel black top.

I was spanked, kicked, beaten in spite of my sickly condition. I witnessed my comrades who tried to resist giving away their mementos. Those falling out of line were clubbed, beaten and sword-whipped and even bayoneted and shot.

The very sick and famished prisoners who fell out of line, straggled frequently and helplessly, moaning on the roadside sometimes trampled or ran over by bike riding Japanese guards.

By daylight, we were to stand under the sun, they called "sun treatment" for a couple of hours and then marched down the road and so on until the 5th day. When we were given a small ball of cooked rice rolled in salt granules but no water. We had to satisfy our thirst by falling out of line when guards are not watching and get some water from the roadside ditches and carabao wallows near the road.

This continued until the 6th day after a forced march of ninety miles or more when we reached the town of San Fernando, Pampanga province, where we were crowded in a big-fenced enclosure with no room to lie down or stretch out. So many death marchers were delirious and died on the spot.

The next day we got again the sun treatment and were herded into box cars packed with no space to move. Diarrhea and dysentery ridden in an unbearable heat and stench with only two almost closed locked doors, I began to wonder, if I would ever survive.

In 1978, my father became terminally ill. I would spend part of my childhood visiting him in the Veterans Hospital near Manila. His siblings in New York City decided to bring him over as a last resort. I was ten years old when I overheard through a hole on the floor that my father was dying. I didn't understand what they meant by "dying." My father, after all, was always sick. But dying, he was not. He always fought. This time, for the very first time, he fought for the rest of my family. America was his last card. My father left us practically indigents. I was entering my teenage years. I would remember everything: the eviction from the house where I lived all my life, my mother taking two jobs, my sister taking a part-time job during college, lacking food, my relatives disappearing on us, lacking water, electricity getting cut off, the shame of poverty, and the front we all put up to face the day. My father, the architect and engineer worked in the U.S. as a messenger. He was in his late fifties. He applied for American citizenship. He petitioned for the rest of us. When we all left, in 1985, I finally said goodbye to the nightmare that was my Philippines.

Upon reaching Capas Train Station in Tarlac Province, we were again herded out of the box cars, got the sun treatment and marched down the road to Camp O'Donnell, Capas, Tarlac, a prison Camp a distance of about 12 miles from the train station.

At the POW Camp O'Donnell, we, survivors of the death march were quartered in two-tiered ramshackle bamboo and nipa roofed shacks with no sanitary facilities, no beddings, no clothing change, etc.

We were so crowded and packed in the sleeping quarters that we had to lie and sleep so close together so much so that sometimes when I woke up in the wee hours of the morning, if ever I was able to sleep. I would discover some of my buddies fellow POWs sleeping beside and nearest to me were already stiff-dead.

I never had a change in my clothing since our capture up to unconditional release due to my complicated illnesses. Never given any POW clothing. This was however a very fertile condition for breeding body lice, etc.

The food was a daily ration of cooked ball of rice rolled in salt. Sometimes accompanied with boiled root crops as sweet potatoes, mung beans mashed to a gravy-like consistency, and at least once a week some limited beef broth without the beef. We got daily ration of a salmon tin can of river water with which we have to satisfy our thirst, wash our lice-infested bodies.

Now, my father uses the term, *Post Traumatic Stress Disorder*, something which he discovered late in his life. Post Traumatic Stress Disorder, and all its manifestations? Is that what it was—the trunk at the foot of our bed full of artifacts from the war, swords, helmets, bayonets, all rusty with time? Is that what it was—the endless days he spent at our window staring into nowhere, counting the days as he peeled the skin off his feet, his daily withdrawals from our world, from our family? Is that what it was—the anger in his eyes at the sight of rats running around the house? Oh, much more, the irritability, the moodiness, the chain smoking, hostility, the shouting—post traumatic stress disorder—while all this time I simply thought that my father didn't know how to love.

Now, I understand. When my family spent the turn of the century with my father in the Veterans hospital in Manhattan, we already knew. A quiet acknowledgment of our *own* survival. His war, our war. His nightmares, our lives. Our history, our lesson.

Our triumphs, souls intact.

Today, April 9, 2000, the Day of Valor, formerly Fall of Bataan, I, Bino A. Realuyo, son of Manila, American immigrant, hereby declare my father, Augusto Roa Realuyo, 79 years old, and all the 60,000 surviving men who fought in Bataan, national heroes of the Philippines.

—BINO A. REALUYO

Solitary in a Strange Land

Rent a video,
buy a six pack,
and say Good night
to the old man in the liquor store. Crossing
streets of night
and silence, hunted
by car lights. In China,
it was easy to break up
with girlfriends. Now
no one else rumples
the neatly-made bed.
Hugging the mattress
on weekends, drinking one beer
after another. The TV
turned up all the way. Easy
to forget oneself. Bottles
lined up, their open mouths
sparkling in the light,
displace the shame
of lovelessness. Always falling
asleep alone in a strange land.
Weekends, crossing the streets
of silence and night, holding
a paper bag and feeling guilty.

—XUE DI
translated by Forrest Gander and Hil Anderson

Five Rice Queens

GWM, 5'11", 170 lbs, Brn/Grn, 8" cut ISO GAM to be my geisha
bun-boy mail-order bride and maybe more! Must be discreet and
disease free. Your photo gets mine.

ISO GAM (18-25) for LTR. I'm a forty-something GWM, 5'8",
average looks, into movies (luv Jackie Chan!), romantic walks,
quiet evenings at home. Let's order-in some take-out!

Well-hung GWM, 6', 200 lbs. seeks smooth GM (Asians a plus!)
for lunchbreak tryst. Into cellophane, peanut oil, duct tape. Shave
my hairy ass and balls during daytime soaps. Serious only.

GBM stud seeks GAM with tiny dick for B & D face-mask fun.
Need not speak good English, only look good with my huge dick
in your mouth and a tight hole I can punish.

Pinkerton looking for Butterfly to suck my Suzie Wong. Versatile
fifty-looks-forty navy officer ISO GAM to service my 10" uncut
pole. You be submissive and suicidal!

—TIMOTHY LIU

When Fidelito Is the New Boy at School

He is a frequent eclipse . . . a shadow on fire. The light breaks over the school-yard and the hallucination of evenly cropped trees in stride moves the glass. As the dark forms of spruce pass his face, he disappears.

He keeps his mouth shut and his palms open despite the steady drum of spit-wads, kid-song, and the long clock's nervous face. Bells refuse to breathe. And the wide hours wait for doors to open.

Fidelito gazes outside. There are other milder distractions: some of the children eat their shirts and some burst into rain. A road burns into a corner. In the power lines above the playground, a grackle's steel eye murders the earth. And the sky, now perfect for flight, is open like the older mouth of our moon.

—OLIVER FRANCISCO DE LA PAZ

The Price of Eggs in China

It was noon when Dean Kaneshiro arrived at Oriental Hair Poet No. 2's house, and as she opened the door, she said, blinking, "Hello. Come in. I'm sorry. I'm not quite awake."

He carried his measuring rig through the living room, noting the red birch floor, the authentic Stickley, the Nakashima table, the Maloof credenza—good craftsmanship, carefully selected, this poet, Marcella Ahn, was a woman who knew wood.

"When you called," she said in her study, "I'd almost forgotten. It's been over two years! I hope I wasn't too difficult to track down."

Immediately Dean was annoyed. When she had ordered the chair, he had been clear about his backlog, and today was the exact date he'd given her for the fitting. And she *had* been difficult to track down, despite his request, two years ago, that she notify him of any changes of address. Her telephone number in San Francisco had been disconnected, and he had had to find her book in the library, then call her publisher in New York, then her agent, only to learn that Marcella Ahn had moved an hour south of San Francisco to the very town, Rosarita Bay, where he himself lived. Never mind that he should have figured this out, having overheard rumors of yet another Asian poet in town with spectacular long hair, rumors which had prompted the references to her and Caroline Yip, his girlfriend of eight months, as the Oriental Hair Poets.

He adjusted his rig. Marcella Ahn was thin and tall, but most of her height was in her torso, not her legs—typical of Koreans. She wore tight midnight-blue velvet pants, lace-up black boots, and a flouncy white Victorian blouse, her tiny waist cinched by a thick leather belt.

"Sit, please," he said. She settled into the measuring rig. He walked around her twice, then said, "Stand up, please." After she got up, he fine-tuned the back supports and armrests and shortened the legs. "Again, please."

She sat down. "Oh, that's much better, infinitely better," she said. "You can do that just by looking?"

Now came the part that Dean always hated. He could use the rig to custom-fit his chairs for every part of the body except for one. "Could you turn around, please?"

"Sorry?"

"Could you turn around? For the saddling of the seat?"

Marcella Ahn's eyes lighted, and the whitewash of her foundation and powder was suddenly broken by the mischievous curl of her lips, which were painted a deep claret. "You mean you want to examine . . . my *buttocks?*"

He could feel sweat popping on his forehead. "Please."

Still smirking, she raised her arms, the ruffled cuffs of her blouse dropping away, followed by the jangling release of two dozen silver bracelets on each wrist. There were silver rings on nearly every digit, too, and with her exquisitely lacquered fingers, she slowly gathered her hair—straight and lambent and hanging to midthigh—and raked it over one shoulder so it lay over her breast. Then she pivoted on her toe, turned around, and daintily lifted the tail of her blouse to expose her butt.

He squatted behind her and stared at it for a full ten seconds. It was a good butt, a firm, StairMastered butt, a shapely, surprisingly protuberant butt.

She peeked over her shoulder. "Need me to bend over a little?" she asked.

He bounced up and moved across the room and pretended to jot down some notes, then looked around. More classic modern furniture, very expensive. And the place was neat, obsessive-compulsive neat. He pointed to her desk. "You'll be using the chair here?"

"Yes."

"To do your writing?"

"Uh-huh."

"I'll watch you, then. For twenty minutes, please."

"What? Right now?"

"It'll help me to see you work, how you sit, maybe slouch."

"It's not that simple," she said.

"No?"

"Of course not. Poets can't write on demand. You know nothing about poetry, do you?"

"No, I don't," Dean said. All he ever read, in fact, were mystery novels. He went through three or four of them a week—anything with a crime, an investigation. He was now so familiar with forensic techniques, he could predict almost any plot twist, but his head still swam in delight at the first hint of a frame-up or a double-cross.

He glanced out the window. Marcella Ahn lived off Skyview Ridge Road, which crested the rolling foothills, and she had one of the few panoramic views of Rosarita Bay—the harbor to the north, the marsh to the south, the town in the middle, and, everywhere beyond, the vast Pacific.

Marcella Ahn had her hands on her hips. "And I don't slouch," she said.

Eventually he did convince her to sit in her present desk chair, an ugly vinyl contraption with pneumatic levers and bulky ergonomic pads. She opened a bound notebook and uncapped a fountain pen, and hovered over the blank page for what seemed like a long time. Then she abruptly set everything aside and booted up her laptop computer. "What do you do with clients who aren't within driving distance?"

"I ask for a videotape, and I talk to their tailor. Try to work, please. Then I'll be out of your way."

"I feel so silly."

"Just pretend I'm not here," he said.

Marcella Ahn continued to stare at the computer screen. She shifted, crossed her legs, and tucked them underneath her. Finally, she set her fingers on the keys and tapped out three words—all she could manage, apparently. She exhaled heavily. "When will the chair be ready?"

"I'll start on it next month, on April twentieth, then three weeks, so May eleventh," he told her, though he required only half that time. He liked to plan for contingencies, and he knew his customers wanted to believe—especially with the prices they were paying—that it took him longer to make the chairs.

"Can I visit your studio?" she asked.

"No, you cannot."

"Ah, you see, you can dish it—"

"It would be very inconvenient."

"For twenty minutes."

"Please don't," he said.

"Seriously. I can't swing by for a couple of minutes?"

"No."

Marcella Ahn let out a dismissive puff. "Artists," she said.

Oriental Hair Poet No. 1 was a slob. Caroline Yip lived in an apartment above the R.B. Feed & Hardware store, one small room with a Pullman kitchen, a cramped bathroom, and no closets. Her only furnishings were a futon, a boom box, and a coffee table, and the floor was littered with clothes, CDs, shoes, books, newspapers, bills, and magazines. There was a thick layer of grease on the stovetop, dust and hair and curdled food on every other surface, and the bathroom was clogged with sixty-two bottles of shampoo and conditioner, some half-filled, most of them empty.

Dean had stayed in the apartment only once—the first time they slept together. He had lain naked on her futon, and Caroline had inspected his erection, baldly surveying it from different angles. "Your penis looks like a fire hydrant," she had said. "Everything about you is short, squat, and thick." It was true. Dean was an avid weightlifter, not an ounce of fat on him, but his musculature was broad and tumescent, absent of definition. His forearms were pickle jars, almost as big as his thighs, and his crewcutted head sat on his shoulders without the relief of a neck. "What am I doing with you?" Caroline said. "This is what it's come down to, this is how far I've sunk. I'm about to fuck a Nipponese fire hydrant with the verbal capacity of tap water."

There were other peculiarities. She didn't sleep well, although she had done almost everything possible short of psychotherapy—which she didn't believe in—to alleviate her insomnia and insistent stress: acupuncture, herbs, yoga, homeopathy, tai chi. She ran five miles a day, and she meditated for twenty minutes each morning and evening, beginning her sessions by trying to relax her face, stretching and contorting it, mouth yowling open, eyes bulging—it was a horrific sight.

Even when she did sleep, it was fitful. Because she ground her teeth, she wore a plastic mouthpiece to bed, and she bit down so hard on it during the night, she left black spots where her fillings were positioned. She had night-mares, a recurring nightmare, of headless baby chickens chasing after her, hundreds of decapitated little chicks tittering in rabid pursuit.

The nightmares, however, didn't stop her from eating chicken, or anything else, for that matter. She was a waif, five-two, barely a hundred pounds. Her hair—luxuriant, butt-length, and naturally kinky, a rarity among Asians—seemed to weigh more than she did. Yet she had a ravenous appetite. She was constantly asking for seconds, picking off Dean's plate. "Where does it all go?" he asked over dinner one night, a month into their courtship.

"What?"

"The food."

"I have a very fast metabolism. You're not going to finish that?"

He scraped the rest of his portion into her bowl, and he watched her eat. He had surprised himself by how fond he'd become of her. He was a disciplined man, one with solitary and fastidious habits, yet Caroline's idiosyncrasies were endearing to him. Maybe this was the true measure of love, he thought—when you willingly tolerate behavior that, in anyone else, would be annoying, even abhorrent to you. Without thinking, he blurted out, "I love you."

"Yikes," Caroline said. She put her chopsticks down and wiped her mouth. "You are the sweetest man I know, Dean. But I worry about you. You're so innocent. Didn't anyone let you out of the house when you were young? Don't you know you're not supposed to say things like that so soon?"

"Do you love me?"

She sighed. "I don't right now," she said. Then she laid her hands on top of his head and shook it. "But I think I will. Okay, you big boob?"

It took her two more months to say that she might, maybe, be a little bit in love with him, too. "Despite everything, I guess I'm still a romantic," she said. "I will never learn."

They were both reclusive by nature, and most of the time were content to sequester themselves in Dean's house, which was tucked in a canyon in the coastal mountains. They watched videos, read, cooked Japanese dishes: *tonkatsu, oyako donburi, tempura, unagi.* It was a quiet life, free of catastrophe, and it had lulled Dean into thinking that there would be no harm in telling her about his encounter with Oriental Hair Poet No. 2.

"That cunt!" Caroline said. "That conniving Korean cunt! She's moved here on purpose!"

It was all she could talk about for three days. Caroline Yip and Marcella Ahn, it turned out, had a history. They had both lived in Cambridge, Massachusetts, in their twenties, and for several years, they had been the best of friends—inseparable, really. But then their first books came out at the same time, Marcella's from a major New York publisher, Caroline's from a small, albeit respected press. Both had very similar jacket photos, the two women looking solemn and precious, hair flowing in full regalia. An unfortunate coincidence. Critics couldn't resist reviewing them together, mocking the pair, even then, as "The Oriental Hair Poets," "The Braids of the East," and "The New Asian Poe-tresses."

But Marcella came away from these barbs relatively unscathed. Her book, *Speak to Desire*, was taken seriously, compared to Marianne Moore and Emily Dickinson. Her poetry was highly erudite, usually beginning with mundane observations about birds or plant life, then slipping into long, abstract meditations on entropy and inertia, the Bible, evolution, and death, punctuated by the briefest mention of personal deprivations—anorexia, depression, abandonment. Or so the critics said. Dean still had the book from the library, but he couldn't make heads or tails of it.

In contrast, Caroline's book, *Chicks of Chinese Descent*, had been skewered. She wrote in a slangy, contemporary voice, full of topical, pop culture allusions. She wrote about masturbation and Marilyn Monroe, about tampons and *moo goo gai pan*, about alien babies and chickens possessed by the devil. She was roundly dispatched as a mediocre talent.

Worse, Caroline said, was what happened afterwards. Marcella began to thwart her at every turn. Teaching jobs, coveted magazine publications, awards, residencies, fellowships—everything Caroline applied for, Marcella got. It didn't hurt that Marcella was a shameless schmoozer, flirting and networking with anyone who might be of use. Yet, the fact was, Marcella was rich. Her father was a shipping tycoon, and she had a trust fund in the millions. She didn't need any of these pitifully small sinecures which would have meant a livelihood to Caroline, and it became obvious that the only reason Marcella was pursuing them at all was to taunt her.

"She's a vulture, a vampire," Caroline told Dean. "You know she won't go out in the light of day? She stays up until four, five in the morning and doesn't wake up until past noon."

And then there was the matter of Evan Paviromo, the English-Italian editor of a literary journal whom Caroline had dated for seven years, waiting patiently for them to get married and have children. He broke it off one day without explanation. She dogged him. Why? Why was he ending it? She refused to let him go without some sort of answer. Finally he complied. "It's something Marcella said," he admitted.

At first Caroline feared they were having an affair, but the truth was more vicious. "Marcella told me she admired me," Evan said, "that I was far more

SCREAMING MONKEYS

generous than she could ever be. She said she just wouldn't be able to stay with someone whose work she didn't really respect. I thought about that, and I decided I'm not that generous. It's something that would eat away at me, that's bothered me all along. It's something I can't abide."

Caroline fled to California, eventually landing in Rosarita Bay. She completely disengaged herself from the poetry world. She was still writing every day, excruciating as it was for her, but she had not attempted to publish anything in six years. She was thirty-seven now, and a waitress—the breakfast shift at a diner, the dinner shift at a barbecue joint. Her feet had grown a full size from standing so much, and she was broke. But she had started to feel like her old self again, healthier, more relaxed, sleeping better. Dean had a lot to do with it, she said. She was happy—or as happy as it was possible for a poet to be. Until now. Until Marcella Ahn suddenly arrived.

"She's come to torment me," Caroline said. "Why else would she move to Rosarita Bay?"

"It's not such a bad place to live."

"Oh, please."

Dean supposed she was right. On the surface, Rosarita Bay looked like a nice seaside town, a rural sanctuary between San Francisco and Santa Cruz. It billed itself as the pumpkin capital of the world, and it had a Main Street lined with gas streetlamps and old-time, clapboarded, saltbox shops and restaurants. Secluded and quiet, it felt like genuine small-town America, and most of the eight thousand residents preferred it that way, voting down every development plan that came down the pike.

Yet the things that gave Rosarita Bay its charm were also killing it. There were only two roads into town, Highway 1 on the coast and Highway 71 through the San Vicente Mountains, both of them just two lanes and prone to landslides. The fishing and farming industries were drying up, there were no new jobs, and, for those who worked in San Francisco or "over the hill" in San Vicente, it was a murderous, traffic-choked commute. The weather was also terrible, rain-soaked and wave-battered in the winter, wind-beaten in the spring, and fog-shrouded all summer long, leaving basically two good months—September and October.

In theory quaint and pretty, Rosarita Bay was actually a no-man's-land, a sleepy, slightly seedy backwater with the gray air of anonymity. People stuck to themselves, as if shied by failure and missed opportunities. You could get lost here, forgotten. It was, when all was said and done, a place of exile. It was not a place for a wealthy, jet-setting artiste and bon vivant like Marcella Ahn. But to come here because of Caroline? No. Dean could not believe it.

"How could she have even known you were here?" he asked Caroline. "You said you're not in touch with any of those people anymore."

"She probably hired a detective."

"Come on."

"You don't understand. I suppose you think if anyone's looking for revenge, it'd be me, that I can't be a threat to her because I'm such a loser."

"I wish you'd stop putting yourself down all the time. You're not a loser."

"Yes I am. You're just too polite to say so. You're so fucking Japanese."

Early on, she had given him her book to read, and he had told her he liked it. But when pressed, he'd had to admit that he didn't really understand the poems. He was not an educated man, he had said.

"You pass yourself off as this simple chairmaker," Caroline said. "You were practically monosyllabic when we began seeing each other. But I know you're not the gallunk you make yourself out to be."

"I think you're talented. I think you're very talented." How could he explain it to her? Something had happened as he'd read her book. The poems, confusing as they were, had made his skin prickle, his throat thicken, random images and words—*kiwi, quiver, belly, maw*—wiggling into his head and taking residence.

"Are you attracted to her?" Caroline asked.

"What?"

"You're not going to make the chair for her, are you?"

"I have to."

"You don't have a contract."

"No, but—"

"You still think it's all a coincidence."

"She ordered the chair *sixteen months* before I met you."

"You see how devious she is?"

Dean couldn't help himself. He laughed.

"She has some sick bond to me," Caroline said. "In all this time, she hasn't published another book, either. She *needs* me. She *needs* my misery. You think I'm being hysterical, but you wait."

It began with candy and flowers, left anonymously behind the hardware store, on the stairs that led up to Caroline's apartment. Dean had not sent them.

"It's her," Caroline said.

The gifts continued, every week or so, then every few days. Chocolates, carnations, stuffed animals, scarves, hairbrushes, barrettes, lingerie. Caroline, increasingly anxious, moved in with Dean, and quickly came down with a horrendous cold.

Hourly he would check on her, administering juice, echinacea, or antihistamines, then would go back to the refuge of his workshop. It was where he was most comfortable—alone with his tools and wood, making chairs that would last hundreds of years. He made only armchairs now, one chair, over and over, the Kaneshiro Chair. Each one was fashioned out of a single board of *keyaki,* Japanese zelkova, and was completely handmade. From the logging to the tung oil finish, the wood never touched a power tool. All of Dean's saws and chisels and planes were hand-forged in Japan, and he shunned vises and clamps of any kind, sometimes holding pieces between his feet to work on them.

On first sight, the chair's design wasn't that special—blocky right angles, thick Mission-style slats—but its beauty lay in the craftsmanship. Dean used no nails or screws, no dowels or even glue. Everything was put together by joints, forty-four delicate, intricate joints, modeled after a traditional method of Japanese joinery dating to the seventeenth century, called *sashimono.* Once coupled, the joints were tenaciously, permanently locked. They would never budge, they would never so much as squeak.

What's more, every surface was finished with a hand plane. Dean would not deign to have sandpaper in his shop. He had apprenticed for four years with a master carpenter in the city of Matsumoto, in Nagano prefecture, spending the first six months just learning how to sharpen his tools. When he returned to California, he could pull a block plane over a board and produce a continuous twelve-foot-long shaving, without a single skip or dig, that was less than a tenth of a millimeter thick—so thin you could read a newspaper through it.

Dean aimed for perfection with each chair. With the first kerf of his *dozuki* saw, with the initial chip of a chisel, he was committed to the truth of the cut. Tradition dictated that any errors could not be repaired, but had to remain untouched to remind the woodworker of his humble nature. More and more, Dean liked to challenge himself. He no longer used a level, square, or marking gauge, relying on his eye, and soon he planned to dispense with rulers altogether, maybe even with pencils and chalk. He wanted to get to the point where he could make a Kaneshiro Chair blindfolded.

But he had a problem. Japanese zelkova, the one- to-two-thousand-year-old variety he needed, was rare and very expensive—amounting to over $150 a pound. There were only three traditional woodcutters left in Japan, and Dean's sawyer, Hayashi Kota, was sixty-nine. Hayashi-san's intuition was irreplaceable. So much of the work was in reading the trees and determining where to begin sawing to reveal the best figuring and grain—like cutting diamonds. Afraid the sawyer might die soon, Dean had begun stockpiling wood five years ago. In his lumber shed, which was climate-controlled to keep the wood at a steady thirty-seven percent humidity, was about two hundred thousand dollars' worth of zelkova. Hayashi-san cut the logs through and through and air-dried them in Japan for a year, and after two weeks of kiln heat, the boards were shipped to Dean, who stacked them on end in *boule* order. When he went into the shed to select a new board, he was always overcome by the beauty of the wood, the smell of it. He'd run his hand over the boards—hardly a check or crack on them—and would want to weep.

Given the expense of the wood and the precision his chairs required, anyone seeing Dean in his shop would have been shocked by the rapidity with which he worked. He never hesitated. He *attacked* the wood, chips flying, shavings whirling into the air, sawdust piling at his feet. He could sustain this ferocity for hours, never letting his concentration flag. No wonder, then, that it took him a few moments to hear the knocking on the door late that afternoon. It took him even longer to comprehend why anyone would be disturbing him in his workshop, his *sanctum sanctorum.*

Caroline swung open the door and stepped inside, looking none too happy. "You have a visitor," she said.

Marcella Ahn sidled past her. "Hello!"

Dean almost dropped his *ryoba* saw.

"Is that my chair?" she asked, pointing to the stack of two-by-twos on his bench. "I know, I know, you told me not to come, but I had to. You won't hold it against me, will you?"

Without warning, Caroline let out a violent sneeze, her hair whiplashing forward.

"Bless you," Dean and Marcella said at the same time.

Caroline snorted up a long string of snot, glaring at Oriental Hair Poet No. 2. They were a study in contrasts, Marcella once again decked out as an Edwardian whore: a corset and bodice, miniskirt and high heels, full makeup, hair glistening. Caroline was wearing her usual threadbare cardigan and flannel shirt, pajama bottoms, and flip-flops. She hadn't bathed in two days, sick in bed the entire time.

"When you get over this cold," Marcella said to her, "we'll have to get together and catch up. I just can't get over seeing you here."

"It *is* incredible, isn't it?" Caroline said. "It must defy all the laws of probability." She walked to the wall and lifted a mortise chisel from the rack. "The chances of your moving here, when you could live anywhere in the world, it's probably more likely for me to shit an egg for breakfast. Why *did* you move here?"

"Pure chance," Marcella told her cheerily. "I happened to stop for coffee on my way to Aptos, and I saw one of those real estate circulars for this house. It looked like an unbelievable bargain. Beautiful woodwork. I thought, What the hell, I might as well see it while I'm here. I was tired of living in cities."

"What have you been doing since you got to town? Buying lots of gifts?"

Dean watched her dig the chisel blade into a piece of scrap. He wished she would put the chisel down. It was very sharp.

Marcella appeared confused. "Gifts? No. Well, unless you count Mr. Kaneshiro's chair as a gift. To myself. You don't have a finished one here? I've actually never seen one except in the Museum of Modern Art."

"Sorry," he told her, nervous now, hoping it would slip by Caroline.

But it did not. "The Museum of Modern Art?" she asked. "In New York?"

Marcella nodded. She absently flicked her hair back with her hand, and one of her bracelets flew off her wrist, pinging against the window and landing on some wood chips.

Caroline speared it up with the chisel and dangled it in front of Marcella, who slid it off somewhat apprehensively. Caroline then turned to Dean. "Your chairs are in the Museum of Modern Art in New York?"

He shrugged. "Just one."

"You didn't know?" Marcella asked Caroline, plainly pleased she didn't. "Your boyfriend's quite famous."

"How famous?"

"I would like to get back to work now," Dean said.

"He's in Cooper-Hewitt's permanent collection, the M.F.A. in Boston, the American Craft Museum."

"I need to work, please."

"Don't you have a piece in the White House?"

"Time is late, please."

"Can I ask you some questions about your process?"

"No." He grabbed the chisel out of Caroline's hand before she could react and ushered Marcella Ahn to the door. "Okay, thank you. Goodbye."

"Caroline, when do you want to get together? Maybe for tea?"

"She'll call you," Dean said, blocking her way back inside.

"You'll give her my number?"

"Yes, yes, thank you," he said, and shut the door.

Caroline was sitting on his planing bench, looking gaunt and exhausted. Through the window behind her, Dean saw it was nearing dusk, the wind calming down, the trees quiet. Marcella Ahn was out of view, but he could hear her starting her car, then driving away. He sat down next to Caroline and rubbed her back. "You should go back to bed. Are you hungry? I could make you something."

"Is there anything else about you I should know? Maybe you've taught at Yale or been on the Pulitzer committee? Maybe you've won a few genius grants?"

He wagged his head. "Just one."

"What?"

He told her everything. Earlier in his career, he had done mostly conceptual woodwork, more sculpture than furniture. His father was indeed a fifth-generation Japanese carpenter, as he'd told her, but Dean had broken with tradition, leaving his family's cabinetmaking business in San Luis Obispo to study studio furniture at the Rhode Island School of Design. After graduating, he had moved to New York, where he was quickly declared a phenomenon, a development that baffled him. People talked about his work with terms like "verticality" and "negation of ego" and "primal tension," and they might as well have been speaking Farsi. He rode it for all it was worth, selling pieces at a record clip. But eventually, he became bored. He didn't experience any of the rivalries that Caroline had, nor was he too bothered by the egos and fatuity that abounded in the art world. He just didn't believe in what he was doing anymore, particularly after his father died of a sudden stroke. Dean wanted to return to the pure craftsmanship and functionality of woodworking, building something people could actually *use*. So he dropped everything to apprentice in Japan. Afterwards, he distilled all of his knowledge into the Kaneshiro Chair, which was regarded as significant a landmark as Frank Lloyd Wright's Willits Chair. Ironically, his work was celebrated anew. He received a five-year genius grant that paid him an annual $50,000, all of which he had put into hoarding the zelkova in his shed.

"How much do you get a chair?" Caroline asked.

"Ten thousand."

"God, you're only thirty-eight."

"It's an inflated market."

"And you never thought to tell me any of this in the eight months we've been going out? I thought you were barely getting by. You live in this crappy little house with cheap furniture, your pickup is ten years old, you never take vacations. I thought it was because you weren't very savvy about your business, making one chair at a time, no advertising or catalogue or anything, no store lines. I thought you were *clueless.*"

"It's not important."

"Not important? Are you insane? Not important? It changes everything."

"Why?"

"You know why, or you wouldn't have kept this secret from me."

"It was an accident. I didn't set out to be famous. It just happened. I'm ashamed of it."

"You should be. You're either pathologically modest, or you were afraid I'd be repelled by how successful you are, compared to me. But you should have told me."

"I just make chairs now," Dean said. "I'm just like you with your poetry. I work hard like you. I don't do it for the money or the fame or to be popular with the critics."

"It's just incidental that you've gotten all of those things without even trying."

"Let's go in the house. I'll make you dinner."

"No. I have to go home. I can't be with you anymore."

"Caroline, please."

"You must think I'm pathetic, you must pity me," she said. "You're not like me at all. You're just like Marcella."

They had had fights before, puzzling affairs where she would walk out in a huff, incensed by an innocuous remark he'd made, a mysterious gaff he'd committed. A day or two would go by, then she would talk to him, peevishly at first, ultimately relenting after she had dressed him down with a pointed lecture on his need to be more sensitive, more supportive, more complimentary, more assertive, more emotive, more sympathetic, above all, more *communicative*. Dean would listen without protest, and, newly educated and humbled, he would always be taken back. But not this time. This time was different. On the telephone the next day, Caroline was cool and resolute—no whining or nagging, no histrionics or ultimatums or room for negotiation. "It's over, Dean," she said.

The following afternoon, he went to her apartment with a gallon of *miso* soup. "For your cold," he said.

She looked down at the tub in his hands. "I'm fine now. I don't need the soup. The cold's gone."

They were standing outside on the stairway landing. "You're not going to let me in?" he asked.

"Dean, didn't you hear what I said yesterday?"

"Just tell me how I should change. I'll change."

"It's not like that."

"What's it like, then? Tell me what you want me to do."

"Nothing," she said. "You can't fix this. Don't come by again, don't call, okay? It'll be easier if we just break it off clean."

He tried to leave her alone, but none of it made any sense to him. Why was she ending it? What had he done wrong? It had to be one of her mood swings, a little hormonal blip, a temporary synaptic disruption, all of which he'd witnessed and weathered before. It had to be more about Marcella Ahn than him. She couldn't really be serious. The best course of action seemed to be to wait it out, while at the same time being solicitous and attentive. So he called—not *too* frequently, maybe once a day or so—and since she wouldn't pick up her phone, he left messages: "I just wanted to see how you're doing. I miss you." He drove to her apartment and knocked on her door, and since she wouldn't answer it, he left care packages: macadamia nuts, coffee, cream, filters, toilet paper, sodas, granola bars, spring water, toothpaste—the everyday staples she always forgot to buy.

Five days passed, and she didn't appear to be weakening. A little desperate, he decided to go to Rae's Diner. When Caroline came out of the kitchen and saw him sitting in her station, she didn't seem surprised, but she was angry. She wouldn't acknowledge him, wouldn't come to his table. After twenty minutes, Dean flagged down Rae, the owner. "Could you tell Caroline to take my order?" he asked.

Rae, a lanky, middle-aged brunette with a fierce sunlamp tan, studied him, then Caroline. "If you two are having a fight, I'm not going to be in the middle of it. You want to stay, you'll have to pay."

"That's what I'm trying to do. She won't take my order."

"Why don't you just move to another station?"

"There aren't any other tables."

"The counter, then."

"I'm a paying customer, I should be able to sit where I want."

Rae shook her head. "Any screaming, one little commotion, and you're out of here. And no dawdling over a cup of coffee, either. The minute your table's cleared, you go."

She had a brief conference with Caroline, who began arguing with her, but in the end Rae won out, and Caroline marched over to Dean's table. She didn't look well—pale and baggy-eyed. She wasn't sleeping or eating much, it was clear. He tried to make pleasantries. "How have you been?" he asked her. She would not say a word, much less look at him. She waited for his order, ballpoint poised over her pad. A few minutes later, when his food was ready, she clattered the plate in front of him and walked away. When he raised his coffee cup for a refill, she slopped the pot, spilling coffee over the brim, almost scorching his crotch. He left her a generous tip.

He came to a similar arrangement with the manager of Da Bones, the barbecue restaurant where Caroline worked nights—as long as he paid, he could stay. He ate meals at every one of Caroline's shifts for a week, at the end of which he had gained eight pounds and was popping antacids as if they were gumballs. It was greasy, artery-busting food. A typical breakfast now consisted of six eggs over easy, sausage, hash browns, blueberry flapjacks, coffee, orange juice, biscuits, and milk gravy. Dinner was the hungry man combo— beef brisket, half a rack of baby backs, kielbasa, blackened chicken, rice, beans, slaw, and cornbread—accompanied by a side of mashed and two plates of conch fritters. But it was worth it. Caroline's resolve, he could tell, was beginning to crack (although the same could be said about her health; she looked awful). One night, as he asked for his fifth glass of water, she actually said something. She said, "You are getting to be a real pain in the ass," and she almost smiled. He was getting to her.

But two days later, he received a strange summons. A sergeant from the sheriff's office, Gene Becklund, requested he come down for a talk concerning Caroline. Mystified, Dean drove over to the sheriff's office on Highway 1 and was escorted into an interrogation room. Gene Becklund was a tall, soft-spoken man with prematurely gray hair. He opened the conversation by saying, "You've been going over to your ex-girlfriend's apartment a lot, dropping off little presents? Even though she told you not to call or visit?"

Unsettled, Dean nodded yes.

"You've also been bothering her at her workplace nearly every day?"

"'Bothering'?"

"And you've been leaving a lot of messages on her machine, haven't you?"

"We haven't really broken up," Dean said. "We're just having a fight."

"Uh-huh."

"I'm not harassing her or anything."

"Okay."

"Did she say I was harassing her?"

"Why don't we listen to something," Becklund said, and turned on a cassette player. On the tape was a garbled, robotic, unidentifiable voice, reciting the vile, evil things that would be done to Caroline—anal penetration, disembowelment. "You think you can treat people the way you've treated me, Miss Mighty High?" the voice said. "Think again. I'm going to enjoy watching you die."

"Jesus," Dean said.

Becklund clicked off the tape. "That's just a sample. There have been other calls—very ugly. The voice is disguised. It's hard to even know whether it's a man or a woman."

"The caller used a voice changer."

"You're familiar with them?"

"I read a lot of crime novels."

"I was surprised how cheap the things are. You can get them off the Internet," Becklund said. "The calls were made from various pay phones, mostly between two and four in the morning. Ms. Yip asked the phone company to begin tracing incoming calls a couple of weeks ago. We can trace where they're being made, but not who's making them." Almost as an afterthought, he asked, "You're not making them, are you?"

"No. Is that what Caroline thinks?"

"Here's what I never understand. She *should* think that, everything in my experience says so, but she doesn't. She thinks it's this woman, Marcella Ahn. I've talked to her, too, but she claims she's only left a couple of messages to invite Ms. Yip to tea, and to see if she would do a poetry reading with her at Beryl's Bookstore."

Dean had never really believed it was Marcella Ahn who was leaving the gifts. Maybe an enamored restaurant customer, or the pimply clerk in the hardware store, but not Marcella. Now, he reconsidered. "Maybe it's not all a coincidence," he said. "Maybe it is her." Suddenly, it almost made sense. "I think it might really be her."

"Maybe," Becklund said. "But my money's on you. Unfortunately, I can't get a restraining order issued without Ms. Yip's cooperation. But I can do this. I can tell you that all the things you did before—the presents, the calls, the workplace visits—weren't prosecutable under the anti-stalking laws until you made a physical threat. You crossed the line with the physical threat. From now on, you make one little slip-up, I can arrest you." He tapped the tabletop with his fingertip. "I suggest you stay away from her."

Dean ignored Becklund. He was frightened for Caroline, and he would do all he could to protect her. The next morning, he waited across the street from the diner for Caroline's shift to finish. When she came outside, he didn't recognize her at first. She had cut off all her hair.

She was walking briskly, carrying a Styrofoam food container, and he had to sprint to catch up to her. "Caroline, please talk to me," he said. "Will you talk to me? Sergeant Becklund told me about the messages."

She stopped but did not turn around. As he stepped in front of her, he saw she was crying. Her hair was shorn to no more than an inch, matted in clumps and tufts, exposing scalp in some places. Evidently she had chopped it off herself in a fit of self-immolation. "Oh, baby," he said, "what have you done?"

She dropped the container, splattering egg salad onto the sidewalk, and collapsed into him. "Do you believe me now?" she asked. "Do you believe it's her?"

"Yes. I do."

"What makes one person want to destroy another?" she asked. "For what? The pettiness, the backstabbing, the meanness—what's the point? Is it fun? She has everything. What more does she want? Why is she doing this to me?"

Dean held her. "I don't know."

"It's such a terrible world, Dean. You can't trust anyone. No matter where you go, there's always someone wishing you ill will. You think they're your friends, and then they're smearing you, trying to ruin you. I can't take this anymore. Why can't she just go away? Can't you make her go away?"

"Is that what you want?"

"Yes," Caroline said.

It was all Dean needed to hear. He took her to his house, put her to bed, and got to work.

It didn't take long to learn her routine. Caroline had been right: Marcella Ahn never left her house until near sunset, when she would go to the newly renovated YMCA to attend a cardioboxing class, topped off with half an hour on the StairMaster. She usually didn't shower at the Y, but would go straight home in her workout clothes. At nine or so, she might emerge and drive to Beryl's Bookstore & Café in town for a magazine and a cappuccino. Once, she went to the Moonside Trading Post for a video. Another time, the Safeway on

Highway 71 at two A.M. She had one guest, a male, dressed in a suit, an O.B./G.Y.N at a San Francisco hospital, according to the parking sticker on his BMW. He spent the night. She didn't go anywhere near Caroline's apartment or make any clandestine calls from pay phones.

Dean didn't try to conceal his stakeouts from Caroline, but he misled her into thinking he wanted to catch Marcella in the act. He had no such expectations. By this time, Marcella had to know that she was—however removed—a suspect, that she might be watched. Dean had an entirely different agenda.

One afternoon, he interrupted his surveillance to go to a spy hobbyist shop in San Francisco. He had found it through the Internet on the Rosarita Bay Library computer—Sergeant Becklund had given him the idea. At the store, he bought a lock pick set, $34.95, and a portable voice changer, $29.95. (The clerk also tried to sell him a 200,000-volt stun gun, on sale for $119.95.) Dean paid cash—no credit card records or bank statements to implicate him later.

In the dead of night, he made a call from a pay phone in the neighboring town of Miramar to his own answering machine, imitating the taunts he'd heard in the sheriff's office with the voice changer. "Hey, Jap boyfriend, you're back together with her, are you? Well, fear not, I know where you live." Before leaving the house, he had switched off his telephone's ringer and turned down the volume on the answering machine. He didn't want to scare Caroline, even though she was likely asleep, knocked out by the sleeping pills prescribed by a doctor he'd taken her to see at the town clinic. Still, in the morning, he had no choice but to play the message for her. Otherwise, she wouldn't have called Becklund in a panic, imploring him to arrest Marcella Ahn. "She's insane," Caroline told him. "She's trying to drive me crazy. She's going to try to kill me. You have to do something."

Becklund came to Dean's house, listened to the tape, and appeared to have a change of heart. Dean and Caroline had reconciled. There was no reason to suspect him anymore. Becklund had to look elsewhere. "Keep your doors and windows locked," he told Dean.

After that, the only question was when. It couldn't be too soon, but each day of waiting became more torturous.

The following Wednesday, before her dinner shift, he drove Caroline to Rummy Creek and parked on the headlands overlooking the ocean. It was another miserable, gray, windy day, Dean's truck buffeted by gusts. Rummy Creek was world-famous for its big waves, and there was supposed to be a monster swell approaching, but the water was flat, a clump of surfers in the distance bobbing gently on the surface like kelp.

"There haven't been any phone calls all week," Caroline said inside his truck.

"I know. Maybe she's decided to stop."

"No," Caroline said, "she'd never stop. Something's going to happen. I can feel it. I'm scared, Dean."

He dropped her off at Da Bones, then drove up Skyview Ridge Road and nestled in the woods outside Marcella's house. On schedule, she left for the YMCA at six P.M. After a few minutes, he strolled to the door as casually as possible. She didn't have a neighbor within a quarter mile, but he worried about the unforeseen—the gynecologist lover, a UPS delivery, Becklund deciding belatedly to serve a restraining order. Wearing latex surgical gloves, Dean inserted a lock pick and tension bar into the keyhole on the front door. The deadbolt opened within twenty seconds. Thankfully she had not installed an alarm system yet. He took off his shoes and walked through the kitchen into the garage. This was the biggest variable in his plan. If he didn't find what he needed there, none of it would work. But to his relief, Marcella Ahn had several cans of motor oil on the shelf, as well as some barbecue lighter fluid—it wasn't gasoline, but it would do. In the recycle bin, there were four empty bottles of pinot grigio. In the kitchen, a funnel and a dishrag. He poured one part motor oil and one part lighter fluid into a bottle, a Molotov cocktail recipe provided by the Internet. In her bedroom, he pulled several strands of hair from her brush, pocketed one of her bracelets, and grabbed a pair of platform-heeled boots from her closet. Then he was out, and he sped to his house in Vasquez Canyon. All he had to do was press in some bootprints in the dirt in front of the lumber shed, but he was running out of time. He drove back to Marcella's, hurriedly washed the soles of the boots in the kitchen sink, careful to leave a little mud, replaced the boots in the closet, checked through the house, and locked up. Then he went to Santa Cruz and tossed the lock pick set and voice changer into a dumpster.

He did nothing more until three A.M. By then, Caroline was unconscious from the sleeping pills. Dean drove to Marcella Ahn's again. He had to make sure she was home, and alone. He walked around her house, peeking into the windows. She was in her study, sitting at her desk in front of her laptop computer. She had her head in her hands, and she seemed to be quietly weeping. Dean was overcome with misgivings for a moment. He had to remind himself that she was at fault here, that she deserved what was coming to her.

He returned to his own property. Barefoot and wearing only the latex gloves and his underwear, he snagged the strands of Marcella's hair along the doorframe of the lumber shed. He threw the bracelet toward the driveway. He twisted the dishrag into the mouth of the wine bottle, then tilted it from side to side to mix the fluids and soak the rag. He started to flick his lighter, but then hesitated, once more stalled by doubt. Were those mystery novels he read really that accurate? Would the Hair & Fiber and Latent Prints teams be deceived at all? Was he being a fool—a complete amateur who would be ferreted out with ease? He didn't know. All he knew was that he loved Caroline, and he had to take this risk for her. If something wasn't done, he

SCREAMING MONKEYS

was certain he would lose her. He lit the rag and smashed the bottle against the first stack of zelkova inside the shed. The fire exploded up the boards. He shut the door and ran back into the house and climbed into bed beside Caroline. In a matter of seconds, the smoke detectors went off. The shed was wired to the house, and the alarm in the hallway rang loud enough to wake Caroline. "What's going on?" she asked.

Dean peered out the window. "I think there's a fire," he said. He pulled on his pants and shoes and ran to the shed. When he kicked open the door, the heat blew him back. Flames had already engulfed three *boules* of wood, the smoke was thick and black, the fire was spreading. Something had gone wrong. The sprinkler system—his expensive, state-of-the-art, dry-pipe sprinkler system—had not activated. He had not planned to sacrifice this much wood, one or two stacks at most, and now he was in danger of losing the entire shed.

There was no investigation, per se. Two deputies took photographs and checked for fingerprints, but that was about all. Dean asked Becklund, "Aren't you going to call the crime lab unit?" and Becklund said, "This is it."

It was simple enough for the fire department to determine that it was arson, but not who set it. The insurance claims adjuster was equally lackadaisical. Within a few days, he signed off for Dean to receive a $75,000 check. Dean and Caroline had kept the blaze contained with extinguishers and garden hoses for the twenty-two minutes it took for the fire trucks to arrive, but nearly half of Dean's wood supply had been consumed, the rest damaged by smoke and water.

No charges were filed against Marcella Ahn. After talking to Becklund and a San Vicente County assistant district attorney, though, she agreed—on the advice of counsel—to move out of Rosarita Bay—which was hardly a great inconvenience for her, since she owned five other houses and condos. Caroline never heard from her again, and, as far as they knew, she never published another book—a one-hit wonder.

Caroline, on the other hand, finally submitted her second book to a publisher. Dean was relentless about making her do so. The book was accepted right away, and when it came out, it caused a brief sensation. Great reviews. Awards and fellowships. Dozens of requests for readings and appearances. Caroline couldn't be bothered. By then, she and Dean had had their first baby, a girl, Anna, and Caroline wanted more children, a baker's dozen if possible. She was transformed. No more nightmares, and she could nap standing up (housekeeping remained elusive). In relation to motherhood, to the larger joys and tragedies that befell people, the poetry world suddenly seemed silly, insignificant. She would continue to write, but only, she said, when she had the time and will. Of course, she ended up producing more than ever.

Marcella Ahn's chair was the last Dean made from the pristine zelkova. He would dry and clean up the boards that were salvageable, and when he exhausted that supply, he would switch to English walnut, a nice wood—pretty, durable, available.

He delivered the chair to Marcella just before she left town, on May 11, as scheduled. She was surprised to see him and the chair, but a promise was a promise. He had never failed to deliver an order, and she had prepaid for half of it.

He set the chair down in the living room—crowded with boxes and crates—and she sat in it. "My God," she said, "I didn't know it would be this comfortable. I could sit here all day."

"I'd like to ask you for a favor," Dean said as she wrote out a check for him. He held an envelope in his hand.

"A favor?"

"Yes. I'd like you to read Caroline's new poems and tell me if they're good."

"You must be joking. After everything she's done?"

"I don't know poetry. You're the only one who can tell me. I need to know."

"Do you realize I could have been sent to state prison for two years? For a crime I didn't commit?"

"It would've never gone to trial. You would've gotten a plea bargain—a suspended sentence and probation."

"How do you know?" Marcella asked. "Your girlfriend is seriously deranged. I only wanted to be her friend, and she devised this insidious plot to frame me and run me out of town. She's diabolical."

"You stalked her."

"I did no such thing. Don't you get it? She faked it. She set me up. *She* was the stalker. Hasn't that occurred to you? Hasn't that gotten through that thick, dimwitted skull of yours? She burned your *wood.*"

"You're lying. You're very clever, but I don't believe you," Dean said. And he didn't, although she made him think for a second. He pulled out the book manuscript from the envelope. "Are you going to read the poems or not?"

"No."

"Aren't you curious what she's been doing for the past six years?" Dean asked. "Isn't this what you came here to find out?"

Marcella slowly hooked her hair behind her ears and took her time to respond. "Give it to me," she finally said.

For the next hour, she sat in his chair in the living room, flipping through the seventy-one pages, and Dean watched her. Her expression was unyielding and contemptuous at first, then it went utterly slack, then taut again. She breathed quickly through her nose, her jaw clamped, her eyes blinked.

"Are they good?" Dean asked when she finished.

She handed the manuscript back to him. "They're pedestrian. They're clunky. There's no music to the language."

"They're good," Dean told her.

"I didn't say that."

"You don't have to. I saw it in your face." He walked to the door and let himself out.

"I didn't say they were good!" Marcella Ahn screamed after him. "Do you hear me? I didn't say that. I didn't say they were good!"

Dean never told Caroline about his last visit with Marcella Ahn, nor did he ever ask her about the stalking, although he was tempted at times. One spring afternoon, they were outside on his deck, Caroline leaning back in the rocker he'd made for her, her eyes closed to the sun, Anna asleep in her lap. It had rained heavily that winter, and the eucalyptus and pine surrounding the house were now in full leaf. They sat silently and listened to the wind bending through the trees. He had rarely seen her so relaxed.

Anna, still asleep, lolled her head, her lips pecking the air in steady rhythm—an infant soliloquy.

"Caroline," he said.

"Hm?"

"What do you think she's dreaming about?"

Caroline looked down at Anna. "Your guess is as good as mine," she said. "Maybe she has a secret. Can babies have secrets?" She ran her hand through her hair, which she had kept short, and she smiled at Dean.

Was it possible that Caroline had fabricated everything about Marcella Ahn? He did not want to know. She would, in turn, never question him about the fire. The truth wouldn't have mattered. They had each done what was necessary to be with the other. Such was the price of love among artists, such was the price of devotion.

—DON LEE

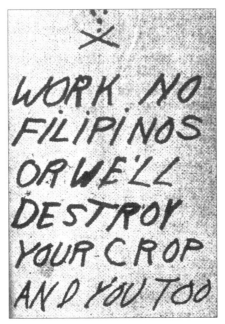

NOVEMBER 1, 1930
An example of the blacklisting of Pinoy laborers in California.
Filipino American National Historical Society Archives and
Filipinos: Forgotten Asian Americans by Fred Cordova.

October 20, 1999
A wall in Palisades Park, New Jersey, vandalized in a predominantly Korean American part of town.
Hanah Journal, Jan/Feb 2000, p.13.

President Theodore Roosevelt's Proclamation Formally Ending the Philippine "Insurrection" and Granting of Pardon and Amnesty

July 4, 1902

WHEREAS, many of the inhabitants of the Philippine Archipelago were in insurrection against the authority and sovereignty of the Kingdom of Spain at diverse times from August, eighteen hundred and ninety-six, until the cession of the archipelago by that Kingdom to the United States of America, and since such cession many of the persons so engaged in insurrection have until recently resisted the authority and sovereignty of the United States; and

WHEREAS, the insurrection against the authority and sovereignty of the United States is now at an end, and peace has been established in all parts of the archipelago except in the country inhabited by Moro tribes, to which this proclamation does not apply; and

WHEREAS, during the course of the insurrection against the Kingdom of Spain and against the Government of the United States, persons engaged therein, or those in sympathy with and abetting them, committed many acts in violation of the laws of civilized warfare, but it is believed that such acts were generally committed in ignorance of those laws, and under orders by the civil or insurrectionary leaders; and

WHEREAS, it is deemed to be wise and humane, in accordance with the beneficent purposes of the Government of the United States towards the Filipino people, and conducive to peace, order, and loyalty among them, that the doers of such acts who have not already suffered punishment shall not be held criminally responsible, but shall be relieved from punishment for participation in these insurrections, and for unlawful acts committed during the course thereof, by a general amnesty and pardon:

Now, therefore, be it known that I, Theodore Roosevelt, President of the United States of America, by virtue of the power and authority vested in me by the Constitution do hereby proclaim and declare, without reservation or condition, except as hereinafter provided, a full and complete pardon and amnesty to all persons in the Philippine Archipelago who have participated in the insurrections aforesaid, or who have given aid and comfort to persons participating in said insurrections, for the offenses of treason or sedition and for all offenses political in their character committed in the course of such insurrections pursuant to orders issued by the civil or military insurrectionary authorities, or which grew out of internal political feuds or dissension between Filipinos and Spaniards or the Spanish authorities, or which resulted from internal political feuds or dissension among the Filipinos themselves, during either of said insurrections:

Provided, however, that the pardon and amnesty hereby granted shall not include such persons committing crimes since May first, nineteen hundred and two, in any province of the archipelago in which at the time civil government was established, nor shall it include such persons as have been heretofore finally convicted of the crimes of murder, rape, arson, or robbery by any military or civil tribunal organized under the authority of Spain, or of the United States of America, but special application may be made to the proper authority for the pardon by any person belonging to the exempted classes, and such clemency as is consistent with humanity and justice will be liberally extended; and

Further provided, That this amnesty and pardon shall not affect the title or right of the Government of the United States, or that of the Philippine Islands, to any property or property rights heretofore used or appropriated by the military or civil authorities of the Government of the United States, or that of the Philippine Islands, organized under the authority of the United States, by way of confiscation or otherwise;

Provided further, that every person who shall seek to avail himself of this proclamation shall take and subscribe the following oath before any authority in the Philippine Archipelago authorized to administer oaths, namely:

"I _____, solemnly swear (or affirm) that I recognize and accept the supreme authority of the United States of America in the Philippine Islands and will maintain true faith and allegiance thereto; that I impose upon myself this obligation voluntarily, without mental reservations or purpose of evasion. So help me God."

Given under my hand at the City of Washington this fourth day of July in the year of our Lord one thousand nine hundred and two, and in the one hundred and twenty-seventh year of the Independence of the United States.

Source: U.S. Senate. The Mabini Case. 57th Congress, 2nd Session. Do. No. III (January 26, 1903).

Voices of Imperialism and War

The Philippines: A Gift from the Gods

"I would like to say just a word about the Philippine business . . . The truth is I don't want the Philippines, and when they came to us as a gift from the gods, I did not know what to do with them . . . "

—William McKinley, explaining to a visiting Methodist clergyman

"The Philippines are ours as much as Louisiana by purchase, or Texas or Alaska."

—McKinley, in a speech to the 10th Pennsylvania Regiment, August 28

Start of Filipino-American Rift

"We purposely gave the insurgents no notice of the attack on Manila, because we did not need their cooperation. We were moved by the fear that they might look, plunder, and possibly murder. Aguinaldo's men and subordinate leaders in conversing with the American officers would frequently say that they intended to cut the throats off all the Spaniards in Manila."

—Major-General Wesley Merritt, commander of U.S. expeditionary forces, quoted by London *Morning Post*, 1898

"To pretend that the American army was solely responsible for the so-called conquest of Manila and Cavite, and to refuse the Filipino troops their share of that work is mean and unfair, and is not the truth."

—Felipe Agoncillo, in a reply to General Merritt's unfounded fear of Filipino revenge against the Spanish

[Note: Felipe Agoncillo was the Philippine envoy to Europe during the pre-war days. He visited President McKinley on October 1, 1898, when the U.S.-Spain peace commission was negotiating for a treaty to lobby for Philippine independence but was turned down by McKinley. When the Treaty of Paris was signed, Agoncillo returned to the U.S. to observe the U.S. Senate debate on treaty ratification for Aguinaldo. He fled to Canada after the outbreak of the war to escape the blame unfairly put on him that he cabled Aguinaldo advising him to start the war in order to derail the treaty ratification process.]

In Search of a New Frontier

"Proponents of expansion had hailed the islands as America's 'new frontier,' and appropriately enough, the men who conquered the Philippines, particularly the volunteers, brought with them a frontier spirit steeped in an individualism that easily degenerated into lawlessness. Virtually every member of the high command had spent most of his career terrorizing Apaches, Comanches, Kiowas, and the Sioux. Some had taken part in the massacre at Wounded Knee. It was easy for such commanders to order similar tactics in the Philippines, particularly when faced with the frustrations of guerrilla warfare. And the men in their command, many of whom were themselves descendants of old Indian fighters, carried out these orders with amazing, if not surprising, alacrity."

—Stuart C. Miller, in his book *Benevolent Assimilation*

"Damn, damn, damn the Filipinos! / Cut-throat Khadiac ladrones! / Underneath the starry flag / Civilize them with a Krag / And return us to our beloved home."

—a popular marching song

For Old Glory and Country

"I am probably growing hard-hearted, for I am in my glory when I can sight my gun on some dark-skin and pull the trigger . . . Tell all my inquiring friends that I am doing everything I can for Old Glory."

—A.A. Barnes, Third Artillery, describing the destruction of Titatia, Batangas

The Ancient Baguio Dead

From Manila's marquees scrimmed
in exhaust past squatter's piss-stained
huts and Spanish Garrison walls past
the provincial church bells circling above
the drunken belches and dogs wandering off
with their ribs through the markets where
women sell the local bottles and boiled
embryonic eggs from buckets
a road winds wide enough for a bus
and the headlong bike
to a mountain city where they wait
stone-colored stiff in glass cases under
museum light the ancient Baguio dead: mummies
naked except for bands
tattooed from ankle to knee and on forearms
like sleeves marks perhaps of a warrior
or wanderer or mother—one whose
elbows pull tight to her sides knees
tucked to her breast as if shivering
in the early morning chill eyes
peer as if her sight could still gash
through the clay that once encased her
as if her sight could wheel through
the canopy of trees tropic cool and dithered
with bird-flits and monkey tails
as if sight could smack
some sky god fattening himself on mist
this woman's lips parted the width of a finger
poised again to suckle to sing to kiss—
one who'll be carrion one who'll carry on

—PATRICK ROSAL

Talking About the Woman
In Cholon

—an excerpt from Magdelena

He wanted to see Magdalena before leaving. He drove to the child care center, bringing with him a small package, his birthday gift for her. He found her seated on a rocking chair, holding a baby in her arms.

He watched quietly by the nursery's doorway. Sunshine was streaming through the open window and a bit of light hit the back of her hair so it shone like ebony. She was playing with the baby. It was a pleasant scene and it evoked happiness in him. More than that it culled up deep feelings of longing to be with her always.

He did not call her; he took in the sight of her whispering nonsensical words to the infant, telling him how sweet he was, sweeter than cane sugar, sweet enough to eat. The baby gurgled and reached up to touch Magdalena's nose. Magdalena pretended to bite the baby's fingers; the baby laughed. Magdalena laughed, throwing her head back, and then she saw him. "You're here," she said, smiling. "Come in."

She got up to meet him, the baby still in her arms. She swung the child in front of her; the baby laughed. "He's just being silly," Magdalena said. "He's not hungry any more. He's just playing."

She glanced around, and seeing no one around, gave him a kiss on the cheek. "Sit down," she said. "I'll be done in just a second." She put the bottle on a table and placed the baby on his belly on a mat on the floor. She patted the baby's back to quiet him down. Two other babies were sleeping, one of them snoring softly.

"I'm glad you're here," she said when the baby settled down.

"I have to leave soon."

"Oh," she said, dejected. "Guam?" she continued, in a hopeful tone.

He shook his head. "Nam."

"And you can't tell me where in Vietnam you're going," she said in a resigned tone. She sat down beside him and glanced out the window at a bougainvillea vine struggling to survive the city's polluted air.

"Top secret." Nathan could not say he would be part of a forty-plane strike into North Vietnam, to the Haiphong harbor, where Russian and Chinese ships docked and which was therefore a major military supply source. He could not tell her that after a briefing, he and his squadron would leave, and then in Nam they would be joined by a number of fighter planes. Some of the fighter planes would fly ahead to knock out SAM sites that might affect the B-52s. Early in the morning, the forty planes would launch against heavily defended Haiphong to hit truck parts, SAM sites, AAA emplacements, storage areas, and other military targets.

"Do you want something cold to drink?" she offered.

He shook his head and glanced at his watch. "I can't stay long."

"When will you be back?"

"I'll try and get back Thursday for your birthday."

"I hate it when you're gone," she said.

"I'll be back soon."

"I always imagine the worse. All the news about Vietnam, I can't help it. But you will be back Thursday—won't you?"

"I'll try." He had been hiding the small package, but now he handed it to her. "This is for you, in case I don't make it back."

She turned the small package in her hands. It was wrapped in red shiny paper with a large gold bow that had been squashed.

"Open it."

"Now?"

"I want to see if you like it."

She removed the ribbon and peeled off the wrapping and opened a jewelry box. Inside lay a gold bracelet with little animal charms. She smiled and lifted the bracelet so the charms dangled and swayed. She had the sensation of being a child and looking at a new toy for the first time.

"Try it on," he said.

"It's not too young for me?" Her eyes sparkled with delight at the little gold animal charms.

"Absolutely not," he said. "The charms remind me of you. See the goldfish? It's jointed. And there's one of a monkey. Of a turtle too. I thought of you when I saw the bracelet. The children will love it," he said, looking at the sleeping infants on the mats on the floor.

The goldfish wobbled and caught the sun's rays. She sucked in her breath. "It's pretty," she said. "Where did you find it?" She put it on her left wrist; he helped her with the clasp.

"Near the Cholon district."

She lifted her left arm in the air and shook the bracelet so the charms scattered little shards of sunlight all around them.

"The last time I was in Saigon, I saw a woman wearing one just like it."

"Where?" she asked, looking at him from the corner of her eyes.

"At the Cercle de Sportiff Club. We were with some USAID guys, talking shop."

"I see."

"Aren't you going to ask what we talked about?"

"Okay, what did you talk about?"

"We had this heavy discussion about why, except for the Civil War, why the United States fights its wars in other people's backyards. Important stuff like that."

"And the woman, was she part of your group?"

"Oh, no. She was with another woman. They were having lunch. We were all out on the terrace, near the pool."

"So that's what you do when you're away? Having lunch by the pool of a club."

"No, that's not what I always do when I'm away." He laughed, chucking her chin.

She smiled, embarrassed at his gesture of intimacy. "So what happened?"

"To what?"

"The woman . . . the bracelet."

"Nothing. She and her friend were eating and I noticed her bracelet."

"You were looking at her."

"Just her bracelet."

"Was she pretty?"

"One question at a time. You asked what happened. When they were having their coffee, I went to their table and asked her where she got it."

"You did not."

"I introduced myself first."

"She may have thought you were picking her up. Was she pretty?"

"Slender, with hair down to her waist. She was wearing a red *oa dais.*"

"A red *oa dais*—how exotic. Was she pretty?"

He paused, puckered his lips as if in deep thought. "If I answer that question, I could get in trouble."

"She was pretty then."

"I was interested only in her bracelet. I went up to her and said, 'I'm sorry to bother you and your friend, but I couldn't help noticing your bracelet. Do you mind if I ask where you got it? I'd like to get one for my fiancée.'"

"Was she . . . beautiful?"

"I'm not going to answer that question."

"Did you really say 'fiancée'?"

"Yes, I did. She spoke French. Her English was not too great, but we managed to communicate. She figured that all I wanted was the name of the store. That same day I went to the Cholon district. Do you like it?"

She lifted her left arm and moved her hands back and forth so the charms clicked together. "It makes me feel sixteen."

"Good."

"I'm not sixteen. Do you know that in the Chinese way of counting, I'll be twenty-seven? How old was the woman in the red *oa dais?*"

"Older than you."

"And pretty, she was pretty, wasn't she? That's why you won't tell me."

"Not pretty at all. She had warts all over her face."

She made a face and laughed. "What's Saigon like? Tell me what it's like."

"Saigon is . . . Saigon. It's a city, and it's crowded. There are motorbikes, jeeps, trucks, taxicabs, and *xich-los.* You have the Cercle de Sportif Club where you can have an elegant chateaubriand meal; and then you have the Thanh-Bich Restaurant where you can eat brown fried rice and a small piece of steak with a large egg over the top, mixed vegetables, a bowl of greens, and *nuoc-mam* fish sauce to pour over everything. It's just Saigon."

"Is it safe there?"

"As safe as Ubec."

"Not that safe then. You have to know where to go and where not to go."

"It's safe enough."

"I'll wait for you Thursday."

"Don't wait for me. I may be late."

"I will wait for you."

"Has anyone ever told you how bullheaded you can be?"

"What time Thursday?"

"I'm not sure. Late, if we leave that day. But I may have to go to Bien-Hoa, so don't wait for me."

"Thursday, then, on my birthday. I'll see you on my birthday."

"I'll try. I'll see you when I get here. I love you. Do you love me?"

"You know I do. Don't kiss me, someone may see us. But I love you. I'll wait for you."

Nathan left, carrying with him the image of Magdalena seated by the window, holding the baby. It was the last image that stayed with him even as the North Vietnamese fighter planes hit his B-52.

—CECILIA BRAINARD

Untitled Art by Kay Chung

Executive Order Number 9066
Franklin D. Roosevelt

Authorizing the Secretary of War to prescribe military areas
Executive Order No. 9066

WHEREAS the successful prosecution of the war requires every possible protection against espionage and against sabotage to national-defense material, national-defense premises, and national-defense utilities as defined in Section 4, Act of April 20, 1918, 40 Stat. 553, as amended by the Act of November 30, 1940, 54 Stat. 1220, and the Act of August 21, 1941, 55 Stat. 655 (U.S.C., Title 50, Sec. 104):

NOW, THEREFORE, by virtue of the authority vested in me as President of the United States, and Commander in Chief of the Army and Navy, I hereby authorize and direct the Secretary of War, and the Military Commanders whom he may from time to time designate, whenever he or any designated Commander deems such actions necessary or desirable, to prescribe military areas in such places and of such extent as he or the appropriate Military Commander may determine, from which any or all persons may be excluded, and with such respect to which, the right of any person to enter, remain in, or leave shall be subject to whatever restrictions the Secretary of War or the appropriate Military Commander may impose in his discretion. The Secretary of War is hereby authorized to provide for residents of any such area who are excluded therefrom, such transportation, food, shelter, and other accommodations as may be necessary, in the judgment of the Secretary of War or the said Military Commander, and until other arrangements are made, to accomplish the purpose of this order. The designation of military areas in any region or locality shall supersede designations of prohibited and restricted areas by the Attorney General under the Proclamations of December 7 and 8, 1941, and shall supersede the responsibility and authority of the Attorney General under the said Proclamations in respect of such prohibited and restricted areas.

I hereby further authorize and direct the Secretary of War and the said Military Commanders to take such other steps as he or the appropriate Military Commander may deem advisable to enforce compliance with the restrictions applicable to each Military area hereinabove authorized to be designated, including the use of Federal troops and other Federal Agencies, with authority to accept assistance of state and local agencies.

I hereby further authorize and direct all Executive Departments, independent establishments and other Federal Agencies, to assist the Secretary of War or the said Military Commanders in carrying out this Executive Order, including the furnishing of medical aid, hospitalization, food, clothing, transportation, use of land, shelter, and other supplies, equipment, utilities, facilities and services.

This order shall not be construed as modifying or limiting in any way the authority heretofore granted under Executive Order No. 8972, dated December 12, 1941, nor shall it be construed as limiting or modifying the duty and responsibility of the Federal Bureau of Investigation, with respect to the investigation of alleged acts of sabotage or the duty and responsibility of the Attorney General and the Department of Justice under the Proclamations of December 7 and 8, 1941, prescribing regulations for the conduct and control of alien enemies, except as such duty and responsibility is superseded by the designation of military areas hereunder.

Franklin D. Roosevelt
February 19, 1942

DRAWING THE LINE

for Yosh Kuromiya

I.
Yosh is drawing the line.
It's a good line, on paper,
and a good morning
for just such an endeavor—

and the line seems to find
its own way, flowing
across the white expanse

like a dark, new river . . .

II.
Yes, Yosh is drawing the line.
And you might say he's simply
following his own nature—

he's always had a good eye,
a fine sense of perspective,
and a sure hand, a gift

for making things ring true,
and come clearer into view.

III.
So the line makes its way,
on paper, charting a clear
course like a signature,
starting from the left
and toward the bottom end,
logically and gradually
and gracefully ascending

to the center, where it takes
a sharp turn upward, straight
toward the top before it
finds itself leveling off
to the right again, descending

slightly for a while before
dropping straight down, coming
to a rest near the bottom,

bending, descending gradually
and gracefully as it began, but
at the other side of the space . . .

IV.
No sooner said than done.
Yosh relaxes for the moment,
blinks his eyes, realizing

his intensity of focus, almost
like prayer, a sunrise meditation.

V.
Ah, another beautiful morning!
Time to move on, see what the day
provides by way of promise . . .

And as for the drawing, well,
the line is drawn, on paper—

other dimensions can come later . . .

VI.
Yosh, although a young man,
a teenager, is naturally
calm and confident by nature.

Thus, when he draws a line,
it tends to stay drawn.
He may make adjustments
but doesn't make mistakes.

That's just the way he is—
trusting his own judgment
as a person, as an artist.

As a result, he is a most
trusted friend, judging

from the many friends who
count on him, rely on him,
respect what he has to say . . .

That's just the way he is—
good-hearted, as they say:
"If you need a favor, ask
Yosh; he'll go out of his way . . . "

VII.
Still, though, you've got to draw the line
somewhere—and as the saying goes,
so goes Yosh. And his friends know
certain things not to ask of him.

What "everybody does" just may not go
with Yosh, the set of beliefs, the sense
of integrity, values, he got from his folks.

VIII.
As for this drawing in his sketchbook,
you might well ask: "What is it?"

At this stage, it's just a line—
a line that goes sideways, up, over,
down, descending to the other margin.

Is it just a line? An abstract design?
Or might it stand for something?

At first glance, it looks to be a line
charting the progress of something

that goes along slowly, rising
a bit to indicate, oh, maybe a normal
growth rate or business-as-usual,

when all of a sudden it jumps, reflecting
a decisive turn of events which lasts
a while before resuming
what might be assumed to be a more
regular course of activity concluding

at what may represent the present
on the journey from the then to the now . . .

That's what graphs show, the flow
of activity, the rise and fall of events
often out of our hands, so it can become
gratifying to simply resume the bottom
line of normalcy again, starting over
at square one, back to the drawing board . . .

That is, it could have been worse.
The line could have been broken, snapped,
or bottomed out into nothing, going
nowhere fast like the slow and steady
line monitoring a silent patient . . .

Or, the line could have turned back
into itself into a dead-end maze,
a meaningless mass of angles and tangles . . .

Ah, but if you asked an observant child,
the answer might be: "Well, it just looks
like the bottom of my baby sister's mouth—
'cause when she smiles, she only has one tooth!"

And if you asked Yosh, he'd simply say,
in his modest way: "Oh, that's just Heart Mountain."

IX.
Maybe you had to be there.
For if you were, you would not only
not have to ask, but you would
appreciate the profile, the likeness

of what looms large in your life
and mind, as large as life staring
you in the face day by day by day

and so on into night, where it is so
implanted in your sight and mind
that the ancient promontory assumes
a prominence in your mildest dreams,

and even when the dust billows, or clouds
cover it, blowing snow and sleet and rain,

you can't avoid it, you can count on it,
Heart Mountain. Heart Mountain
is still there. And you're here.

X.
Ah, but it is, after all,
just a mountain—one of many,
actually, in this region,
in this range, and if anything
distinguishes it, it's just
its individual shape and name.

And the fact that it stands
rising up out of the plains
so close you can touch it,
you can almost but not quite
get there on a Sunday picnic,
your voices echoing in the ever-
green forest on its slopes . . .

As it stands, it is a remote
monument to, a testament to
something that stands to be
respected from a distance,

accessible only in dreams,
those airy, carefree moments
before the truth comes crashing
home to your home in the camp . . .

XI.
Yosh can take you there, though,
by drawing the line, on paper.

And Yosh, with his own given name,
is somewhat like the mountain—

an individual, certainly, but also
rather common to this region.

He's just so-and-so's kid,
or just another regular teenager
engaged in whatever it takes these days . . .

But this morning, it was different.
He was out there at the crack of dawn,
pacing around over by the fence,
blowing into his hands, rubbing
his hands, slapping, clapping
his hands together as if in preparation
to undertake something special
instead of doing the nothing he did—

that is, he just got to his knees
and knelt there, facing the mountain.

Knelt there. Knelt there. Is he praying?
But now he's writing. But writing what?

Then, as sunlight struck the mountain,
and the ordinary idle elder
and the regular bored child
approached Yosh, they could tell
from the size of the wide sketchpad
that he was drawing—but drawing
what? Well, that's obvious—but what for?

XII.
Seeing the drawing was its own reward.
Boy, look at that! He's got it right!
You've got to admire him for that.

And, boy, if you really look at it—
in this sunrise light, under this
wide, blue sky—why, it really is
a beautiful sight, that majestic
hunk of rock they call Heart Mountain.

And to top it off, this talented guy
sure accentuates the positive, because
he *didn't* include the posts and wire.

was going to happen to Hanh. I hoped he would be all right. I thought it was much better for me to take this risk rather than stay on the boat holding onto the fake papers and trying to persuade them to believe in me, only to end up dead. Water babbled and whispered in my ears as if someone was chanting along with the echoing gong of a temple. I did not know which way the current would take me. I thought of my parents and family and remembered that the Buddha would help me, for I had my hidden virtues from my past life. I said my prayers.

I changed my position on the container. I saw a light move up and down. It got clearer. I knew I was getting closer to the land. The night sky was darker. I kept floating on the water until I hit something in front of me. I extended my arm like a blind person feeling his way in the dark. I touched something cold that I had never touched before, especially in the water, but my curiosity kept my hand moving along the object until it ended at the head. I knew it was a dead body. I pushed it and swam fast away from it. Then another hit my back. It felt slippery. I pushed the can harder and harder, breathing heavily. The waves seemed like they were rolling over me, like someone rolling a carpet. I slowed down; my whole body was falling apart, my energy was gone. Suddenly my feet touched the ground. It was a wonderful feeling; I was on land. I stumbled, stubbed my toes on rocks. When I reached the sand I couldn't stand up anymore. I fell down, blacking out.

—JADE NGOC QUANG HUỲNH

XIII.

Yosh, smiling, greeting, is striding
toward the barracks. There's a line
at the mess hall, a line at the toilets.

Better check in with the folks. Mom's
all right, but Dad's never adjusted.
I may or may not show him the drawing.

It depends. He likes me to stay active,
but this might be the wrong subject.
It might rub him wrong, get him
in a mountain-mood of reminiscing
about California, the mountains of home.

And, heck, those were just hills
by comparison, but they've taken on
size in his eyes; still, when I fill in
the shading, the forest, tonight, maybe
he can appreciate it for just what it is:

Heart Mountain, in Wyoming, a drawing
by his dutiful son here with the family
doing its duties—kitchen duty, latrine duty . . .

I'll do my duties; and I've got my own duty, my
right, to do what I can, to see this through . . .

XIV.

The sketchbook drops to the cot.
Brrr, better go get some coal.
It's the least I can do—not worth
much else, me, without a real line
of work. But this art might get me
someplace—maybe even a career
in here. Doing portraits of inmates.

But out there is *in here* too, related—
it's a matter of perspective, like lines
of lineage and history, like the line
between me and the fencepost, between

me and the flagpole, between stars,
stripes, the searchlight, and the guy
on duty in the guard tower, maybe
like me, from California, looking
up at the airplane making a line
of sound in the sky, searching
for the right place in a time of peace . . .

Yes, if I had a big enough piece
of paper, I'd draw the line
tracing the way we came, smooth
as tracks clear back to California,

and in the other direction, the line
clean out to the city of Philadelphia
and the Liberty Bell ringing testimony
over Independence Hall and the framing
of the Constitution. Yes, it's there,
and I can see it, in the right frame of mind . . .

XV.
No, you have no right
to imprison my parents.

No, you have no right
to deny us our liberty.

Yes, I have my right
to stand for our justice.

Yes, I have my right
to stand for our freedom.

XVI.
And this is where Yosh
drew the line—

on paper, on the pages
of the Constitution.

XVII.
The rest is history.

SCREAMING MONKEYS

Arrested, judged,
sentenced, imprisoned

for two years
for refusing
induction under

such conditions:
"as long as my
family is in here . . ."

Eventually arrives
a few sentences
of presidential

pardon, period.
But history
doesn't rest,

as Yosh gives
testimony,
drawing the line,
on paper, again.

XVII.

This time, though, he's a free man
with a free mind and a very clear
conscience, having come full circle
to this clear spring at Heart Mountain.

And Heart Mountain, of course,
is still here, timeless and ever-
changing in the seasons, the light,
standing, withstanding the test of time.

And this time Yosh is free to roam
his home range like an antelope,
circling the mountain, seeing all sides
with new visions, wide perspectives:

from here, it comes to a narrow peak;
from here, it presents the profile

of a cherished parent, strong, serene;
from here, yes, it could be a tooth;
and from anywhere, forever, a heart.

Yes, that's about the truth of it—
once a heart, always a heart—

a monumental testament under the sky.

This time, though, Yosh is strolling
over a freshly plowed and fenceless field
with that very same sketchbook, searching
through the decades to find that rightful
place in relation to the mountain, wanting
to show his wife where the drawing happened,

where that quiet young man sank to his knees
in reverence for the mountain, in silent
celebration for that vision of beauty
that evoked such wonder, such a sunrise
of inspiration, wisdom, and compassion

that the line drew itself, making its way
with conviction in the direction it knew
to be right across the space, on paper,

and yes, yes, the heart, the eye, the mind
testify this is right, here, Yosh, hold
up the drawing, behold the mountain, trust
the judgment upholding truth through time
as the man, the mountain, the profile make
a perfect fit in this right place and time
for Yosh to kneel again, feel again, raise
his radiant eyes in peace to face the radiant
mountain, Heart Mountain, Heart Mountain—

and begin, again, with confidence, to draw the line!

—LAWSON INADA

THE WHITE HOUSE
WASHINGTON

October 1, 1993

Over fifty years ago, the United States Government unjustly interned, evacuated, or relocated you and many other Japanese Americans. Today, on behalf of your fellow Americans, I offer a sincere apology to you for the actions that unfairly denied Japanese Americans and their families fundamental liberties during World War II.

In passing the Civil Liberties Act of 1988, we acknowledge the wrongs of the past and offer redress to those who endured such grave injustice. In retrospect, we understand that the nation's actions were rooted deeply in racial prejudice, wartime hysteria, and a lack of political leadership. We must learn from the past and dedicate ourselves as a nation to renewing the spirit of equality and our love of freedom. Together, we can guarantee a future with liberty and justice for all. You and your family have my best wishes for the future.

Bill Clinton

Honor, 1946

In birdsong my father strolled the Presidio
of San Francisco, a Filipino in the US

Army, sharp in parade dress, lieutenant's
bars riding his shoulders like sun cresting
clouds. A corporal in dingy fatigues walked

past my father, snickered, kept his right
hand by his hip. "Hold it right there, soldier!"

my father barked. "Where's that goddamn salute?"
The corporal smirked, looked him in the eye and said
nothing, but my father could read it in his face—

*I'll be damned before I salute a little brown
monkey who ought to be climbing a fucking tree.*

My father growled an order. The soldier jerked
to attention. My father slipped off his jacket, draped it
on a hedge. The rainbow of ribbons reminded him

not of crossfire and the soldier he saved on patrol,
not of the forced retreat to Corregidor,

not of the weeks evading Japanese capture,
not even of the Bataan death march,
nor of the concentration camp. Instead

he recalled the American jeep that tried to run
him down in a rainstorm. *Get out of the road, monkey!*

My father said, "You might not want to salute *me,*
young man, but you *will* salute this jacket, these bars.
Do it!" Birds sang. "Again." Sun shone. "Again."

The corporal's arm swept the air, a wiper blade
trying to swipe brown mud from a windshield.

—VINCE GOTERA

Justifying U.S. Assistance to Filipino War Veterans, an address to Congress by Senator Daniel Inouye

Following is the text of U.S. Senator Daniel Inouye's June 14, 2001 speech from the Congressional Record: S. 1042. A bill to amend title 38, United States Code, to improve benefits for Filipino veterans of World War II, and for other purposes; to the Committee on Veterans' Affairs.

Mr. President, I rise to introduce to Filipino Veterans' Benefits Improvement Act of 2001. This bill provides our country the opportunity to right a wrong committed decades ago, by providing Philippine-born veterans of World War II who served in the United States Armed Forces their hard-earned, due compensation.

Our Nation is now at peace, and our prosperity has reached levels never before seen by any Nation in history. We are on top of the world in terms of economic power and military might, and much of this unprecedented success is due to the tremendous sacrifices made by our fighting forces during World War II. We trampled tyranny in Europe and in the Pacific, and when we raised our flag proudly over hostile lands, we were greeted enthusiastically by the millions we liberated from the grasp of terrible aggression.

I take this opportunity today to remind everyone of an injustice that persists as a blemish on one of history's greatest success stories.

The Philippines became a United States possession in 1898, when it was ceded from Spain following the Spanish-American War. In 1934, the Congress enacted the Philippine Independence Act, Public Law 73-127, which provided a 10-year time frame for the independence of the Philippines. Between 1934 and final independence in 1946, the United States retained certain powers over the Philippines, including the right to call all military forces organized by the newly-formed Commonwealth government into the service of the United States Armed Forces.

On July 26, 1941, President Roosevelt issued an Executive Order calling members of the Philippine Commonwealth Army into the service of the United States Armed Forces of the Far East. Under this order, Filipinos were entitled to full veterans' benefits. More than 100,000 Filipinos volunteered for the Philippine Commonwealth Army and fought alongside the United States Armed Forces.

The United States Armed Forces of the Far East fought to reclaim control of the entire Western Pacific. Filipinos, under the command of General

Douglas MacArthur, fought in the front lines of the Battle of Corregidor and at Bataan. They served in Okinawa, on occupied mainland Japan, and in Guam. They were part of what became known as the Bataan Death March, and were held and tortured as prisoners of war. Through these hardships, the men of the Philippine Commonwealth Army remained loyal to the United States during the Japanese occupation of the Philippines, and the valiant guerrilla war they waged against the Japanese helped delay the Japanese advance across the Pacific.

Despite all of their sacrifices, on February 18, 1946, Congress betrayed these veterans by enacting the Rescission Act of 1946 and declaring this service performed by the Philippine Commonwealth Army veterans as not "active service," thus denying many benefits to which these veterans were entitled.

Then, shortly after Japan's surrender, Congress enacted the Armed Forces Voluntary Recruitments Act of 1945 for the purpose of sending American troops to occupy enemy lands, and to oversee military installations at various overseas locations. A provision included in the Recruitment Act called for the enlistment of Philippine citizens to constitute a new body of Philippine Scouts. The New Scouts were authorized to receive pay and allowances for services performed throughout the Western Pacific. Although hostilities had ceased, wartime service of the New Philippine Scouts continued as a matter of law until the end of 1946.

On May 27, 1946, the Congress enacted the Second Supplemental Surplus Appropriation Rescission Act, which included a provision to limit veterans' benefits to Filipinos. This provision duplicated the language that had eliminated veterans' benefits under the First Scout Rescission Act, and placed similar restrictions on veterans of the New Philippine Scouts. Thus, the Filipino veterans that fought in the service of the United States during World War II have been precluded from receiving most veterans' benefits that had been available to them before 1946, and that are available to all other veterans of our armed forces regardless of race, national origin, or citizenship status.

The Congress tried to rectify the wrong committed against the Filipino veterans of World War II by amending the Nationality Act of 1940 to grant the veterans the privilege of becoming United States citizens for having served in the United States Armed Forces of the Far East.

The law expired at the end of 1946, but not before the United States had withdrawn its sole naturalization examiner from the Philippines for a nine-month period. This effectively denied Filipino veterans the opportunity to become citizens during this nine-month period. Forty-five years later, under the Immigration Act of 1990, certain Filipino veterans who served during World War II became eligible for United States Citizenship. Between November, 1990 and February, 1995, approximately 24,000 veterans took advantage of this opportunity and became United States citizens.

For many years, Filipino veterans of World War II, who are now in their twilight years, have sought to correct the injustice caused by the Rescission Act by seeking equal treatment of their valiant military service in our Armed Forces. They stood up to the same aggression that American-born soldiers did, and many Filipinos sacrificed their lives in the war for democracy and liberty.

Heroes should never be forgotten or ignored, so let us not turn our backs on those who have sacrificed so much. Many of the Filipinos who have fought so hard for us have been honored with American citizenship, but let us now work to repay all the brave men for their sacrifices by providing them the full veterans' benefits they have earned.

"More Fun Than a Turkey Shoot"

said the soldiers from Nebraska
charging across San Juan bridge—
Two rebels fallen   Hundreds more
trying to cross the Pasig river
Women and children among them
But who knows they're all
alike   Shifty eyes   Nigger-dark
hides   Filipinos are so absolutely different from us
in mind body and soul
Ladrones Bandits Tedious
months in mosquito-infested camps
Tropical shadows   No relief from rain
turning heat to steam   Smell of piss
in trenches   Something inevitable
condensed over the paddy fields
Willie Grayson were you dreaming
too of turkeys that evening
One buffalo soldier from the south
was telling stories   At Thanksgiving they
pounced upon the largest bird in the yard
while the Master and his family watched
If you were a guest you did the honors
grasping the bearded neck   Swinging your arm
in ever-widening arcs until something snapped
then shudders feathered downward
Here we go   Flush the turkeys out
of their hiding places   Our torches
lit up night with gaudy brilliance
Fragile thatch houses burned delicately
like wings of paper   The churches
took longer   Later I wrote home to Kansas
Dear father and mother with my own hand
hand I set fire to over fifty Filipino
houses   Caloocan   Guiguinto   Santa Ana
Pandacan and south as far as Laguna
My corporal says we should get out
as soon as we can with honor
but not until we've beaten these monkeys
into submission   *This is a harsh*

but philanthropic war
The heat alternates with storms
and we collapse from exhaustion
I dislike walking in the mud
because a hike takes hours and
I begin to question difficult
things like my convictions
Sometimes we are forced to fill
our canteens at pools where water
buffaloes have wallowed
Nevertheless
this is the way I endure
The rest of this country
I have not seen

—LUISA A. IGLORIA

SOUTH WIND CHANGING

—an excerpt

Book III, Chapter 9

As we ran along the river to Cho Lach, I remembered they used this way to get to the ocean by Ba Dong. In the boat I recognized Phuoc's wife and two children, and the lady I had met at the connection family in Vinh Binh with her children, along with five other people. We looked at each other nervously because we had the same thoughts. We saw in each other's eyes that we might never return, or might die on the water. But at least there was a little hope in searching for our freedom. The children looked at us and felt something was wrong; one child cried out, then another, and then they all started crying. We watched them but didn't stop them. I wondered if it might be good to shed some tears for our ancestors, or maybe for ourselves.

Along the river there were small canoes that ran close to the shore where some of the people were fishing. There were many cork trees in the mud on the little island along the river. The wind blew the leaves, making them wave like someone saying goodbye to us. The afternoon was mild. I inhaled the fresh air, feeling as if I had been released from a tunnel under the water. We arrived in Cho Lach about two hours later. The ride was smooth but the children seemed sick. The clouds were clear up in the sky, red and orange shades that were scattered at the end of the water where the horizon met and the waves moved.

From time to time I saw a dead tree or some grass floating from the current. We passed some poles that people used to hang fishing nets on. When it was dark, we turned into the small branch of the river. We went on for another half hour and then heard the engine of a big boat running along the river. Our driver stopped the engine, signaled three times with the lighter, and waited. We saw a light in the middle of the river flash back three times. We paddled our boat quickly to the middle of the river. When our boat got close to the big boat Hanh and I jumped on, then began to help the rest of our group get on. The children were crying.

Cover their mouths," someone whispered.

The crying was hushed, then loud again when someone released a hand from a mouth. The night was tranquil. We tried to be very quiet, but you could hear tiny voices here and there in the front and back of the boat. When our whole group was almost on, the captain of the big boat asked us, "Did you catch any fish?"

"No, we didn't. We prefer chicken."

"Wrong group. Go back."

Chaos broke out. Some people yelled to others to shut up before the police heard anything. We grabbed the children, passing them back to the small boat. I jumped off the big boat. I heard someone cursing because I stepped on them in the cramped dinghy. We pushed away, rowed our small boat back to the side of the river to hide ourselves in the thickets, and waited for our boat to come. Teacher Phuoc suggested, "I have some sleeping pills. Let the children take them so they can sleep. It will be much safer for us."

We passed the pills along to the adults to give to the children. About ten minutes later they all fell asleep. We kept our eyes and ears open but nothing came. Another half an hour passed. The taxi person kept demanding that we pay him in advance because he said when we saw the big boat we would forget to pay him and jump on. We told him to shut up. If he made any noise and the police spotted us, we would kill him. He was quiet but still mumbling. Hanh gave him a bar of gold.

"We will give you the rest when the big boat arrives."

He seemed satisfied and didn't say another word. The mosquitoes attacked us, and our slaps pricked the night air. Bats twittered, looking for cork fruit, and occasionally the fruit fell into the water, making a little noise, just enough to notice. There was no sound at all except the mosquitoes, birds, bats, water lapping into the bushes, and occasionally an unexplained rattle of leaves. High in the sky stars scattered about in different shapes, creating their own groups, beaming and dimming. There were no clouds. We waited and waited. Suddenly, from the middle of the river, the sound of an engine moved toward us.

"Don't be in a hurry. Watch out for the police boat," I whispered softly.

We waited for the boat to come closer. The taxi person signaled with his lighter, and was answered by a lighter signal on the big boat. We held on to the branches, pushed our boat out into the current. Everyone was paddling, some of us using our hands because we didn't have any paddles. The big boat turned the engine down low and stood still. We approached it cautiously.

"Do you have any white chickens?" I asked.

"Yes, we have white chickens!" a voice from the big boat called back.

We moved our boat faster in their direction as the taxi driver shouted.

"Give me the money now! It's the right boat!"

Some of us pulled out the money and gold and gave them to him. He didn't say anything more.

"Give me your hand," someone on the big boat whispered.

We began to climb aboard the big boat. The children were still asleep, and we passed them up. It was packed on the boat. When they placed the children on they split them up, away from their mother or father; since it was dark, people didn't recognize one another and there was no one spot for an entire family to settle.

"Teacher, give me your money. You haven't given it to me yet," the bargee whined, trying to squeeze some more money out of us.

"I'm the middleman. I arrange the customers and owners. So I get my family's fare free," teacher Phuoc answered while I climbed onto the boat.

"That's right, taxi!" a voice shouted from the cabin. I recognized this voice as my connection, the fat man to whom I had paid the gold.

The bargee pushed his boat away from the big boat and started his engine. I could hear the propellers churning. We filed down below the deck, into the dark hold of the wooden hull. Hanh and I sat near the engine room where several plastic containers of food and water were located. They revved the engine louder as the boat moved off. I heard the captain ask the organizer, "Are they our last group?"

"Yes. We can go now. It's all yours now. One hundred twenty-four people."

The unwieldy boat moved like an old man. People squatted on the leaking wooden floor, on the deck, on the cabin; every inch of the boat packed.

It was very hard to breathe because there were only two holes on the deck above us where the air could get in. Besides the engine's odor, gasoline fumes from the exhaust also circulated, making us nauseated and lightheaded. I couldn't see any stars or breathe the fresh air anymore. I began to vomit and pass out. I woke up with a heavy head, like a bad hangover. I felt the boat slapping against the water, shaking it like a huge wave. We were on the ocean. A little light came in and I saw vague human forms everywhere, sitting, lying, and breathing. We were squeezed in like so many flowers in a small vase.

"Is it safe to come up yet?" I shouted. "People are dying down here."

The cover from another hole was removed and more light came in with a little air. I crawled over people, climbed up on the deck. When I speak of a big boat one may think it was a ship, but it was not. It was a shabby wooden boat, four meters wide by fourteen meters long. It had to carry 124 people including food, water, oil, gas, and the engine. But it was amazing how valuable a small piece of wood was in the big ocean. We began to help people crawl up onto the deck to breathe some good air. The scent from the water drifted in the wind like a miracle medicine to cure all of us. How wonderful an ocean mist is on a hot day! Just like fresh coconut water to drink. The children were still knocked out with the sleeping pills. Someone asked for water. The engine ran smoothly and all around us now was water. Further away there were some dinghies scattered about. I looked ahead and saw the sun rising slowly. There were no obstacles between us. The water, rippled with the sun's reflection in a crimson background. The sky was like a huge canvas on which were painted many bright colors on this clear, blue day. I was thinking about my family, wondering if I would have a chance to see them again. I remembered this kind of morning when I was in Vung Tau waterfront on my school vacation. It was totally different now as I looked back. Was I really free

386   SCREAMING MONKEYS

now? The boat kept moving farther away from the shore, the water becoming a darker blue. The surface of the water was gentle now, like a cotton blanket that my mother used to put over me on a chilly night. The seagulls began flying back to the land, no longer circling us in the sky. I looked in front of the boat to where it crushed the water, creating a foam mass running along both sides of the boat and disappearing at the end. Suddenly I saw some kind of fish diving in and out of the water in front of our boat. Someone shouted.

"Come on, race with us, *ong nuoc!*" we all clamored in excitement. Everyone forgot about their sickness as the whole clan of fish jumped up and down ahead of and alongside our boat, their fins glimmering.

"It's very good weather. It will be an excellent day today because we have had some *ong nuoc* show up," the captain smiled. The fish flashed on, their silver jumps leading us into the dark blue sea.

Book III, Chapter 10

The children began to recover from the sleeping pills, and cried now for water and food. The people in the cabin started to pass out food and water for each person. It was only a few teaspoons of food and one teaspoon of water. I looked at Hanh as if to ask him, "Do we have enough supplies for 124 people?" He shook his head, not knowing. Our course was for Thailand, which was over 4,000 miles away. Families tried to get together in one spot with their children, but it was so cramped that it was hard even to straighten our legs, let alone move. After people had something to eat they were happier but still had a little doubt in their eyes, wondering where they were going. The heat became more powerful; people started sweating. Some of the men took off their shirts, made little umbrellas over their heads for their children. The day went by.

When the night came the waves were stronger and the sky seemed dark, without any stars. I tried to locate the *sao ham* star. This was the star used at night to find directions. But I couldn't find it. People got inside beneath the deck because we knew a storm was coming. An hour later the boat was tossing up and down in the water, riding with the waves. Every time it went down I felt it would sink all the way to the bottom, like a little fish in the big ocean who couldn't struggle but let the current carry it away. I held on tight to the deck like everyone else; the water poured over us as if we were taking a shower. It was so loud that I couldn't hear if the engine was running or not. The storm went on for half an hour, then flattened out. I felt chilly, exhausted, and dreamed about a new land. The sky turned bright as the stars came out. We could see a little phantom boat in the dim night, the engine groaning like a sick person. Dawn came, and I found the *sao mai* star. It only shows up at daybreak; we used it for directions. It hung in the sky beautifully, outshining the other stars. The night turned bright, the sun rose, and another day passed with a little food and a little water. People were seasick; the children were crying and vomiting. The parents couldn't help them because they were sick too.

"Where are we now, captain?" People gathered their last energy to call into the cabin, but there was no answer. The boat kept putting along in an ocean of nowhere. Another storm struck in the afternoon before the sun went down. This time it was more violent; one of the children fell into the ocean. The captain couldn't stop to look for him. The parents yelled for help, but there was no hope. His mother wanted to jump off the boat but people held her back. I heard the water pump working harder; there was a lot of water in the boat. The engine broke down, the mechanic labored to fix it. Finally the storm ended. The ocean was so gentle after its anger. The engine began running again. One more night passed but there was no sign of land anywhere. The food was running out and the water was all gone. We had used up all of our energy. We realized what was going on around us but could do nothing to prevent it. The boat moved on. The heat came again and the engine broke. People were losing hope. In the afternoon, we saw a fisherman's boat coming closer to us. Our spirits lifted when I saw a sign on the boat that said, *Tau Danh Ca Quoc Doanh*. It was a government fishing boat. Men stood on the deck with machine guns and AK-47s aimed at our boat.

"Where is your captain? " they shouted.

The captain came out from his cabin.

"I'm the captain."

"How many people are in your boat?"

"I don't know, comrade. It's over 100."

"Tie the rope on your boat. We will tow you back. If anybody tries to escape, we will shoot."

"We don't have any more food or water. Can we have some for our people?"

"I'll send someone over."

They got closer to our boat, and one man carried a jug of water over.

"Captain, why don't we negotiate with them; maybe they'll let us go?" people shouted to the captain.

The captain spoke with the other man, but he didn't say anything and went back to his boat. Then a northerner came over. After the Communists invaded, they took over all the fishermen's boats and put one northerner and one vc on each boat every time they went fishing on the ocean. They carried machine guns with them.

"How much do you have?" the northerner asked the captain. He was thin, wearing an army-colored shirt.

"We have only thirty bars of gold left. Would you take that?" the captain pleaded.

"Over 100 people for only thirty bars. Too little. I'll take fifty in exchange for food and water."

"We don't have that much, comrade."

The northerner pointed his AK-47 as he turned around to inspect us. The captain asked all of us to take off all our jewelry and give it to him, plus the thirty bars of gold.

"That's all we have, comrade. Please let us go."

"I don't think it's enough, but I'll take it and think about it."

He took the bag, went back to his boat, and started its engines. The line stretched tight, towing our boat back toward the shore. A VC stood on the deck with his gun, watching over us every minute. People started to argue, saying why didn't we try to fight back when they came onto our boat? When we arrived back on shore they would execute us or put us in a labor camp. We had a chance to escape if we fought back.

"Do you think you can win with that machine gun?" said the captain. "It's lucky for us that they towed our boat back since our engine broke. We ran out of food and water. We would die in the middle of the ocean anyway. We may have a chance if we come back to shore."

"I think it's our captain's fault because we were on the ocean two days and two nights and we didn't get anywhere. That's enough time to get to Malaysia. I think he was just driving in circles."

"Yeah, I think he's right!" someone yelled. "The captain's on their side!"

"Why don't we throw him in the ocean?" someone called.

"He let them rob us and we will be put in jail when we get to shore."

People were muttering but they weren't doing anything. I still felt sick, but better for having drunk some water. Hanh and I looked at each other without saying a word because we saw our future. They towed us about half a day. Then we saw a boat just like our boat with many people sitting on the deck. Suddenly the fishermen's boat released the rope, turned around and chased that boat, calling to them to stop. The boat kept running and the shooting began. The government boat went after them for about twenty minutes but the small boat ran faster. Finally they gave up and came back. The man shot at the water near our boat to threaten us, to show us that they dominated the ocean. He ordered us to throw the rope back to them. Our boat followed their boat under the fiery sun without resistance. I saw a little line showing up at the end of the water—the land, I guessed. The seagulls were flying around in the air and landed on one of the poles that had a string on it. They made their own sound, pecked at each other, then flew up in the air. They seemed so carefree, looking down at us like we were prisoners. I wondered if they had any sympathy or felt the way we felt. I wished I had wings to fly. The kids were bawling because of the sun and were asking for food but we had nothing to give them except some water. The line at the end of the horizon became clearer, a shoreline. The VC still held on to their machine guns and stared at us. From my pocket, I pulled a small plastic bag in which I had carefully folded all my papers. I opened it, took them out one at a time and slid my hand along the side of the boat to let each one drop into the ocean. I kept only the fake police paper, folding it back into the plastic bag, which I handed to Hanh.

"Save it for me, so we don't have to buy it again."

He took it, and put it into his pocket.

"What are you going to do? Are you going to jump off the boat now?" he murmured.

"It's better for you to stay because you have nothing to lose. You are handicapped; you have the police papers. You can fool them, saying that these people forced you to escape with them. Then just take a ride back to your grandfather in Cho Lach. I think they will release you in a matter of days when you get on shore. Go back home and wait for me."

"Don't tell me you are going to jump?" He looked at me like he was shocked.

"No, you think I'm stupid or something?"

Hanh looked at me.

"What else can you do?"

"Wait for the dark."

He nodded his head as if he understood.

"After three weeks, if you don't see me come back, I'm finished. Burn some incense for my cold soul."

His eyes were watery, looking to the side.

"Don't let my family know. I don't think my mama could stand it if . . . "

The afternoon came to a close. The breeze was nice, carrying a little mist as if it were baptizing a new life. The sun was gone, but Hanh kept watching the guard holding the machine gun on the back of the towboat. I spotted a large plastic container which I planned to use. I saw a light flashing on shore. I waited a little longer for it to get darker. I squeezed Hanh's shoulder, held on to the side of the boat, and slipped into the water gently. I held on to the plastic container, then heard a sound as if someone else had jumped into the water. The waves pushed me away from the boat as it moved on its way. I didn't know where all my energy came from, but it felt so good. I took my shirt off and tied it to the buoyant container. I couldn't see anything in the dark, only the waves, with a flicker of light in the distance, bobbing up and down.

I held the container for about ten minutes, but I felt like I was struggling with its bulk, rather than getting much benefit from it. I opened the lid and let some water in until it sank down just enough for me to stay on it comfortably. I kicked my feet slowly to save my energy, drifting with the current. The water was warm; I didn't know how far it was from there to the shore, but I didn't want to think about it. Once in a while I felt a little fish nipping me as if I were bait. I was scared but pretended not to be. I wondered what

Dictee

—an excerpt

Honolulu, T.H.
July 12, 1905

To His Excellency, The President of the United States

Your Excellency,—The undersigned have been authorised by the 8,000 Koreans now residing in the territory of Hawaii at a special mass meeting held in the city of Honolulu, on July 12, 1905, to present to your Excellency the following appeal:—

We, the Koreans of the Hawaiian Islands, voicing the sentiments of twelve millions of our countrymen, humbly lay before your Excellency the following facts:—

Soon after the commencement of the war between Russia and Japan, our Government made a treaty of alliance with Japan for offensive and defensive purposes. By virtue of this treaty the whole of Korea was opened to the Japanese, and both the Government and the people have been assisting the Japanese authorities in their military operations in and about Korea.

The contents of this treaty are undoubtedly known to your Excellency, therefore we need not embody them in this appeal. Suffice it to state, however, the object of the treaty was to preserve the independence of Korea and Japan and to protect Eastern Asia from Russia's aggression.

Korea, in return for Japan's friendship and protection against Russia, has rendered services to the Japanese by permitting them to use the country as a base of their military operations.

When this treaty was concluded, the Koreans fully expected that Japan would introduce reforms into the governmental administration along the line of the modern civilization of Europe and America, and that she would advise and counsel our people in a friendly manner, but to our disappointment and regret the Japanese Government has not done a single thing in the way of improving the condition of the Korean people. On the contrary, she turned loose several thousand rough and disorderly men of her nationals in Korea, who are treating the inoffensive Koreans in a most outrageous manner. The Koreans are by nature not a quarrelsome or aggressive people, but deeply resent the high-handed action of the Japanese towards them. We can scarcely believe that the Japanese Government approves the outrages committed by its people in Korea, but it has done nothing to prevent this state of affairs.

They have been, during the last eighteen months, forcibly obtaining all the special privileges and concessions from our Government, so that to-day they practically own everything that is worth having in Korea.

We, the common people of Korea, have lost confidence in the promises Japan made at the time of concluding the treaty of alliance, and we doubt seriously the good intentions which she professes to have towards our people. For geographical, racial, and commercial reasons we want to be friendly to Japan, and we are even willing to have her as our guide and example in the matters of internal reforms and education, but the continuous policy of self-exploitation at the expense of the Koreans has shaken our confidence in her, and we are now afraid that she will not keep her promise of preserving our independence as a nation, nor assisting us in reforming internal administration. In other words, her policy in Korea seems to be exactly the same as that of Russia prior to the war.

The United States has many interests in our country. The industrial, commercial, and religious enterprises under American management, have attained such proportions that we believe the Government and people of the United States ought to know the true conditions of Korea and the result of the Japanese becoming paramount in our country. We know that the people of America love fair play and advocate justice towards all men. We also know that your Excellency is the ardent exponent of a square deal between individuals as well as nations, therefore we come to you with this memorial with the hope that Your Excellency may help our country at this critical period of our national life.

We fully appreciate the fact that during the conference between the Russian and Japanese peace envoys, Your Excellency may not care to make any suggestion to either party as to the conditions of their settlement, but we earnestly hope that Your Excellency will see to it that Korea may preserve her autonomous Government and that other Powers shall not oppress or maltreat our people. The clause in the treaty between the United States and Korea gives us a claim upon the United States for assistance, and this is the time when we need it most.

Very respectfully, Your obedient servants,

(Sgd.) P.K. Yoon

Syngman Rhee

* * *

March 1, 1919. Everyone knows to carry inside themselves, the national flag. Everyone knows equally the punishment that follows this gesture. The march begins, the flags are taken out, made visible, waved, every individual crying out the independence the freedom to the people of this nation.

Knowing equally the punishment. Her parents leading the procession fell. Her brothers. Countless others were fired at and stabbed indiscriminately by the enemy soldiers. Guan Soon is arrested as a leader of the revolution, with punishment deserving of such a rank. She is stabbed in the chest, and subjected to questioning to which she reveals no names. She is given seven years prison sentence to which her reply is that the nation itself is imprisoned. Child revolutionary child patriot woman soldier deliverer of nation. The eternity of one act. Is the completion of one existence. One martyrdom. For the history of one nation. Of one people.

Some will not know age. Some not age. Time stops. Time will stop for some. For them especially. Eternal time. No age. Time fixes for some. Their image, the memory of them is not given to deterioration, unlike the captured image that extracts from the soul precisely by reproducing, multiplying itself. Their countenance evokes not the hallowed beauty, beauty from seasonal decay, evokes not the inevitable, not death, but the dy-ing.

Face to face with the memory, it misses. It's missing. Still. What of time. Does not move. Remains there. Misses nothing. Time, that is. All else. All things else. All other, subject to time. Must answer to time, except. Still born. Aborted. Barely. Infant. Seed, germ, sprout, less even. Dormant. Stagnant. Missing.

The decapitated forms. Worn. Marred, recording a past, of previous forms. The present form face to face reveals the missing, the absent. Would-be-said remnant, memory. But the remnant is the whole.

The memory is the entire. The longing in the face of the lost. Maintains the missing. Fixed between the wax and wane indefinite not a sign of progress. All else age, in time. Except. Some are without.

—THERESA HAK KYUNG CHA

Black Korea

"Or your little chop-suey ass will be a target . . ."
—Ice Cube

Last summer, four black cops arrested me because I was "dat chinese man." You want proof? Get me the money I need for a lawyer—I'll pay you back extra after I win.

We do win.

* * *

EPISODE: After an afternoon of collecting quotations, diagrams, and photos for an essay on *DICTEE* (the masterpiece by a Korean American murdered by a security guard in SoHo), a night in the Library of Congress's basement video dungeon, two of First District's finest holding cages, and Central Cell Block.

For being "dat chinese man."

* * *

IN THE BASEMENT OF THE LIBRARY OF CONGRESS: Sat for two hours while Mudbrain and crew tried to figure out forms and sign their names. "Do they want our weight or his?" "I don't know—that's a tough one. You better go ask the captain." Don't they have to read me Miranda rights or something? What are one's rights when there's no witness but four empowered gook-grillers? Twenty more minutes pass.

"Do we put in his birthdate or ours?"

"I don't know. That's a tough one."

"I guess I'll go ask the captain. Man, these are tough."

Then it's time for handcuffs and hauling me again for the ride to First District. Young admirer driving the cruiser coos to Mudbrain, "Jeez, I didn't know you had it in you." Badge no.31 *thirty-one, thirty- one, 7 P.M.* I repeat like a mantra. His name, too—Not mine.

AT FIRST DISTRICT: Crew congratulates itself, "This is good—it sets a precedent." Denied release on citation by Metro PD because "You mean dat chinese man? He hasn't been in the country long enough," despite my documents, sister, and a *Business Week* reporter saying I was born & raised in Baltimore, 60 miles away, despite my Bawl'mer English. "Do we put in his birthplace or our birthplace?" Aint Chinee, you shitheads, r u F.O.B. from the congo?

No ancestral pine and guardian-graced hillock in Baltimore, 200 ri away, quaked at all this. Sleep, grandfathers grandmothers: I know you sigh already from your own history.

TWO HOURS LATER, STILL AT FIRST DISTRICT: Mudbrain and his fat crew shuffle out of station, smiling, assuring my sister and journalist friend (family name: Hong) that I will be free in minutes. Just working for the public goode, ma'am. *They have a dream! They have a dreeeam. That from a gook corpse on the proud flank of Capitol Hill, even morons can one day feast in the glad tidings of proMOtion and like the permed asshole with the citizen's achievement awards covering his left tit who got a hard-on-all-ovah-his-body whenever he pushed me around* ("Stand behind me and put your thUMB out") *even the lowly He and All the Righteous Rest may rejoice as they trample over fallen yellars and ba-baloneyans, always holding high the colors of our world-champion Killah-nation in the cause of of . . . Liberty and Freedom for All . . . No, I mean the NEW WORD ODOR! Hail to the . . . I have SEEN the Glory of the*

Now solely Metro PD's meat, yours Truly, Lew.

Half-nelsoned and shoved away from my sister pleading beyond the door that my rights be honored. Hong notes down names and badge numbers. Dried blood-smears all over the cell's lemon brick.

FOLLOW THE YELLOW BRICK WALL: *DICTEE*, I remember your second image: last wishes carved in the wall of a mine by starving Korean slave children (All for the goode of Japan, ma'am.): *Ŏmŏni pogoship'ŏ Pae-ga kop'ayo Kohyang-e kagŏship'ta* I look down at the steel bench and, after idly glancing along the scattered initials and dates there, discern in the dim fluorescent light that, near the middle, a few *Korean* letters have also been scratched into it. After fifteen minutes of staring and studying, I still cannot make them form a complete word. First syllable: *Mu* probably meaning "non-," "without-," "not," or maybe it's the *mu* of "soldier, weapon, martial." Then a *ch* and *n*, but there are no vowels in between to make a full syllable. I conjecture that, since one cannot have anything in the cell except the minimum of clothing—even my shoelaces have been confiscated—maybe police came at that point and took the stylus or the prisoner away.

Mu ch n

OFF TO CENTRAL CELL BLOCK: The whole airless paddy wagon to myself, wire tight around the wrists, doubled through my beltloops, marking more flesh each time we bounce through a rut and I'm bumped around on the metal plank, window so small and dull I don't know where the hell I am, back-and-forth around the city cuz brainchild forgot my papers.

"You're spending the night here in CCB, no matter what you say." Three hours to frisk, photograph, and fingerprint me for the third time (I think—I've lost track), tortured by "Married with Children" and Arnold S.'s "Commando" on the one-finger-typing officer's tube, though I enjoy the scene where Arnoould's high-heeled sidekick blasts open a paddy wagon with an anti-tank bazooka.

Some Latino and Black youngsters I'm being processed with complain about their treatment.

"So sue us, go ahead and sue the whole fuckin department," the sandwich munching officer grins. "Do you know how HIGH the stack of cases waiting to be heard is?"

He lifts his free hand about four feet above the desk. (Me? I just want his fuckin sandwich.)

"Yeah, maybe you'll get heard 2 or 3 years from now. And you'd better have a good LAWYER too! We're the Federal government!"

Here we go. Just like a Bronson film. Big beautiful belaying pin switches to open and shut cages from a distance, brass showing through where the paint's chipped.

"Officer, put him in here with me, I'm LONEsome,"

"Sorry, I don't assign the cells."

Mine is number 22, Jim Palmer's old number! The officer performs his most helpful service of the day: passing single cigarettes back and forth like lacing up a high-top as he walks along between the two rows of cages, 25 cents each.

IN CELL 22: To my surprise, I find my brothers of this evening in the many-throated, constantly thrusting and sighing conversation rolling like a wave up and down between the cages. A red bandanna'd member ("He's a SCHOLAR!") asks me into their banter, and I quickly conjoin my own solos of sympathetic cluck. They laugh and I laugh: we share our stories of false apprehending.

After a cup of Hi-C (orange color) for dinner, I lay down on a perforated metal frame (my bunk) in water and cigarette ash. For a night of conjuring poems—but for whom? I have no listening *volk*. For the bantering brothers here, then, endlessly joking black boys and brown boys, all sad inside if you listen close enough, but most of all the invisible one with the Korean blade who has drifted along with me from First District's yellow brick, forever lay-ing the dark puzzle out before me like a scarred nameplate or gravestone so broad it blocks off the whole field of vision..

Mu ch__ n

Answer this, s/he pleads, *I too don know what I'm spelling out Please complete for me so I* short bars of light flicker in the cigarette smoke *free of this pain of writ-ing what I don know that etches itself into bones of my arm my hand*

mu ch n

* * *

MAYBE SINCE THEN I have passed a brother or sister on the street, that very pattern of scarring weight and need altering a bit the swing of his or her arm on one side, slowing by just the width-of-a-moment the acceleration with which a hand lifts or "warms itself around a cup of coffee"

MU CH N

   I guess and gaze, present it to others
Ajŏshi, i kŏs-ul chom pwa chuseyo!
Still have not made up our mind.

        —WALTER LEW

Blue Dreams

—an excerpt

The Los Angeles Riots, the Korean American Story
The focused destruction of Korean American businesses and the dramatic image of armed Korean Americans on Los Angeles rooftops during the L.A. riots piqued public attention. Koreans? Why are they in Los Angeles? Are they hated? Are they hateful? The mayhem of fire, looting, and vigilantism seemed to augur an apocalyptic vision of a race war, a real-life preview of Ridley Scott's film *Blade Runner.* Frank Chin, an Asian American writer, saw Korean Americans with Uzis and AK-47s guarding their own and compatriots' shops, and wondered: "The Alamo in Koreatown was a mini-mall. In the race war that's started, are we all going to choose up sides and appear at the appropriate mini-mall to man the barricades?"

In the media barrage during and after the riots, Korean Americans came to occupy a particular place in the American ideological landscape. They were often invoked to support one point or another about the L.A. riots. Imagined variously as quintessential or exceptional immigrants, as culturally legible or inscrutable, as racist or oppressed, Korean Americans emerged at the crossroads of conflicting social reflections over the L.A. riots. Through the Korean American story, observers decried the "death of the immigrant dream," underscored intra-minority racism, and again and again offered formulaic cultural contrasts between Korean Americans and African Americans. *Blue Dreams* presents the Korean American story against the backdrop of the L.A. riots, media bafflement, and the contentious American debates over capitalism, race, and community.

Making Sense of the L.A. Riots
On March 3, 1991, Rodney King, a twenty-five-year-old African American living in Altadena, California, was speeding down a highway in San Fernando Valley, when he was stopped, shot by a stun gun, and repeatedly kicked and beaten by police officers. What distinguished this episode of police brutality was that the excessive force used against King was videotaped by George Holliday, a nearby resident, and repeatedly shown on television news shows throughout the United States. Whether the grainy imagery confirmed suspicions of police brutality and racism or shattered myths of police civility and fairness, very few doubted that the worst offenders in the King beating would stand accused and be duly punished. Yet, on April 29, 1992, twelve Simi Valley jurors—ten European Americans, one Latino, and one Asian American—acquitted all four officers standing trial: Stacey Koon, Laurence Powell, Timothy Wind, and Theodore Briseno.

The dissonance between the manifest guilt and the innocent verdict stunned virtually the whole country. As the *Los Angeles Times* reported:

> Mayor Bradley appeared at a press conference, saying he was stunned, shocked and outraged: "I was speechless when I heard that verdict. Today this jury told the world that what we saw with our own eyes is not a crime." Joseph Lowery, president of the Southern Christian Leadership Conference, expressed fear for the nation. Even in South Africa, he said, white police officers are punished for beating blacks. Benjamin Hooks, the executive director of the NAACP, called the verdicts outrageous: "Given the evidence, it is difficult to see how the jurors will ever live with their consciences."

In many parts of the United States, angry demonstrations, civil disobedience, rioting, and looting broke out. In San Francisco, a curfew was declared for the first time since the 1906 earthquake; in Las Vegas, uprisings occurred four weekends in a row; in Seattle, Atlanta, and other cities around the country, demonstrations and disturbances rocked urban centers. Nowhere was the violence more pronounced than in Los Angeles. After three days of what came to be known as the L.A. riots, there were an estimated "1,158 dead, 2,400 injured, 11,700 arrested, [and] $717 million in damages." It was the worst urban upheaval since the 1965 Watts riots, and perhaps since the 1863 New York City Draft Riots. The social historian Mike Davis commented: "It is becoming clear that the King case may be almost as much of a watershed in American history as Dred Scott, a test of the very meaning of the citizenship for which African Americans have struggled for 400 years."

An event of such magnitude, not surprisingly, became an occasion for multifarious reactions and reflections. Perhaps the only consensus was that something seemed deeply wrong with Los Angeles and the United States. The British journalist Martin Walker remarked: "One of the world's richest cities, for so long the ultimate lure in the land of opportunity, has torn itself apart. America's free market has its costs, its democracy fails to embrace so many of its poor, and the high temple of consumer capitalism has been pillaged by its own excluded worshippers." *Understanding the Riots*, written by the staff of the *Los Angeles Times*, concluded its narrative with: "Los Angeles had come to symbolize an ugly side of the American dream—hatred among races, a widening gap between rich and poor, the rise in urban violence and the seeming impotence of society's institutions." Whether one was black or white, Korean or Latino, poor or rich, on the left or right, the L.A. riots were a symptom of a deeper malaise afflicting Los Angeles in particular and the United States in general.

Beyond the universal acknowledgment of this malaise, the understanding of the L.A. riots spanned the full range of the U.S. political spectrum. Perhaps it is the most trite of truisms to say that most people saw what they wanted to see in the L.A. riots. Indeed, many people's analyses were shaped by their preconceptions and political perspectives. For some radicals, they were the beginning of a much-awaited revolution by the oppressed, a "black intifada"; for liberals, they denoted the failure of Republican domestic policy; for some conservatives, they were the outbreak of a paroxysm of violence and nihilism of the underclass. Coming as they did in an election year, politicians jumped to explain the "problems" and offer "solutions."

For progressives and radicals, particularly among African Americans, the "fire" of Los Angeles was not a "riot" but a "rebellion" or even the beginning of a "revolution," not "mindless" violence but an "organized insurrection." The poet June Jordan saw in "fire everywhere" a simmering sentiment for social justice and a hope for a political movement against racism and oppression: "I am beginning to sense a victory of spirit risen from the death of self-hatred. I am beginning to envision our collective turning to the long-term tasks of justice and equal rights to life, liberty, and the pursuit of happiness right inside this country that has betrayed our trust repeatedly. Behold the fire everywhere!" Robin D.G. Kelley, a professor at the University of Michigan, wrote: "As I watched 'on the ground' videotape of the black and Latino poor seizing property and destroying what many regarded as symbols of domination, I could not help but notice the joy and sense of empowerment expressed in their faces. It strengthened my belief that the inner cities are the logical place for a new radical movement in post-cold war America."

More prosaically, the U.S. Representative from South Central Los Angeles, Maxine Waters, said: "The fact of the matter is, whether we like it or not, riot is the voice of the unheard." The Detroit-based journal *Against the Current* proclaimed: "The first and essential response to the explosion in Los Angeles must be: *This rebellion was justified, as was the 1965 uprising in Watts and those in between.*" The journalist James Ridgeway concurred: "The looting in the streets of Los Angeles was nothing compared to the massive theft openly conducted over the past 12 years by political officials of the Reagan and Bush administrations."

Yet some African Americans, particularly of the middle class, were deeply ambivalent. While understanding the motivation, some nonetheless remained critical of the rioting and looting. Dympna Ugwu-Oju, a professor at Middlesex County College, asked: "Could I tell [my children] that I understand the senseless actions of those black youths and not misdirect them? Could I tell them that while I do not condone their violence, I forgive it?" An African American manager of a law firm explained: "I don't agree with the looting, but I understand the frustration." Myra Bauman, managing partner of a public relations firm, responded: "I don't condone the riots. I understand the riots. I understand them as being a result of people who are looking to vent what is pent-up frustration. In some cases, people who don't have, didn't have clothing or didn't have certain household items. . . . Some who were just simply crying out in frustration." Gary Phillips, active for the last 20 years in African American community organizing, wrote:

> The wellspring of the riot—police abuse, lack of economic equity, underserved schools, years of neglect—were understood. They were the same conditions that led to Watts 27 years ago. But I had no romanticized view that the people were in the streets taking justice into their own hands. Otherwise, Black-owned businesses . . . would not have been gutted. The oldest continuously operated Black bookstore in America (opened in 1941), the Aquarian Book Shop . . . was burned down because it had the misfortune of being in a strip mall that was looted and then firebombed. . . . The mob ruled, not politics.

Among mainstream liberals, the L.A. riots offered an occasion to criticize twelve years of Republican presidency. Senator Bill Bradley, for instance, reasoned that the "tragedy" of Los Angeles resulted from the public and politicians' "distortion and silence" on "the issue of race and urban America." He stressed the need for a "new democratic movement," which "must start with the acknowledgment that slavery was America's original sin and race remains our unresolved dilemma." The solution "can occur only by winning over all segments of urban life to a new politics of change, empowerment, and common effort." Similarly, Jesse Jackson noted that "the riots in Los Angeles and elsewhere remind us just how incalculable the costs of neglect are." Like Bradley, the charismatic African American politician spoke of the need "to rebuild our cities, to invest in people, to provide hope." Bill Clinton, then a Democratic presidential hopeful, echoed Bradley and Jackson in blaming the riots on "twelve years of denial and neglect" by the Reagan and Bush administrations.

At the other end of the American political spectrum, the conservative writer Mark Horowitz simply found the riots humorous: "Not many people thought the Los Angeles Riot was funny, but I did. I freely admit it. I enjoyed great sweeps of it. I suppose you could say I had a good riot." More ominously, Patrick Buchanan sounded an apocalyptic note. Comparing the looters to Brown Shirts and Red Guards, he warned that "what we saw in Los Angeles was evil exultant and triumphant." While Bradley and Jackson spoke of racism and poverty, Buchanan invoked "a religious war going on for the soul of America." In contrast to the progressive prescription of anti-racism, empowerment, and the economic rejuvenation of inner cities, Buchanan's remedy was religious: "The war for the soul of America will only be won with basic truths [which] are spelled out explicitly in the Old and New Testaments."

Most conservatives, like Buchanan, condemned what they perceived as the mindless anarchy and pathological violence of the poor. They attempted to find the source of the riots in the moral depravity of the rioters and the larger society. The California Senator John Seymour, who was later defeated in the 1992 U.S. Senate election, observed: "Finally, there must be a return to family values and community respect." In keeping with his bashing of the television program *Murphy Brown* for positively depicting a single mother, Vice President Dan Quayle said of the riots: "I believe the lawless social anarchy which we saw is directly related to the breakdown of family structure, personal responsibility and social order in too many areas of our society." President George Bush, after his spokesperson Marlin Fitzwater blamed the riots on social welfare programs since the 1960s, noted: "What we saw in Los Angeles is not about civil rights. It is not about the great cause of equality that all Americans must uphold. It is not a message of protest. It has been the brutality of a mob, pure and simple."

No doubt the memory of the burning flames in Los Angeles played its part in overturning twelve years of Republican rule, as most voters emphasized the sluggish economy over "family values" at the polls. Yet it should be noted that poverty and inner-city problems remained virtually taboo topics in the 1992 presidential election campaign. The national debate on the origins and meanings of the L.A. riots reached no specific consensus or conclusions.

The Riots in Black and White

The 1992 Los Angeles riots were originally reported as a reprise of the 1965 Watts Rebellion. The 1965 civil disturbance, which resulted in 34 dead, over 1,000 injured, and nearly 4,000 arrested (the vast majority of them African Americans), epitomized the twin failures of liberal social reforms and moderate civil rights movements. As televised images of African Americans rioting and looting—"Burn, Baby, Burn!" became etched in the American memory, Watts came to signify "black race riots," which raged across the United States in 1965. While these riots revealed rising expectations of urban African Americans and their frustration with the Johnson administration and the "nonviolent" civil rights movement, they also prompted Republicans to unleash "a full-scale assault on liberal social policies." The "race riots" thus set the stage for burning political debates over race, city, poverty, and welfare—central issues in the United States since the 1970s.

The disparate responses to the 1992 riots represented, at first glance, a continuation of the debates unleashed by the 1960s "race riots." For many, the 1992 L.A. riots reconfirmed the 1968 Kerner Commission report, which stated: "To continue our present policies is to make permanent the division of our country into two societies; one, largely Negro and poor, located in central cities; the other, predominantly white and affluent, located in the suburbs and in outlying areas." *The Economist* expressed its opinion on its editorial page: "An apparently racist verdict, followed by black riots, seems to have confirmed both blacks and whites in an instinctive distrust of each other." *Time* wrote:

"As Los Angeles smolders, black and white Americans and the country try to comprehend the verdict and the future of social relations." In discussing the beating of the truck driver Reginald Denny during the riots, Lance Morrow commented: "The truck-driver video accomplished the amazing task of nullifying the Rodney King video. . . . On that level of discussion, if Americans choose to stay there, there can only be a gridlock of rage: blacks make demons of whites, whites make demons of blacks."

Yet the facile imagery of the black race riot, 1992 as a reprise of 1965, belied what was obvious to most eyes: the multiethnic composition of looters and victims. Indeed, the L.A. riots have come to be widely characterized as "the nation's first multiethnic urban riot." Along with the Denny beating, "the pictures of Korean boys with Uzis keeping watch from a rooftop and the shots of several buildings in full frame, constituted the main iconography of the first 36 or so hours of the riot." As television viewers and journalists in Los Angeles came to appreciate the multiethnic character of the L.A. riots, simple parallels with the 1965 Watts upheaval no longer seemed adequate. It turned out, for example, that one of the "white" police officers, Theodore Briseno, was part Latino. No longer were African Americans the only rioters; Latinos constituted over half of the arrested. Many of the victims were not "white"; Korean Americans were the single most visible group of victims. More than half of the 3,100 Korean American businesses in Los Angeles suffered damages, totaling $350 million. When the L.A. riots are viewed as essentially "black and white," a variation on the saga of "race" in the United States—slavery, civil war, Jim Crow, civil rights—Korean Americans and other ethnic populations are rendered invisible and irrelevant.

The Curious Role of Korean Americans

The multiethnic reality of Los Angeles struck us forcefully on one of our first days of fieldwork in Los Angeles. When a Korean American man addressed in English a seemingly African American guard at a mini-mall in Koreatown, the guard replied in Korean: "I am Korean; don't speak to me in English." The son of an African American military man stationed in South Korea and a South Korean mother, he in fact preferred to use Korean. On the same day, a middle-aged Korean American we had just interviewed in his jewelry shop encouraged us to interview his sister-in-law. A long drive took us to an affluent suburb and a sprawling home, where a Korean American woman was giving orders in Spanish to a Latina maid who was taking care of the woman's four children. Losing our way home around the interminable surface streets of Los Angeles, we stopped at one of the few unburned and unlooted "swap meets"—modeled after open-air markets in South Korea—to ask for directions. When Abelmann, a European American woman, asked one of the seemingly Latino guards in

English, he spoke in Korean to a middle-aged Korean American woman, "Come here, she is asking a question." When Abelmann then asked again, this time in Korean, the woman was unfazed and simply gave her directions in Korean. In Los Angeles, nothing seemed obvious; certainly things were not black and white.

The broadcasted images of the multiethnic riot featured Korean Americans in unexpected places and in surprising poses. The prevalence of Korean language signs near downtown Los Angeles—indeed, the very existence of Koreatown—must have been news for some viewers. More striking, armed Korean Americans on rooftops and in cruising vehicles overturned the stereotype of meek and diffident Asian Americans.

For those who explored beneath the surface of the L.A. riots, then, the curious but crucial role of the Korean Americans became inescapable. Some saw a simmering and seething interethnic conflict between African Americans and Korean Americans as one of the significant stories behind the riots. They noted that the ferocity of African American anger against the "Rodney King verdict" could be understood only in the context of the earlier light sentence against Soon Ja Du. Du, a Korean American grocer, shot and killed Latasha Harlins, a fifteen-year-old African American girl, after an in-store squabble over a shoplifting charge. The shooting, in cold blood, was videotaped by an anti-theft camera. "Latasha Harlins. A name that was scarcely mentioned on television was the key to the catastrophic collapse of relations between L.A.'s black and Korean communities" Richard Rodriguez wrote: "We cannot settle for black and white conclusions when one of the most important conflicts was the tension between Koreans and African-Americans." Thus the "black-Korean conflict" was sometimes presented as one of the key factors of the L.A. riots. Many Korean Americans, as we shall see, disagreed vehemently; we too criticize the "black-Korean conflict" frame in Chapter 6.

Like the responses to the L.A. riots, media portrayal of Korean Americans varied widely. In accounts decrying the mob violence, Korean Americans emerged as the model minority, immigrant entrepreneurs who had realized the American dream. The conservative author William Murchison wrote: "For Korean merchants the looters reserved a special fury. I should ask parenthetically, isn't it time our society showed some concern over the well-being of these honest, hard-working, lovable people, the Koreans, who prosper in the black ghettos only to arouse their customers' wrath when they prosper too well?"

In contrast, Korean Americans played a more ambiguous role in other accounts, as part exploiter and part victim. John Edgar Wideman offers what might be a canonical progressive interpretation of Korean Americans' role in the L.A. riots:

Koreans arrived determined to be merchants, buying failing businesses in Hispanic and black neighborhoods. The function of such businesses in the larger economic picture is to snatch back the few dollars that trickle down into the hands of the working poor, the unemployed, mothers on welfare, the elderly on social security, exploiting segments of the public that big business no longer deems worth the trouble to service. Since labor is expensive, Korean businesses tended to be family concerns. Long hours, hard work, minimal overhead, streamlined services were survival strategies. Korean businesses monopolized the cash coming into the community and eventually turned a profit, prospering and expanding while the neighborhoods supporting them languished. An explosion was inevitable, a systemic failure whose symptom, not cause, was racial animosity between Koreans and other people of color.

Even in Wideman's considered response, however, Korean Americans merely fill a particular niche in his interpretation of the L.A. riots. With a few exceptions—such as the lawyer Angela Oh's appearance on Ted Koppel's *Nightline* after a campaign waged by Korean Americans—Korean Americans were virtually shut out of the mainstream media in the United States. They were widely discussed but largely silent.

None of the portraits of Korean Americans across the American ideological spectrum captured the complex realities of Korean American lives. In part this was because writers mobilized Korean Americans for one or another interpretation of the riots. There are, of course, glimpses of truth in many of these accounts. Yet we must be mindful both of the transnational dimension of Korean Americans and of their irreducible diversity. In turn, understanding their situations and listening to their voices challenges some of the dominant assumptions about the United States.

—NANCY ABELMANN AND JOHN LIE

Caught Prey

Gunner Lindberg, 21, and Dominic Christopher, 17, were arrested for the murder of Thien Minh Ly, based in part on a letter believed to be penned by Lindberg. Italicized sections taken from his account, which originally appeared in the Los Angeles Times, *Orange County Edition, March 7, 1996.*

First, finger the prey,
Oh I killed a jap a while ago.
Dominic was with me.

Secure your position,
We walked into the tennis court
where he was. I walked up to him.

Bait the hook
I looked at him and said, "Oh I thought I knew you."
Then I hit him . . .

Cast out the line,
I pulled out the knife, a butcher knife,
and he said "no." I put the knife to his throat,

Reel in the catch,
And he looked at me, so I stomped on his head
3 times and each time said, "Stop looking at me."

The catch will flail,
Then he was kinda knocked out,
dazed,

Subdue the catch,
Then I stabbed him in the side about 7 or 8 times; he rolled over
a little, so I stabbed his back out 18 or 19 times.

Commence cleaning,
Then he lay flat and I slit
one side of his throat on his jugular vein.

Let your dinner companion assist,
Then Dominic said, "Do it again,"
so I cut his other jugular vein.

Marinate fillets in red wine,
Dominic said, "Stab him in the heart."
So I stabbed him about 20 or 21 times in the heart. . . .

Survey the preparation,
I wanted to go back and look, so we did,
and he was dying just then.

While cooking, offer your companion a taste,
I told Dominic to kick him,
so he kicked the f _ _ _ out of his face,

Clean up,
Then I ditched the knife, after wiping it
clean on the side of the 5 freeway.

—JOHNSON CHEU

Body Search

From the feet up, as the security guys do
it to you in airports at some pre-flights,

I've inspected my body on a regular
basis for concealed dangerous weapons

and bit by bit over these many years
I've discovered more than just a few

ominous items: from between the toes
I pulled out sharp stainless steel spikes

and from behind both well-shaped kneecaps
several antique Oriental throwing knives.

The crotch yielded the most deadly treasure:
a machine gun, sticks of dynamite and letter

bombs, one of which went off from mishandling.
I still carry nasty scars from that nice blast.

Hidden in the armpits were ropes of old-
fashioned hand grenades, pins half-pulled.

A heavy-gauge shotgun with sawed-off barrels
I recovered from the belly button's hollow.

A considerable cache of explosive chemicals
and powders was expertly stashed deep

in the shadowy cavities of the nose, ears,
mouth and down the hatch of the throat

which gives a clue to more powerful arsenals
kept in the dark crevices of the brain vicinity—

but more smartly hidden: all the recent and
thorough head scans revealed nothing unusual.

—LUIS CABALQUINTO

On the Other Side of Granite

—*in defense of Maya Lin*

"Brought to a sharp awareness of such a loss, it is up to each individual to resolve or come to terms with this loss. For death is in the end a personal and private matter, and the area contained with this memorial is a quiet place, meant for personal reflection and private reckoning. The black granite walls . . ."
—Statement by Maya Ying Lin, March, 1981

damn da-damn damn damn!
you wanna ride that chink in you?
that gee-golly gook in you?
yes you can, be cam-bod-jan.
wok on da wild side with buddist brothas
to the other side of the granite—
don't panic

five-eight-three-zero-five heroes—
that's over fifty-eight thousand flag mans and woe-mans
chiseled like the armor that should have been theirs
like the dropzone that should have been dropped altogether
like the escalation that should have been deceleration
colonial desecration as is
puppeteers and pawn generals playing kids
all taking a back-alley yellow whiz
to the tune of a southeast danang fix-asian

damn damn da-da-da-damn!
you wanna crown maya limb from lin
queen of the mekong delta
the 17th parallel prophet
model minority by design
architect of resolution
for her piece for peace and salutations
after a two-bit worthless confrontation
damn damn da-damn damn damn!
don't tread on me and my demilitarized zone
please just max out your agent orange exhalations
and dreams of a republican elephant brahma

in red, white and blue
boo fuckin' hoo!

but maya made it all better
you say that chink made it all better

damn damn da-damn danang
danang danang danang
to do the abacus arithmetic
on the other side of the black granite
two decades between g.i.—
that's government issued genocides
always one away from one too many
military junta homicides—
five-eight-three-zero-five killed will never
equal two million brown brothas and sistas with no memorial
except cheap tickets to miss saigon
a free refugee ride to the capitalist machine
and your own killing fields of uptown
twin-cities gooktown
respectfully called g-town
like it's goddamn good ol' georgetown.

and here you are contemplating the validity
of an itemized gritblasted memory
forever half-remembered
always half-ass articulated
please correct yourself—
carry the one right back to the south china sea
back to the gulf of tonkin
back to the other side of the black granite—

where the names of my people
are written.

—MARLON UNAS ESGUERRA

December 8, 1941
A grocery store owned by a University of California graduate of Japanese descent.
Bridge, Volume 7, No.4, Winter 1981–1982, p.16.

October 20, 1999
A Korean American-owned computer store front,
vandalized in Palisades Park, New Jersey.
Hanah Journal, Jan/Feb 2000, p.13.

Wilshire Bus

Wilshire Boulevard begins somewhere near the heart of downtown Los Angeles and, except for a few digressions scarcely worth mentioning, goes straight out to the edge of the Pacific Ocean. It is a wide boulevard and traffic on it is fairly fast. For the most part, it is bordered on either side with examples of the recent stark architecture which favors a great deal of glass. As the boulevard approaches the sea, however, the landscape becomes a bit more pastoral, so that the university and the soldiers' home there give the appearance of being huge country estates.

Esther Kuroiwa got to know this stretch of territory quite well while her husband Buro was in one of the hospitals at the soldiers' home. They had been married less than a year when his back, injured in the war, began troubling him again, and he was forced to take three months of treatments at Sawtelle before he was able to go back to work. During this time, Esther was permitted to visit him twice a week and she usually took the yellow bus out on Wednesdays because she did not know the first thing about driving and because her friends were not able to take her except on Sundays. She always enjoyed the long bus ride very much because her seat companions usually turned out to be amiable, and if they did not, she took vicarious pleasure in gazing out at the almost unmitigated elegance along the fabulous street.

It was on one of these Wednesday trips that Esther committed a grave sin of omission which caused her later to burst into tears and which caused her acute discomfort for a long time afterwards whenever something reminded her of it.

The man came on the bus quite early and Esther noticed him briefly as he entered because he said gaily to the driver, "You robber. All you guys do is take money from me every day, just for giving me a short lift!"

Handsome in a red-faced way, greying, medium of height, and dressed in a dark grey sport suit with a yellow-and-black flowered shirt, he said this in a nice, resonant, carrying voice which got the response of a scattering of titters from the bus. Esther, somewhat amused and classifying him as a somatotonic, promptly forgot about him. And since she was sitting alone in the first regular seat, facing the back of the driver and the two front benches facing each other, she returned to looking out the window.

At the next stop, a considerable mass of people piled on and the last two climbing up were an elderly Oriental man and his wife. Both were neatly and somberly clothed and the woman, who wore her hair in a bun and carried a bunch of yellow and dark red chrysanthemums, came to sit with Esther. Esther turned her head to smile a greeting (well, here we are, Orientals together on a bus), but the woman was watching, with some concern, her husband who was asking directions of the driver.

His faint English was inflected in such a way as to make Esther decide he was probably Chinese, and she noted that he had to repeat his question several times before the driver could answer it. Then he came to sit in the seat across the aisle from his wife. It was about then that a man's voice, which Esther recognized soon as belonging to the somatotonic, began a loud monologue in the seat just behind her. It was not really a monologue, since he seemed to be addressing his seat companion, but this person was not heard to give a single answer. The man's subject was a figure in the local sporting world who had a nice fortune invested in several of the shining buildings the bus was just passing.

"He's as tight-fisted as they make them, as tight-fisted as they come," the man said. "Why, he wouldn't give you the sweat of his . . ." He paused here to rephrase his metaphor, ". . . wouldn't give you the sweat off his palm!"

And he continued in this vein, discussing the private life of the famous man so frankly that Esther knew he must be quite drunk. But she listened with interest, wondering how much of this diatribe was true, because the public legend about the famous man was emphatic about his charity. Suddenly, the woman with the chrysanthemums jerked around to get a look at the speaker and Esther felt her giving him a quick but thorough examination before she turned back around.

"So you don't like it?" the man inquired, and it was a moment before Esther realized that he was now directing his attention to her seat neighbor.

"Well, if you don't like it," he continued, "why don't you get off this bus, why don't you go back where you came from? Why don't you go back to China?"

Then, his voice growing jovial, as though he were certain of the support of the bus in this at least, he embroidered on this theme with a new eloquence, "Why don't you go back to China, where you can be coolies working in your bare feet out in the rice fields? You can let your pigtails grow and grow in China. Alla samee, mama, no tickee no shirtee. Ha, pretty good, no tickee no shirtee!"

He chortled with delight and seemed to be looking around the bus for approval. Then some memory caused him to launch on a new idea: "Or why don't you go back to Trinidad? They got Chinks running the whole she-bang in Trinidad. Every place you go in Trinidad . . ."

As he talked on, Esther, pretending to look out the window, felt the tenseness in the body of the woman beside her. The only movement from her was the trembling of the chrysanthemums with the motion of the bus. Without turning her head, Esther was also aware that a man, a mild-looking man with thinning hair and glasses, on one of the front benches was smiling at the woman and shaking his head mournfully in sympathy, but she doubted whether the woman saw.

Esther herself, while believing herself properly annoyed with the speaker and sorry for the old couple, felt quite detached. She found herself wondering whether the man meant her in his exclusion order or whether she was identifiably Japanese. Of course, he was not sober enough to be interested in such fine distinctions, but it did matter, she decided, because she was Japanese, not Chinese, and therefore in the present case immune. Then she was startled to realize that what she was actually doing was gloating over the fact that the drunken man had specified the Chinese as the unwanted.

Briefly, there bobbled on her memory the face of an elderly Oriental man whom she had once seen from a streetcar on her way home from work. (This was not long after she had returned to Los Angeles from the concentration camp in Arkansas and been lucky enough to get a clerical job with the Community Chest.) The old man was on a concrete island at Seventh and Broadway, waiting for his streetcar. She had looked down on him benignly as a fellow Oriental, from her seat by the window, then been suddenly thrown for a loop by the legend on a large lapel button on his jacket. I AM KOREAN, said the button.

Heat suddenly rising to her throat, she had felt angry, then desolate and betrayed. True, reason had returned to ask whether she might not, under the circumstances, have worn such a button herself. She had heard rumors of I AM CHINESE buttons. So it was true then; why not I AM KOREAN buttons, too? Wryly, she wished for an I AM JAPANESE button, just to be able to call the man's attention to it, "Look at me!" But perhaps the man didn't even read English, perhaps he had been actually threatened, perhaps it was not his doing—his solicitous children perhaps had urged him to wear the badge.

Trying now to make up for her moral shabbiness, she turned towards the little woman and smiled at her across the chrysanthemums, shaking her head a little to get across her message (don't pay any attention to that stupid old drunk, he doesn't know what he's saying, let's take things like this in our stride). But the woman, in turn looking at her, presented a face so impassive yet cold, and eyes so expressionless yet hostile, that Esther's overture fell quite flat.

Okay, okay, if that's the way you feel about it, she thought to herself. Then the bus made another stop and she heard the man proclaim ringingly, "So clear out, all of you, and remember to take every last one of your slant-eyed pickaninnies with you!" This was his final advice as he stepped down from the middle door. The bus remained at the stop long enough for Esther to watch the man cross the street with a slightly exploring step. Then, as it started up again, the bespectacled man in front stood up to go and made a clumsy speech to the Chinese couple and possibly to Esther. "I want you to know," he said, "that we aren't all like that man. We don't all feel the way he does.

We believe in an America that is a melting pot of all sorts of people. I'm originally Scotch and French myself." With that, he came over and shook the hand of the Chinese man.

"And you, young lady," he said to the girl behind Esther, "you deserve a Purple Heart or something for having to put up with that sitting beside you."

Then he, too, got off.

The rest of the ride was uneventful and Esther stared out the window with eyes that did not see. Getting off at last at the soldiers' home, she was aware of the Chinese couple getting off after her, but she avoided looking at them. Then, while she was walking towards Buro's hospital very quickly, there arose in her mind some words she had once read and let stick in her craw: People say, do not regard what he says, now he is in liquor. Perhaps it is the only time he ought to be regarded.

These words repeated themselves until her saving detachment was gone every bit and she was filled once again in her life with the infuriatingly helpless, insidiously sickening sensation of there being in the world nothing solid she could put her finger on, nothing solid she could come to grips with, nothing solid she could sink her teeth into, nothing solid.

When she reached Buro's room and caught sight of his welcoming face, she ran to his bed and broke into sobs that she could not control. Buro was amazed because it was hardly her first visit and she had never shown such weakness before, but solving the mystery handily, he patted her head, looked around smugly at his roommates, and asked tenderly, "What's the matter? You've been missing me a whole lot, huh?" And she, finally drying her eyes, sniffed and nodded and bravely smiled and answered him with the question, yes, weren't women silly?

—HISAYE YAMAMOTO

Antiwar Statement of
Filipino Educators

"Más resistencia, más esperanza."
—From flyers sent out by the Katipunan during the Philippine-American War, circa 1899 (LITERARY DIGEST).

We are educators, teachers and scholars of Filipino descent in the Philippines, the u.s. and the world, who strongly oppose any act of u.s. preemptive military aggression or support for such aggression against Iraq or against any other country. We believe that the false evidence that the u.s. president has peddled regarding Iraq's imminent threat to the u.s., together with the u.s. government and media's manipulation of the American public's grief over last year's 9/11 tragedy, mask a deceptive and wholly undemocratic campaign to coerce the American people and the peoples of the world into accepting the unlawful and unwarranted u.s. invasion of other countries. We furthermore note that u.s. taxpayers are being forced to divert the money originally allocated to health care, education, and social security, to the indiscriminate bombing of civilian populations and the anticipated economic exploitation of Iraq by u.s. oil companies and big business.

We speak as the sons and daughters of a nation systematically decimated and brutalized by u.s. imperialism since the turn of the twentieth century—first, through the decimation of 1/10 of the Philippine population through murder and concentration camps; and later, through the active promotion of economic underdevelopment and political corruption at the highest levels of Philippine government. As witnesses to the recent return of u.s. military troops and stations to the Philippines, in flagrant violation of the 1991 Philippine congressional act effectively reinstating the country's territorial sovereignty against foreign military occupation; and as concerned respondents to the mounting tension between the Philippine government and various groups branded by the u.s. as "terrorist," we denounce the escalation of violence in the Philippines as a direct consequence of the u.s. war campaign against the Arab peoples of the world. While the stain of prostitution, environmental pollution, and economic exploitation spread by the u.s. military bases in the Philippines has become our legacy of colonial subjection, we join our hands and hearts in an unequivocal opposition and resistance to u.s. unilateralism and its self-proclaimed right to violence—in Iraq, in the Philippines, and in every part of the world.

Signed, FILIPINO CONVENORS AND SIGNATORIES OF THE ANTI-WAR STATEMENT CONVENORS:

1. Dr. John David Blanco, Comparative Literature, U of California-San Diego 2. Dr. Sarita See, English and American Studies, U of Michigan 3. Dr. Nerissa S. Balce, Postdoctoral Fellow, U of Oregon 4. Dr. Dylan Rodriguez, Ethnic Studies, U of California-Riverside 5. Dr. Bliss Lim, Film Studies, U of California-Irvine 6. Dr. Maria Josephine Barrios, Visiting faculty, U of California-Irvine 7. Dr. Roland Tolentino, Visiting faculty, Osaka U, Japan; Associate Professor, U of the Philippines-Diliman 8. Dr. Kimberly A. Alidio, History and Asian American studies, U of Texas-Austin 9. Dr. Peter Chua, Sociology, San Jose State U 10. Dr. Rick Baldoz, Sociology, U of Hawaii-Manoa 11. Dr. Leny Strobel, Lecturer, Sonoma State U 12. Jeffrey Santa Ana, Doctoral candidate, U of California-Berkeley 13. Vernadette Gonzalez, Doctoral candidate, U of California-Berkeley 14. Robyn Rodriguez, Doctoral candidate, U of California-Berkeley 15. Lucy Burns, Doctoral candidate, U of Massachusetts and Lecturer, Women's studies, U of Califonia-Santa Cruz 16. Tony Tiongson, Doctoral candidate, U of California-San Diego and Lecturer, Ethnic Studies, U of California-Berkeley 17. Benito Vergara, Assistant Professor, Asian American Studies, San Francisco State University 18. Dr. Lily Mendoza, University of Denver 19. Dr. Ellen Fernandez-Sacco, History of Science and Technology, U of California, Berkeley 20. Luisa A. Igloria, Associate Professor, English Department, Old Dominion U 21. Dr. E. San Juan, Jr., Director, Philippines Cultural Studies Center 22. Dr. Delia D. Aguilar, Women's Studies Program, U of Connecticut-Storrs 23. Luis Francia, Lecturer, Asian/Pacific/American Studies, New York U 24. Luis V. Teodoro, Professor of Journalism, U of the Philippines 25. Patrick Rosal, Lecturer, Bloomfield College 26. M. Evelina Galang, Assistant Professor of English, University of Miami 27. Dr. Theodore S. Gonzalves, American Studies, U of Hawaii-Manoa 28. Helen Toribio, Lecturer, Asian American Studies, San Francisco State U and City College of San Francisco 29. Wendell Capili, Professor, Associate Dean for Administration/ Dev. Arts and Letters, U of the Philippines 30. Dr. Ramon P. Santos, Composer/Musicologist and Professor, University of the Philippines 31. Angela Dyan T. Giron, student, Ateneo de Manila University, Philippines 32. Oscar Peñaranda, Writer and Educator, San Francisco 33. Arnel F. de Guzman, Executive Director Education for All Resource Colloquium, Philippines 34. Dr. Raul Pertierra, School of Sociology, University of New South Wales, Sydney, Australia 35. Dr. Ruth Elynia S. Mabanglo, Coordinator, Filipino and Philippine Literature Program, University of Hawaii-at-Manoa 36. Dr. Elmer A. Ordonez, Professor of English, University of the Philippines 37. Elenita S. Ordonez, M.A., Professor of Art studies, University of the Philippines 38. Dr. Fidel

Nemenzo, Mathematics, University of the Philippines 39. Jing Panganiban, Filipino Department, Ateneo de Manila University 40. Rev. Dr. Elizabeth S. Tapia, Lecturer in Missiology, Bossey Ecumenical Institute, Celigny, Switzerland 41. Dr. Nenita Pambid Domingo, Lecturer, South and Southeast Asian Languages and Cultures Program, East Asian Languages and Cultures Department, U of California-Los Angeles 42. Dr. Neferti Tadiar, Department of History of Consciousness, U of California-Santa Cruz 43. Lorenzo Paran III, Assistant Professor, Department of English and Comparative Literature, U of the Philippines-Diliman 44. Ma. Luisa Reyes, Associate Professor, Ateneo de Manila University 45. Danilo A. Arao, Assistant Professor, Department of Journalism, U of the Philippines in Diliman, Quezon City 46. Elizabeth H. Pisares, Ph.D., English, DePaul University 47. Adelwisa L. Agas Weller, Filipino Language and Culture, University of Michigan 48. Dr. Rowena T. Torrevillas, Visiting Assistant Professor, Department of English, University of Iowa 49. Dr. Teresita V. Ramos, Professor and Chair, Department of Hawaiian and Indo-Pacific Languages 50. Christine Bacareza Balance, Doctoral Candidate, New York University Performance Studies & Asian/Pacific/American Studies 51. Dr. Jose V. Abueva, Kalayaan College and University of the Philippines 52. Muriel Orevillo-Montenegro, Doctoral candidate, Union Theological Seminary, New York 53. Marcelo Estrada, Lecturer, Lacanian School of Psychoanalysis, Berkeley 54. Dr. Rick Bonus, American Ethnic Studies, University of Washington 55. Dr. Dean T. Alegado, Chair, Ethnic Studies Department, University of Hawai'i 56. Eleanor Eme E. Hermosa, Professor of Education, University of the Philippines 57. Marivi Soliven Blanco, Development Assistant/Writer, La Jolla Chamber Music Society

Nerissa S. Balce
Ph.D. Postdoctoral Research Fellow 2002-2003
Center on Diversity and Community University of Oregon

Anti-Asian Incidents

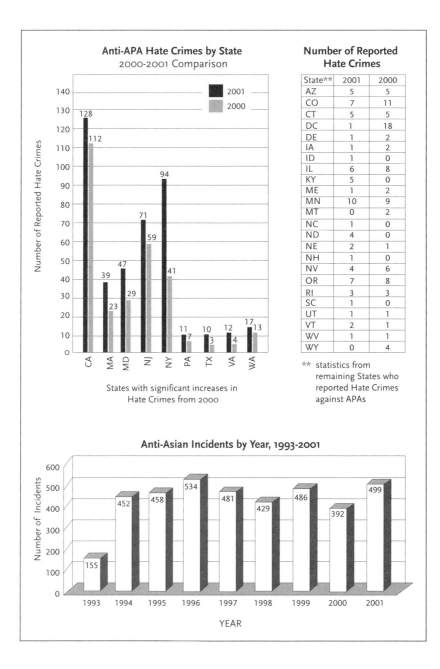

Anti-APA Hate Crimes by State
2000-2001 Comparison

Number of Reported Hate Crimes

- 2001
- 2000

State	2001	2000
CA	128	112
MA	39	23
MD	47	29
NJ	71	59
NY	94	41
PA	11	7
TX	10	3
VA	12	4
WA	17	13

States with significant increases in Hate Crimes from 2000

Number of Reported Hate Crimes

State**	2001	2000
AZ	5	5
CO	7	11
CT	5	5
DC	1	18
DE	1	2
IA	1	2
ID	1	0
IL	6	8
KY	5	0
ME	1	2
MN	10	9
MT	0	2
NC	1	0
ND	4	0
NE	2	1
NH	1	0
NV	4	6
OR	7	8
RI	3	3
SC	1	0
UT	1	1
VT	2	1
WV	1	1
WY	0	4

** statistics from remaining States who reported Hate Crimes against APAs

Anti-Asian Incidents by Year, 1993-2001

Year	Number of Incidents
1993	155
1994	452
1995	458
1996	534
1997	481
1998	429
1999	486
2000	392
2001	499

YEAR

Above charts created from data provided by the National Pacific American Legal Consortium's
2000 *Audit of Violence Against Asian Pacific Americans* and
the Asian Pacific American Legal Center's *Audit 2001 Data Analysis Update.*
Compiled by found images/text editor Anida Yoeu Esguerra.

A History of Anti-Asian Violence

Vincent Chin   June 19, 1982
In Highland Park, Michigan, a Chinese American engineer, Vincent Chin, was bludg-
eoned with a baseball bat by two White autoworkers who had mistaken him for a
Japanese and blamed him for their plight. The killers were sentenced to 3 years probation and a $3,780 fine after their trial. A subsequent conviction in a federal civil rights
prosecution was overturned on appeal, thus neither killer ever served a day in prison.

An Pech   July 22, 1983
47-year-old Cambodian Pech, while sitting outside his apartment in Dallas, Texas, was
beaten with a baseball bat by an unidentified African American man in an attack witnesses said was spurred by racial tension. Mr. Pech died several hours later.
Subsequently most Cambodians moved out of the neighborhood as anti-Asian violence increased.

Ly Yung Cheung   February 29, 1984
19-year-old Cheung was pushed to her death in front of a subway train in New York City
by a white public school teacher. The mentally unstable killer apparently believed that
he was pursued by Asian demons and stated, "Now we're even" as Ms. Cheung died.

Jean Har-Kaw Fewel   January 30, 1985
8-year-old Chinese orphan Fewel, a native of Hong Kong, was found dead hanging from
a tree in Chapel Hill, North Carolina. On February 3, a man was arrested and charged
with kidnapping, rape and murder.

Cleveland Elementary School   January 17, 1989
Raphanor Or (age 9), Ram Chun (8), Sokhim An (6), Thuy Tran (6), Oeun Lim (8)
were among five Southeast Asian-American children killed. One Vietnamese and
four Cambodian children were killed and twenty-nine others (including 22 Asians)
were wounded, when Patrick Purdy fired one hundred rounds from an assault rifle
into a crowded schoolyard, in Stockton, California. Police and media did not catego-
rize the attack as bias-related, although Purdy dressed in fatigues and apparently
resented Asians. California's Attorney General later determined that the shooting
was racially motivated.

Heng Lim   June 16, 1990
37-year-old Lim was struck over the head with a 2'x3' piece of lumber by Timothy
Meitzler, a White man, in Philadelphia, Pennsylvania. The altercation started with
Meitzler saying to Lim, who was in a van with his family, "Come on out you fucking
Chinese." Police took the family into custody and refused to allow them to leave for
four hours. In the meantime, Heng Lim died.

Nakashima Family   August 13, 1992
Junko Nakashima, wife of prominent Watsonville nurseryman Doug Nakashima, a
Nakashima cousin, and an unidentified third victim were killed when Mark Cleaver,
heavily armed and clad in military camouflage fatigues, shot his way into the
Nakashima household in Watsonville, California. He hunted down family members in
the house and adjacent nurseries wounding several other people before killing himself.

Yulee Turner, the killer's half-brother stated that Cleaver felt "ripped off" by the Japanese who came to this country, bought up a lot of land, and got rich while "Americans" remained poor.

Thien Minh Ly   March 3, 1996
A 24-year-old Vietnamese American was brutally murdered while rollerblading on a high school tennis court in Tustin, California. He was kicked, stomped on and stabbed more than a dozen times allegedly by two White supremacists, Gunner Lindberg and Domenic Christopher. Investigators say one suspect, Lindberg even bragged to a friend about killing a "Jap."

Kuanchung Kao   April 29,1997
In Rohnert Park, California a 33-year old father of three children was standing in his own property inebriated when the police arrived in response to a neighbor's complaint that Kao was disturbing the peace. Within 34 seconds of arrival, the police shot Kao and prohibited his wife, a registered nurse, to tend to his aid. Kao died within 10 minutes. The police said they feared Kao to be a martial arts expert.

Kanu Patel, Mukesh Patek   October 15, 1998
In Camp Springs, Maryland three South Asian immigrants were working at an all-night Dunkin' Donuts when a robber, Trone Tyrone Ashford, entered and assaulted them with his shotgun. He taunted them about their poor fluency in English. The men were shot at point blank range as they lay on the floor of the back room. The gunman, together with two other alleged suspects, doused the shop with gasoline and left the store in flames. They took less than $100. Only one of the victims survived after being rescued by firefighters.

Won-Joon Yoon   July 4, 1999
A graduate student of Indiana University, Yoon, age 26, was killed during a shooting spree over the July 4th weekend. The shooter, Benjamin Nathaniel Smith, was a member of the World Church of the Creator, a White supremacist group. In nine separate stops across Illinois and Indiana, Smith targeted several Jews, Blacks and Asians. Yoon was shot outside of his church in Bloomington, Indiana as members of the congregation, predominantly Korean, were leaving the service.

Joseph Santos Ileto   August 10, 1999
White supremacist Buford Furrow wounded five people at a Jewish Community Center in the Los Angeles area, before gunning down Filipino American postman Joseph Ileto. Allegedly, the suspect said he targeted Ileto because he was Non-White and was wearing a federal letter carrier's uniform, making Ileto a "good target of opportunity." Buford is a member of the Aryan Nation, an organization premised on the ideology that a race war rages between "Aryan Whites" and Non-Christians and Non-Whites.

Anil Thakur, Thao Q. Pham, Ji-Ye Sun, Gary Lee   April 28, 2000
In Pittsburgh, Richard Baumhammer, a white former immigration attorney who professed to hate immigrants went on a shooting rampage that killed four Asian Americans, one African American, one Jewish woman and critically wounded another South Asian American. Baumhammer had formed a political party to end Third World immigration and affirmative action and once wrote of his fear that "traditional" Americans will live in isolated suburbs outnumbered by Third World immigrants.

Chicago Serial Rapes   April–July 2000

Between April and July of 2000, Mark Anthony Lewis, an African American male sexually assaulted nine women in Chicago and the north and northwest suburbs. Seven of the nine victims were Asian Pacific American women, and there is evidence to show that Lewis may have believed that the other two victims were also of Asian descent. Of the 212 crimes with which Lewis has been charged, eight are hate crimes. The other charges include rape, aggravated criminal sexual assault, kidnapping and home invasion.

Thung Phetakoune   July 14, 2001

On July 14, 2001 Thung Phetakoune, who is believed to be in his 70s, was struck by Richard Labbe, 35, and hit his head on the pavement. Labbe pushed the elderly man who was passing by an apartment complex. The victim suffered severe head trauma and died two days later. According to news reports, Labbe said that he hated Vietnamese people, and called for "payback" for the deaths of his relatives in the Vietnam War. When interviewed by the police, Labbe reportedly said, "What's going on is that those Asians killed Americans, and you won't do anything about it, so I will." Ironically, Phetakoune had fought alongside Americans as a soldier in Laos during the Vietnam War.

Balbir Singh Sodhi   September 15, 2001

A gunman shot and killed 49-year-old Balbir Singh Sodhi as he was outside doing landscaping work at a gas station. The gunman fired several shots at the victim while shouting, "I stand for America all the way!" Sodhis's death is one of the first known bias-motivated murders related to the September 11th terrorist attacks. The same gunman then drove to a second gas station and shot at a Lebanese American clerk. Next, he drove to the residence of a family of Afghan descent and fired several shots. No one was injured in these two shooting incidents.

Lili Wang   October 12, 2002

Lili Wang, a 31-year-old graduate student at North Carolina State University, was shot four times in the head and knees by Richard Borrelli Anderson. Anderson, a white classmate who had become "infatuated" with Wang, walked onto a tennis court and shot Wang four times in the head and knees before turning the gun on himself. Wang was already married, but this fact did nothing to deter Anderson's advances, which appear to have been racially motivated. According to press reports, Anderson had confided to a colleague that he liked Asian women because "they study hard, and they're very nice, soft speaking."

This is a partial list of anti-Asian violence as compiled from the National Asian Pacific American Legal Consortium's 1998, 1999, 2000 *Audit of Violence Against Asian Pacific Americans*, *A Timeline of Hate* from *Asianweek.com*, and the Committee Against Anti-AsianViolence's list of Bias-Motivated or Related Killings since 1981. Compiled by found images/text editor Anida Yoeu Esguerra.

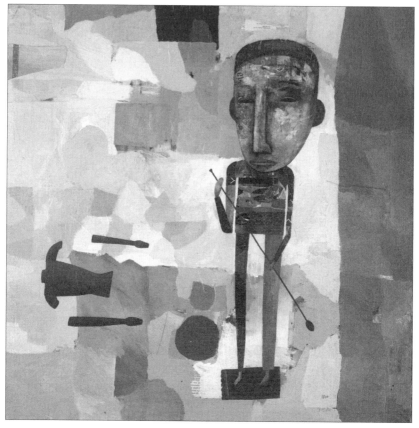

Untitled Art by Jordin Isip, art editor

Nobility

. . . as a wave is a force and not the water of which it is composed, . . . so nobility is a force and not the manifestations of which it is composed . . . .
—Wallace Stevens

She opens her silk robe before lying, face down, on the stone floor. The surface is rough against her breasts, cold against her brow. Her tears do not help. She wills herself in that position for the hours that her adoring public believes she wallows in a bubble bath (champagne and strawberries presumably within reach). Suffering never counts when it is shared.

After chaining a diamond necklace around her neck, her lover walked out of the door. She never saw him again, and will recall forever how he never broke his stride with a single look back. Diamonds never complete a bed. She sheathed herself in a black gown trimmed by purple feathers and ordered a limousine towards Long Island. Digging her satin pumps into the sand, she flung the diamond necklace over the surf as if she pitied a mermaid pleading for it. She did not begin her chosen act with the presumption of a prayer. Introductions are inherently insufficient.

She no longer questions why the fall of snow reminds her of Africa. She once straddled a man there for the access to his blanket woven from threads dyed in brilliant hues of red, blue, green and yellow. The fabric was gritty against her knees and she welcomed that more than the clench of his teeth below her breasts. She was determined to live out the rest of her life in technicolor. In New York, the snow is never pure. She likes the effect of contamination on white.

Nor has she experienced surprise since a young poet told her that he writes from "a position of happiness." *It is my way of continuing tradition*, he said calmly, *and is very much an aesthetic consideration.* When she dropped her eyes before the stark nudity of his sincerity, her gaze snagged on the ending of a poem he was offering from an outstretched hand. The young poet's words concluded: *The physical reality of revolution is decadence. The aftermath is what transcends.*

—EILEEN TABIOS
poetry editor

Genghis Chan: Private Eye XXIX

(Fourteen Ink Drawings)

Mirror   film   stain

Gown   tiger   glass

Canopy   powder   bell

Mulberry   blister   festival

Boat   portrait   box

Vermillion   chestnut   cloud

Milk   shadow   moon

Breeze   identical   face

Ink   ladder   jar

Orchid   chimney   tongue

Parachute   word   wave

Groom   motel   coffee

Anvil   clock   hair

Condom   audience   dog

—JOHN YAU

Genghis Chan: Private Eye XXX

shoo war
torn talk

ping towel
pong toy

salted sap
yellow credit

hubba doggo
bubba patootie

wig maw
mustard tongue

—JOHN YAU

After *My Chronology* by Peter Lorre

The splattered flag of an idiot scavenger; this was how
I sailed beyond the perfect faces of the coming storm.
Many times, almost as many as in your shabby arenas,
their walls of baritone shadows, their stream of flailing ants.
I was rolled beneath a couch. Stuffed in a trunk. Drooled
down a box (complete with fishing tackle,
their silvery tangle and heap of pink wigglers).
Flopped into a crumpled cup. A semi-anonymous heap,
shorn of all but secondary features, some of which
were legendary; petals of manufactured smoke
erasing butterflies shivering in the branches of
    my material remains.
Did you try and insert me in a pile of juggled lumps?
Was I part of a column of figures? Or was I
a figural column surrendering sky's black roof?
Who traces the umbilicus of these outbursts of frenzy
back to its mouth, my carriage of sagging carbon
cries out? Who embraces these hummingbird sparks
    of lateral agitation?
A monogrammed hanky steeped in sepulchral vapors?
Pathetic this monaural chivalry.

Once I even crawled around a lake resting in
the crevice of a porcelain saucer, before being
swatted into diaphanous mulch, leaving only
an inky signature on the lard inflated plains.
What is chronology, but detachable hands
sifting for condensation collectivized in an earlier era?
Could I not have arrived before you opened your eyes,
found your axial culmination seated in the upper registers
of a Babylonian balcony or Sumerian wing chair,
optically registering disturbances flooding through
the illuminated window? Or were you always there,

always perfectly poised, stored among the glass roses
you will be requested to accompany to the heated antechamber?
Always waiting for the mirror to begin reciting the contents of
    its solid lake?

—JOHN YAU

LITANY NO. M

tonal	in	may
limn	on	lint
tin	litany	lay
mat	nation	yam
my	lion	ton
many	any	nil
omit	omni	lot

Trying to figure out your tonal calculations of color and sound I forgot the precise parameters for normal chit chat in our cold November. "The maypops stuck in your hair remind me of eating flowers during recess," seemed inappropriate. Instead, a limned message stealthily left behind on the table or in the tip cup, maybe taped to the bathroom mirror. Lint shimmies off my spontaneous mechanisms. You make tinny smiles melt into genuine sweet by calling a litany of ambiguous desire filled with hey, hey, hey.

I want to lay my eyes on the sticky floor, let them roll about to find you on children's mats with words like lust and lost scribbled on them. A mass fantasy of an earnest nation of short haired, regendered kids. How about you and me and some purple yam ice cream on Sunday night after work, my usual seduction. I have a lion's nature obscured by a cotillion charm. My face weighs a ton, heavied by flirting contortions and biting lips.

How many girls whisper your name before they go to sleep? You cure any sour phase of maturation with emotive sighs and of course, ingenuitive fingers. Hanging around, nil smoke provides a nimble explanation, I am here for addiction, my posture declares, omit my omnifarious affection for you. Let it dissipate in the air as we exhale. A crush stranges me a lot, like uncanny dreams.

—MICHELLA RIVERA-GRAVAGE

They Grew Up to Be Lovely

Poise, with this supple back, the arch it makes, the spending the reduction the instant of love of fingers down the slender throat the humane velvet of tongue. Poise as the others wait the expectation the running water the hand towel the chewing gum, serenity in exhalation, these clean teeth this sweet bile, the ease of smiles, so pretty in my dress. Walking. Invisible books weighting each move.

Beauty, leaning out the tower, the long hair, the pitch of song, the sell the sale the buyer, equity in each step, the years the planning, the collecting of this beauty the string my hair makes the spinning of yarn, between ears, the collision, strength inside the elegant figure, my dignified I don't know, the bow of the head, the window shades drawn: What do you think? The long hair holding its crocheted purse lips tightened. Good Smile.

Grace, of these shaking hands a push and through these revolving doors between offices the turning and sending of myself back out again the uncertainty the censorship the retracing of memory remember where I'm going, to meet anticipation and more shaking of hands the bitten nails their yellow ridges the burning home, going there, seeming there, the sobbing drunk, solipsismal, crying to me I'm sorry I'm sorry I'm sorry, those hearts drawn of my own blood my own skin the wearing down the wearing of arms heavy with no touch, tears, the pull of revolving doors the shaking of my own hands.

—LUBA HALICKI

Labandera

Washing

Lola Malaya squats at the bottom of the hill, a plastic tub of dirty linen flushed against her thighs. Seven A.M. and a jackhammer rips the sky open, grates against the bellow of jeepney horns, of bells on motor tricycles. This early in the morning and diesel trucks belch into the hot air. Water spills from the edge of the tub, cooling her callused feet. Old lola looks over her shoulder to a row of cardboard houses and aluminum rooftops. She eyes her window. A bed sheet flutters light as butterfly wings. She squints, searching for her granddaughter.

"Are you ready, anak? You'll be late."

She yanks at the collar of a white cotton shirt. Lipstick bleeds from its corners. She wonders who has done this, the Sir's wife or the Sir's mistress? She often dreams the stories behind the stains of other people's clothing. She likes to imagine life is hidden in the way people dirty their garments. The sun heats the sidewalk and the hot tar road. The vendors have pulled their bushels of fruit out into the open—and the colors of mangos, of bright bananas and light green santol wash Manila's polluted air. From where she sits she sees bundles of lychees, red and round pulled together like grapes hanging by their branches. She glances at the stack of clothing next to her and calculates how long it will take her to finish the work.

Ernesto Reynaldo calls to her, pushing his cart of corn up the narrow hill. He waves, and under the brim of his straw hat she catches his smile as he displays a mouthful of missing teeth. "Kamusta ka, Lola Malaya?" he asks.

She nods at him, says, "Good, good." Handsome, she thinks, not bad for his age. He winks at her and all the lines of his face collapse like the folds of a beautiful Spanish fan. "You will be home later?"

"Sa gabi," she tells him, after her work is finished and dinner has been cleared away.

Then moving past her he calls his wears, crying, "Mah—eeese. Mah—eeese." She watches his body moving slowly, the calves of his legs bulging from all the years he's spent pushing that cart up and down the streets of Metro Manila. Naku, she thinks, feeling sorry for Ernesto, ang hirap ng buhay. How hard the life.

Her mother named her freedom and she understands that this is not the life God meant for her. "I was at the wrong place, at the wrong time—what can I say?" she says out loud.

She calls again to her grandchild, thirteen-year-old Maria Elena, also born for the finer things in life. Lola Malaya often catches the child daydreaming, dancing, and staring at the sky. "I'm telling you, anak, if you don't hurry up, you will be tardy again and then the principle will bring you home herself. You will be officially expelled and you will be destined to this life—a labandera. And tell me anak, why would you want to do that when you could be a doctor, a lawyer, maybe even a writer."

Malaya washes each garment and thinks of her apo, the troubles of their relationship, the future Maria Elena could have if only she'd behave. Something different than this, she thinks, rubbing her forehead with her skinny elbow. She could have a better life. People skirt about the lola. They cover their mouths with kerchiefs to keep the waste of diesel from their lungs. Somebody bumps her. Soap suds knock her so she comes crashing like the Pacific at high tide. Dirt, wet from the suds, paints her bare legs like the streak of a child's dirty hand. Lola Malaya pushes herself back up, her arms moving like grasshopper limbs. Her joints ache. She feels old. Looking up, she sees the perpetrator, a young woman in a cotton housedress bearing a child on one hip, and dragging another at her side. The woman moves away, unaware of her actions. Children in white and blue uniforms run past her, head toward school. A jeepney of twenty riders zooms past Lola Malaya, drowns her voice as she reprimands the woman. "Respect your elders," she calls after her, "Watch what you do!" Then turning her head to the house she continues, this time at the deaf Maria Elena.

"You cannot afford to be this way, anak. If you were born rich, they'd say you are a lady in waiting, but you are here and here we call you lazy. Move faster, child. Move faster."

* * *

Lola Malaya scrubs the blood from a white pair of panties. The blood is thick and has hardened like mud. She looks up from her work and tells one of the children on the street to call her grandchild. "Tell her I mean business." She wipes the sweat from her brow. The humidity clings to her body, coats her damp and sticky. A shadow creeps over her, and for a moment the sun is gone. The lola keeps scrubbing.

"That's sickening, Lola," Maria Elena says. "How can you touch that?"

"You do what you do to put food on the table, hija," says Lola Malaya. "Now hurry up before you're late again."

Maria Elena stands still and vacant. The old woman dips the panties back under the basin of water, rubs vigorously. The suds tumble out onto the hot pavement, wash everything white. Finally the child says, "Aalis na ako, po." She's leaving now. The old woman nods her head. She reaches into her pocket and hands the girl five pesos and Maria Elena leans over to kiss her. In this moment Lola Malaya looks into her granddaughter's face, and sees herself as a girl. The child bears the same square jaw, lips full and soft as petals, and a tiny black mole at the tip of her left eyebrow. Like Lola Malaya, Maria Elena speaks her mind. Too often, Lola thinks and sighing she leans into the girl and sniffs—Pinay kisses born of every lola. Her apo smells like a baby, with talcum powder showering her neck and back. Ang sarap, Lola thinks. How delicious.

"Dahan, dahan, ha?" the lola warns Maria Elena. "Be careful today. Stay out of trouble."

* * *

When Malaya was fourteen, her mother sent her to the market to buy a sack of rice. "Be quick," said her mother, kissing her on the forehead. "Dahan dahan," There were rumors of war, of soldiers and fighting. "No more playing around, just get the bigas and come home right away."

She walked the back roads, watching the sky which was full of orange light. The cicadas seemed to have gathered on all the branches of the banana trees, whirling its song to meet the setting sun. The sound mesmerized the girl, made her feel enchanted and floating high into the purple red sky. She didn't see them coming, didn't hear them. A jeep full of soldiers rode past her, backed up. Called to her. But she was gazing at the trees, looking for cicadas, wondering how they found this perfect pitch. In a moment the soldiers had taken her away. Six little men, yellow as overripe bananas. Noisy and abrupt. Speaking words that were not words.

Hanging

Lola Malaya pulls a rope across the patch of dirt behind squatter's row. Her oldest friend, Lola Imelda, sits on an empty crate, watching Malaya tie the rope onto a street lamp and the other to a sickly looking palm tree.

"Did you hear," Lola Imelda asks.

"Gossip again?" Lola Malaya answers. "I'm not like you, I don't have two sons and a grandson to work and earn my keep. I don't have a daughter to cook my meals. I don't have time for gossip."

Lola Imelda shoos her words away. "This affects you, Lola, listen," she says.

"Do I have a choice? You'll talk no matter what—listen or not." She glances at Lola Imelda, gray-haired woman, toothless woman, round as a mushroom with fat hands and feet. Imelda crosses her arms, closes her eyes. After a long moment she opens her eyes wide and pointing her finger she castigates Lola Malaya.

"No matter how old you are, I am still older than you. Still your ate. You should not talk to me like that," scolds Lola Imelda.

"Artista!" Lola Malaya says. "Ano," she gives in. "Tell me what."

Imelda leans forward, slapping her knees. "The police want to tear down the houses. They are coming soon. Where are we going to go?"

"Rumor," hisses Lola Malaya.

"Truth," answers Lola Imelda. "Talaga, lola. Talaga."

"So what," Lola Malaya says. She picks up a shirt, wrings it dry and shakes it open. The sleeves sail like two wings. From her pockets she pulls wooden pins, begins to hang the laundry. "Where did we go when the lahar hit the houses?" She pictures Mount Pinatubo shouting at them, at the volcano's angry black snow showering her sky, her house, burying her life in ash. "Where did we go when our mothers sent us away?" She bends over and grabs another garment. "No problem."

"Your mother," Lola Imelda corrects. "My husband."

"Same thing. We survived."

"How can you talk like that old woman?" Lola Imelda holds an open palm to Malaya and closes it swiftly into a fist.

"What's the use, Imelda? You can't change it, no matter what. So stop worrying."

The noise from the streets rises in a clutter of horns and bells. Traffic must have halted, or a caribou drawn cart must be defecating on the streets of Manila, she thinks. The sharp ping of a rock hits the white sheet she has hung, leaves a black mark. Naku, she thinks, not this again. Soon a battery of rocks come flying over the rooftops of the makeshift houses, and the cries of nasty children pitch insults at the old women. "Tira!" she hears them caw. "Tira! Ng Hapones."

Tira, leftovers, used goods. Japanese waste.

Lola Imelda curls her arms up around her head, folds her feet up close to her fat tummy. Shuts down. The taunting continues. The rocks fly over the rooftops, come from the edge of the streets. Lola Malaya runs around the corner of the houses, picking up rocks as she goes, tossing them as she runs, hurling words at the children.

"Demonio!" she screams. Her heart thumps and fills up her chest. "Pang ba hira!" she says. "Show your faces you little bastards!"

* * *

At their age, she was living in a war-torn chapel with fifty other hostages—girls and young women stolen in the midst of eating family dinner, or harvesting rice, or hanging clothes to dry.

What do these devil children know of that life—to spend your nights lying in makeshift cubicles, your legs spread so far apart you fear your limbs will snap. She was taken before she had desire, before she understood the difference between love and sex, before she knew the art of flirting. She was taken before she understood the beauty of men. She did what she did to survive. And what would they have done? How would they feel about servicing foreign men who smelled of war—of guns and blood and rotting flesh?

The soldiers stood in line, like waiting for a bathroom stall. The pews had been removed and laundry lines hung in narrow rows to give the men some privacy. They used sheets taken from houses Japanese had raided. Curtains or bed spreads—sometimes dirty laundry—divided the garrison into space just large enough to fit one cot, one girl, one soldier. Sometimes the girl next to her would claw at the curtains or kick at her stall. Hands and feet would punch at the curtains the way the unborn kick inside their mothers' bellies. Then came the sounds of bayonets ripping into flesh, slicing resistance away, and the noise would end. This is how she learned not to fight back.

Perhaps the devil children are right. Tira ng Hapones. So what about it? Even if it's true, what does she get for surviving it?

* * *

By the time she gets to the street, all she hears are echoes of laughter, the ghost of hate slipping from the sidewalks. Nothing there, no one.

When she returns to the line of laundry, Lola Imelda is sobbing, uttering a mantra, "Ay naku, naku, ang hirap ng buhay. Hirap ng buhay." She pounds a brown fist onto her chest, "Ang sakit ng puso," How painful the heart.

"Stop it," Lola Malaya says, tearing down the newly soiled wash. "You make it worse."

"Ay, Lola, ang tigas ng puso mo."

But Lola Malaya knows better. Her heart isn't hard, just practical. "You can't let them get to you," she tells Lola Imelda. "Every week those devil children come by, every week they do the same thing. Ignore them."

"You don't ignore them. You chase them and they laugh even harder," Lola Imelda says.

"Don't let them get to you, I mean. Don't let them see."

Lola Imelda shakes her head, beats her chest with the fist.

They spend the rest of the morning re-washing the garments that have been marred with dirt, re-wringing the sheets, re-hanging everything. Above them, the sun continues to burn through the haze and as they move, now in silence, the heat from their bodies intensifies like a halo of white.

Ironing

She stands in Ma'am's kitchen, underneath the air con's blower. This steady wind calms her, dries her damp skin. All day, the heat. No respite, no breath. Until now, she thinks, sighing. Steam floats white and breathy from the mouth of a hot iron. On hot days like this, she looks forward to pressing laundry, eating leftovers from the family's afternoon merienda, while Emma the housemaid teases her about Ernesto. The white tile feels cool against Lola Malaya's tired feet.

"Naku, Emma," she sighs, "Ang hirap ng buhay." She smoothes a range of creases and darts the iron's nose against the T-shirt's chest.

"A man of commerce," Emma says, clicking her tongue. "Not bad, Lola Malaya." Emma stands at the kitchen sink, cleaning milkfish and bitter melon.

"A corn vendor," Lola Malaya corrects. "He's lucky I notice his old body."

"You look at his body?" Emma rubs the fish with salt and places it on a pan to fry.

"Only notice."

A silence falls in between their bursts of laughter. Just beyond the kitchen, they can hear the children chasing after Hollywood, the family dog. While they continue their tasks, the two trade little jokes, and nibble on rolls of pan de cocoa. Emma pours cold glasses of kalamansi juice.

"It's tart," she warns Lola Malaya.

Lola's fast with the iron. In this light, against clean white cotton, her hands look hard as earth, with veins—blue mountains—tunneling just beneath her skin. She presses imperfection out of wrinkled limbs and torsos, out from darts that billow slight curves at the hips and bust of Ma'am's skirts and blouses. She hangs the clothing on gold hangers wrapped in silk. She folds linen in perfect rectangles and stacks them in a basket made of bamboo.

Ma'am charges into the kitchen, past the white double doors with a newspaper rolled up in her hand. She waves it at Lola Malaya like a wand. She brings with her the fragrance of expensive perfume, and the energy of a tiny typhoon.

"Kita mo, Lola?" she asks. "Did you see? Wowee, naman." Ma'am's hair falls straight across her shoulders and collarbone. Smiling, she winks at Lola Malaya, beams. "Ang litrato ni Lola sa front page," she coos, holding the paper up in front of the women.

In the photograph, Lola and her comares hold up picket signs before the president's motorcade. In the foreground a blur of big black cars with red lights travel unaware of the protestors. A smattering of Philippine National Police dots the photo in white helmets and blue short-sleeved shirts. An officer stands just to the left of the lolas, his white teeth popping out of shadow, his arm waving at the camera, cheering.

Purple scarves wrap the old women's shoulders and cover their thinning scalps. They hold their free hands up, shape them like the letter "L." Their bodies are poised to charge invisible foes. The hand-painted signs read "Justice" and "Laban" and "Never Again."

Lola Malaya studies the photo and smiles. The faces of her fellow survivors scrunch up and all the wrinkles in their skin make them look mean and old.

Warriors. Their graying brows rise up in reprimand. The mouths have been caught in the midst of their battle cry. "LABAN!" You'd never know, she thinks, how weak the hearts, how frail the bones. In the middle of the photo, she casts her arms like wings, the purple scarf sailing from her shoulders, swiping the sky lavender.

"Lola," Ma'am says. "Your granddaughter must be so proud."

Lola only smiles at Ma'am, as if she's lost her words.

"Let me see," Emma says, peaking over the young housewife's shoulder. "Wow, Lola," she sings. "Movie star."

* * *

Every time Lola Malaya shows up on television, or on the front page or every time some American comes to interview the lolas about the war, Maria Elena stops eating. She stops speaking. Sometimes she goes about her business as if her grandmother weren't around at all. Her face takes on the look of the lost souls. No expression. No reaction. No life. Silence enters their home, a breeze through the window, a little draft from impending monsoon rains. She'd rather Maria Elena scream at her. Thinking of her apo, a chamber somewhere in her chest closes up. The beat, she thinks, it's like I skip a beat. She presses her iron heavy on the dress.

How will she make Maria Elena understand her actions. Sometimes when the child sleeps, Lola studies her face, the slope of her cheek and the dark lashes resting like tired butterfly wings. She traces the little mole, rising like a star upon Maria Elena's brow. How easy to mistake the child for Malaya as a girl. Because Maria Elena shuts Lola out, the old woman waits for night to open up the distance between them. She whispers stories into the child's hands, into her ear, telling her, "I do this so you will never have to, anak. I do this so never again. Never again."

She cannot sleep at night. Even after fifty years, the dreams keep her awake. Each night the soldiers come to her and she remembers the nights, the shadows looming over her, blocking light from stained glass windows. During those times she closed her eyes and focused on the image of Mary, a mahogany statue stained brown to match the people's skin. The artist carved intricate details of the Virgin and in her terror Malaya saw the lilt of a breast, the shade of hips. The soldiers overlooked God's mother, left her standing, so that Malaya would only need to close her eyes, and the image of the Virgin would appear. She uttered prayers to sustain her.

She has forgotten the blur of faces—or maybe Mother Mary saved her from seeing them. What stays with her is the stench of death and war painted on men's bodies—hot sweat, fresh blood—hers, or his, or maybe some dead American soldier's. What stays with her are the sounds in the church. The echoes of other Filipinas begging for grace, the calling out at night. What she hears even now are the voices of the men—"Kura, Kura!" Garbage words. Angry nonsense words. The groaning of their bodies. The howling.

* * *

"Talaga," Ma'am is saying. She spreads the paper down on the kitchen table, her painted fingernails gleam pearly pink, her rings shimmer gold. "You are so courageous, Lola. Think of what you're doing."

Ma'am pulls a sack of clothing out of a cupboard and hands it to her. "These are dresses," she tells her. "For Maria Elena, Lola."

The dresses are fancy linen cut sleek to fit the body. Light colors—pale yellows, pinks and baby blues—they'll pick up dirt too easily. "I've grown too fat for those," Ma'am tells her. "Such a waste to throw them out."

Lola Malaya nods her head, whispers thank you, irons a cotton camisole a little more vigorously.

From the other room, Ma'am's children yell at one another. Hollywood barks. Something crashes. Ma'am stands up and sighs. "Ay, Emma, can you stop them? Did you bathe Hollywood today?"

"Not yet, Ma'am," Emma tells her.

"Wash the dog," she tells her.

"Yes, Ma'am," Emma answers.

"And don't forget to dry him really good—so he doesn't smell."

"Yes, Ma'am."

Lola Malaya hangs a child's dress on a silk covered hanger. She sighs, thinking about that spoiled little Hollywood running the house. Washed every day like a baby, she thinks, then blow-dried like a beauty. What a life, she thinks, what a hard life.

Gathering

She makes 500 pesos at Ma'am and Sir's house. Closing the gate behind her, she slips the money into her pocket, pulls out her pinaypay, a bamboo fan covered with blue and white fabric. She whips the pinaypay open and fans herself. "Naku," she utters. "Init."

She walks among the people, keeping one hand in her pocket, clutching the fist of pesos, while the other hand gracefully flutters her fan. She steps around children, past hens and caribou, in between parked motor trikes and stalled jeepneys. Now and then she spits on the ground, relieves her mouth of diesel fumes.

When she arrives at Santa Maria she walks to the back and opens the door, stepping into another kitchen. This one, hot and filled with steam, thick with cooking grease and the aroma of freshly cooked rice. She walks past Manang

Tess who fries fish for Father Anacleto. Despite the heat, Manang Tess sings loud and off key.

"If you're hoping to woo the young priest that way, Manang," Lola says, "Forget it."

Manang Tess raises the volume of her song and her voice cracks above the popping grease. When it's clear that she's not interested in speaking with Lola Malaya, Malaya asks her, "Is his laundry ready?"

"Sa hallway," Manang Tess answers, pointing her finger to the door.

Lola steps out of the kitchen and walks down a long marble hall. On the wall, portraits of Santa Maria pastors hang. She glances up at the photos walking past black and white and sepia-toned priests—some of them American, some of them Spanish, some of them Filipino. At the end of the hallway she winks at the portrait of Father Anacleto. His image lives within an ornate frame, golden and full of intricate carving. He has the first color photograph. His black robes flow from a tall and lean body and she must crane her neck to see his beautiful young face, his large eyes, high cheekbones. His thick hair has been carefully combed back with pomade. Guapo, she thinks, with his brown, brown skin and his gentle voice. He would make a good lover, a good one for a beautiful young dalaga. A girl with equally long legs. They could have beautiful children. Too bad.

She spies an open door, and peeks into a bathroom where every surface is marble—the floors, the walls, the ceilings. And every fixture etched in gold. Walking over to the toilet bowl, she fingers the handle. How beautiful, she thinks. How nice to live a life where waste is flushed away with something as beautiful and gold as this. She flushes the bowl and watches the water swirl in circles, slipping quietly away. How nice.

"Afternoon, Lola Malaya," calls a voice loud as God's.

She looks up and the young priest stands at the doorway with his hands folded under his arms. He is out of his priestly garments, wearing a faded Coca-Cola T-shirt and running shorts. He looks too young, she thinks. Just a boy.

"Staying out of trouble?" he asks.

"Depends what you mean by trouble, Father," she says, flirting. She walks past him and gathers five plastic grocery bags of laundry tied up neat like sack lunches.

He tells her they prayed for the lolas in mass today. "I'm sorry I couldn't make the rally, La," he says.

"So kay," she says slipping the handles around her wrists. "Is this all of it?" He nods.

How was it, he wants to know. And she draws for him a picture of farmers and workers and squatters gathered for miles down Commonwealth Avenue. She saves the comfort women for last. Banners skipped over their heads, like sails in an ocean—red and purple flags, yellow and green. "Many souls," she tells him, "looking for justice." The lolas waited for six hours without the shade of a tree. Some of them took to bickering with one another. "You know the lolas," she tells him, "always tsmis, always gossip." When the president drove past, it seemed the motorcade sped up. Father Anacleto shakes his head, clucks his tongue. He reminds her of the unclean woman who touched the hem of Jesus. It was crowded and people pushed their way forward, reaching out their hands, hoping to hold onto Him.

"Her faith stopped the bleeding," he says.

She considers this a moment. Sighs. "Is that any way for a priest to dress?" she asks him, tugging on his shirt.

"Exercising, Lola," he says. "You know how it goes."

"Someday," she tells him, "you'll find out it's better to make trouble than stay out of it. Di ba?"

He walks her to the front door, makes mano, placing the old woman's hand to his forehead.

"Naku," she says. "It's me who should be paying you respect. Not the other way around." She waves her free hand at him and begins walking down the gated yard to the streets.

She wonders how Father Anacleto grew to be beautiful and kind and spiritual too. How did his mommy do that, she wonders. Maria Elena has potential, but she's so ma sungit, so mean.

Naku, she thinks, I must lecture her all the time. And she always does the exact opposite thing. Laging Contravida naman.

She walks to two other homes and gathers their dirty laundry, placing the little plastic sacks in a large duffel bag she has sewn from old sheets. She swings the bag over her shoulder, bends at the waist and walks toward home. Maybe, she thinks, I will bring her Jollie Bee for dinner. Hamburger and rice. After all, Lola thinks, didn't Ma'am just pay me? We will start over, she thinks, start happy. She digs into the bag Ma'am gave her, wonders if the dresses will fit her apo, if she will like them at all.

When she gets to the corner, she weaves her way about a disarray of parked cars. The bag weighs heavy on her back and she must be careful to bend her knees as she climbs the curb. She pushes her way through the glass door, wondering where the security guard is who usually greets customers. Naku, she thinks, if something happens, where is he? The burger joint, with its red and yellow walls and giant bumblebee, has little room for Lola Malaya and her sack of dirty laundry. She must shove her way through people who seem planted to their spots. No one moves out of her way. She finds a place in line and waits like all the others. When she gets to the counter, the girl in the baseball cap and polo shirt smiles, looks past the lola and says, "Can I help you sir?" Lola Malaya turns and sees a young man in a blue suit and wire rim glasses pulling out his wallet.

"Excuse," says Lola Malaya to the clerk. But the young man has stepped forward and is trying to get around Lola's sack. "Excuse me," she says a little louder, swinging her bag into the man. "Young lady. I was here first." She blocks the young man. "Take my order."

* * *

Outside, she balances the dirty laundry on her back, and clutches a white paper bag of French fries, rice, and hamburger. She walks along the shade of the building's alley, stepping around old bottles and discarded paper cups. The air smells of rotting vegetables. Dogs run past her, chase one another for leftovers from nearby garbage cans. Near the end of the building, behind the dumpster, she sees the back of the Jollie Bee security guard leaning on a schoolgirl. He must be twice her age, she thinks. People crowd even this alley, crisscross the lovers like curtains, reveal their shape like flashes of lightning. His arms are spread wide, and he holds her down against the brick. Her head is thrown back and she cannot tell if the girl enjoys this or is being held against her will. The brim of his hat covers her face. His rifle has fallen to the ground, rests next to her stack of books. Lola sees schoolgirl shoes and the gleam of white anklet socks. The girl places one foot firmly on the ground and the other she presses against the wall. Her skirt—blue and black plaid— rises up. Her leg is lean and beautiful in the light. No wonder, Lola Malaya thinks, he was not at the door. He's taking a break. As Lola nears the two, she casts her gaze at her feet.

* * *

The memory recurs in the way her flesh aches. When her husband was alive, the nightmares began each time he drew himself in and out of her. Though he was gentle, her skin remembered soldiers who were rough and left her swollen, raw. It took her body a very long time to learn that acts of kindness included kissing and touching, appeared in the chaos of arms and legs gripping one another.

She was too small and the soldiers had a hard time entering her. They'd get mad at her. Hit her. Shout words like thunder. When they grew frustrated the soldiers spat on her. They took knives and little flames from matches and scarred her navel, the nape of her neck, the inside of her thigh. One soldier branded the soft flesh of her breast, marked her for life.

* * *

Lola Malaya cannot help it. She walks past them and she glances their way, wants to know if the girl needs help. Not that there is much she can do. The girl moans and Lola's heart beats fast. "Naku!" she yells, running at the two. She yanks the girl by the hair. "This is how you behave?" she says. She knows this girl, worries over her safety every moment of her old life. "Have you learned nothing?" she asks Maria Elena who is screaming now, and pulling herself away from Lola.

"Pick up those books," the lola tells her. "Pull down your skirt."

The guard zips up his pants, straightens his hat, grabs the gun. He turns away from the women, like he is not a part of the scene.

"Let me go," Maria Elena says.

"Never," Lola tells her as she gathers herself, the sack, the laundry, the girl, and carries her burden across Manila.

Sorting

The clothes lie in piles across straw mats. Lola has ordered her granddaughter to sit in the room and listen. She goes through the bags of dirty clothes, counts the number of shirts, the camisetas, the socks, the pantalones.

"In broad daylight?" Lola says.

Maria Elena sits in a corner of the house, her legs drawn up, her skirt pulled over her knees. A trail of smoke curls its way up into the stuffy house. She holds the cigarette loosely between her slender fingers.

"Is there no shame?" Lola Malaya asks her. Walang hiya. She tosses a dark pair of socks into a pile. "Has my life meant nothing to you?"

She glances over her shoulder at the girl. Maria Elena's eyes are wide open, round saucers, polished stone. They are vacant as a doll's. Lola tosses Ma'am's hand-me-downs at Maria Elena. "For you," she mutters, not looking at her.

"Do you not understand," Lola asks, "Ang hirap na hirap ng buhay." She waves at the granddaughter. "He wasn't even handsome. Pangit naman."

"No kidding," Maria Elena says.

And here Maria Elena breaks her silence, utters every ugly thought she has ever had. Tells her lola, "Shame, ano ba? Who should be ashamed? Not me. You started this, old woman. You cursed us. Me, ang nanay ko. Where is my mother now? She has left you too." Every day the lola speaks to her, plants the history of sex into her skin like lotion on a body. If men want them so badly, why not use it? And what would have happened, the girl wants to know, if you would have said no? Escaped? Refused this curse? "I follow your example, La." She can no longer bear the shame, the way her grandmother announces her private life to all the Philippines.

The child rains words onto the old woman. Lola Malaya considers her name. Freedom. Considers her life. Considers the child. Her heart weakens. The tears fall. A pain shoots through her and she has lost her breath. Outside she hears the rooster crowing. She takes the beads from her nightstand and storms out of the house. On a rock, Lola settles herself and conjures up Mother Mary—her serene face, her full lips. This Blessed Mother is the Pinay version of the Mother of God and Lola sees the dark grain of mahogany that is her very complexion.

Maria Elena yells through the window, cannot stop now that she's begun. Cannot understand how airing the past can bring Lola justice. "What makes you think those politicians even see you?" she calls. "Why can't you stay quiet?" she wants to know.

Lola Malaya watches the Manila sky, utters Hail Marys and dreams about another life.

* * *

After three months, rebels from the mountains sneaked into the garrison and killed all the guards. The women lined up, weeping silently, and tiptoed out of the church. Lola found her way to the house where she was born, but when she got there, the door remained locked. Her mother called from behind a screen. "You are dead, hija," she said. "It's better to go to the city, start a new life."

That first night, Malaya slept at the foot of the door, waiting. She woke to the sound of dirt, hitting aluminum, to a shower of earth falling upon her. She looked below, down the ladder that led to their nipa hut, and a group of men called to her, threw fistfuls of dirt at her. "Tira," they chanted. "Tira."

Her father came to the door, and shook his head. She saw his tears and wanted to put her arms around him, but he held her off. "Go," he said. "We will never have peace, and you will always have shame unless you go."

* * *

The sun has stained what was blue with red and purple, with vibrant orange. The cityscape mars a beautiful sky and brings Lola Malaya to the streets again. Ernesto makes his way down the hill, a sack of corn at his side. He waves at Lola Malaya, begins to run to her.

The sight of the old fool only makes the pain worse. Her tears fall and fall, do not stop. He nears her, smiling wide and toothless. Stretching, he offers the gift. "Tira lang," he tells her. "Still fresh today, but tomorrow no good." He takes a handkerchief out of his pocket, wipes the tears from her face. "So kay," he whispers. "So kay." Her hands shake. The rosary rattles like wind chimes. He takes a seat on the ground next to her, and covers her free hand with his.

"Ay, Ernesto," she whispers. "Talaga. Ang hirap na hirap ng buhay ko."

The prayers wash over the old couple. She circles the rosary in her hand three times, fifteen decades of Hail Marys, before the moon rises above the tall buildings and the sound of car horns blink like stars. She stretches her fingers, and curls them over Ernesto's battered hand. Like this they point to moonlight sailing high above like hope.

—M. EVELINA GALANG
fiction editor

Axolotl

I may practice divination with the bones
of an eel, but the world would be
just as cruel were it within my will.

The yellowing leaves of the honey locust
would still be yellowing, and a woman
riding in a hearse would still grieve and grieve.

We don't live in a hypothetical world,
and yet the world would be nothing
without hypothetical dreaming. I hope no

ultimate set of laws to nature exists;
maybe, instead, there's only layering.
Maybe you look in a store window and see

twenty-four televisions with twenty-four images:
now the explosion of a napalm bomb,
now the face of an axolotl.

—ARTHUR SZE

In Your Honor

In your honor, a man presents a sea bass
tied to a black-lacquered dish by green-spun seaweed.

"Ah" is heard throughout the room:
you are unsure what is about to happen.

You might look through a telescope at the full
bright moon against deep space,

see from the Bay of Dew to the Sea of Nectar,
but, no, this beauty of naming is a subterfuge.

What are the thoughts of hunters driving
home on a Sunday afternoon empty-handed?

Their conception of honor may coincide
with your conception of cruelty? The slant

of light as sun declines is a knife
separating will and act into infinitely thin

and lucid slices. You look at the sea bass's eye,
clear and luminous. The gills appear to move

ever so slightly. The sea bass smells
of dream, but this is no dream. "Ah,

such delicacy" is heard throughout the room,
and the sea bass suddenly flaps. It

bleeds and flaps, bleeds and flaps as
the host slices slice after slice of glistening sashimi.

—ARTHUR SZE

Time for Pause

How can you say it's all superstition?
We're made of ferrous dust, supernovas
coursing the jugular, heart, carotid veins.
Amethysts *could* remagnetize blood.
One clear blue disc in the sky shakes down every day.
It is indeed a miracle, identical discs
shaking the blood, salt and air, perspiration,
the last few miles. Tired forests heave
into themselves. Cinders. Two minutes after
I run back with a birdbook, the warblers
gone. Pages flickering in early wind. Leafless
willows, red sap sugars gone taffy, bark-hard.
You just never know what the faces waiting
in crumpled paper, chert-stone, bark
will say. Why just yesterday a cherry-chested sunbird
explained dry winters, sipping diaphanous
strings of water, the foliage thick, enwebbed.
And bright with memory.

These are the ways. How wings shook out of
the trees, warned him. How the circle of bloody feathers
blotted grass, how cat-tails hummed cucumber songs one spring. You
just never know. So, when forty fire-flecked warblers
whir up, taking the shape their tree aspired
for years, you know it's time for pause.

—MAYA RANI KHOSLA

I'm Still Warm

Maybe I shouldn't have done it
but I wanted to see it happen

I shouldn't have written
that song for the dove
but I wanted to see it fly
wanted to hear it
sing

I shouldn't have flung my
heart so readily to the world
but its sadness begged me

(for the world tells the truth
when it is sure there is a listener
and that is only to make
certain
that you will believe it the next time
it tells a lie)

Yet I am not bitter; I'm still warm, I still blush
I am yet another who's had
a lover's quarrel
with the world and planted a rose
where only
the cactus grows, that's all

—OSCAR PEÑARANDA

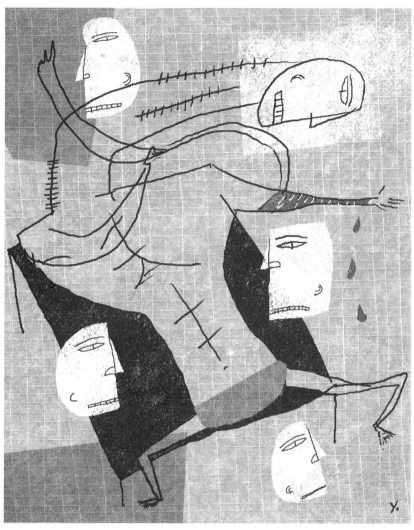

Untitled Art by James Yang

One-Man Show

—an excerpt from Tripmaster Monkey

It came to you to be yourself. Your fellow-actors' courage failed; as if they had been caged with a pantheress, they crept along the wings and spoke what they had to, only not to irritate you. But you drew them forward, and you posed them and dealt with them as if they were real. Those limp doors, those simulated curtains, those objects that had no reverse side, drove you to protest. You felt how your heart intensified unceasingly toward an immense reality and, frightened, you tried once more to take people's gaze off you like long gossamer threads—: but now, in their fear of the worst, they were already breaking into applause: as though at the last moment to ward off something that would compel them to change their life.
—Rilke, *The Notebooks of Malte Laurids Brigge*

I. I. I.
I. I. I.
I. I. I.
—Monkey's aria, THE JOURNEY TO THE WEST

Of Course, Wittman Ah Sing didn't really burn down the Association house and the theater. It was an illusion of fire. Good monkey. He kept control of the explosives, and of his arsonist's delight in flames. He wasn't crazy; he was a monkey. What's crazy is the idea that revolutionaries must shoot and bomb and kill, that revolution is the same as war. We keep losing our way on the short cut—killing for freedom and liberty and community and a better economy. Wittman could have torched the curtains and the dry flowers; he could have downpoured the oil lamps onto the chairs and fruit crates. He'd been envying that Japanese-American guy that got shot allegedly helping to set the Watts fires, yelling, "Burn, baby, burn." But, no, Wittman would not have tried to burn the City. It's all too beautiful to burn.

The world was splitting up. Tolstoy had noted the surprising gaiety of war. During his time, picnickers and fighters took to the same field. We'd gotten more schizzy. The dying was on the Asian side of the planet while the playing—the love-ins and the be-ins—were on the other, American side. Whatever there is when there isn't war has to be invented. What do people do in peace? Peace has barely been thought.

Our monkey, master of change, staged a fake war, which might very well be displacing some real war. Wittman was learning that one big bang-up show has to be followed up with a second show, a third show, shows until something takes hold. He was defining a community, which will meet every night for a season. Community is not built once-and-for-all; people have to imagine, practice, and re-create it. His community surrounding him, then, we're going to reward and bless Wittman with our listening while he talks to his heart's content. Let him get it all out, and we hear what he has to say direct. Blasting and blazing are too wordless.

On the third night, the one hundred and eight bandits climbed the stairs to become stars in the sky, except for some of the Juan brothers. They escape westward, that is, to Southeast Asia. They shunt their skiffs through the tule fog and shoot out in Viet Nam. Juan II, Juan V, and Juan VII (pronounced the Hispanic way, not like Don Quick-set and Don Jew-On the way we learned at Berkeley), played by Chicanos, become the One Hundred Children who are the ancestors of the Vietnamese. Though Vietnamese will deny that. Everybody would rather be the indigenous people of a place than be its immigrants. Another Indian punchline: "Are they going back where they came from yet?" A door like two golden trays opens up for a moment in the sky, which tears like blue silk, and a hundred and five bandits go to Heaven and three start a new country. The audience clapped loud, bone-proud of our boys and our girls, just like graduation, where we take the hardest awards, math and science. The End.

Except: A Chinese-minded audience likes the moral of the story told in so many words. And the American theater was rejoicing in scoldings; Blacks were breaking through the fourth wall. Whites were going to the theater and paying good money to be yelled at by Blacks, and loving them for it. Wittman Ah Sing waited for the audience to stop applauding, whistling, calling out names—"Kamiyama!" "Shaw!" "Nanci!"—a kabuki tradition. The actors had taken solo bows after arias and scenes and acts. He held up his hands— enough, enough already—turned his chair around, lit a cigarette, smoked, straddled the chair. He wanted to address the world as the shouting Daruma, fists upthrust pulling force up from lotus butt base, his body a triangle of power, and hairy mouth wide open and roaring. Not the Daruma doll that you knock around but Daruma the Shouter.

"I want to talk to you," said Wittman. "I'm Wittman Ah Sing, the playwright." The audience clapped for the playwright. He further introduced himself by giving them the melee of his name. "I'm one of the American Ah Sings. Probably there are no Ah Sings in China. You may laugh behind my family's back, that we keep the Ah and think it means something. I know it's just a sound. A vocative that goes in front of everyone's names. Ah Smith. Ah Jones. Everyone has an ah, only our family writes ours down. In that Ah, you can hear we had an ancestor who left a country where the language has sounds that don't mean anything—la and ma and wa—like music. Alone and illiterate, he went where not one other Chinese was. Nobody to set him straight. When his new friends asked him his name, he remembered that those who wanted him had called, 'Ah Sing.' So he told the schoolmarm, 'Ah Sing, ma'am,' and she wrote down for him the two syllables of a new American name."

Wittman waved the newspapers in his hand, and whacked them against his knee. "The reviews have come out. You've seen the reviews, haven't you?" The audience, which now included the actors, gave the reviews a round of applause. "I want to talk," he said. They gave him another hand, welcoming him to go ahead, talk. "So. You were entertained. You liked the show, huh? I myself have some complaints and notes but. Let me discuss with you what the *Chron* and the *Examiner* said, and the *Oakland Tribune*, and *The Daily Cal* and the *Berkeley Gazette*, and the *Shopping News*, and the *Barb*. They've reviewed us already, thinking that opening night is no different from the second night and tonight. You like the reviews? I am sore and disappointed. Come on, you can't like these reviews. Don't be too easily made happy. Look. Look. 'East meets West.' 'Exotic.' 'Sino-American theater.' 'Snaps, crackles and pops like singing rice.' 'Sweet and sour.' Quit clapping. Stop it. What's to cheer about? You like being compared to Rice Krispies? Cut it out. Let me show you, you've been insulted. They sent their food critics. They wrote us up like they were tasting Chinese food. Rice, get it? 'Savor beauteous Nanci Lee,' it says here. That's like saying that LeRoi Jones is as good as a watermelon. 'Yum yum, authentic watermelon.' They wouldn't write a headline for *Raisin in the Sun:* 'America meets Africa.' They want us to go back to China where we belong. They think that Americans are either white or Black. I can't wear that civil-rights button with the Black hand and the white hand shaking each other. I have a nightmare— after duking it out, someday Blacks and whites will shake hands over my head. I'm the little yellow man beneath the bridge of their hands and overlooked. Have you been at a demonstration where they sing:

> *Black and white together.*
> *Black and white together.*
> *Black and white together*
> *someda-a-a-ay.*

Deep in my heart, I do believe we have to be of further outrage to stop this chanting about us, that 'East is east and west is west.' Here's one that keeps quoting longer, like more learned. I won't read it to you. My mouth doesn't want to say any more wog-hater non-American Kipling. 'Twain shall.' Shit. Nobody says 'twain shall,' except in reference to us. We've failed with our magnificence of explosions to bust through their Kipling. I'm having to give instruction. There is no East here. West is meeting West. This was all West. All you saw was West. This is The Journey *In* the West. I am so fucking offended. Why aren't you offended? Let me help you get offended. Always be careful to take offense. These sinophiles dig us so much, they're drooling over us. That kind of favorableness we can do without. They think they know us—the wide range of us from sweet to sour—because they eat in Chinese restaurants. They're the ones who order the sweet-and-sour pork and the sweet-and-sour spare ribs and the sweet-and-sour shrimp. I've read my Aristotle and Agee, I've been to college; they have ways to criticize theater besides for sweetness and sourness. They could do laundry reviews, clean or dirty. Come on. What's so 'exotic'? We're about as exotic as shit. Nobody soo-pecial here. No sweet-and-sour shit. No exotic chop suey shit. So this variety show had too much motley; they didn't have to call it 'chop-suey vaudeville.' I am so pissed off. But. This other piece says that we are *not* exotic. 'Easily understood and not too exotic for the American audience.' Do I have to explain why 'exotic' pisses me off, and 'not exotic' pisses me off? They've got us in a bag, which we aren't punching our way out of. To be exotic or to be not-exotic is not a question about Americans or about humans. Okay, okay. Take me, for example. I'm common ordinary. Plain black sweater. Blue jeans. Tennis shoes ordinaire. Clean soo mun shaven. What's so exotic? My hair's too long, huh? Is that it? It's the hair? Does anybody have a pair of scissors? Here, help me spread these newspapers on the floor. I'm cutting my hair. If I bend over like this, I can see it, and cut it fairly straight. What's so funny? It ought to be the same around each ear? No need for symmetrical, huh? I don't want to snip off my ears. Earless Oichi. I'll lean over this way, and off comes this side. And this side too. And the top. The do-it-yourself haircut. Can be done without mirrors or friends. Whatever you get, you wear. Natural. Fast. Cheap. Just cut until you yourself can't see any more hair. Go by feel. I like the feel of sharp blades sandily closing through hairs. Sure, it's my real hair. I'm not wearing a wig, I'm honest. Wow, I didn't know I was carrying so much hair on my head."

Winging it, the monkey was indeed cutting off his actual hair. Black hair covered the newspapers. Wittman was performing an unpremeditated on-the-spot happening, unrepeatable tomorrow night. His prickly pear head cracked the audience up. The hair down his collar kept him in aggravation.

Wittman turned the chair flush toward the audience, sat up straight facing them, classic talk-story pose, and said: "We should have done a soap opera that takes place in a kitchen about your average domestic love agonies and money agonies. The leading lady is in hair curlers and an apron, and her husband, who has a home haircut like mine, stomps in, home from work. He knocks the mud off his workboots. He lets down the bib of his farmer or mechanic overalls. He drinks his beer while kneading his toes. She empties his lunchbucket, and they argue about whether a napkin does or does not count as one lunch item. A radio is on, and it's tuned to some popular station broadcasting whatever happens to be on, show tunes or a ball game or the news. No ching-chong music, no epic costumes, you understand? The high-point will be the family eating and discussing around the table—where the dramatic confrontations of real life take place; that's why meals are the hardest scenes to block. You know what the *Tribune* will say? 'Exotic.' Or they'll say, 'Whaddya know? Not exotic. The inscrutables are explaining themselves at last. We are allowed into their mysterious oriental world.'" Pause for the thinkers to think. "Okay, let's say in this soap opera, they hear bad news about their only son—killed in war. (Don't you whites get confused; he's killed fighting for *our* side. Nobody here but us Americans.) The mom is weeping big sobs with nose-blowing, and the dad howls, 'Aiya! Aiya! Aaaaaaa! Say, la! Naygamagahai! Aaaargh! Say, la! Say, la! Aiyaaaah!' and like in the funnies, 'Aieeeee!'"

Wittman stood and vocalesed a wail of pain that a dad might cry who'd given his only kid to his country. His eyebrows screwed toward each other, and his mouth was bent into the sign for infinity. Some audience members laughed.

"And guess how too many people will react? They'll say, 'Inscrutable.' We do tears. We do ejaculations. We do laffs. And they call us inscrutable.

"I have an idea how to make them cut that inscrutable shit out. Our next task is to crack the heart of the soap opera."

"I've gotten work on the soaps," said Charley. "They're starting to hire minorities now."

"Me too," said Nanci. "I played a nurse."

"Did you play the lab tech again, Charley? Or the court stenographer? You guys are too grateful. The job of the characters they let you play gets upgraded from criminal or servant to semi-professional, and you're fooled that we're doing better. Just because you get to wear a nurse's uniform rather than a Suzie Wong dress doesn't mean you're getting anywhere nearer to the heart of that soap. You're not the ones they tune in every day to weep over. We need to be part of the daily love life of the country, to be shown and loved continuously until we're not inscrutable anymore.

"Wait a minute. Let me try that again. We're not inscrutable at all. We are not inherently unknowable. That's a trip they're laying on us. Because they are willfully innocent. Willful innocence is a perversion. It's like that other perversion where people fly to Japan or Denmark to have their ex-hymen sewn shut. People who call us inscrutable get their brains sewn shut. Then they run around saying, 'We don't know you. And it's your fault. You're inscrutable.' They willfully do not learn us, and blame that on us, that we have an essential unknowableness. I was reading in a book by a Black man who travels far from America to this snowy village in the Alps. No Black man had set foot on that part of the Earth before. The villagers are innocent of slavery and of standing in the schoolhouse door and even of having ever seen a Black person. Their innocence pisses him off. On his walks, the kids call to him, innocently, 'Neger. Neger,' which makes echoes of another word to his American ears. He doesn't make a scary face and chase those kids, and he doesn't lecture them. He is a very quiet guy, who thinks at them: 'People are trapped in history and history is trapped in them . . . and hence all Black men have toward all white men an attitude which is designed, really, either to rob the white man of the jewel of his näiveté, or else to make it cost him dear.'"

Wittman was quoting from "Stranger in the Village," which is in *Notes of a Native Son* by James Baldwin. After getting educated, a graduate has to find ways to talk to his family and regular people again. It helps, when you want to tell them about your reading, to leave out the title and author. Just start, "I was reading in a book . . ."

"We have a story about what to do to those who try to hang on to the jewel of their näiveté. Cho Cho will get them. Once after losing a battle, Cho Cho hides out in a farmhouse with a well-meaning family. So many kids of various sizes run all over the place, they seem like the hundred children. The farm folks are going about their chores and speaking ordinarily, but all is fraught; the birds are stirring and beating their wings. Cho Cho walks here and there, peeping through doors and windows. What are these people up to, treating him so well? They say they are not political; they welcome the stranger as a guest. They certainly laugh a lot. Cho Cho steps into the wine cellar; a tall boy ducks into a jar. 'Aren't you too old to be playing hide-and-go-seek?' And where did the father go? Cho Cho strolls in the fields and orchards. No father. 'Where is he?' he asks this kid and that kid. 'He went to market to buy a fat pig.' The same answer from everybody. Had they had a meeting, and rehearsed that answer? Some kind of code? They say, 'He went to market to buy a fat pig,' and look at one another and laugh. Grandma brings a butcher knife, and a sister brings a boning knife. The mother sharpens them. 'Why are you sharpening the knives?' 'We're going to slaughter the fat pig that Father is bringing home from market.' Did she say 'pig' like she meant *him?* Why's everybody giggling? A brother and a cousin are talking behind a tree. What are they laughing at? What's so funny? There were eight of them—they could gang up on him. Nothing for it but to pick them off one by one. He catches a brother alone in a lean-to, and quietly kills him, and hides the body behind the storage. Kills the mother, and hides her in the loft above the kitchen. Kills the grandma with her own knife, tucks her behind the grain jars. The rest of the family goes about their routine, not missing the others. He kills them one and all. Got a sister in the courtyard, a brother in the fields, another brother in the barn. Very neatly.

No fights, no hysteria. Killed that family clean. Got them from behind, a hand over their eyes, fast. They didn't know what hit them. Nobody suffered.

"He leaves the farm, and meets the father on the road. He is trundling a fat pig bundled upside down in a basket. The rattan binds against its human-like skin. A pig's eye looks out between wickerwork bands. One has to look closely to see that it is a pig and not a naked man; sometimes there are naked men trussed up like this as a punishment for adultery, adulterer in a pigpoke. So the family had been acting secretive and excited because they had been planning a surprise party. The father says, 'The party's for you. You'll act surprised when the ladies tell you, won't you?' 'I'll do that, yes,' says Cho Cho. The father will have to go too, a quick stab in the back. The poor man is spared the suffering of finding his family slaughtered. Cho Cho takes the pig and continues his journey."

The listeners did not applaud this tale of paranoia. They were not ready to slaughter innocents. The white people were probably getting uncomfortable. The others were watching to see Wittman get struck mute.

"I think," he tried explaining, "that history being trapped in people means that history is embodied in physical characteristics, such as skin colors. And do you know what part of our bodies they find so mysteriously inscrutable? It's our little eyes. They think they can't see into these little squinny eyes. They think we're sneaky, squinnying at them through spy eyes. They can't see inside here past these slits. And that's why you girls are slicing your eyelids open, isn't it? Poor girls. I understand. And you glue on the false eyelashes to give your scant eyes some definition. I could sell all this hair for eyelashes. Make a bundle."

The girls and women who were wearing them did not lower their eyelashes in abashment. Wittman was just part of a show, which did not upset them; he's talking about other girls. Bad Wittman did not let up. "I have been requesting my actresses to take off their false eyelashes, to go on bare-face and show what we look like. I promise, they will find a new beauty. But every one of them draw on eyeliner, top and bottom rims, and also up here on the bone to make like deep sockets. Then mascara, then—clamp, clamp. They kink their stubby lashes with this metal pincher that looks like a little plow. With spirit gum and tape, they glue on a couple of rows per eye of fake-hair falsies. A bulge of fat swells out over the tape—a crease, a fold—allthesame Caucasoid. That is too much weight for an eyelid to carry. There's droop. Allthesame Minnie Mouse. Allthesame Daisy Duck." Wittman held the backs of his hands over his eyes, and opened and shut his fingers, getting laffs.

Judy, the awfully beautiful pigwoman, was agreeing with him, nodding her natural head. And Taña, who did not have an eye problem, also understood.

She will let that tactless husband of hers have it later in private. The ladies with the mink eyelashes ought to speak up for themselves. But through the make-up they did not feel assaults on their looks.

"Worse than make-up," said Wittman, "is the eye operation. There's an actress who dropped out of the show because she was having it done—the first Chinese-American I know to cut herself up like an A.J.A., who have a thing about knives. I won't tell you her name. Too shame. She's hiding out in a Booth home for girls during double-eye post-op. She didn't want to show her face with black stitches across her reddish swollen Vaselined eyelids X'ed across like cut along the dotted line. You girls shouldn't do that to yourselves. It's supposed to make you more attractive to men, right? Speaking as a man, I don't want to kiss eyes that have been cut and sewn; I'd be thinking Bride of Frankenstein. But I guess you're not trying to attract my type. I can tell when somebody's had her lids done. After she gets her stitches pulled and the puffiness goes down, she doesn't have a fold ex-actly, it's a scar line across each roundish lid. And her mien has been like lifted. Like she ate something too hot. The jalapeño look. She'll have to meet new guys who will believe she was born like that. She'll draw black lines on top of the scars, and date white guys, who don't care one way or the other single-lid double-lid."

Several pioneer showgirls were present who had secretly had that operation done long ago. They were laughing at the girl with the jalapeño expression. They did not admit that all you have to do is leave your eyes alone, and grow old; the lids will naturally develop a nice wrinkle.

"As a responsible director, as a man, I try to stop my actresses from mutilating themselves. I take them for coffee one at a time, and talk to them. You guys need to help me out, there's too many beautiful girls who think they're ugly. You're friends of a raccoon-eyed girl, tell her how beautiful she might be without make-up. She says, 'No, I look washed out. I look sick.' You say, 'You shouldn't wear stage make-up out in the street. Will you take it off for me? I want to see what you look like. Go to the ladies' room with this jar of Abolene cream, and come out with a nude face. Be brave. Go about bareface. Find your face. You have enormous eyes, not enormous-for-a-Chinese but for anyone. I want to kiss your naked eyelids, and not feel false eyelashes on my lips.' Okay, I get nowhere. Maybe I say it wrong, you laugh, they laugh. But you guys who get chicks to listen to you better than I do should give them a talking to.

"Please don't end up like a wife of some military dictator of a nowhere Southeast Asian country. Trip out on the before-and-after Madame Su-karno and Madame Thieu and Madame Ky and Madame Nhu. Their eyes have been Americanized. They wear shades, like everything is cool, man. They've been hiding stitches or maybe a botch job. They have round noses but

Madame Nhu's is the roundest, hardly enough bridge to hang her glasses on. Any Mongolian type you see fucking with their eyes, you know they've got big problems. You girls ought to step right up here, and peel those false eyelashes off, and cast them down amongst this other hair."

Nobody took him up on that, but they didn't walk out either, and Wittman went on:

"Speaking of plastic surgery, did you see on t.v. this dentist named Dr. Angle, D.D.S., who invented a way to straighten buckteeth? He's fixed thousands of people—the champion bucktooth fixer in the world. He brought along audio-visual aids, shots of make-overs. The interviewer asked him what his standards are for a good bite. He said, 'That's a good question. I thought hard about that very question.' His answer did not have to do with chewing, or being able to talk better, or teeth in relation to the rest of the face. He said, 'I use my own teeth as the model. Because they're perfect. I've got perfect teeth.' And he does. Dr. Angle looks just right. Regular eyes, regular nose, regular teeth. No mole or birthmark or crookedness I can use to describe him so's you'd recognize him.

"Like Dr. Angle, I declare my looks—teeth, eyes, nose, profile—perfect. Take a good look at these eyes. Check them out in profile too. And the other profile. Dig the three-quarter view. So it's not Mount Rushmore, but it's an American face. Notice as I profile, you can see both my eyes at once. I see more than most people—no bridge that blocks the view between the eyes. I have a wide-angle windshield. Take a good look. These are the type of eyes most preferred for the movies. Eyes like mine sight along rifles and scan the plains and squint up into the high noon sun from under a Stetson. Yes, these are movie-star eyes. Picture extreme close-ups of the following cowboys: Roy Rogers. Buck Jones. John Wayne. John Payne. Randolph Scott. Hopalong Cassidy. Rex Allen. John Huston. John Carradine. Gabby Hayes. Donald O'Connor, if *Francis the Talking Mule* counts as a western. Chinese eyes. Chinese eyes. Like mine, Like yours. These eyes are cowboy eyes with which I'm looking at you, and you are looking back at me with cowboy eyes. We have the eyes that won the West."

Now, Wittman was giving out what he thought was his craziest riff, the weirdest take of his life at the movies. But the audience stayed with him. His community was madder than he was. They named more cowboys with Chi-nese eyes—Lee Marvin, Steve McQueen, Gary Cooper. And more— Alan Ladd and Jack Palance in *Shane,* a movie about a Chinese against a Chi-nese. Gregory Peck. Robert Mitchum. Richard Boone. Have you heard: James Coburn is taking Chinese lessons from Bruce Lee, his "little brother." There's this guy, Clint Eastwood, who can't get work in Hollywood because of Chinese eyes, working in Italian westerns now. Some are traitors to their Chinese heritage. Richard Widmark took a role as a U.S. Cavalry expert on Indians in *Two Rode Together*, where he says, "I've lived among the Apache. They don't feel pain." The Lone Ranger masks Chinese eyes. So does Cato.

The poets who sit zazen get Japanese eyes: Philip Whalen and Gary Snyder.

The ladies refused to be left out. They found for themselves actresses who have Chinese fox eyes: Luise Rainer and Myrna Loy and Merle Oberon and Gene Tierney and Bette Davis and Jennifer Jones and Katharine Hepburn and Shirley MacLaine. Rita Hayworth is Chinese. The showgirls have a souvenir program of the Forbidden City's All-Chinese Review, and there she is, Rita Hayworth, in the middle of the front row.

"Marlon Brando," said Wittman, "is not Chinese, and he's not Japanese either. To turn him Japanese, they pulled back his hair and skin and clamped the sides of his head with clips. They shaved his eyebrows clean off, and drew antennae like an insect's, like an elf's. Sekiya scoot-scoots about, procuring his sisters for the all-white American armed services."

Lance Kamiyama stood up from the throne-chair where he was sitting at the back of the room. Sunny sat in the other one. He held up a banana, and made as if to throw it. "For you," he said. He tried to walk with it up to the stage area, but the floor was too crowded. He handed the banana off, "Pass it on, no pass back." It went from hand to hand up to Wittman. What signifies a banana? If I were Black, would I be getting an Oreo? If I were a red man, a radish?

"'Is this a dagger which I see before me, the handle toward my hand?' " said Shakespearean Wittman. "No, it's a banana. My pay? Thank you. Just like olden days—two streetcar tokens, two sandwiches, one dollar, and one banana—pay movie star allthesame pay railroad man. Oh, I get it—top banana. Thank you. Ladies and gentlemen of the Academy, I thank you. Hello. Hello. Nobody home in either ear. I feel like Krapp. I mean, the Krapp of *Krapp's Last Tape* by Ah Bik Giht. He wears his banana sticking out of his waistcoat pocket. I'm going to wear mine down in my pants. Have you heard the one about these two oriental guys who saved enough money for a vacation at the seashore? They're walking on the beach and desiring all the bathing beauties. They make no eye contact with bullies who kick sand in faces. The smaller oriental says, 'I strike out with the chicks. I try and I try but. How you do it?' The bigger oriental says, 'I been studying your situation, brother. I recommend, you put one banana in your bathing suit.' 'Ah, so that be the secret. I'll go buy a banana and try it.' He does that, and too soon returns in disappointment. 'I don't understand. I buy one big ripe banana. I stick it in my swimsuit. I walk on the beach—and the chicks laugh at me. What be wrong?' The big oriental says, 'I think you're supposed to wear the banana in front.'

"Seriously, folks, this banana suggests two parts of the anatomy that are deficient in orientals. The nose and the penis. Do you think if I attached it between my eyes I'd get to be a movie star? Do you think if I attach it between my legs, I'd get the girls?

"I ought to unzip and show you—one penis. Large. Star Quality. Larger than this banana. Let me whip out the evidence that belies smallness. Nah. Nah. Nah. Just kidding, la. I'd only be able to astound the front rows; the people in back will tell everybody they didn't see much. I've got to get it up on the big screen. The stage is not the medium for the penis or for the details of this face. For the appreciation of eyelids, double-eye or single-eye, we need movie close-ups. So you can learn to love this face.

"Is there anybody out there who's heard the joke all the way through that has the line, 'The chinaman don't dig that shit either!'? That may be the punchline. All my life, I've heard pieces of jokes—maybe the same joke in fragments—that they quit telling when I walk in. They're trying to drive me pre-psychotic. I'm already getting paranoid. I'm wishing for a cloak of invisibility. I want to hear the jokes they tell at the parties that I'm not invited to. Americans celebrate business and holidays with orgies of race jokes. A white friend of mine has volunteered to hear for me what comes before 'The chinaman don't dig that shit either!' Don't dig what shit?"

"It's about this horny bushy guy who comes down out of the Arctic Circle," said Lance.

"He wants a girl for fifty cents," said Zeppelin. "But she costs too much—one dollar."

"No," said Lance. "No girls available, but for one dollar, you can have the chinaman. This manly guy doesn't want the chinaman. He says, 'I don't dig that shit.' "

"No, no, that's not the way it goes," said Zeppelin. "He can afford fifty cents but they up it on him to one dollar."

"The exact amount of money," said Charley, "is beside the point. Whatever they say the cost is, this guy thinks it's too much, especially since he wouldn't even be getting a girl. He goes away. He's very horny, so comes back for the deal on the chinaman. But now they want to charge three times as much. Let's make it simple, three dollars."

"Three dollars?!" said Zeppelin. "How come three dollars. Awhile ago, you offered one dollar. I don't dig that shit."

"One dollar for the chinaman, and two dollars for the two guys to hold him down," said Lance. "The chinaman don't dig that shit either."

"American jokes too dry," said Siew Loong.

"No wonder they call you inscrutable, you don't laugh at jokes," said Wittman.

"You guys feel so sorry for youself," said Auntie Dolly. "But you tell tit twat cunt chick hom sup low jokes."

"All you joke experts be here, why don't you men tell us, 'Is it true what they say about Chinese girls?' " said Auntie Bessie. "Is *what* true?"

"The full line," said Wittman, "is, 'Is it true what they say about Chinese girls' twats?' They think they're sideways, that they slant like eyes. As in *Chi*nese *Jap*anese *Kor*ean." He put his fingers on the tails of his eyes, and pulled them up, "*Chi*nese," pulled them down, "*Jap*anese," pulled them sideways, "*Kor*ean." He felt immediately sorry. He had pulled tears of anger and sorrow up into his eyes. White men let little yellow men overhear that twat joke to make them littler and yellower. And they fuck over the women too. Kick ass, Wittman. "The King of Monkeys hereby announces: I'm crashing parties wherever these jokes are told, and I'm going to do some spoilsporting. Let me educate you, Mr. and Mrs. Potato Head, on what isn't funny. Never ask me or anyone who looks like me, 'Are you *Chi*nese or *Jap*anese?' I know what they're after who ask that question. They want to hear me answer something obscene, something bodily. Some disgusting admission about our anatomy. About daikon legs and short waist or long waist, and that the twat goes sideways, slanting like her eyes. They want me to show them the Mongoloidian spot on my ass. They want to measure the length of my ape arms and compare them to Negers' arms.

"And don't ask: 'Where do you come from?' I deign to retort, 'Sacramento,' or 'Hanford,' or 'Bakersfield,' I'm being sarcastic, get it? And don't ask: 'How long have you been in the country?' 'How do you like our country?'"

"The answer to that," said Lance, "is 'Fine. How do *you* like it?'"

"The one that drives me craziest is 'Do you speak English?' Particularly after I've been talking for hours, don't ask, 'Do you speak English?' The voice doesn't go with the face, they don't hear it. On the phone I sound like anybody, I get the interview, but I get downtown, they see my face, they ask, 'Do you speak English?' Watch, as I leave this stage tonight after my filibuster, somebody's going to ask me, 'You speak the language?'

"In the tradition of stand-up comics—I'm a stand-up tragic—I want to pass on to you a true story that Wellington Koo told to Doctor Ng, who told it to me. Wellington Koo was at a state dinner in Washington, D.C. The leaders of the free world were meeting to figure out how to win World War II. Koo was talking to his dinner partners, the ladies on his left and right, when the diplomat across from him says, 'Likee soupee?' Wellington nods, slubs his soup, gets up, and delivers the keynote address. The leaders of the free world and their wives give him a standing ovation. He says to the diplomat, 'Likee speechee?' After a putdown like that, wouldn't you think Mr. and Mrs. Potato Head would stop saying, 'You speakee English?'

"And I don't want to hear any more food shit out of anybody. I'm warn-ing you, you ask me food shit, I'll recommend a dog-shit restaurant. Once when I was in high school, I met one of the great American Beat writers—I'm not saying which one because of protecting his reputation. He's the one who looks like two of the lohats, beard and eyebrows all over the place. He was standing next to me during a break at the *Howl* trial. I told him I wanted to be a playwright. I was a kid playwright who could've used a guru. While he was shaking my hand, he said, 'What's a good Chinese restaurant around here?' I tell you, my feelings were hurt bad. Here was a poet, he's got right politics, anti-war, anti-segregation, he writes good, riding all over America making up the words for it, but on me he turned trite. Watch out for him, he's giving out a fake North Beach. He doesn't know his Chinatown, he doesn't know his North Beach. I thought about straightening him out, and almost invited him for crab with black-bean sauce, and long bean with foo yee, and hot-and-sour soup, but I didn't want to hear him say, 'I likee soupee. You likee?'

"I know why they ask those questions. They expect us to go into our Charlie Chan Fu Manchu act. Don't you hate it when they ask, 'How about saying something in Chinese?' If you refuse, you feel stupid, and what-samatter, you're ashamed? But if you think of something Chinese to say, and you say it, noises come out of you that are not part of this civilization. Your face contorts out of context. They say, 'What?' Like do it again. They want to watch you turn strange and foreign. When I speak my mind, I spill my guts, I want to be understood, I want to be answered. Peter Sellers, starting with the Ying Tong Goon Show and continuing throughout his bucktoof career to this day, and Mickey Rooney in *Breakfast at Tiffany's* and Warner Oland and Jerry Lewis and Lon Chaney are cutting off our balls linguistically. 'Me no likee.' 'Me find clue to identity of murderer.' 'Ming of Mongo conquers the Earth and the universe,' says Ming of Mongo. 'Confucius say,' says Confucius. 'Me name-um Li'l Beaver,' says Li'l Beaver. They depict us with an inability to say 'I.' They're taking the 'I' away from us. 'Me'—that's the fucked over, the fuckee. 'I'—that's the mean-ass motherfucker first-person pronoun of the active voice, and they don't want us to have it.

"We used to have a mighty 'I,' but we lost it. At one time whenever we said 'I,' we said 'I-warrior.' You don't know about it, you lost it. 'I-warrior' was the same whether subject or object, 'I-warrior' whether the actor or the receiver of action. When the turtles brought writing on their shells, the word for 'I' looked like this." Wittman wrote on the blackboard:

我

"It looks almost like 'Ngo' today, huh? 'Wo' to you Mandarins. This word, maybe pronounced 'ge,' was also the word for long weapons such as spears and lances and Ah Monkey's pole and the longsword. This longest stroke must be the weapon. And 'ge' also meant 'fight.' To say 'I' was to say 'I fight.' This isn't a Rorschach craziness on my part. I'll bet somewhere in China, a museum has collected that turtle shell in the same exhibit with the longswords. To this day, words to do with fighting and chopping off heads and for long weapons have this component:

戈丶

as does the word for 'I.' We are the grandchildren of Gwan the Warrior. Don't let them take the fight out of our spirit and language. I. I. I. I. I. I. I. I. I. I-warrior win the West and the Earth and the universe.

"They have an enslavement wish for us, and they have a death wish, that we die. They use the movies to brainwash us into suicide. They started in on us with the first movies, and they're still at it. D.W. Griffith's *Broken Blossoms*, originally entitled *The Chink and the Child:* Lillian Gish as the pure White Child, Richard Barthelmess as the Chink, also called The Yel-low Man. They were actually about the same age. The Child has a drunken father, so the Chink takes her into his house to protect her. One moonlit night, she seems to be asleep in a silk Chinese gown. He yearns for her. Ripped on opium, he looks at her out of stoned, taped eyes. His fingernailed hand quivers out for her, and barely touches a wisp of her gossamer hair, lacy and a-splay and golden in the moonbeams. The audience is in nasty anticipation of perversions, but before he can do some sexy oriental fetishy thing to her, his yellow hand stops. He kills himself. The Yellow Man lusts after a white girl, he has to kill himself—that's a tradition they've made up for us. We have this suicide urge and suicide code. They don't have to bloody their hands. Don't ever kill yourself. You kill yourself, you play into their hands."

Nanci was saying something to Auntie Marleese. "Poor Wittman." The two of them shook their heads. "He's so oversensitive."

"I am not oversensitive," he said. "You ought to be hurting too. You're dead to be insensitive, which is what they wish for you. You think you're looking good; you think you're doing fine, they re-run another one of those movies at you. And the morning cartoons get you wearing that pigtail again. And Hop Sing chases after the white man, and begs, 'Me be your slave. Please let me be your slave.' John Wayne has a Hop Sing, and the Cartwrights have a Hop Sing. They name him Hop Sing on purpose, the name of the powerful tong, to put us down. Here's another custom for orientals: Deranged by gratitude, an oriental has to have a master, and will tail after a white man until enslaved. In *Vertigo*, which could have been my favorite movie, James Stewart dives into the Bay and saves Kim Novak. He brings her back to his apartment that has a railing with the ideograms for joy. He lives within sight of Coit Tower. He tells Kim Novak, who's wearing his clothes and drying her hair by the fire, 'Chinese say if you rescue someone, you're responsible for them forever.' Think carefully; you've never heard a real Chinese say that; the ones in the movies and on t.v. say it over and over again. Every few days they show us a movie or a t.v. episode about us owing them, therefore thankfully doing their laundry and waiting on them, cooking and serving and washing and sewing for John Wayne and the Cartwright boys at the Ponderosa. The way Hop Sing shuffles, I want to hit him. Sock him an uppercut to straighten him up—stand up like a man.

"I want to punch Charlie Chan too in his pregnant stomach that bellies out his white linen maternity suit. And he's got a widow's hump from bowing with humbleness. He has never caught a criminal by fistfighting him. And he doesn't grab his client-in-distress and kiss her hard, pressing her boobs against his gun. He shuffles up to a clue and hunches over it, holding his own hand behind his back. He mulls in Martian over the clues. Martians from outer space and Chinese monks talk alike. Old futs talking fustian. Confucius say this. Confucius say that. Too clean and too good for sex. The Good Mensch runs all over Setzuan in a dress, then in pants, and fools everybody because Chinese look so alike, we ourselves can't tell the difference between a man and a woman. We're de-balled and other-worldly, we don't have the natural fucking urges of the average, that is, the white human being.

"Next time you watch insomnia television, you can see their dreams about us. A racist movie is always running on some channel. Just the other night, I saw another one that kills off the Chinese guy for loving a white lady. I'm not spoiling it by giving away the ending. They always end like that. Barbara Stanwyck is the bride of a missionary, and she is interested in converting this guy with tape on his eyes named General Yin, played by Nils Asther. He talks to himself, rubbing his hands together, plotting, 'I will convert a missionary.' Which is racially and religiously very fucked up. Chinese don't convert white people but vice versa. (Someday I'll tell you my theory about how everyone is already a Buddhist, only they don't know it. You're all Buddhas whether you know it or not, whether you like it or not.) General Yin's religion has to do with burning incense in braziers and torturing slavegirls. He keeps faking wise sayings about conquering the Earth. I liked him. He seemed intelligent. Whatever his cause, he's lost. He's fought his last battle, and lost his army and friends. He's alone in his palace with Barbara Stanwyck and one last slavegirl, Anna May Wong, whom he has locked up and plans to kill slowly. The right couple would have been General Yin and Anna May, coming to an understanding of each other and living happily ever after. However, Barbara enters his throne/bedroom to plead with him for the life of the poor slavegirl. This is an emergency, and she didn't have time to dress. She's wearing her satin nightgown that flows like a bridal train down the stairs of the dais. He's sitting enthroned, and she kneels at his feet to beg him. Her face comes up to his knee. She asks him for mercy while holding back tears, an actress's trick that gets to the viewer more than her weeping outright. He denies her pleas. The tears well up and up, and spill. She lifts her face to his face, her lips trembling, eyes, cheeks, and lips moist, her head almost touching a knee of his spread legs, which are draped with the silk of his smoking robe. They don't touch each other, but they tantalize and agonize nearer and nearer. Smoky snakes of incense entwine them. But she's a woman of God. She says, crying softly, looking up, looking down, pulsating, daring to teach this general, 'It's good to do something when there is no advantage to you, not even gratitude.' He has no morals; as we were taught from grammar school, life is cheap in Asia. Listening, he moves closer, she moves closer. Two-shots of their heads nearing. He slides past her lips, and gives her a hug. She allows it, her motivation being that she feels sorry for him. They hug, and they part. 'I will think over what you have said,' he says. She rushes back to her room, where she takes off her satin nightgown and puts on one of those spangly mermaid-skin evening dresses. She has to try another plea in a different outfit. The general could've looked down, as the camera does, and seen pretty far down her décolletage. She's wet with tears again. This time he touches her. He wipes her eyes and cheeks with a silk hanky. More tear well and fall. He wipes her off again, and again. The audience is catching thrills. Are they going to make out? Are the tails of that silk handkerchief tickling her neck and the tops of her tits? Are his lips going to land on her lips in an inter-racial kiss? Will her heavy head come to rest in his crotch? And he peel off her mermaid skin and carry her to the canopy bed? Which has all along been a large part of the ravishing decor. Will its lush curtains open for them, and close, and two masculine feet and two feminine feet thrash out, his on top of hers, and their four feet kick and stiffen? I saw that once in a Hong Kong movie; he was a demigod and she was a mortal. The wedding bed was in a garden among the flowers and under the sky. The bed was like a chamber or a stage, you could live in there. The actor who played the demigod had Star Quality, not just good-looking-for-a-Chinese—a thin straight nose, eyes which beheld his lover's ways so that from then on she's wonderful, even when she's alone, because watched from the sky whatever she does and wherever she goes. Whatever she asks, he answers, 'Forever.' But back to Barbara Stanwyck and General Yin. Are they going to get it on? Or neck or what? He picks up his teacup and drinks, and quietly leans back in his throne. And dies. He has poisoned himself before he can defile her. The name of that movie was *The Bitter Tea of General Yin.* They named him that to castrate us. General Yin instead of General Yang, get it? Again the chinaman made into a woman."

Making Sense of Screaming:
A Monkey's Companion

"She's great. She's like a friend."
"I see that. She lets you cook and guard the cars."
—David Wong Louie (pg. 303)

> *servility made him sinister*
> *his buck teeth were glowing mirrors*
> *and he shined his shit at me*
> *hoping i'd see myself and quiver*

—Dennis Sangmin Kim (pg. 314)

You've just completed reading—or reading around in—*Screaming Monkeys: Critiques of Asian American Images.* You probably enjoyed some pieces, laughed out loud, or learned something new. Other works might have left you angry or defensive, wanting to start an argument. In any case, these pieces might provoke you to pose questions that you might not have considered or investigate histories that you did not previously know about. Now what? How do you make sense of the whole from reading these fragments of what could be called the "Asian American experience"? Is there such a thing? All of these pieces are produced out of such diverse viewpoints, what do they total up to be? Beyond the individual perspective of each author, what can be taken away?

What follows is intended to help you construct a bigger picture to frame your reading. It poses more questions than it provides neat summaries: it asks you to debate the authors, to take them on, to investigate their meanings. It includes "found" quotations that are meant to inspire, provoke, or amuse. In some cases, it pushes you to seek other avenues of inquiry beyond this printed page.

> *Don't blame me for racism, that stuff happened a long time ago, and anyway, I can't be racist! My girlfriend is white and so are some of my best friends and servants!*

—Thien-Bao Thuc Phi (pg. 154)

Thin-skinned . . . and That's a Compliment

This anthology takes its title from a restaurant review in which an Amerasian boy is called a "rambunctious little monkey." When confronted with community charges of racism, the editor of *Milwaukee Magazine* prints a weak apology setting off a storm of letters and e-mails, some of which are reprinted in this volume. And now,

"No, no," said Charley Bogard Shaw. "That's Yen. *The Bitter Tea of General Yen.*"

"Yen Shmen," said Wittman. "That movie was a death-wish that Confucius and Lin Yutang take poison as co-operatively as Socrates."

Stepgrandfather Lincoln Fong raised his hand. You had to let the old guy talk, and once started, take over. "Yes, Ah Goong," said good Wittman.

Mr. Fong stood, waited for attention, and addressed each dignitary, "President Ah Sing"—that is, Grand Opening Ah Sing—"Mr. Chairman" —that's Wittman—"ladies and gentlemen, Lin Tse Hsü was General Commissioner of Canton Against Narcotics. He stopped the opium from coming in for five months. He arrested two thousand Chinese dealers. He executed addicts. Nine out of ten Cantonese were addicted to opium. He wrote to Queen Victoria, held meetings with the British and American Tobacco Company, and led a raid on a factory, confiscated the shit, and detained the British manufacturers for seven weeks. There are paintings of Lin burying opium in trenches half a football field long and seventy-five feet wide and seven feet deep. The Queen fired Lin from his office, and sent her navy to enforce opium sales. Your grandmothers and grandfathers, using Cho Cho's tactic, chained sixty junks across the Boca Tigris. Ten thousand of our Cantonese relatives fought with hoes, pitchforks, and two hundred new guns. They dumped opium into Canton Harbor like the Boston Tea Party. The British broke through into the Pearl River Delta and up the Yangtze to the rest of China. The famous joke of the nineteenth century: the West brought three lights—Fiat Lux, Standard Oil, and the British and American Tobacco Company. Why China went communist was to build an economy that does not run on opium."

"Thank you, Ah Goong," said Wittman. "Let's give Mr. Lincoln Fong a big hand." PoPo's old man took his bows and sat down. Please, don't another competitive old fut get up, and another, orating through all the wars, war after war, won and lost. "I'm doing dope no more, no, sir. Lest our grandparents dumped Brit shit in vain. We don't need dope because we're naturally high. We come from a race of opium heads. Nine out of ten—wow!—of our immediate ancestors were stoned heads. We're naturally hip. Trippiness is in our genes and blood. In fact, we need kung fu for coming down to Earth, and kung fu is all we need for flight. I'm quitting cigarettes too. Ah Goong, you have given me the political strength to take a stand against the American Tobacco Company." Wittman turned his pack upside down, and strewed cigarettes amongst the hair.

"The Delta they're blowing us out of nowadays is the San Joaquin Delta. The footage of John Wayne beating his way through the hordes on Blood River, they shot on the San Joaquin River. They keep celebrating that they won the Opium Wars. All we do in the movies is die. I watch for you,

Charley; your face appears, but before I can barely admire you, they've shot you dead. Our actors have careers of getting killed and playing dead bodies. You're targets for James Bond to blow to pieces. Did you know that J.F.K.'s favorite *reading* is James Bond *books?* The books are worse than the movies. Have you read one? You should, and dig what the President gets off on. He has ideas for what you can do for your country, and empire. There are these 'Chigroes'—what you get when you crossbreed a Chinese and a Negro—mule men with flat noses and cho cho lips and little eyes and yellow-black skin. They're avid to be killer-slaves. 'Chigroes.' It makes my mouth sick to say that out loud. You actresses have got to refuse to play pearl divers in love with James Bond. You have to get together with Odd Job. That's where the love story ought to be. That's not funny. A face as big as Odd Job's should star on the Cinerama screen for the audience to fall in love with, for girls to kiss, for the nation to cherish, for me to learn how to hold my face. Take seven pictures of a face, take twelve, twenty of any face, hold it up there, you will fall in love with it. Mako got his face up there, filling the screen with shades of oak and gold, this-color wongsky skin, and these eyes, and this nose, and his cho cho lips. What should be done with a face in close-up is to behold and adore it. They skin Mako alive. They peel him alive. He's skinned by his fellow Chinese. Hearing their voices making vulture-like sounds of an inhuman language, and watching Mako's screaming face, you imagine the skinning. You don't see it on camera. Where's my banana? Here, I'll show you, like so—peeling yellow skin. A strip, another yellow strip. And Mako is screaming, 'AAaaa! AaaAAagh! AAaaaaiyaaa!' His solo screams fill the sound track. 'AaaaaAAAaah! Aaaaaieeeeee!' We've been watching his face directly, then we watch it through the crosshairs of Steve McQueen's rifle. The audience wants to kill him so badly. We're in an agony of mercy to shoot him out of his pain. Steve McQueen, to whom he has been a faithful sidekick, does him the favor. Bang! Here's what they really think of their little buddy. Squanto and Tonto and Li'l Beaver. They have skinned and shot their loyal little tagalong buddy. Die, Hop Sing, Wing Ding, Chop Chop, Charlie Two Shoes, Tan Sing. Skin that cute li'l Sherpa. Like the banana he is! And no Pocahontas to save him. She's busy sticking her neck out for John Smith."

Wittman held the banana in his fist so the peelings flapped out like two arms and two wings. "Mako got nominated Best Supporting Actor for his role as the banana. He didn't win the Oscar but. None of us gets an Oscar except James Wong Howe—for the cinematography on *Hud.* You guys have got to get your asses out from behind the camera. You're the most all-around talents in Hollywood, but they don't give Oscars for what you do best. There ought to be an Oscar for the One Actor Best at Playing a Horde. You run around and around the camera and back and forth across the set. Clutch guts, twitch, spazz out—the bullets hit here and here—fall like trip-wire ankles, roll downhill, dead with face up to the sky and camera. The director sends you back in there for the second-wave attack. 'I was killed already in the last scene,' says the conscientious supernumerary. 'That's all right,' says the director: 'Nobody can tell you apart.' I accept this Oscar for Most Reincarnations." Again and again, we're shot, stabbed, kicked, socked, skinned, machine-gunned, blown up. But not kissed. Nancy Kwan and France Nuyen and Nobu McCarthy kiss white boys. The likes of you and me are unstomachable. The only hands we get to hold are our own up our sleeves. Charlie Chan doesn't kiss And Keye Luke doesn't kiss. And Richard Look doesn't kiss. We've got to kiss and fuck and breed in the streets."

Poor Wittman Ah Sing, Ah Star. It's going to get worse. He could spend the rest of his life advocating our stardom. When the *Planet of the Apes* series begins, the Asian American actors will say, "Here's our chance. You can look like anything under those ape costumes." But the roles will go to those who have to wear brown contact lenses. Pat Suzuki, after singing so well in *Flower Drum Song,* will play an ape-girl in *Skullduggery;* she roots in the dirt and grunts and squeals, and points, jumping up and down. And John Lone will play the title role in *Iceman,* a grunting, gesturing Neanderthal; his forehead is built up, his jaw juts prognathously, you won't recognize a Chinese-American of any kind under there. And when he gets to show his face in *Year of the Dragon,* John Lone, who has the most classic face amongst us, will have to have it broken on camera, and his eyes beaten shut. The last third of the movie his expressions are indecipherably covered with blood. He begs to be killed, and his co-star cradles his head, then point-blank shoots it off. The U.S. will lose the war in Viet Nam; then the Asian faces large on the screen will be shot, blown up, decapitated, bloodied, mutilated. No more tasteful off-camera deaths. We're going to have a President who has favorite movies rather than favorite books. The British actor who will bring back Fu Manchu claims not to be a racist because he doles money to the boat people. The actress who plays the dragon lady says that if you people picketing the set want movies from your p.o.v., "make your own movies." She doesn't understand that her movies are our movies, and that those horde-like picketers are her fellow SAG members.

"Thank you," said Wittman, eating the banana, no waste. "You feed the artist—thank you." He dropped the peel among the hair and cigarettes. "If there were Oscars for Improvisation and for Directing Oneself, you guys would sweep them. You made four hundred films about some kind of Chinese, whose roles were barely scripted. Maydene Lam and Richard Look and Keye Luke, all of you, you sized up the scene, and invented the dialogue with appropriate dialects and business. You keep giving your name to the character you're playing. Whenever the name on the left in the credits is the same as the name on the right, you aren't getting credit for acting. You just be the oriental you are. They think you behave oriental without having to act.

'Just say something Chinese,' says the director, throwing you into the movie. 'Do something Chinese.'

"Which gives me an idea. You have the set-up to do some sabotage. Go ahead, take whatever stereotype part. They ask you to do Chinese shtick, make free to say whatever you want. True things. Pass messages. 'Eat shit, James Bond. Kiss my yellow ass.' 'Fuck off, John Wayne. I love Joang Fu.' 'Ban the Bomb.' 'C.I.A. out of Southeast Asia.' Gwan's grandchildren—take over the movies.

"And say who we are. You say our name enough, make them stop asking, 'Are you *Chi*nese or *Jap*anese?' That is a straightman's line, asking for it. Where's our knockout comeback putdown punchline? Who *are* we? Where's our name that shows that we aren't from anywhere but America? We're so out of it. It's our fault they call us gook and chinky chinaman. We've been here all this time, before Columbus, and haven't named ourselves. Look at the Blacks beautifully defining themselves. 'Black' is perfect. But we can't be 'Yellows.' 'Me? I'm Yellow.' 'I'm a Gold. We're Golds.' Nah, too evocative of tight-fisted Chang. Red's our color. But the red-hot communists have appropriated red. Even Fruit of Islam, though too fruity like Fruit of the Loom, is catchier than anything we've got. The image of a black bulge in the jockey shorts scares the daylights out of the ofay. We want a name like that, not some anthropological sociological name. American of Chinese extraction—bucktoof ethnick. A.J.A. is good—sharp, accurate, symmetrical. The long version sounds good too. Americans of Japanese Ancestry. Makes up for 'jap.' And the emphasis is right—'American,' the noun in front, and 'Japanese,' an adjective, behind. They had the advantage of Relocation Camp to make them think themselves up a name. We don't have like 'Americans of Chinese Ancestry.' Like 'A.C.A.' We are not named, and we're disappearing already. We want a name we can take out in the street and on any occasion. We can't go by what we call ourselves when we're among ourselves. Chinese and Hans and Tangs are other people of other times and another place. We can't go to the passport office and say, 'I'm a Han Ngun,' or 'I'm a Tang Ngun.' I'll bet that Tang Ngun are gone anymore even from that red Asiatic country on the opposite side of the planet. Try telling the census taker, 'I'm a Good Native Papers Boy.'

"For a moment a hundred years ago, we were China Men. After all, the other people in the new world were Englishmen and Frenchmen and Dutchmen. But they changed themselves into Americans, and wouldn't let us change into Americans. And they slurred 'China Man.' 'Chinaman,' they said dactylically. One of the actresses who is giving me a bad time—I'm forsaking her—said, 'Is China Man like china doll? Like fragile?' Here I'm trying to give us a Sierra-climbing name, a tree-riding name, a train-building name, and she said, 'You're fragile like china?' She's a Mississippi Delta Chinese, and says 'fragile' like 'honey chile.' 'China Man' makes echoes of another word.

"Once and for all: I am not oriental. An oriental is antipodal. I am a human being standing right here on land which I belong to and which belongs to me. I am not an oriental antipode.

"Without a born-and-belong-in-the-U.S.A name, they can't praise us correctly. There's a favorable review here of our 'Sino-American' theater. When the U.S. doesn't recognize a foreign communist country, that's Sino-American. There is no such *person* as a Sino-American."

"They used to call us Celestials," said PoPo, "because at one time they glorified us so."

"But you never called yourself a Celestial, did you?" said Wittman. "They called you Celestial hoping that you'd go to heaven rather than stay in America. You called yourselves Wah Q and Gum Sahn Hock and Gum Sahn How."

PoPo said, "Gum Sahn Po. Gum Sahn Lo Po Nigh. Sahm Yup Po. Say Yup Po." The old fut names for Gold Mountain Ladies made people laugh.

Wittman said, "Sojourners no more but. Immigration got fooled already. You not be Overseas Chinese. You be here. You're here to stay. I am deeply, indigenously here. And my mother and father are indigenous, and most of my grandparents and great-grandparents, indigenous. Native Sons and Daughters of the Golden State. Which was a name our ancestors made up to counteract those racists, the Native Sons and Daughters of the Golden West. We want a name somewhat like that but shorter and more than California, the entire U.S.A.—ours.

"They get us so wrong. 'Sun Ch'üan, the king of Wu, played by an American. . . .' Of course, he's an American. As opposed to what? We're all of us Americans here. Why single out the white guy? How come I didn't get 'an American' after my name? How come no 'American' in apposition with my parents and my grandma? An all-American cast here. No un-American activity going on. Not us.

"When I hear you call yourselves 'Chinese,' I take you to mean American-understood, but too lazy to say it. You do mean 'Chinese' as short for 'Chinese-American,' don't you? We mustn't call ourselves 'Chinese' among those who are ready to send us back to where they think we came from. But 'Chinese-American' takes too long. Nobody says or hears past the first part. And 'Chinese-American' is inaccurate—as if we could have two countries. We need to take the hyphen out—'Chinese American.' 'American,' the noun, and 'Chinese,' the adjective. From now on: 'Chinese Americans.' However. Not okay yet. 'Chinese hyphen American' sounds exactly the same as 'Chinese no hyphen American.' No revolution takes place in the mouth or in the ear.

"I've got to tell you about this experiment I volunteered for in college. I answered an ad for 'Chinese-Americans' to take a test for fifty bucks an hour, more per hour than I've ever made—but hazard pay. So we Chinese-hyphen-ated-schizoid-dichotomous-Americans were gathered in this lab, which was a classroom. The shrink or lab assistant asked us to fold a piece of paper in half and write 'Chinese' at the top of one half and 'American' at the top of the other. Then he read off a list of words. Like 'Daring.' 'Reticent.' 'Laughter.' 'Fearful.' 'Easygoing.' 'Conscientious.' 'Direct.' 'Devious.' 'Affectionate.' 'Standoffish.' 'Adventurous.' 'Cautious.' 'Insouciant.' 'Painstaking.' 'Open.' 'Closed.' 'Generous.' 'Austere.' 'Expressive.' 'Inexpressive.' 'Playful.' 'Studious.' 'Athletic.' 'Industrious.' 'Extroverted.' 'Introverted.' 'Subtle.' 'Outgoing.' We were to write each word either in the left-hand column or the right-hand column. I should have torn up my paper, and other people's papers, stopped the test. But I went along. Working from the inside, I gave the Chinese side 'Daring' and 'Laughter' and 'Spontaneous' and 'Easygoing,' some Star Quality items. But my bold answers were deviated away in the standard deviation. The American side got all the fun traits. It's scientifically factual truth now—I have a stripe down my back. Here, let me take off my shirt. Check out the yellow side, and the American side. I'm not the same after they experimented on me. I have aftereffects—acid flashbacks. I got imprinted. They treated me no better than any lab animal, who doesn't get the journals nor invited to the conferences that announce the findings. I happened to pick up the weekly science section of the newspaper, and saw a double-decker headline: 'Oriental Frosh Stay Virgins Longest/Caucasian Boys Get Most Sex Soonest.' When I thought they were testing my smarts, élan vital and spelling, they were checking out my virginity. There was this other test where they squeezed my Achilles tendons with calipers. I was to rate the pain from discomfort to unbearable, which level I never reached. I thought it was a pain tolerance test, but maybe they were test-ing for inscrutability. I'm not making this up. I tell you, there's a lot of Nazi shit going on in the laboratories. Don't fall into their castrating hands. Even if you don't go off into longterm or side effects physically or chemically, you're fucked philosophically. I'm never going to know what my straight head would have thought unaltered. I'm off, like the roosters you hear crow any time of day or night that you walk past the labs. No more lab gigs.

"I *am* this tall. I didn't get this tall by being experimented on by scientists try-ing to find the secret of height. They're looking for a time hormone in the pitu-itary gland; maybe the chronons are up there. Speeding them up (or slowing them down) may fool the body into growing more. They're taking unused time from the brains of cadavers and injecting it into the brains of short little orien-tals. You Sansei kids, stop going to height doctors to fuck with your hypothal-amus. How many inches anyway between short and tall? Two. Three. Not many. The price of size—your mind. Don't be a generation of height freaks.

"It has to do with looks, doesn't it? They use 'American' interchangeably with 'white.' The clean-cut all-American look. This hairless body—I mean, this chest is unhairy; plenty hairy elsewhere—is cleaner than most. I bathe, I dress up; all I get is soo mun and sah chun.

"Which is not translated 'Star Quality.' Do you see it? Is my Star Quality showing nakedly yet? I've been trying to acquire it through education, attitude, right words, right work. Don't trust the movies, that stars are born. In a democracy, Star Quality can be achieved. And it can be conferred; I can love anybody. I'm learning to kiss everyone equally. Do you want to learn too? There's this theater game we play for warming up. Everybody goes around the circle and kisses everybody else. I judge who gets the title—Best Kisser in All the Land. The kissing contest is too good to keep backstage. Ladies and gentlemen, do I have some volunteers for free kisses? Step right up. That beautiful girl over there, Nanci, holds the title of Best Kisser and all the rights, duties, obligations, and privileges pertaining thereto. She'll participate. Now do I have some volunteers? Here's your chance. Come on up and take the championship away from her. Old futs too, come on, come on. I'll hug and kiss you myself. Nah, nah, nah, just kidding, la. I don't dig that shit either. But I challenge you old futs. You've been scolding me too much for the flagrancies of hugging and kissing going on in this play. You need to be taught a lesson, accusing me of affection. I'm going to unbrainwash you from believing anymore that we're a people who don't kiss and don't hug."

Led by PoPo, quite a few old futs stepped right on up. Nanci and Tãna volunteered, the show-offs, and Sunny and Lance, good at parties, fielded a contingent—"We're game"—including Caucasians who had tuned out during the racial business.

To help everybody over shyness, Wittman went first. He kissed his wife, and got ready to kiss this girl he'd had a crush on, an obsession for, wanted but can't have, quite a few girls of the unattainable type, and a girl that was always making him puzzle over her physicality, and his mother, and his grandmother. Test his rule: Kiss the one you love for as many seconds—five six seven eight—as you kiss anyone you can't stand, an ugly girl the same hardness you kiss a pretty one. Equality in food, jobs, and amount of loving. He touched a rough complexion, pores all wrecked by too much stage make-up, hot lights and late hours, and liked the feel of zits on his fingertips. A man of principle kisses everybody as though they're the same beautiful. Everybody was getting the same kiss off of him. This girl he was trying to forget put her hand on his face and her other hand on his naked, feeling chest, maneuvering. Is this going to be a cheek smack, or are we going to land on the lips? They kissed mouth to mouth, she turning aside, imperceptible to onlookers but felt by him, her move away from him. All he had to do was prolong that kiss, pull her to him for half a second too long, and it would slide into another meaning. He put his hands on her waist, and tickled her. He pounced on the next girl, and tickled her in the armpits. And somebody ambushed him from behind, Tãna tickling him. Wittman laughed. Whereby his community shouted out a title for him—Most Laughable.

To cheers and comments, each man went around and kissed each of the ladies, and each lady kissed all the men. Because everybody excelled at kissing, Wittman gave all of them titles—Most Juicy Kisser, Most Sincere, Best Technique, Most Succulent, Most Experienced, Most Passionate, Mr. and Miss Congeniality, Most Promising, Most Style, Coolest, Hottest, the One Who Causes the Most Dreams, Most Motherly (not won by Ruby Long Legs), Most Sisterly, Most Brotherly, Most Troublemaker, Most Suave, Most Dangerous. Those whom Wittman didn't personally kiss, he dubbed-thee by observation.

So these champion kissers were practicing a custom of a country they were intuiting. If ever it happens that the Government lets us take vacations to China, we're going to find: everywhere friends and relatives who will embrace us in welcome. Everywhere demonstrative customs of affection—holding hands, sitting in laps, pats and strokes, on heads and backs, arms around waists, fingers and cheeks touching cheeks. It has to be that way. Chinese live crowded, don't have enough chairs, or space on the sofa, so sit close and all sleep together in the one bed at inns and at home. In a land where words are pictures and have tones, there's music everywhere all the time, and a party going on. Whenever they need affection during the labor of the day or the insomnia of the night, why, they betake themselves publicly, and the crowds receive them with camaraderie and food. The whole country—on all its streets—is an outdoor café. Commadres and compadres are always around for some talk, a card game, and a midnight snack. A billion communalists eating and discussing. They're never lonely. Men are brothers holding hands, and women hold hands, and mothers and fathers kiss children. We see evidence of their practices here: The day people from that country step off the boat, or off the plane, they walk up and down Grant Avenue holding hands with one another, or arm in arm, or one's arm around the other's neck and the other's arm around the waist, walking and talking close face-to-face. You have to look fast. The next time you see them, they're walking apart. They've learned not to go about 'so queer. They have come to a lonely country, where men get killed for holding hands. Well, let them start a new country where such opposite creatures as a man and a woman might go about the streets holding each other's hand in friendship.

Given heart by a loving community, Wittman confided to them his marriage. "While off guard, I got married, she married me. I have a wife to support. I'm having a bad time of it. I've been looking for a job. The other day I was at an interview, and trying not to smoke, I set my socks on fire. I had my foot over my knee like this. I was rubbing up the fuzz on my new socks. Gotta match? My face and your ass. I mean your ass and my face. I mean, nevermind. The next thing I knew, I'd lit my match on the bottom of my shoe, and touched it to my sock, like so. Whoosh. Flambé. Flaming foot of fire. Flash fire." As he talked, Wittman did what he was saying, and for a moment looked like Prince Na Zhen, the malicious baby, who runs on wheels of fire. Fire rushed around his ankle and leg. The kids yelled for an encore. The mothers yelled at him for burning himself. "I'm all right. It doesn't hurt. I'm okay. See? My ankle's fine. Flame out so fast, it didn't burn through. I didn't feel a thing. The interviewer probably thought he was seeing things. No, I can't do fire socks again. You can only do it once per sock. This other sock I fired up already. I didn't get the job.

"I applied at the insurance company where my wife works. Don't worry, I knew better than to use her as a reference. Does anyone know why it is that at certain jobs such as insurance and teaching, they won't hire husband and wife? Family fights and family sex in front of the customers? I dressed straight-arrow. I treated the receptionist like she's boss. I applied myself, and filled out the forms without wedging any wisecracks or opinions into the answer spaces. I'm trying to be a Young Affordable, like you; then I'll buy my own shoes and new socks. I borrowed these shoes from the costume shop. They're too big for me." He lifted his foot over his knee. The shoe, too heavy, kept going, pulling him over with it. "I took an arithmetic test in these shoes. I matched rows of long numbers with other rows of long numbers, digit for digit the same. For example, is 68759312 exactly the same or not the same as 68759312? I did not add, did not subtract, just read horizontally and vertically. What for I went to college? I did pretty well, got everything right. And this personnel guy says to me, 'You people are good at figures, aren't you?' I can't think of how to answer right off. I should take that as a compliment? It's within his realm of *in*surance to recognize in me one of a tribe of born mathematicals, like Japanese? I say, 'Who, me? Not me, man. I come from the group with no sense of direction. I'm more the artistic type. What do you have in the creative line?' I didn't get a callback.

"At a corporation that I don't know what they actually produce, I told the interviewer about having organized a sales campaign before. And he says, 'Made fifty cents on the dollar?' I think I heard right. I say, 'What you say?' He says, 'Made a dollar out of fifty cents.' I let him have it on the immorality of profits. 'I'm against profits,' I say; 'I won't work for a corporation that profits from making shit. And if you're making something worthwhile, you should be giving it away.'

"What they always ask is, 'Why do you want to join our firm, Mr. Ah—Ah Sing?' They don't understand, I don't want to. I have to. And I don't join; I rule. But the most they'll let me do is the filing. How I answer, I say, 'I be-leaf in high high finance. I be-leaf in credit. Lend money; get interesting. Smallkidtime, I like bang money like Scrooge McDuck. I also likee bad Beagle Boys—follow map and dig under city into fault. No, not San Andreas Fault. Bang fault. Safu.' I was up for teller—I'm pretty smart—passed typing, passed adding machine—but when they call the tellers 'our girls,' I can tell they're not about to hire me.

"I'm unfit for office work. I'm facing up to that. And I can't write sales anymore. It fucks me up bad to sell anything to anybody. I have no attitude against blue collar, just so long as they make fruit cocktail instead of bombs, but I hate to lie that I'm not too overeducated. At this hiring hall for Fruit-vale, guess what the guy says to me? He says, 'Do you have your green card?' My skin turning browner, my back getting wet, my moustache drooping, I say the truth, 'I don't have to show you no steenking green card.' And I don't, don't have to show it, and don't have one. I get so fucking offended.

"Unemployed and looking, my task is to spook out prejudice. They'll say any kind of thing to the unemployed. In Angel tradition, let me pass on to you the trick question they're asking: 'What would you say your weak point is?' They ask in a terribly understanding manner, but don't you confide dick. You tell them you have no weak point. Zip. 'None that I can think of,' you say. 'Weak point?' you say. 'What you mean weak point? I only have strong points.' They get you to inform on yourself, then write you up, 'Hates business,' 'Can't add,' 'Shy with customers.'

"My caseworker at the Employment Office, that is, the Office of Human Development—he's right over there—give him a hand—stand up—take a bow-Mr. Leroy Sanchez—advised me to get a haircut, and sent me to this shopping-news office on the Peninsula. On the bus, I thought out the power that would he mine peacemongering the shoppers with an aboveground grass-roots press. I'd be practicing right politics among locals who buy and sell. A radical can't accuse me, 'Poet, aussi, get your ass streetward,' that is, aux barricades et rues of Burlingame. I'd already be out on the block. Dig: the shopping news taking a stand on zoning—zoning can change society—re-seating the draft board and ex-locating the recruiting office. We'll sponsor contests with trips to Russia and Cuba and China for exchange workers and exchange soldiers. They will feel possessive of the Alameda shipyards, and can't bear to bomb them. We'll join one another's Friends of the Library and League of Women Voters and Audubon Society and food co-op and Sierra Club and S.P.C.A. and SANE and cornea bank. We exchange families and pets and recipes and civil servants. Like Leadership. Day in high school, we hand over the running of the Government and everything to them, and vice versa. We do one another's work and keep up one another's social invitations. Sister cities conduct the foreign policy. Pretty soon we'll be all miscegenated and intermarried, we'll be patriotic to more than one place. By the time I got off the bus, I wanted the gig a lot. I was on time for my appointment. I gave my plan for world peace to the editor. I hope he appropriates my ideas. And you appropriate them too. Please. He asked, 'How old are you?' They think we look young. I told him nicely that I wasn't a short and young Chinese boy. He didn't hire me. I'll make my own shopping news. I'm passing the hat. Will you please put some money in it toward offset printing of my shopping news?"

As you may imagine, when Wittman promised a love story, but it was turning into a between-gigs story, he was losing some audience. He didn't try to stop them. Go ahead, leave. He did notice when this one and that one cut out. It's all right. Go. Go. Squeeze out between the knees and the chairbacks. (There are two types of audience members when they're excuse-me-leaving-excuse-me—some turn their ass and some their genitals toward the faces in a row.) They love fight scenes; they love firecrackers. But during a soliloquy when a human being is thinking out how to live, everybody walks about, goes to the can, eats, visits. O audience. For those who stayed with him, those with hungry ears but nobody has read to them since bedtime stories, he kept on talking. Those kind people were putting money and red envelopes into the hat.

"Readers will be able to pick up my shopping news for free. I'm going to give ideas on how to live on barely anything. From experiments in living, I know that three thousand dollars a year is plenty enough to live on and to sock some away as back-up for eventualities, and for projects such as this play. Our editorial policy will be that Congress has to pass Walter Reuther's plan for a guaranteed annual minimum living wage for United Auto Workers and everybody—three thousand dollars, which will bring every American up to the official poverty level. A married couple could pool their money—six thousand dollars. Two couples—twelve thousand dollars, a ten-percent down payment on a hundred and twenty thousand dollars worth of communal land. Life is possible.

"I want to run an information exchange on how to live like a China Man. Whenever you buy a newspaper, whenever you spend a dime for a pay toilet, you leave the door of the dispenser or the can open—don't slam it—for the next guy on voluntary poverty who comes along. I've found a route of newspaper dispensers where somebody's being regularly thoughtful of me. I hardly buy anything. I use the bathroom at Pam Pam's without being a customer, and they're okay about it. Lately I order pizza, and leave an unbitten wedge for some hungry person to grab ahead of the busboy. Do the same with club sandwiches. I'm going to make a listing of cafés where you may sit for a long time over one cup of coffee, and they don't say, 'There's a dead one at table eleven.' Sticks and stones. Just be sure to tip the waitress extra well. The Christian Science Reading Room is a private club for yourself alone, no other readers ever in there. Old St. Mary's has a reading room too, and the church part is open day and night seven days a week; in the middle of the night when you're freaking out, it's a quiet dark place to come down, sniffing the India Imports smells. Sometime in our lives, everyone ought to live on just what nature and society leave for us. Loquats dropping off the park trees bid us who know they're not poisonous, 'Eat me. Eat me.' To live on leavings, we find out just how inhabitable this planet, this country is. I pick up stuff off the street that I don't even need. I have to think up uses for what's there. If you sit on the seawall at Baker Beach or Aquatic Park for quite some time, you'll see the shoes and socks that nobody is coming back for. You'll not be wearing a drowned man's shoes; he went out into the water or walked along the shore and lost his landmarks. If they're still there after your own long walk, they're yours. Take them or the tide will. Of course, later, you will lose those shoes, and the watch that was inside one of them; there's a losing karma to things that you find. Like there's a stealing karma to hot stuff. When a Chinatown coot gets his unregistered gun stolen from under his pillow, and another old coot gives him his, that gun gets stolen too. My free shopping news will help every human being survive as an artist. If you hadn't helped me put on this show, I was going to drop Xeroxed copies of scripts into Goodwill bins. Painters can use the Salvation Army thrift shop for a gallery. Shoppers who buy art there would also buy playscripts, and read them and perform them.

"Among the ads about the price of bananas and birthday clowns and other odd jobs, I plan to keep running my idea for an anti-war ritual: Cut off the trigger finger instead of circumcision for all the boy babies, and all the girl babies too. Chop. I'll volunteer to have mine done first. On the other hand, the people who love shooting, they'll use their toes, they'll use their noses. It's more difficult to make peace than war. You take war away from human beings, you have to surrogate them with projects that haven't been thought up yet. Workers at weapons factories could keep their jobs making missiles but out of papier-mâché, and install them in the landscape for admiration. They're launchable. We let ourselves go at long last, drop them on Russia and Cuba, and invite them to drop theirs on us.

"You didn't come to the theater on your night off to think about jobs and war; you came to be entertained. For my last bit, I'll tell you about marriage. I was learning to live poor—for one only. Then I got married. But. I have mixed feelings about that. About her. I may be getting a divorce. I have a marital problem. I married my second-best girl. I like her. She started the marital problem. She said that she's not in love with me. 'I'm not in love with you, Wittman,' is how she put it. I answered, 'Well, I'm not in love with you either, but. It's okay.' If I were in love with her, or vice versa, we should go to a shrink. Shrink the *ro*mance out of us. She—my wife—said, 'We haven't been romantic about each other. I never fantasized about you. And I said, 'That's good. I don't want anybody fantasizing about anybody.' And she said, 'Out there somewhere is the soul chick you're going to fall in love with and leave me for. She's waiting for you, and you're waiting for her. The prosaic things you do, Wittman, will be interesting in her eyes. You'll become brave showing off for her. You better start regretting our marriage now so you won't regret everything when you're old, and it's too late.' One of the things I like best about my wife, she'll face a bad trip head on.

"I am sometimes somewhat in love with her. But it's not fate or magic. There's a specialness about her that is photographable. She has an expression on her face like she's appreciating whomever she's looking at. All she has to do is regard me, behold me like that, and I won't be able to leave her. She's listening; I hope she doesn't get self-conscious on me; I hope she isn't acting. The way her top lip upcurves with a dip in the center—she can't act that. She can't make mean lips. She smiles sideways. Quite a few movie stars have a sideways smile and beholding eyes, and we fans want them to keep reacting like that—to us, to everything. And she's got long blonde hair. I wouldn't mind a shrink immunizing me to it. I don't like being taken in by movie-star eyes and movie-star hair and movie-star lips.

"She admitted to me how she got this guy. Before she met me. On a rainy night, she went with her girlfriend and this guy into a coffeeshop. He held the umbrella and the door for this other girl to go ahead; he went in next. Water poured off the umbrella onto the girl in back, that is, her, my wife. He had made his choice. She said to herself, 'I'm going to get him.' At the next party, she let her hair down all clean and dry, a-tumble and curly, cascades of it down her back and shoulders, parted to the side, the way bad girls part hair, for a hank to fall over one eye and have to be seductively pushed back. That guy didn't have a chance. He was mesmerized in love, and the only thing changed about her was her hair. She's told me her magic. I've seen her with her hair wet and in a rubber band and in curlers. I'm not taken in. I'm not under her blonde power.

"She's not Chinese, I'll admit, but those girls are all out with white guys. What am I to do, huh? I don't want a Hong Kong wife marrying me for a green card. I've been testing my wife out. There was this sofa game in *Life* magazine a long time ago, where the guy sits at one end of the sofa and the girl at the other. They look into each other's eyes. In the next frame, they move closer together. 'Irresistibly,' said the caption, they meet in the middle. In the last frame, they're in each other's arms, kissing. A time clock at the corners of the pictures marked off minutes and seconds. There were three test couples in a series of long photographs. I've wondered, what happens if you mix the couples up, or pair strangers at random? My wife and I tried it. She can resist forever. She kept talking; she recited love poems; she read. So I read back to her Thomas Hardy, where Sergeant Troy says, 'Probably some one man on an average falls in love with each ordinary woman. She can marry him; he is content, and leads a useful life. Such a woman as you a hundred men always covet—your eyes will bewitch scores on scores into an unavailing fancy for you—you can only marry one of that many. . . . The rest may try to get over their passion with more or less success. But all these men will be saddened. And not only those ninety-nine men, but the ninety-nine women they might have married are saddened with them. There's my tale.' 'We don't want to be part of a system like that,' I told her. We're going to prove that any two random people can get together and learn to care for each other. I'm against magic; I go into despair over things happening that skip causation. The superior man loves anyone he sets his mind to. Otherwise, we're fucked.

"From the day that I made my explanations to my wife, she hasn't cleaned the apartment. I noticed before long that we'd gone through the dishes. Some of them have turned into ashtrays. I can trace the mess beginning at when I took my Hardyesque stand against *ro*mance. There are coffee cups all over the place with mold growing out of them. I can hear the dregs festering and bubbling. Her cups are especially disgusting because she uses cream. But black coffee grows mold too. Even non-dairy coffee creamer grows mold. Coffee must be nutritious, it can cultivate that much life. You have to watch where you step or sit. You kick aside newspapers, and the coffee cups underneath spill coins of mold that blend with the rug. All the doorknobs have towels and coats on them. I don't know where so much stuff comes from. It doesn't belong to me. It probably used to be in the drawers and closets, and she isn't putting it back. The place smells of cat piss and cat shit. My sense of smell is shot from smoking, but the cat is getting through to my nose. She got this S.P.C.A. cat and made it into a flealess indoor cat. The vet de-fleaed it the same day the fumigator came. The cat never goes outdoors again. She didn't have a cat when I married her. She does clean out the cat box and refill the kitty litter. But that fucking disoriented cat's been shitting in the clothes and newspapers. You don't want to step or sit for the cat turds.

"At meals, we clear off two spots at the table for her setting and my setting. The centerpiece is growing—rib bones from Emil Villa's Hickory Pit, a broken wineglass and candlewax and shrimp shells from an October candlelight dinner, plates from our last evening of clean dishes, movie popcorn boxes and used paper plates. I eat amongst mementos of other breakfasts, other suppers, naked lunches.

"The water standing in the kitchen sink started out as a soak for the pots and pans. Some are soaking in the bathtub too, and the skillet is in the living room from when we ate out of it. She can't wash dishes anymore because you can't run clean water without delving your arm through the scum and knives to unclog the drain. I wish, were I to flip the dispose-all on, a rotation would vortically twirl the room including the cat, and grind everything down and away.

"To be honest, one of my wife's attractions is that she's got a coin-operated washer and dryer in the garage. She did some laundry the other day; she picked her clothes out of the piles, and washed them, and ironed them. She does outfits to go to work in. I tossed in a pair of my skivvies, which didn't come back. As long as she's running a wash, she could do an item of another person's, right? I don't give her a full load. It's not as if she has to get depressed at the laundromat." Wittman put on his shirt; *he* didn't have the habit of dropping dirty clothes on top of piles of newspapers and banana peels and hair and cigarettes.

"We've been running all over the apartment churning up the newspapers and cat shit, yelling at each other, looking for a shoe and car fare and the phone. The off-the-hook noise is driving me nuts. I fell down slipping on a phonograph record under newspaper. She's always late for work because she can't find her car keys, or the house keys. They'll fire her, then the two of us on Unemployment, she can stay home and clean up. I was almost late myself tonight. The keys to the place were in the toaster oven. I don't know how they got there. Like the gravity has been acting up. She does cook. She's been standing at the stove and eating over the saucepan. If I want any, I have to eat her leftovers. We're leaving the front door unlocked, which the bags of garbage and the bags of groceries are shoving against. Anybody who would want to do some thieving in there, clean us out. Please. The ironing board unfolded out of the wall and dropped across the doorway.

"In the bathroom, I drape my washcloth on the rim of the sink, flat and neat, and she puts hers on top of it. Mine never dries. It took me days to detect that the mildew I was smelling was coming off of me. The newspapers for reading on the john get wet and print the tiles black. The black in the shower stall is an alga, and a strain of red alga is growing too.

"On Wednesdays, she says, 'Tonight's garbage night.' She knows the schedule. On her way to her car for work, she could pick up a bag of garbage and beat the scavengers to the cans. I've never believed the stereotype that Caucasians are dirty, but. Her place wasn't a dumpyard when I first went over there. Cleaned up for visitors, I guess. Good thing I haven't given up my own apartment until she learns better habits. The broom is missing. We need to hose the place out, or burn it down—a good fire—and start over. She isn't house-proud. I won't ask her to clean up. Our conversation has got to transcend garbage and laundry and cat shit. I don't want to live for garbage night. Domesticity is fucked. I am in a state of fucked domesticity. I am trying for a marriage of convenience, which you would think would make life convenient at least.

"Each of us announces to the other which room he's walking to. 'Well, I think I'll watch t.v. while I eat this t.v. dinner.' 'I'm going to read in the bathroom.' We don't want to lose track of each other's whereabouts. Things sure don't feel like they're about to end up in sex again. Yet how am I going to leave her? I ought to go out the door with my laundrybag and my toothbrush, and keep walking." He held his thumb and forefinger in a downward ring, as if holding his toothbrush by a suitcase-type handle.

"I had thought that one advantage of marrying a white chick would be that she'd say, 'I love you,' easily and often. It's part of their culture. They say 'I love you' like 'Hi, there,' nothing to it, to any friend, neighbor, family member, husband. You know how verbal they are. No skin off their pointy noses to say 'I love you.' But all I'm getting is, 'I'm not in love with you, Wittman.'

SCREAMING MONKEYS

"The marriage is about two months old. I know what will happen next. I'm going to stay married to her; we're going to grow old. At our deathbed scene, whoever's not too gone to talk—she, I hope—will say at last, 'I love you.' I'll hear her. (The ears are the last to go.) And I'll think, Do you mean *in* love with me? Have you now or at any time in our life together ever loved me? Did you finally fall in love with me for a few moments during our long marriage? And since she has E.S.P. on me, she'll answer, 'Sure. Do you love me back? If you love me back, nod or blink.' I'll die suspicious and being suspected of loving and loving back. I'll nod, I'll blink. So I lied.

"Taña, if you're listening in the wings, you're free to leave if you want to leave me. But I'll always love you unromantically. I'll clean up the place, I get the hint. You don't have to be the housewife. I'll do one-half of the housewife stuff. But you can't call me your wife. You don't have to be the wife either. See how much I love you? Unromantically but."

Out of all that mess of talk, people heard "I love you" and "I'll always love you" and that about dying and still loving after a lifelong marriage. They took Wittman to mean that he was announcing his marriage to Taña, and doing so with a new clever wedding ritual of his own making. His community and family applauded. They congratulated him. They pushed and pulled the shy bride on stage, and shot pictures of her and of the couple. They hugged the groom, and kissed the bride. They teased them into kissing each other. More cameras flashed and popped. They threw rice. They congratulated their parents and grandparents. Their parents congratulated one another. Friends were carrying tables of food through the doors, and spreading a cast party and wedding banquet. And more firecrackers went off. And champagne corks popped. To Wittman and Taña—long life, happy marriage, many children. Taña and Wittman Ah Sing were stars in a lavish, generous wedding celebration. To drums and horns, the dragons and lions were dancing again, a bunny-hopping conga line that danced out of the house and into the street. Wittman's community was blessing him, whether he liked it or not.

And he was having a good time. He still had choices of action, more maybe. If he wanted to drop out and hide out, he had heard of the tunnel that goes under a hill between the old Army Presidio and the Marina for a subway never built. And somewhere in Fresno, there's an underground garden of fifty rooms. And he himself had been beneath the Merced Theater in Los Angeles. He had memories of dug-out dressing rooms that were part of an underground city where Chinese Americans lived and did business after the L.A. Massacre, nineteen killed. He and other draft dodgers could hide in such places until the war was over. But better yet, now that he had Taña—she could be the paper-wife escort who will run him across the U.S.-Canada border at Niagara Falls. He had made up his mind: he will not go to Viet Nam or to any war. He had staged the War of the Three Kingdoms as heroically as he could, which made him start to understand: The three brothers and Cho Cho were masters of war; they had worked out strategies and justifications for war so brilliantly that their policies and their tactics are used today, even by governments with nuclear-powered weapons. And they *lost*. The clanging and banging fooled us, but now we know—they lost. Studying the mightiest war epic of all time, Wittman changed—beeen!—into a pacifist. Dear American monkey, don't be afraid. Here, let us tweak your ear, and kiss your other ear.

—MAXINE HONG KINGSTON

MAKING SENSE OF SCREAMING

A MONKEY'S COMPANION

The Top Ten list of Obvious Objections to this example:

10. What's the big deal? It's a restaurant review for chrissake.
9. The storeowner was not offended. Why should you be?
8. The only offense in this review is bad writing.
7. The author of the review did not **intend** to disparage Filipinos.
6. To me, all kids are monkeys. I like monkeys.
5. That review was complimentary; after all, she *praised* the food.
4. Some people are just overly sensitive. This is just overreacting.
3. There are certainly more important things to protest.
2. Some of my best friends are Chinese food.

The number one response from the Top Ten list of Obvious Objections:

1. **If we had to watch our language all the time, we'd never say anything.**

Now, this volume exists in defiance of this Top Ten list; it came into being to counter both the petty ignorances and the larger histories of oppression that Asians face in the u.s. It indicates different screaming thresholds, some activated by incidents like Wen Ho Lee's arrest, and others in which the seemingly banal—a restaurant review, a billboard, an article in *Newsweek*—indicates larger cultural anxieties about Asian Americans. Do the pieces in this volume successfully counter the sentiments expressed in this Top Ten list? Do they make urgent, immediate, and significant the grievances detailed in these pages? Can these objections be applied to other instances in which Asian American authors analyze the social implications of culture, for example, Sunaina Maira's point that marketing trends appropriating Asian culture are fetishistic and exploitative?

No doubt some might refuse to see Madonna's channeling her inner geisha to be implicitly racist. Does this resistance arise from the belief that Asians do not suffer from racial oppression? Perhaps part of the answer is that positing difference is never neutral; difference will always be placed in an evaluative hierarchy. This leads to the following discussion . . .

I can't be a Filipino. I don't want to be a Filipino because the only Filipino everyone knows is the Filipino that eats dogs or the Filipino that walks around with a broom in his hands.
—R. Zamora Linmark (pg. 322)

Colonization of the imagination is a two-way street.
—Jessica Hagedorn (pg. 210)

Dogeaters Alla Same: Cultural Relativism

At a dinner party, a guest discoursing on her son's trip to China took the time to inform me that the Chinese eat dogs. This is, as can be imagined, a loaded thing to say to a Chinese American. Upon taking the look on my face as a sign of incredulity, she pressed her point: "The Chinese really DO eat dogs."

OK, so the Chinese eat dogs. I accept this as a fact. But was it only information being exchanged at that moment? After all, the French eat horses, don't they? But we don't conjure up this image—eater of horse flesh—when we think, "French."

The trope of the dogeater—like that of the monkey—is a historically laden image. As Catherine Ceniza Choy, R. Zamora Linmark, and Dindo Llana and others in this volume attest, the image portrays Asians not merely as culturally different but as barbaric, backward, pre-modern.

What is at stake in describing Asian culture or Asians as different from what one takes to be the norm?

A more complicated question concerns the issue of cultural relativism embedded within any discussion of representation. "Dogeater" is a stereotype, by which one implies that it is a false perception. But if the image of the dogeater—or for that matter, the monkey, the geek, the model minority, the Lotus Blossom—were dispelled, would the truth about Asian Americans then emerge? The image of Asian Americans as alien, FOBs, or perpetual foreigners poses a more pressing question. Such portrayals deny Asian American participation in the public sphere as full citizens—the headline, "American Beats Out Kwan" in this volume is a case in point. Nevertheless, one cannot merely repudiate Asian "foreignness" as simple stereotype because doing so might ignore the significance of immigration policy, ESL initiatives, or theories of flexible citizenship—all addressed to "foreigners"— for Asian Americans as a group.

What are the politics embedded within any cultural comparison? Consider, for example, Arthur Sze's poem, "In Your Honor." Its dominant image is that of a fish being sliced alive at the table. Delicacy or cruelty? "Stereotype" or neutral fact of Asian cultural practice? Consider, too, Gish Jen's "Chin," which witnesses, in faux naïf fashion, a child's beating. Necessary discipline or child abuse? Confirmation of harsh Asian parenting? Or important spotlight on one form of social injustice? How do the pieces in this volume depict cultural comparisons that force us to come to ethical or political judgments that reflect our own cultural locations?

> jackie kicks the bad
> guy's ass sets the vase
> back on its rosewood
> stand in the next

shot a stray
bullet smashes
it into a thousand pieces
—Lori Tsang (pg. 250)

Hello Kitty, and What do You Have to Do with Asian America?

In writing about the trend of Indo-chic—examples of which can be found in this volume—Sunaina Maira writes, "Cultural appropriation of Asian artifacts and images is always a charged issue, because it is the tip of the deeper coagulation of histories of anti-Asian racism, anxieties about changing demographics, and exploitation of cheap Third World labor, the turn-of-the-millennium version of Orientalization" (pg. 229). For her, this American re-circulation of Asian images goes hand in hand with other forms of exploitation, both mutually enforcing and producing them. Popular culture is a medium of social control intrinsically connected to the maintenance of a status quo that includes hierarchies based on race and class.

"So," asks Maira, "what kinds of representations do we, and can we, construct in response?" The answer is partly to be found in this volume. It is not only that American commodity culture appropriates and abstracts Asian culture, the reverse is also true: references to American popular culture abound in the work of these Asian American authors and the "found" images selected by the editors. In wresting these cultural references away from their contexts, the writers force new meanings upon them, produce alternative interpretations.

Consider the following:

Pluto

Hello Kitty

Bruce Lee

Dixie cups

Midas muffler

Princess Amidala

Miss Saigon

In taking on popular culture in their art, Asian Americans are not merely consumers of commodity culture, but producers of alternative signs. How are these icons perceived in American culture? How do they resonate for Asian Americans? How are they revised in this volume and for what reason?

How, for instance, does race factor in attraction? A popular answer says love sees no color.

I don't believe that. We're taught to see race early on. The culture teaches us a racial hierarchy even before we're conscious of being taught.
—David Mura (pg. 297)

Pinkerton looking for Butterfly to suck my Suzie Wong.
—Timothy Liu (pg. 330)

Becoming Visible: Is it *Enough?*
Some questions about the limits of liberal multiculturalism
From this anthology, you learn that Asian Americans invented the nectarine in 1921.

Okay.

I forgot to tell my niece that piece of info. She's doing a report for school and has a budding social consciousness, the same kind of consciousness that provoked Helen Zia to seek out original scholarship in Asian American Studies that documented "our lost history." She sought and found stories that gave "faces and names to Asian American pioneers, and . . . place[d] them in history books with George Washington, Columbus, and the *Mayflower*" (pg. 98). Like Zia, my niece's teacher wants to know,

Q: What contributions did Asians bring to American society?

Certainly there is value in bringing a repressed history to light, as Zia notes, value in finally uncovering those "dramatic moments in the nation's history with Asian Americans at center stage." Before, there was only erasure and invisibility.

There was a time in which any Asian representation in American popular culture, however perverted, was cause for celebration. As Jessica Hagedorn writes about white actors portraying Asians in film, "Back then, not many thought to ask why [whites in yellowface]; they were all too busy being grateful to see anyone in the movies remotely like themselves" (pg. 204). It's true. My dad used to call us to come look at the TV when he thought he saw an "Oriental" (for some reason, usually a *Solid Gold* dancer). This would cause us all to run in and take a look. My mother would then scoff, more often than not, "Dad thinks a *black* girl is Oriental." I don't think he was exactly grateful for the representation, I think he just enjoyed looking at the girls. Allan Issac diagnoses this desire to see oneself somewhere in America as the source of his fascination with Andrew Cunanan: "Perhaps, my perverse compulsion stemmed from a longing to be reflected in the small screen in this American media sensation. Filipinos would in some manner be part of an American drama. Any American drama" (pg. 87). If African Americans have O.J., we could have at least *one* killer, dang it.

This anthology raises a broader question about representing ethnic experience in the u.s. We want to see ourselves in culture—but does that change anything? Does it make a difference? One could say that these pieces contribute to the project of making visible what was once repressed and marginalized. They shed light not only on contributions that Asians have made here, but on the very ways in which our history **is** that of the nation and its involvement in global processes—from American imperial endeavors at the turn of the century and those leading up to the Cold War, to the suspension of civil liberties upon the incarceration of Japanese Americans, to American claims to be an immigrant nation. M. Evelina Galang begins the volume with this leap of faith: "What if Ann Christenson had studied the history of the first wave of Filipino u.s. nationals? What if her editors at *Milwaukee Magazine* had been as familiar with the history of Asian immigrants in America as they are with the history of immigrants on the *Mayflower?* Someone would have seen the mistake, caught it, erased it, and never let it see the printed page" (pg. 5–6). *Knowing*, she implies, stops racism before it happens. It kills bugs dead.

This belief is foundational to the Asian American Movement that spawned the scholarship Zia discovered in college. Nevertheless, it prompts a critical question about how this aim might have been co-opted once "diversity" became a catch-word in American national self-conception. Vijay Prashad notes that American racial representation in the post-Civil Rights era is dominated—and contained—by the logic of liberal multiculturalism:

> The anti-racist struggle . . . fought against the arrogance of white supremacy, but the United States' response to the struggle was simply to adopt the liberal patina of multiculturalism to fend off the challenge. Despite multiculturalism's roots in anti-racism, it now seems to be restricted to the promotion of an ahistorical diversity and the pedagogy of sensitivity. (pg. 257)

One could say that the very presence of anthologies like this one unwittingly contributes to that "liberal patina of multiculturalism." *Screaming Monkeys* gives voice to a "primal scream" that attests to Asian American presence and anger, but is it merely content to render visible what was previously invisible? Does it do more—if so, what? Can it transcend the moment of its own emergence?

Open-ended Questions:

If acknowledgement of marginalized populations is the goal of multi-culturalism, then anthologies like this one function as its horizon; they make it possible to have access to diversity at any Barnes & Noble. Does the very existence of the multicultural anthology become a sign of social progress? Or is it merely a superficial indication of change that substitutes for more meaningful social transformation? Can one abstract the existence of such an anthology, its physical presence and the historical circumstances that bring it into being, from its content?

What would a rigorous concept of multiculturalism look like? Do any pieces in this volume suggest avenues of radical, systemic critique?

A: The nectarine was invented in the U.S. by two Koreans in 1921.
This is immensely important.

Or not.

> *danang danang danang*
> *to do the abacus arithmetic*
> *on the other side of the black granite*
> —Marlon Unas Esguerra (pg. 411)

The Other Side of Black Granite: America's Repressed Colonial History
In leading us behind the Vietnam War Memorial, Marlon Unas Esguerra leads us to the obscured history of American imperialism. As a number of authors here note, this legacy reflects "historical amnesia about America's violent imperialism" (pg. 37), a willful incomprehension of a past that is "everywhere and nowhere." (pg. 90).

Why the repression of imperial history, in particular to the concerns of this volume, the history of American annexation of the Philippines? At one level, it is clear that democracy is antithetical to colonialism; military control is seen as incommensurate with representative democratic politics. In regard to this history, the acute parallel may not be to other Asian groups in the u.s. but to Native Americans. How, for example, do depictions of Filipino savagery or innocence addressed here reflect portrayals of the Indian? How is the language of paternalism or conquest similar?

Screaming Monkeys forces us to consider how American involvement overseas has affected Asian American representation. Often, the only trace of that repressed history exists in those displaced populations—war brides, refugees, migrant labor, domestic workers sending money home, retired servicemen—whose presence is a direct result of imperialism and who thereby figure ambivalently in national memory. As students of American history discover the other side of black granite, how does our national self-conception change? How does Asian American literature pull us to that place?

Literary Interpretation as Historical Interpretation

Literary and historical interpretation are not dichotomous acts. Knowing history becomes key to interpreting a number of pieces in this anthology. For example, Ricco Villanueava Siasoco's "The Rules of the Game" depicts a conflict over a game of mah-jongg between Filipinos and their white boss: how is it resolved and why? How do the histories of Philippine conquest and the Filipino diaspora influence your reading? By the same token, in Hisaye Yamamoto's "Wilshire Bus," we learn in an aside that Esther has just returned to Los Angeles after being released from a concentration camp in Arkansas. How does this explain her reaction to the incident on the bus? Is knowledge of Japanese American internment necessary for a full understanding of the story?

For Further Research Google This
—comfort women
—Bataan Death March
—Heart Mountain, Wyoming
—Wen Ho Lee
—Vincent Chin
—Executive Order 9066
—*United States v. Bhagat Singh Thind*
—Chinese Exclusion Act
—Los Angeles Riots or Los Angeles Rebellion
—Maya Lin
—Corregidor
—Gentleman's Agreement, 1907
—Philippine Insurrection or Philippine American War

> *[Our] common oppression should be the basis of sympathy and solidarity, yet it often inspires the opposite: superhuman attempts to differentiate ourselves—the good, assimilated, upwardly mobile Asians—from those undesirable and unruly Others.*
> —Lynn Lu (pg. 267)

Ambivalent Assimilation, or Can Two Wongs Make a White?
A number of authors in this anthology present views of assimilation that are marked by ambivalence. That is, it is unclear whether or not increasing acculturation is a positive thing. On one hand, authors inscribe characters or speakers who are apparently eager to win acceptance and entry into

American society and who view the loss of ethnic culture as a fair trade for Americanization. On the other hand, they may also represent this process as fraught with violence or ultimately impossible for people of color. How do any of these texts provide contrasting representations of assimilation?

Geeta Kothari's "Meena's Curse" (pg. 214)
Bienvenidos Santos's "The Day the Dancers Came" (pg. 126)
Robbi Sethi's "Fifty-Fifty" (pg. 181)
Thaddeus Rutkowski's "White and Wong" (pg. 142)

How could we write poetry in a time like this?
—Marilyn Chin (pg. 192)

The Ultimate Test

The ability to make the connection between the injustice we have faced as Asian Americans and the injustice that others face is the ultimate test . . . I believe our Asian-American coalition will live or die by our choice in that regard.
—Mari Matsuda (pg. 160)

Asian American identity is a coalitional one: we come together as Asian Americans not because we have "natural" racial affinities, but because we share a common and continuing history in the u.s. This volume stands in testimony to that commonality, for better or worse, a commonality based on threats of violence and acts of exclusion as well as fellowship and solidarity. Marlon Unas Esguerra leads us angrily, lyrically, behind the Vietnam War Memorial forcing us to acknowledge what is not inscribed there, "the names of *my* people," the Vietnamese who likewise died in battle (emphasis mine). I don't know whether Marlon Unas Esguerra is Vietnamese or not. To paraphrase Thaddeus Rutkowski in this volume, no matter, you get the picture.

These testimonies of Asian solidarity—seeing oneself in the fate of others and acting upon it—are not limited by an affinity based solely on race. If we accept what Matsuda recognizes as the desire for justice underlying something called "Asian America" then there are no boundaries to conceiving alternative affinities, no claims of unity based on simple likeness.

The writers in this volume have re-imagined the sometimes tenuous, sometimes expedient bonds that link people. An airplane flight becomes the occasion for one such ephemeral community:

We are on an island. Suspended above the clouds, we are a nation of our own. We can forget who we are, where we come from and where we are going until we get there. (pg. 224)

So writes S.L. Kim. The passengers' commonality is only fleeting—the duration of one flight—and fragile, held together only by the hull of machinery. They share one identity: the fact of being a passenger on this one flight, at this one time, might be the only identity that matters. 9/11 has shown us how truly this image can resonate. "[W]e are a nation," but national unity is only one means of imagining some shared collectivity.

Writers in this anthology have focused on global linkages between working class peoples, Asian or no, who occupy similar positions within the processes of global capital. Sonia Shah, for example, suggests that "attempting to understand our place in the world" is the only way that Asian American awareness can "[step] outside the narrow confines of identity politics" to become "something much broader and long lasting" (pg. 277). To that end, she links the West's reliance on exploitable Asian labor to be the most significant cause of anti-Asian bias. Bino A. Realuyo's poem invoking Flor Contemplacion and Sarah Balabagan, Filipina maids accused of crimes while working abroad, draws a connection between Filipino diasporas. Tara Agtarap's "A Lavender Army" questions commodified notions of femininity imported from the West and its relevance to Third World women. These concerns are all Asian concerns.

What other pieces inscribe coalition? How is coalition imagined beyond race and ethnicity?

As importantly, a number of authors inscribe ambivalent or missed opportunities for solidarity; they are attune to how corrections become denied whether due to shame, fear, or indifference. Where is it refused? In Hisaye Yamamoto's "Wilshire Bus," shared racial oppression is the cause of the characters' repudiation of each other: an "I Am Korean" button greets the Japanese American narrator like a slap in the face, but it is only different in degree from her own detachment when she is faced with a white man's diatribe against Chinese Americans. Similarly, while the granddaughter in M. Evelina Galang's "Labandera" could show pride in her grandmother's activism on behalf of comfort women, instead she experiences only shame and refuses to claim solidarity as a woman. Likewise, Abelmann and Lie's treatment of the Los Angeles Riots highlights the competitive economic structure that governs Korean American and African American interaction in South Central L.A.

How does coalition figure in the following pieces? Does it presume likeness? What possibilities are affirmed or denied?

"Chin"

"Fifty-Fifty"

"Summer of Bruce"

"The Price of Eggs in China"

"Honor, 1946"

The authors, speakers, and characters in this anthology forge connections across multiple boundaries and for multiple reasons. Can we imagine political alliances that transcend a shared condition of social vulnerability, a common relation to social injury? Can we think of coalitions that articulate other forms of shared subjectivity?

> *I believe the key defining element of Asian-American identity is the quest for justice.*
> —Mari Matsuda (pg. 160)

—LESLIE BOW

Contributors' Notes

Nancy Abelmann (Ph.D. UC-Berkeley, 1990) is the author *Blue Dreams: Korean Americans and the Los Angeles Riots* (with John Lie). Harvard University Press, 1995.

Tara Agtarap (and, yes, you can find her first name in her last name too) thinks words are sometimes easier to deal with when written in Word because if they come out her mouth, she can't press backspace for a fresh start. She currently resides in San Francisco.

Hil Anderson, a native of Georgia, has lived in Taiwan researching contemporary poetry. He is currently pursuing a joint degree at Harvard University and Georgetown Law Center.

Mei-mei Berssenbrugge was born in Beijing in 1947 and grew up in Massachusetts. Her books include *Empathy* from Station Hill Press, *The Four Year Old Girl* and, forthcoming, *Nest*, both from Kelsey Street Press. She lives in New York City and New Mexico with her husband, Richard Tuttle, and their daughter.

Rick Bonus is the author of *Locating Filipino Americans: Ethnicity and Cultural Politics of Space* (Temple University Press, 2000). He is an assistant professor of American Ethnic Studies at the University of Washington, Seattle.

Leslie Bow is Associate Professor of English and Asian American Studies at the University of Wisconsin, Madison. Her work has appeared in the *Berkeley Fiction Review, Cultural Critique, Profession, Prose Studies*, and *Dispositio*, as well as a number of critical anthologies. She is the author of *Betrayal and Other Acts of Subversion: Feminism, Sexual Politics, Asian American Women's Literature* (Princeton, 2001).

Cecilia Brainard is the author and editor of ten books including *When the Rainbow Goddess Wept, Magdalena, Acapulco at Sunset and Other Stories, Philippine Woman in America*, and *Woman With Horns and Other Stories*. She edited *Fiction by Filipinos in America, Contemporary Fiction by Filipinos in America*, and *Growing Up Filipino: Stories for Young Adults* (2003). She co-edited two children's books and *Journey of 100 Years: Reflections on the Centennial of Philippine Independence*. Her book, *Cecilia's Diary 1962-1968*, will be released in 2003.

Carlos Bulosan emigrated from the Philippines in 1931. The horrendous conditions of Filipino laborers were fictionalized in his book *America Is in the Heart* (1946). Excerpts of his 1944 book, *Laughter of My Father*, were published in *The New Yorker* and *Harper's Bazaar*. Bulosan was commissioned by President Franklin Roosevelt in 1945 to write the essay "Four Freedoms," and was later blacklisted by Sen. Joseph McCarthy during the anti-Communist movement of the 1950s. His other books include *Letter from America* (1942), *Chorus from America* (1942), *The Voice of Bataan* (1943), *The Cry and the Dedication* (published posthumously in 1995), and *The Sound of Falling Light* (1960).

Luis Cabalquinto writes in three languages (English, Tagalog, Bikol) and his poetry has appeared in numerous publications in nine countries. His fourth poetry book, *Bridgeable Shores*, was published last year by Kaya Press (New York). *Moon Over Magarao: New and Selected Poems* is forthcoming from the University of the Philippines Press (2003).

Nick Carbó is the author of *El Grupo McDonald's* (1995) and *Secret Asian Man* (2000). He is the editor of *Returning a Borrowed Tongue* (1996) and co-editor with Eileen Tabios of *Babaylan: An Anthology of Filipina and Filipina American Writers* (2000). Among his awards are fellowships in poetry from the NEA and NYFA.

Theresa Hak Kyung Cha, the third of five children, was born on March 4, 1951, in Pusan, Korea, outside of Seoul. The primary theme of her artistic output was the dislocation—cultural, geographic, and social—embodied by immigration. Cha's best-known work, *Dictee*, is the story of several women: the Korean revolutionary Yu Guan Soon, Joan of Arc, Cha's mother, Demeter and Persephone, Hyung Soon Huo (a Korean born in Manchuria to first-generation Korean exiles), and Cha herself. Cha was murdered at the age of thirty-one by a stranger in New York City on November 5, 1982, just seven days after the publication of *Dictee*.

Johnson Cheu's poetry has appeared in anthologies such as *Staring Back: The Disability Experience from the Inside Out* (Plume, 1997), as well as periodicals such as *Blue Fifth Review, Disability Studies Quarterly, Midwest Poetry Review, North American Review, The Progressive, Red River Review*, and *Witness*.

Marilyn Chin's books include *Rhapsody in Plain Yellow, The Phoenix Gone, the Terrace Empty*, and *Dwarf Bamboo*. She has won many awards for her poetry, including two NEA grants, a Lannan Residency, two Fulbright

Fellowships, and the Stegner Fellowship. Her poems are anthologized widely and are taught in universities nationally. She teaches in the M.F.A. program at San Diego State University.

David Choe is a Korean American artist. He is awesome, cool, and rad, in that order. He wrecks shit.

Saiman Chow immigrated to the U.S. from Hong Kong when he was fifteen years old. He has a B.F.A from Art Center of Design in Pasadena and has exhibited with renowned artists like Barry McGee and Shepard Fairey. Despite many opinions that he has fused East and West, Chow says, "When I create stuff, I didn't intentionally dig through my memory or even think about East/West stuff. I don't really see the difference between them." Rather, he says the obvious influence in his work is in cartoons.

Catherine Ceniza Choy is the author of *Empire of Care: Nursing and Migration in Filipino American History (American Encounters/Global Interactions)* (Duke University Press, 2003). As a 2002-03 Association of American University Postdoctoral Research Fellow, she is beginning a second book project that will focus on the history of the international adoption of Asian children in the United States.

Kay Chung's work can be seen at www.kayolaswan.com.

Oliver de la Paz is the author of *Names Above Houses*, a winner of the 2000 Crab Orchard Awards Series in poetry. His work has appeared in journals such as *North American Review, Quarterly West, Cream City Review*. He has taught creative writing at Arizona State University, Gettysburg College, and Utica College.

Edward del Rosario has been making drawings by hand for the last sixteen years. He lives in a virtually rodent-free apartment in Manhattan.

Brian Komei Dempster's poems have appeared in *The Asian Pacific American Journal, Crab Orchard Review, Fourteen Hill's Green Mountains Review, Gulf Coast, Ploughshares, Post Road, Prairie Schooner,* and *Quarterly West*. He is the editor of *From Our Side of the Fence: Growing Up in America's Concentration Camps* (Kearny Street Workshop, 2001).

Xue Di was born in Beijing in 1957. His published works include *An Ordinary Day, Circumstances, Heart Into Soil, Flames, Trembling,* and *Dream Talk*. Xue Di is a two-time recipient of the Hellman/Hammet Award. Since shortly after the Tiananmen Square Massacre in 1989, he has been a fellow in Brown University's Freedom to Write Program in Providence, Rhode Island.

Denise Duhamel is the author of eleven books and chapbooks, the most recent of which are *The Star-Spangled Banner* (winner of the Crab Orchard Award in Poetry, Southern Illinois University Press, 1999) and *Oyl* (a collaborative chapbook with Maureen Seaton, Pearl Edition, 2000). Her poems have appeared in four issues of *The Best American Poetry* (2000, 1998, 1994, and 1993). She teaches in the M.F.A. program at Florida International University in Miami.

Phoebe Eng is a national lecturer and author of *Warrior Lessons* (Simon & Schuster, March 1999). Eng has been featured in the *New York Times,* the *Wall Street Journal, CNN, PBS, NPR, Crain's Business Reports,* and *Great Day America,* as well as in several media industry and legal trade publications for her perspectives on race and gender dynamics.

Anida Yoeu Esguerra seeks an artistic, spiritual, and political exploration of her identity as a non-hyphenated Cambodian Muslim American woman. Esguerra has performed across North America with I Was Born With Two Tongues, The Yellow Technicolor Tour, and Mango Tribe. At the heart of her work as a visual artist, writer, performer, and motivator is the lesson: *No one else can tell her story. Every one has a story to tell and everyone's story is worth telling.*

Marlon Unas Esguerra is Chicago born and bred. As a program coordinator and creative writing teacher for Young Chicago Authors, Marlon works with teens in the Chicago Public Schools, the Alternative High Schools, Cook County Juvenile Detention Center, and Gallery 37. He is a founder of the Asian American Artists Collective-Chicago, APIA Spoken Word & Poetry Summit, I Was Born With Two Tongues, and YAWP: Young Asians with Power APIA youth group.

M. Evelina Galang is the author of *Her Wild American Self,* a collection of short fiction from Coffee House Press (1996). She has been widely published and her collection's title story has been short-listed by both *Best American Short Stories* and *Pushcart Prize.* She has recently completed her novel, *One Tribe,* and has been researching the lives of surviving Filipina Comfort Women of WWII for her book of essays, *Lolas' House.* Galang teaches in the M.F.A. Creative Writing program at the University of Miami where she is an assistant professor.

Forrest Gander was born in Barstow, in the Mojave Desert, in 1956. He is the editor of *Mouth to Mouth* (Milkweed Editions) a bilingual anthology of contemporary Mexican poets, and the author of four books, most recent of which is *Science & Steepleflower* from New Directions. His other titles include *Rush to the Lake* (Alice James Books); *Lynchburg* (University of Pittsburgh Press); and *Deeds of Utmost Kindness* (Wesleyan University Press).

Vince Gotera serves as editor of the *North American Review,* and as an English professor at the University of Northern Iowa. Gotera's books include a book of poems, *Dragonfly,* a book of criticism, *Radical Visions: Poetry by Vietnam Veterans,* and *Ghost Wars.* He is co-founder with Nick Carbó of the e-group for Filipino writers, FLIPS, http://www.uni.edu/gotera/flips.

Michella Rivera-Gravage is a writer and filmmaker. Her work has been published in literary journals such as *Shellac, Maganda* and can be found in *Babaylan: An Anthology of Filipina and Filipina American Writers.* As a filmmaker, Michella's short film has screened at the NY Mix Festival, Visual Communications Festival, and the San Francisco International Asian American Film Festival.

Jessica Hagedorn is the author of two novels, *Ganster of Love* and *Dogeaters,* and a collection of poetry and prose, *Danger and Beauty.* She is also editor of *Charlie Chan Is Dead: An Anthology of Contemporary Asian American Fiction.* Her most recent book is a collaboration with photo-journalist Marissa Roth, *Burning Heart: A Portrait of the Philippines.* Her plays and collaborative multimedia theater pieces include "Airport Music" (with Han Ong) and the recent theatrical adaptation of *Dogeaters.*

Luba Halicki received an M.F.A. in Creative Writing from the School of the Art Institute of Chicago and a B.A. in Spanish from the University of Illinois-Chicago. She teaches English and Writing at Columbia College and Truman College in Chicago. More of her work can be found in *Babaylan* (Aunt Lute Books), as well as heard at frequent readings and sound performances in Chicago.

Wennie Huang is a mixed-media installation/performance artist. Born in 1972 in Cortland, New York, she is a second-generation Taiwanese American. She received her B.F.A from the Pratt Institute and her M.F.A. from The University of Michigan. Huang has received awards and residencies from the Bronx Museum of Art, New York Foundation for the Arts, Ragdale Foundation, Lower East Side Printshop, and Dieu Donne Papermill. Huang lives in New Rochelle, New York, with her husband, composer, Manly Romero.

Jade Ngoc Quang Huỳnh survived the war in Vinh Binh, Vietnam. He became a university student in 1974 and was consequently sent to labor camps for "education in communist ideology, psychological, and physical retraining." He escaped in 1977, first to Thailand, then the U.S. He spent six years working at fast food restaurants, cleaning bathrooms, washing dishes, and working in factories. He received his B.A. degree from Bennington College in 1987, and his M.F.A. from Brown University in 1992. His memoir *South Wind Changing* tells the story of his family being torn apart by war, his surviving prison camp, and his struggle to resettle in the United States.

Phung Huynh was born in Vietnam in 1977. Her father is Cambodian and her mother is Chinese. Her family stayed in a Thai refugee camp for about six months until they immigrated to Mt. Pleasant, Michigan, in 1978. Most of her childhood was spent in Los Angeles's Chinatown after the family moved in 1982. She is currently at New York University to complete her masters in painting, and she freelance illustrates.

Luisa A. Igloria is the author of six books*: Blood Sacrifice* (University of the Philippines Press, 1998); *In the Garden of the Three Islands* (Moyer Bell/Asphodel, 1995); *Encanto* (Anvil Press, 1994); *Cartography* (Anvil Press, 1992); *Cordillera Tales* (New Day Publishers, 1990); and *Songs for the Beginning of the Millennium* (De La Salle University Press, 1999). She co-edited, with Renee Olander, the anthology *Turnings: Writing on Women's Transformations*, published in March 2000 by the Friends of Women's Studies at Old Dominion University, Norfolk, Virginia.

In 1971, **Lawson Fusao Inada**'s *Before the War* became the first volume of poetry by an Asian American to be released by a New York publishing house. He has since edited two major Asian American anthologies, and pioneered the creation of multicultural curriculums for high school and college teachers. His last book, *Legends from Camp,* won an American Book Award and was featured on CBS *Sunday Morning.* He is also the author of *Drawing the Line.*

Allan Punzalan Isaac is assistant professor of English at Wesleyan University. His forthcoming book is entitled *American Tropics: U.S. Imperial Grammar and Asian American Postcoloniality.*

Jordin Isip was born and raised in Queens, New York. He received a B.F.A. from Rhode Island School of Design in 1990. His work has appeared in numerous periodicals, including a cover for *Time Magazine.* He has received many awards for his work and has been exhibited in galleries internationally.

Isip is currently teaching at the School of Visual Arts, Tyler School of Art, and Rhode Island School of Design.

A second-generation Chinese American, **Gish Jen** was raised in the large Jewish community of Scarsdale, New York. She published her first novel, *In the American Society*, in 1986. The quirky Chang family first appeared in her novel *Typical American* (1991), and again in the sequel, *Mona in the Promised Land* (1996). One of the short stories from *Who's Irish?* (1999) also appeared in *The Best American Short Stories of the Century*.

Maya Rani Khosla has been published in the *Seneca Review*, *America's Poetry Review*, and others. She has written a collection of poetry, *Heart of the Tearing* (Red Dust Press) and is working on a collection of essays, entitled *Marin Headlands: Notes from the Field*. Her book, *Web of Water*, will soon be published by the Golden Gate National Park Association.

Dennis Sangmin Kim was born in 1978 in Fairfax, Virginia to immigrant Korean parents. He is perpetually touring with pan-Asian spoken word phenomenon, I Was Born With Two Tongues, and the feared and respected hip-hop unit, Typical Cats.

S.L. Kim was born in Seoul, South Korea, but spent most of her childhood in Nairobi, Kenya. She worked as a flight attendant while completing her M.F.A. in writing at The School of the Art Institute of Chicago. She is currently working on her first novel.

Hiroshi Kimura was born in Hakodate, Hokkaido, Japan, and studied in Tokyo. In 1992, Kimura moved to the U.S. and has been living in New York City since 1997.

Maxine Hong Kingston, for her memoirs and fiction, *The Woman Warrior, China Men, Tripmaster Monkey,* and *Hawai'i One Summer,* Kingston has earned numerous awards, among them the National Book Award, the National Book Critics Circle Award for Nonfiction, the Pen West Award for Fiction, an American Academy and Institute of Arts and Letters Award, and a National Humanities Medal from the National Endowment for the Humanities, as well as the rare title of "Living Treasure of Hawai'i."

Geeta Kothari teaches at the University of Pittsburgh. Her writing has appeared in various journals and anthologies, including *The Kenyon Review, The Pittsburgh Quarterly*, and *The New England Review*. She is the editor of *Did My Mama Like to Dance and Other Stories about Mothers and Daughters* (Avon).

Betty Kung's style is influenced by her mixed cultural background. She has lived in Taiwan and the U.S. She graduated from Pasadena Art Center in 1999, and is currently working in Tokyo, Japan.

Don Lee is the author of the short story collection *Yellow*, which won the Sue Kaufman Prize for First Fiction from the American Academy of Arts and Letters. He has received a Pushcart Prize and an O. Henry Award, and his stories have been published in *GQ, Bamboo Ridge, The Gettysburg Review*, and elsewhere. Currently he lives in Cambridge, Massachusetts, and is the editor of the literary journal *Ploughshares*. His novel, *Country of Origin*, will be published by W.W. Norton in the fall of 2004.

Li-Young Lee was born in 1957 in Jakarta, Indonesia, of Chinese parents. Lee is the author of *Book of My Nights* (BOA Editions, 2001); *The City in Which I Love You* (1991), which was the 1990 Lamont Poetry Selection; and *Rose* (1986), which won the Delmore Schwartz Memorial Poetry Award; as well as a memoir entitled *The Winged Seed: A Remembrance* (Simon and Schuster, 1995), which received an American Book Award from the Before Columbus Foundation. He lives in Chicago, Illinois, with his wife, Donna, and their two sons.

Wen Ho Lee is the author of *My Country versus Me: The First-Hand Account by the Los Alamos Scientist Who Was Falsely Accused* (Hyperion, 2002). He lives with his wife in Los Alamos, New Mexico.

Walter Lew has been an active editor, *(Premonitions: The Kaya Anthology of New Asian American Poetry*, Kaya Press), critic, and multimedia artist in the Asian American literary community for years.

John Lie is a contributor to *Blue Dreams: Korean Americans and the Los Angeles Riots* (Harvard University Press). He is a professor of sociology at University of Michigan.

R. Zamora Linmark has lived in Manila, London, Madrid, and Honolulu, and presently makes his home in San Francisco. His work has appeared in *The Best Gay Fiction of 1997, Premonitions: The Kaya Anthology of Asian North American Poetry*, and *Charlie Chan Is Dead: An Anthology of Asian American Contemporary Fiction*, edited by Jessica Hagedorn. *Rolling the R's* is his first novel.

Dindo Llana won the bronze medal in the Art Association of the Philippines

Art Competition in 1995. For his illustration *Anna Learns to Swim,* he was listed both by the White Ravens of the International Youth Library in Munich and the 1996 Philippine National Book Awards. He was one of the artists selected for the At Home and Abroad exhibition at the Asian Art Museum of San Francisco, University of Hawai'i Art Gallery, Contemporary Arts Museum of Houston, and Metropolitan Museum of Manila in 1999.

Timothy Liu is the author of four books of poems, most recently *Hard Evidence* (Talisman House, 2001). Two new books are forthcoming: *Of Thee I Sing* (University of Georgia, 2004) and *E Pluribus Unum A.K.A. Kamikaze Pilots in Paradise* (Southern Illinois University, 2005). An associate professor at William Paterson University, Liu lives in Hoboken, New Jersey.

David Wong Louie was born and raised in New York. He received a bachelor's degree in English from Vassar College and an M.F.A. from the University of Iowa. He is the author of two books of fiction. *Pangs of Love,* a story collection and his novel, *The Barbarians Are Coming.* Louie teaches in the Department of English and the Asian-American Studies Center at UCLA.

Lynn Lu is a freelance writer whose work has also appeared in *Dragon Ladies: Asian American Feminists Breathe Fire* (South End Press, 1997) and *Talking Back and Acting Out: Women Negotiating the Media Across Cultures* (Peter Lang, 2002).

Sunaina Maira teaches Asian American studies at the University of California, Davis. She is the co-editor of *Contours of the Heart: South Asians Map North America* (Asian American Writers' Workshop), a literary anthology that won the American Book Award in 1997. Her short stories have appeared in the *Asian Pacific American Journal, India Currents, Asian American Renaissance, Her Mothers' Ashes 2,* and the *NuyorAsian Anthology.* She is currently doing a project on the commodification of Indo-chic.

Eugenio Matibag has published two books of cultural criticism: *Afro-Cuban Religious Experience* (Florida, 1996) and *Haitian-Dominican Counterpoint* (Palgrave Macmillan, 2003). An associate professor of Spanish at Iowa State University, he is currently chairing a committee on Asian American Studies and writing a book on Philippine Hispanic literature.

Mari Matsuda was a professor of law at the University of California at Los Angeles School of Law before joining the Law Center. Her books include *Called From Within* (University of Hawai'i Press); *Words that Wound* (Westview Press); and *We Won't Go Back, Making a Case for Affirmative Action* (coauthored, Houghton Mifflin) and *Where is Your Body?* (Beacon Press, 1997). She serves on the national advisory boards of *Ms. Magazine;* the American Civil Liberties Union; and the National Asian Pacific Legal Consortium.

Barry McGee received a B.F.A. in painting and printmaking from the San Francisco Art Institute in 1991. He has had solo exhibitions at the UCLA Hammer Museum; Walker Art Center, Minneapolis; Yerba Buena Center for the Arts; and the Atelie Museum Lasar Segall, Sao Paulo. McGee received a Louis Comfort Tiffany Foundation Award in 1999, a SECA award from the San Francisco Museum of Modern Art in 1996, and a Lila Wallace-Reader's Digest International Artist's Fellowship in 1993.

Molly McQuade's books include *Barbarism, Stealing Glimpses,* and *By Herself.* Her poem "Sumo-esque" is one in a series about Asia and the Middle East. Other poems in the series have appeared or will appear in *The Paris Review, Parnassus,* and *TriQuarterly.*

maiana minahal's is one of the founding members of the Queer Pin@y Kreatibo collective. She has been published in June Jordan's *Poetry for the People: A Revolutionary Blueprint; Take Out: Queer Writings from Asian and Pacific America;* in *Vasian: Asian Sisters Represent; maganda magazine;* and in the upcoming anthology, *Going Home to a Landscape;* and is featured on the spoken word CD *Infliptration: A Youngblood Revolution.* Her first book of poetry will be published by Monkey Press in November.

David Mura has written two memoirs: *Turning Japanese: Memoirs of a Sansei* (Anchor-Random), and *Where the Body Meets Memory: An Odyssey of Race, Sexuality and Identity* (Anchor, 1996). Mura's second book of poetry, *The Colors of Desire* (Anchor, 1995), won the Carl Sandburg Literary Award from the Friends of the Chicago Public Library. His first, *After We Lost Our Way* (Carnegie Mellon University Press), won the 1989 National Poetry Series Contest.

Oscar Peñaranda was born in the Philippines and grew up in Manila. In 1956, when he was twelve years old, his family moved to Vancouver, Canada, and then moved to San Francisco in 1961. He has resided in the Bay Area ever since. His piece in *Screaming Monkeys* was written while he was vacationing in Mexico in the midst of the Vietnam War, civil rights struggles, and ethnic studies activism.

Thien-Bao Thuc Phi was born in Sai Gon, Vietnam and raised in the Phillips neighborhood in Minneapolis. He has been a performance poet since 1991, and has had the fortune of reading his work all over the country, and has been included in numerous anthologies. His new CD, *Refugeography*, will be released in the Fall of 2003. www.baophi.com.

Jon Pineda studied at James Madison University and in the M.F.A. program in Creative Writing at Virginia Commonwealth University. He is a recipient of a Virginia Commission for the Arts Individual Artist Fellowship and his first poetry collection, *Birthmark*, was chosen by Ralph Burns as the winner of the 2003 Crab Orchard Award Series Open Competition and will be published by Southern Illinois University Press in April 2004.

Vijay Prashad teaches international studies at Trinity College in Hartford, and is the author of *Untouchable Freedom: A Social History of a Dalit Community* (Oxford University Press, 2000) and *Karma of Brown Folk* (University of Minnesota Press, 2000). Prashad is the editor of *Satyagraha in American: The Political Culture of South Asians,* a special issue of *Amerasia Journal* (Spring 2000), and also writes columns in *Colorlines* (Oakland), *Frontline* (Chennai), *People's Democracy* (New Delhi), and ZNET (www.zmag.org).

Bino A. Realuyo was raised in Manila and studied international relations in the U.S. and South America. His poetry has appeared in *The Kenyon Review, Manoa, New Letters,* and *The Nation*. He received the 1998 Lucille Medwick Memorial Award from the Poetry Society of America. He guest edited *The Literary Review's* special Philippine Literature issue (Spring 2000). His first novel, *The Umbrella Country*, was cited by *Booklist* as one of the "Top 10 First Novels of 1999."

Patrick Rosal is the author of the poetry collection *Uprock Headspin Scramble and Dive* (Persea Books) and the chapbook *Uncommon Denominations*, which won the Palanquin Poetry Series Award. His poems have appeared in *Columbia, The Literary Review, Footwork,* and the anthologies *The NuyorAsian Anthology* (ed. Bino Realuyo), *The Beacon Best 2001* (ed. Junot Diaz), and *Eros Pinoy* (ed. Alfred Yusoon et al). He was appointed 2001 emerging writer in residence at Penn State Altoona. He teaches literature and creative writing at Bloomfield College.

Thaddeus Rutkowski's novel, *Roughhouse* (Kaya Production) was a finalist for the Member's Choice of the Asian American Literary Awards. His work has been anthologized in *The Outlaw Bible of American Poetry* (Thunder's Mouth) and has appeared in *Fiction, American Letters and Commentary,* and other magazines.

Bienvenido Santos earned a B.A. from the University of the Philippines in 1932. His first two novels, *Villa Magdalena* and *The Volcano*, were published in the Philippines in 1965. Santos became an American citizen in 1976. One year later, the Marcos regime banned his novel about government corruption, *The Praying Man*, and he and his wife remained in San Francisco. *Scent of Apples* (1980), his only book to be published in the United States, won the American Book Award from the Before Columbus Foundation. He wrote more than a dozen books about exiles in both of his adopted countries, including the short story collections including *You Lovely People* (1955) and *Brother, My Brother* (1960).

Robbie Clipper Sethi is a professor of English, Russian, and creative writing at Rider University in Lawrenceville, New Jersey. Her novel in stories, *The Bride Wore Red*, was a Barnes & Noble Discover Great New Writers selection. She has won fellowships from the New Jersey State Council on the Arts and the National Endowment for the Arts. Her stories have appeared in *Atlantic, Mademoiselle,* and many literary magazines and anthologies. Three stories have been translated into Italian and Marathi. A second novel in stories, *Fifty-Fifty*, was published in 2003 by Silicon Press.

Purvi Shah is the executive director at Sakhi for South Asian Women, an antiviolence organization in New York City. She was born in Ahmedabad, India, but came to the United States at two. Her poetry has been published in *Borderlands: Texas Poetry Review, Crab Orchard Review, Descant,* and *Weber Studies,* as well as anthologies such as *Contours of the Heart* and *NuyorAsian.* Since 1997, she has served as a poetry editor for *The Asian Pacific American Journal.* She is pursuing a doctorate in English at Rutgers University, and in her free time learns Kathak, a North Indian classical dance form.

Sonia Shah, a freelance journalist, is author of *Crude: The Story of Oil* (Seven Stories, 2004) and editor of *Dragon Ladies: Asian American Feminists Breathe Fire* (South End Press, 1997). Her articles have appeared in *The Nation, The Progressive, Knight-Ridder,* and elsewhere. Her book on the globalization of clinical trials is forthcoming from The New Press.

Ricco Villanueava Siasoco has published fiction in *The North American Review, Genre Magazine,* and *The Boston Phoenix* as well as numerous anthologies. He has received fellowships from the LEF Foundation, Fine Arts Work Center in Provincetown, and the Institute of Asian American Studies. In 1998, he was the recipient of a PEN New England Discovery Award. Ricco teaches creative writing at Boston College. He is completing his first novel.

Arthur Sze is the author of seven books of poetry, including *The Redshifting Web: Poems 1970-1998* (Copper Canyon Press, 1998) and *The Silk Dragon: Translations from the Chinese* (Copper Canyon Press, 2001). He is the recipient of a Lannan Literary Award for Poetry, a Lila Wallace-Reader's Digest Writer's Award, a Guggenheim Fellowship, and teaches at the Institute of American Indian Arts in Santa Fe, New Mexico.

Eileen Tabios writes poetry, fiction, essays and criticism. Her books include *Beyond Life Sentences* (Anvil, 1998), which received the Philippines National Book Award for Poetry; *Black Lightning: Poetry-in-Progress* (AAWW/Temple, 1998), which received a Witter Bynner Poetry Grant; *The Anchored Angel: Selected Writings of Jose Garcia Villa* (Kaya, 1999); and (with co-editor Nick Carbó) *Babaylan: Poetry and Fiction by Filipina and Filipina American Women Writers* (Aunt Lute Press, 2000). Her most recent poetry collection is *Reproductions of the Empty Flagpole* (Marsh Hawk Press, 2002), and forthcoming is *Menage a Trois with the 21st Century* (xPressed, Winter 2003–4).

Lori Tsang was raised by a Chinese Jamaican mother and an "American" Chinese father in Connecticut and Indiana. Her poems have been published in *dISorient, Controlled Burn, Amerasia Journal, WordWrights, phati'tude, Crab Orchard Review, The Journal of Asian American Renaissance, Drumvoices,* and the *Asian Pacific American Journal.* Her essays and reviews have been published in the *MultiCultural Review, The Washington Post Book World, Women's Review of Books,* and *Amerasia Journal.*

Hisaye DeSoto Yamamoto was born in Redondo Beach, California, in 1921. She attended Compton Junior College where she majored in languages. During World War II she was moved to an internment camp. Currently, she lives in Los Angeles. Yamamoto writes poetry and short stories and is the author of *Seventeen Syllables and Other Stories* (Kitchen Table: Women of Color Press).

Lois-Ann Yamanaka is a Japanese-American writer who grew up in Hawai'i. With a unique voice that often uses pidgin English, Yamanaka's novels tackle themes of Asian American families and local Hawaiian culture. Her books include *Saturday Night at the Pahala Theatre* (1993), *Wild Meat and the Bully Burgers* (1996), *Blu's Hanging* (1997), *Heads by Harry* (1999), and *Father of the Four Passages* (2001). Yamanaka is also the recipient of a 1998 Lannan Literary Award and two Pushcart Prizes.

James Yang's work has appeared in some of the most prestigious trade publications in the United States, including *Communication Arts Design Annual,*

Communications Arts Illustration Annual, Print Magazine, Graphis, and the *Society of Publications Designers Annual*. One of his many posters was featured at the Hiroshima Museum of Art. He has also designed a sculpture titled "Clockman," which is a part of a permanent exhibit at the Smithsonian's national Museum of American History. James currently lives and works in New York City.

John Yau was born in Lynn, Massachusetts, in 1950, shortly after his parents fled Shanghai. He received his B.A. from Bard College in 1972 and his M.F.A. from Brooklyn College in 1978. His collections of poetry include *Borrowed Love Poems* (Penguin, 2002), *Forbidden Entries* (1996), *Berlin Diptychon* (1995), *Edificio Sayonara* (1992), and *Corpse and Mirror* (1983), a National Poetry Series book selected by John Ashbery. His books of art criticism include *The United States of Jasper Johns* (1996) and *In the Realm of Appearances: The Art of Andy Warhol* (1993).

Helen Zia is the author of *Asian American Dreams*. She has covered Asian American communities and social and political movements for more than twenty years. Born in New Jersey and a graduate of Princeton's first co-educational class, she lives in the San Francisco Bay Area.

Acknowledgments

Abelmann, Nancy and Lie, John, from *Blue Dreams: Korean Americans and the Los Angeles Riots*. Copyright © 1995 by The President and Fellows of Harvard College. Reprinted with permission of the publisher. For details and notes on this piece please refer to the above edition.

Agtarap, Tara, "A Lavender Army." First printed with the permission of the author.

Berssenbrugge, Mei-mei, "Chronicle." Reprinted with the permission of the author.

Bonus, Rick, "Homeland Memories . . ." Reprinted with the permission of the author.

Brainard, Cecilia Manguerra, "Talking About the Woman in Cholon," from *Magdalena* (Austin: Plain View Press, 2002). Copyright © 2002 by Cecilia Brainard. Reprinted with the permission of the author.

Bulosan, Carlos from *America Is in the Heart*. Copyright © 1943 by Carlos Bulosan. Reprinted with permission of University of Washington Press.

Cabalquinto, Luis, "Body Search." Reprinted with the permission of the author.

Carbó, Nick, "Assignment," reprinted with the permission of the author.

Cha, Theresa Hak Kyung, from *Dictee*. Copyright © 2001 by the Regents of The University of California Press. Used with permission of the University of California Press.

Cheu, Johnson, "Caught Prey." First printed with the permission of the author.

Chin, Marilyn, "Rhapsody in Plain Yellow" from *Rhapsody in Plain Yellow*. Copyright © 2002 by Marilyn Chin. Reprinted with the permission of W. W. Norton & Company, Inc.

Choe, David, art printed with permission of the artist.

Chow, Saiman, art printed with permission of the artist.

Choy, Catherine Ceniza, "Salvaging the Savage: On Representing Filipinos and Remembering American Empire." First printed with the permission of the author.

Chung Kay, art printed with permission of the artist.

de la Paz, Oliver Francisco, "When Fidelito Is the New Boy at School." Reprinted with the permission of the author.

del Rosario, Edward, art printed with permission of the artist.

Dempster, Brian Komei, an earlier version of "Transaction" was published in the Spring/Summer 1997 (vol. 6, no. 1) issue of *The Asian Pacific American Journal*.

Di, Xue, "Solitary in a Strange Land," translated by Forrest Gander and Hil Anderson. Reprinted with the permission of the translators and author.

Duhamel, Denise, "Hello Kitty (A Double Sestina)." First printed with the permission of the author.

Eng, Phoebe, "She Casts Off Expectations" from *Warrior Lessons: An Asian American Woman's Journey into Power*. Copyright © 1999 by Phoebe Eng. Reprinted with the permission of Simon & Schuster Adult Publishing Group and the Elaine Markson Agency.

esguerra, marlon unas, "On the Other Side of Granite." First printed with the permission of the author.

Galang, M. Evelina, "Labandera," reprinted with permission of *Prairie Schooner* and the author.

Gotera, Vince, "Honor, 1946." First printed with the permission of the author.

Gravage, Michella Rivera, "litany no. m." First printed with the permission of the author.

Hagedorn, Jessica, "Asian Women in Film: No Joy, No Luck." Copyright © 2003 by Jessica Hagedorn. An earlier version of this essay was originally published in *Ms. Magazine*. Reprinted with the permission of the author.

Halicki, Luba, "They Grew Up to Be Lovely." First printed with the permission of the author.

Huang, Wennie, art printed with permission of the artist.

Huỳnh, Jade Ngoc Quang, excerpt from *South Wind Changing*. Copyright © 1994 by Jade Ngoc Quang Huỳnh. Reprinted with the permission of Graywolf Press, Saint Paul, Minnesota.

Huynh, Phung, art printed with permission of the artist.

Igloria, Luisa A., "'More Fun Than a Turkey Shoot.'" First printed with the permission of the author.

Inada, Lawson, "Drawing the Line" from *Drawing the Line*. Copyright © 1997 by Lawson Fusao Inada. Reprinted with the permission of the author and Coffee House Press, Minneapolis, Minnesota.

Isaac, Allan, "Andrew Cunanan or the Manhunt for Philippine America." First printed with the permission of the author.

Isip, Jordin, art printed with permission of the artist.

Jen, Gish, "Chin" from *Who's Irish?* (New York: Alfred A. Knopf, 1999). Copyright © 1999 by Gish Jen. Reprinted with the permission of the author.

Khosla, Maya Rani, "Time for Pause." First printed with the permission of the author.

Kim, Dennis Sangmin, "Satta Massagana." First printed with the permission of the author.

Kim, S.L., "Red Lines Across the Map." First printed with permission of the author.

Kimura, Hiroshi, art printed with permission of the artist.

Kingston, Maxine Hong, "One-Man Show" from *Tripmaster Monkey: His Fake Book*. Copyright © 1989 by Maxine Hong Kingston. Reprinted with the permission of Alfred A. Knopf, a division of Random House, Inc.

Kothari, Geeta, "Meena's Curse." First printed with the permission of the author.

Kung, Betty, art printed with permission of the artist.

Lee, Don, "The Price of Eggs in China." Reprinted with the permission of the author.

Lee, Li-Young, "The Cleaving" from *The City in Which I Love You*. Copyright © 1990 by Li-Young Lee. Reprinted with the permission of BOA Editions, Ltd.

Lee, Wen Ho, excerpt from *My Country Versus Me: The First-Hand Account by the Los Alamos Scientist Who Was Falsely Accused of Being a Spy*. Copyright © 2003 by Wen Ho Lee. Reprinted with the permission of Hyperion.

Lew, Walter K., "Black Korea" from *Amerasia Journal* (IAMJ) 19 no. 2 (1993): 171–174. Reprinted with the permission of the author.

Linmark, R. Zamora, "The Two Filipinos," from *Rolling the R's*, Copyright © 1995 by R. Zamora Linmark. Used with permission of the author and Kaya Press.

Llana, Dindo, art printed with permission of the artist.

Liu, Timothy, "Five Rice Queens." First printed with the permission of the author.

Louie, David Wong, Chapter 3 from *The Barbarians Are Coming: A Novel*. Copyright © 2000 by David Wong Louie. Reprinted with the permission of G.P. Putnam's Sons, a division of Penguin Group (USA) Inc.

Lu, Lynn, "Ancient Chinese Secrets and Little White Lies." First printed with the permission of the author.

Maira, Sunaina, "Mirror Mirror Tea Tea." First printed with the permission of the author.

Matibag, Eugenio, "Findings of a Recent Inquiry into the Background and Causes of a Dissociative Identity Disorder in the Case of an American Subject of Filipino Descent." First printed with the permission of the author.

Matsuda, Mari J., "Why Are We Here? Thoughts on Asian-American Identity and Honoring Asian-Americans in Congress" from *Where Is Your Body and Other Essays on Race, Gender, and the Law*. Copyright © 1996 by Mari J. Matsuda. Reprinted with the permission of Beacon Press, Boston.

McGee, Barry, art reprinted with permission of the artist.

McQuade, Molly, "Sumo-esque." Reprinted with permission from *Mississippi River*, Vol. 31, No. 3. Copyright © 2003.

minahal, maiana, "you bring out the filipina in me." Printed with the permission of the author.

Mura, David, *"Fargo* and the Asian American Male." Reprinted with the permission of the author.

Peñaranda, Oscar, "I'm Still Warm." Reprinted with the permission of the author.

Phi, Thien-Bao Thuc, "Reverse Racism." Printed with the permission of the author.

Pineda, Jon, "A Few Words on Rome, or The Neighbor Who Never Waves." Reprinted with the permission of the author.

Prashad, Vijay, "Summer of Bruce" originally published in *Everybody Was Kung Fu Fighting: Afro-Asian Connections and the Myth of Cultural Purity* (Beacon Press). Copyright © 2002 by Vijay Prashad. Reprinted with permission of the author. For details and notes on this piece please refer to the above edition.

Realuyo, Bino A., "When Heroes Are Not Dead," and "Four Million." All reprinted with the permission of the author.

Rosal, Pat, "The Ancient Baguio Dead." Reprinted with the permission of Pat Rosal.

Rutkowski, Thaddeus, "White and Wong" and "Hello, Nuremberg." Reprinted with the permission of the author.

Santos, Bienvenido, "The Day the Dancers Came" from *Scent of Apples*. Copyright © 1997 by the University of Washington Press. Reprinted with the permission of the University of Washington Press.

Sethi, Robbie Clipper, "Fifty-Fifty." Reprinted with the permission of the author.

Shah, Purvi, "A Blue Boy in a Picasso Painting" First printed with the permission of the author.

Shah, Sonia, "Race and Representation: Asian Americans." First printed with the permission of the author.

Siasoco, Ricco Villanueava, "The Rules of the Game." First printed with the permission of the author.

Sze, Arthur, "Axolotl" and "In Your Honor" from *The Redshifting Web: Poems 1970–1998*. Copyright © 1998 by Arthur Sze. Reprinted with the permission of the author and Copper Canyon Press, P. O. Box 271, Port Townsend, WA 98368-0271.

Tabios, Eileen, "Nobility," from *Reproductions of the Empty Flagpole* (Marsh Hawk Press). Copyright © 2002. Reprinted with permission of the author and Marsh Hawk Press.

Tsang, Lori, "gridlock." Reprinted with the permission of the author.

Yamamoto, Hisaye, "Wilshire Bus" from *Seventeen Syllables and Other Stories*. Copyright © 1988 by Hisaye Yamamoto. Reprinted with the permission of Rutgers University Press.

Yamanaka, Lois-Ann, "I Wanna Marry a Haole So I Can Have a Haole Last Name" from *Wild Meat and the Bully Burgers*. Copyright © 1996 by Lois-Ann Yamanaka. Reprinted with the permission of Farrar, Straus & Giroux, LLC.

Yang, James, art reprinted with permission of the artist.

Yau, John, "Genghis Chan: Private Eye xxix," "Genghis Chan: Private Eye xxx," and "After *My Chronology* by Peter Lorre." All reprinted with the permission of the author.

Zia, Helen, "Surrogate Slaves to American Dreamers" from *Asian American Dreams: The Emergence of an American People*. Copyright © 2000 by Helen Zia. Reprinted with the permission of Farrar, Straus & Giroux, LLC.

Coffee House Press Anthologies

Returning a Borrowed Tongue: an Anthology of Filipino & Filipino American Poetry
NICK CARBÓ, EDITOR

This major collection features celebrated contemporary poets and writers whose work is not readily available elsewhere. Contributors include Mila D. Aguilar, Luis Cabalquinto, Luis H. Francia, Eric Gamalinda, N.V.M. Gonzalez, Vince Gotera, Jessica Hagedorn, Bino A. Realuyo, and many more...

Moment's Notice: Jazz in Poetry and Prose
ART LANGE & NATHANIEL MACKEY, EDITORS

Jazz-influenced prose and poetry from over fifty writers ranging from Langston Hughes, James Baldwin, Jack Kerouac, Jayne Cortez, and Ntozake Shange to musicians such as Abdullah Ibrahim and Cecil Taylor. This eclectic collection also features full-page photographs of jazz musicians at work and in the moment. A must-have for lovers of words and jazz.

Visit Teepee Town: Native Writings After the Detours
DIANE GLANCY & MARK NOWAK, EDITORS

The first anthology dedicated to postmodern Native poetry and poetics. Featuring both new and established authors, including James Thomas Stevens, Gerald Vizenor, Rosmarie Waldrop, Linda Hogan, Wendy Rose, Maurice Kenny, Hachavi Edgar Heap of Birds, Allison Adelle Hedge Coke, Phil Young, Larry Evers and Felipe Molina, Juan Felipe Herrera, Peter Blue Cloud, Louise Bernice Halfe, and Sherman Alexie.

Available at fine bookstores everywhere.

Coffee House Press is a nonprofit literary publisher supported in part by the generosity of readers like you. We hope the spirit of our books makes you seek out and enjoy additional titles on our list.
For information on how you can help bring great literature onto the page, visit coffeehousepress.org.

Coffee House Press

The coffee house of seventeenth-century England was a place of fellowship where ideas could be freely exchanged. The coffee house of 1950s America was a place of refuge and tremendous literary energy. Today, coffee house culture abounds at corner shops and online.

Coffee House Press continues these rich traditions. We envision all our authors and all our readers—be they in their living room chairs, at the beach, or in their beds—joining us around an ever-expandable table, drinking coffee and telling tales. And in the process of exchanging the stories of our many peoples and cultures, we see the American mosaic being reinvented, and reinvigorated.

We invite you to our table, and to the tales told in the pages of Coffee House Press books. Please continue to purchase our fine books or consider making a donation to our nonprofit literary press at www.coffeehousepress.org.

Funder Acknowledgments

Coffee House Press is an independent nonprofit literary publisher. Our books are made possible through the generous support of grants and gifts from many foundations, corporate giving programs, individuals, and through state and federal support. This project received major funding from the National Endowment for the Arts, a federal agency, and the Medtronic Corporation. Coffee House Press also received support from the Minnesota State Arts Board, through an appropriation by the Minnesota State Legislature; and from grants from the Buuck Family Foundation; the Bush Foundation; the Patrick and Aimee Butler Family Foundation; Lerner Family Foundation; the McKnight Foundation; the Outagamie Foundation; the law firm of Schwegman, Lundberg, Woessner & Kluth, P.A.; Target, Marshall Field's, and Mervyn's with support from the Target Foundation; James R. Thorpe Foundation; West Group; the Woessner Freeman Foundation; and many individual donors.

This activity is made possible in part by a grant from the Minnesota State Arts Board, through an appropriation by the Minnesota State Legislature and a grant from the National Endowment for the Arts.

MINNESOTA
STATE ARTS BOARD

NATIONAL
ENDOWMENT
FOR THE ARTS

To you and our many readers across the country, we send our thanks for your continuing support.

Good books are brewing at coffeehousepress.org

MAKIBAKA!
A tagalog command that means "Join the struggle!"
Often used by grassroots movements in the Philippines to rally the masses.